MASTERPLOTS II

WORLD FICTION
SERIES

MASTERPLOTS II

WORLD FICTION SERIES

3

Mag-Sec

Edited by

FRANK N. MAGILL

SALEM PRESS

Pasadena, California   Englewood Cliffs, New Jersey

Library of Congress Cataloging-in-Publication Data
Masterplots II: world fiction series.
  Bibliography: p.
  Includes index.
  Summary: Examines the themes, characters,
plots, style, and technique of 347 works by authors
from the non-English speaking countries of the
world, including Poland, France, Czechoslovakia,
Austria, Germany, and Russia.
  1. Fiction—19th century—Stories, plots, etc. 2.
Fiction—19th century—History and criticism. 3.
Fiction—20th century—Stories, plots, etc. 4. Fic-
tion—20th century—History and criticism. [1. Fic-
tion—Stories, plots, etc. 2. Fiction—History and
criticism] I. Magill, Frank Northen, 1907-   . II.
Title: Masterplots 2. III. Title: Masterplots two.
PN3326.M28 1988   809.3   87-33695
ISBN 0-89356-473-7 (set)
ISBN 0-89356-476-1 (volume 3)

PRINTED IN THE UNITED STATES OF AMERICA

90-2970

LIST OF TITLES IN VOLUME 3

THE MAGICIAN OF LUBLIN

Author: Isaac Bashevis Singer (1904-   )
Type of plot: Moral picaresque
Time of plot: Around 1900
Locale: Lublin, Piask, and Warsaw
First published: Der Kuntsnmakher fun Lublin, 1959 (English translation, 1960)

> *Principal characters:*
> YASHA MAZUR, the protagonist, a traveling magician
> ESTHER, his wife
> MAGDA ZBARSKI, his assistant and mistress
> ZEFTEL LEKACH, a deserted wife from Piask, also his mistress
> EMILIA CHRABOTZKY, a once-wealthy but now-impoverished widow, also his mistress

The Novel

As the novel begins, Yasha Mazur, a magician "religious and heretical, good and evil, false and sincere," has just returned from a series of performances in the country; he has come home to spend the holidays with his wife, Esther. One evening while he is out walking, he has a vision of Emilia Chrabotzky, his mistress in Warsaw. The next morning, Pentecost, Yasha sleeps late, and when Esther returns from synagogue, he takes her to bed.

The holiday over, Yasha readies his horses and wagon and leaves for Warsaw. On the way, he stops outside Piask to pick up Magda Zbarski, his assistant and mistress. Because Yasha supports their family, Elzbieta Zbarski, Magda's mother, obliges him to stay with them overnight. Passing through Piask the next day, Yasha visits Zeftel Lekach, another of his mistresses, who begs him to take her to Warsaw with him. A central idea of the book underlies Yasha's numerous and complicated affairs: By seeing many women and being a different Yasha to each of them, he hopes to forestall the inevitable responsibilities that accompany a choice—but the complexities of his promiscuity become too great.

Once in Warsaw, he drops Magda off in the apartment he maintains there and visits Emilia. Significantly, although exuding confidence in himself and his skills everywhere else, Yasha loses confidence whenever he visits Emilia. During the visit, her daughter Halina enters, and Yasha begins to recognize increasing feelings of desire for her in addition to those he already has for her mother. Emilia wishes to marry Yasha and wants them to go to Italy, where his talents will earn for him the money and acclaim he deserves.

Before he can do this, however, he must get enough money to finance the move. Robbery seems the only choice, and when Emilia's maid innocently mentions a rich old miser who lives alone and who has a reputation of keeping great sums of cash at home, Yasha makes up his mind.

After this point things go from bad to worse. During the robbery attempt, which is unsuccessful, Yasha falls and breaks his foot. On returning to Magda, he discovers that she has found out about his plans to marry Emilia. They argue and Yasha leaves. He goes to Emilia, who throws him out. He returns to Magda, only to find that she has killed herself. Turning finally to Zeftel, who has followed him to Warsaw, he finds her in bed with a pimp.

Three years pass, during which time Yasha has returned to Lublin and Esther, a broken man. After several more months have passed, Yasha orders masons to build a cell in his yard, with a small window but no door, in which he imprisons himself. Word soon spreads of the penitent Yasha, now known as Rabbi Jacob, and pilgrims begin to visit him at his cell, hoping for a blessing from the mad holy man. One day Esther, who brings Yasha his meals and necessities, brings him a letter from Emilia. In it she tells him that her daughter Halina has been confined to a sanatorium and that she herself has married.

The Characters

Yasha Mazur is a character for whom a reader may feel at once great distaste and great sympathy. Who has not often felt the desire for both stability and freedom? Yet how despicable is the man who causes so much pain to those nearest him, out of his own selfish pursuit of pleasure. In Yasha, Isaac Bashevis Singer has created a most appealing demon and an almost fatally flawed hero. In his evaluation of himself and his skills, Yasha is clearly a victim of hubris. Yet in his tender concessions to his wife and Magda at the beginning of the book, he reveals a genuinely caring facet of his nature.

Singer portrays Yasha's women with restraint but also with important characteristic touches. Esther is, significantly, childless. Magda, his longest-running mistress, is "in her late twenties but appeared younger; audiences thought her no more than eighteen." Zeftel is in her forties, has wide hips and abundant breasts, and Yasha regards her as sometimes motherly. Emilia, although she is superficially loving and caring to Yasha, is essentially compassionless: Before they can marry, she insists, he must convert, and when he appeals to her after his burglary attempt, she shuns him.

Even the most minor characters benefit from Singer's sure use of detail. Bolek, Magda's brother, is a terrifying and constant reminder to Yasha (and to the reader) of his sin with Magda, even though he is never actually seen. Halina's clearly nonsexual adoration of her "Uncle Yasha" makes all the more repellent his incestuous feelings toward her.

Themes and Meanings

The principal themes are symbolized by the novel's most repeated image: the tightrope. Yasha walks a tightrope as part of his performance, and he aspires to new and always more dangerous stunts. He also figuratively walks a tightrope between faith and moral degeneration. Early in the book, driving along a road in early spring, he exclaims, "Oh, God Almighty, you are the magician, not I!" Yet on his trip to Piask and Warsaw, he readily betrays his wife with three mistresses. After his bungled burglary attempt, he finds refuge in a synagogue. Although he has been in synagogues before, mostly for his wife's sake, this time he prays in earnest and concludes, "I must be a Jew! . . . A Jew like all the others!" His newfound orthodoxy, however, is short-lived. Shunned by Emilia, finding Magda dead and Zeftel in bed with a pimp, he realizes that for him forgiveness can come not from God but only from his now-inaccessible victims.

For Yasha, not even God is exempt from the image of the tightrope. During that first outburst in early spring, God was Yasha's own, personal, immediate companion; again in the synagogue, Yasha feels His presence as a real and vital one. Yet he always returns to his skepticism toward the Jewish God, who reveals Himself to no one, who gives no indication of what is permitted or forbidden.

Even in his self-imposed prison, Yasha walks a tightrope. He believes that through his asceticism he may expiate his sins—indeed, penitents soon come to him, believing him to be a holy man. Yet his prison really still protects him from having to choose between faith and freedom. From his cell, Yasha admits, "No, the temptations never cease."

Critical Context

The Magician of Lublin is one of the most widely read and perhaps the best book by the Nobel Prize-winning Singer. In this book as in many of his other works, he considers the nature of faith and the existence of God; he establishes the traditional tenets of the Jewish faith—belief in one personal God and service to Him through *Halakah*—as the accepted background for his characters. Yet this book is more easily accessible than some of Singer's other works. It relies not on an intensely violent backdrop such as that found in *Satan in Goray* (1935; English translation, 1955) or on the all-accepting attitude of a character such as Gimpel the Fool. Rather, it poses for its protagonist a very basic, modern dilemma: Should he maintain faith in a God in whom he believes yet whom he views as an unconcerned observer, or should he cling to his freedom, knowing he risks falling into a moral abyss?

Though widely acclaimed, *The Magician of Lublin* has been criticized on the grounds that it overemphasizes the sexual aspect of Yasha's temptations. Nevertheless, that aspect is a valid and necessary one. Particularly, Yasha desires Gentile women, who symbolize not only sexual taboo but also that world of wealth and social status into which he hopes to escape through his marriage to Emilia.

Sources for Further Study
Allentuck, Marcia, ed. *The Achievement of Isaac Bashevis Singer*, 1969.
Buchen, Irving. *Isaac Bashevis Singer and the Eternal Past*, 1968.
Malin, Irving, ed. *Critical Views of Isaac Bashevis Singer*, 1969.

David W. Kent

THE MAKEPEACE EXPERIMENT

Author: Andrei Sinyavsky (as Abram Tertz, 1925-   )
Type of plot: Satire
Time of plot: The early 1960's
Locale: Lyubimov, a fictitious small Russian town
First published: Lubimow, 1963 (English translation, 1965)

> *Principal characters:*
> SAVELY KUZMICH PROFERANSOV, the narrator, the town
>   librarian
> SAMSON SAMSONOVICH PROFERANSOV, an ancestor of Savely
>   Proferansov who directs Savely's writing, at times becom-
>   ing the narrator himself, and who also appeared to Savely
>   as the Professor
> LEONARD "LENNY" MAKEPEACE (LEONID TIKHOMIROV), a
>   bicycle repairman who becomes the leader of Lyubimov
> SERAFIMA PETROVNA, his wife, a teacher
> VITALY KOCHETOV, a government spy, later a loyal supporter
>   of Makepeace

The Novel

In the Prologue, the first narrator, Savely Kuzmich Proferansov, sets the stage by describing the town of Lyubimov as small but progressive, with a number of intellectuals, and characterizes himself as rational and literate, although his timid asides and conclusions reveal his own cowardice and superstitiousness. An avid reader of governmentally approved literature, he finds beginning the narrative difficult and describes his writing as though it were something he is impelled to do.

The first chapter tells how at a May Day parade, the leader Comrade Tishchenko installs Leonard Makepeace (Leonid Tikhomirov), a simple bicycle repairman, as the supreme ruler. No one questions the sudden change; Lenny promises peace and freedom. Tishchenko attempts to escape but is subdued by Makepeace, a struggle which later became a folk legend that the narrator discounts, even though he presents the folk legend rather than the true account.

In the second chapter, the narrator reveals the background of Lenny's rise to power. To win the love of the beautiful Serafima Petrovna, Makepeace agrees to lay the city at her feet. He begins reading voraciously, and one day a book, *The Magnet of the Soul*, falls to his feet from the ceiling. The book tells him how to gain mental control over others; Makepeace sees this gift not only as a means to power but also as an opportunity to do good for the town, and, through mind control, he has himself installed as ruler. At this point in his storytelling, the narrator is interrupted by a voice that first appears in the footnotes and eventually dominates the main text. The voice reveals itself as that of the Professor, an acquaintance of Savely who in 1926 urged him to write the story of Lyubimov. The Professor now tells Savely that he is also Samson Samsonovich Proferansov, an ancestor of the narrator and the author of the book that enabled Makepeace to rise to power. From this point forward, Samson controls the narrative, often becoming the narrator himself.

In the regional center of X, Lieutenant Colonel Almazov receives a report from the Secret Police chief Maryamov telling of the revolution. Almazov leads an expedition, disguised as fishermen on vacation, to Lyubimov. Meanwhile, Lenny prepares for his wedding; lacking adequate provisions for the ceremony, Lenny transforms surplus mineral water, pickles, and red pepper into alcohol, salami, and steak (in reality, he merely changes the people's perception of these substances, using mind control). In a grand gesture, he temporarily turns the local river into champagne. The celebration, however, is marred by the death of a thief who has drunk too much of the spurious alcohol. Lenny's inability to understand how the man could have died from what was only water, or why, given freedom, a man would want to drink himself to death, hints at the ultimate weakness of his plan to make the people happy by attending to all of their needs. Still, through willpower, Makepeace makes Almazov and others believe that the city of Lyubimov has disappeared, and so he is able to continue with his utopian reforms.

At first Lenny's reforms and modernization succeed, in spite of the presence of a spy, Vitaly Kochetov, and the attempts of a greedy capitalist journalist to corrupt Lenny's lofty ideals. Even Lenny's devout mother accepts his godless zeal, though only to avoid displeasing her son. One day Samson confronts Lenny, and Lenny, befuddled by the specter, asks Savely to explain who this figure is. Savely tells how his ancestor, an amateur scientist and intellectual, had traveled to India, where he obtained a sacred book revealing the purpose of life; unfortunately, Samson died before revealing this truth, but his spirit survived, haunting the estate until it burned in the Russian Revolution.

An unforeseen airplane attack nearly kills Lenny, but he escapes harm and convinces the pilots that they have destroyed the city. The spy Vitaly Kochetov reveals himself, apologizing for his role as informer, for now he sees the superiority of Lenny's method of reform over traditional governmental methods. Impressed by Vitaly's sincerity, Lenny makes him Chief Deputy.

Gradually, however, Lenny's reforms begin to fail. The people are unhappy with their substitute vodka, now rationed, because it cannot give them hangovers, and eventually they start brewing their own. Lenny discovers that his wife has been married before, and he forces her to tell him the truth about her background. Wanting to seem truthful, Serafima fabricates an elaborate history of lovers. Although Lenny had previously ignored his wife while pursuing his reforms, his love now turns into an irrational jealousy. Failing to seduce Lenny's one faithful companion, Vitaly, Serafima leaves Lyubimov. Samson apparently takes back the book from which Lenny gets his powers, and Lenny begins to lose his control; distraught, he wanders through the town, his random musings and curses wreaking havoc on the villagers. Tanks storm the city, and Vitaly is its only defender, losing his life in the process; Lenny simply wanders off, hoping to set up a bicycle repair shop one day. The old order returns to Lyubimov, with the same figures in command, though demoted. The novel ends with Savely once again in control as narrator; fearing that the authorities will discover his manuscript, he asks the Professor to help him keep the book safe.

The Characters

While *The Makepeace Experiment*, as a satire on utopian ideals, depicts the conflict between ideology and reality, it does so through its portrayal of conflicts between individualized characters who never become merely representations of abstract ideas; nor does the novel present its characters as morally one-dimensional, simply good or bad. The protagonist of the central struggle, Lenny Makepeace, does at times embody the single-minded fervor of the utopian reformer (a character criticized in the nineteenth century by Fyodor Dostoevski and in the twentieth century by Yevgeny Zamyatin); nevertheless, Lenny is also a complex and contradictory figure. His zeal is essentially benevolent, but in spite of his generosity, he cannot see that the people do not really want an ideal state. His love for Serafima is apparently genuine, but he easily forgets her while working on his programs. His jealousy contradicts all of his assumptions about how easily people can be controlled, for he cannot control either Serafima's past or his own irrational behavior.

The main narrator, Savely Proferansov, suffers from other contradictions, embracing both a smug rationalism and a cautious superstitiousness, wanting to write an important history and yet fearful of offending the authorities; he is also prone to hypocrisy, moralizing but self-serving, loyal to Lenny but only while Lenny is clearly in charge. In these and other ways he represents many of the forces in the Russian character (and in human nature in general) that perpetually thwart the realization of idealistic schemes such as those of Lenny. Savely also serves as a counterpoint to Andrei Sinyavsky, who seeks in his work to investigate the spiritual nature of the world, and who, by publishing his writings internationally, risks the sort of punishment that Savely avoids at all costs.

To some extent, Serafima Petrovna also represents a selfishness that undermines utopian reform, and at the same time she is an individualized character, sympathetically portrayed as needing the love and attention that

Lenny ignores in order to pursue his political goals. The unquestioned loyalty of Vitaly, on the other hand, proves fatal and futile; his hero Lenny remains unaware that Vitaly has given his life for Lenny's goals.

Perhaps the most ambiguous figure is the mysterious Samson Samsonovich Proferansov. Like his biblical namesake, he is able to confound Soviet philistinism; yet ultimately all of his intervention in the life of Lyubimov is for naught. At best, Samson has inspired his descendant with a bit of courage, but he provides no final solution, even though he has supposedly learned "the purpose of life." In his endeavors to bring about a utopian state based on the satisfaction of needs, Samson embodies the goals of nineteenth century rationalism, from which Marxism and other reforming philosophies have descended. Makepeace's failure underscores the futility of such a program in the face of the basic irrationality of the human temperament. At the same time, the more specific political satire on the Soviet government adds another dimension to Samson's significance: As an uncontrollable and elusive force, Samson Samsonovich also represents the limitations of the materialistic perspective of Vladimir Ilich Lenin and Karl Marx. Any government that fails to acknowledge the spiritual realm will appear shortsighted and ridiculous, as do the bumbling attempts of the Soviet bureaucrats. Still, the ease with which Vitaly Kochetov changes from an orthodox Marxist to a follower of Makepeace, paralleled by the narrator Savely Proferansov's immediate repudiation of Makepeace's philosophy once the cause proves futile, shows how willingly people embrace a dogma rather than seek to understand the complex reality of the spiritual world.

Themes and Meanings

The Makepeace Experiment develops simultaneously two sets of themes, one based on the specific political satire of the novel and the other based on the more universal commentary on human nature; over these two groups, the author superimposes a third type of theme by reflecting on the nature of literature itself.

The political satire ridicules the tendency of a government to reduce the needs of its citizens to the material level and to use those needs to control the people. The bungling of the Soviet bureaucrats, their selfish infighting, and their ludicrous attempts to quash the Makepeace revolution reveal in comic fashion the ignorant but savage workings of a totalitarian state. The novel does not attack one system of government in order to promote another, however, for the attempt of the American journalist and spy Harry Jackson to buy out and capitalize on Lenny's secret suggests that both capitalist and Communist states seek to manipulate their citizens. No political ideology can conquer or outlast the irrational side of the human personality. This irrational element may take the form of the self-destructive tendency toward greed, drunkenness, and superstition, or it may surface as the soul's need to love and be loved and its desire to understand its own spiritual nature. In either case, any government that tries to control human nature by satisfying its material needs through reason, no matter how benign this reform may seem, will inevitably fall prey to the irrational impulse.

The novel's political satire underscores its general depiction of human nature. Offered a program that would guarantee them continual happiness, the citizens of Lyubimov eventually reject Lenny's utopian system, preferring a drunkenness that leaves them with hangovers to one that is painless. As a guide for life, reason will always indicate which choice is best for people, but reason precludes what people want most—to make their own choices, even if freedom means making the wrong choice.

The form of *The Makepeace Experiment* reflects its preference for the irrational over the rational, for freedom over happiness. Rather than following the conventional formula of the nineteenth century realistic novel, Sinyavsky undermines the stability of point of view and plot by interrupting Savely's complacent narrative with the comments by Samson and the numerous digressive footnotes, frequently parodying scholarly erudition. By undercutting the reader's certainty of what is happening, the author suggests that the traditional view of what can happen is also limited when one concentrates only on the physical world. Whereas Savely sets out to write a history of the village of Lyubimov, his account turns out to be mysterious and perplexing, a record of the difficulty of writing, particularly in a totalitarian state, and at the same time a tribute to the power of the imaginative over the prosaic.

Critical Context

Like Sinyavsky's first novel, *Sud idyot* (1960, as Abram Tertz; *The Trial Begins*, 1960), *The Makepeace Experiment* treats complex political and artistic themes with satire and irony. Less conventional in form, however, *The Makepeace Experiment* develops in more detail the problem of art and the role of the artist in the modern world. Sinyavsky's first critical work, the book-length essay *Chto takoe sotsialisticheskii realizm* (1959; *On Socialist Realism*, 1960), had pointed out the contradictions and limitations of Socialist Realism, such as its preference for ideology (especially the positive hero) over true realism; the essay proposed a new art, one which would reveal truth through fantasy and the grotesque, as does *The Makepeace Experiment*. The collection of aphorisms and sketches *Mysli vrasplokh* (1966; *Unguarded Thoughts*, 1972) continues Sinyavsky's experimentation with form, and at the same time it represents a step forward in the spiritual search begun in *The Makepeace Experiment*. *Golos iz khora* (1973; *A Voice from the Chorus*, 1976), written during Sinyavsky's imprisonment for heretical writings, combines and contrasts various phrases and sayings from his fellow prisoners with the fragments from the more literary and self-conscious letters to his wife; *A Voice from the Chorus*, in its search for form and meaning, also signals the author's move toward Christianity.

As an anti-utopian satire and an attack on the preference for happiness over freedom, *The Makepeace Experiment* recalls the short novels of Fyodor Dostoevski; its more specific criticism of Soviet ideology also owes much to Yevgeny Zamyatin's *My* (1952, written 1920-1921; *We*, 1924). Whereas its philosophy is clearly in the tradition of Russian anti-utopian literature, the novel's innovation with structure and its complex layers of meaning mark it as an important step forward in the modern novel's quest for a form that can capture the complexity and variety of the twentieth century experience.

Sources for Further Study

Aucouturier, Michel. "Writer and Text in the Works of Abram Terc," in *Fiction and Drama in Eastern and Southeastern Europe: Evolution and Experiment in the Postwar Period*, 1980. Edited by Henrik Birnbaum and Thomas Eekman.

Brown, Deming. "The Art of Andrei Siniavsky," in *Slavic Review*. XXIX (1970), pp. 663-681.

_____ . *Soviet Russian Literature Since Stalin*, 1978.

Dalton, Margaret. *Andrei Siniavskii and Julii Daniel': Two Soviet "Heretical" Writers*, 1973.

Lourie, Richard. *Letters to the Future: An Approach to Sinyavsky-Tertz*, 1975.

Steven L. Hale

THE MAKIOKA SISTERS

Author: Jun'ichirō Tanizaki (1886-1965)
Type of plot: Social and psychological realism
Time of plot: 1938-1941
Locale: Kobe-Osaka district and Tokyo
First published: Sasame-yuki, 1943-1948, serial; 1949, book (English
  translation, 1957)

Principal characters:

TSURUKO, the mistress of the senior or "main" house in Osaka
SACHIKO, her sister, the mistress of the junior house in
    Ashiya, a small city just outside Osaka
YUKIKO, their sister, thirty and still unmarried, shy and
    retiring, now not much sought after
TAEKO "KOI-SAN," their sister, willful and sophisticated
    beyond her twenty-five years
TATSUO, Tsuruko's husband, a cautious bank employee who
    has taken the Makioka name and who has become the
    active head of the family
TEINOSUKE, Sachiko's husband, an accountant with
    remarkable literary inclinations
ETSUKO, Sachiko's precocious daughter
O-HARU, Sachiko's lazy, untidy maid
OKUBATA "KEI-BOY," the man with whom Taeko tried to elope
    at nineteen, and whom she still secretly sees
ITAKURA, a man of no background to whom Taeko is attracted
    after her betrothal to Okubata is too long delayed

The Novel

The Makioka Sisters is the saga of a proud, refined Japanese family that
declines in fortune. The novel re-creates the sumptuous and pleasure-filled
upper-class life of Osaka—the commercial center of Japan—just before and
during World War II. Jun'ichirō Tanizaki carefully creates a detailed portrait
of four once-rich and haughty sisters, whose lives encompass a wide area of
joys and sorrows, and he provides simultaneously a satirically accurate description of the whims and fancies of a vanished era.

The novel opens with a marriage prospect for the third sister, Yukiko, and
ends with preparations and emblems for this sister's ultimate wedding years
later. Between these rituals lies a sequence of passions that fuse nostalgia and
bitterness, tragedy and comedy. The Makioka sisters, although still proud
and refined, have lost status in their society, for the luxury of their father's
last years and the dignity of ancestral reputation have been long reduced by

extravagance and bad management of the family business. Consequently, it is now difficult to find acceptable suitors for Yukiko—especially as she is in the habit of rejecting men, has a blemish over her left eye, and is maligned in the local press for a scandal which really concerned Taeko, the youngest, most capricious sister.

The novel is divided into three parts. In the first, there is little dramatic incident beyond marriage proposals and negotiations, Sachiko's attack of jaundice, the nervous prostration of Etsuko, a cherry blossom viewing, and Yukiko's return to Tsuruko's control in Tokyo. The second part opens a year later, and the action increases, particularly with the harrowing experience of a terrible flood, from which Etsuko and Taeko are miraculously saved. The third section begins with yet another marriage proposal for Yukiko who, at thirty-three, is still a cause of anxiety for her two eldest sisters. The Makiokas no longer enter a marriage negotiation with the former feeling of social superiority, and, indeed, for the first time in their history fail to satisfy the prospective groom's family with their credentials. Although old rituals continue—a firefly hunt, visits in spring to Nara, commemorative services for their dead parents—family honor slides. Tsuruko threatens to expel Taeko from the family unless she returns to the senior house in Tokyo. Taeko, however, earns sympathy rather than reproof when she falls gravely ill and loses her youthful appearance. She looks like a fallen woman—the very thing her detractors always considered her to be—and she suffers from nightmares about deceased Itakura.

Human destiny, the Makiokas learn, is unpredictable—the very lesson that world events repeat. The Stolzes, former neighbors, have returned to Nazi Germany, where they cultivate an unrealistic optimism for the future. Taeko recovers from her illness to inherit more trouble. Yukiko, even in her wedding preparations, shows signs of having a nervous disorder. Nothing can be entirely harmonious or beautiful for the once-enviable Makioka sisters.

The Characters

The special beauty of this novel is the way in which Tanizaki evokes the very different personalities of the four sisters. There is a palpable sense of family heritage and pride, for the Makiokas are an old family, well-known in Osaka. Its best days, however, lasted only into the mid-1920's, when extravagance and bad business management cut into its fortunes. The four sisters are in thrall to their family name, preserving their nostalgia with almost sacred zeal.

Tsuruko has six children and resembles her mother, a Kyoto woman. Lacking Yukiko's delicate beauty, she has a certain hardness to her personality, although she is not as self-contained as she appears. In times of crisis, she stares vacantly into space, then busies herself in manic activity. During these hectic periods, she looks selfless, but is really too excited to know better. A manipulator, she uses Aunt Tominaga as a messenger to influence Sachiko in dealings with the two youngest sisters. Tsuruko is the most tradition-bound of the sisters.

Sachiko, more sympathetic than Tsuruko, dominates much of the book, simply because the two youngest sisters live with her for much of the time. The tallest, most strikingly beautiful Makioka, she is really more vulnerable than she appears—suffering as she does from a vitamin deficiency. She tires easily amid all the domestic complications created by Taeko and Yukiko, and she is almost as spoiled as her own daughter Etsuko. Yet Sachiko almost seems to exist to bring compassion to others. She wants desperately to give her husband a son, and when she suffers a miscarriage she is devastated. Like Taeko and Yukiko, she does not like Tokyo (except for the Palace and pine-covered grounds), and she aligns herself spiritually with the old ancestral place in Osaka. While Tsuruko is relatively authoritarian, Yukiko is diplomatic.

Diplomacy, however, does not go very far with the two youngest sisters. Yukiko, who looks like the most delicate one in the family, is the toughest physically. Docile and gentle on the surface, she is hard underneath. The most Japanese in appearance, she is really Westernized in her taste for French and music. Without a real home of her own, she is dependent on Sachiko. A mysterious blemish over her left eye is a handicap as far as marital prospects are concerned—as is her reluctance to please her suitors. Yukiko's closest Western correspondence is probably to medieval maidens in ivory towers, because there is purity in her idealization of beauty, and she is distanced from much of the common life around her.

The least nostalgic or sentimental, as far as family pride is concerned, is Taeko. At age nineteen she eloped with a son of the Okubatas, an old Semba family and owners of a jewelry store. She was able to escape public notoriety only because her identity was mixed up with Yukiko's in the newspaper report. Taeko, the most Western of the sisters, throws caution to the winds in her passionate affairs with Itakura and Okubata. In her quest for independence, she criticizes her family for its social prejudice and old-fashioned views. Her candor and open mind are sometimes tinged with rudeness and vulgarity, but she has no sense of nostalgia for the Makioka past, not having known much of her father's prosperous past and not having anything but the dimmest memories of her mother who died just as Taeko was starting school. Basically good-natured, her quest for independence makes her risk all respectability and she becomes the scapegrace. When she is struck by illness, her beauty vanishes and she acquires the look of a fallen woman. She has nightmares of Itakura, her deceased lover. Taeko is a complicated character, whose failings are offset by her virtues—not the least of which are her ability to read people correctly, and her fascination with beauty via doll-making, dance, and fashion.

There are numerous subsidiary characters: Yukiko's suitors; the various female go-betweens; O-haru, the lazy, untidy maid; the anxious brothers-in-law; the Stolzes; Taeko's boyfriends. All these characters have roles to play in the great story. They are foils to the main characters and show how close or how far the sisters are from beauty, truth, and happiness.

Themes and Meanings

Saturated with humdrum events and bourgeois life, *The Makioka Sisters* could well be misread as simply a realistic chronicle of family fortunes, but its original title, *Sasame-yuki*, means "delicate snow," and this poetic symbol points to a more aesthetic purpose. There is a direct poetry in the novel— through verse and song—and there is also an indirect poetry of psychological yearning, unhappiness, and exaltation. Events accumulate, but their effects wane—as do the delicate snows of yesteryear. There are flood, typhoon, sex scandal, illness, death, family dishonor, but all these things pass in the flow of time and human purpose. Characters remember old geishas (with blackened teeth and green lipstick), great *kabuki* actors, and *sushi* experts. Yet these are ghosts seen, as it were, by candlelight—evanescent presences that leave memories of sensuous beauty.

The four Makiokas cherish beauty in different ways and degrees. As the world rolls toward the madness of war, the sisters look back fondly at the past when life was less rushed, anxious, or embarrassing. In an attempt to preserve some continuity of the old honorable way of life, the sisters participate in firefly hunts, dance exhibitions, cherry-blossom viewings, and pilgrimages to Nara in springtime. Beauty is much sought after, and assaults upon it are resisted. The beautiful, whole world of the past is cracking— Adolf Hitler and Dunkirk haunt the background, and Japan is falling behind the West in science and art—so the Makiokas stick to their individual concepts of what is beautiful, true, and whole.

Critical Context

Although his early novels suggest a bohemian spirit and appear to have been influenced by Edgar Allan Poe, Charles Baudelaire, and Oscar Wilde, Jun'ichirō Tanizaki is not a mannerist writer. A much-honored novelist—who won the Imperial Prize in Literature in 1949, and who was the first Japanese to be elected an Honorary Member of the American Academy and the National Institute of Arts and Letters in 1964—Tanizaki became absorbed in the Japanese past, abandoning his superficial Westernization. Some of his novels—such as *Kagi* (1956; *The Key*, 1960) and *Fūten rōjin nikki* (1961-1962; *Diary of a Mad Old Man*, 1965)—are about sexual desire and the will to live, but *The Makioka Sisters* is, perhaps, the most representative of his deepest themes. Its length shows Tanizaki's marathon energy, concentration, and control. Some critics have asserted that he works on readers almost as much as he does on his characters. Yet despite the length of his novel, its painstaking fidelity to events and the surfaces of things, and its depiction of natural forces, Tanizaki is not a naturalistic writer. Cultural and social factors are not massive forces to be scientifically analyzed, but nagging irritants. The chronicling of society is undisturbed by the episodic nature of the writing.

Tanizaki's art is subtler than it first appears. The blow-by-blow narrative gets bogged down in trivia and extraneous material, and the digressions on a variety of subjects appear to weaken the flow of the story. Yet there is a method to this arduous realism, and there is a commitment to the facts and truths of existence. Small talk is recorded with as much fervor as are major exchanges among characters. Clinical details of illness and disease are not curtailed. Tanizaki's novel is loaded with conversations. His characters speak directly and freely, and reveal themselves in what and how they speak.

The often-colorless diction looks flat at times, but it demonstrates Tanizaki's refusal to differentiate between practical and artistic language. His sentences are often long, sometimes dull, but always aimed at the revelation of character and society. The persuasiveness of the writing is finally indisputable.

Western readers will be most charmed by the satire and the almost courtly manners of the sisters at times. These qualities of comic charm and decorum have a distinctly Oriental flavor.

Sources for Further Study

Falke, Wayne. "Tanizaki: Opponent of Naturalism," in *Critique: Studies in Modern Fiction.* VIII, no. 3 (1966), pp. 19-25.

Petersen, Gwenn Boardman. "Tanizaki Jun'ichirō," in *The Moon in the Water: Understanding Tanizaki, Kawabata, and Mishima,* 1979.

Ueda, Makoto. "Tanizaki Jun'ichirō," in *Modern Japanese Writers and the Nature of Literature,* 1976.

Keith Garebian

MAN IN THE HOLOCENE

Author: Max Frisch (1911-   )
Type of plot: Psychological realism
Time of plot: The 1970's
Locale: Ticino, a canton of Switzerland in the Alps near Italy
First published: Der Mensch erscheint im Holozän, 1979 (English translation, 1980)

> *Principal character:*
> GEISER, a retired businessman, age seventy-three, living alone in an Alpine village

The Novel

Man in the Holocene takes place during the last few days of a major rainstorm which has caused a road blockage and some interruptions of power and telephone service. The story records the protagonist's response to his isolation during the storm and to the broader isolation of old age.

In the opening scene of the novel, Geiser attempts to ignore the sound of the rain as he builds a pagoda out of crisp bread, but he finds himself turning to the encyclopedia, reading the entries on lightning and thunder and making lists of the nine types of thunder he has been able to distinguish. Although he continually reads the books in his house for distraction, his reading inevitably returns to subjects that relate to weather, local geography, and geology. These topics reinforce his concern with landslides and avalanches, which historically have recurred in the Alps. His obsessive reading also becomes a way for him to test his memory, which he fears is fading. In fact, some of the articles he reads in his encyclopedia have to do with memory loss and other dimensions of aging. In addition, he does some research on Iceland, dinosaurs, and the human condition. Many short excerpts from Geiser's reading are included verbatim in the novel, and the author includes sources for the quotations as if to assure the reader that they, too, are not fictional.

For a period, Geiser makes notes on his reading, but finally he decides that it will be more efficient simply to cut the relevant pages out of his books and tack them to the walls of his house. He reflects that his wife, who has been dead for some years, would not have approved of the holes in the plaster. Soon every available space on his walls is masked by clippings. He even takes down a portrait of his wife at nineteen in order to find more space to cover with the clipped pages that quickly begin to curl up in the humid air. When neighbors come to check on him or offer soup, he refuses to answer the doorbell because he does not want to reveal his transformed house.

Geiser finds that the evening passes with excruciating slowness, and he understands why someone would consider suicide to escape the sound of his own footsteps. In the morning, he picks up his rucksack, raincoat, and umbrella and embarks on a hiking expedition along a mountain path he has traveled in previous years. The footing is tentative and in places running water blocks the path, but Geiser presses on. Initially, the reader does not know why he has taken this hike. Only when Geiser decides to turn back is it clear that the town toward which he was heading would have provided means of transportation to the city Basel, his former home and the present home of his daughter and son-in-law. In turning back, Geiser accepts the isolation of his mountain home, and once he has returned, he ignores the ringing telephone, which he presumes signals calls from his daughter.

Geiser discovers himself lying on the floor beside an overturned chair, feeling dizziness and a numbness in part of his face. His thoughts and actions become erratic: He imagines that he resembles a newt, and he roasts his pet cat as if to eat it for dinner. He cannot bring himself to eat the cat, however, and buries her in the garden. As he drifts into a long reminiscence of a perilous mountain climb that he made fifty years earlier, his daughter, Corinne, arrives from Basel to make sure that he is all right and to restore order to the strangely altered household. The sun has come out again, and Geiser's final reflections suggest that his world has returned to normal, that he recognizes the reassuring continuity of life in the valley, from earlier historical epochs to the present day. Nevertheless, it is evident that his fears and meditations during the past few days have reinforced his sense that individual human beings are essentially alone and essentially inconsequential compared to the grandeur and longevity of nature.

The Characters

Man in the Holocene is a one-character novel, and its action occurs mainly inside the protagonist's mind as he awaits catastrophe caused by the interminable rain. The novel is written in a very limited third-person point of view, almost as if its reflections were confined strictly to Geiser's own mind. Because of this technique, the reader is sometimes forced to extrapolate information about what has happened to Geiser when Geiser himself is disoriented or unaware. This is particularly true toward the end of the novel when Geiser begins to behave eccentrically. The evidence of his behavior and physical symptoms suggests that he has had a stroke. Near the final page, this intuition is confirmed by the final quotation, an excerpt on the subject of apoplectic stroke. Evidently, Geiser himself was sufficiently aware of his changing condition to do some medical research in the same encyclopedia which had provided his clippings about dinosaurs and geology.

Despite the close connection between the point of view and Geiser's mind, the narration is spare and objective. The reader sees only what Geiser sees but is rarely told how the protagonist feels about his experiences, his memories, or his reading. The dominant emotion in the book is Geiser's fear that an avalanche will destroy his house or his village, but even this fear is conveyed indirectly—for example, by the collapsing pagoda of crisp bread that Geiser is constructing when the book begins. Later, he watches the rock cliffs that surround the village, searching for cracks. Shadows, snakes, or running water may momentarily seem to him to be a fatal crack in the earth.

Oddly, the most emotional moments in the book come neither in connection with Geiser's present fears nor with respect to any memories relating to his wife and children but in his description of the long-ago climb of the Matterhorn, undertaken with his brother, Klaus. The two men managed the ascent with ease, but they made an error in descending, trapping themselves on a narrow ridge of snow. It was decided that Klaus, as the elder, would take the risk of climbing back upward to surer ground from which a rope could be lowered to his brother. If this plan did not work, Klaus would descend by himself and go for help. Geiser knew that he could not wait for hours on the narrow ledge and that he would allow himself to fall before he could endure the long, cold isolation. Luckily, Geiser was rescued within short order by this method. About the experience, he tersely remarks that Klaus was a good brother. Yet, from this episode, the reader understands Geiser's love and admiration for his brother as well as Geiser's own physical courage. It is also apparent that Geiser is willing to confront the loneliness and potential death inflicted by the world of ice which surrounds and underlies his Alpine homeland. He recognizes, too, the thin line between life and oblivion.

Themes and Meanings

Images of ice, of loneliness, and of the long, slow, passage of history dominate *Man in the Holocene*. The novel is set amid the glacial architecture of the Alps, and one of the few books that Geiser reads during his isolation is a guidebook to Iceland. The rain that forms the novel's backdrop turns without warning to icy hail, destroying Geiser's garden. Geiser's most significant memory is of his near death during his descent from the Matterhorn.

Given this pattern of images, it is plausible to interpret *Man in the Holocene* as an existential parable about the status of man in the universe. Although Geiser evidently loved his brother, wife, and daughter, Max Frisch chooses not to emphasize Geiser's place in a network of human bonds. Instead, Geiser is placed in the context of geological time. The reader is reminded, by Geiser's clippings on dinosaurs, that man has not always existed and that beings larger and stronger than man have thrived on earth only to become extinct. Other clippings dwell on the passing of civilizations or species. Overall, the novel portrays man as a temporary inhabitant of a world which will continue well after his extinction.

Despite the potentially grim message implied in the idea that man is insignificant in the grand scheme of time, *Man in the Holocene* is not entirely a pessimistic work. It is certainly not a denunciation of man or a warning that man is destroying the world. On the contrary, the novel pays homage to the enduring power of nature itself, a force that predates man and, perhaps most significant, is not dependent on him. Although Geiser's valley changes physically as man erects buildings or fells diseased trees, his world has changed little from the Middle Ages—or even from the Stone Age. Twentieth century man has much in common with prehistoric man, man in the Holocene.

In addition to offering a parable for man's status in the universe, *Man in the Holocene* also reflects on the changes that man undergoes as he ages. It is partly Geiser's advanced age that permits him to view the world from a historical and geological perspective, because the passing of time has loosened his connections with his immediate surroundings. He realizes, for example, that he cannot remember the names of his grandchildren and that a portrait of his wife holds no sentimental value. As he sheds the particular memories that have defined his identity, Geiser becomes more of an Everyman figure. Even his specific Alpine surroundings may symbolize the relatively cold and unyielding world faced by the solitary elderly.

Critical Context

Man in the Holocene has two distinctive features: It is peppered with excerpts from reference works and it is very short. Both of these features place the work outside the realm of the traditional novel, edging it closer to a genre sometimes called antifiction. Antifiction characteristically uses devices that call attention to the structure of the work or to the authorial presence behind the text. Traditional fiction, on the other hand, tries to create a fully imaginative world or alternative reality in which the reader can lose himself. For the writer of antifiction, the very idea of fiction as an escape is romantic and inappropriate. The style of *Man in the Holocene*, then, is consistent with its theme; both the form and the content of the book are rigorously unsentimental and economical. No doubt some readers would also find that these adjectives seem appropriate for the work of a Swiss writer.

In the context of Frisch's other work, *Man in the Holocene* perpetuates the theme of the quest for identity found in his earlier works. Whereas earlier works explored the possibility of adopting a new identity as easily as a new name, *Man in the Holocene* ultimately repudiates the very meaning of identity in the face of eternity.

Man in the Holocene is likely to remain one of the most widely read of Frisch's novels; it is an important contribution to the relatively small canon of Swiss writings known outside the German-speaking community.

Sources for Further Study

Butler, Michael. *The Novels of Max Frisch*, 1976.
Petersen, Carol. *Max Frisch*, 1972.

Probst, Gerhard F., and Jay F. Bodine, eds. *Perspectives on Max Frisch*, 1982.
Weisstein, Ulrich. *Max Frisch*, 1967.
The Yale Review. Review. LXX (Winter, 1981), pp. 273-283.

Diane M. Ross

THE MAN WHO WATCHED THE TRAINS GO BY

Author: Georges Simenon (1903-   )
Type of plot: Psychological realism
Time of plot: The 1930's
Locale: Gronigen, Amsterdam, and Paris
First published: L'Homme qui regardait passer les trains, 1938 (English
   translation, 1958)

        Principal characters:
            KEES POPINGA, the managing clerk for the firm of Julius de
               Coster and Son, ship chandlers; a model husband and
               father, later a murderer and lunatic
            "MUMS," his wife, the mother of Frida and Karl, a good
               Dutch housewife
            JULIUS DE COSTER, Kees's employer, the head of an
               apparently well-established firm, actually a crook and a
               bankrupt
            PAMELA MACKINSEN, de Coster's mistress, a cabaret
               entertainer and later a murder victim
            LOUIS, the head of a gang of car thieves
            JEANNE ROZIER, Louis' mistress, a prostitute
            GOIN, the owner of the garage in Juvisy where stolen cars are
               given new identities
            ROSE, Goin's sister
            INSPECTOR LUCAS, a member of the *Police Judiciare* who is in
               charge of the hunt for Kees

The Novel

   The novel opens on December 22. Kees Popinga is bored by the evening
routine in his respectable household: children doing homework, wife pasting
cards from chocolate packages in an album, stove making the air heavy. He
goes out to check whether the shipping firm for which he works has outfitted
the *Ocean III* properly. Nothing ordered has been delivered; his employer,
de Coster, is getting drunk in a bar and confides that he plans to abscond,
faking suicide. The firm is based on fraud: Kees's job is gone, his savings are
lost. De Coster gives him five hundred crowns and Kees aids in his employer's disappearance, then goes home to bed, refusing to get up the next morning. Whenever he is plagued by thoughts of work, he rehearses the meeting
that he plans to have with de Coster's luscious mistress, Pamela. At nightfall,
Kees takes the train, leaving his family and his former conformist-self behind
in Gronigen.

   He whiles away the journey with amused recollections of the time he
dropped a (winning) opponent's chessman into a tankard of beer, of the

evening when he added sugar to his host's oxtail soup because the maid had repulsed him. In Amsterdam, Pamela repulses him, too; worse, she laughs at him. Kees silences her with a towel and leaves on the Paris train, unaware that he has committed murder.

In Paris he picks up Jeanne and spends the night with her. She persuades her boyfriend, Louis, to admit Kees to his gang. Under Louis' direction, Kees steals a car and drives it to Juvisy where he hides out at Goin's garage. When Inspector Lucas, who is in charge of the hunt for Kees, questions Jeanne and the papers publish Kees's crime, the gang considers turning him over to the police. Kees escapes and returns to Paris to see Jeanne, who refuses to sleep with him. Kees beats her unconscious with a revolver butt and returns to the streets of Paris, moving from hotel to hotel, café to café, picking up a different woman each night, reading about himself in the papers each day. He writes to the newspapers and to the police, correcting their view of him and giving information about Louis and his gang. Though the police arrest the car thieves, they are released to set the underworld hunting for Kees.

By New Year's Eve, Kees feels hunted. His habits must be broken because they will betray him. He cannot rest. A psychiatrist is reported to have called him paranoiac. The papers claim that he will soon be caught. He wants to announce himself to the world. Then all his money is stolen and he realizes that he is only an amateur in crime. He can neither outfit himself as a tramp and sleep under bridges nor afford a hotel. Clad in only a raincoat, he places his head on the railway line and waits for the train.

The train stops in time, and Kees is captured and taken to the police. He finds interrogation boring, refuses to answer, and pretends not to recognize his wife, Mums. Finally, he is returned to Holland and placed in an asylum where Mums visits him regularly once a month, bringing news of the biscuit factory where she pastes on labels, of their son Karl's scholarship, of their daughter Frida's leaving school to work in an office, where her employer's nephew has proposed marriage to her. Kees does not care. Contentedly, he considers the way in which he has himself proved himself superior to the police. The doctor wants to play chess. Kees drops a chessman in the teacup. His memoirs, "The Truth About the Kees Popinga Case," remain unwritten. "Really, there isn't any truth about it, is there doctor?" says Kees, at the conclusion of the book.

The Characters

In a sense, Georges Simenon has written the book that Kees did not write, but the truth contained in it remains subject to question. The title suggests that Kees Popinga watched longingly as life passed him by. His stifling home and rigid respectability enable the reader to sympathize with his wish to escape and to comprehend his dream of being a different Kees, his feeling that the rascally de Coster is the man who does what another, deeply buried Kees would like to do.

Yet even in the first chapter there are warning notes: "Kees tended to over-play his part . . . were he to give way in the smallest point there were no lengths to which he would not go." The rigidity of his life has kept him safe. Associated with his love of night trains is "the streak of wildness latent in his mental make-up," the longing for the improper, the idea that anyone leaving on the night train is gone forever. The distance from himself and from reality suggested by his vision of himself, playing himself, grows stronger as Kees's mental illness increases.

The shattering of his illusions about his employer, the end of his security and respectability, are represented by Kees as the advent of freedom. Paradoxically, Simenon insists that free choice ended when Kees left home on December 22: "Then destiny took charge."

Simenon is always concerned with the relation of environment to character, and he has said that he is interested in what a man shows himself to be when he is stretched to the limit. *The Man Who Watched the Trains Go By* shows how a shock unhinges a man who has spent his life conforming. Yet this shock does not make Kees a different being: It merely brings into play characteristics already present, though hidden.

The coincidence of person and circumstance produces the apparently uncharacteristic act with its predictable and inexorable consequences. Thus while Simenon seems to chronicle the decline into criminality of a conventional man who "lets go," he also takes care to present the paranoid characteristics which increase during the course of the narrative. For example, de Coster remarks that his managing clerk has always had a high opinion of himself though he is unaware of the frauds perpetrated under his nose. Previously, Kees revenged himself in petty ways on those who attacked his image of himself. Both these characteristics, like his detachment from reality, become increasingly evident as the novel progresses. By the end of the novel, the world and everyone in it are unworthy of his attention, are merely comic. His wife's concern for their children makes him discover her inferiority to a "man of wide experience like himself."

The Man Who Watched the Trains Go By is essentially the study of one character. Certainly Mums, with her flannel drawers, her solid figure, her pasting, her stifling domesticity, is easy to picture and easy to understand. She is not belittled for the competence she brings to dealing with financial disaster, which underlines her husband's irresponsibility, and her regular visits to him in the asylum indicate her family loyalty.

Jeanne, the Parisian prostitute, is presented with clear, neutral understanding. Her reactions to Kees as a client, her relationship to Louis, and her reactions to police questioning provide the reader with a coherent system of antisocial reactions and relations. The gang members are differentiated only in superficial ways; for example, Louis is merely a function. De Coster has solidity: He is an engaging rascal as he cheerfully reveals his years of skulduggery, his family's tradition of fraud, his own established infidelities, and those of his wife. De Coster exists to provide both motive and example for Kees's escape, but he exists quite vividly in the reader's mind, perhaps because he is present in Kees's own mind.

Although the novel is written in the third person, Simenon inhabits Kees; indeed, he knows more of Kees than Kees knows of himself. Thus the reader sees characters and events from Kees's point of view, feels the stifling routine of his home, chuckles over the sugared soup and the drowned chessman. Kees appeals to the universal wish to break out of the traces: "I am not crazy. . . . I am merely a man who at the age of forty has determined to live as he thinks fit, without bothering about convention or the laws; for I have discovered, if somewhat late in life, that I was the dupe of appearance."

Nevertheless, Simenon's technical skill is evident in his management of the reader's sympathy. As Kees becomes divorced from reality, the reader becomes divorced from Kees. Although he is clearheaded, can eat, sleep, plan, and play chess, yet his enjoyment of his notoriety, his view of his own behavior as justified and reasonable, his increasing sense of superiority all limit the reader's identification with him. Thus, by the end of the novel, Kees has withdrawn from reality and the reader has withdrawn from Kees.

Themes and Meanings

If *The Man Who Watched the Trains Go By* merely traces the development of an idiosyncratic and abnormal mind, its truth is hardly general enough to remain interesting. The dominance of trains as an image in the book suggests, however, that the paradoxical nature of freedom is at the heart of the novel. In Gronigen, the passing trains symbolize for Kees a world of freedom that he has never known. Simenon, however, uses the image less simply. Train journeys mark all stages of the narrative: The evening train takes Kees to the fatal interview with Pamela; on the night train, he escapes to Paris. He returns to Paris by train to confront and assault Jeanne. A train is at the center of his plan to escape by suicide, but instead it takes him to captivity in Paris. Another train carries him to confinement in Holland.

The train is therefore a paradoxical image of freedom, for Kees is no freer than was Oedipus. Trains run on predetermined paths, and derailment is disaster. So it is with Kees. What seems to him to be an escape from his fate leads him back to it, for humans run the ways determined by their innate selves and by the laws, conventions, and habits which dictate the relationships of society. Even those outside the law are not exempt. Kees himself observes that Louis' gang is tied to the garage at Juvisy as Mums is to the house in Gronigen. Total freedom is at best a figment of the imagination and at worst a destructive dream.

Critical Context

Simenon's first novel was published in 1922; the Maigret series was begun in 1931. Thus *The Man Who Watched the Trains Go By* is an early novel, but it is not apprentice work; Simenon was a full-time writer of pulp fiction during the 1920's and had already published more than fifty novels under various names and written nineteen of the Inspector Maigret stories before writing *The Man Who Watched the Trains Go By*. The novel lacks the sophistication of some of Simenon's later narratives in that it is linear and uncomplicated and contains only one character of any depth. Nevertheless, its unobtrusive neatness of line, its realism, its particularity, and its grimness are characteristic of later and better-known works. The psychological, not the factual, emphasis which marks Inspector Maigret is evident even in those novels in which he does not appear. Perhaps Simenon may be compared to Arthur Conan Doyle, who also created a fictional detective so fascinating that he overshadowed his creator's other works. Maigret aside, Simenon is a vastly prolific craftsman who can make comprehensible the apparently bizarre psyche with conviction and economy. He is a novelist whose success has paradoxically overshadowed his achievement.

Sources for Further Study

Becker, Lucille F. *Georges Simenon*, 1977.

Bresler, Fenton S. *The Mystery of Georges Simenon: A Biography*, 1983.

Lambert, Gavin. *The Dangerous Edge*, 1976.

Narcejac, Thomas. *The Art of Simenon*, 1952.

Raymond, John. *Simenon in Court*, 1968.

Jocelyn Creigh Cass

THE MAN WITHOUT QUALITIES

Author: Robert Musil (1880-1942)
Type of plot: Social criticism
Time of plot: c. 1913
Locale: Kakania, a fictionalization of the Austro-Hungarian Empire, just before World War I
First published: Der Mann ohne Eigenschaften, 1930-1943, 3 volumes; revised, 1952; revised, 1978 (English translation, 1953-1960, 3 volumes)

>   *Principal characters:*
>   ULRICH, the man without qualities
>   WALTER, his paranoiac friend, a pianist
>   CLARISSE, Walter's wife and Ulrich's friend
>   COUNT LEINSDORF, the honorary sponsor of the Collateral
>   Campaign
>   ARNHEIM, an industrialist and a leader of the Collateral
>   Campaign
>   DIOTIMA, the spiritual guide to the Collateral Campaign
>   MOOSBRUGGER, a murderer
>   AGATHE, Ulrich's sister

The Novel

   To call Robert Musil's *The Man Without Qualities* a novel is to reduce it to a whim. It is actually a life's work, a massive, comprehensive statement of philosophical, social, and political response to an entire epoch of modern European history characterized by the decadence of the Habsburg Empire. Written during and after the empire's collapse, during the rise of National Socialism, the novel is both an indictment of the indifference of the masses to Adolf Hitler's rise to power and a personal observation about the indifference of all peoples to the political structure that they allow to stand through ennui and self-interest. At the same time, it is the receptacle of a vast range of ideas, speculations, observations, and conjectures by an obsessive note-taker, covering three huge volumes in which the plot itself moves through only one year in the characters' lives.

   Beginning in 1913, near the end of an era known for its attention to finery, sport, luxuries, and gentility, the text follows the monumental planning for a great celebration of the dual monarchy of Austria and Germany. This celebration, known as the Collateral Campaign, gives the novel a spine, as the story describes the life of a man known only as Ulrich, a "man without qualities," who takes a year away from his day-to-day life to observe his existence from the outside. This premise allows the narrator to describe Ulrich watching the active characters in the story, who hurry from idea to idea, from pro-

ject to project, busily establishing their "qualities," wasting energies on meaningless activities that occasionally attract Ulrich, as passive as a piece of drift-
wood in a whirlpool. By his stillness, by his refusal to act on qualities, Ulrich
accidentally assumes leadership of the Campaign, finds himself in love affairs
neither sought after nor avoided, and begins to follow the fortunes and misfortunes of Moosbrugger, a murderer. Plans for the Collateral Campaign
proceed, made all the more ironic by the reader's knowledge that the entire
Austro-Hungarian Empire will collapse years before the planned celebration.

The novel's plot is interrupted at every turn by philosophical observations,
sometimes from characters qualified to make them and sometimes by the
narrator explaining the naïveté or moral indecisiveness of less introspective
personalities in Ulrich's life. Through family and governmental connections,
Ulrich's father, decidedly a man of qualities, has found a position for Ulrich,
a position that suits Ulrich well, since no actual activity is required, only the
outward signs of activity: He is to present himself to certain salons, where his
ideas will be considered, along with myriad others, in a search for a "Great
Idea" which will inform the entire occasion of the Collateral Campaign.

The tone of the novel is ironic throughout, a kind of detachment and musing "observership" that accurately depicts the society of the time, which was
more concerned with appearances than with substance. The temperament of
the main character, Ulrich, is also suited to nonaction, so that his search for
what he calls a "narrative order" in his life is at the same time Musil's structural device: a plot interrupted by contemplation, philosophical inquiry, and
speculation.

While at the center of the outward plot of *The Man Without Qualities* is
the planning of the Collateral Campaign, this campaign is never articulated
in the novel except in the most general terms, because it serves as a receptacle for any and all hidden agendas, political favors, social jostling, and other
human activities without meaning or purpose. The Great Idea is a metaphor
for the great idea of living from day to day as if there were a Great Plan moving humankind forward, when in fact the only great idea is the idea that
there is such a plan. In other words, Musil is discussing how human beings
somehow manage to keep busy and deluded about the importance of their
lives, in service to a Great Idea too lofty and too comprehensive to submit to
any closer scrutiny. To deny the Great Idea, to question it, to ask to have it
defined, are crimes against the unwritten moral code by which humans live
without question.

The Collateral Campaign represents the narrative order of daily activities,
all seemingly addressing some larger blueprint, despite the lack of any sub-
stantive measurement or proof that the idea exists. This construct is the modern existential dilemma transformed into a campaign of statesmen to justify
the existence of boundaries, borders, governments, rules, manifestos, con-
stitutions, and calendars.

As Ulrich finds himself almost accidentally named the honorary secretary of the Collateral Campaign, the plot moves through a series of relationships with virtually no active events interfering with the opportunities to philosophize seized by all the characters. From General Stumm, who makes lengthy observations about libraries, to Moosbrugger the murderer, whose mildness contradicts the violent crimes to which he readily admits, the inhabitants of Kakania (a clever contraction of *kaiserlich und königlich*, literally "kaiser-like and king-like") are taken to living their lives in spite of the meaninglessness perceived by Ulrich and the narrative voice. At various points throughout the novel, Ulrich walks through the city, making observations, trying to sort out his year's experiences as a man without qualities, and reaching few conclusions. These interludes, together with each character's long disquisitions on every social and aesthetic subject, give the novel its eclectic, unfocused quality.

The final plot resolution can only be imagined, as Musil died leaving behind sheaves of notes, many of them contradictory, regarding the resolution of Ulrich's "vacation from life." Scholars have disputed the "only logical" conclusion to the novel, but it remained for Musil's widow, Martha Musil, to publish the remnants in volume 3, leaving to history one of the most intriguing puzzles in modern literature.

The Characters

Ulrich may be the most difficult character to define, since the essence of his character is the avoidance of all qualities, all properties, all definable features. He leaves himself open to the social structure, without prejudgment, without a plan, without a narrative order in his life. Ulrich has tried several careers—as military man, as engineer, and as a mathematician. Each attempt has ended in his dissatisfaction with the limitations of any career, any series of choices, in the light of what he calls the "possibilities." In Ulrich's mind, the concept of possibilities is an actual philosophy, in which the unlimited nature of man's potential actually disables the choice-making facility, defusing the cause-and-effect relationships of choice-making and obfuscating the directions one might take, as though all paths lead everywhere and therefore none can be chosen. Thus his character is passive, more a receiver of events than a seeker of events. In this configuration, Ulrich is European man himself, faced with a future of mechanistic high technology with unlimited potential and thereby frozen into inaction. Events take over the choice-making process, a process which requires qualities. Ulrich's father has such qualities and can make decisions, even for Ulrich. It is Ulrich's fate, however, simply to allow events to occur.

Although she does not appear until the third volume of this massive unfinished work, Ulrich's twin sister, Agathe, is an important figure in the total construction, because she serves as a partner to Ulrich as he tries to find meaning in his life. The German idea of *Doppelgänger* applies here: Agathe was reared apart from Ulrich, but when they meet, Ulrich is completed, in much the same way as intellect and passion form one whole person. Agathe, who forged their father's will in a real act of criminality, is like Moosbrugger as well: quiet, undemonstrative, yet capable of serious crime. Ulrich, then, is three characters, since Moosbrugger is a manifestation of Ulrich's possibilities, just as Agathe is Ulrich's completing element.

Important, too, is the married couple Walter and Clarisse, both friends of Ulrich. Their marriage is no marriage at all, but rather a competition. Clarisse wants no children, but Walter does. Playing the music of Richard Wagner together seems to substitute for a real relationship, and as the novel progresses, Clarisse becomes more demonstrative in her affection for Ulrich, until she finally asks him to give her a child; at the same time, she is driven insane, gradually becoming obsessed with Wagner, Moosbrugger, and Ulrich. Walter, meanwhile, sensing the limitations of his talent as a pianist, sulks jealously, watching the unfolding of Clarisse's madness and Ulrich's passive acceptance of her friendship, unable to become part of it, although he, too, is Ulrich's friend.

The other major characters are somehow involved with the formulating of the Great Idea. The official leader of the Collateral Campaign is Count Leinsdorf, the embodiment of aristocracy without purpose. The very act of combining two celebrations into one grand one is an example of the kind of high-spirited but unrealistic planning best left to titled personages. For spirituality, Leinsdorf enlists the aid of Diotima, a sort of soullike character who provides an abstract ideal to the enterprise. For practicality, the successful industrialist Arnheim is added to the team. Diotima's platonic yet passionate affair with Arnheim completes this portrait of Europe before the world wars. Each character represents one facet of the society that awaited Hitler and, through their indifference, allowed him to demonstrate his "qualities," however sinister.

Themes and Meanings

Musil's total philosophy is expressed in this novel, composed of a complex weaving of ideas, related and contrasting. Order, soul, morality, and love are the themes. What is Musil's intention as he weaves them throughout the text? Details in the novel, developments and relationships, point to this intention in the end. For example, Ulrich's early resolve to take a "vacation from life" for a year is emblematic of Musil's own attitude toward the novel. Here is the direction that the main character is taking: a suspension from the common narrative order, from the serial progression of events that one calls one's life, a period of pure examination. It is in this suspended atmosphere that the events of the novel take place. Thus the first clue to Musil's intentions is that the ideas presented are contemplative ones, ideas designed to be viewed in the abstract, away from the demands of pragmatism. The reader would be in error, then, to question the efficacy, the practicality, of any suggestions that the author-narrator makes. They are ideas only. This approach itself is revealing of the author's intent: He wishes to investigate what can be, not what is. In this respect, the novel is utopian, but without a concrete resolution to offer in place of the real world.

The novel's themes are condensed in the male-female relationships. These relationships are presented in detail, from outside the relationship and from the points of view of each participant. All the relationships are imperfect, all the relationships echo one another, and in every pair the similarities between the two participants are a force of exterior combination, as though narrative order brings them together but abstract ideas keep them apart. Walter and Clarisse are childless, by Clarisse's wishes and against Walter's. They both play Wagner, they both have Ulrich for a friend. Rachel and Soliman are both servants, both devoted (on the surface) to a greater authority and both demonstrating basically romantic tendencies. They are in the shadow of the far greater, superficially purer, relationship between their masters, Arnheim and Diotima. The servant pair and the master pair are pitiable echoes of each other in the idealistic nonsense of the Good, the True, and the Beautiful in the women and the outwardly gentlemanly but inwardly conniving natures of the men. Soliman is a small, black version of Arnheim, as Rachel is a stupid, lower-class version of Diotima.

Another pair that reflects all the others in a frightening way is the pair made up by Moosbrugger and his victim. On the animal level where prostitutes and itinerant carpenters survive, Moosbrugger and his victim perform the same *pas de deux* performed by the other pairs—the vague, often-imperceptible sense of "right living" snuffed out suddenly by the "frothing lunacy" which seems eternally to threaten the moral sanity of every man (and here Musil refers to the polarities of love and sex as well). Moosbrugger is plagued by his victim just as Ulrich is plagued by the series of women who throw themselves at his feet. Ulrich's seduction of Gerda, for example, bears so many of the same motivations as Moosbrugger's murder that the reader is astonished at the brazen admission that the episode implies. Ulrich seduces Gerda to rid himself of her, despite his disgust for her plainness, despite his "moral" code which forbade it. Gerda is as persistent and as gnawing as the poor prostitute who dies at Moosbrugger's hands.

One specific passage demonstrates the complexity of the novel's plot, always tied to inaction or the inability to act. Clarisse visits Moosbrugger in the insane asylum, where she herself will be eventually. Before this visit, Clarisse has attempted to force Ulrich into fathering her child. She goes to his room, does all she can to arouse him, and fails. Her desire to see Moosbrugger is a sublimation and a symbolic fulfillment of that same wish— the wish to see man reduced to animal by his passions, passions (like so many of Wagner's themes) which underlie and negate all lofty moral propositions, all order, and all concepts of some other reality in which the soul dares to be defined.

Moosbrugger, on the other hand, does not articulate his feelings, and the nature of the relationship between Moosbrugger and Ulrich poses an interesting question. On the surface, the answer is simple: Ulrich, in his contemplation of what is "right living," sees Moosbrugger's plight as a rent in the pious, legal, or social definition. Ulrich's father spent much energy trying to determine the degree of guilt in a madman, but his father was a man of qualities, who was clear about the nature of morality and whose life had a narrative order. Moosbrugger attracts Ulrich because of his honest face, in marked contrast to the shackles which bind him. Yet this surface attraction does not fully explain the blatant comparisons of Moosbrugger and Ulrich. One cannot help thinking that Ulrich sees a Moosbrugger in himself, in all people. Ulrich and Moosbrugger are personifications, perhaps, of two sides of a human being: the ideal and the real, the mind and the body. This duality is incomplete, however, because neither one of the pair is exclusively one or the other.

"Musical," Clarisse's word to describe Moosbrugger, means harmonious, expressive of human passion, Wagnerian in power and action. Moosbrugger has acted, has pounded out the last heavy chords of his masterwork. Ulrich refuses to play; he merely reads the music silently, to himself. There is something "other" than either Moosbrugger or Ulrich, something that lies between them. That "something," the most difficult abstraction with which Musil had to contend, is no more definable than Musil's final theme itself, but it can be encircled by an examination of the major symbol in the novel: the relationship between Ulrich and Agathe.

On one level, Agathe is Ulrich's soul, his other half in a mystical or even physiological sense, but this view is a screen to Musil's real intentions. Ulrich and Agathe, as a pair, do not form a complete person, and it is not Musil's contention that a man need only find his soul to be happy. Aside from the complicated possibilities in defining the soul and the very real question in the mind of Musil (as echoed in his characters' discussions of the soul) as to whether a soul even exists, there is the distressing fact that Ulrich and Agathe are not happy, do not make a complete person, and are not the end point at which Ulrich-Agathe can resume "life" after a long vacation from it. It is true that Ulrich realizes that, by allowing Agathe to move in with him, he is giving up his "vacation." That admission, however, is not from Ulrich's conscious mind so much as from his unconscious understanding of what that "vacation" implies—a suspension of feeling, a suspension of love, and an exchange of self. Thus, Agathe is not the soul of Ulrich, but rather the vexing impediment that prevents Ulrich from suspending the narrative order of everyday life.

What makes the point for this view (that Agathe is not Ulrich's soul, simply and purely) is that Ulrich is all too aware of imperfections in Agathe: She is married to Hagaeur, she forges their father's will, and she changes the medals on his coat before burial. In the symbolic matrix of this novel, these features relate back to the fact that their father was a man of qualities, and his will and his medals (that is, his public reputation) are jeopardized by Ulrich and Agathe. She is willing to have lovers other than Ulrich, and she carries around her neck (although he does not realize it) a picture of her first love and a capsule of poison for her own destruction, another way to be free of decision making. While Ulrich may not take note of the locket, Musil wants the reader to do so, inserting the theme of suicide, the final act of a man without qualities. Musil wants the reader to see the romantic attitude in Agathe that precludes her identity as a soul. Her suicidal impulse gives her a character more complex than a mere psychelike personification of spiritual life. The fact that Agathe can kill her husband or herself means that she is not Ulrich's soul but Moosbrugger in female disguise, a counterpart of Ulrich that is denied an existence by dint of Ulrich's temporary suspension from "life." In other words, when Agathe enters Ulrich's life, Ulrich must act, and it is only action that separates Ulrich from Moosbrugger. This imperative to act explains why Agathe enters the novel so late and why Musil never finished his novel—it would have meant an engagement with the world that Musil refused to admit.

Anton Chekhov, in his play *Dyadya Vanya* (1897; *Uncle Vanya*, 1914), makes the statement, through the character of Astrov (who shares with Ulrich his inability to act on the moment), that, without a guiding light somewhere outside the forest, the stumbling of humankind in the dark is unbearable, but when even one light outside the forest can be seen, the wanderer no longer feels the twigs snapping against his face. Ulrich, in this analogy, has chosen to stop in the forest, to get his bearings, to look for a light, and, perhaps, to discover some path (narrative order) in the forest. If he chooses, as Moosbrugger did, to live in the forest instead of trying to leave it, he will have relieved himself of all moral choice, by making the choice to become an animal without moral responsibility.

The implications of the novel's themes are many, but a consensus of scholars' speculations about how Musil wanted the novel to end can be attempted. Musil's Ulrich will "make history" by "acting on his baser qualities." Ulrich will reach that point in his investigation when he will no longer be able to say "not yet" to life but must either say yes to it, by admitting to his soul that it exists, or say no to it, thereby denying forever the existence of an order greater than the artificial one imposed by man in society. By saying no, Ulrich will deny that morality exists, that right and wrong exist. In this respect, Musil's novel is a modernist novel, in which the entire spectrum of man's decision making is reduced to the question of meaning versus meaninglessness. What makes the novel rich in implication, however, is the reasoning which allows the reader to conclude that saying no to life is the only truly moral act Ulrich can possibly perform. It is easy to understand why finishing the novel was so difficult for Musil.

When a man denies all morality, when he will not acknowledge any written or unwritten code of action as being right and any other code of action as being wrong, that man moves from the order of the soul into the order of the Nietzschean Will. To answer to no morality is to answer to the only morality: self-will, choice.

What was Musil's intention in writing *The Man Without Qualities*? The question is made more intriguing by the absence of an available conclusion by Musil himself: His random notes, unedited and untranslated, may either support or confuse what has gone before, but no simple explanation is available. The novel has led to the very absence of qualities that Musil uses as his premise.

It is possible that Musil planned to have Ulrich commit some antisocial, sexual, perhaps even bestial act—perhaps the murder of Hagaeur (Agathe's husband), perhaps the incestuous union with his sister, or (allowing for certain plot developments) perhaps some confrontation with Moosbrugger that would lead to a double suicide of Ulrich and Agathe. It seems clear that Musil intended Ulrich to transcend the earthly boundaries of morality and love, freeing himself from the temporary inaction of his "vacation from life" and, in doing so, resolving the perplexing problem of what constitutes "right living." From a moral standpoint, Ulrich must reconcile the superficially atrocious actions of Moosbrugger with Moosbrugger's innocence. Ulrich must complete himself by denying both his male, active self and Agathe, his soi-disant passive self. His final act must be a real act in the real world and absolutely unpardonable in the eyes of common morality, but this act must be the final anguished declaration of his own humanity, the resolution of his most vital doubt: whether the soul exists and how it makes itself known.

Critical Context

This novel ranks with Thomas Mann's *Der Zauberberg* (1924; *The Magic Mountain*, 1927) and James Joyce's *Finnegans Wake* (1939) as a study in the total modern sensibility and, as such, deserves a more prominent place in modern world literature. Musil completed other works, notably *Die Verwirrungen des Zöglings Törless* (1906; *Young Törless*, 1955) and several short stories, but *The Man Without Qualities* is his major contribution to modern literature. Perhaps because it was not finished, it has not met with the same kind of success, but it deserves more recognition, not only as a portrait of Europe in the twentieth century but also as a careful study of the nature of man's duality. The ontological question of meaning and meaninglessness pervades other great works, such as Samuel Beckett's The Trilogy (1951-1953),

Hermann Broch's *Die Schlafwandler* (1931-1932; *The Sleepwalkers*, 1932), and Fyodor Dostoevski's *Besy* (1871-1872; *The Possessed*, 1913).

There is another reason Musil's masterpiece should be examined more thoroughly by readers of modern fiction: as a warning to ivory-tower humanists and scholars who think the world will run itself without the intervention of moral people. The novel scathingly condemns the inertia of the European intelligensia, who, by taking a "vacation from life" and choosing to ignore the rise of Fascism as a harmless variation on age-old political campaigns, remained silent in the face of Hitler's advances—until it was too late.

Sources for Further Study

Hickman, Hannah. *Robert Musil and the Culture of Vienna*, 1984.
Luft, David S. *Robert Musil and the Crisis of European Culture, 1880-1942*, 1980.
Morton, Frederic. Review in *Saturday Review*. XXXVII (December 11, 1954), p. 52.
The New Yorker. Review. XXX (December 11, 1954), p. 202.
Peters, Frederick G. *Robert Musil, Master of the Hovering Life: A Study of the Major Fiction*, 1978.
Pike, Burton. *Robert Musil: An Introduction to His Work*, 1961.
Time. Review. LXIV (November 15, 1954), p. 64.

Thomas J. Taylor

A MAN'S BLESSING

Author: Leonardo Sciascia (1921-   )
Type of plot: Detective/sociological realism
Time of plot: From August, 1964, to September, 1965
Locale: A village in western Sicily, near Agrigento
First published: A ciascuno il suo, 1966 (English translation, 1968)

> *Principal characters:*
> PAOLO LAURANA, a professor of Italian and history at the liceo
>   Agrigento
> MANNO, a pharmacist, assassinated while hunting
> ROSCIO, a doctor, killed at the same time as his friend, Manno
> LUISA, Roscio's wife and Rosello's lover
> ROSELLO, a lawyer, a Christian Democratic politician, a
>   cousin of Luisa and also her lover

The Novel

The bodies of Manno and Roscio are found lying in a field, shot to death at close range. The victims had been out hunting that day; their game is now spilled out on the ground. The clues are sparse: Practically none exist save for a Branca cigar stub found near the bodies.

Several days before the murder, Manno had received a threatening letter, pasted together with words from a newspaper. People naturally assume that the crime is one of passion and speculate that Manno either seduced a girl or had an extramarital affair. It is unfortunate that his hunting companion Roscio was also killed; he simply happened to be in the wrong place at the wrong time. The police make a full investigation, gather a list of suspects, and even film everybody that attends the victims' funerals; but ultimately, they give up.

Yet the crime intrigues Paolo Laurana, a high-school teacher, who embarks on his own investigation, fueled by intellectual curiosity. Laurana has little desire to bring the guilty parties to trial, much less denounce them to the police: "Laurana had a kind of obscure pride which made him decisively reject the idea that just punishment should be administered to the guilty one through any intervention of his." Laurana deduces that the printed words pasted on the anonymous letter had been clipped from the Vatican newspaper, *L'osservatore Romano*, and he discovers that only two people in town receive subscriptions to the publication. Both are churchmen: one a dean, the other a rector. Since many others had access to these editions or could have obtained copies elsewhere, however, the clue, although interesting, leads to a dead end.

Hoping to obtain a suggestive reaction, Laurana reveals what he has discovered at an informal gathering at a local men's club that he frequents, but all that his announcement does is to alert the unknown guilty party to Laurana's activities. Laurana continues his investigation. He is convinced that the person who arranged the killing was somebody well-known to one of the victims, because hunters usually keep the place where they are planning to go hunting secret, especially on the opening day of the season. The murderer was therefore a friend, and a nonhunting friend at that.

The next important bit of information comes to Laurana by chance. The following month, he happens to be in Palermo supervising school examinations when he runs into an old school friend, a Communist legislator, who tells him about a visit he received from Roscio several weeks before the murders. Roscio had wanted to find out if the politician would officially denounce, on the floor of the Parliament and in his party's newspapers, a prominent person from his village, one who "made men, unmade them, stole, bribed, swindled." From this conversation, Laurana deduces that the assassination of Manno was merely a smoke screen for the real target. In a subsequent conversation with the rector of the church of Sant'Anna, he discovers that the man who most fits Roscio's description is Rosello, the lawyer. The possibility is confirmed when, again by chance, Laurana runs into Rosello outside the Palace of Justice in the company of a politician and a rather suspicious-looking character who smokes Branca cigars, the brand discovered at the scene of the crime. Laurana investigates the identity of the stranger and finds that he is a professional hit man named Raganà.

Laurana no longer doubts the identity of the guilty man, but he is still unsure of the motive. Most plausibly, it seems that Rosello and his victim's wife are lovers, not merely cousins, and that her husband's death would clear the way for a marriage to reunite the family fortunes. Still, Laurana cannot bring himself to believe that such an attractive woman as Luisa could be part of such a horrendous scheme. With great relief, he welcomes her confidence, which is made in the course of a supposedly chance encounter on the bus going to Agrigento, that she also has suspicions of Rosello and believes that he played a part in killing her husband. Luisa tells Laurana that she wants to meet him secretly to discuss what they should do, and they arrange to meet in Agrigento at the Café Romeris, an out-of-the-way restaurant.

Laurana arrives early, but Roscio's widow never appears. Finally, after more than two hours of fruitless waiting, he leaves in order to catch the last train back to his village. On the way to the station, a car driven by somebody he recognizes from his village offers him a ride. It is a set up, and Laurana is killed. His body is thrown down an abandoned sulfur mine, halfway between the county seat and his town.

After the customary year of mourning, Luisa announces her betrothal to Rosello. The arrangement merely confirms the suspicions of the town about

Rosello's role in the murder. These villagers already knew what Laurana had merely suspected, that Rosello and Luisa had been having an affair and that Roscio had caught them in bed together. In addition, they had been informed that Roscio had threatened to make public incriminating evidence of Rosello's illegal activities. The outraged husband had also delivered an ultimatum that Rosello should leave the village and never return. Laurana's mysterious disappearance did not surprise them either, because he obviously did not know enough to keep silent. He was clearly a fool.

The Characters

Laurana is not the stereotypical detective. Although he shares with his fictional counterparts a talent for organization and persistence, he has taken to sleuthing primarily out of a sense of academic arrogance and a need for diversion. He has lived in his village his entire life, in a house with his mother—an imposing woman who still rules over her offspring—whom he refuses to leave even to move closer to the school where he teaches. Despite being a local, it is clear that he does not know much about the community in which he lives, specifically about the village's power structure or about the personal relations of its inhabitants, common knowledge in a community of that sort.

Although Laurana's prime suspect is someone whom he encounters routinely in his daily life, the detective has to be told about Rosello's activities by a priest. His criminal investigation is a model of the scholarly detachment befitting his occupation, but it lacks comprehension of human nature. It becomes a manifestation of hubris that, as in Greek tragedy, leads to fatal consequences. Laurana is in over his head and completely unable to appreciate the villainy of such a man as Rosello or the languorous amoral complicity of Rosello's mistress, Luisa. This village, after all, is a society in which the women are not actors but do the bidding of men. Laurana's search for truth comes too late to save him or affect the society of which he is a victim.

Rosello is more attuned to reality than is Laurana: The lawyer best epitomizes Sicily's "madmen, its high-noon and nocturnal demons, its oranges and its sulphur and its booted up corpses." He is a person whom others in the village can respect and to whom they can closely relate. He is ruthless, powerful, and active. He serves on the board of directors of an important company; as a legal consultant for yet another; as a corporation president; and as the Christian Democratic representative on the provincial council who was instrumental in torpedoing an alliance with the Fascists and promoting one with the Socialists.

Rosello remains as murky and distant but as ever-present, as the landscape in which he operates and the village over which he holds sway. He is a man of great personal charm and intellect, equally at home with a hired assassin such as Raganà and men of breeding such as that "eternal fountain of culture" the Honorable Abello, who bests Laurana in a bit of literary rep-artee, much to Rosello's amusement.

Rosello is a great dissembler who remains friendly with Roscio even while plotting his murder. His neglect in covering his tracks comes from his confidence that nobody would dare give him away or that if somebody were stupid enough to investigate him, that person could always be eliminated. His is a different kind of willful pride, but one based on reality.

These two central characters—Laurana and Rosello—are different aspects of the Sicilian personality: the timid, intellectual, aloof scholar; the hard, cruel, practical politician. They pose for the others the fundamental question of what a decent man should do in an immoral situation. The answer suggested by the outcome is that people should keep their mouths shut, trust nobody, and have more reverence for killers than for their victims.

Themes and Meanings

Although Leonardo Sciascia's choice of protagonist seems foreign to the genre of detective fiction, his careful attention to setting is not. For example, it would be as difficult to divorce Raymond Chandler's novels from the sleazy mores and glitz of Southern California as it would be to take Scaiscia away from the backwardness and routine squalor of a dried-out Sicilian town, with its obligatory statue of some past dignitary embellishing the main square. In the genre of detective fiction, the hero's ability to abide by a certain personal code of conduct is an element essential to his success; in Sciascia, the characters must abide by the collective rules of society in order to survive at all.

The husband who finds his wife in bed with her cousin violates society's canons in deciding to use outside help to obtain his revenge. Thus, he signs his own death warrant. Roscio should have confronted the interloper and settled the matter man to man: "the highest right and truest justice, if one really cares about it, if one is not prepared to entrust its execution to fate or to God, can come only from the barrels of a gun."

Laurana also pays with his life for his transgressions and deficiencies, especially those involving ignorance about the people with whom he is dealing. Although he is the most decent character in the book, he is judged pitilessly by the others. His disappearance draws no sympathy; he is viewed more as the village idiot than as a victim of barbarity.

Sciascia's commentary on the land of his birth is a picture without either hope or redemption. The author suggests that those who expect Sicily to be otherwise or who anticipate change are as naïve as Laurana. The title of the book reflects this immutability. "One man's trouble is another man's blessing," according to the old saying. Nothing will change, because it is in the interest of a few that it remain the same, even though the beneficiaries are often the least deserving, most disreputable, cruelest members of society.

A murderer is able to get away with his crime because a large part of his society shares his values, or because, as one character says, the whole society is going under and therefore what difference is the fate of the few: "A half-million emigrants, which is to say, almost the entire able-bodied population; an agriculture that is completely abandoned; sulphur mines that are closed; salt mines that are about to close; a petroleum industry that is a joke; regional authorities each more addlepated than the next; a national government that lets us stew in our own juice.... We are drowning, my friend, drowning." The suspicion that the more things change, the more they stay the same becomes in Sciascia even more disquieting, less paradoxical: The more things stay the same, the more things stay the same.

Critical Context

If the greater sin produces a greater redemption, Sciascia seems to be saying that Sicilian society will go no further than the sin. He is not alone in pointing out this aspect of Sicily, which forms the theme of much of the literature to come from that unhappy island.

In his book *Il gattopardo* (1958; *The Leopard*, 1960), Sciascia's fellow countryman Giuseppe Tomasi di Lampedusa has his main character, Don Fabrizio, decline an offer made to him by an official of the new government to become a senator, by explaining that the Sicilian mentality is conditioned by a death wish, that Sicilians never want to improve because "they think themselves perfect," that they want to sleep and will always "hate anyone who tries to wake them, even in order to bring them the most wonderful of gifts."

Sciascia perpetuates this attitude, but in doing so, he has taken the older literary styles and reinterpreted them in a modern idiom. In *A Man's Blessing*, he has presented the sociology of a small Sicilian town in the form of a detective novel, making strong use of the local idiom, underlining the closeness of the society, its superstitions, and the prevalence of the community's fear, solitude, and lack of trust. *A Man's Blessing* avoids the direct mention of poverty and deprivation, unlike *Le parrocchie di Regalpetra* (1956; *Salt in the Wound*, 1969). His characters are well-placed members of society; nevertheless, they are captives of the island's misery and backwardness.

Similarly, the Mafia, although not central to the book's theme, as it is in *Il giorno della civetta* (1961; *Mafia Vendetta*, 1963), is present as a state of mind, a synonym for corruption and indifference, and an example of the dead hand of the past controlling the future. Consequently, one mafioso—Rosello—is sufficient to terrorize an entire town.

Benito Mussolini's prefect, Mori, who waged relentless war against the Mafia during the Fascist period, admitted that with a few battalions of Blackshirts he had driven the Mafia underground, but that this effort was not enough to eradicate its influence: "How can you stamp out what's in a peoples blood?" In trying to explain what is in his people's blood, Sciascia has been considered a spokesman for those who, unlike his characters, do not keep silent when they know the truth.

Sources for Further Study
Cattanei, Luigi. *Leonardo Sciascia*, 1979.
Jackson, Giovanna. *Leonardo Sciascia, 1956-1976: A Thematic and Structural Study*, 1981.
Mauro, Walter. *Sciascia*, 1970.
Mitgang, H. Review in *The New York Times Book Review*. LXX (May 12, 1968), p. 40.
Motta, Antonio. *Leonardo Sciascia: La verità, L'aspra verità*, 1985.

Wm. Laird Kleine-Ahlbrandt

MAN'S HOPE

Author: André Malraux (1901-1976)
Type of plot: Epic
Time of plot: 1936-1937
Locale: Spain
First published: L'Espoir, 1937; revised, 1947 (*Days of Hope*, 1938; better
  known as *Man's Hope*)

> *Principal characters:*
> MANUEL, a Communist soldier in the Spanish Republican
>   army
> MAGNIN, a French aviator, the leader of the Republic's
>   International Squadron
> GARCIA, an officer in Spanish Intelligence
> CAPTAIN HERNANDEZ, who is in charge of the siege at Toledo
> COLONEL XIMENES, the Civil Guard commander in Barcelona
> SCALI, an Italian volunteer in the International Squadron
> NEGUS, a leader of the Anarchists

The Novel

Man's Hope is an epic novel about the Spanish Civil War of 1936-1939.
During this bloody conflict, sometimes regarded as a dress rehearsal for
World War II, the Fascist elements of the Spanish military and the Catholic
church, under the leadership of the Falangist dictator Francisco Franco, were
supported vigorously by Benito Mussolini's Italy and Adolf Hitler's Germany
and overthrew the leftist Republican government of Spain which was supported by the Soviet Union and by individual citizens of the Western European nations.

André Malraux was among many anti-Fascist Europeans who volunteered
to fight for the Republicans, and he played a significant role as an organizer
of the International Squadron of aircraft for the Republic. Malraux's experiences in Spain went into the writing of *Man's Hope*, which contains more
than seventy named characters and provides a panoramic view of the war
from the Republican vantage. Written in the heat of battle and published
while the war was still raging, it depicts the events of 1936-1937 as an adventure of the human spirit within a framework of historical, political, and philosophical ideas.

The novel is divided into three parts, and the first two of these parts are
themselves divided into two sections. The first part is titled "Careless Rapture" and its first section bears the same title. This title keynotes the optimistic and carefree mood of the Republican militia and their international volunteer comrades during the first summer of the Civil War. The action begins in

Madrid on July 18, 1936, and the reader follows the adventures of Manuel, a neophyte Communist, as he participates rather unthinkingly though successfully in the anti-Fascist fighting. This fighting takes place amid fists clenched in the leftist salute and street singing that keynotes the lyric impulse of a folk movement against tyranny.

The scene swiftly shifts from Madrid to Barcelona, where the Anarchists form a surprising coalition with the Civil Guard (commanded by Colonel Ximenes, a devout Christian) to defeat the Falangists. In Barcelona, the singing of Madrid is replaced by the no-less lyrical strains of the factory sirens, symbolic of the workers' power. The further successes of the Republicans are relayed to the reader through Manuel, fighting in the countryside, and through Colonel Magnin (the French volunteer who organizes the Republicans' International Squadron) as he successfully recruits volunteers and leads a raid on Medellín.

Beneath the surface of this uprising, Malraux also strikes a more sober note, pointing to a need for structuring and organizing the elation of a popular movement. There is too much carelessness and waste of life, as shown in Manuel's smoking as he drives a car loaded with explosives, in the unnecessary kamikaze tactics of the Anarchists, in the boyish antics of some of Magnin's airmen, in the insensitivity of a youngster who dips his finger into the blood of an executed Falangist to write Republican slogans on a wall.

This sobriety deepens in the second section of part 1, entitled "Prelude to Apocalypse," which concerns the mismanagement of the emotions of the Republican movement. The illusionary nature of the lyric impulse is primarily shown through the failure of the Republican siege of the Alcazar (castle) of Toledo. Seasonally, summer has changed to autumn, and the dominant atmosphere is no longer that of singing but of funereal flamencos and Wagnerian Valkyrie wailings heard amid the stench of decomposing flesh. The first failure of Magnin's squadron occurs as Jaime Alvear, a most likable member, is blinded during a sortie.

Malraux focuses on Captain Hernandez, who is apparently in charge of the siege of the Alcazar. Hernandez is a former Alcazar cadet and professional soldier who chooses the Republican side because of his ideology, which is rooted in a conviction about individual freedoms. He is unable to organize the besiegers, especially the Anarchists, into a disciplined force, and his characteristic gesture becomes a shrug of the shoulders. When the Falangist relief column approaches the Alcazar, Hernandez's men abandon their posts and retreat hastily to Madrid, but Hernandez, playing the part of a sacrificial victim, fights a gallant delaying action with a few good soldiers and is captured and executed. Hernandez's death underlines the analysis of Spanish Intelligence Officer García (an erstwhile professor of ethnology), who has pronounced that the energies of the people's movement will have to become organized or else die—even though organization is antithetical to the movement's spirit. To Garcia, the party discipline of the Communists seems best suited to achieve that organization. Malraux, however, tempers Garcia's assertions with the viewpoints and examples of Negus, an admirably brave Anarchist leader, and of Colonel Ximenes, the model of an efficient Christian soldier.

The second part of *Man's Hope* is entitled "The Manzanares" (named for the river flowing through Madrid), and its sections are entitled "Action and Reaction" and "Comrades' Blood." "The Manzanares" begins with the rout of the Republicans from Toledo in September, continues with the siege and bombing of the Republicans in Madrid (now a hard-pressed city in flames), and ends in December with the Republican counterattack on Guadarrama. Describing this perilous time for the Republicans, each section of "The Manzanares" contrasts the ethic of intellection against that of action. "Action and Reaction" dramatizes the historical and military action of the siege of Madrid, but in his original French title "Être et Faire," Malraux also counterpoints the intellectual and individualistic urge *to be* and to fulfill an identity (*être*) against an activist's communal need *to make* (*faire*) a society. For this purpose, Malraux embeds in this section a despairing discussion between two intellectuals: Scali, an Italian art scholar who has joined the International Squadron, and Alvear, a Spanish art historian whose son was blinded during a bombing mission.

In the second section, "Comrades' Blood," the Republican plight becomes even grimmer as Madrid is subjected to saturation bombing, and there is hand-to-hand fighting in the West Park and on the University campus. Again, Malraux embeds a contemplative discussion, this time about Miguel de Unamuno y Jugo, a real-life intellectual and writer who dies after being placed under house arrest by General Millan Astray (who is notorious for his slogan of "Death to intelligence! Long live death!"). While these intellectuals either are frozen in despairing inaction (Alvear) or suffer death (Unamuno), however, Malraux shows that those engaged in political action are succeeding. In "Action and Reaction," Manuel becomes a lieutenant colonel as he transforms the rabble retreating from Toledo into troops to defend Madrid. In "Comrades' Blood," he becomes the brigade commander in the successful Republican counterattack at Guadarrama, having learned well from Colonel Ximenes and General Heinrich, a German with the International Brigade. Similarly, Magnin is able to overcome the demoralization and lack of material that had set in at the beginning of "Action and Reaction," and in "Comrades' Blood," his men fly newly assembled planes from the Soviet Union and successfully protect Madrid from bombing by German-made Junkers.

The final part of the novel was originally entitled "The Peasants," but Malraux changed the title to "Hope" in his definitive 1947 revision—probably to underscore its importance for the work as a whole. In the first chapter, Malraux raises the problems of dehumanization, efficiency, and intellectualism in a confrontation between the machine-gun expert Karlitch and the humanist scholar Scali. Karlitch has become progressively more bloodthirsty as the war progresses, even commenting that hanged men do not look right because of the lack of bloodshed. Scali, who has watched this degeneration, is plunged into despair by it. Counterbalancing Scali's gloom is the hope in Jaime Alvear's recovering eyesight as he begins to make out the lights of a merry-go-round. Thus Malraux sets up his rhythm of antithetical oppositions, despair and hope.

The experience of Attignies, a bombardier, adumbrates this rhythm as his plane is shot down and crashes in the sea. The survivors are rescued by the militia and join a group of peasants who make their way through a tunnel. As Attignies passes into the bowels of the earth and reemerges on the other side, he undergoes a symbolic death and resurrection. He is made to feel the mystery of life and a profound fraternity with the peasants for whom he fights.

Magnin experiences the same vision, only more intensely, as he goes to a mountain (in contrast to Attignies' tunnel) to bring down the survivors and the bodies from one of his planes. Among the crew is Scali, whose foot has been destroyed. As the cortege of wounded and dead are borne down the mountain, Scali sees Spain as a region dominated by death and symbolized by the twisted machine gun that he sees lying on top of a coffin. Magnin, however, catches sight of an apple tree surrounded by a ring of dead fruit; as he looks, Magnin realizes that the decomposing fruit also contain seeds that will regenerate life. Magnin's consciousness is thus filled with this circular, cyclical symbol, a vision of regeneration and hope. When he looks at the same twisted machine gun, Magnin's imagination sees it metaphorically as a living tree branch.

A similar and possibly more complex epiphany is experienced by Manuel. In the course of the novel, Manuel has become a more disciplined person, an efficient soldier, and an astonishingly effective leader of men. He has not achieved this maturity without paying a price. At the beginning of the novel, Manuel is a carefree cinema sound technician whose greatest love is music. After the Republican victory at Guadalajara against forty thousand Italian troops, followed by a similar success at Brihuega, Manuel enters a church and plays a *Kyrie* composed by Giovanni Pierluigi da Palestrina for Ximenes. As Manuel plays, he is suddenly desolated by the feeling that music belongs to another existence from which he is now excluded by his combat career. Ximenes predicts that the young man will be a general before he reaches the age of thirty-five.

In the final chapter of the novel, however, Manuel happens to hear, amid the sounds of the spring thaw, a militiaman picking out a tune on an abandoned piano. Manuel returns to his quarters and listens to Beethoven records, finding that his old love for music has not deserted him. On the contrary, he discovers that this music enables him to recover and resurrect his past self, a self which he had thought was dead. The undulations of the musical phrases tell him that life is not a state but a flux. The state of war and warrior is not permanent but only a phase in life's rhythm of change; the rhythm itself is what is permanent. As he looks out onto the fields of Spain, where Christians and Moors once fought on ground now trod by a new generation of losers and victors, Manuel discovers that the tramp of the men and murmur of the streams are as profound and as permanent as the beat of the human heart.

The Characters

Although there are dozens of characters in this epic novel, Manuel may be seen as its protagonist. In fact, the book could be read as Manuel's *Bildungsroman*, showing his transformation from a rather irresponsible and playboyish sound technician into a lieutenant colonel in nine months' time. In Manuel, the reader watches an individual's love of adventure deepen into an appreciation of fraternity in communal risk-taking and turn into a realization that structure and organization are essential for military and political victory. Malraux also uses Manuel's development to illustrate the potential loss of humanistic values that may accompany the gain in ability to act efficiently. Manuel himself is acutely aware of this problem. He himself overcomes the virtuous scruples of a woman whom he has loved for several years and efficiently seduces her, but finds that he can no longer feel for her. Again, after he court-martials some deserters and sends them to a firing squad, Manuel loses his voice. Thus Malraux explores some excruciating problems attendant upon the evolution of a character from carefree artist to efficient military commander.

Magnin, too, is a prominent character, present in many scenes of the book. Superficially, he could be thought of as a projection of Malraux himself. Nevertheless, although intelligent and aware, Magnin is not so deeply troubled as are Manuel and several of the other characters. Magnin is generally cheerful, practical, and an effective leader, and his vision of the life-renewing apple tree is a symbol central to the novel.

Several other characters, perhaps representing aspects of Malraux's own thinking, may be pointed out for special note. Negus, the leader of the Anarchists, revels in the early days of the popular uprising, seeing it as the apocalypse of romantic, individual action; as the war wears on, however, he realizes that Anarchism must increasingly give way to the better organized, if soulless, ethic of Communism. Garcia, the ethnology professor turned Intelligence officer, is an intellectual and landowner who commands the love and respect of peasants and soldiers alike. Observant, intelligent, and understanding, he is a clarifying element in the ideological debates that intersperse this book. He often formulates intellectual positions lucidly, summing up an argument memorably. While Garcia and Magnin are examples of intelligence that can be transformed into action, other intellectuals, such as Scali and Alvear, are examples of intelligence that ends in paralysis. Both these latter men are humanists by calling, men of good will, and the brutality of war fills them with despair and a vision of the futility of the human endeavor.

Themes and Meanings

One main theme of the novel concerns the nature of a revolution or popular uprising. As Malraux sees it, a revolution comes into being under the impetus of a lyric burst of feeling, the best of which is found in freedom and fraternity. At this stage, Anarchism sorts well with a revolution. For a revolution to be sustained, however, these feelings have to be disciplined and organized; hence the need for a political machinery such as that of the Communist Party (which will, ironically, destroy the lyric impulses of revolution).

On a political level, then, *Man's Hope* dramatizes the self-defining process of a revolution. As it does so, Malraux also explores the meaning of being human. When humanist intellectuals such as Scali are confronted with the brutalities of war and carefree individuals such as Manuel evolve into effective military leaders, they have to come to terms with the meaning of humanity—their own as well as others'. By means of the symbolic epiphanies of Attignies' death-birth passage through a tunnel, of Magnin's decomposition-regeneration vision of the apple tree, and of Manuel's loss-recovery of self through music, Malraux resolves the problematics of these themes in an assurance of hope in the endurance of fundamental humanity.

Critical Context

Man's Hope has had a mixed reception. Some readers have found it to be too journalistic, diffuse, and even propagandistic—a disappointment after Malraux's earlier success in *La Condition humaine* (1933; *Man's Fate*, 1934). Malraux thought of *Man's Hope* as his highest achievement, however, and later critical opinion came around to this view, praising *Man's Hope* for its masterly blend of emotion and intellect, its treatment of individualized characters in a mass movement, its penetration into the problematics of Communism and existentialism, its profound use of authentic detail and meaningful metaphor.

Because of its historical background, *Man's Hope* can be usefully compared to other well-known books about the Spanish Civil War: Ernest Hemingway's *For Whom the Bell Tolls* (1940) and George Orwell's *Homage to Catalonia* (1938). Interesting comparisons can also be made between *Man's Hope* and the 1947 film of the same title that Malraux made from it, which is also known as *Sierra de Teruel*.

Sources for Further Study

Boak, Denis. *André Malraux*, 1968.

Chua, Cheng Lok. "Nature and Art in the Aesthetics of Malraux's *L'Espoir*," in *Symposium*. XXVI (1972), pp. 114-127.

Frohock, Wilbur Merrill. *André Malraux and the Tragic Imagination*, 1952.

Horvath, Violet. *André Malraux: The Human Adventure*, 1969.

Thompson, Brian, and Carl Viggiani, eds. *Witnessing André Malraux: Visions and Re-visions*, 1984.

C. L. Chua

MARBOT
A Biography

Author: Wolfgang Hildesheimer (1916-   )
Type of plot: Historical realism
Time of plot: 1801-1830
Locale: England, Germany, Switzerland, France, and Italy
First published: Marbot: Eine Biographie, 1981 (English translation, 1983)

>*Principal characters:*
>   SIR ANDREW MARBOT, an aesthete and an art theorist
>   LADY CATHERINE, his mother
>   FATHER GERARD VAN ROSSUM, his German-speaking tutor

The Novel

Marbot opens with Sir Andrew Marbot, age twenty-four and on his second Grand Tour of the Continent, conversing in flawless German with Johann Wolfgang von Goethe. Not awed in the least by the elderly German poet, Andrew had made it his life's work to conduct research into the inner lives of gifted artists and writers. He had spent the first nineteen years of his life on his family's estates in the north of England, where he came to hate his father and love his mother with a passion that was later to become incestuous. A melancholic and pessimist, Marbot saw art as the only creative response to the otherwise senselessness of life. As much as he longed to be an artist, Marbot apparently had no artistic talent and remained a critical observer of painting, past and present, until his suicide in Italy in 1830.

Marbot acquired his aesthetic interests from his maternal grandfather, Lord Claverton, a foreign diplomat who retired in 1797 to his estate, Redmond Manor, seventy miles from Marbot Hall. Catherine, Lord Claverton's only child, was born in 1781, grew up in Italy, was converted with her parents to Catholicism in Rome in 1790, and was married to Sir Francis Marbot in 1799. Sir Francis, unlike his cosmopolitan and cultivated wife, was not intellectual and devoted himself instead to hunting, fishing, raising cattle, and looking after his holdings. The three months each summer that Lady Catherine would spend at Redmond Manor with her children (Andrew and his younger brother and sister, Matthew and Jane) but without her husband gave Andrew ample opportunity to acquaint himself with Lord Claverton's collection of Venetian masters. Writers and artists were frequent guests at Redmond Manor, as was Father Gerard van Rossum, a Dutch priest who converted the Clavertons. He joined them in England and became the Marbot family chaplain and the children's tutor. Father van Rossum, fluent in German and Italian and well-versed in literature, art, theology, and philosophy, was the boy's only teacher and a very liberal and tolerant one.

Among his grandfather's paintings, Tintoretto's *Origin of the Milky Way* was particularly mysterious to the young Andrew. In it, Hercules sucks so strongly from Juno's breast that a stream of milk shoots into the heavens, thereby creating the Milky Way. The five-year-old child asked his mother to explain the painting and, especially, to show him the parts of her body that corresponded to those of the naked Juno. She refused, but she held him in her arms in such a way that he might feel "this mysterious territory" with his body. In one of the first of the entries that became his secret diary, Marbot notes that this experience was his earliest, and most wonderful, conscious memory.

Marbot left on his first Grand Tour of the Continent in the spring of 1820, when he was nineteen. His mother accompanied him to London, where both stayed in her parents' townhouse. It was here, shortly before his departure for the Continent, that the consummation of their forbidden love took place. This "unnameable deed" would shape Marbot's emotional and intellectual development: "[W]ithout giving him a lasting and universal vision, it nonetheless [made] him look in all his future encounters for hidden or suppressed forces beneath the surface." During his stay in London, he began to record these investigations into the deeper truths in art and the artists themselves in three leather-bound quarto volumes that he had made. His notes and observations, compiled by Father van Rossum under the assumed name of Gerald Ross, would eventually be published posthumously in England in 1834 under the title *Art and Life*. Father van Rossum, under the assumed name of Gerald Ross, was the compiler and editor. Marbot's first Grand Tour, now in part an exercise in renunciation for both him and his mother, lasted two years. He traveled simply and lightly, first to Paris for several months, then on to Padua, Venice, Pisa, Siena, Urbino, and finally Florence. In August, 1822, he arrived in Florence, where he learned of his father's death in the autumn.

Between the winter of 1822 and the spring of 1825, Marbot and Lady Catherine pursued their love without interruption, hindered only by the threat of discovery. Before their final separation, which had been planned all along, the lovers paid a final visit to Redmond Hall. In May, Marbot left for London, where he renounced his claim to both family estates. Lady Catherine returned to Marbot Hall in the fall and confessed the illicit affair to Father van Rossum, who with superhuman grace would remain her friend and supporter until her death in 1832. Before Marbot's departure to Hamburg on June 23, he vigorously resumed his intellectual pursuits as compensation for the loss of his beloved.

Marbot spent the summer and fall in Germany and Switzerland. In Weimar, not only did he converse with Goethe, but he also had a brief affair with Goethe's daughter-in-law, Ottilie, the first of three liaisons that he would have in the next five years. At some point during the fall, Marbot received a letter from Lady Catherine in which she told of her confession and Father van Rossum's stern compassion. In October in Splügen, Switzerland, Marbot became very ill, probably with pneumonia, and was unable to cross the Splügen Pass into Italy until mid-November. Crossing the pass during a wild snowstorm seemed to him a purifying experience, "both link and dividing line between two sections of his life." He would spend almost all of his remaining years in Italy, engrossed in his observation and criticism of art.

Marbot settled in Urbino, which provided for him sufficient cultural atmosphere and "a retreat from the world." He rented a large house from a wealthy widower, Anna Maria Baiardi. It was she who was primarily responsible for keeping the memory of Marbot alive, for after his death, she sent all of his notes, letters, and papers to Lady Catherine, who in turn, after editing out intimacies, passed them on to Father van Rossum. In April of 1826, Marbot visited Rome for the first time and stayed on until November. There he had his second affair, with Teresa Guiccioli, a flamboyant woman with a penchant for Englishmen. Back in Urbino, he found the "calm and equilibrium" needed for his studies and fell in love with Anna Maria. He traveled only twice more, to Paris for two months in the fall of 1827 and to Rome in December, 1828, to visit the poet Giacomo Leopardi.

In his own house he was an affable host who welcomed guests and enjoyed the respect of the townspeople. Convinced of the futility of his research and lacking the artist's creative solutions to life, he chose his "free death" (he abhorred the word suicide) in February, 1830, at a time "when he considered that the register of his receptivity and potentialities was exhausted and foresaw a future full of necessary repetition." With the mystery of artistic inspiration still unsolved, his notebooks end with the question: "The artist plays on our soul, but who plays on the soul of the artist?"

The Characters

Sir Andrew Marbot never lived. The massive scholarly documentation—quotations, footnotes, index, interpretive digressions, refutation of Marbot's previous biographer, announcement of a new critical edition of Marbot's notes and letters—is merely the playful structure of what Wolfgang Hildesheimer called a "perfect biography," that of a purely artificial figure. *Marbot* is the fictional counterpart of Hildesheimer's *Mozart* (1977; English translation, 1982)—the similarity of the names is an indication of the mirror-like nature of the two projects—whose four essays deny any possibility of an understanding of the nature of Wolfgang Amadeus Mozart's genius. Other than establishing dates and facts, the biographer of a real person, Hildesheimer claims, can only speculate on the connections between his subject's life and work. In the extreme case of Wolfgang Amadeus Mozart, there is an unknowable chasm between his stormy life and his sublime music.

In Marbot's case, the biographer has no such scruples. Marbot's own investigations into the souls of artists have but a single motivation: They are the sublimation of his sexual desire for his mother. Indeed, Marbot's biographer so overinterprets his character that Marbot is reduced to little more than the Oedipal pawn of his creator, a schematic vehicle for numerous encounters with famous painters and writers of the time. Marbot's biographer condemns "those terrible simplifiers, who draw lopsided and therefore false pictures" of their biographical heroes by repressing their scandalous secret practices or who, he adds with a note of unself-conscious irony, "take care that they are perpetuated in intensified form." Marbot's incestuous relationship with his mother dominates the biography to such a degree that it undermines the biographer's psychoanalytic explanations and shifts attention away from Marbot's life to what is the ultimate focus of the author's interest: Marbot's writings.

These writings reveal a man who exhibited great self-control and yet had "something of the darkness of the fallen angel" in him. Outwardly reserved, taciturn, independent, dignified, and unobtrusive, Marbot betrayed a violent "urge to create everything afresh." His greatest misfortune was that he was not able to turn his inner turmoil into creative activity, and yet, the biographer artfully notes, "In contrast to so many bunglers at failure, Marbot had mastered his." He had natural insight into people and was an astute critic of contemporary art. His self-imposed roles of outsider and nonconformist allowed him the distance to take unfashionable stands within the aristocratic world of taste and privilege into which he was born. In literature, he preferred the melancholy negations of life in William Shakespeare's tragedies to the poetry of the English Romantics, most of whom he met. In painting, he sought out those works which displayed the greatest degree of subjective truth, that is, in which the image of the artist's inner self was embedded most strongly.

Although, like her son, Lady Catherine was susceptible to the "charms of the forbidden," she was a devoutly religious woman who suffered far more than he for their illicit relationship. Her overpowering sense of guilt and sinfulness persisted until her confession to Father van Rossum, after which, without her son and increasingly isolated from the outside world, she languished at Marbot Hall until her early death of a broken heart two years after Marbot's death. Father van Rossum remained her faithful friend to the end despite the heavy burden that he was forced to share with her. Liberal and compassionate, he forgave Marbot his shortcomings and agnosticism and continued to correspond with him up until his death. As editor of Marbot's papers, he was scrupulously thorough in assembling the materials at his disposal despite the fact that he was no match for their intellectual content.

Themes and Meanings

Besides providing a scholarly tour of the cultural circles of late Romanticism, *Marbot* is an ingeniously constructed expression of Hildesheimer's own notions of art and artistic productivity. An artist as well as a writer and a former resident of Marbot's chosen home of Urbino, Italy, Hildesheimer clearly shares much of his subject's vision of life and art; yet, at the same time, he distances himself from Marbot's excesses through the novel's multiple ironic refractions. The biographer's stuffy pedantry, the elaborate pretense of biographical truth, and the flat, psychological representation of Marbot's life prevent any simple identification of Hildesheimer with his alter ego. Nevertheless, Marbot's unsystematic notes, deftly interwoven throughout the narrative, complement perfectly Hildesheimer's own loose, aphoristic style.

Marbot's keen observations of specific artworks (Antoine Watteau's *Gilles*, Giotto di Bondone's frescoes in Padua, Sandro Botticelli's *Primavera*, Jan van Eyck's *The Anolfini Marriage*, Giorgione's *Self-Portrait*, and Eugene Delacroix's *Death of Sardanapalus*) are, in Hildesheimer's opinion, more important than Marbot's prophetic anticipation of Sigmund Freud's psychoanalytical theories of art. What is unique to Marbot's theories is the weight he gives to the subjective truth of the work of art, that is, the truth of the artist and not of the subject matter. Marbot defended William Turner, whose work he greatly admired, by stating, "The true artist does not portray nature but his own image of her essence: not nature itself, but his own nature." He reserved his sharpest criticism for allegorical and narrative art, which merely reproduced reality without inventing or creating it anew. His modernist, anti-Romantic bent is revealed in his preference for what he termed "reflective painting," which "discloses the depths of the inner life of its subject," as opposed to "descriptive painting," which reinterprets old myths and stories. The former is primarily visual, spiritual, and pictorial, the latter, intellectual, derivative, and representational. After Turner's visit to Urbino in January, 1829, Marbot noted that the English artist was "on the way to dissolving the concrete objectivity of Nature into forms of manifestation. Gradually all firm outlines vanish, becoming atmosphere, air, mist, he is no longing painting creation, he is himself creating." Condemned merely to be objective, describe, and reproduce, Marbot scribbled in the margin: "Happy is he who lives in his objects and thus becomes his object."

Critical Context

In 1983, two years after the publication of *Marbot*, Hildesheimer announced that he was giving up literature in order to devote himself fully to his painting. Already in 1975, in an essay titled "The End of Fiction," he had expressed his doubts about the ability of the writer of fiction to deal with contemporary reality, a reality over which people had no control and which threatened them with extinction. His two "biographies," *Mozart* and *Marbot*, both escapes into history and historiography, postponed Hildesheimer's inevitable turning away from a successful career as a writer of satires, comedies, radio plays, and novels. His first collection of stories, *Lieblose Legenden*

(1952; loveless legends) contains playful, ironic, parodic, absurd, or grotesque satires on postwar German culture. In one of them, a writer and critic named Gottfried Theodor Pilz (1789-1856), who successfully fought against the cultural overzealousness of his age by persuading artists and musicians to curtail their production, is a cheerfully portrayed predecessor of Andrew Marbot. In both works, history and fiction are intricately intermingled, yet Hildesheimer identifies far more closely with the struggles of the protagonist of the later work. Hildesheimer's other major novels, *Tynset* (1965) and *Masante* (1973), are lengthy monologues of melancholic narrators who have withdrawn from the world in order to contemplate in endless variations the absurdity of their failed lives.

Marbot is an intriguing yet flawed work that can be best read and appreciated in conjunction with the critically acclaimed *Mozart*. Its brilliant forgery of documents and pretensions to authenticity are unique among the numerous German biographical novels. The fact that Hildesheimer himself was wrestling with many of his hero's questions and yet sought an answer not in suicide but in a renunciation of fiction and a renewed commitment to art lends the novel a curiously ironic fascination.

Sources for Further Study
Art in America. Review. LXXII (February, 1984), p. 21.
Weisstein, Ulrich. "Wolfgang Hildesheimer's *Marbot*: Fictional Biography and Treatise on Comparative Literature," in *Yearbook of Comparative and General Literature*. XXXII (1983), pp. 23-38.
World Literature Today. Review. LVI (Autumn, 1982), p. 676.

Peter West Nutting

MARKS OF IDENTITY, COUNT JULIAN, and JUAN THE LANDLESS

Author: Juan Goytisolo (1931-   )
Type of plot: Psychological realism
Time of plot: 1963 to 1975
Locale: Spain, France, and Morocco
First published: Señas de identidad, 1966 (*Marks of Identity,* 1969);
Reinvindicación del conde Don Julián, 1970 (*Count Julian,* 1974); *Juan sin tierra,* 1975 (*Juan the Landless,* 1977)

> *Principal characters:*
> ALVARO MENDIOLA, the narrator and central character
> ALVARO PERANZULES (THE GREAT FIGUREHEAD, alias SENECA),
>   the leader of the Spanish people
> TARIQ, the Arab invader of the Spanish Peninsula
> JULIAN, the Spanish traitor who collaborates with Tariq in the
>   Arab invasion
> FATHER FOUCAULD, the priest who promulgates a message of
>   hedonism
> FATHER VOSK, the priest who preaches the virtues of
>   asceticism

The Novels

These three novels are frequently referred to as Juan Goytisolo's Exile Trilogy, because of their thematic unity and the numerous references within the text of each novel to the fictional reality of the others. The novels portray three stages in Alvaro Mendiola's search for his "marks of identity"—the significant characteristics of his existence, identified in *Juan the Landless* as "race, profession, class, family, homeland."

Marks of Identity begins in 1963, as Alvaro returns to Barcelona from his exile in France to search for an understanding of his experience at the university in the 1950's. Renewing his friendship with his fellow students and with Dolores, his former lover, Alvaro examines the relics of his past—family photograph albums, police reports on his underground political activities, places that he frequented during his student days. As he engages in lengthy conversations with his friends, Alvaro remembers and narrates episodes from his youth in Barcelona. At every point, the memories and the present experiences are narrated against the background of the repressive Spanish society of 1963. In the last scene of the novel, as Alvaro prepares to return to his exile in France, he goes to the Castle of Montjuich to look out over the city in which he spent his youth. In the presence of the tourists and the surveillance of the police, he experiences an overwhelming feeling of despair and disillusionment.

Count Julian is the narrative of a typical day in the life of Alvaro Mendiola, who now lives in exile in Tangiers. He gets up in the morning and looks out his window across the straits at his homeland. He sweeps up the dead bugs in his kitchen, takes them to the library, and crushes them between the pages of the volumes of Spanish literary masterpieces, obliterating the sacred words of his cultural heritage. Alvaro then spends the day first in the company of Tariq, the Arab, who takes him to an opium den, and then with the Great Figurehead, Alvaro Peranzules, alias Seneca. The narrator relates a series of hallucinatory scenes which detail a fantasized destruction of traditional Western morals. A tourist, whom the narrator calls the D. A. R. lady, is bitten by a snake charmer's serpent. As she lies writhing on the ground, bloated by the poison, the Arabs who witness the scene pull up her dress and urinate on her body. The narrator recalls his experience as a child in the biology laboratory with insects that inject poison into one another, then imagines contaminating the blood supply of Spain by donating his own blood after suffering an attack by a rabid dog.

The Great Figurehead extols the virtues of the asceticism of his namesake, the Stoic philosopher Seneca, then takes Alvaro to meet his mother, the devout Queen Isabel *la Católica*. Isabel takes Alvaro aside and performs a lewd striptease, while the Great Figurehead, attacked by flying insects after delivering a speech on the beauties of the Spanish literary tradition, dies trying, in vain, to pronounce an obscene word. His funeral cortege is led by a young man with a cross, who is transformed into Julian, the traitor, as the procession becomes an unbridled orgy from which the Hispanic populace flees in terror, pursued by the licentious African invaders.

The Great Figurehead is transformed into a bullfighter, who is run through by the horns of Tariq, the Arab bull, and then into a child, Little Red Riding Hood. His grandmother, Julian, turns him over to Tariq, who rapes him with his enormous serpent. The narrative of *Count Julian* ends at sunset, once again in the room of the narrator Alvaro Mendiola, who looks across the straits at his mother country and vows that tomorrow the invasion will begin again.

The text of *Juan the Landless* begins, still in Morocco, with an examination of photographs that evoke the origin of the narrator, Alvaro Mendiola, a white child born of the sexual union between a black slave woman and Changó, the enormous gorilla-god of the slaves of Cuba. The narrative continues as a contemplation of the significance of the Spanish experience, developed through a series of metaphorical scenes. The child Alvaro sits on the toilet while the forces of evil encourage him to defecate and the forces of good urge him to emit only sweet perfume. The black Cuban slaves and the Arabs relieve their bowels in open sewer ditches while Western society first invents the chamberpot, then develops the flush toilet, and finally evolves to the point of not having to expel their body waste at all. The slaves rebel by practicing witchcraft, which makes the whites sweat and smell and menstruate and defecate in the presence of the blacks.

The narrator becomes an Arab watching a perfect Spanish husband and wife copulating in a store window. Then he is King Kong, whose enormous penis intimidates the poorly endowed Spanish bridegrooms and disillusions their innocent brides. The narrator moves the scene to France for a consideration of the role of the Arabs in the 1968 revolution and then passes throughout the Arab world portraying the gradual domination of Western society by the licentiousness of Arab culture.

A dissertation on the ascetic ideals of Spanish culture is transformed into a scene in which the *auto-da-fé* becomes a spectacle staged for tourists. The king and queen of Spain deliver a speech, pointing out with great pride that they do not defecate. Father Vosk preaches a sermon on the path to perfection, which is a process of becoming immune to the need to empty the bowels. That is followed by a passage which proclaims the virtues of elimination of body wastes and the democratization of all people through the removal of all restrictions on defecation, through a worship of the eye of the Devil—the anus—and through a glorification of the enormous penis of King Kong.

Father Vosk berates the narrator for his departure from the realistic tradition and laments the destruction of modern literature by the invasion of the alienated novel. The novel ends with a discussion of literature and textuality, in which the narrator describes the development of the plotless discourse that becomes a text operating as an autonomous object. In the final pages of the novel, the language breaks down into an incoherent series of words, then a jumble of letters, a passage in transliterated Arabic, and finally, several lines of Arabic script.

The Characters

Only in *Marks of Identity* is it appropriate to speak of characters in the traditional fictional sense. In this first novel of the trilogy, the characterization of Alvaro Mendiola is developed through an approach that is primarily sociohistorical. His discontent and despair are identified as grounded in his early childhood experiences and in the facts of the cultural and historical milieu of mid-century Spain. This interpretation of Alvaro's identity is clear in the first scene of the novel, in which he searches for the roots of his rebellion against his marks of identity in the photographs that he finds in his family album. He was born of parents whose grandparents owned a sugar plantation in Cuba worked by hundreds of black slaves, and his most vivid image of childhood is the strict prohibition against any kind of erotic expression. Thus, the conflict of the cultural stereotype of the African as the incarnation of sexual freedom and the restraints on sexual expression in Western society, reflected in Alvaro Mendiola's political activities and in his reactions to his homeland when he returns in 1963, become the central motifs of the Exile Trilogy.

The other characters in *Marks of Identity*, the university friends of Alvaro, serve primarily as stimuli to the memory process, evoking narratives of Alvaro's life in Barcelona during the time he was a student. Not until the second novel, *Count Julian*, do the secondary characters gain significance. Their elaboration is grounded in the conflict of Senecan stoicism and African hedonism that is first suggested in *Marks of Identity*.

The secondary characters are either metaphorical portrayals of actual persons of historical significance or personified myths of the Spanish cultural tradition. The Great Figurehead, Alvaro Peranzules, whom the narrator presents at times as the perfect boy child and at times as the revered leader of the country, is a fictionalization of the Fascist Generalissimo Francisco Franco. Julian and Tariq are elaborations of the myth of the Spanish traitor and his Arab coconspirator who opened the doors of the Iberian Peninsula to the Arab invaders to avenge the rape of Julian's daughter by the Spanish king.

The characters appear again in *Juan the Landless*, along with others that function as metaphorical representations of the conflict of Western asceticism and African hedonism. The great gorilla-god of the black Cuban slaves, Changó, who also appears in the form of King Kong and as a personified, phallic mosque turret in Ghardaia, is the incarnation of the myth of the enormous African penis. Father Foucauld, obsessed with unbridled, hedonistic carnality, is the counterpoint of Father Vosk, who proclaims the gospel of perfection of the flesh, of evolving to a purer state of righteousness characterized by the absence of the need to defecate.

Throughout the narrative, the identity of Alvaro Mendiola merges at times with the identity of each of these symbolic characters. Alvaro becomes the Great Figurehead, or Tariq, or Julian, thus acknowledging the historical and cultural origins of his marks of identity, as he moves in and out of his fantasies and hallucinations. Because the characters other than Alvaro Mendiola are employed, in *Marks of Identity*, primarily as means of stimulating the narrator's memory, and in the two later novels, primarily as fantastic, irrational inventions, the narrative is dominated by the presence of one consciousness, that of Alvaro Mendiola, the narrator and creator of the perverted, obscene vision of contemporary Spanish reality.

Themes and Meanings

The most remarkable aspect of Goytisolo's Exile Trilogy is the disparity between the more traditional narrative approach of the first novel and the chaotic stylistic features of *Count Julian* and *Juan the Landless*. The narrator of *Marks of Identity* makes use of the diverse points of view and narrative devices typical of European and Latin American fiction of the 1960's. The two later novels, however, are much more unusual and innovative in their approach to the fictional representation of the narrator's experience. *Count Julian* is narrated entirely from what may be called a second-person perspective. The narrator, who is also the central character, refers to himself as "you"—you get up in the morning, you sweep up the bugs, you go out on the street.

Alvaro Mendiola maintains this point of view in *Juan the Landless*, but in this last novel, he shifts from an implied telling of the experience to a clear portrayal of writing the narrative. This is an important distinction, for novelistic fiction has traditionally been characterized by an illusion that it is not written text. The traditional realistic novel, for example, attempts to create an impression of verisimilitude, employing various techniques calculated to make the text transparent and provide direct access, in an objective manner, to a sociohistorical reality. Novels which do not follow this approach are usually characterized as experimental, for they do not do what the novel has always done.

Count Julian is experimental primarily because it calls attention to itself as a linguistic artifact, and in doing this establishes itself as an intermediary between the reader and the fictional experience. Goytisolo uses semicolons in the place of periods, visual-linguistic signals such as dollar signs in the place of the word "dollar," and irregular line lengths on the page that interrupt the flow of the text and require the reader to pay attention to the linguistic act of reading. In *Juan the Landless*, the narrator further exploits the concept of the text as a written linguistic act as he analyzes the process of putting the words on the paper.

There is a very clear development of narrative perspective in the trilogy, a development that gradually intensifies the interpretation of the text as language that exists for its own sake. This linguistic theme is directly related to the conflict between hedonism and asceticism through the metaphorical representation of writing as masturbation. The pen is the penis, and the ink is the seminal fluid flowing on the page, the product of a nonprocreative, sterile exercise of purely solipsistic self-indulgence with no redeeming social value. Writing fiction, then, has the same potential as masturbation, the flaunting of every restrictive Western taboo, the destruction of all traditional moral values, the exercise of one's individual freedom despite all attempts to suppress the will to self-expression.

Critical Context

Goytisolo's early novels, *Juego de manos* (1954; *The Young Assassins*, 1959), *Duelo en el paraíso* (1955; *Children of Chaos*, 1958), and *Fiestas* (1958; English translation, 1960), attacked the repression and psychological deprivation of Franco's Spain in a conventional narrative style typical of social realism. The publication of *Marks of Identity* represents a significant shift in the development of Goytisolo's fiction. His disillusionment with the possibilities of traditional fiction, and with the values and mores of Western society, becomes evident in the first novel of the Exile Trilogy and then more pronounced in *Count Julian* and *Juan the Landless*. His disenchantment with the repressive society created by the regime of Franco, his pessimism, and his experimentation with narrative form are not unique for his time. They are also evident in the work of other Spanish novelists of the postwar period, such as Carmen Laforet, Luis Martín-Santos, Juan Marsé, and, most of all, Juan Benet. Goytisolo's view of the corrupted, obscenely degenerate nature of Western society, however, is the most disturbing. It is a nihilistic vision that offers no hope for redemption within the boundaries of Western concepts of morality.

The novelist's emphasis on the analysis of the role of language is one of the significant aspects of the trilogy, for it makes coherent the maze of obscene, perverted portrayals of a wide range of cultural and historical signs. Goytisolo is destroying an intricate complex of myths associated with Western culture and Hispanic tradition, myths that are entrenched in and inseparable from the language that has conveyed them and kept them entrenched in the European experience for centuries. The "marks of identity" of Alvaro Mendiola—his race, profession, class, family, and homeland—can be conceptualized only in terms of language. The destruction of those marks is possible only through the annihilation of language itself.

The theme of the trilogy, then, is closely linked with the cultural context in which it was created. The destruction of the myths of Western society and, more specifically, of Spanish society is effected through the destruction of the language that embodies them. The trilogy presents the process of annihilation through an innovative historical metaphor—the Arab invasion of Spain, reenacted in its most terrible form, as the subjugation of the sexually repressed Spanish society to the violent, licentious carnality of the Arab world. The perverted fantasies of the narrator in *Count Julian* and *Juan the Landless* become a demythologizing of Hispanic culture. The traditional Spanish themes of purity of the blood and of the spirit are contaminated by visions of penis worship, anal intercourse, sodomy, defecation, vaginal fixations, masturbation, and by the prevailing theme of the pollution of Spanish blood with the poisonous semen of the African.

Sources for Further Study
Fuentes, Carlos. Preface to *Count Julian*, 1974.
Schwartz, Kessel. "Juan Goytisolo's Non-fiction Views on *La España sagrada*," in *Revista de estudios hispánicos*. XVI (October, 1982), pp. 323-332.
Spires, Robert C. "From Neorealism and the New Novel to the Self-referen-

tial Novel: Juan Goytisolo's *Juan sin tierra*," in *Anales de la Narrativa Española Contemporánea*. V (1980), pp. 73-82.

Ugarte, Michael. *Trilogy of Treason: An Intertextual Study of Juan Goytisolo*, 1982.

Gilbert Smith

MARY

Author: Vladimir Nabokov (1899-1977)
Type of plot: Ironic romance
Time of plot: 1924
Locale: Berlin
First published: Mashenka, 1926 (English translation, 1970)

> *Principal characters:*
> LEV GLEBOVICH GANIN (an alias), a twenty-four-year-old
> Russian émigré, who is planning to leave Berlin
> ALEXSEY IVANOVICH ALFYOROV, another fugitive from
> Communist Russia, living in the same pension as Ganin
> and expecting his wife to arrive from Russia
> ANTON SERGEYEVICH PODTYAGIN, an elderly Russian poet,
> trying to get to Paris
> KLARA, a twenty-six-year-old Russian woman, working as a
> typist, who is attracted to Ganin and is a friend of Ganin's
> mistress

The Novel

Ganin, stuck in a dark elevator with Alfyorov, a boring, well-meaning fellow refugee, learns that Alfyorov's wife, from whom he has been separated for some time, has finally managed to leave Russia and will be arriving in a few days. Ganin, who is thinking of leaving Berlin on the day of her arrival, is uninterested and is more concerned about how he can tell his mistress that he is no longer in love with her and is leaving the city, by himself.

The pension is occupied by a small group of Russian refugees of various occupations. Ganin, gloomily preoccupied by his problems, listens while Alfyorov chatters on about his wife at the communal lunch. Podtyagin, who wants to go to Paris, is cheered that the French have sent him an exit visa, but he complains that the German officials are making things difficult for him. Alfyorov sees the confusion as an example of German efficiency, as opposed to the inefficiency of Russia. Only Russian women are exempt from his scorn, and he suggests that Podtyagin write a poem praising them. Ganin, disgusted and unhappy, goes to his room and thinks of how briefly his love for Lyudmila Rubanski has lasted and of what a nuisance she has become for him.

At the cinema that night with Lyudmila and Klara, Ganin is depressed further by seeing himself as an extra in a film (he makes occasional money by acting in crowd scenes); he regards his image on the screen as a symbol of the transitory nature of human life. Later that night he learns that Alfyorov's wife is, in fact, the first love of his life, but he says nothing to Alfyorov, who is offended by Ganin's suddenly leaving the room after being shown a picture of her.

Upset by this revelation, Ganin wanders the streets through the night. The next morning, surprisingly full of energy and purpose, he tells Lyudmila that he loves someone else and is going away. He walks through the city, thinking of when he was fifteen years old and first met Mary, who is now Alfyorov's wife. On returning to the pension, he slips into Alfyorov's room, determined to find photographs of Mary. Klara catches him rifling through the desk and believes that he is looking for money. Ganin offers to explain but then does not. Klara is left mystified, pitying him. He almost tells Podtyagin of the exciting rediscovery of his old love, but the old man is so depressed and ill that Ganin desists. He thinks tenderly of that summer in which he first met Mary near his father's country estate. For some time he was too shy to approach her and had to be satisfied with riding past her on his bicycle, but eventually they did meet, and their sweet affair began.

On Wednesday, Ganin receives a letter from Lyudmila but he refuses to read it. Podtyagin returns from another unsuccessful visit to the government offices, disillusioned and depressed. Ganin offers to accompany him the next time. Ganin listens to Alfyorov talk about his wife with new interest now that he knows the woman is Mary, and he wonders how she could have married such a silly man.

Ganin again turns to his memories of the affair with Mary and how happy they were together through the remaining weeks of that summer. In the middle of the night, Podtyagin comes to him suffering a mild heart attack, and Ganin manages to calm him. They decide not to go to the government offices until Friday.

Alfyorov, who wants to take over Ganin's room when his wife arrives, disturbs Ganin by asking him for assurance that he will be gone by Saturday, but Ganin's irritation turns into another memory of his time with Mary: how they carried on their affair over the next two years until they drifted apart in the summer of 1917.

On Friday, Ganin and Podtyagin go to the police offices and complete Podtyagin's application, but they fail to make further progress, because the old man loses his passport. Returning to the pension, Podtyagin has a minor heart attack. He is now certain that he will never leave Berlin alive.

Ganin, packing to leave, rereads five letters that Mary wrote to him during the last stages of the war, urging him to come back to her. He, however, was obliged to leave Russia quickly, and has not seen or heard from her since. He is now determined to steal her from her husband. At a farewell party that night, Podtyagin has another, serious attack, and Alfyorov gets helplessly drunk. Ganin puts him to bed, says good-bye to the dying Podtyagin, and leaves a tearful Klara at the door. He has set Alfyorov's alarm incorrectly to delay him and is on his way to meet Mary at the station. Watching a group of workmen erect a new building, he suddenly realizes that Mary is an ideal image of the past and that they have no future together. He takes a train from another station, determined to make his way to the south of France and the sea.

The Characters

There is a piquancy to the use of a third-party narrator in *Mary*, as the love story is based, at least modestly, on Vladimir Nabokov's own adolescent love affair with a girl named Tamara. That affair was ended by the intrusion of the Russian Revolution. The third-party voice is used to enter the minds of other characters, but in the main the narrator remains very close to Ganin and manifests much of his tonal and intellectual attitude toward the events of the novel.

Ganin, in many ways, is a precursor of the major male character as he is developed in much of Nabokov's work. He is intelligent, perceptive, often coldly aristocratic, and distanced from those with whom he associates. Certainly part of his attraction for Klara lies in his ambiguous hauteur, his self-contained confidence. There is, however, an aspect of his character which is only occasionally seen by the other characters. He has been, in the past, a young man of feeling, and his memory of the affair is charged with tenderness and an eye for the beauty of the Russia he has left behind. Now his emotions seem limited to the satisfying of his sexual appetites and he is restrained, if not icily cool, in his relations with others. He can, however, be gratuitously kind, as he is to Podtyagin and in the way he senses the lovelorn despair of Klara.

Perhaps the best thing about Nabokov's methods of characterization in this novel lies in the ease with which he conveys their feelings. *Mary* is, in part, a novel about lost, confused, emotionally bruised creatures, all driven from their homeland, all trying to make some sense of their new lives, and often failing to do so. Klara's tentative, fumbling desire for Ganin is presented with great sensitivity. Nabokov, who is an ironic writer usually, deals here with two homosexual ballet dancers without patronizing them. It is significant that Ganin, for all of his toughness is equally unjudging in his dealings with them. The desultory conversations, the details of dress and gesture, and the subtle movements of this pathetic but likable group flood the work with considerable tenderness. Ganin's last moments in the pension as he takes leave of Podtyagin and is taken to the door by Klara are an example. Nabokov's third-party narrator is always clear-eyed; here that eye is admirably understanding, almost caressing in its restraint.

Themes and Meanings

The most obvious way to read the novel, as several critics have suggested, is to see Mary as Russia and Ganin and the others as those Russians who can never go home again. Ganin, with his history of fighting in the Crimea in 1919, suggests an anti-Bolshevik attempt to retrieve Russia from Communism. His final repudiation of Mary can be read as a recognition that the old czarist Russia is lost forever.

This narrowly symbolic reading is aesthetically thin, however, and does little justice to the richness of the work. *Mary* has also been seen as one of the best novels on the plight of Russian émigrés, often at loose, inconsequential ends in the early 1920's. The economy with which Nabokov fleshes out the secondary characters in their maundering fragilities shows in this, his first novel, the promise that would culminate in his formidable reputation.

Old Russia is a theme in *Mary*, but a minor theme which forms the background to Ganin's exploration of his past as an innocent lover whose love has been lost. He must arrive, through reliving the experience in his memory, at that mature, if sad, awareness that the past is no more than memory, however idyllic it still seems to be. If Ganin dare not go home again physically, he also learns that he cannot go home again emotionally.

The most unformed aspect of Nabokov's gift lies in the rather blatant way in which symbolic motifs and patterns are used. The novel begins with two men in the dark who are closer than they know, and ends with Ganin making his decision not to meet Mary as he watches a group of carpenters erect a new building. That he decides to leave for the south has equally obvious suggestions of new life, of emotional renewal and fructification. The setting of the novel in April and occasional references to rebirth in the plant life of the city provide a background for the refugees who are attempting to renew themselves.

Nabokov is successful in conveying that peculiar air of hopelessness, ennui, and somewhat limp angst and frustration in this group of admirably civilized outcasts which reminds the reader of the Chekhovian exploration of the prerevolutionary Russians in their failures to make sense of lives of self-pity and fecklessness. Ganin, at least, escapes, not only the hothouse enfeeblement of the pension but the past as well, and he attempts to do it without going back for passport or visa, repudiating the old identities.

Critical Context

This first novel looks so much simpler than Nabokov's mature work that it may be easy to ignore the obvious signs of connection which are here, as in a five-finger exercise. Ganin has the marks of the later protagonists, not only in his "apartness" but also in his inclination toward mild forms of outlaw conduct: The reader never learns his real name, and he is determined to cross the borders illegally. The male-female love triangle appears repeatedly in Nabokov's work. Even his sometimes extravagant use of coincidence is evident in Ganin and Alfyorov living in the same boardinghouse, Mary arriving just as Ganin is to leave, and in a reference to Alfyorov and Podtyagin in one of Mary's last letters to Ganin.

Mary's generous evocation of young love and its celebration of sexual innocence and ardor seem somewhat too conservative for the Nabokov known through his later works. The ending, which may be read as a sentimental rejection of anything less than the ideal world, which can never be retrieved, may also be read as Nabokov's ironic refusal to give readers what they want: the happy ending. The overall tone may be bittersweet, but there are intimations of acridity in the novel which anticipate stronger work to come.

Sources for Further Study
Field, Andrew. *Nabokov: His Life in Art*, 1967.
Lee, L. L. *Vladimir Nabokov*, 1976.
Morton, Donald E. *Vladimir Nabokov*, 1974.
Proffer, Carl, ed. *A Book of Things About Vladimir Nabokov*, 1973.
Rowe, William Woodin. *Nabokov's Deceptive World*, 1971.

Charles Pullen

MASKS

Author: Fumiko Enchi (1905-1986)
Type of plot: Romantic realism
Time of plot: The mid-1950's
Locale: Kyoto and Tokyo, both cities in Japan
First published: Onnamen, 1958 (English translation, 1983)

Principal characters:

MIEKO TOGANŌ, a poet, a teacher of poetry, and an amateur
    student of spirit possession in classical Japanese literature
YASUKO TOGANŌ, her daughter-in-law, the widow of Mieko's
    son Akio
HARUMÉ TOGANŌ, Akio's twin sister, who is severely
    mentally retarded
TSUNEO IBUKI, age thirty-three, a professor of Japanese
    literature; he is married and the father of a three-year-
    old daughter, yet briefly the lover of Yasuko Toganō
TOYOKI MIKAMÉ, also thirty-three, a bachelor; he holds a
    doctoral degree in psychology and is an amateur authority
    on Japanese folklore

The Novel

Masks opens with the chance encounter of Tsuneo Ibuki, a specialist in
Heian period Japanese literature, and his friend Toyoki Mikamé in a coffee
shop in Kyoto's main train station. Mikamé is a physician who holds a doc-
toral degree in psychology, and he is on his way back to Tokyo from Osaka,
where he attended a medical convention. Ibuki is in Kyoto to deliver special
lectures at a university, and he is in the coffee shop waiting for Mieko Toganō
and her daughter-in-law Yasuko. They have invited him to join them in calling at the home of the famous Nō performer Yorihito Yakushiji. The actor's
daughter is studying the writing of poetry under Mieko, and Yakushiji has invited the Toganō ladies to inspect the ancient costumes and masks in his
collection. Ibuki asks Mikamé, who knows both women, to join the group.

Both Mikamé and Ibuki are in love with Yasuko Toganō. Four years after
the death of her husband in an avalanche on Mount Fuji, Yasuko still lives in
the home of her mother-in-law. Akio Toganō was Ibuki's younger colleague;
as a scholar, he was interested in the phenomenon of spirit possession as it is
revealed in the literature of the Heian period. With Mieko's encouragement,
Yasuko has continued Akio's research, attending Ibuki's classes and bringing
into the Toganō home people such as Mikamé, whose interest in Japanese
folklore complements her study of spirit possession. Central to a particular
kind of Nō play is the motif of the vengeful spirit or ghost, often in the form

of a beautiful woman. The visit to the Yakushiji collection suggests the relevance of these elements to the Toganō family's story.

During the train ride from Kyoto to Tokyo, Yasuko confesses to Ibuki that she would like to escape Mieko Toganō's control. It is not the fact that her mother-in-law depends on her help in editing a poetry magazine or that she actively encourages her to continue Akio's research into the phenomenon of spirit possession that bothers Yasuko. Perhaps without knowing it, Mieko is throwing Yasuko at Mikamé and Ibuki, and at the same time she encourages Yasuko's emotional dependence on herself. Ibuki and Mikamé have already discussed the emotional relationship of the Toganō ladies, using for the purpose of comparison the example of a seance that both men had attended with Yasuko some time before the meeting in Kyoto. If Yasuko is the medium, the two men agree, Mieko is the spirit who inhabits her body and speaks through it.

Yasuko suggests that the two men are right when she reminds Ibuki of the fact that Mikamé and he, earlier in the summer, encountered in the garden of Mieko's Tokyo home a mysterious, beautiful woman. The two were part of a group invited to the Toganō residence, a remnant of the large estate the family had occupied before World War II, to view fireflies in the moonlit garden. The mysterious woman, who disappeared when they approached her in the garden, was Akio's twin sister, Harumé. Supposedly kicked in the head by her male sibling while they were in the womb, Harumé is severely retarded. Sent to the home of Mieko's parents as an infant (the Toganō family subscribing to the Japanese superstition that twins are unlucky), Harumé returned to Mieko's house only after Akio's death. Even then, her presence and identity remained a secret. Harumé's childlike mind and woman's body make her a medium through whom Mieko can, and does, act as well. Indeed, she uses both Harumé and Yasuko to work out the final step in an elaborate revenge upon the memory of her dead husband.

Akio and Harumé are not the children of Mieko Toganō's husband. They are the offspring of a man she took as a lover, and who died in the Sino-Japanese War after failing to persuade Mieko to leave Toganō and bring the children to him. Mieko had taken this lover in response to the fact that when she came to the Toganō household as a bride of nineteen, her husband's mistress Aguri was installed in the house as a maid. Aguri was a village girl from the district in Niigata prefecture, in which the Toganō family had large agricultural holdings. She had come to young Toganō's bed, as generations of peasant girls had come into those of earlier Toganō males, to provide him with the services required by an upper-class gentleman. Pregnant twice, she had consented to Toganō's orders that she abort both children. When the young bride Mieko had become pregnant, Aguri became jealous and planted a nail in a strategic spot on a flight of stairs, catching Mieko's kimono and causing her to fall and lose her first child. Aware of the fact that Aguri was

Toganō's mistress, Mieko's parents opposed her decision to remain in her husband's house. She went back, however, on the condition that Aguri be sent away, and she extracted the further revenge of giving Toganō children that were not his and of concealing the fact from him through the remainder of his life.

When Akio died in the accident on Mount Fuji, having been married a year but failing to father a child of his own, Mieko felt thwarted again in her revenge upon her husband. She encouraged Yasuko's involvement with Mikamé and Ibuki. When her daughter-in-law took Ibuki as a lover, Mieko condoned the relationship in order to persuade Yasuko to cooperate in the plan to pass Harumé off as Yasuko and thereby obtain a child who had Akio's blood and that of Mieko's own lover in his veins. As an accomplice in this plot, endangering the life of the childlike Harumé in the process, Yasuko was drawn into a bond of complicity with Mieko so strong that she would never be able, despite her engagement to Mikamé, to leave the Toganō house. She has come to want this child as fiercely as Mieko does.

The Characters

It is typical of Fumiko Enchi's treatment of women that the novel *Masks* focuses on the unconscious processes by means of which Mieko Toganō gains control of the minds of her daughter Harumé and daughter-in-law Yasuko. It is also characteristic that Enchi does not approach the material from the perspective of clinical psychology. The irony is intentional that the psychologist Mikamé is less perceptive than Ibuki, the scholar of literature, about Mieko's motives and actions. Both men are essential, however, to the reader's gradual acceptance of the premise on which Enchi bases her characterizations of the three women at the novel's center. That premise is that Mieko, Yasuko, and Harumé are a valid instance of the spirit possession which many of the characters study in Japanese folklore, classical poetry, and the Nō drama. Enchi's handling of the material, however, has nothing of the self-consciousness of deliberate archaism. Her emphasis is resolutely feminist, in a sense, for in Harumé, Yasuko, and Mieko, she portrays the efforts of women to be free of the male domination which causes them so much pain.

Enchi's statement that Harumé was beaten about the head by the feet of her brother while both were in Mieko's womb may seem strident, but it also conveys the novelist's conviction that Harumé is a victim of her own femaleness. Her retardation is so extreme, for example, that Harumé is not conscious of the significance of her menstrual periods. Like an animal in heat, she is excited and restless during the early part of the cycle and leaves a trail of blood spots about the house during the later stage. Mieko arranges for Harumé to take Yasuko's place in bed with Ibuki at the point in her menstrual cycle at which she is most likely to conceive. Harumé is unaware that her physical nature betrays her dependence on the male, but Yasuko is conscious of the degree of her physical and emotional victimization. Like so many Japanese women, she defines herself chiefly in terms of her relationships with men. Struggling to escape Mieko's gradually unfolding plot, Yasuko turns to Ibuki and Mikamé in her effort to escape. She encourages the bachelor Mikamé to approach her mother-in-law for permission to ask Yasuko to marry him, and she embarks, at first secretly, on the affair with Ibuki. Both actions, ironically, meet with Mieko's approval.

The characterization of Mieko Toganō is the most complex portrait of a woman in Enchi's *Masks*. Outwardly passive and uninterested in Yasuko's emotional life, Mieko manipulates her daughter-in-law in accordance with a half-conscious plan to regain for the Toganō family a male heir totally free of the Toganō blood. Nevertheless, Mieko also represses her own awareness of what she is doing. When she comforts Yasuko, awakened from a recurring nightmare in which she sees Akio's face disfigured by the avalanche, she does not recognize that she encourages both Yasuko's guilt over Akio's death and her feeling of relief that he is gone. Here Mieko projects onto her daughter-in-law the feelings she had for Akio's nominal father. These are the impulses which prompt Yasuko to betray Akio's memory by considering marriage to Mikamé and an affair with Ibuki. These options, which Yasuko exercises openly because of her status as a widow, are those Mieko considered, perhaps toyed with half fearfully, in her involvement with the man who fathered Harumé and Akio.

Themes and Meanings

Awareness of the enormous price in human suffering that her need for revenge has exacted comes to Mieko Toganō at the end of *Masks*. After the birth of Harumé's infant son, the daughter of the Kyoto Nō performer Yorihito Yakushiji calls upon Mieko with the gift of one of her late father's Nō masks. It is that of a female character named Fukai, and when Mieko holds it in her hand, she recalls the faces of Akio and Harumé and the revenge she has sought so long. Harumé's baby cries in the next room, and the juxtaposition of his voice and the face of Fukai brings home to Mieko just what she has done: "In a trance she reached out and covered the face on the mask with her hand, while her right arm, as if suddenly paralyzed, hung frozen, immobile, in space." The gesture is unconsciously theatrical, but it brings home the enormity of her treatment of son, daughter, and daughter-in-law.

Enchi uses the masks examined at Yakushiji's home early in the novel to reveal the personalities of her characters. She also uses three of them as subtitles for the three sections of *Masks*. The first part of the novel bears the name "Ryō no Onna," referring to the vengeful face of a coldly beautiful woman. The second is entitled "Masugami," referring to a mask depicting the face of a madwoman; and the third bears the name "Fukai." Hers is the face of a middle-aged woman, a mother, and it is that element in the mask that Mieko is given that causes her to recognize the pain she has inflicted on her children. All three masks describe Mieko at different stages of her life. She is the young woman driven mad by the painful betrayal of her husband and his mistress. She is the coldly vengeful Ryō no Onna, a woman intent on repaying pain with pain. At the end of the novel, by means of the gesture of the dead Kyoto actor, she realizes the mother in herself. Significantly, at the beginning of *Masks*, the mask which is handed to Yasuko to examine is that of "Magojirō," the face of a young woman at the peak of her mature beauty. The masks Enchi uses as the subtitles of the sections of *Masks* reflect the changing identities of Yasuko and Harumé as well as that of Mieko. Clearly, Harumé's is the face of a madwoman, and Yasuko, as she comes under Mieko's influence, becomes the cold, vengeful beauty.

Enchi extends the motif of the mask into the fabric of the novel by describing the faces of actual people as masks. The woman who acts as medium at the seance that Mikamé, Ibuki, and Yasuko attend, a woman whose voice is that of a dead Frenchman, is one such mask. Another is the recurring nightmare Yasuko and Mieko share of Akio's damaged face under the snow on Mount Fuji. Enchi fills *Masks* with references to Japanese folk beliefs concerning spirit possession, to the literature of the Heian period dealing with the phenomenon, and specifically to that period's prose masterpiece, Lady Murasaki's *Genji monogatari* (c. 1004; *The Tale of Genji*, 1925-1933). The chief of these is to a chapter recounting the unconscious possession of the body of Prince Genji's wife by the spirit of his jealous mistress, the Rokujo Lady. Mikamé and Ibuki discover that Mieko had written an essay on this episode and published it in 1937.

Critical Context

Fumiko Enchi herself spent more than ten years translating *The Tale of Genji* into modern Japanese, so it comes as no surprise that she draws upon it in the construction of her own fiction. Her novel *Onnazaka* (1957; *The Waiting Years*, 1971) shows the influence of Murasaki's work. Like *Masks*, this novel deals with three women struggling against the paternalistic family structure of Japan, but it deals with nineteenth rather than twentieth century Japan.

Masks is among Enchi's most challenging works. It rises above the preoccupation with social and political conditions limiting the expression of Japanese women that characterizes her work since the 1920's. It also transcends the overtly feminist twist Enchi gives characters and plot. While the proposition that Mieko Toganō suffered at the hands of an insensitive husband and his jealous mistress does not need to be challenged, Enchi cannot justify Mieko's response except by giving it the plausibility of a case of spirit possession. In the context of the folk beliefs and ancient texts to which Enchi alludes, Mieko's conduct takes on the authenticity of archetype.

Sources for Further Study
Kearns, George. "World Well Lost," in *The Hudson Review*. XXXVI (1983), pp. 551-552.
Updike, John. "As Others See Us," in *The New Yorker*. LIX (January 2, 1984), pp. 88-89.

Robert C. Petersen

THE MASTER AND MARGARITA

Author: Mikhail Bulgakov (1891-1940)
Type of plot: Satirical fantasy/historical realism
Time of plot: A.D. 30 and 1920
Locale: First century Jerusalem and postrevolutionary Moscow
First published: Master i Margarita, 1966-1967, expurgated; 1973, unexpurgated (English translation, 1967)

> *Principal characters:*
> WOLAND, the Devil, who arrives in Moscow as a foreign expert in theater
> PONTIUS PILATE, the Roman Procurator of Judaea
> YESHUA HA-NOTSRI, an accused rabble-rouser from Galilee
> THE MASTER, a Soviet writer who has written a novel about Jesus and Pilate
> MARGARITA, the Master's beloved and the wife of a successful Soviet scientist

The Novel

The Master and Margarita presents three interlaced lines of action, which are integrated and are mutually enlightening: a visit by Satan to Moscow, a Faustian love story of a writer and his Margarita, and Pilate's condemnation of Jesus to execution. The Moscow and Jerusalem episodes have parallels, and the love story connects the two.

In the first story, Satan, in the form of a foreign expert in theater (magic is his specialty), visits Moscow in the spring of 1920. Satan takes the German name of Woland. He and his minions—a black cat named Behemoth, a naked maid named Hella, a disreputable clown named Koroviev-Faggot, and an evil trickster called Azazello—play tricks on the Soviet literary and theatrical establishments and on the ordinary people of Moscow in order to reveal their victims' anti-Soviet greed for material things. A magic show in a theater and a series of destructive tricks around town reveal and satirize real elements of Soviet life in the 1920's and 1930's: the hunger for consumer goods; gold-hoarding; sexual hanky-panky; the jockeying for special treatment; the suppression of literature; the humorlessness of the bureaucracy; and the pervasive informing on friends, neighbors, and acquaintances.

The satanic crew finds a writer's girlfriend and persuades her to serve as the hostess for the annual Satan's ball, which she agrees to do in order to earn the freedom of her lover, who is in a mental institution. Woland then demonstrates his links with the timeless supernatural world when he produces a copy of the Master's burned manuscript. The Devil knows its contents and says that he has talked to Pilate himself. According to Woland, "Manuscripts don't burn."

The action of the Master's novel constitutes the second plot of Mikhail Bulgakov's novel. Interpolated in the Moscow sequence, this novel-within-a-novel relates in fresh terms the New Testament account of the Passion in first century Jerusalem. Yeshua (Jesus) has been betrayed to the Jews by Judas. Pilate, while submitting to his role as Roman procurator and to the political pressure of Caiaphas and the Sanhedrin, nevertheless tries to keep Yeshua from incriminating himself. Yeshua, while not in the least eager to suffer or die, refuses to admit that any temporal power has jurisdiction over him. He tells Pilate that "all power is a form of violence exercised over people and . . . the time will come when there will be no rule by Caesar nor any other form of rule. Man will pass into the kingdom of truth and justice where no sort of power will be needed." The procurator naturally cannot release a man who so challenges Caesar, and the execution of Yeshua is accomplished in a moving chapter featuring Matthew the Levite's arrival too late to relieve Yeshua's pain, just as Margarita came too late to keep the Master from destroying his manuscript and taking himself off to the asylum. Diverging from the biblical story, Arthanius, chief of the Roman secret police, attempts to assuage Pilate's guilt for his part in the execution of Yeshua by arranging the murder of Judas. The frustrated Pilate wishes to speak further to the strangely comforting Yeshua but must wait until the end of the novel and his own death before their conversation can be continued.

The love story of the writer and Margarita is the third line of action, one with resonances of Faust's being saved by his Marguerite, though here it is the Marguerite figure, not the Faust figure, who sells her soul to the Devil. Margarita, unhappy in her materialistic life with her successful Soviet technocrat husband, meets and falls in love with the writer she comes to call the Master. His novel is written only because he wins from a lottery enough money to quit his museum job. Nevertheless, his novel is rejected before publication, and then he becomes the victim of vicious literary attacks, which culminate in his madness. He goes to the asylum willingly, realizing that he is ill. Late in the book, the truth emerges that his persecution is in fact the result of a secret denunciation by a man who wanted the writer's apartment.

In the asylum, the Master meets Ivan Bezdomny, a young poet who has similar problems with critics because he has written a poem depicting a life-like Jesus, as if he had really existed, when the official policy is atheist. Bezdomny is in the asylum, however, because of his account of his unbelievable encounter with Woland and his accomplices. Woland has predicted the death of a high-ranking member of the literary elite, and the man dies as scheduled. (Bezdomny is engaged in a discussion of atheism with the official when Satan appears at the beginning of the novel.) The cohorts of Satan lead the poet on a wild chase across town. Only writers and lovers can see the satanic figures for what they are; the melee is seen by ordinary people as a series of incomprehensible events. In a society based on reason, there is no

Devil, and no God, and Bezdomny must be judged insane. In an epilogue, Bezdomny recovers his freedom, but he never writes again.

Margarita makes her deal with the Devil in order to be able to find and ransom her beloved. She becomes a witch and does some joyous damage of her own to the malevolent critics before meeting her commitment at Satan's ball. While presiding over the ball, she encounters the pain of all human misdeeds throughout history. In her compassion for a woman who has murdered her own child, Margarita yields her right to ask Woland for the Master's release, but Woland nevertheless grants that wish as well and allows the lovers rest and peace and life together in death at the end of the novel. Soviet agencies achieve a rational explanation for all the irrational events, and only the full moon troubles the spirits of the imaginative ones left to live in the Soviet world.

The Characters

The characters represent a mixture of those transcending time and the history-bound residents of twentieth century Moscow. Woland and his attendants are transcendental figures taking on local form to explore human evils in contemporary terms. By tempting citizens (as the Devil's conventional task), Woland establishes the encroachment of the very values that the Soviet state has declared outlived. The interest of the character lies in the Faustian epigraph which introduces the novel: "'Say at last—who art thou?'/ 'That power I serve/ Which wills forever evil/ Yet does forever good.'"

Woland appears at first like the seedy devil in Ivan Karamazov's nightmare in Fyodor Dostoevski's *The Brothers Karamazov* (1879-1880). He grows in stature, as the novel progresses, becoming a figure as impressive and ambiguous as John Milton's Satan in *Paradise Lost* (1667, 1674). Woland is the means by which moral order is asserted on earth, a sort of agent for good who works by exposing evil. He is linked with death, and just as, in the medieval mystery play, God sends Satan to call Everyman to account, Woland calls the venal Muscovites to account and brings rest if not absolution to the heroes. The disorder that he allows his assistants to create is irrelevant to his main purpose, serving the transcendental function that implies a kind of order which the state does not admit. Woland's aristocracy arises from his own creative function: He is himself an artist, in tune with truth like all real artists. It is the falsity of Soviet institutions and the desertion of the search for truth that he punishes. He judges weak human beings as Yeshua will not.

Pilate in the novel-within-the-novel uneasily represents earthly power and demonstrates the despair that the earthly power without commitment to a moral order brings. Pilate's headaches; his dependence on his dog for loyalty and affection; his hatred of Jerusalem, the city that he is condemned to rule; the cowardice which makes him unable to follow his own insights; and his guilt all help to mitigate the image of the elegant and cruel ruler who sends

Yeshua to his death. Pilate has memories of his own past cruelties to haunt him, and he is a lonely, suffering man. Only Yeshua can reach through to the soul of the man. Pilate therefore tries to save Yeshua, who is too innocent politically to take the procurator's hints. When the document is presented showing the prophet's unwillingness to support Caesar, Pilate "has no choice" and must allow the Sanhedrin to have him. He cannot challenge the system that has produced him; political circumstance makes him unable to tell the Sanhedrin to withdraw the spurious charges against Yeshua. Yet "the greatest crime is cowardice," and when rulers are not free to prevent injustice, they must learn from figures such as Yeshua.

Yeshua's characterization is of great interest because of its humanization of the figure of Jesus. Bulgakov emphasizes the historical Jesus rather than the biblical image (Yeshua repeatedly says that the Gospels do not represent accurately what he said and did), but the author portrays a man of extraordinary insight and prescience. Only at the end of the novel is it made clear that Yeshua is a transcendental figure. Pilate cannot help but respond to him, when Yeshua treats the procurator as a man with a headache rather than as the awesome official holding all Jerusalem in his grip.

Yeshua's assumption is that all men are good men, a view demonstrably untrue: The novel shows examples in Jerusalem and Moscow of people who have lost their humanity through persistent misuse of power or through over-reaching self-interest. Yeshua feels pity for those who cannot be the good people he is convinced that they essentially are. The distinguishing characteristic of this very human Jesus, who feels fear and pain like anyone, is the courage not to violate his conscience.

This courage links him with the Master. In the corrupt Moscow society, in which Woland catches everyone violating what he or she knows to be right, the image of Yeshua's accepting death rather than submission to a violent state is a powerful one. It is Yeshua who is able at the end of the novel to forgive the man who has condemned him. Abiblical as the characterization of Yeshua is, the moral influence of Jesus is nevertheless brilliantly communicated in his simple actions and words. He belongs to the transcendental group, though so human in his depiction. At the end, he and Pilate continue their conversation. The polar figures of state and conscience are left in dialogue: "Perhaps they can work something out."

The Master is, in his commitment to truth and the freedom of the artist, a dropout from Soviet society but, worse from Bulgakov's point of view, he is a dropout from his commitment to continue writing. While hostile criticism and cowardly censorship do not in themselves crush the Master, he begins to break when he realizes that the whole campaign against him is false: The people who write against him are not saying what they believe. This response strikes fear into his heart and makes him feel that "some very cold, supple octopus was fastening its tentacles round my heart"; in despair, he burns his manuscript. He overcomes his fear and despair only with Woland's help, saying that he has been through everything that a man can go through and that nothing can frighten him any longer. "Where else can such wrecks as you and I find help except from the supernatural?" he asks Margarita. The Master is prescient throughout, as Yeshua is, and as the young poet Bezdomny increasingly is: All the creative characters are linked. Though a man of this world and time, the Master can, through his art, guess at enduring realities.

Compassion is Margarita's dominant characteristic, and her pity touches all those damaged by the difficulties of life, both in the underworld at Satan's ball and in Moscow. In the ironic twist that only by bargaining with the Devil is a person able to help anyone in Moscow, she becomes not the passive Marguerite in Johann Wolfgang von Goethe's *Faust* (1808, 1833) but the Faustian figure itself: She becomes a witch in order to gain the power to help her beloved. While not herself prescient, her sympathy, loyalty, and appreciation of excellence enable her to join the heroic group. She becomes, by the end of the novel, a mater dolorosa, like Mary in an icon, because she has suffered herself, borne the suffering of others, and yielded her hard-earned wish to a woman suffering more than she.

It is appropriate to consider Griboyedov a sort of collective character in the novel. The building for the support and entertainment of the literary establishment in Moscow summarizes the value system to which the major characters are opposed: greed, bourgeois luxurious living, toadying, lying, stupidity, jealousy, self-interest, cowardice, disloyalty, atheistic amorality. Bulgakov puts into the image of the arts community everything that the octopus in the Master's fearful dream implies about state control of the arts and the self-satisfied vulgarity resulting from the power of the mediocre over the gifted. When the building burns at the end of the book, the villain is defeated as surely as in any melodrama.

Themes and Meanings

Multiple plots yield multiple meanings. Mikhail Bulgakov's enduring topics, brought to their greatest formulation in this novel, are many. They include the connection between the real artist and transcendental truth (the Master's novel is known to the transcendental figures); the fate of the artist, who is ordinarily at odds with society (the Master and Bezdomny suffer in society, but "manuscripts don't burn," and their work will last, though the artists themselves die); the necessity for perseverance in one's work (the Master may achieve only rest, not absolution, because he ceases his writing); the failure of the idealistic aims of the revolution (the magic show reveals that the Soviet people are greedy for consumer goods); the importance of loyalty, generosity, love, and compassion in a world of suffering (Margarita's choices represent ideal love); the imperative for courage in challenging violence (Pilate suffers purgatory for his failure); the abuse of power which is not based on faith (Mark Muribellum, Pilate's strong man, has become inhuman in his practice of violence); the true creator's hatred of hypocrisy, fanaticism, self-seeking, and lying (the man who informs on the Master is the nadir of human character); the acceptance of one's fate and death (the lyrical epilogue on the coming of death communicates tragic acceptance); and humanity's freedom of will (each of the characters chooses his behavior; responsibility always remains with the individual). Such a list suggests the diversity of theme in this extraordinarily rich novel, but it by no means exhausts the possible meanings. The reader comes away from the novel with an appreciation of the nature of Soviet society's shortcomings, the value of art, Bulgakov's definition of morality and faith, an image of the good life, and a complex reaction to evil and suffering.

In the ambiguous figure of Woland, Bulgakov goes beyond the purely social and moral issues to express his painful acceptance of the necessity of evil in the world to generate an appreciation of truth, which alone can lead to justice and faith. The epigraph from *Faust* invites the reader to see the dark as a part of the light, death and suffering as an inevitable part of life. Since Bulgakov continued to revise the novel until his own long-foreseen death, the coming to terms with death resonates deeply, and the philosophical dimension of the novel emerges. Yet Bulgakov rejected systematic philosophical positions; indeed, the novel is his ultimate rejection of the rationalist, materialist approach to reality that the Bolsheviks brought into Russian life.

Critical Context

Bulgakov's novel is his masterpiece, containing all the themes he had developed in a variety of genres, as well as a dazzling compendium of stylistic devices developed over the years of his productive life. The writer did not belong to any one group of Soviet artists, and he has roots in the great Russian writers of the past—Fyodor Dostoevski, Leo Tolstoy, Nikolai Leskov. Nevertheless, he participated in the great experimental upsurge of the 1920's; his friends included all the best Soviet writers, many of whom also suffered repeatedly from censorship during Joseph Stalin's rule. Bulgakov's own struggles for artistic freedom provide a contest for the themes of hypocrisy, cowardice, mediocrity, truth, power of art, ills of Soviet society—and in the long run, of the way even efforts at good generate evil, and even triumphant evil generates good.

Sources for Further Study

Barratt, Andrew. *Between Two Worlds: A Critical Introduction to "The Master and Margarita,"* 1987.
Mihailovich, Vasa D., ed. *Modern Slavic Literatures: A Library of Literary Criticism,* 1972.
Natov, Nadine. *Mikhail Bulgakov,* 1985.

Proffer, Ellendea. *Mikhail Bulgakov: Life and Work*, 1984.
Russian Literature Triquarterly. XV (1978). Special Bulgakov issue.
Wright, A. Colin. *Mikhail Bulgakov: Life and Interpretations*, 1978.

Martha Manheim

THE MASTER OF GO

Author: Yasunari Kawabata (1899-1972)
Type of plot: Chronicle novel
Time of plot: June, 1938, to January, 1940
Locale: Tokyo and Itō, Japan
First published: Meijin, 1942-1954, serial; 1954, book (English translation, 1972)

>Principal characters:
>HONNIMBŌ SHŪSAI, the master of Go
>OTAKÉ, the challenger in Shūsai's last match
>URAGAMI, the narrator, a news reporter assigned to cover the Go match

The Novel

The Master of Go is a fictional rendering of an actual Go match that occurred in Japan in 1938 on which Yasunari Kawabata reported for the *Tokyo Nichinichi Shimbun*. The details from the game are factual as are the interactions of the players. Kawabata, who himself referred to *The Master of Go* as a "chronicle novel," has fictionalized the story only in his delineation of the protagonist and in his interpretive comments on the action. In this literary rendering, the Go match is a metaphoric battlefield, in which the warriors pit themselves against their own limits, illness, time, and death.

The narrative is in the first person, in the voice of the news reporter Uragami. The novel opens at the end of the story with an account of the death of the protagonist, Honnimbō Shūsai, the master of Go, and a description of events surrounding the end of the master's last match. The game is then reported chronologically, with occasional digressions, from the elaborate opening ceremonies to the game's conclusion six months later. Events in the lives of the contestants, negotiations for alterations in the game's schedule, commentary on the game, and key moves of the game (which lasts 237 moves) make up the materials of the story.

On June 26, 1938, at the Kōyōkan Restaurant in Tokyo, each player makes his first move amid the ceremonies that convey the importance of the game and the high respect that it receives. The next day, the players complete up to move 12, and the game moves to another location, at Hakone, where, in the following month and a half, the next eighty-eight moves take place. Shūsai's weak health deteriorates rapidly as his heart begins to fail him, and the game recesses for three months, to resume in Itō, where it continues from move 100 to the close of the game. With comments on the game's outcome and Shūsai's death a year later, the novel ends where it began.

Though the focus of *The Master of Go* is on the characters of the competing players, drama is also provided by the moves of the game and the players' negotiations over their schedules. The game of Go is extremely complex in strategy—so much so that the relative strengths of the players' moves are frequently open to much debate, even among experts, and the final tallying of the points is a lengthy and difficult matter. As chronicler of the game, Uragami does not attempt to teach even the game's basics but instead describes the players' reactions to key moves to give a sense of their significance. The most dramatic of these is move 121 by Otaké, the challenger. Each session of play ends with a "sealed in" play, one in which the last player, rather than playing his move, records it for storage until the opening of the next session. The purpose of the sealed play is to avoid giving an advantage to either player during a recess from the game. Play 121 is such a sealed play, but one that Otaké makes on an area of the board remote from the tense series of previous moves that are determining the fates of the players at the center of the board. Once the play is unsealed, even expert analysts have trouble finding it on the board, not guessing that Otaké would have broken the thematic thread the previous plays had established. For Shūsai, move 121 destroys the harmony of the game and degrades it. To a master of the old school that regards each game as a carefully wrought work of art with its own unique rhythms and patterns, governed by the competing yet mutually appreciating intelligences of the players, move 121 is a blotch, or intentional smear, on a masterpiece. It destroys the game's tension at its height of play. The thought that Otaké might have played it intentionally to throw his opponent off balance makes the move even more offensive. As a result, Shūsai loses some of his commitment to the match. Soon after, in the equally controversial move 130, he moves with unnecessary haste and ensures his defeat. The dramatic tension surrounding moves 121 and 130—a tension made more complex by various levels of ambiguity—typifies all elements of this game, including the consequences of the players' illnesses and arrangements to accommodate the dying master.

The Characters

The Master of Go is an excellent example of Kawabata's technique of revealing character indirectly, through observations of gesture, small details, and brief, telling moments of dialogue. Though this narrative's focus is clearly on the master, Shūsai (which offers much opportunity for a conventional revelation of character through dramatic action), odd bits of detail are still important. Two chapters are devoted to a set of photographs Uragami takes of Shūsai after his death, at the request of the master's wife. Fastidious in taking the photographs, and in keeping them secret until he has examined them, Uragami studies them with equal care and discovers material for a character study. Though moved initially by the unattractiveness of Shūsai's face, with its grotesquely unbalanced features—small eyes, overly large nose and mouth, flattened earlobes—Uragami also notes how the images represent a face rich in feeling, unlike the man who in life was so cool and aloof. Uragami decides that this might be the revelation of a secret that was intended not to be disclosed and has second thoughts about releasing the photographs. In another chapter, similar attention is given to one very long hair of Shūsai's left eyebrow. Uragami learns from Shūsai's wife that Shūsai was flattered by the reporter's observation of the hair which Uragami made in a newspaper article. Significant to Shūsai as a promise of long life, and to Uragami as a welcome aberration observed at a moment of unrelenting tension in the game, the hair becomes a vehicle for revealing the relationships that exist among the principal players and their close scrutiny of each other during the drama of the Go match.

Kawabata's attention to character in *The Master of Go* is devoted almost entirely to Shūsai and Otaké. Other characters—the players' wives and high-ranking players who are observing the game—are described, often vividly, but primarily to underscore characteristics of the two principals. Otaké, for whom Uragami has great respect and affection, is depicted as a brilliant opponent, in some ways ideally suited to be the austere master's adversary. Otaké has a good sense of humor, an intense drive to succeed in Go equal to that of Shūsai, humaneness, and a determination to be treated respectfully and fairly—even in the face of Shūsai's illness, which forces him occasionally to accept undesirable changes in their playing schedule. Most significant, he is a foil to Shūsai as a representative of a younger generation of Go players, and, by extension, of postwar Japanese modernism pitted against the Meiji world represented by the master. Otaké lives and plays by rational laws and their loopholes, by mathematical calculations that determine a competitor's standing; Shūsai lives and plays in a world in which Go is regarded as the ancient warrior's way, in which age and hard-won authority earn respect, in which Go is surrounded by an aura of elegance and mystery. In Shūsai's Meiji world, action is governed by reverence rather than by equality. In this clash over the ancient game of Go, what transpires is not only the defeat of the master but also the overthrow of Meiji refinement by modern rationalism.

Themes and Meanings

After Japan's fall in 1945, Kawabata announced that thereafter he would write only elegies. *The Master of Go*, as it comments on a changing order and the sad defeat of a Meiji master, is one such elegy, in tone as well as in theme. With this theme of a fallen world is woven another of Kawabata's themes, that of the pursuit of ideal beauty.

Shūsai and Otaké, tangled in their battle at the Go board, take on symbolic significance as representatives of two epochs of Japanese history. The nostalgia and sadness in the tone of the novel arise from Kawabata's sympathies as he unravels the tale. In spite of Uragami's affection for Otaké and the comfort he derives from Otaké's openness and accessibility (much in contrast to Shūsai's aloofness), his sympathy is consistently with Shūsai, and he records Shūsai's fall with unambiguous expressions of loss.

Most notably, the sadness is conveyed by Uragami's direct comments about the beauty and elegance of the old style that is represented by Shūsai. It is also conveyed by the attention paid to small details that suggest symbolic action. After his hospitalization and three-month recess from the match, the ailing Shūsai returns, determined to overcome pain and the infirmities of age. Just before reentering the match, he has his hair dyed black. The action suggests layers of meaning: On the one hand, it is an attempt to lift his own spirits by denying his age, while on the other, it can be seen as an attempt to relieve the anxieties of his opponent and the judges, all of whom are feeling responsible for his deterioration. Thus the act, though undoubtedly issuing from self-pride, nevertheless goes beyond mere vanity and expresses a sense of honor characteristic of the era Shūsai represents. On the last day of the match, by which time his defeat is certain, Shūsai appears with his hair cropped short, like that of a priest. He appears youthful at this last confrontation, as he faces the winning Otaké. At the board, "breath came more rapidly, as if two warriors were parrying with dirks; fires of knowledge and wisdom seemed to blaze up." Such is the setting—echoing epics and legends, beginning with inspired calm—in which Shūsai makes his last pose before the rapid decline that brings about his eventual death. It is beauty poised, frozen in an image, before time reduces its elements to the mundane or defeated. Significantly, Uragami notes that throughout the last sessions of the match at Itō, Shūsai was constantly looking at his watch.

The fundamental beauty of *The Master of Go*, however, is that which Shūsai pursues in the game. In the trance state that he achieves when playing, he pursues a beauty in its purest form for him—the abstract, elegant paintings of the intellect that he perceives in Go. The reality to which he escapes when the rest of the world is shut off by his stern concentration is similar to that of any devotee of beauty; the search is for an ideal that is beyond the ordinary and is alone in deserving such pure devotion. In *The Master of Go*, such a beauty is not unobtainable, though its pursuit is not long isolated from an awareness of degeneration and death.

Critical Context

Though uncharacteristic in its absence of the erotic or of deeply probed relationships between men and women, *The Master of Go* nevertheless remains similar to much of Kawabata's writing. From the beginning of his literary career, in the mid-1920's, Kawabata demonstrated an interest in sensations and details that are described for their own sakes, which undoubtedly trained him for the observation of small, telling details in *The Master of Go*.

Also characteristic of his writing is loose plot construction, as exemplified in the circular presentation of chronology in *The Master of Go*, which begins and ends at the same point and contains within it many abrupt jumps in time.

The Master of Go was published in book form in 1954, the same year as was *Yama no oto* (1954; *The Sound of the Mountain*, 1970), which many consider to be Kawabata's most important work. Common to the two books is the theme of postwar spiritual chaos. In both, traditional Japanese sensibility takes a stand against modernism.

Kawabata's creation of unique worlds as settings for his stories is another characteristic that distinguishes many of the works for which he is best known. The setting of *Yukiguni* (1947; *Snow Country*, 1956) is a winter resort, remote from the environs to which its main characters are accustomed. *Sembazuru* (1952; *Thousand Cranes*, 1958) isolates itself in the world of the tea ceremony. *Nemureru bijo* (1961; *The House of the Sleeping Beauties*, 1969) takes place in a brothel catering to old men. The worlds of these books, like the world of Go at the level of masters, are rarefied and abnormally focused, which lends intensity to their action.

Most significant, *The Master of Go* is the elegiac masterpiece of a writer so taken with eulogies and obituaries that in his lifetime he was dubbed "the undertaker." In this novel, Kawabata uses the freedom of the form to go beyond conventional elegiac writing. He expands his meditation to include commentary on the era that was ushered in with the defeat of his country and the deaths of all his immediate family. Kawabata began the novel during World War II and completed it nine years after the war's end. It can be fairly regarded as his major work on the theme of the loss that he observed in the historic change.

Sources for Further Study

Barry, P. "Citizens of a Lost Country: Kawabata's *The Master of Go* and James's 'The Lesson of the Master,'" in *Comparative Literature Studies*. XX (Spring, 1983), pp. 77-93.

Keene, Donald. *Dawn to the West: Japanese Literature of the Modern Era*, 1984.

Rogers, W. N. "Hero's Defense: The Lost Positions of Nabokov's Luzhin and Kawabata's Shūsai," in *Comparative Literature Studies*. XX (Summer, 1983), pp. 217-230.

Swann, Thomas. "The Master of Go," in *Approaches to the Modern Japanese Novel*, 1976. Edited by Kinya Tsuruta and Thomas Swann.

Ueda, Makoto. "Kawabata Yasunari," in *Modern Japanese Writers and the Nature of Literature*, 1976.

Dennis C. Chowenhill

A MEDITATION

Author: Juan Benet (1927-   )
Type of plot: Antistory
Time of plot: The 1920's through the 1960's
Locale: Región, a fictional town in northwest Spain, and its environs
First published: Una meditación, 1970 (English translation, 1982)

> *Principal character:*
> THE NARRATOR, a mature man trying to recall the events of the
>   last forty years

The Novel

A Meditation consists of one long, rambling paragraph, without divisions, in which the narrator sets forth his memories of growing up in Región and the outlying area. There is no coherent plot. Instead, the work consists of isolated scenes, philosophical meanderings, fragments of speech, parts of a letter, and diverse reflections, all arranged in no particular order. Through recollection and reflection, the narrator hopes to understand better his own life, as well as the lives of his family and acquaintances. Memory becomes a tool in the process of existential self-creation, which serves to give meaning to the existence of the individual. As Región is a symbol of Spain and a microcosm of the world, the narrator's meditation is an ambitious search for the meaning of not only his own life but also that of his nation and of human beings in general. At the end, however, the narrator is no closer to an understanding of reality than he was at the beginning.

Although memory is the operating force of the narrative, there is an element of will that assigns greater or lesser importance to every recollection. Will is not necessarily subject to reason or logic: It "has its own predilections." For will, "the death of a blood aunt can be much less a reason for concern than the loss of a cigarette lighter." Thus, memory dredges up and dwells on those incidents for which the individual feels a particular passion or interest. That is why seemingly unimportant details sometimes occupy pages, while major events may be mentioned only in passing. For example, on one occasion, the narrator's family sends his cousin to pick hazelnuts outside the house of a prestigious clan with which his aunts have become obsessed, in the hope that the girl will be invited inside. On the way, the narrator, then a young child who is fascinated with his cousin, falls and scratches his knee, then runs to catch up with the group, so that he will not miss Mary's entry onto the terrace. The episode is described in great detail. "I don't know why I keep that entry so engraved in my memory, why I remember it with such insistence and precision, and why at times I see myself trying to inquire into its most insignificant details, as if the discovery of one of them might change the

whole balance of the system remembered," the narrator muses. Then he realizes that falling, shedding blood, and pushing himself to go on had taken on
"heroic characteristics" in his then-childish mind. He had subconsciously
transformed the incident into a sort of sacrifice, a proof of valor, that he
must make on behalf of Mary, whom he greatly admired. On the other hand,
when the narrator refers to Emilio Ruiz, a self-righteous, hypocritical man
who hopes to marry into the narrator's family, he remembers the name only
vaguely, referring to him as "Emilio something Ruiz something."

Illogically, an event as cataclysmic as the outbreak of the Spanish Civil
War takes on importance only because it allowed the narrator more freedom
as a child, for, as the adults became more concerned with the war, their
preoccupation with the children's behavior diminished. The Civil War is the
focal point of the novel. It is the chronological referent for all other events,
which are often described as having occurred before, after, or during the war.
Yet *A Meditation* is not a political novel. Juan Benet is interested in the effect of the war—and other occurrences—on the psyche of the individual.

The narrator's recollections range from the humorous to the grotesque,
from the trivial to the repugnant. Often, there is a note of irony. When his
Uncle Alonso appears with an unmarried couple posing as husband and wife,
the narrator's scandalized family, which suspects the truth, entertains the pair
only with reluctance. After raising eyebrows by retreating into the bedroom
for a long period, during which time they make a shockingly loud racket, the
guests further upset the family by splitting up for dinner. The lady pleads
exhaustion and stays in her room, while the gentleman dines with the adults.
(The children have been shooed away to protect them from corruption.) In
spite of their prejudices, the staid aunts and uncles find their guest to be
highly entertaining and soon are laughing and joking with him—much to
their embarrassment when he is gone.

In another episode, a missionary with a reputation for saintliness gets his
beard caught in a drawer. When one of the nephews suggests that the beard
be cut in order to free the man, the missionary hurls a series of oaths and
curses at him.

Much of the humor of the novel revolves around a liqueur created by the
narrator's grandfather. The potion is so strong and unsavory that guests routinely pour it into plants, which die shortly thereafter. Yet Mr. Hocher, a
stubborn Swiss gentleman who is anxious to marry into the family, drinks it
with apparent pleasure and compliments the grandfather on it constantly,
thereby irritating the old man. These episodes not only relieve the tedium of
Benet's wordiness but also serve to point out the hypocrisy of society.

Other episodes jolt the reader by reducing the characters to grotesque,
repulsive, animalistic beings. For example, one night, Jorge Ruan goes to the
room of a woman known as Camila. As he ejaculates, he bites her earlobe,
causing blood to run out of her ear at the same time that his own secretions

flow from his body. Afterward, he places a dead rat on the pillow beside her. Later that night, a woman whom Camila desires and for whom she had been waiting, appears and places the dead rat between the girl's legs. This episode underscores the spiritual ruin of the characters, who, alienated and frightened, seek temporary escape in sex, only to sink back into the depths of their misery after the act. Typically, Benet's characters are emotionally uninvolved, even distant, during sex. Often they are nameless. The narrator is deliberately vague about the woman's name: "I don't think [she] was called Camila, as the few friends who knew her and dealt with her said." The effect is to distance and dehumanize the participants. With irony, the narrator refers to the "cadaver" of the rat, thereby humanizing the animal and insinuating that it is more human than the people who handle it.

The Characters

A Meditation is filled with characters who are governed by strange fixations. For example, the grandfather is so obsessed with his liqueur that he is certain that Carlos Bonaval has stolen and commercially exploited the recipe. Cayetano Corral spends his entire life in his workshop tinkering with clocks. Jorge is fixated on rats. The Indian, who killed his father, masturbates incessantly in front of a picture of his mother. These traits serve to distinguish the characters, who hardly have identities apart from their manias.

Benet's female characters are distinctly sexual beings. Mary, who left for America with her exiled husband, bore children, and returned with a new mate, is representative of the woman who seeks her authentic self by disregarding society's norms and following her passions. Instead of finding freedom and happiness, however, Mary degenerates physically and emotionally.

No character acquires depth or develops through the course of the novel. Most are vague. For example, no one knows why the man called the Indian is known by that name; he is not, in fact, an Indian. Many of the characters are easily confused with one another, among them Mary, Leo, and Laura. Nor do the characters communicate with one another. Although there are fragments of speech throughout the novel, there is no real dialogue. There is no "I-you" relationship, but only one "I" existing alongside another. Even the letter from Cayetano Corral to Carlos Bonaval is more a treatise on psychology and physics than a personal letter, and it leads nowhere, for it is interrupted midway.

Only one voice emerges from the morass of words, that of the narrator. He is the existential "I" who confronts an amorphous world composed of "others." Throughout the novel, he struggles to recall, as precisely as possible, those pertinent incidents and people that influenced the development of his "self." The frequency of expressions such as "perhaps," "I imagine," "how can I know," "I don't remember," and "I can't visualize it" indicates that he is groping for accuracy. Others, such as "I am sure" and "I can still see it," indicate that he is sure of his facts. At times, he contradicts or corrects himself. For example, he begins a scene: "The outbreak of the civil war caught us celebrating a birthday, under the wisteria." Later, he thinks better of it and adds, "Excuse me, a baptism. Cousin Celia had given birth to her second son." Yet it is not through words that he can capture the essence of his existence, for words convert experience into an "objective narration" that pulls together all the loose ends, destroying the chaos and incongruence that are the core of human reality. Cayetano Corral understands that thought cannot be fixed in words. That is why, although he makes notes constantly, he writes only with chalk and erases everything.

Gonzalo Sobejano has written that Región is the real protagonist of *A Meditation*. Indeed, the town suffers from the same disintegration that plagues all the characters; it is "a mummified Región, wrapped in decay, boredom, and solitude." The narrator describes the trash around the trees as "a rotting offer to rottenness." The rotting of trees—which are a traditional symbol of hope—conveys the despair that permeates Región.

Themes and Meanings

The theme that dominates *A Meditation* is the search for the self. Yet this search is doomed from the beginning, because it is expressed through words, and words are inadequate tools of communication: "two people who talk and understand each other by making use of the same words often see two different spectacles inside themselves, neither of which emerges into the other's view and only occasionally giving origin to an emotion that is analogous and shared." Furthermore, the I who remembers is not the same person who experienced the incident, for the individual is ever changing; he feels "as if between my I and my memory of the I there always existed a distance that was . . . unbridgeable." The narrator is alienated not only from society but also from himself. He looks at himself, especially the self that was, as though he were looking at another.

What time does to the narrator, illness does to Mary: "[S]he walks feeling her way behind herself, concerned only with herself and rather alien to all that is going on around her; instead of sitting down to contemplate the countryside or the street she sinks into a hammock, in order, through a pair of dark glasses, to consider her impotent and painful I; and so she remains, converted into a dog of her own I." Mary is so immersed in her own pain that she sniffs around it like a dog, observing it and examining it until "it" becomes a separate entity and "the solution of continuity between beast and fear disappears." Once the primal fear is gone, Mary "is no longer a person of this world," for existential terror is at the center of human existence.

If self-analysis offers no solutions, neither does science. Cayetano Corral observes that "psychology with the pretext of a better precision and differentiation of the elements it is analyzing, does nothing but introduce a radical confusion and seek what belongs to the syntactical in the analogous realm." The knowledge that the individual desires so desperately—the knowledge of the self—constantly eludes him. In fact, there is no real knowledge, because "all knowledge is nothing but the substitute of an experience." Thus, there is no such thing as intellectual certainty, for life is experiential, not intellectual. Self-realization requires breaking with reason and yielding to passion: "there is no true living without passion."

Society's role is to hold in check the passions, which, if given free rein, would lead to anarchy. Society invents rules to maintain order. Public morality is essentially a web of hypocrisy, for while the social man openly supports society's values, the inner man constantly struggles to get free. Thus, "moral history is nothing but a chain of chimeras that go along devouring each other and subrogating their power so as never to give entry to the Individual." Unlike adults, children readily act on impulse, without hypocrisy. The children of the Ruan clan and those of the narrator's play together freely, while their elders invent barriers to separate the two families. It is because the authentic self is buried under the layers of hypocrisy which society imposes that the narrator dwells on his childhood, attempting to strip away the deceptions in order to approximate his early experiences.

There can be no chronological time in the novel because chronology is an ordering device, while memory conjures up images randomly. The intensity of a recollection depends on the intensity with which it was experienced; events that caused no impression fade from the memory. Time is a major preoccupation of the narrator and an obsession of Cayetano Corral. Cayetano understands that "time isn't engendered either by stars or by clocks, but by tears," by the pain of the individual experience that leaves its indelible mark on the memory.

Pain is at the center of all the narrator's recollections, even the humorous ones. There are no completely happy, carefree moments in the novel. There is no real bonding between human beings, even family members. There is no real love. The relationship between father and son is defined by hatred, fear, and resentment. The biblical story of Abraham and Isaac obsesses the narrator, who repeatedly analyzes Isaac's anger toward the father who was willing to sacrifice him. The Indian provides the archetype: "He had killed his father, as his father had done to his grandfather, as his grandfather had done to his great-grandfather; it wasn't a matter of a tradition or a family custom, not even of a curse, but a fate repeated three or four times . . . nor was it, seemingly, taken into consideration by him in order to avoid engendering a son." Alongside man's primal dread is a destructive impulse that is directed at the father, who is the first to impose order and discipline, and also the first to inspire fear. The animosity between Jorge Ruan and his father reveals a profound resentment that takes the form of a literary rivalry between father and son.

For the writer Jorge, art, like sex, is a release from inner anguish. It is a means of getting even with his father by outperforming him. Nevertheless, writing affords Jorge no lasting joy. On the contrary, he is so negative and self-destructive that he cannot bear to talk about his work. He feels contempt for those who worship the word, for he believes, as Benet does, that words serve only to conceal that primal fear that festers below the surface.

Critical Context

Benet is considered one of Spain's premier existentialist writers. Many critics consider *A Meditation*, Benet's second novel, to be his best work. Benet's previous novel, *Volverás a Región* (1967; *Return to Región*, 1985), had failed to attract critical attention, but in 1969, when *A Meditation* received the Biblioteca Breve literary award, the prize attracted readers' attention toward *Return to Región* and *Nunca llegarás a nada* (1959; you will never get anywhere), an early collection of novellas.

Benet has written stories, novellas, plays, and essays in addition to his novels. Yet his work defies classification, for it consistently breaks with traditional boundaries of genre. In his fiction, he has cultivated a circuitous, wordy narrative almost devoid of plot and characterization. The first four— *Return to Región*, *A Meditation*, *Un viaje de invierno* (1972; a winter journey), and *La otra casa de Mazón* (1973; the Mazóns' other house)—take place in Región and have been customarily referred to as the Región cycle. Another novel, *En el estado* (1977, in the state), takes place in La Portada, an area similar to Región. Yet this last novel is different from Benet's previous works in form and style. Nevertheless, in all of his fiction, Benet's vision is one of man alone in an absurd and hostile universe, forced to reinvent himself in order to give meaning to his life.

Sources for Further Study

Cabrera, Vicente. *Juan Benet*, 1983.

Compitello, Malcolm. *Ordering the Evidence: Volverás a Región and Civil War Fiction*, 1983.

Herzberger, David K. "The Emergence of Juan Benet: A New Alternative for the Spanish Novel," in *American Hispanist*. I, no. 3 (1975), pp. 6-12.

_____. *The Novelistic World of Juan Benet*, 1976.

Mantiega, Robert C., David K. Herzberger, and Malcolm Alan Compitello, eds. *Critical Approaches to the Writings of Juan Benet*, 1984.

Barbara Mujica

THE MEETING AT TELGTE

Author: Günter Grass (1927-   )
Type of plot: Historical fiction
Time of plot: 1647, at the close of the Thirty Years' War
Locale: The town of Telgte in Westphalia, Germany
First published: Das Treffen in Telgte, 1979 (English translation, 1981)

> *Principal characters:*
> SIMON DACH, the organizer of the meeting, a prominent
> seventeenth century German poet
> CHRISTOFFEL GELNHAUSEN (modeled after Jakob Christoffel
> Grimmelshausen), a regimental secretary and, later, the
> greatest German novelist of the seventeenth century
> LIBUSHKA, the landlady of the Bridge Tavern at Telgte and
> Grimmelshausen's former mistress
> HEINRICH SCHÜTZ, a great seventeenth century composer

The Novel

Compared to the longer, more monumental works of Günter Grass, *The Meeting at Telgte* is a short novel. It is the story of a fictional 1647 meeting of major figures of the German literary world who actually existed. Poets, prose writers, preachers, musicians, and publishers travel at considerable risk through a Germany ravaged by the Thirty Years' War (1618-1648). This war was the most destructive in German history prior to World War II. By 1647, the year of the meeting, peace was at hand, but much of Germany was decimated, fragmented, and dominated by a caste of authoritarian princes and nobles. Furthermore, the German language had been corrupted by the invading armies of the European powers and was in danger of descending into hideous jargon.

The original goal of these German intellectuals was to meet in Osnabrück, a site of peace negotiations between the Catholic and Protestant European powers and the rival princes of Germany who had fought the German emperor to a standstill. Since Osnabrück remained occupied by the Swedes, however, the writers hold their conclave in the small town of Telgte, a site of pilgrimage midway between Osnabrück and Münster, the two cities in which the Peace Conference of Westphalia will be held.

The noble goal of the writers is to revive, purify, and strengthen the last remaining bond of the German nation, its language and literature. They also aspire to influence the politicians by issuing a manifesto for peace. They meet in the Bridge Tavern. Room and board are secured by Christoffel Gelnhausen, a regimental secretary and aspiring novelist. His former mistress, Libushka, is the obliging landlady of the tavern. Gelnhausen clears out the tavern for the writers by announcing the presence of the plague (a widespread cause of death at the time).

The writers settle in and embark on their patriotic literary projects. They soon squabble over the proper use of dactylic words, the essence of irony and humor, and the applicability of classical models. They separate into factions: optimists against pessimists, purists against pragmatists, and Catholics against Protestants. Such is the irony of their unifying goal. Their sessions are a combination of serious discussions and the comic, bawdy, grotesque, and chaotic happenings characteristic of Grass's novels. While the older writers draft their high-flown manifestos, the younger ones fornicate with the serving maids. Then, all settle down to a great feast, forcibly procured by the soldier Gelnhausen.

At the end of this short novel, the writers finally agree on a lengthy statement exhorting peace, religious toleration, the reform of the German language, and efforts at political unity. Though their appeal would have gone unheeded anyway, says the narrator, the tavern catches fire and the declaration is destroyed. The writers set off for their diverse destinations, harboring the dream that their noble words and goals will live on. The novel ends on a note of resignation and ambiguity, for no one, including the omniscient narrator, knows who set fire to the tavern. The results of the best efforts of the writers are left to the imagination of the reader.

The Characters

Although the meeting at Telgte so vividly described by Grass never took place, the characters of the novel actually existed and made some important efforts to salvage German language, literature, and culture. The twenty major and minor characters represent a blend of the realistic and fantastic typical of Grass. The identity of the narrator is never revealed. He is omniscient; he evidences a great knowledge of seventeenth century German Baroque literature and a familiarity with the writers themselves. He even knows the details of their physical appearance. The narrator uses indirect statements to distance himself from the story. This is the technique used in *Die Blechtrommel* (1959; *The Tin Drum*, 1961), Grass's picaresque novel about World War II. Finally, the narrator is clearly writing from the perspective of the present: He begins the book by saying that yesterday will be what tomorrow has been. Thus, the narrator's role is in part to link the seventeenth with the twentieth century.

The rest of the characters are a collection of most of the major German literary and cultural figures of the seventeenth century. They represent a great variety of regions, ages, temperaments, and literary forms. Some are self-made men of action such as the soldier Gelnhausen and the civil servant Georg Rudolf Weckherlin, who has left Germany for London to become John Milton's predecessor as Latin secretary under the British Puritan

Commonwealth. The characters include dour preachers and hymn writers, such as Paul Gerhardt and Johann Rist, and the satirists Johann Michel Moscherosch and Friedrich von Logau. Philipp von Zesen represents the literary theorists and Andreas Gryphius is present as the greatest German dramatist of the seventeenth century. The great and aging composer of the first German opera and of fine religious music, Heinrich Schütz, is cast as a man of great wisdom. The organizer of the conference is the venerable poet Simon Dach, a man of tolerance and benevolence.

The figures come from every part of Germany. Most are Protestant Lutherans. A few are Catholic. Some, such as the satirist Logau, are skeptics. Many have founded regional language and literary societies to purify and preserve the German language. They disagree over such matters as the use of dialect, matters of form, and the definition of what is "German." All, however, are cultural and literary patriots and exhibit a love for the art, something the politicians have abdicated. They wish to revitalize German language and culture, the only force of unity left in their fragmented and demoralized country. In that sense, they see themselves as the center of national consciousness, the "true Germany." Grass portrays their efforts sympathetically, but ironically.

The characters are torn between their idealism and their rivalries and physical needs. They find themselves implicated in the war they condemn when their feast is procured by violence and plunder. Then, they have the temerity to try Gelnhausen when he reveals his desire to become a writer of the realistic school. The satirist Logau defends Gelnhausen and berates his fellow writers for serving and praising the very princes who are responsible for the war. It is clear that the author's sympathy lies with Gelnhausen and Logau. Nicknamed "Courage," the landlady and former prostitute Libushka is also portrayed as honest and humane. Grimmelshausen wrote a drama about a similar "Courage," and Bertolt Brecht celebrated her in his play *Mutter Courage und ihre Kinder* (1940; *Mother Courage and Her Children*, 1941). Grass obviously has only contempt for such literary snobs as Zesen, who witnesses two entwined corpses floating in a river and wonders how he will feature them in his next romance. In contrast, Gelnhausen will write about life as it really is.

Toward the end of the novel, the characters grow humbler about their political limitations, and they part amicably. They have become more realistic about the place and the power of the writer, and they feel less isolated than before.

Most of the literary figures will be unfamiliar to the general reader. Although the names of the characters remain obscure and the influence on their contemporaries was minimal, their impact was ultimately important. Their dreams of German unity and greatness remained frustrated but lived on. Their resentment of foreigners, their bombastic praise of a narrow

"Germanness," their attempt to compensate for national fragmentation by glorification of the language, national traits, and a great past occurred in the absence of a viable political structure. The historical obsession with German national identity would continue and eventually become disastrous three hundred years later.

Themes and Meanings

The connection between 1647 and 1947 is a major theme of *The Meeting at Telgte*. The fictitious meeting of 1647 is the counterpart of a real meeting of German poets and writers known as Gruppe 47. They met in 1947, at the end of the most devastating war in modern history. As was the case in 1647, the community of concerned German writers was faced with the repair of the language, this time after twelve years of Nazi barbarism and propaganda. As in 1647, the German writers strove to reassert the humane values of enlightenment, tolerance, and humanism. Grass dedicated *The Meeting at Telgte* to commemorate the seventieth birthday of Hans Werner Richter, the founder of Gruppe 47. Grass was to join the group as a young writer and was given its literary prize for his first great novel, *The Tin Drum*.

As with all of his novels, Grass designed the book jacket of *The Meeting at Telgte*. As a reminder of Baroque symbolism, it depicts a writer's hand holding a frayed goose-quill pen. The hand is rising triumphantly like a phoenix from the rubble below, symbolizing the struggle of the writer to give meaning and to create values for his age even in the aftermath of the worst war and destruction.

The parallels between past and present may apply to at least two of the characters in the novel. Simon Dach is reminiscent of Hans Werner Richter, while Christoffel Gelnhausen, the self-educated picaresque novelist and lover of life in all of its forms, comes close to the outlook of Günter Grass himself.

The novel reveals other levels of meaning. It can be read as a parody of the pretensions of writers, intellectuals, and literary gatherings. It also deals with the tension between reality and ideals. The characters who meet at Telgte seek to create a new Germany; yet they also readily escape into feasting, drinking, and fornicating. Their literary aims are somewhat humbled by the scenes of horror they witness. They begin to recognize that their lofty ideals cannot be realized in an immoral world.

If *The Meeting at Telgte* is a parody, it is also an elegy to the writer as a national figure. Grass presents the problems that writers have in trying to influence the politics and the events of their time.

As historical fiction, the novel succeeds brilliantly. The stylistic devices run the usual Grassian gamut from comedy, ribaldry, and irony to horror, stark realism, and back to idealism and finally material concerns. As in Grass's previous novels, the imagery of food is important. The last fish dinner the writers settle down to eat is reminiscent of the Last Supper. The thistle is also an important image; it is a German baroque symbol of patriotic linguistic purity. In a fit of rage, one of the characters smashes a potted thistle, symbolizing what has become of the Germany tongue. Yet the thistle remains intact, a sign that the consciousness of the nation lives on in the minds of its writers.

Critical Context

Compared to Grass's greatest works, *The Meeting at Telgte* is a modest novel. Still, it is fascinating in its depiction of a remote but vital epoch of German history. It is also a stimulating and entertaining book. It challenges the reader to reflect on the role of the writer in national affairs, politics, and war. In addition, it affirms Grass's belief that writers have a strong obligation to their society, no matter how limited their influence may seem. The novel serves as a reminder that the German problem still exists.

Where the imaginary meeting of 1647 failed, Günter Grass has succeeded. He was the product of the real Gruppe 47 and remains a strong public conscience, a classic German author of today.

Sources for Further Study

Grass, Günter. *On Writing and Politics, 1967-1983*, 1985.
Hollington, Michael. *Günter Grass: The Writer in a Pluralist Society*, 1980.
Lawson, Richard H. *Günter Grass*, 1985.
Leonard, Irène. *Günter Grass*, 1974.
Miles, Keith. *Günter Grass*, 1975.

Leon Stein

MEMED, MY HAWK

Author: Yashar Kemal (Yaşar Kemal Gökçeli, 1922-   )
Type of plot: Adventure/folktale
Time of plot: Probably the 1940's
Locale: The Çukurova region of Turkey, in south-central Anatolia
First published: İnce Memed, 1955 (English translation, 1961)

> *Principal characters:*
> İNCE MEMED (SLIM MEMED), a young man who has turned to
>   banditry
> DEUNEH, his mother
> HATÇE, a girl from the neighborhood who becomes Memed's
>   wife
> ABDİ AĞA, a powerful local landowner
> VELİ, Abdi's nephew
> MAD DURDU, a well-known brigand from the area
> SERGEANT RECEP, a police officer who has turned outlaw
> KERİMOĞLU, the leader of an outlaw band that sometimes
>   works with Durdu's group
> ALİ SAFA BEY, one of Abdi's associates
> KALAYCI OSMAN, a local thug employed by Abdi
> IRAZ, Hatçe's aunt
> SERGEANT ASIM, a law enforcement officer from the area

The Novel

A young boy's entrance into full-fledged manhood is accompanied by social realizations that lead him onto what, by official standards, are wayward paths; still, most people in his native village regard him as a local hero. Eventually his name takes on semilegendary connotations. Along the way a number of odd encounters take place which dramatize the distinctions between formally constituted authority and the basic notions of justice that common people in Turkey actually hold. The story begins with İnce (Slim) Memed, who has grown up without a father and has spent much of his time with his mother, Deuneh, or with other relatives in nearby villages. Rather early, his relationship with Hatçe, a neighbor girl, blossoms into a full-scale love affair; she finds a way around every obstacle her family puts in the way of their courtship. Soon her songs to him have become known throughout the area. It is not long before they become engaged, and in a breathless fit of passion they make love under the open sky. In other ways, however, their lives are complicated by the grasping intrigues of Abdi Ağa, a dubious character whom the others disparage as a sallow, goat-bearded old man. This local grandee insists upon returning a smaller share of the wheat crop to Memed's mother than he allows the other villagers to retain; he routinely beats those he considers to be beneath him, and he mishandles Memed severely. One of his ambitions is to have Hatçe married to his nephew Veli. By a ruse Memed thwarts this plan before the arrangements can be completed and spirits away Hatçe. Abdi sets his men to tracking them as they would wild animals. When they catch up with Memed, he opens fire with his rifle on Abdi and leaves him badly wounded. During the same exchange of shots, Veli is left dead; the others capture Hatçe while Memed is making his escape. After Hatçe is thrown into prison, Abdi, in an effort that amounts to the subornation of perjury, has his men testify that it was she who fired the fatal shots.

Memed joins that peculiar informal brotherhood of outlaws which seems to flourish perennially in the region. In the course of a rough-and-ready existence he comes across some rather picturesque individuals. For a time he joins the band of Mad Durdu, a highwayman who specializes in forcing travelers to divest themselves of all of their clothing, including their underwear. Memed also becomes acquainted with Sergeant Recep, a renegade policeman who has often been on the wrong side of the law, and who seems to want to assist the younger man. In time Memed turns away from the wholesale and senseless aggression Durdu practices: When the notorious bandit turns on another old gang leader, Kerimoğlu, and threatens him, Memed and Recep force Durdu at gunpoint to back away. Memed is more concerned with combating the injustices perpetrated by village officials; in the process, however, he and Recep agree not to kill bystanders or those who have acted honorably, notwithstanding their association with Abdi. In a bold assault on their primary antagonist, Memed and his men set fire to Abdi's house and leave a charred trail in their wake. Although during this time Recep falls dead after a confrontation with the police, the villagers begin to side more openly with the young outlaw leader. After a while they begin to call Memed their "hawk," a man who fights oppression by swooping down mysteriously and unexpectedly upon unjust local potentates.

Although Memed and his outlaws may act according to standards of basic decency, their opponents have few reservations about the tactics they use in the effort to preserve their own sway. Indeed, Abdi Ağa draws up a cutthroat band of his own, including some individuals suspected of violent and destructive acts during their careers on either side of the law. A certain Ali Safa Bey offers to obtain stocks of ammunition for Abdi; they also open conversations with Kalaycı Osman, an unsavory character who was once involved in the wanton shooting of a man at his wedding. By some estimates he may have killed forty people in all during his career. On the other hand, there are some defections from Abdi's forces, as men who previously had collaborated with him begin to supply information to Memed and his followers. The common people, far from assisting their nominal leaders, begin instead to regard the outlaws as the real government of the area.

Memed's homecoming leads to a final denouement of violence. Stealthily he enters the town's prison and manages to visit Hatçe; later, when she is being transferred to another location, he helps her escape. They are joined by Iraz, Hatçe's aunt, as they make their way about the rocky mountain redoubts nearby. Much hiding and seeking takes place as various police forces are brought to the scene. The authorities turn to measures of wholesale intimidation to obtain information about Memed from the villagers; in the process, an elderly man and his wife are beaten senseless, and others are similarly mistreated. It is learned that at some point Deuneh has died, after being trampled unmercifully by Abdi's men during the early stages of the manhunt. During that winter, the peasants are inspired by Memed's acts of defiance and begin to appropriate lands and goods for themselves. For his part Memed is able to find refuge in one of the craggy lairs in the towering peaks around him. In a series of climactic confrontations, he is surrounded by the police; though he cannot be forced into the open, he is torn between his inclination to keep fighting and his responsibilities to others, for during this time he and Hatçe have become married. At one juncture Hatçe gives birth to a baby son, and Memed surprises his adversaries by offering to surrender to a certain Sergeant Asım. This proposal is refused—the lawman believes that he cannot honorably apprehend the celebrated brigand under such circumstances—but in a later encounter Hatçe is killed during another burst of fighting. In one final bold gesture Memed rides into his native village, goes straight up to the house of a startled Abdi Ağa, and shoots his opponent dead; he then goes off, leaving the local people to marvel at his audacity in ridding them of one of the most hated and feared officials in the area.

The Characters

The extreme polarization of social relations in the region described in *Memed, My Hawk* makes it possible to regard the major characters as essentially of several types. To be sure, there are some variations, and there are cases in which some individuals seem to act on one and then on another side of various disputes, but for the most part the struggle between the forces of an unjust order and the brigands imposes distinctions that are acknowledged all around by the various figures in this novel. At the same time, the elements of ambivalence that exist in some characters impart added interest to them, though in other cases there are some who simply are not so fully developed as others. At times as well, the author seems reticent in tracing the thoughts and inner lives of various individuals, even as changes of scene and action would otherwise seem to bring them into focus.

At the outset Memed is portrayed as a tough, simple, hardworking youth who is grimly conscious that he has been grievously wronged by Abdi and his henchmen. His frustration and bitterness are likely to flare up all at once; it is particularly significant that, very much in addition to resentment at the reign of injustice in his village, it is a quarrel over Hatçe that goads him finally into becoming an outlaw. He seems mercurial and is given sometimes to feats of derring-do for their own sake; this propensity is demonstrated notably during some gun battles and in his agile manner of scaling rocky slopes when he is in flight from the authorities. The motive of vengeance evidently weighs heavily upon him; many of his exploits are directed specifically at bringing down his adversary. He does, however, have some sense of fair play, and he possesses some discernment about the actual loyalties and intentions of other characters. Memed's own basic scruples lead him to abandon Durdu and his accomplices; for that matter Memed is careful to recognize those from the other camp who have assisted him as well. Unlike some other bandits, Memed does not turn to indiscriminate pillage and looting for their own sake; though this question is taken up more conclusively in a later work, it is not clear at the end of this novel whether he intends to continue with his activities as a sort of free-lance outlaw.

Among those who in one way or another have acted outside the law, there are some who are decidedly less sympathetic than others. Durdu seems possessed by some strange compulsion to subject others to gross indignities; it does not matter to him whether his intended victims are harmless wayfarers or his own partners in crime. Kerimoğlu, himself an outlaw leader of note, earns some favor from the others when he protests against Durdu's attempts to demean him. Sergeant Recep appears to share many of Memed's values, and indeed supports the younger man when they take their leave of Durdu; Recep is also more than willing to expose himself to danger for the sake of Memed. On the other hand, with few exceptions the tactics adopted by the authorities provide caustic commentary on the forms of corruption that power seems to spawn in rural Turkey.

There is little that can be said in extenuation of Abdi Ağa's vicious and self-serving schemes; indeed, it could be maintained that the author has not really attempted to elucidate the inner workings of this most unappealing character. Not much is revealed about his past or his personal life. Among the charges laid against him are peculation, dishonesty, willful perversion of justice, gross brutality, and conspiracy to bring about the violent deaths of his opponents. For that matter, though he is a fairly good shot, he does not have any particular courage in his own right. Others who are drawn into the fray include Ali Safa Bey, who had studied law before involving himself in some rather devious schemes to gain title to vast tracts of land. Kalaycı Osman is a psychopathic type who seems to have few qualms about vicious and violent undertakings. Their part in the ongoing manhunt reflects the essential lack of scruples which Abdi Ağa has displayed all along. Of a different sort, however, is Sergeant Asım, who should receive some passing honorable mention for refusing to take advantage of Memed's preoccupation with his newborn child. It is significant that Memed has more respect for him than he does for others who work more directly with Abdi.

The love interests that surface from time to time in this work necessarily are muted by the stark and gripping conflicts that set Memed against his pursuers. There is, however, little fundamental doubt of Hatçe's ultimate devotion to Memed. Her early attraction to him, over and against Abdi's efforts to foist Veli upon her, seems genuinely felt. Even under the tribulations of her imprisonment, she will not turn upon him or collaborate with the authorities. As a final measure of her trust in him she follows Memed into his lair, under rather harrowing circumstances. For his part, it would seem that her death toward the end of the novel is a shattering experience, which uproots many of his remaining ties with his native village.

Themes and Meanings

There has been in Turkey a long and cherished tradition of banditry, where outlaws felt called upon to express popular dissatisfaction with the prevailing order. Often political upheaval, weakening the powers of the central government, permitted local chieftains to assert themselves in various parts of Anatolia. During such times there was sometimes admiration or sympathy for noted brigands; songs and folktales sprang up celebrating the audacity and exploits of various outlaw leaders. It was from this tradition that Yashar Kemal's first novel was drawn. At various places in *Memed, My Hawk* there are references to outlaw leaders from the past, some fictitious and some real. It may be contended that the characterization is overly romanticized and that it depends upon ideal types which are essentially based upon the author's efforts to recapture the more heroic elements in the outlaw tradition. Kemal's interest in folklore, which portrays bandits in a guise that is larger than life, may have affected his fictional creations; on the other hand, this conception may have produced a more gripping and evocative work than would have resulted from efforts at a more balanced and even-handed narrative. All the same, this novel should be read for the sense of action and adventure it conveys. As social commentary its effect may suffer somewhat from the author's stereotypical approach.

The undercurrents of violence that run through this work illustrate another aspect of Kemal's social vision. According to the author, village life in Turkey is conditioned to a great extent by violence and responses to brutality. Orderly processes for settling disputes do not really seem to exist; even those who exercise some legal functions ally themselves with those who can bring the use of force to bear on any outstanding issues. In some respects the author may have generalized from certain egregious examples. It may be asked, for example, whether the savage beatings and intimidation Abdi and his minions dispense necessarily are typical of practices in all rural communities throughout Turkey. In some ways, indeed, it could be contended that, for Memed and his companions to be cast in a glowing light, it is corresponding necessary for their opponents to be depicted in the darkest possible hues. Thus the demands of plot and narrative functions may have produced contrasts that conceivably may be unnecessarily severe.

Critical Context

As Yashar Kemal's first novel, *Memed, My Hawk* created a literary sensation when it was first published, and the author was acclaimed as a major new talent. He won his country's prestigious Varlık Prize for this work and, as translations appeared, he became one of the most widely recognized Turkish writers. Even after a number of subsequent efforts have appeared, his literary reputation is still derived to some significant extent from this novel. To be sure, the thematic concerns or locales of his later productions have shifted. Other works, such as the trilogy beginning with *Ortadirek* (1960; *The Wind from the Plain*, 1963) and concluding with *Ölmez otu* (1968; *The Undying Grass*, 1977), present a much broader vision of social life in the Çukurova region. In this series there are some interesting mentions of İnce Memed's story. Yashar Kemal brought back his first major protagonist in another offering, as a sort of sequel, *İnce Memed II* (1969; *They Burn the Thistles*, 1973), in which there are references to Memed's original exploits in the context of another sharply drawn conflict between brigands and scheming local officials. In that work the successors to Abdi Ağa are confronted in some dramatic and violent encounters before Memed finally rides off into the distance. Other settings and characters appear in novels drawn from folktales of the regions around Mount Ararat and Mount Binboğa. Maritime locales are utilized in efforts such as *Al gözüm seyreyle Salih* (1976; *Seagull*, 1981) and *Deniz küstü* (1979; *The Sea-Crossed Fisherman*, 1985), which take up themes of youth and criminal activity in the greater Istanbul area.

The common elements in most of Yashar Kemal's works, notably the use of folk motifs in studies of crime and violence, reveal the various combinations that in this way are open to the writer. It would seem that in some respects *Memed, My Hawk* is more melodramatic than other offerings; this very quality, however, may account for the widespread acceptance of this novel. It could in this regard be considered as a gripping story well told. In this sense, it may be contended that, quite apart from the efforts at social realism found in some of Kemal's other novels, the elements of adventure and high drama are attractive features in the kind of narrative he has produced.

Sources for Further Study

Al'kaeva, Leila Osmanovna. "*İnce Memed*," in *Edebiyat*. V, nos. 1/2 (1980), pp. 69-82.
Başgöz, İlhan. "Yaşar Kemal and Turkish Folk Literature," in *Edebiyat*. V,

nos. 1/2 (1980), pp. 37-47.

Hickman, William C. "Traditional Themes in the Work of Yaşar Kemal: *İnce Memed*," in *Edebiyat*. V, nos. 1/2 (1980), pp. 55-68.

Karpat, Kemal H. "Contemporary Turkish Literature," in *The Literary Review*. IV, no. 2 (1960/1961), pp. 287-302.

_____. "Social Themes in Contemporary Turkish Literature," in *The Middle East Journal*. XIV, nos. 1/2 (1960), pp. 29-44, 153-168.

Ötüş-Baskett, Belma. "Yaşar Kemal's Dream of Social Change: The Fable of the Hawk and the Goatbeard," in *Edebiyat*. V, nos. 1/2 (1980), pp. 87-93.

Rathbun, Carole. *The Village in the Turkish Novel and Short Story, 1920 to 1955*, 1972.

J. R. Broadus

A MINOR APOCALYPSE

Author: Tadeusz Konwicki (1926-　　)
Type of plot: Historical fantasy
Time of plot: Sometime in the not-too-distant future
Locale: Poland
First published: Mała apokalipsa, 1979 (English translation, 1983)

> *Principal characters:*
> KONWICKI, the narrator
> HUBERT and RYSIO, two Polish dissidents who ask Konwicki
> to set himself on fire in protest against the Polish
> government
> NADEZHDA, a beautiful Russian woman who is attracted to
> Konwicki
> COMRADE KOBIALKA, Konwicki's neighbor and a high-ranking
> Polish politician who takes his clothes off on television as a
> protest against the system
> COMRADE SACHER, a Politburo member who once threw
> Konwicki out of the Communist Party but who now
> befriends the narrator
> TADZIO SKORKO, a young Pole from the provinces who
> befriends Konwicki but who is also a police informer
> JAN, a revered dissident who is exhausted and depressed by
> his years of opposition to the government

The Novel

A Minor Apocalypse takes place sometime in the not-too-distant future. The author makes himself the narrator and protagonist who is importuned by two dissident friends to set himself on fire as a protest against the inhumanity of the Polish government. Hubert and Rysio suggest that Tadeusz Konwicki should sacrifice himself because he is a prominent writer—but not so valuable that his loss would do irreparable damage to the nation. Konwicki would like to ridicule their proposition, yet he is forced to take it seriously because of his own stymied creativity and the demoralizing stasis of the country as a whole. As he says to Jan, whom he has regarded as a moral beacon of the culture, "someone has to break this lethargy. . . . To wake the sleepers with a wild cry."

Much of *A Minor Apocalypse* is taken up with Konwicki's efforts to prepare himself for his immolation in the service of the Polish quest for freedom. During his daylong journey around Warsaw, he meets several figures who are representative of the culture, of both the authorities and the Polish underground. Much of the narrator's own past is also revealed. He is, himself, a compromised figure, having once been a Party member. What strikes him now is how long both the government and its opponents have put up with a stalemated situation. If the Communists have not built a better world through socialism, the opposition has become almost comfortable with its lack of effectiveness. At times, it seems more like a weary game the two sides are playing.

Indeed, Poland has been under the Russian hammer for ages, it seems, and the result is that no one is sure of the country's own history. Dates vary in the novel, and the narrator is never quite certain which anniversary of the victory of socialism is being celebrated. Time itself has become a political tool. In such vague and ambiguous circumstances, Konwicki wonders—right up to the end of the novel—whether his sacrifice will have meaning.

The Characters

Although the Konwicki character of *A Minor Apocalypse* bears a striking resemblance to the novelist, author and narrator are not the same. If Konwicki did at one time collaborate with the Polish Stalinist state in the late 1940's and early 1950's, he has also had a much more successful career in opposition than his namesake in the novel. After 1954, the novelist turned against the government and authored several significant novels and directed several important films. While he may feel the weariness of his narrator and rue the seeming futility of Polish history, his art has been steadfastly witty and energetic—hardly the sign of an exhausted talent.

A Minor Apocalypse abounds in interesting characters. Hubert and Rysio, for example, present the bizarre plan for Konwicki's sacrifice in rational, well-articulated terms. They are men in the business of dissidence. Even though Konwicki wants to discount what they say, he recognizes the impulse behind their extremism. They want to galvanize a country slipping away into acquiescence to the status quo. Moreover, Konwicki realizes that something is afoot (perhaps a change in the *Zeitgeist*?) when Comrade Kobialka strips on nationwide television and addresses Party members as Comrade Swine. The totalitarian system is itself victimized by an unreality that some of its members occasionally acknowledge.

It is extraordinary how much good fellow-feeling Poles on opposite sides of the political fence have for each other in this novel. Even when Konwicki is tortured with a sophisticated drug that makes the slightest touch of his flesh excruciatingly painful, he is entertained by a tormentor who tacitly acknowledges that all Poles are in the same historical boat. The question is not whether to compromise with the Russians, but rather the limits to which the individual will go in compromising. Thus the young Tadzio Skorko is a genuine admirer of Konwicki, the dissident, yet informs on Konwicki nevertheless. Similarly, Konwicki turns on Tadzio and threatens physical violence, but no harm is actually done to the informer because the narrator surely knows that Tadzio is an aspect of himself—or at least of his former self. Konwicki makes a point of noting that he is from the provinces, and Tadzio is repeatedly described as a young man from the provinces. Tadzio, too, is another form of the narrator's own name, Tadeusz.

Comrade Sacher is perfectly expressive of the absurd Polish situation, in which characters have a way of turning into their opposites. He has been a Party hack, responsible for expelling Konwicki from the Party. Now in old age Sacher turns to painting and would like to view himself and Konwicki as fellow artists. In this pre-Solidarity novel, Poles are, in other words, divided against themselves and suspicious of one another's motivations. Rysio, the dissident, is opposed by his brother, a government official, who calls him an idiot and accuses him of "dreams of a career on a world scale. That's why he writes that unpunctuated, dissident prose."

The Russians—traditionally viewed as the source of most of Poland's misfortunes—are presented sympathetically in the figure of Nadezhda. She falls in love with Konwicki but reveals how little the Russians know about Poles. Konwicki is fascinated with her and not about to give her up. Time after time, the individuality of the novel's characters makes them larger than the opinions they express. Konwicki does not care much for Russians, yet he cannot seem to help his attraction to Nadezhda. The contradictions that Konwicki finds are the contradictions not simply of socialism but also of humanity as a whole.

Themes and Meanings

"Apocalypse" is not usually associated with the word "minor." "Apocalypse" means some kind of prophetic disclosure or revelation. If Konwicki's self-immolation is a "minor apocalypse" in that it involves only one person, it is also, perhaps, an ironic recognition of what is true for all human beings, who have their self-destructive urges. Near the beginning of the novel, he lights a cigarette and notes, "Everybody shortens their existence on the sly." By putting a match to himself in public, the narrator acknowledges what he knows to be true of people in private.

As he walks around Warsaw, the narrator sees over and over again signs reading WE HAVE BUILT SOCIALISM! These ludicrous, self-congratulatory messages seem more amusing every time they are mentioned, since no one behaves as though anything has been accomplished. On the contrary, the system seems to be dying of its own inanition. Comrade Kobialka finds himself in the same torture chamber as Konwicki and asks the novelist if he believes that the Communist government is coming to an end. "Everything's coming to an end. Water, coal, the whole world," Konwicki replies, for this is a world that has lost faith in itself.

Except for Jan, who serves as a reminder that even the most stalwart humanists may succumb to disappointment and old age, Konwicki's characters, including himself, approach the seeming hopelessness of the Polish situation with incredible zest. Konwicki has time for a love affair on the last day of his life and goes through several police interrogations with most of his humor and resilience intact. Tadzio doggedly follows Konwicki, gas can at the ready, to do his literary master's bidding. Somehow the act of stripping has made Comrade Kobialka quite lively in his delineation of Polish entropy. There is, in the end, something irrepressible about the human temperament that compensates for the catastrophe of Polish life. As Jaroslaw Anders puts it in his review of the novel in *The New Republic*: "Konwicki's protagonist clings to the belief in the immortality of the world, and this belief makes him accept his own, seemingly absurd death as the only human conclusion of the day of humiliations and reckonings."

Critical Context

A *Minor Apocalypse* quickly became a controversial novel when it appeared in 1979. Konwicki seemed to be attacking everyone—not simply the Russians and the Polish government but also dissidents and the West. Like several other critics of the novel, its American translator, Richard Lourie, identifies certain characters as based on prominent Polish artists and intellectuals. He suggests in his translator's introduction that Konwicki is settling scores with many of his Polish colleagues, including the famous film director Andrzej Wajda. While there is little doubt that certain characters have their origins in real-life models, it seems misguided to call *A Minor Apocalypse* a *roman à clef*; that is, the author has more in mind than immediate political realities. The characters in his novel, like the character of Konwicki himself, are fully imagined figures in a fable of history. As Anders concludes, "By placing his story in an indefinite future, where time has almost ceased to exist, Konwicki captures this repetitive character of the Polish drama, giving us not Poland in a particular moment but a summa of Polish history."

A *Minor Apocalypse* is one of those novels that is particularly sensitive to the changing currents of history. It was written just before the Solidarity strikes in August of 1980. At that time, Polish society seemed particularly stagnant and divisive. The standard of living was rapidly dropping, the political opposition to the government seemed hapless, and the country seemed to be drifting toward the apathy that is so acutely present in the novel. The stunning success of Solidarity then seemed to prove Konwicki wrong, for the country aroused itself in a massive movement in favor of democracy and human rights. Yet the subsequent suppression of Solidarity supports his skeptical vision about the possibilities of a permanent change for the better. Whether anything more than a "minor apocalypse" is possible in Poland is an open question, a question Konwicki has posed with great wit, humor, and tolerance.

Sources for Further Study

Anders, Jaroslaw. Review in *The New Republic*. CLXXXIX (November 21, 1983), pp. 43-45.

Fuksiewicz, J. *Tadeusz Konwicki*, 1967.

Krzyżanowski, J. R. "The Haunted World of Tadeusz Konwicki," in *Books Abroad*, XLVIII (1974), p. 3.

The New York Review of Books. Review. XXX (October 13, 1983), pp. 19-20.

The New York Times Book Review. Review. LXXXVIII (October 23, 1983), p. 13.

The New Yorker. Review. LIX (January 2, 1984), pp. 89-90.

Newsweek. Review. CII (August 8, 1983), p. 72.

Rostropowicz, Clark J. "Introduction," in *The Polish Complex*, 1984.

Wegner, J. *Konwicki*, 1973.

Carl E. Rollyson, Jr.

MIRACLE OF THE ROSE

Author: Jean Genet (1910-1986)
Type of plot: Inverted romanticism
Time of plot: Approximately the first thirty years of the narrator's life
Locale: A boys' reformatory at Mettray and the Fontevrault Prison
First published: Miracle de la rose, 1946; revised, 1951 (English translation, 1966)

Principal characters:

THE NARRATOR, a prisoner in the prison at Fontevrault

HARCAMONE, a condemned man who is in a death cell at Fontevrault

BULKAEN, a young weakling who is covered with tattoos

VILLEROY, the boy who plays "big shot" to the narrator's "chicken" at Mettray

DIVERS, Villeroy's successor, who "marries" the narrator at Mettray and then reappears fifteen years later at the prison

VAN ROY, the "big shot" to whom the narrator is sold by Villeroy

The Novel

Confined to prison for stealing a ring, the narrator begins to relive his wonderful memories of the reformatory at Mettray and the prison at Fontevrault, which was, for the boys, "the sanctuary to which our childhood dreams aspired." To the narrator, the prison becomes the "universe for which I am meant."

The narrator tells of sexual assaults made upon him by the older boys at Mettray, of his being a concubine to Villeroy, whom he adored, and to Van Roy, whom he did not. He tells of his one-day "marriage" to Divers (they do not see each other again until fifteen years later, in the disciplinary hall at Fontevrault). He tells of his seduction by Divers; of his desire for Bulkaen, another prisoner at Fontevrault, whom he invested with manly virtues in order to find him worthy of love. Between their assigned tasks, the prisoners develop friendships and love affairs, concoct small comforts, and set up elaborate means of communication.

The miracle of the novel is connected with Harcamone, already at the prison awaiting execution. He is the hero of convict society. "I thus," says the narrator, "aspired to heavenly glory, and Harcamone had attained it before me, quietly, as the result of murdering a little girl. . . ." Only sixteen years old at the time, Harcamone had raped the frightened child ("the shuddering little bitch"), then strangled her—an act which grants the narrator "the vision of an ascension to the paradise that is offered me."

The narrator haunts the vicinity of the condemned man's cell and sees "the burden of saintliness" on Harcamone's chain transformed "into a garland of white flowers." As Harcamone approaches death, the narrator has a succession of dream visions, the most impressive of which reveals the center of Harcamone's heart as "a red rose of monstrous size and beauty." The action of the book culminates in the execution of one convict, Harcamone, and the shooting of another for trying to escape.

The Characters

The narrator of *Miracle of the Rose* is an autobiographical figure. Like him, Jean Genet spent his childhood and adolescence in a reformatory and was later sentenced to prison. *Miracle of the Rose* was written while Genet was incarcerated at La Sante and Tourelles prisons.

The characters are criminals, often with exotic names; all speak the French argot. The narrator refers to different boys and men by name, but it is impossible to get an individualized picture of any of them. They have no personal idiosyncrasies or ambitions. In a sense, they are all the same, moving between fidelity and betrayal, courage and cowardice, possibly because Genet is only concerned with their sexuality.

Harcamone becomes a sacrificial figure. He sees death as "the only way of shortening his captivity." That escape comes with "a rather trivial act"; he cuts the throat of the one guard who had shown any kindness to him at the beginning of his life sentence, "a man insolent with mildness." Luckily, this murder differed from his first; "all too often people overlook the sufferings of the murderer who always kills in the same way."

The narrator's accounts of events and his complicated loves dovetail with the memories of little boy "big shots," "chickens," and "jerks" in the hierarchical world of Mettray. The prison society is equally and intensely as snobbish. It is dominated by the "toughs," hard cases who exact tribute in the form of sex and tobacco from the other criminals. "Crashers" (burglars) will not talk to pimps. Influence is based on length of term. France outside the walls practically ceases to exist: A war is going on somewhere; the prisoners are making camouflage nets for the Germans rather than mailbags.

Genet makes a religion of evil. Pimps, crashers, big shots, and chickens exist primarily as angels and archangels in this inverted heaven of prison. Out of pity for another, one prisoner will attack a third, although he knows it means additional punishment for him. It is a world where all feelings, pity, anger, and cruelty are on the surface and produce instant action. In this atmosphere, the detailed homosexual encounters become routine.

Themes and Meanings

There is no ordered narration to the novel. It moves back and forth within a vague time frame from the reformatory to Fontevrault. The ideals and code of the reformatory set those for the prison.

Genet traces a change from "feminine" to "masculine" homosexual love in a most credible fashion. When ordered to keep his mouth open so that seven of the prison's "big shots" can take turns spitting into it, the narrator believes that he is being covered "with roses that had been tossed at me. . . . I was the object of an amorous rite. I wanted them to spit more and thicker slime."

There is a twisting of piety that allows a vision in which the chains of a condemned murderer become roses of utmost purity and scent. The narrator expresses strong emotions and wants to change every situation with noble terms. Robberies symbolize heroic and religious acts. Burglary becomes a form of sexual excitement. The murderer who commits rape and pays for it with his life is raised to the level of saint and martyr.

The narrator seems to have gone through a profound mystical experience in prison. He learns that his path is one of inner searching. Consequently, when he arrives at the prison, the fountain becomes a symbol that indicates his inner transformation is about to begin. He gives Bulkaen the characteristics that he likes and in so doing, the narrator activates his deepest unconscious. The ship image symbolizes his freedom to escape the confines of the prison atmosphere. Genet moves into a moral realm different from that of ordinary people. "War was beautiful in the past because in shedding blood it produced glory. It is even more beautiful now because it creates pain, violence, and despair. It breeds sobbing widows, who take comfort or weep in the arms of the conquerors. I love the war that devoured my handsomest friends."

Miracle of the Rose is a complex narrative which has as its ultimate object the elevation of Harcamone, who is introduced early in the book and then disappears until near the end. He becomes a sacrificial figure. The narrator betrays Harcamone by sleeping with Divers, the man who denounced Harcamone to the police for an earlier crime. Thus the narrator becomes Divers' accomplice and betrays one whom he really loves. At the same time, however, by despising himself for his betrayal, he frees himself from his own love for Harcamone. In doing so, he increases his love for Divers.

A new emotional attitude evolves. Harcamone is a god (Christ)—free of guilt. The narrator, submerged in guilt feelings, always sacrificing and doing penance, thereby pays for the sin of being born. The most important miracle occurs just before Harcamone's execution. The four men who slowly descend into his body see what only God should see—the depths of man. Harcamone's execution symbolizes the sacrificial death and resurrection of Christ.

Critical Context

Miracle of the Rose was Jean Genet's second novel, written after *Notre-*

Dame des Fleurs (1944; revised, 1951; *Our Lady of the Flowers*, 1949; revised, 1963) but before *Journal d'un voleur* (1949; *The Thief's Journal*, 1954). It is related to *The Thief's Journal* in its prison milieu and to *Our Lady of the Flowers* in its glorification of homosexuality. Thus *Miracle of the Rose* is a most powerful contribution to the field of inverted romanticism.

According to Jean-Paul Sartre, Genet was a saint who made a religion of evil. Throughout his works, Genet glorified the beauty of crime and turned cowardice, betrayal, and murder into theological virtues. Sartre asserts that Genet was always obsessed with the concept of superiority. Consequently, Genet chose evil because that is the realm in which he could achieve it. This worship of evil has led to comparisons with Charles Baudelaire. Genet's long history as a thief has also produced comparison with François Villon. Yet Jean Cocteau, the first writer to discover and admire him, considered Genet to be a moralist.

Throughout his works and plays, it is clear that Genet felt alienated from the modern world, guilty for simply being. With his writing, which in later years included poetry, fiction, and plays, such as *Le Balcon* (1956, revised 1961; *The Balcony*, 1957), he achieved intellectual freedom, and freedom from restricting loyalties and theories.

Sources for Further Study

Dobrez, L. A. C. *The Existential and Its Exits: Literary and Philosophical Perspectives on the Works of Beckett, Ionesco, Genet, and Pinter*, 1986.

Grebanier, Bernard. Review in *The New York Times Book Review*. LXXII (February 19, 1967), p. 5.

Hassan, Ihab. *The Dismemberment of Orpheus: Toward a Postmodern Literature*, 1971.

Knapp, Bettina. *Jean Genet*, 1968.

Sartre, Jean-Paul. *Saint Genet, Actor and Martyr*, 1963.

Updike, John. Review in *The New Yorker*. XLIII (November 4, 1967), pp. 230-234.

Weightman, John. *The Concept of the Avant-garde: Explorations in Modernism*, 1973.

Rita E. Loos

MR. PALOMAR

Author: Italo Calvino (1923-1985)
Type of plot: Psychological meditations
Time of plot: The 1980's
Locale: Europe, Japan, and Mexico
First published: Palomar, 1983 (English translation, 1985)

> *Principal character:*
> MR. PALOMAR, who lives in Rome with his wife and daughter

The Novel

Mr. Palomar is a group of twenty-seven mostly benign meditations on— or, more accurately, observations of—the natural world. There is no connected story line, though the novel culminates in the death of the central character, yet each thoughtful vignette does proffer some insight via Palomar himself. These are the observations of a man temperamentally unsuited for any scientific enterprise, anguished over the disconnectedness he feels between himself and the rest of the universe, and eager to discover some appropriate relationship. The reader is also part of that alien universe, since the only access to Mr. Palomar is through the third-person narrative; the reader is the observer of the observer.

It is left to the reader to notice a thematic index at the conclusion of the novel. Italo Calvino explains that each chapter contains various admixtures of three themes, and that its position in the index indicates the proportion. Primarily visual descriptions are indicated by "1"; those chapters which are most narrative are labeled "2"; "3" indicates speculative meditation. Each of the three major divisions of the book ("1. Mr. Palomar's Vacation"; "2. Mr. Palomar in the City"; and "3. The Silences of Mr. Palomar") is further divided into three groups of three chapters. The first chapter (labeled 1.1.1., "Reading a Wave") is ostensibly the most visually oriented. The sixth chapter (1.2.3., "The Infinite Lawn") is a mixture of description, story, and meditation. The fifth chapter of the second division (2.2.2., "The Cheese Museum") is mostly narrative, and the final chapter of the third division (3.3.3., "Learning to Be Dead") is the most speculative.

Is this index descriptive or prescriptive? If the former, there is after all a kind of movement in the novel, as if, in fits and starts, Mr. Palomar finds that he needs more and more abstract speculation to achieve harmony with the universe. In "Serpents and Skulls" (3.1.2.), Mr. Palomar visits the remains of a pre-Columbian civilization in Mexico. His unnamed Mexican friend spins artful tales of the god Quetzalcoatl while nearby a group of schoolchildren is told by their instructor that, though the ancient carvings can be described and even dated, no one knows what they mean. Mr. Palomar observes that somehow his friend has translated mere descriptions (facts) into something living (meaning). Mr. Palomar sees in himself "the need to translate, to move from one language to another, from concrete figures to abstract words, to weave and reweave a network of analogies. Not to interpret is impossible, as refraining from thinking is impossible." When Mr. Palomar considers his own place in the universe, mere observation is not enough.

If the index is prescriptive, it may be that Calvino is having a little joke on his own creation. In the third section of the book, the twenty-fifth chapter is entitled "The World Looks at the World" (3.3.1.). In this meditation Mr. Palomar realizes that his own ego is preventing him from seeing what the world wants him to see. He determines to become the eyes of the world, by an act of will observing everything from "outside." Yet nothing changes, and Mr. Palomar begins to understand that in order for meaning to occur, "From the mute distance of things a sign must come, a summons, a wink: one thing detaches itself from the other things with the intention of signifying some-thing. . . ." At some unforeseen moment, some part of the universe must want to be seen just at the time Mr. Palomar is looking. The joke here is that in Mr. Palomar's anguish to find meaning and connection for his life, the author of the story has been precisely ordering and juxtaposing events and making connections ("signifying something"), of which poor Mr. Palomar seems all too unaware.

Mr. Palomar begins quietly enough with Mr. Palomar on the beach, ob-serving the waves, trying to take in all there is to see of a small portion of the waterfront, and, having looked, to move on to yet other patches of the beach. The waves have been looked at, but they do not divulge their mean-ing. What is vexing for Mr. Palomar is not the change in the waves, but that for him to comprehend what he is seeing he must understand himself as a particular person watching the waves and then interpret this understanding, which in turn must become part of a larger system interpreting the inter-pretation. At another time, watching an albino gorilla in the Barcelona Zoo grasp a rubber tire,

> Mr. Palomar feels he understands the gorilla perfectly, his need for something to hold tight while everything eludes him, a thing with which to allay the an-guish of isolation, . . . of the sentence of being always considered a living phenomenon. . . . We all turn in our hands an old, empty tire through which we try to reach some final meaning, which words cannot achieve.

The third and final major section of the novel, "The Silences of Mr. Palomar," is in effect Mr. Palomar's working out of the lesson learned from the gorilla. The world has little need for Mr. Palomar's words and can get along just as well without them, and without him. Therefore he will with-draw his attention from the world, acting as if he were dead. This has the beneficial effect of providing Mr. Palomar with an absolute to hold on to, namely himself-as-dead, unchanging, and unchanged by the prickly interactions with the rest of the universe. In his silence Mr. Palomar will have himself: an old, empty tire. By drawing the end of his life, Mr. Palomar can then begin to catalog the collection of each of his life experiences. Since he was unable to place bounds on the universe and catalog its moments, he will turn to himself as a project. His inner architecture will be fixed as he learns to be dead, and his catalog will in the end provide the text for a full understanding of himself. Yet only a living Mr. Palomar can catalog himself. Pressed with the paradox of the same person being both living observer (ever changing as he observes his own observations) and an unchanging, bounded object, Mr. Palomar dies.

The Characters

Mr. Palomar lives with his wife, identified only as Mrs. Palomar, and unnamed daughter in Rome. He is a kind of urban Everyman who becomes increasingly worried over the rather tenuous connection between him and the rest of the world. Mr. Palomar himself is a nervous and anxious man, by turns haughty, evenhanded, and depressive, doubtful of his own significance, caught up in his own interior monologue. He wears glasses to correct myopia and ironically trusts only his own limited eyesight to provide certitude in a frenzied world. Even the ability of science to provide certainty must be doubted: Science cannot explain the most common of natural events, the migration of starlings.

Palomar, edgy and absentminded, introverted and fickle, is presented in the novel not as a fleshed-out individual, but rather as a collection of moods and attitudes, whose passion lies in making collections. He groups a blackbird's song into trills, whistlings, and gurgles; he sees his lawn as a collection of this blade and that weed, and the universe as a collection of galaxies, dust particles, and force fields. He observes a flock of starlings, the foods in a Paris gourmet store, and he draws and measures the cheeses in a cheese shop, attempting to place each kind of cheese in some kind of context: historical, social, psychological. He thinks of the cheese shop as a dictionary.

Yet when Palomar observes the waves, the animals at the zoo, or the planets and stars, definitions fail him because there, unlike the manufactured cheeses, there is no history, no biography. The stars will not yield up their secrets; they can only be observed and cataloged. Palomar knows that is not enough. Somehow he must move from the surface of things to their interpretation. This is humorously expressed in the second meditation in the book, "The Naked Bosom" (1.1.2.), as Mr. Palomar repeatedly passes a sunbather who has bared her breasts. He is striving to achieve just the right kind of glance; averting his eyes would be to acquiesce in overzealous prudery, yet viewing the bared bosom as he would view a sand dune or an ocean wave is to do disservice to the significance of the female breast. Finally, certain that he has achieved a "detached encouragement," Palomar once again crosses near the woman, who promptly leaves in a huff.

Mr. Palomar would like nothing better than to deduce the meaning of his own life, but his first principles, or axioms, are hazy at best. All of his models of reality disintegrate until he must face reality directly, and with that his inability to give it order or to explain it.

Themes and Meanings

Mr. Palomar is a novel about meaning. As the two-hundred-inch telescope on Southern California's Mount Palomar pulls in the light from distant galaxies, so the novel pulls the reader into its text as an inescapable link in the infinite chain of observers observing observers. In the very act of reading the novel the reader must perpetuate Mr. Palomar's attempt to draw meaning from his observations, to make connections between things, or events, or chapters. Though Calvino provides a structuring concept for the twenty-seven meditations, he never reveals the significance behind the triple triadic arrangement. Is it a Trinity of Trinities, an intimation of something godlike? Or is the author having his little joke with readers who find that they, too, cannot avoid interpretation?

Calvino's prose, translated from the Italian by William Weaver, is deceptively forthright. Each short meditation is well crafted, seemingly translucent. Yet the reader comes to realize that any understanding of Mr. Palomar has come not through the detail of the text but through the connection and interpretation that the novel forces the reader to supply, with the help of Calvino, the fellow observer. The reader is wooed into believing that such connections must be found for the story to have the significance "intended" by the author, and with that, the trap is sprung. The reader becomes Mr. Palomar's accomplice.

The meditations themselves are quietly human documents, blessed with a touching humor and a recognition of the pull of contrary desires. The visit to a Paris cheese shop raises cheese choices to the level of metaphysics: "Mr. Palomar's spirit vacillates between contrasting urges: the one that aims at complete, exhaustive knowledge and could be satisfied only by tasting all the varieties; and the one that tends toward an absolute choice, the identification of the cheese that is his alone. . . ." His deep interest in the edibles displayed before him perplexes the other customers. When Mr. Palomar is shaken from his reverie by the salesperson in front of him, the first words out of his mouth refer to a mundane and popular variety. With sadness, Mr. Palomar realizes that the consumer culture around him has triumphed again. There had been no opportunity to step back from the hubbub in the shop to learn the names and natures of the cheeses so that Mr. Palomar could place himself in the appropriate stream of cheese history. Mr. Palomar seems forever an outsider: At the zoo, the civilized-looking penguins make him shudder. He is attracted to the giraffe, symbolizing in its crazy-quilt appearance the kind of disharmony and uncoordination at large in the world.

Most of Mr. Palomar's meditations begin with the unspoken assumption that the natural world, or at least its surface as Mr. Palomar observes it, has something to "say," though he is never certain of the message. Written in the present tense, each chapter promises imminent discovery: Tortoise sex, so outwardly dumpy, must signal the existence of an inner life of crystalline clarity; reptiles must be immersed in crocodile time, unhurried, geologic. Mr. Palomar, however, is overwhelmed with things to observe. Observation becomes obsessive. He longs for stability, the cessation of change which is death. Yet, ironically, even what one is in death is altered by the changing thoughts of others.

Critical Context

Mr. Palomar was the last novel published by Calvino before his death in 1985. In one sense, it harks back to a realism present in his first novel, *Il sentiero dei nidi di ragno* (1947; *The Path to the Nest of Spiders*, 1956), but in structure it is more closely related to the tales-within-tales of *Se una notte d'inverno un viaggiatore* (1979; *If on a Winter's Night a Traveler*, 1981) and the mathematical arrangement of *Le città invisibili* (1972; *Invisible Cities*, 1974). As Calvino wrote in 1976, explaining his earlier turn away from social realism toward tales of allegorical fantasy and scientific wit, such as in *Le cosmicomiche* (1965; *Cosmicomics*, 1968), "now we can no longer neglect the fact that books are made of words, of signs, of methods of construction. We can never forget that what books communicate often remains unknown to the author himself, . . . that in any book there is a part that is the author's and a part that is a collective and anonymous work." It is not for literature to express a political order or even to teach the values of society; rather, literature must bring something new into the world by a partnership with the reader in co-creation. Calvino is widely recognized as one of the great modern writers, in the stream of Jorge Luis Borges, Stanisław Lem, and Vladimir Nabokov.

Like Palomar, Calvino left a wife and daughter at his death. Locations in *Mr. Palomar*—the beach, the apartment in Rome, the Paris shops—were Calvino haunts. It is tempting to count the novel as autobiography, and the last chapter, "Learning to Be Dead," as Calvino's envoi. Yet it would be more fitting to say that, while Calvino evoked Mr. Palomar's aspects within himself, new directions surely lay ahead for his creative insight. Calvino's literary legacy is difficult to characterize, but that too is fitting. Only through time, as readers are provoked into making connections within the gaps left by the novelist, will the fruit of his labors be realized. For Mr. Palomar, "Before, by 'world' he meant the world plus himself; now it is a question of himself plus the world minus him." This may well describe Calvino's estate. It is in his precarious silences that he is most profound.

Sources for Further Study

Adler, Sara Maria. *Calvino: The Writer as Fablemaker*, 1979.

Andrews, Richard. "Italo Calvino," in *Writers and Society in Contemporary Italy: A Collection of Essays*, 1984. Edited by Michael Caesar and Peter Hainsworth.

Calvino, Italo. *The Uses of Literature*, 1986.

Carter, Albert Howard. *Italo Calvino: Metamorphoses of Fantasy*, 1987.

Dan Barnett

MOBILE
Study for the Representation of the United States

Author: Michel Butor (1926-   )
Type of plot: Antinovel
Time of plot: From the precolonial period to the early 1960's
Locale: The United States
First published: Mobile: Étude pour une représentation des États-Unis, 1962
   (English translation, 1963)

> *Principal character:*
> THE UNITED STATES, its land and its people

The Novel

   Mobile: Study for the Representation of the United States has fifty chapters, and each chapter is more or less devoted to a different state, in alphabetical order, of the United States. The novel does not tell a story or relate a sequence of events. Instead, the disjointed details, mostly about small-town America, consist of information usually found in history books, atlases, encyclopedias, tourist brochures, and Howard Johnson menus. Some continuity is provided by a series of repetitions which are designed to illustrate the scope and diversity of the United States. For example, the first chapter is entitled "pitch dark in CORDOVA, ALABAMA, the Deep South" and that is all. The first word is not capitalized, nor is there a period at the end. The second chapter reads "pitch dark in CORDOVA, ALASKA, the Far North" and continues with a brief, nightmarish description of the land around Cordova. With no apparent connection, the book next lists Douglas, a small town near Juneau, Alaska. The third chapter begins "pitch dark in DOUGLAS, Mountain Time, ARIZONA, the Far West." Running through the entire book is a seemingly endless catalog of tiny towns whose names are repeated in state after state. For example, there is Concord, California; Concord, North Carolina; Concord, Georgia; and Concord, Florida. Interestingly, Concord, Massachusetts, a town of great importance to both American history and American literature, is omitted.
   Nevertheless, there are a number of linking devices. Each of the fifty chapters has the name of a different state, in alphabetical order from Alabama through Wyoming. Twenty-six chapters begin with "WELCOME TO" and end with the name of a state. The first of the twenty-six is entitled "WELCOME TO NORTH CAROLINA," which would be alphabetized as "Carolina, North" in French. The chapter on North Carolina, however, is almost equally divided between lists of doves, cuckoos, conchs, clams, rivers, and mountains which the narrator places in Georgia, Florida, South Caro-

lina, and Virginia, as well as in North Carolina. There is no apparent reason for omitting the "WELCOME TO" for the remaining twenty-four states, although each state does appear in the chapter title, somewhere on the first page of each new chapter. Despite the quirks of North Carolina's chapter, in most chapters the discussion is limited to the state listed in the heading.

Another pattern that runs throughout the book alludes to both the importance that Americans attach to their automobiles and the melting-pot quality of the United States. Periodically in the text, fragmentary sentences appear describing the color and make of a particular car, followed by a brief, unflattering description of its driver and a record of how fast it is going. Here is a sample: "A tomato-colored Buick driven by a fat young Japanese in a green shirt (65 miles)."

Another motif concerns the American love for ice cream and the Howard Johnson restaurant chain's catering to that taste with the company's famous thirty-two exotic flavors, beginning with apricot ice cream in Concord, North Carolina. In Bristol, Connecticut, the preferred ice cream flavor is pineapple. It is raspberry ice cream at the Howard Johnson's in Manchester, New Hampshire, and gooseberry ice cream at the Howard Johnson's in Manchester, Connecticut.

Another recurring theme is established by a series of brief descriptions of various Indian tribes and the various ways in which the Indians have been mistreated. Michael Butor notes that English missionaries had difficulty teaching the ways of civilization to the Cherokee because the missionaries believed that the Cherokee language could not be given written form. The fate of the Calusas and Seminoles was to be driven from their Florida lands and sent to "Indian Territory" in what is now Oklahoma. The Choctaw indians who lived along the Gulf of Mexico were also forced to emigrate to Indian Territory. Then, the narrator reveals that after the Indians were all gathered in Oklahoma, the federal government declared that Oklahoma was no longer Indian Territory. In addition, the Delaware Indians never had a chance to emigrate. In spite of their treaty of friendship with William Penn in 1682, they were exterminated one hundred years later by new settlers who probably had never even heard of the Penn treaty.

Juxtaposed to the unfair treatment of Indians is an account of the absurd accusations against Susanna Martin, who was tried for witchcraft in Salem, Massachusetts, in 1692. Portions of the transcript show that Martin was accused of changing into a cat, of causing rain to fall at inconvenient moments, and of causing a puppy to fly.

The narrator also quotes extensively from Benjamin Franklin and Thomas Jefferson, two of America's most respected men of letters. The excerpts focus on Franklin's and Jefferson's unenlightened views of blacks, in which they equate blacks with horses, oxen, and other beasts of burden.

In addition to the major motifs, there are many minor ones. State birds, state flowers, state flags, service stations, foreign-language newspapers, time zones, and department stores which were designed to serve rural America are only some of the many types of lists. The culminating effect is that of a country of vast but repetitious proportions.

The Characters

Since there is no story or sequential narrative in *Mobile*, there is no character or single person around whom the story revolves. Butor is, in a sense, characterizing the huge expanse of the United States from its beginnings to the 1960's, when the novel was published. Written in French by a native Frenchman, it is a rather unflattering portrait of the United States and its inhabitants. The United States is noted for its great cultural and business centers, such as New York, Chicago, San Francisco, and New Orleans, yet Butor concentrates on the country's endless supply of forgotten and for the most part forgettable small towns scattered across five time zones. The references to New York focus on a tawdry theme park called "Freedomland" rather than on the internationally famous Statue of Liberty and Empire State Building.

Another characteristic to which the citizens of the United States point with pride is the large number of national monuments. The narrator observes, however, that what Americans like to call a national monument is nothing more than an "archaeological curiosity," one of the worst examples being Mount Rushmore, which he describes as having "enormous, clumsily carved faces of Washington, Jefferson, Lincoln and Theodore Roosevelt."

National pride in early leaders is another facet of the American character that Butor ridicules. Blasphemous reverence for George Washington, Thomas Jefferson, and Abraham Lincoln turns them into the "three divinities," and the chief "god [Washington] is represented in the form of an enormous obelisk." On the other hand, Benjamin Franklin's "principle temple" is located in Philadelphia rather than in "the sacred city of Washington."

Having debunked elements of the United States of which its residents are proud, Butor devotes even more space to an aspect of which they are not proud: racial prejudice. Interspersed with letters from William Penn to the Indians in which Penn promised unending love and peace are accounts of Indians from all over the country being forced off their ancestral lands and being controlled by addiction to peyote, a stimulant drug extracted from cactus plants. Although less space is devoted to prejudice against blacks, Butor selects Thomas Jefferson as the main spokesman on the issue. As the chief framer of the Declaration of Independence, Jefferson is considered the champion of freedom. Excerpts from other writings by Jefferson make it clear, however, that he does not see those freedoms being extended to blacks. Also appearing throughout the novel is a list of towns and counties where blacks are not welcome.

Themes and Meanings

The fact that *Mobile* is dedicated to the memory of Jackson Pollock is a clue to Butor's technique as well as to his theme. The abstract expressionist painter is best known for his technique of pouring and spattering of paint across his canvases instead of using the more common method of applying paint with a brush. Butor throws words across the page in somewhat the same manner that Pollock threw paint. The words seem to tumble around like so many blobs of acrylic. While there are many small patterns to be seen, the series of patterns does not lead to any kind of coherent whole. Sentences do not necessarily begin with capital letters, nor do they always observe the traditional boundaries of commas and periods. The chapter headings are all capitalized, but the headings may be buried in the middle of the page. Sometimes the states' names are written out, and sometimes, for no apparent reason, they are abbreviated. The typography, or the way that the words appear on the page, is unpredictable. Some sentences begin at the right-hand side of the page and work backward; other sentences or fragments begin in the middle of the page. A large portion of the book, approximately one-third, is printed in italics. All the excerpts from Penn, Franklin, and Jefferson are italicized, but other italicized portions are not attributed. Therefore, it is not possible to determine whether those portions come from anonymous writers or from the objective narrator. Transitions from one thought to the other are provided by only a series of repetitions or variations of repetitions.

Another clue to Butor's method lies in the title. A mobile in artistic terms is a kinetic sculpture which is usually made from metal wire. The metal wire or other material is delicately balanced so that a slight breath of air can cause the sculpture to move. The reader is invited to view the panorama of the United States as Butor's details revolve slowly from page to page in a way similar to that in which an art lover sees a mobile. Reinforcing the artistic imagery is the subtitle, "Study for a Representation of the United States." This phraseology is usually associated with drawing and painting rather than with writing.

Mobiles are, by their very nature, both unpredictable and ever-changing, just as Butor's America is constantly on the move. In addition to the movement of automobiles, the narrator catalogs the comings and goings of trains and airplanes as they move in and out of stations and airports. On the other hand, mobiles never really change the various parts that make up the whole; the elements that make up the sculpture remain the same. The mobile, then, becomes a metaphor for the United States. Although the lack of commentary in relation to the specific details seems to lend an air of objectivity to the novel, the selection of details makes it clear that in Butor's mind the forces that motivate the American character are vast, repetitious, contradictory, sinister, and vulgar.

Critical Context

Butor is a widely respected French writer who is best known for his experimentation with the novel form. His novels are, for the most part, not novels at all but antinovels. The antinovel, essentially a French form, aims to destroy narrative structure by fragmenting events and nonevents and by dislocating logical time frames. This technique makes enormous demands on the reader to make sense of the words by mentally constructing some kind of order. Reading such a novel, then, becomes an active rather than a passive exercise. Butor brings to his theories about the role and purpose of fiction a love and knowledge of art. The result is an innovative work in which the content of writing is fused with the form of visual art.

Degrés (1960; *Degrees*, 1963), *L'Emploi du temps* (1956; *Passing Time*, 1960), and *La Modification* (1957; *A Change of Heart*, 1959), all novels which are set in Europe, have elicited more critical attention than *Mobile*, Butor's first novel set in the United States. His most experimental work, *Mobile* completely does away with characterization and narrative in the traditional sense, as it sets out to capture in one novel the essence of the history, geography, and people of the United States. As a result, Butor creates 319 pages of seemingly endless lists, which give the book a kind of epic quality. One is reminded of John Milton's famous catalog of bad angels in *Paradise Lost* (1667, 1674). While the list takes the better part of one of the epic's twelve books, each angel is portrayed with a separate and distinct personality in vignette form. Milton's range and genius enabled him to create new interest with every line. Butor, however, is not Milton, and his experiments with form seem to contradict rather than enhance content and thereby make his lists seem merely interminable.

Sources for Further Study

Albérès, R. *Michel Butor*, 1964.

McWilliams, Dean. *The Narratives of Michel Butor: The Writer as Janus*, 1978.

O'Donnell, Thomas D. "Michel Butor and the Tradition of Alchemy," in *The International Fiction Review*. 1975, pp. 150-153.

Roudiez, Leon S. *Michel Butor*, 1965.

Sturrock, John. *The French New Novel: Claude Simon, Michel Butor, Alain Robbe-Grillet*, 1969.

Sandra Hanby Harris

A MOMENT OF TRUE FEELING

Author: Peter Handke (1942-   )
Type of plot: Philosophical realism
Time of plot: The mid-1970's
Locale: Paris, France
First published: Die Stunde der wahren Empfindung, 1975 (English
   translation, 1977)

Principal characters:
   GREGOR KEUSCHNIG, a press attaché at the Austrian Embassy
      in Paris
   THE WRITER, a friend of Keuschnig

The Novel

Gregor Keuschnig, a press attaché with the Austrian Embassy in Paris, is
married and has a four-year-old daughter. One morning, he has a dream in
which he murders someone. From that point onward, his inner life is in upheaval, although he pretends to be normal and to go about his everyday business. He is often in an extremely agitated state, and he believes that he has
fundamentally changed. Keuschnig realizes that he is divorced from his own
"true feelings." In this alienated condition, he wanders around the streets of
Paris. As in Peter Handke's earlier novel *Die Angst des Tormanns beim
Elfmeter* (1970; *The Goalie's Anxiety at the Penalty Kick*, 1972), there is little
overt plot. The narrative focuses primarily on Keuschnig's perceptions of himself and others.

Keuschnig goes to work but leaves soon after arriving. He finds a phone
number, written on the sidewalk, which he then calls. A woman answers, and
he makes a date to meet her the next evening. He visits an old girlfriend but
is constantly plagued by feelings of estrangement. Returning to the office, he
has sex with a woman worker whom he hardly knows. He has a strong desire
to disrobe in public. Keuschnig's behavior is the extreme opposite of his
actions prior to his dream. He seems to exist in an almost schizophrenic, disoriented state. Random objects that he sees on the street suggest strong feelings to him. He longs for a new "system" of perception, to be able to experience life in a new way.

This longing for a change in the way he perceives reality is satisfied in a
section toward the middle of the novel. He is sitting on a park bench at sun-
down and sees three objects on the ground before him: a chestnut leaf, a
piece of a broken pocket mirror, and a child's hairclip. Suddenly these insignificant items become miraculous objects that give him a sense of well-
being and harmony with the world. He experiences a kind of semimystical
epiphany or revelation and realizes that he has the power to change his life.

Keuschnig returns home, where he and his wife have a dinner party with several friends, including a writer who always seems to be taking notes on Keuschnig's behavior. Keuschnig becomes increasingly paranoid during the dinner; overcome by a sense of alienation, he spits at the writer and then begins to undress, smears his own face with food, and starts fighting with the guests. Later, Keuschnig and the writer go for a walk. He continues to perceive objects as representing his subjective visions. Dreams of his mother also haunt him. He again becomes so desperate that he feels like committing suicide. He grasps the meaning of his experience with the three objects in the park: Insofar as the world can become "mysterious" for him—as opposed to routine and typical—he can connect himself to it. At the end of the novel, he decides that he must find a new kind of work, a new perspective on life. He begins to experience himself as if he were a character in a novel. He goes to a café to meet the strange woman whose number he had called. The text ends with a paragraph that suggests the beginning of a new novel.

The Characters

As with all Handke's characters, the figure of Keuschnig is a fictionalized projection of the author himself. In an interview, Handke once remarked that this text was the most personal that he had written up to that point. As does his character, the author lived for a number of years in Paris during the 1970's. The extreme alienation experienced by Keuschnig is a reflection of the estrangement that Handke has also discussed in interviews on several occasions. The author writes from a strongly autobiographical standpoint, and the figure of Keuschnig is an excellent example of this approach to character.

Although Keuschnig remains a projection of his author's inner life, the character is not typical of those found in the traditional modern novel, in which authorial comment often provides the reader with insight into the motivation of the characters. Influenced by postmodernist authors such as the French writer Alain Robbe-Grillet, Handke does not provide the reader with an in-depth narrative discussion of his protagonist's psychology but rather remains on the surface of the character's consciousness, giving the content of the individual's behavior but little explanation for it. What Keuschnig does and thinks is reported without psychological analysis of its significance. Thus the character appears somewhat opaque, and the reader is forced to create an interpretation of the individual's situation. This is consistent with Handke's thematic intentions, which emphasize the postmodernist view that "reality" is a construction, the product of an individual perspective that is expressed primarily through language.

In *A Moment of True Feeling*, the figure of the writer—who is always silently taking notes on Keuschnig's actions but never offering comment—is also a reflection of the author himself. Handke the author (the writer) reflects here upon himself as human being (Keuschnig); his analytical-creative self confronts his experiential self. For Handke, the creation of character becomes a mode of literary self-analysis, a way of orienting himself in the real world through the reflection of fictions.

Themes and Meanings

Handke's *A Moment of True Feeling* is typical of his many novels and is closest in theme and style to his earlier *The Goalie's Anxiety at the Penalty Kick*. These works stand in close yet clearly fictionalized relation to the author's biography. The starting point of the work is similar to that of his other narrative texts: A man experiences a shock or jolt to his consciousness and suddenly becomes aware of his estrangement from those around him. Like the character of Joseph Bloch in *The Goalie's Anxiety at the Penalty Kick*, Keuschnig seems schizophrenic. The random objects in his environment (a baby carriage or a peach pit lying on the street, for example) suggest messages or secret meanings to him. He is an individual in whom the daily routine of life has produced a deep sense of alienation and who is seeking a new significance for his existence, a revitalized sense of connection to the world around him. This is representative of the existential thrust of Handke's texts.

The dream of murder that signals Keuschnig's breakdown suggests the repressed or estranged dimension of his self, his antisocial and destructive feelings of violence. Such extreme experiences occur frequently in Handke's writings. The fact that he must now acknowledge this aspect in himself means that he can no longer live in the manner he had in the past. He must now begin a quest to seek a new identity or, as Handke phrases it in the text, a new "system" of meaning in which he will make sense to himself. In order for Keuschnig to be able to experience reality again, his world must become "mysterious," not routine and typical. In contrast to the author's previous works, the journey in this novel begins to assume a quasi-mystical direction that becomes more pronounced in the later writings.

The mystical aspect is clear in the experience that Keuschnig has with the three "miraculous" objects in the park. This is the pivotal scene in the novel. What occurs is similar to a religious epiphany. Yet this is not a manifestation of the traditional vision of the divine but rather a secular revelation of the role of the aesthetic dimension of human consciousness. Not unlike the figure of Bloch in *The Goalie's Anxiety at the Penalty Kick*, Keuschnig manifests a kind of metaphoric or poetic vision in which these objects become signs or symbols for subjective states. Both Bloch and Keuschnig begin to view reality as if it were almost a literary "text" of which they are the authors. For Handke, the poetic act assumes a quasi-religious dimension; it becomes a form of secular salvation.

After Keuschnig sees the three things, he contemplates their meaning and says to himself: "What names cannot accomplish as CONCEPTS, they do as IDEAS." Handke is fond of inserting quotes from the writings of other authors and philosophers, and this is from the German-Jewish intellectual Walter Benjamin's *Der Ursprung des deutschen Trauerspiels* (1928; *The Origin of German Tragic Drama*, 1977), a dense and abstract treatise. Benjamin argues that concepts, signs representing intellectual abstractions of experience, are falsifications of reality; they ultimately alienate the individual from his feelings. That is precisely the situation in which Keuschnig finds himself. His job in the Austrian Embassy, for example, is to serve as press attaché; he collects newspaper articles that present a certain notion of Austria to the public, and he must monitor these signs.

In order to be connected to his own "true feelings," Keuschnig needs to find a language that does not falsify, that is authentic. He hopes to find it in words that are "IDEAS," that is, in aesthetic images. The Greek root of the word "idea," *eidos*, means visual image or picture. Handke's program as author revolves around the theme of art as a mode of transcendence for the alienated self. The creative imagination allows the individual to visualize other possible ways of living, other possible realities, and, as such, gives him the vision to change a reality that is unbearable. Art serves as a mode of liberation for estranged consciousness. The central paradox of Handke's project as creative writer is revealed here: Fiction or the "unreal" serves as the means by which the self comes to experience reality.

Keuschnig seems to come to this realization, and one might surmise that his decision to seek a new occupation at the end of the novel involves becoming an author himself. Indeed, the beginning of a new narrative at the end of Handke's text might be that "composed" by Keuschnig himself. In any case, Keuschnig's secular epiphany relates to his search for an authentic language that can again connect him to existence. It is significant that even after his experience in the park, he is still plagued by feelings of anxiety and dislocation. This suggests the existential nature of his epiphany, that no form of transcendence is absolute or permanent; the salvation of art and the imagination is momentary at best and must be renewed again and again.

Critical Context

A Moment of True Feeling stands in the tradition of modern existential literature. Handke is well aware of this, and it is no mere coincidence that the first name of the novel's character is Gregor. The association is to one of the most famous alienated figures in modern literature: Gregor Samsa in Franz Kafka's novella *Die Verwandlung* (1915; *The Metamorphosis*, 1936). In both stories, a dream signals the awakening of the figure's true self, and both characters undergo tranformations in which their estranged consciousnesses are revealed. Kafka's story presents this theme in a more grotesque and dreamlike style. Handke's theme also links his novel with other major existential writings of the twentieth century, such as Rainer Maria Rilke's *Die Aufzeich-nungen des Malte Laurids Brigge* (1910; *The Notebooks of Malte Laurids Brigge*, 1930, 1958), Jean-Paul Sartre's *La Nausée* (1938; *Nausea*, 1949), and Albert Camus's *L'Étranger* (1942; *The Stranger*, 1946). The novels of the Austrian writer Thomas Bernhard also treat the same issues developed in Handke's texts. All these existential writers view art as a mode of momentary transcendence for estranged consciousness.

What distinguishes Handke from the writers cited above is his awareness of the semiotic processes that condition the perception of "reality." The ideas and theories of structuralism and semiology inform all of his works. Language and sign systems become, in the course of time, routine, automatized, and eventually mistaken for real experience. As Handke suggests in one of his early essays, human beings confuse nature (reality as it is) with the forms of their language ("reality" as they construct it). This confusion becomes a major source of the alienation that plagues his characters and is certainly the case with Gregor Keuschnig. He feels like "a prisoner in Disneyland," confined in a prisonhouse of signs that are ultimately artificial and divorced from his experience. His moment of liberation or "true feeling" comes when he can create unique signs—such as the three objects in the park—that speak to his own existence.

Sources for Further Study

Hansen, Olaf. "Exorcising Reality," in *New Boston Review*. IV (Summer, 1978), p. 5.

Jurgensen, Manfred, ed. *Peter Handke: Ansätze-Analysen-Anmerkungen*, 1979.

Klinkowitz, Jerome, and James Knowlton. *Peter Handke and the Postmodern Transformation*, 1983.

Renner, Rolf Günter. *Peter Handke*, 1985.

Schlueter, June. *The Plays and Novels of Peter Handke*, 1981.

Wilkie, Brian, and James Hurt. "Peter Handke," in *Literature of the Western World*, 1984.

Thomas F. Barry

THE MONKEY'S WRENCH

Author: Primo Levi (1919-1987)
Type of plot: Philosophical realism
Time of plot: The 1970's, with reminiscences from previous decades
Locale: The Soviet Union, India, Africa, Alaska, and Italy
First published: La chiave a stella, 1978 (English translation, 1986)

Principal characters:

THE NARRATOR, an Italian industrial chemist in late middle age
who has a second profession as a writer

LIBERTINO FAUSSONE, a thirty-five-year-old Italian steel rigger
who travels the world erecting bridges, cranes, derricks,
and other heavy installations

The Novel

In *The Monkey's Wrench*, a series of discursive anecdotes are recounted to an unnamed narrator by Libertino Faussone, a steel rigger whose work takes him all over the world. The stories are about work—the problems, the disasters, the exhilaration when everything finally comes out right. In the final chapters, the narrator, a paint chemist who is also a professional writer, tells his own work story to Faussone.

When the book opens, the narrator explains that he has recently arrived at a factory in a remote area of the Soviet Union and has met Faussone, the only other Italian on the site, in the dining room for foreign visitors. Over a huge plate of roast beef, Faussone recalls a visit to an African port to erect a dockside crane. When the task was completed he expected everyone to celebrate with him, but the workers were in an angry mood. They had been campaigning for the canteen to serve food conforming to their religion, but the boss, who was of another religion, had adamantly refused. At a mass meeting, they put a curse on the boss by ceremonially mutilating his photograph. He became ill and died. His wealthy family took the workers to court, accusing them of "homicide with malice aforethought." The narrator asks how the trial ended. "You're kidding," says Faussone, "it's still going on. . . ."

Faussone's second story, set in Italy, gives the first of his many vivid and absorbing descriptions of the technological processes of construction—in this case, the building of a distillation plant. Soon after this immensely complex undertaking was completed, the installation became "sick." It heaved and groaned like a man in the grip of illness. A design fault was identified and Faussone had to modify the structure by slowly working his way upward for two days inside a vertical pipe. He was overcome by claustrophobia but forced himself to continue. The modification was successful, but he now calls himself a "concave" rigger and leaves the "convex" jobs to others.

Over tea and vodka in his room, Faussone talks about one of the best friends he has ever had—a monkey, which arrived while he was erecting a derrick in a forest clearing and learned to do modest tasks. In its over-enthusiasm for button-pressing, however, it almost destroyed the derrick.

On a Sunday walk in a forest, Faussone tells his companion about the only woman whom he has ever considered marrying—a tall, strapping forklift driver who could corner "better than Nikki Lauda." Fausonne recalls their lovemaking with uncharacteristic tenderness and confesses that he still yearns for her.

One evening Faussone is unexpectedly befuddled by wine. In a key dialogue, the rigger and the writer discuss the advantages and disadvantages of constructing with metals and constructing with words.

Faussone's Alaska story is interspersed with recollections of shrimp for breakfast, lunch, and dinner. His task was to finish the assembly of a mammoth derrick, load it onto pontoons, and install it some way out to sea. In another of his breathtaking descriptive passages, Fausonne recalls how, perched on the derrick arm, high above the turbulent ocean, he became seasick. Ashamed at this loss of personal style, he nevertheless gamely finished the job.

On a hot September Sunday, the two men take a boat trip on the Volga. Faussone launches into a description of the building of a bridge in Calabria. His India story is also about a bridge: the construction of a suspension bridge across a river. When the piers had been erected, ready for the final span, the river suddenly veered to the left, breaching the embankment, rooting up trees, flooding adjacent fields, and damaging part of the installation. There was nothing Faussone could do except wait until the torrent subsided. Faussone's enthusiastic description of the drawing of the suspension cables, an extraordinarily complicated and demanding task, is one of the most fascinating passages in the book.

In a confidential mood, Faussone talks about his aunts in Turin. They fuss over him and try to make matches for him. He reminisces, too, about his early working life, when he was a welder.

On a snowy winter's day, Faussone describes the rigging of a crane in icy conditions in the Soviet Union. On inspection day everything went like clockwork until the inspector tested the rotation. The gigantic steel arm creaked and shuddered. The inspector declared the machine "kaput," but Faussone discovered that the bevel gear had been sabotaged, probably by someone from a rival French firm. There was a lawsuit. Years passed; the matter is still before the courts, and Faussone is pessimistic about the outcome. "I know what happens," he says, "when things of iron becomes things of paper."

In his own story, the narrator explains that he is in the Soviet Union to investigate a complaint that a specialized enamel, supplied by his firm for coating the inside of food tins, becomes lumpy when used for anchovies. Through an ingenious process of deduction, he has discovered that the lumps have been caused by tiny fragments of fiber from the rags used by a Russian official with a mania for cleanliness. The paint contract is saved, and he can return to Italy.

The Characters

Each of the two main characters is absorbed by the demands of his own profession, but while the narrator's relationship to his work is mainly intellectual, Faussone's is physical and emotional. Faussone is inspired by the handling of tangible objects and the creation of massive working structures from them, by the poetry of motion when something which he has helped to construct functions elegantly. "It seemed to walk the sky, smooth as silk," he says, recapturing the moment when the bridge crane began to function. "I felt like they'd made me a duke, and I bought drinks for everyone."

Faussone has learned his sensitivity to the properties of metals and his fierce spirit of independence from his coppersmith father. In the postwar period, his father refused many lucrative offers of industrial work in order to remain his own boss.

Faussone enjoys good food and wine and a night with a woman. He understands his own nature well enough, however, to know that he will always be ready to give up these pleasures for the supreme achievements offered by his work. Whatever his feelings for the forklift driver, who first attracts him because of her boldness of spirit and her pride in her driving skills, he knows that he will never settle down. He evaluates others in his own terms and even expresses a grudging praise for the artistry of the men who sabotaged the bevel gear. By the same token, he is scornful of "imbeciles" and idlers, salesmen and bureaucrats, and designers who fail to anticipate problems. He is also ashamed of his own weaknesses: his failure to learn to swim, his claustrophobia, and his propensity for seasickness.

Faussone is a fictional character, a "mosaic," writes the author in a short endpiece, "of numerous men I have met, similar to Faussone and similar among themselves in personality, virtue, individuality, and in their view of work and the world." The narrator, on the other hand, although unnamed in the book, is not fictional. He is clearly identifiable with Primo Levi himself, possessing the same background, professional experience, and general outlook. He is an older, more scholarly man than Faussone and can illustrate his point with examples from Greek legend as well as from his own life.

One of his functions in the book is to mediate between Faussone and the reader, setting straight the chaotic deviations in his stories, interrupting on behalf of the reader to ask for elucidation, and addressing the reader directly with his own opinions and questions. Having a "real" narrator mediating for a fictitious storyteller is a delightfully ingenious literary device, enabling Levi to characterize the rigger's narrative style as rough-and-ready while present-ing it in readable literary form. It also strengthens the book's realism—the realism not only of its stories but also of the stories' underlying humanistic truths.

Themes and Meanings

"Perhaps the most acceptable form of freedom," says the narrator in one of his asides to the reader, "the most subjectively enjoyed, and the most use-ful to human society consists of being good at your job and therefore taking pleasure in doing it."

This definition encapsulates the spirit of *The Monkey's Wrench*, which, in effect, is a paean to skilled work done with flair and pride. One of its most remarkable aspects is Primo Levi's ability, through the medium of Faussone, to describe a highly complex technological process with such clarity and pa-nache that the most unscientific reader can understand and visualize it and even become emotionally involved in its progress. Underlying every story is an ongoing dialogue on the philosophy of work, a dialogue which becomes explicit in the key discussion between the two men about the relative merits of working with words or with tangible objects.

The narrator points out that writing is a lonely profession and that when things go wrong the writer alone is to blame. The failure, however, does not become apparent until the reader notices it, and then it is too late to correct it. Faussone is struck by this unique burden on the writer. "Just think," he says, "if they'd never invented control instruments, and we had to do the job by guesswork . . . it'd be enough to drive you crazy."

On the other hand, he reminds the narrator of the dangers of the rigger's work, both the physical risks and the strain on the nervous system. "A man can't get sick from writing," he says; "at worst, if he writes with a ballpoint, he gets a callus."

The rigger-writer dialogue becomes three-cornered when, in the "anchovy story," the narrator talks about his profession as an industrial scientist. He draws an analogy between the microscopic building blocks of paint chemistry and the massive constituents of the rigger's trade, and, to gain Faussone's understanding and to refine the analogy, he refers to himself as "a rigger-chemist."

Critical Context

During World War II, Primo Levi suffered the horrors of Auschwitz, and most of his books written before *The Monkey's Wrench* stem directly from this experience. The relationship between people and their work, however, has always been integral to his depiction of character, and it is a major theme in *Il sistema periodica* (1975; *The Periodic Table*, 1984); the anchovy story in *The Monkey's Wrench* is, in fact, a partial reworking of one of the chapters of *The Periodic Table*. In *The Monkey's Wrench*, wartime events are mentioned only in passing and the work theme is wholly dominant.

Levi always considered himself to be more of a chemist than a writer. *The Monkey's Wrench* was published a year after he had retired from his scientific post and had begun to devote himself to writing. Its interior argument about the relative advantages of working with materials or words reflects his own struggle of that time.

At the end of the book, after listening to the narrator's anchovy story, Faussone urges him not to give up his work as a chemist: "Doing things that you can touch with your hands," he says, "has an advantage; you can make comparisons and understand how much you're worth. You make a mistake, you correct it, and next time you don't make it. But you are older than me," he adds, "and maybe you've already seen enough things in your life."

In retrospect, there is a sadness about these final words. Levi's death in May, 1987, was attributed to suicide. Perhaps he had, indeed, "seen enough things" in his life.

Sources for Further Study

Denby, David. "The Humanist and the Holocaust," in *The New Republic*. CXCV (July 28, 1986), pp. 27-33.

Hughes, H. Stuart. *Prisoners of Hope: The Silver Age of the Italian Jews, 1924-1974*, 1983.

King, Francis. "The Romance of Labour," in *The Spectator*. CCLVIII (May 9, 1987), p. 39.

Library Journal. Review. CXI (October 15, 1986), p. 110.

The New York Times Book Review. Review. XCI (October 12, 1986), p. 1.

Thomson, Ian. "Mapping the World of Work," in *The Times Literary Supplement*. June 5, 1987, p. 610.

Time. Review. CXXVIII (November 17, 1986), pp. 92-93.

Nina Hibbin

THE MOON AND THE BONFIRES

Author: Cesare Pavese (1908-1950)
Type of plot: Neorealism
Time of plot: The late 1940's and, in retrospect, the period between World
   War I and World War II
Locale: Gaminella and neighboring villages in the Piedmont region of Italy
First published: La luna e i falò, 1950 (English translation, 1952)

> *Principal characters:*
> THE NARRATOR, whose name and occupation are undisclosed
> NUTO, his best friend, a carpenter and a musician
> CINTO, a lame boy whom the narrator befriends
> SILVIA,
> IRENE, and
> SANTINA, the daughters of Sor Matteo, the landowner for
>   whom the narrator worked as a boy

The Novel

The story of *The Moon and the Bonfires* unfolds on three levels of the
narrator's experience. On the first level—that of the present—the narrator
has returned from America to his native village. Here he seeks out the old
places and friends of his boyhood, among whom is Nuto, now married, a car-
penter and local musician living quietly on his own land. It is several years
after World War II, when memories of betrayal and death are still fresh and
the body of a Fascist, a German soldier, or a partisan may wash out from a
shallow grave in the next rain.

The narrator and Nuto renew their friendship, walking about the countryside and stopping at remembered places. Some of the townsmen and land-
owners are convinced that the narrator has returned from America rich
enough to buy their lands, but the narrator admits to being neither rich nor
desirous of buying their farms.

On one such visit he meets Cinto, Valino's son, a lame, sickly boy who becomes fascinated with this man who has traveled to America and has come
back in possession of another world. For his part, the narrator takes a liking
to the boy, who reminds him of his own youth.

Here, the story reaches a second level of experience—the narrator's past,
a quiet, sometimes lonely boyhood spent in the countryside. These memories
form the bulk of the novel, not only complementing and explaining the first
level of action in the present but also shedding light on the narrator's character. His earliest memories are not pleasant: He recounts his painful awareness of being illegitimate, farmed out as a young boy to work on Sor
Matteo's lands, and brought up always just outside the familial unit.

Central to his experience are his memories of Sor Matteo's daughters and the ultimate unhappiness of their lives. Irene, the oldest, married a man she did not love and lived in a one-room flat where her husband beat her. Sylvia, more vibrant than her older sister, teased village expectations with several love affairs, but a bungled abortion at the hands of a midwife caused her to hemorrhage. She died in her bed. Santina, the youngest, sold herself to the Fascist cause, changed sides when defeat was imminent and lived with a partisan leader, then changed sides again. Captured by the partisans, she was executed. Out of love for her, the partisan leader ordered her body consigned to a bonfire so it would never be found.

The sisters' histories span both levels of the narrative. The sisters are seen in the narrator's youth and young manhood, and their ultimate fates are told to him by Nuto as the two stand on a hill overlooking the vineyards and the valley. They thus serve to connect the narrator's distant past with the present and help to reinforce the perception of life as basically sad, even tragic.

The third level of the story deals also with the narrator's past—his more recent one, in America. This range of experiences is the narrowest, the most tenuous in the book. The American experience is dreamlike in its vagueness. Places are identified by name, but they lack the hard, earthbound solidity of soil and valley and tree that forms a large part of the narrator's feel for his native Italy. America (whose literature, significantly, Cesare Pavese had studied and written about, but whose land he had never seen) is a lonely place, a nameless desert in which the narrator had once spent a night sleeping in the cab of a truck.

The narrator's other major experience of America was his relationship with Rosanne, a woman with whom he had lived for a time. Like him, Rosanne was rootless, pathetically holding to a vague ambition of becoming a film star. Both realized that their relationship was too fragile and that they had no future together. One morning Rosanne left him, and the narrator never saw her again.

These three levels of experience, which emerge and recede in a seemingly arbitrary pattern throughout the book, form an emotional context of loneliness, melancholy nostalgia, and hopelessness. The novel ends not with the narrator's present situation, which would suggest at least a continuum and the possibility of a future, but with Santina's execution, suggesting a sudden stop, a cessation of the will on the part of the narrator himself.

The Characters

Like the heroes of many classic novels, the narrator returns to his native place to find those elements in his past which will give meaning to his identity as a human being and assure him of his place in the scheme of existence. The narrator, however, receives no nourishment from his return. His sojourn in his native village gains for him no serenity. He speaks of events in a flat, unemotional tone, as if afraid to let down his guard and risk being wounded. His psychological wound—the knowledge that he is illegitimate—prevents him from giving himself completely to the joys of life, although his feel for the land and his attraction to Nuto and the boy Cinto prove his yearning to do so.

Nuto embodies that serenity and self-assuredness which the narrator finds attractive, even enviable. Nuto is a realist. He is not disillusioned by the course of life but at the same time understands the need for holding on to ideals, as when he tells the narrator that he believes in the moon, in its power as a force of nature and as a symbol. Proof of Nuto's hardihood is that he has survived the war. Living quietly and contentedly, he helps the narrator remember the past and has no regrets.

Clever yet vulnerable, Cinto is drawn to the narrator as to a symbol of romance—the exciting life of travel and adventure in the new world. Cinto's own boyhood, like the narrator's, is filled with loneliness and even fear. Cinto's father, Valino, is a violent man, frustrated and unhappy. More than once he threatens his son and ultimately burns down his house, killing the entire family except for Cinto, who has run off. Life has thus become a serious affair: violent, dangerous, and inexpressibly sad.

For the three sisters who fill a central place in the mind and heart of the narrator, life is not only sad but also too quickly gone. As the oldest of the three, Irene is the quietest and most even-tempered. Discreet in her relationships with men, she is the most self-possessed, though she is capable of jealousy when she notes the interest one of her callers has taken in her younger sister, Sylvia.

Sylvia is everything that Irene is not. Where blonde Irene is meek and ladylike, dark-haired Sylvia is outspoken and flirtatious. Where Irene plays the piano and drives with her boyfriend in a carriage, Sylvia chatters teasingly and rides with her boyfriend on the back of a motorcycle.

Santina, "the baby," is perceived by the narrator as the most angelic; her name suggests a saintlike quality. Santina matures, however, into an earthy, passionate creature, ready to assume the political cause that most appeals to her at the time. She is, in a symbolic way, the image of Italy itself.

The three weird sisters of Greek mythology who determine the fates of men are here given flesh and blood, yet instead of controlling destiny they are themselves the victims of it. Their short, unhappy lives are a testament to the narrator's bleak view of existence.

Themes and Meanings

The symbols of moon and bonfire which pervade the book serve as a counterbalance to the narrator's grim view of life, providing a context of ambiguity which suggests a point of view wider than despair, one that embraces hope and affirms the value of the mystery of life. The symbols first appear in a conversation between the narrator and Nuto. The farmers, the reader learns, light bonfires on St. John's Eve as a way of renewing the fertility of the land.

The narrator scoffs at the practice, dismissing it as peasant superstition. Nuto, the realist, gently scolds him, reminding him that he has been away too long to understand truly these customs and traditions. The moon, like the bonfires, brings the good things in life, forcing the people to live according to natural cycles and thus become part of the earth's mysterious process of regeneration.

His cynicism toward the value of these symbols is a reflection of the narrator's hardened attitude toward life, his inability to believe in the inherent spirituality and mystery of the world. This faith is difficult to maintain in the face of the violence and death which form the core of the narrator's experience.

Critical Context

The Moon and the Bonfires was the last work Cesare Pavese wrote before committing suicide in 1950. As such, it is the most interesting of his novels for those readers seeking autobiographical clues to the writer's state of mind. On a more critical level, however, the book is considered Pavese's masterpiece because of his successful use of the vernacular style and the integrated use of natural symbols.

Influenced by such American writers as Ernest Hemingway and William Faulkner—spending much of his career in the 1930's translating their works, as well as those of Walt Whitman and Herman Melville—Pavese experimented in his own novels with a vernacular style: plain, elliptical, idiomatic, and new to Italian literature. *Paesi tuoi* (1941; *The Harvesters*, 1961) was his first attempt with the vernacular form in a novel, but the book was obviously experimental and derivative, the style not yet fully accommodated to the action. In *The Moon and the Bonfires*, Pavese achieved his most successful fusion of the vernacular style with theme and meaning, creating a work which has influenced a generation of Italian novelists.

The images of moon and bonfire suffuse the novel as natural cultural symbols, commenting on action and deepening meaning without calling attention to themselves. Like the vernacular, these natural images are nonliterary and rhetorically simple, emerging organically from the action rather than being imposed upon it.

Sources for Further Study

Fiedler, Leslie. "Introducing Cesare Pavese," in *The Kenyon Review*. XVI (1954), pp. 536-553.

Heiney, Donald. "Cesare Pavese," in *Three Italian Novelists: Moravia, Pavese, Vittorini*, 1968.

Sontag, Susan. "The Artist as Exemplary Sufferer," in *Against Interpretation*, 1966.
Thompson, Doug. *Cesare Pavese: A Study of the Major Novels and Poems*, 1982.

Edward Fiorelli

MOONRISE, MOONSET

Author: Tadeusz Konwicki (1926-   )
Type of plot: Journal-novel
Time of plot: 1981
Locale: Warsaw; fictional passages take place in northeastern Poland, in and around the city of Wilno, and in the newly acquired western territories in postwar Poland
First published: Wschody i zachody księżyca, 1982 (English translation, 1987)

> *Principal characters:*
> THE NARRATOR, the authorial persona of Tadeusz Konwicki who relates the tumultuous events of 1981 and re-creates his adolescent World War II and postwar experiences in fictional passages that are interjected into the narrative
> POLISH SOCIETY, a collective character and presence from which issue Solidarity members, prominent political figures, Konwicki's fellow writers, the Communist Party, and various younger individuals from Warsaw's artistic and dissident circles

The Novel

Moonrise, Moonset—a journal-novel encapsulating a year created "from juicy life and unfettered fantasy," to use the author's words—records events witnessed by the author-narrator during 1981 in Poland, in the aftermath of the "bloodless revolution" effected in the summer of 1980 by Solidarity, the union that became a social movement. The first chapters find the narrator musing on the hard-won freedoms and the strange melancholy accompanying Solidarity's attainments, as well as on the Party's embittering humiliation and its isolation from the new movement. The book closes with the declaration of martial law in Poland in December of 1981, the suppression of Solidarity, and the narrator's interrogation by the police. Tadeusz Konwicki's wide-ranging narrative—bursting with the daily minutiae of the author's life, his reflections on Polish-Russian and Polish-Western relations, recollections of fellow writers (living and deceased), adolescent memories, confessions of weakness for various notorious public figures, fictional passages and remarks directed at his cat Ivan, to mention only a few of his subjects—is enclosed within these two startling moments in Polish history: Solidarity's ascent and its sudden and violent deposition.

Within *Moonrise, Moonset*'s stream of observations, opinions, reminiscences, incisive political commentary ("The West has the subconscious desire to be raped by Russia"), remarks to the reader, complaints about the narrator's health, and erotic adventures rise islands of historical fiction and fragments of unpublished novels which the author offers to the reader in answer to, in one case, the beloved Polish dissident Adam Michnik's request that Konwicki write about his role as a young guerrilla fighter in the Home Army during World War II. In these passages, Konwicki describes his armed struggles against the invading German army and, later, against the Soviet "liberator."

In the tradition of Polish writers Józef Mackiewicz and Czesław Miłosz, Konwicki's pulse quickens as he depicts the landscapes in and around Wilno. The Polish-Lithuanian countryside is rendered with astounding plasticity and precision, lending these segments of the book an immediacy and emotional resonance unmatched elsewhere in the work:

> I have dreamed of that strange little town so many times, so many times has a sudden stillness reminded me of that place at the bend of the Wilia, so often has a paroxysm of metaphysical dread summoned up from dark oblivion those dozen or so months I spent in that little town not so far from Wilno, where there were three Catholic homes, a presbytery, a police station, my Grandmother Helena's inn, as well as three or four Jewish homes, a little store, a blacksmith's shop, and probably a bakery that made challah.

The Characters

The narrator is an aging writer and film director constructed by Konwicki as an obviously autobiographical authorial persona that is both intimate and detached. His is the all-seeing eye, the filtering presence which conducts a dialogue with the reader, shares its observations of "the Polish earthquake" (the Solidarity movement), bemoans Poland's history as "a mound of graves," and bares old Communist sympathies. The narrator describes the travails of making a film of Miłosz's book *Dolina Issy* (1955; *The Issa Valley*, 1981) and dissects relationships with fellow writers—Stanisław Lem, Jerzy Putrament, Stanisław Dygat—and with actor Zbigniew Cybulski, the Polish James Dean. Through observation, confession, reminiscence, and fictional remnant, Konwicki tries to grasp the many Konwickis, his own elusive essence.

Polish society also figures as a character and subject of this work as it is the workings of the Solidarity trade union, its battles, achievements, and aspirations (and the narrator's marveling at them) that feed and underlie the narrator's skeptical yet hopeful musings: "To exist, other countries need good borders, sensible alliances, disciplined societies, but a decent miracle will do us just fine. . . ."

In the fictional passages of *Moonrise, Moonset*, the reader also encounters the character of Adam (named in honor of Adam Michnik). It is through this character that Konwicki's narrator strives to create a bridge between the World War II experiences of his generation and those of Michnik's. The aging writer wants to shift the Adam of today to that scorching summer and have him experience that chain of episodes in my life. . . . I wanted to give Adam a little piece of my youth so that he too would have a war record. . . . I wanted to see how he, the darling of salons and temporary arrests, would bear up to that first burst of machine-gun fire, how he would take the sight of blood, and how he would react to the resurrection of freedom wearing the coarse-cloth uniform of slavery.

Themes and Meanings

Ostensibly, Konwicki's *Moonrise, Moonset* is a book that records daily events, catalogs friendships, reveals collective complexes and personal feelings of guilt and skepticism, and throughout appears to be an exposé of one specific historical time and one individual sensibility. The more profound underlying current, however, is Konwicki's search for his true self. The question unposed yet constantly present is: Who is the real Konwicki—child-guerrilla, Communist, writer, director, father, Polish tourist, or senior citizen-student? Which role encases his true essence? How does each become just another facet of the self, incomprehensible in its many, self-contradictory manifestations?

Konwicki's calm but searching, not to mention witty, authorial voice is the taut lifeline that guides the reader through the maelstrom of historical upheavals, deforming collective experiences, realizations of his worst nightmares, fluid political creeds, nagging doubts, abiding skepticism, and ever-present guilt. It is this voice—so painfully conscious of its own flaws and unreliability—and its striving to witness and articulate, even to its own detriment, that becomes a value. Konwicki's measure of faith in the face of despair becomes his offering to the reader.

Moonrise, Moonset illustrates effectively how a hybrid, "mongrel" form can expand the more conventional journal form to convey rich, complex, emotion-ridden experience in an attempt to grasp a single reality. Because Konwicki's work is not bound by constrictions of genre or chronology (the interspersed fictional fragments are set in World War II and immediate postwar Poland), one year of life in modern-day Poland conveys decades of collective and individual experience. Many modern Polish writers claim that "pure" forms are no longer adequate to convey human experience in the twentieth century because this experience is too bewildering and raw to be expressed in a form too refined and polished. Konwicki explodes the journal form to render the life surrounding him in all of its dynamic multiplicity, simultaneously frivolous and profound, and to extract, from these mountains of everyday minutiae, one mote of authentic experience.

Critical Context

Within the context of Konwicki's own writing, *Moonrise, Moonset* is a return to the hybrid and congenial form introduced to readers in *Kalendarz i klepsydra* (1976; the calendar and the hourglass), which Konwicki describes in *Moonrise, Moonset* as "a diary, a pseudo-memoir, autobiographical apocrypha . . . a stretch of life in calendar time, the novel as a chunk of life." Unlike the novel form, in which Konwicki is well-versed—*Sennik współczesny* (1963; *A Dreambook for Our Time*, 1969), *Kompleks polski* (1977; *The Polish Complex*, 1981), and *Mała apokalipsa* (1979; *A Minor Apocalypse*, 1983)—the journal-memoir-confession-diary-novel hybrid form of *Moonrise, Moonset* allows Konwicki to record life "on the wing," without the exclusion of "the garbage of life," usually refined out of existence in a work of art.

Within the context of Polish literature, Konwicki's attempt to get at the truth of experience and his own essence by shuttling between the lofty and the trite is not new. It is preceded by the more selective masterpieces of this nongenre which includes Witold Gombrowicz's *Dziennik* (1957, 1962, 1966, 3 volumes; diary) and Kazimierz Brandys' *Wiesiące* (1981-1982; *A Warsaw Diary, 1978-1981*, 1983). Polish writers acknowledge that this form graciously accommodates the large doses of current events, political commentary, critical opinion, and effluvia that constitute a writer's life. It allows the writer more freedom to alternate the everyday with the extraordinary. From the perspective of world literature, Konwicki's voice has joined those of other Central Europeans such as Milan Kundera, Miłosz, and Gombrowicz in creating universal value through exacting yet relaxed analyses of individual and collective complexes, historical defeat, and the miraculous resilience of the human spirit in its struggle to wrest itself free of all man-made forms.

Sources for Further Study
The New York Times. Review. CXXXVI (August 13, 1987), p. C28.
The New York Times Book Review. Review. XCII (August 30, 1987), p. 3.
Publishers Weekly. Review. CCXXXI (June 26, 1987), pp. 66-67.

Lillian Vallee

MOUCHETTE

Author: Georges Bernanos (1888-1948)
Type of plot: Philosophical realism
Time of plot: Unspecified
Locale: The Artois region of northern France, near the Belgian border
First published: Nouvelle Histoire de Mouchette, 1937 (English translation, 1966)

> *Principal characters:*
> MOUCHETTE, a fourteen-year-old peasant girl
> ARSÈNE, a local poacher and liar, who rapes her
> MOUCHETTE'S MOTHER, who dies before she can hear of Mouchette's rape
> MATHIEU, the game warden
> PHILOMÈNE, the village sitter-with-the-dead
> MÉNÉTRIER, a local farmer
> THE NARRATOR, a priest

The Novel

Mouchette is the brief story of a humble girl's last miserable hours. It is a tale told with a marvelous economy of words and in a limpid style, taking the reader through the series of encounters the child experiences in her misery. The tale begins as Mouchette slips away from the singing class at the village primary school, where she has been rejected both by the teacher and by the other students. She takes to the road. Having cut across the *taillis* (a stunted wood, periodically cut back for charcoal making), she takes refuge between two trees to shelter from a rainstorm. By this time, she has lost both a shoe and her scarf. (Even the finest of details Georges Bernanos makes reverberate meaningfully in subsequent stages of her wandering and loss.)

Mouchette is then found by a friend of her smuggler-father, the drunk poacher Arsène, who takes her to his hut. There he gives her a drink from his small remaining stock of alcohol. He boasts graphically of having saved her from the "cyclone" raging outside, confesses in detail to killing the game-keeper, Mathieu, and falls unconscious in an epileptic fit. Mouchette cradles his head and, though she hates music at school, sings lovingly and beautifully to him. When he recovers, Arsène rapes her. A brief glimmering of hope is thus extinguished. The small fire in the hut has become ashes. Mouchette takes to the road again.

At dawn, she arrives at the hovel where she lives only to find her father and brothers snoring drunkenly, the neglected baby crying, and her mother lying mortally ill. Mouchette succors the baby as she did Arsène and learns from her mother that the poacher lied to her about the storm the previous night. Mouchette's mother dies before she can hear her daughter's confession of her secret, however, and the girl again flees, alone, any dream of happiness or even of tenderness gone.

A Sunday-morning encounter with the gamekeeper, Mathieu, and his wife confirms Arsène's deception. A savage in the eyes of the close-knit villagers, a miserable outcast in her own fumbling imagination, Mouchette defiantly announces to Mathieu that Arsène is her lover and then leaves.

The girl is invited into the house of the ancient, macabre Philomène, the professional watcher over the dead in the community, who has had her eye on Mouchette for some time. Philomène, it seems, thrives on death. She gives the fragile dress of a long-dead young lady whom she looked after in her early days of domestic service to Mouchette as a present.

Mouchette, now filled with ideas of her own death, goes to a local pond alone, where she leaves a strand of the torn muslin dress. A farmer, Ménétrier, observes her and then goes on his way. Mouchette realizes that no caresses are ever going to come her way here, not from her family, not from Arsène, not from the village community, not from the Church. A voiceless voice speaks in her head, and she slides into the water, glances once at the sky, and drowns. Such is Georges Bernanos' view of man's inhumanity to man, or here to a young girl, on the road of life.

The Characters

The summary of events, sketched above, gives a most inadequate rendering of the power of this elegantly crafted tale. It also does little more than suggest the complex responses aroused in a reader by Bernanos' rendering of his innocent heroine's death following a series of rejections on all fronts. The book's focus is exclusively on the inarticulate Mouchette in her few moments of joy and in her lifetime of suffering. At least (such is Bernanos' skill), it seems like a lifetime; in fact, however, it cannot be more than eighteen hours from the start to the finish of the action. No other characters' motives are examined by the omniscient narrator.

The reader follows with increasing sympathy Mouchette's growing confidence in her abductor, her half-desirous, half-terrified involvement in her rape, and her painful realization that she has lost her virginity to a liar. Such is the potent effect of the stunted landscape, the incessant downpour, and the closed rural society that the reader comes to sympathize deeply with Mouchette and even to feel like something of an accomplice in her suicide. People do not understand her, she is unable to express herself adequately, and so she is rejected. Her life is miserable. With all the stubbornness, timidity, and incomprehension of a small animal, she is hunted from place to place, from person to person, increasingly degraded with each encounter. From the potentially life-giving meeting with Arsène, she travels to her ominous encounter with a devotee of Death (in the person of the wake-goer, Philomène).

The minor characters in the story are developed only insofar as they have an impact on the "chase," to use Bernanos' hunting metaphor; they are the dogs who pursue the game to its death.

Themes and Meanings

Following his exclusively Catholic education, Georges Bernanos never faltered in promoting his idea that what is not God-centered does not satisfy. All of his fiction is directed to demonstrating that end. In his extended metaphor of the road traveled by an innocent, the reader has a model for his life and receives more than a hint of his responsibility as keeper of his brothers and sisters.

Mouchette is a revelation of the despair that results from the absence of God. Bernanos' child heroine is the archetypal symbol of crushed innocence in the pervasive evil of the world. She, in her antipathetic community, becomes a symbol for everyone in the larger and no less antipathetic world with its moral horrors, which Bernanos observed at first hand from the trenches in World War I and in Francisco Franco's Spain. Surrounded by drunken unfeelingness and violence, and driven to her death, she is a symbol for all in the larger world, which is equally bent on mass suicide. Pursued to her various stations, for Bernanos Mouchette parallels Christ's expiatory suffering and death in a world alien to Him.

The physical setting in the novel clearly supports this dominant theme. In the hallucinatory wet, stunted growth of the Artois woods, Mouchette's muddy minidrama is acted out among at best uncomprehending neighbors; at worst, they are drunkenly perverted. Evil surrounds her and tracks her down in a Manichaean world where the forces of Satan flourish and kill. Bernanos' novel as a whole is a cry of horror against such a world, one that brutalizes the spirit of childhood in Mouchette and in all human beings.

After the deafening silence which comes to surround her, the water finally fills her ears with a "joyous murmur." Bernanos extends only this small hope from her suffering and death, the single meaning to be extracted from a world given over to the power of Satan, where the voice of the narrator is the solitary sacerdotal presence.

Critical Context

Mouchette is the archetypal, suffering adolescent found in many of Bernanos' fictions, but here, in his last conceived novel—*Monsieur Ouine* (1943, revised 1955; *The Open Mind*, 1945), a later novel, was started in 1931 but not finished until 1940—she is also a fully realized individual. Mouchette and her thoughts and feelings are the constant center of attention in this remarkably compressed work. Bernanos, fresh from the spectacular success of his *Journal d'un curé de campagne* (1936; *Diary of a Country Priest*, 1937) is here at the top of his stylistic bent.

He portrayed in Mouchette yet another of his self-giving saint-heroines. She is one, however, for whom, in her poverty, there is no exit except in suicide and God. In an interview, the author said that the inception of the novel came from his being struck by the sight of a truckload of Spanish peasants going uncomprehendingly to their deaths at the hands of one of Franco's firing squads. Bernanos had already written in his early *Sous le soleil de Satan* (1926; *The Star of Satan*, 1927; also known as *Under the Sun of Satan*) of a character named Mouchette who killed herself. Bernanos stated, however, that the two girls have nothing in common except the same tragic loneliness in which they lived and died. It was his fervent hope that God would have mercy on both of them.

This simple Christian avowal is typical of Bernanos in all of his works and in his life. What is unusual here is that no priest figure is present, beyond the narrator. The reader is told that no one in the village is attending Mass now, including the Sunday on which Mouchette dies. The pattern of the humiliation, rejection, and death of Christ is played out only by her. She needs love and sympathy to realize herself; they are not available. Such, more than in the writings of other well-known French Catholic novelists, such as François Mauriac, is Bernanos' sympathetic position as he views the wretchedness and poverty of much of humanity. As long as communication remains a problem for individuals, Bernanos deserves to be read for the compassionate voice that sings in *Mouchette*.

Sources for Further Study

Asti, F. D. "Failures in Communication in *La Nouvelle Histoire de Mouchette*," in *Nottingham French Studies*. XX (1981), pp. 42-62.

Blumenthal, Gerda. *The Poetic Imagination of Georges Bernanos: An Essay in Interpretation*, 1965.

Bush, William. *Georges Bernanos*, 1969.

Hebblethwaite, Peter. *Bernanos: An Introduction*, 1965.

Speaight, Robert. *Georges Bernanos: A Study of the Man and the Writer*, 1974.

Archibald E. Irwin

MUDUN AL-MILH

Author: 'Abd al-Raḥmān Munīf
Type of plot: Naturalism
Time of plot: Cities of Salt, from World War I to 1953; *al-Ukhdūd*, from 1953 to 1962
Locale: Saudi Arabia
First published: al-Tīh, 1984 (*Cities of Salt*, 1988); *al-Ukhdūd*, 1985; "Taqāsīm al-layl wa-al-nahār," forthcoming

> *Principal characters:*
> *Cities of Salt*
> Mut 'ib al-Hadhdhāl, a Bedouin patriarch living in the oasis
> The prince
> Ibn Rāshid, the prince's deputy
>
> *al-Ukhdūd*
> Khaz 'al, the sultan of the oil-rich sultanate
> Subḥī al-Maḥmaljī, his personal physician and adviser
> Hammād, the head of the secret service of the sultanate
> Wadād, Subḥī's wife
> Samīr, an Egyptian journalist and sometime lover of Wadād

The Novel

Mudun al-milh (cities of salt) narrates the story of the discovery of oil in the Arabian Peninsula and the radical impact of that discovery on the physical and human landscape. Although the kingdom in which the action takes place is never mentioned by name, it is clear that the reference is to the kingdom of Saudi Arabia. In the novel, the cities of Ḥarrān and Mūrān represent the major Saudi Arabian cities that developed in the aftermath of the discovery of oil during the first decades of the twentieth century.

The action of volume 1 spans the period from World War I to the early 1950's. No specific dates are given in the novel itself. The time frame, however, can be readily established from the transparent correspondence between internal narrative events and actual historical events. Thus, the reign of Sultan Khuraybiṭ, founder of the fictional kingdom in the novel, corresponds to the reign of Sultan 'Abd al-'Azīz (1902-1953), founder of the Saudi kingdom.

Volume 2 begins with the ascent of Khaz 'al, Khuraybiṭ's eldest son, to the throne and ends with his overthrow by his younger brother on charges of inefficiency and corruption. Sultan Khaz 'al stands for King Sa'ūd, who ruled Saudi Arabia from 1953 until 1962, when he was deposed by his younger brother, Fayṣal, who then became sultan. (The forthcoming third volume, entitled "Taqāsīm al-layl wa-al-nahār," "divisions of day and night," will presumably dramatize subsequent historical events that occurred during the reign of Sultan Fayṣal and his successors.)

Although sultans, kings, and princes exercise significant control in the novel, they are not its immediate or primary subject. The focus of attention throughout volume 1 is on the gradual transformation of a desert oasis from pristine simplicity to a bustling metropolis. What sets this process of transformation in motion is the sudden, unannounced appearance of three American petroleum engineers in this idyllic landscape. Having had no previous exposure to foreigners, the indigenous Bedouin population views the three American engineers with curiosity and apprehension as they go about surveying the desert landscape in search of oil. In the manner of nineteenth century European and American naturalist fiction, the slow-paced narrative attempts to capture in minute detail the reaction of the Bedouins to this unprecedented encroachment on their desert habitat.

The Americans' presence in the desert begins to take a more permanent nature with the arrival of prefabricated houses, heavy landscaping and drilling equipment, and other technological wonders such as binoculars, radios, tape recorders, and television sets. The apprehension of the indigenous population turns to forthright hostility. Initially, this hostility is passive and finds expression in the withdrawal of Mut 'ib al-Hadhdhāl, the patriarch of the oasis, from the encounter with the new reality. When he fails to persuade the prince to put a halt to the surveying and drilling and to order the Americans out, the patriarch simply rides his camel into the desert one night and disappears. Although no physical trace of him is ever found, he becomes a symbol of resistance to the new epoch and occasionally returns to haunt the prince and local representatives of the government. When, toward the end of volume 1, the Bedouins stage a strike against the American oil company and someone sets the entire oil field and camp ablaze, all fingers point to the ghost of Mut 'ib al-Hadhdhāl.

The focus of volume 2 shifts from the physical landscape of the remote oasis and the city of Ḥarrān that was built around it to the new capital in the interior, Mūrān (presumably Riyāḍ, the actual capital of Saudi Arabia). Unlike Ḥarrān, the nucleus of the capital consists of a cluster of palaces built with oil revenues for members of the royal family. The sultan's main palace houses his ever-increasing harem and serves as the locus of much of the narrative in this volume.

A still greater portion of this volume is devoted to describing the personality, motives, concerns, and life-style of the sultan's physician and main adviser, Subḥī al-Maḥmaljī. While not a member of the royal family by blood, "the physician," as he is called in the novel, is the actual founder of the kingdom. It is he who creates the governmental institutions and offices on which the nascent state stands. Foremost among these are the secret service and the propaganda department, for which he handpicks the most loyal and efficient among the sultan's subjects. To immortalize his own name, the physician envisions writing a historical and philosophical treatise about the nature of government based on his actual experience in the service of the sultan. As he indulges his illusions of grandeur in this manner, control over the affairs of state slips imperceptibly from his hands and passes into the hands of his subordinates, especially Ḥammād, the head of the sultanate's secret service whom the CIA had been cultivating for many years without the physician's knowledge.

Totally engrossed in his quest for financial and political power, the physician also neglects the emotional and sexual needs of his wife, Wadād. She avenges herself by maintaining regular illicit relations with his various subordinates and business partners. Just when the physician's lifelong wish to become the sultan's exclusive adviser and confidant appears within reach, events take an unexpected turn. Shortly after the aging sultan marries the physician's sixteen-year-old daughter and departs for Europe on their honeymoon, he is deposed by his younger brother and the physician is ordered by the new ruler to leave the country immediately.

The Characters

Characterization in this novel serves the primary objective of providing a panoramic view of Bedouin society as it undergoes radical transformation. To realize this intention, the narrative point of view constantly shifts from one scene to another, describing each barely long enough to record the effects of the cataclysmic change on the face of the desert and its dwellers. The net result is akin to a set of group photographs as opposed to individual portraits. No Bedouin character displays any significant psychological depth, and none is given to introspection. In fact, no clear line appears to separate the private from the public realm in the life of this nomadic society. The characters who display any degree of roundedness stand out as typical, rather than unique, individuals.

This may explain, at least in part, Mut 'ib's disappearance at the end of volume 1. The Bedouin patriarch tries to stem the ravishing of the desert through the only means available to him, namely, public remonstration with the prince. When that fails, there is little else he can do as an individual. Disappearance into the desert in the thick of night invests him with mythic qualities and enables him to carry on the fight.

The same strategy of characterization is applied to the American engineers and personnel. They always appear together and are described as a group. The reader never gets a direct glimpse of their personalities and conduct. Instead, 'Abd al-Raḥmān Munīf shows the reaction of the indigenous population to the presence of the Americans. From such a distance, all the characters appear to be stereotypes rather than realized individuals.

Among the major characters of the novel, only the physician appears as a well-rounded character. For this reason, he, and not the sultan, should be considered the main character of the novel. This is particularly true of volume 2, which dramatizes his methodical and painstaking pursuit of power and his sudden fall from it.

There is evidence to suggest that the physician may be a composite of a number of historical figures who served in various capacities under Sultan 'Abd al-'Azīz, the founder of the Saudi monarchy. As a fictional character, however, the physician is interesting because he simultaneously combines in his personality the omnipotence of every creator over his creation and the ability to subordinate himself completely to the will of those whom he installs in power. His obscure origins and mysterious arrival into the nascent desert kingdom and his admiration for "the German way of doing things" are also intriguing.

Ḥammād, the Bedouin whom the physician handpicks to head the secret service of the new state, develops to full stature in the course of the novel's action. His character demonstrates precisely how knowledge can be transmuted into power. While the physician was the first to detect Ḥammād's talent, it is the CIA which cultivates it for systematic application. Ḥammād's initiation into the sophisticated methods of intelligence-gathering and the effective wielding of knowledge and power takes place during his first trip to the United States. From that point on, his visits to the United States increase steadily in frequency and length. Toward the end of volume 2, he emerges as the undisputed power behind the throne.

Themes and Meanings

The overriding thematic concern of *Mudun al-milh* is to chronicle the passing of one historical epoch and the onset of another. As is often the case in human history, the transition from one phase of civilization to another occasions a clash between the old and the new. In this novel, the arrival of machines, cars, and boats in the desert announces the start of the conflict between the traditional nomadic life-style of the indigenous Bedouin population and modernity.

This universal theme takes the form of a cultural conflict in the novel because the agents of transformation are foreigners. That these foreigners are non-Muslims adds a religious dimension to the conflict. For the indigenous population, the American land surveyors and engineers appear as the very embodiment of the Devil. Their looks, indiscreet dress code, lax manners, and especially the technology they bring, strike a note of terror in the hearts of the locals. The vast knowledge they display about the history, geography, social customs, and mores of the Bedouins (including the genealogy of their numerous and diverse tribes) arouses the suspicion and hostility of the locals. When they hear the Americans speak fluent Arabic and discourse knowledgeably about Islam, the Bedouins' suspicions acquire even more compelling weight. They ask in sincere bewilderment, "Why don't they convert to Islam, if they are not devils?"

The status of women is another major theme in this novel. In a highly segregated society such as Saudi Arabia, the women's quarters are carefully shielded from public view. The omniscient third-person narrator of this novel carries the reader right into these quarters, to observe the hierarchy among the sultan's harem in the palace, the preparation of new brides for the sultan, and the ways in which women pass their time behind their veils.

Critical Context

Mudun al-milh is Munīf's seventh and undoubtedly most important novel. It is the first, however, set in the writer's native land of Saudi Arabia. His earlier novels dealt with more general Arabian concerns as he perceived them from his self-imposed exile, initially in Iraq, where he worked for many years as a petroleum engineer, and later in Paris, which he made his home. Most of Munīf's fiction is written in the traditional styles of naturalism and social realism, both of which were fashionable in the 1940's and 1950's in Arabic fiction but which have become somewhat archaic since then.

The naturalistic mode is exceptionally appropriate, however, for the purposes of this novel: namely, to evoke in minute detail the plenitude of a world that once was and is no more. This is an undertaking of epic proportions, and, like all epics, it describes and explains everything in full, leaving nothing to chance. It is unquestionably the most important Arabic novel in decades and will probably have an impact far beyond literature.

Sources for Further Study

Allen, Roger. *The Arabic Novel: An Historical and Critical Introduction*, 1982.

_____. *Modern Arabic Literature*, 1987.

Siddiq, Muhammad. "The Contemporary Arabic Novel in Perspective," in *World Literature Today*. LX, no. 2 (Spring, 1986), pp. 206-211.

Muhammad Siddiq

MY MICHAEL

Author: Amos Oz (1939-   )
Type of plot: Psychological realism
Time of plot: The 1950's
Locale: Jerusalem, Israel
First published: Mikha'el sheli, 1968 (English translation, 1972)

>   *Principal characters:*
>   HANNAH GONEN, the narrator of the novel, whose journal
>   entries reveal the disintegration of her inner world
>   MICHAEL GONEN, Hannah's geologist husband, whose
>   ineffectuality as husband and father lead Hannah to
>   despair
>   YAIR GONEN, Hannah and Michael's precocious, sometimes
>   insolent son
>   YEHEZEK GONEN, Michael's brooding, depressed father

The Novel

   My Michael begins as an epistolary novel set in Jerusalem in the 1950's, a place and time which constituted, as Amos Oz has said, "a Jewish anticlimax after the tragedies and achievements of the forties." The novel consists of the journal entries of Hannah Gonen, a despairing Israeli housewife retracing the important events and aspirations of her young life. From the beginning, she tells the reader mysteriously that she is keeping her record specifically "because people I loved have died . . . because when I was young I was full of the power of loving, and now that power of loving is dying. I do not want to die." Her power to love and to live becomes inextricably interwoven with her ability to separate dream from reality in her journal, an ability which fails her as the novel moves to its denouement.

   What begins as a seemingly straightforward, dispassionate chronology of events soon devolves into an idiosyncratic, often fragmentary account of Hannah's mental life as she walks through the ruins of her adulthood and her disintegrating marriage. Hannah attempts to forge a coherent pattern to her life. Yet she discovers not only "a sameness in the days and a sameness in me" but also "something which is not the same. I do not know its name." Hannah begins her attempt at naming this vague discomfort by recording the facts of her marriage to Michael Gonen. Hannah had met Michael, to whom she constantly refers as "my Michael," by chance, while an undergraduate literature student at Hebrew University in Jerusalem. His dry, pragmatic pursuit of a Ph.D. in geology contrasts with Hannah's passionate and lyrical literary tastes. Michael is neither witty nor particularly imaginative, yet Hannah is drawn to his stability and settledness.

Their courtship and eventual wedding are described in precise but ironically unromantic terms as something inevitable, a relationship which neither exactly chose but which seemed somehow appropriate to them. The matter-of-factness and ambivalence with which Hannah recounts these events foreshadow her eventual estrangement from her husband and their mode of life. Hovering over their budding relationship is the brooding, divided city of Jerusalem, whose "villages and suburbs surround it in a close circle like curious bystanders surrounding a wounded woman lying in the road." Thus, Jerusalem itself emerges in her imagination as a haunting presence and a competing rival for Michael's attention and devotion.

From the concreteness of this early episode, Hannah's narrative soon shuttles violently between her inner and outer life; reminiscence, daydream, and the banal details of her "real" existence coalesce, and she is increasingly unable to distinguish between sleeping and waking. She thinks often of her childhood, remembering fondly her bout with diphtheria, which offered "a state of freedom," a dose of attention from her parents and doctors that gave her a sense of worth. Upon recovering from the illness, she felt "exiled," and she carried away from her childhood a "vague longing to fall seriously ill." Her most alarming preoccupation, however, stems from the innocent but problematic relationship she recalls with the twin Arab boys of her adolescence, Halil and Aziz. Her frequent reveries of sexual debasement at their hands temporarily distract her from the empty, unfulfilled life she lives with Michael but underscore her disturbing disengagement from the events of her everyday existence.

As Michael climbs the ladder of moderate academic success, the amiability that has characterized their marriage turns to mere tolerance, precluding true intimacy or friendship. Even the birth of her son, Yair, provides no meaningful entry into a more public world for Hannah; at an early age, Yair becomes enamored of his father and paternal grandfather, Yehezek Gonen, sharing his greatest confidences with them. In one incident, emblematic of their growing mistrust of each other, Michael childishly intimates that she is responsible for the disappearance of a cat he has brought home for Yair. Dishonoring Hannah in front of their obviously spoiled son, Michael implies that Yair may get his way by learning to bully and throw tantrums.

As his career is eclipsed by the discrediting of his geological theories and their money dwindles, Michael becomes a more sulking, insensitive partner. In defense, Hannah submerses herself in her private fears and secret dreams. Disengaged from her past by her father's death and from the present by Michael's aloofness, Hannah resigns herself to the death of their marriage ("without touching each other") and resolves to find her release in sleep. The frenzied climax of the novel finds Hannah in a familiar daydream, her mind drifting to a now grown-up Halil and Aziz, whom she accompanies on a guerrilla mission to disrupt the daily lives of Jerusalem's population.

The Characters

Oz's Hannah Gonen is a cultured, intense young woman whose control of her inner and outer life is in question throughout the narrative. While she succumbs to the chaos of her dreamworld toward the end of the novel, her journal's remarkable evocation of the past and how it has affected her present life is startling in its precision and psychological realism. This is a testimony to Oz's narrative skill, which in many ways overshadows the minor plot structure of *My Michael*. Hannah exemplifies Oz's consistent thematic concern for the fate of the individual consciousness struggling with rather than embracing the political currents of his or her society. His strategy for highlighting the personal crisis of individual protagonists is what some critics have labeled "Magical Realism," a juxtaposition of everyday, mundane events with fantasy, dream, or startling metaphor. Here Oz uses this device to lay bare Hannah's psyche, exposing her innermost thoughts and flights of fancy as clues to her disorientation and paranoia.

The reader first becomes aware that Hannah is not merely cataloging daily occurrences when she begins to allude to latent feelings and vague recollections of a distant past without an accompanying context. Memories of childhood begin to surface quite randomly in her narrative, eventually displacing the chronological structure with which the novel begins. Hannah's pretentiousness about writing in the journal emerges as a running theme: "I have written somewhere in these pages: 'There is an alchemy in things which is also the inner melody of my life.' I am inclined to reject this statement now because it is too high-flown." The more aware she becomes that she is melodramatizing her experiences, the more detached from reality she gets, finally confessing that only fiction can give her life any semblance of order.

Hannah's Michael emerges as a well-meaning but ineffectual academic, one more at home in scholastic debate and naming prehistoric rocks than in the arms of a loving wife. Her constant reference to him as "my Michael" becomes an ironic counterpoint to their actual relationship. Instead of an affectionate term playfully implying spousal possession, "my Michael" looms as an invective measuring the chasm that has erupted between the two. His surname, Gonen, which means "protector" in Hebrew, is another irony in the novel; while Michael provides all the necessary worldly goods the family needs to survive, he cannot meet Hannah's spiritual and psychological needs and cannot protect her from herself and the dissolving tension between her dreams and reality.

In the skilled hands of Amos Oz, Jerusalem itself assumes the role of a character, standing in the background as a spiritual fortress guarding many secrets and longings across Arab, Jewish, and Christian cultures. As Jerusalem is a city ostensibly "normal" but divided by hostile camps, so Hannah's consciousness is a battlefield of unfulfilled ambitions and spousal duties. Implicitly, Hannah's disengagement from the world at large is as much an escape from the city as it is from her husband. In her dreamy world of shadows, "Jerusalem was far away and could not haunt her" and is transformed as the lost playground for her and the twins. "[T]hrowing hand grenades before dawn among the ravines of the Judean desert . . . ," they bridge the gulf between the irreconcilable cultures.

Themes and Meanings

Oz has said that "one should present the great and simple things, like desire and death," in fiction writing, and *My Michael* follows that statement in its treatment of Hannah and the Israeli culture in which she is immersed. While on the surface *My Michael* deals with the mundane details of middle-class life in postwar Jerusalem and the disintegrating marriage of a disillusioned young woman, Hannah's experiences clearly become a metaphor for the dualistic lives many contemporary Israelis feel compelled to lead. Several American critics have thus read it as an Israeli version of *Madame Bovary*, the elaborate depiction of a private life amid great social turmoil. Read as such, *My Michael* is one of the more remarkable evocations of a protagonist's psychological disintegration in contemporary literature.

Still, it is important to point out that Oz's characters rarely escape a close identification with their environment, and in *My Michael* the problems of Hannah and Michael are clearly interwoven with the heterogeneity of Jerusalem. During one early encounter with Michael, Hannah observes, "Maybe it's a pity that Jerusalem is such a small city that you can't get lost in it." The reader presumes this to mean that one can never escape Jerusalem's paradoxes and tensions; one either learns to live with them or chooses to merge with them. As the critic Hana Wirth-Nesher has remarked, "It is clear that Oz is using Hannah to depict the isolation and alienation that many Israelis feel partially as a country in a state of siege and partially as a small enclave of Western culture in a vast area of cultures and landscapes unlike what they have known."

Thus, *My Michael* also can be read as a diagnosis of the malaise in Israeli culture following its statehood and years of military triumph in the late 1960's: a clash between postindependence militarism and the newer generation's ambivalence toward such a stance. Despite Michael's blithe optimism and willingness to fight in the Six Day War, Hannah remains skeptical, wondering if the loss of her husband and the father of her son is worth the price of the victory. This more political reading, in fact, has been characteristic of Israeli critics, who regarded *My Michael* as "little short of seditious" when it first appeared, citing its implication that the new, inordinately militaristic Israel is at least as responsible for Middle Eastern instability as the peoples it has displaced. Despite Hannah's waking fantasies, the reality of Jerusalem's divisiveness cannot be wished away. This attitude would simply condemn its residents to a city that is both native to them and strangely alien.

Critical Context

Oz's thematic concerns are quite different from the kind of celebration of Jewish culture often associated with Israeli writers. These better-known themes are reflected, for example, in the work of Isaac Bashevis Singer, Israel's most revered modern writer, who is spiritually attuned to and respectful of the "old ways" and writes expressly to preserve a tradition for later generations. Oz, though writing in Hebrew, is less interested in preserving than in challenging the social and religious mores of modern Israel. For this reason, *My Michael*, his first novel, written when was he was twenty-eight years old, was an immediate *cause célèbre* in Israel. In a society whose Hebrew-reading public numbers less than a million, *My Michael* sold a remarkable forty thousand copies. Following Israel's wild success in the Six Day War, the novel was widely read as an attack on Israel's new arrogance; Hannah Gonen's deliberate, undisguised ambivalence toward what Oz conceives as the political imperialism of his countrymen shocked and disturbed many readers.

Oz belongs to the postindependence generation of novelists, whose outlook was significantly shaped by the fact that, unlike their families, they were part of a country they could call their own. Distanced from his parents' "longing for a return home," Oz is thus unchained from a borrowed past that might limit or dictate his narrative themes and strategies. Regarding himself as a "secular Zionist" who is not particularly religious, he still embues his characters and settings with the age-old piety of this "holy land."

This religious temperament resonates in *My Michael* not only because Oz writes in Hebrew but also because he knows that, no matter how secularized Israel becomes, the ancient religion of the Jews—with all of its ambiguities and tribulations—still haunts the modern Israeli landscape. Oz's narrative style and focus has helped displace the nostalgia of pre-independence fiction with a problematic, self-questioning mode of writing and has energized political soul-searching in Israel, earning for him a prominent place in international letters as one of Israel's leading novelists and social critics.

Sources for Further Study

Alter, Robert. Review in *The New York Times Book Review*. LXXVII (May 21, 1972), p. 5.

Baker, A. T. Review in *Time*. C (July 3, 1972), p. 63.

Stern, David. "Morality Tale," in *Commonweal*. C (July, 1974), pp. 100-101.

Wirth-Nesher, Hana. "The Modern Jewish Novel and the City: Franz Kafka, Henry Roth, and Amos Oz," in *Modern Fiction Studies*. XXIV (1978), pp. 91-104.

Bruce L. Edwards

MYSTERIES

Author: Knut Hamsun (Knut Pedersen, 1859-1952)
Type of plot: Psychological realism
Time of plot: 1891
Locale: A small Norwegian coastal town
First published: Mysterier, 1892 (English translation, 1927)

> *Principal characters:*
> JOHAN NILSEN NAGEL, an eccentric and mysterious outsider,
> supposedly an agronomist
> JOHANNES GRØGAARD, THE MIDGET
> DAGNY KIELLAND, a parson's daughter who is engaged to a
> naval officer
> MARTHA GUDE, a humble older woman to whom Nagel
> proposes

The Novel

When Johan Nilsen Nagel disembarks from a steamer one midsummer evening, wearing a loud yellow suit and an oversized cap and carrying only a suitcase, a violin case, and a huge fur coat, he inevitably becomes an object of curiosity in the small Norwegian coastal town to which he has come. His eccentric appearance, his unusual behavior, and his lack of any discernible purpose for being in the town make him a bizarre and mysterious stranger. The only thing that the hotelkeeper is able to learn about his guest is that he is supposedly an agronomist who just returned from abroad and plans to spend some weeks in their town.

Nagel's first act is to befriend Johannes Grøgaard, the Midget, a grotesque but likable character who survives by playing the fool for the town sadists. One night, Nagel intervenes when the Midget is being ordered by his tormentor, the deputy Reinert, to drink a glass of beer which has been used as an ashtray and to dance and grind his teeth loudly for the amusement of the hotel café's patrons. Nagel beats Reinert, drives him from the hotel, and, to the astonishment of the easily astonished townspeople, invites the Midget to his room for champagne and cigars. The Midget reveals that he is from a good family (the son of a parson and a relative of one of the authors of the country's constitution), but since an accident (a fall from the ship's rigging while he was a sailor), he has lived with and worked for his uncle, a coal dealer. Nagel gives him money and admonishes him to remember his family name and breeding and not to accept "clown money" any longer.

Nagel uses his friendship with the Midget to extract information from him about the townspeople who interest him. He asks about Karlsen, a young divinity student who recently committed suicide, and he asks about Dagny

Kielland, whom Nagel has already encountered and frightened by his aggressive behavior. He learns that Dagny is the parson's daughter and is engaged
to a naval officer currently on duty in Malta, the son of a wealthy businessman. He manipulates the Midget into confessing that he carried a letter
from Karlsen to Dagny, thus giving added weight to the rumor that the unfortunate Karlsen killed himself because of his unrequited love for her. Nagel
also inquires about a woman, prematurely gray, whose eyes remind him of a
woman he once loved. He learns that she is Martha Gude, a respectable spin-
ster, the daughter of a deceased sea captain, now reduced to selling eggs for
her meager living.

Nagel is invited by Dr. and Mrs. Stenersen to a party at their home, where
he distinguishes himself by his loquacity and his iconoclastic views. He dismisses the Christiania (Oslo) of which they are so proud as a cultural backwater; he characterizes the celebrated Grand Café, gathering place of great
artists, as a place where nobodies are "elated because other nobodies
acknowledge them." He is arrogant and insolent but also intriguing, particularly to Dagny Kielland, whom he walks home. When Nagel totally misrepre-
sents his quarrel with Reinert, making himself out to be in the wrong,
Dagny, who has heard of Nagel's noble defense of the Midget, cannot understand why Nagel is lying. He confesses that it is all part of a strategy:
Through such false self-denigration, he hopes eventually to appear better
than he is; further, he would do anything to make her pay attention to him.
At the evening's end, Dagny's only response is that now at least she will have
something interesting to write her fiancé, but Nagel has fallen deeply in love
with her. He begins spending evenings near her home, hoping for a glimpse
of her, and nights in the woods nearby, praying for her (or perhaps to her).
When at length he confesses his passion, Dagny angrily accuses him of
destroying their friendship and tells him that she wishes never to see him
again.

Nagel attempts to divert himself from his obsession with Dagny by inviting
Dr. Stenersen, Hansen the lawyer, Holtan the schoolmaster, Øien the student, and the Midget to a stag party. As alcohol flows freely, discussion of
writers, politics, and religion becomes heated. Nagel denounces Leo Tolstoy
as a mediocrity and attacks Guy de Maupassant, Victor Hugo, and particularly Henrik Ibsen. The doctor, a liberal, attacks the socialist views of the
lawyer. When the talk turns to suicide, Nagel shows the group a vial of prus-
sic acid that he keeps in a vest pocket in case of need but confesses that he
lacks the courage to use it. The evening ends with everyone smashing
glasses—a successful party overall, but for Nagel, unsuccessful as a diversion
from his self-destructive passion for Dagny. He begins to think of Martha
Gude.

Despite Nagel's diatribes against the false nobility of charity and philan-
thropy, much of his time is spent in being a secret benefactor to people in

need. He gives money and clothes to the Midget, always swearing him to secrecy. Posing as an antique dealer, he cultivates Martha's friendship and tries to push a large sum of money on her in payment for a worthless broken chair. He invites her to the town bazaar. He lavishes his attention on her (at the same time looking for Dagny), dazzles her with his garrulous storytelling, awes the crowd by playing a borrowed violin, escorts her home, and proposes to her. The elaborate fantasy that he sketches for her of a cottage in the woods, a simple Edenic existence, and unending happiness seems so real and so appealing that she begins to believe him and agrees to marry him. When she changes her mind the next day, Nagel realizes that Dagny turned her against him and thus ended his only hope of tolerable life.

He throws the mysterious iron ring that he wears into the sea, goes to the woods near Dagny's house, and drinks from his vial. When at length he finds himself still alive, he realizes that the Midget has removed the poison and substituted water. For a short time, he is ecstatic at being alive, but this mood soon gives way to depression and despair. Instead of being grateful to the Midget, Nagel is enraged to find on his return to town that the Midget has reverted to his former ways, self-abasement for money. Nagel calls him a scoundrel, accuses him of secret depravity beneath his surface goodness, and vows to rip off his mask and expose the evil which is there. Nagel falls ill and suffers Dostoevskian nightmares and hallucinations. Shaking with fever, disoriented, and desperately needing (for some unknown reason) to recover the strange ring that he threw away, he rushes to the pier, throws himself into the sea, and drowns.

The following April, Dagny and Martha talk as they return from a party where the strange story of Johan Nagel was evidently a topic of discussion. Their conversation reveals that Nagel's intuitions about the Midget's secret sin are correct: He was guilty of some unspecified but evil behavior toward Martha. Since Martha had told no one, Dagny marvels at how Nagel could have known.

The Characters

Nagel appears nearly as mysterious to readers as he does to the townspeople. Despite two long monologues which narrate Nagel's chaotic thoughts directly, little of substance is conveyed; the remainder of the book, a third-person narrative, reveals remarkably little about his past, his true identity, or even his real name. A woman known as "Kamma," with whom he was previously involved briefly, visits him in his hotel room, calls him "Simonsen," is amused by his assumed identity of agronomist, tearfully declares that she still loves him (although she knows he no longer cares for her), accepts the money he proffers, and leaves on the next steamer.

Nagel's character is mercurial, paradoxical, and exasperating. He alternates between ecstasy and despair, clarity and confusion, impulse and contemplation, self-abasement and self-exaltation, and loathing and love of his fellow human beings. He contemptuously denounces charity as a form of egoism but continually gives away money. In his flights of fancy, his stories of the supernatural, and his fantasies, he appears to be a poet, but he is also given to an incomprehensible garrulousness which embarrasses even him. There are other inconsistencies: The violin case he so prominently displays in his room contains nothing but dirty linen; he denies that he is a rich man but consistently behaves as one; and his luggage appears costly, but he wears a cheap iron ring of some mysterious significance. His strategy of causing others to believe the worst of him is another perplexity. He lies about a medal that he carries, bestowed to him for saving a drowning man, and tells Dagny that he bought it. The truth is that he did earn the medal, but he has doubts about how heroic it may be to save a man who wants to drown.

The Midget is equally problematic. He appears to accept with exemplary Christian submission the many cruelties and humiliations the townspeople (and life) have heaped upon him. He appears to be all forgiveness to his enemies and all gratitude to his benefactor. Yet Nagel comes to believe that the Midget's behavior is an act beneath which lurks a scoundrel. Inexplicably, Nagel for a time even suspects the Midget of having murdered Karlsen, the divinity student, although the evidence clearly indicates suicide and the Midget's motive would be difficult to fathom. Knut Hamsun once said that the Midget was Nagel's alter ego, but this idea does not seem well developed. The powerful influence of Fyodor Dostoevski, with his interest in doubles and divided selves, however, is apparent here as elsewhere in the novel. "Your virtue brings out the brute in me," Nagel shouts at the Midget, recalling Dostoevski's perception that the higher part of the soul calls forth the lower part.

Dagny Kielland and Martha Gude appear as opposites: the one, proudly beautiful, self-assured, much sought-after; the other, awkward, plain, and looking older than she is. The two correspond to a story that Nagel tells about the beautiful Klara and her hunchbacked sister (although Martha is by no means deformed or repulsive). True to that story, Dagny does not want Nagel, but she also does not want Martha to have him. Thus she intervenes, successfully destroying his chances with Martha and, ultimately, his hope and his life. It is important to realize, however, that at no point does Hamsun make use of the possibilities of third-person narrative technique to reveal the inner thoughts of his female characters or of any character other than Nagel. Thus, all judgments about character are necessarily colored by Nagel's view.

Themes and Meanings

Hamsun's purpose in *Mysteries* is to depart as far as possible from "ordinary fiction about dances and engagements and excursions and marriages [which] is nothing but reading for sea captains and coachmen looking for an hour's entertainment." What Hamsun wishes to explore is human psychology, the mysteries, depths, paradoxes, and irrationalities of human behavior, personality, and identity, the same areas he perceived Dostoevski and August Strindberg to have explored. In an essay entitled "From the Unconscious Life of the Mind," Hamsun wrote of the need for writers to be concerned with the ineffable:

> . . . the secret stirrings that go on unnoticed in the remote parts of the mind, the incalculable chaos of impressions, the delicate life of the imagination seen under the magnifying glass; the random wanderings of those thoughts and feelings; untrodden trackless journeyings by brain and heart, strange workings of the nerves, the whisper of the blood, the entreaty of the bone, all the unconscious life of the mind.

Viewed from this perspective, the novel appears slightly less bewildering. Hamsun has gone some distance toward conveying the mysterious aspects of human consciousness. For example, how is Nagel able to know about the Midget's secret depravity? He is certainly not able to know by the usual methods of observation, interrogation, logic, or deduction. Even his dreams seem to contradict this view of the Midget. Still, he somehow knows with certainty, and in the end he is proved right. Nagel laughingly derides the inadequacy of the doctor's materialist view of that "infinite mystery," the human brain: "so many inches high and so many inches broad, something you can hold in your fist, a lump of thick grayish matter." The entire concept of rational, empirical knowledge is brought into question as Nagel asks: "What do people really know about life? We fall in line, follow the pattern established by our mentors. Everything is based on assumptions; even time, space, motion, and matter are nothing but supposition. The world has no new knowledge to impart; it merely accepts what is there."

The novel is filled with mysteries, from the small (how could Nagel have known that the Midget's name was Johannes?) to the much larger—the five suicide victims, Nagel's futile passion for Dagny, Kamma's equally futile passion for Nagel, the strange emptiness of Martha's life, and the shadowy woman who twice warns Nagel of death.

Critical Context

Mysteries is in part a reaction against the work of older realist writers, such as Ibsen, who tend to represent people as basically rational, understandable beings whose social problems are presented for a reader's edification. Hamsun is less interested in abstractions such as "society" and "social problems" and more interested in individual psychological analysis, particularly of exceptional people—eccentrics, outsiders, and wanderers such as Nagel. The so-called outcast from society is a type which appears in other early Hamsun novels, such as *Sult* (1890; *Hunger*, 1899) and *Pan* (1894; English translation,

1920). His preference for such protagonists seems to derive from his belief that unusual, iconoclastic types are more interesting and more important than ordinary, bourgeois people. Hamsun is no Democrat (a fact which became scandalously obvious with the revelation of his pro-Nazi views). As critics have noted, there is in much of his work a Nietzschean contempt for the average person and especially for what the average person regards as a truly great man. Hamsun confessed, "I am completely incapable of writing for the masses; novels with betrothals and dances and childbirth, overlaid with an external apparatus, are a bit too cheap for me and have no interest for me. . . . I address myself to an intellectual elite, and it is the appreciation of this elite that I value." Clearly, Nagel's scorn for what he calls "the carnivores," the commonplace, the average, and for all merely received ideas (a telling phrase), accords well with his creator's views. Still, it is important to acknowledge that later, in *Markens grøde* (1917; *Growth of the Soil*, 1920), Hamsun created strong, positive characters whose simplicity, commonness, and even primitiveness are their greatest virtues.

Mysteries prefigures much that became insistent in the twentieth century novel: the reaction against realism and naturalism, the turn toward the inner life and the resultant disintegration of an earlier, more stable and coherent sense of self, the preoccupation with the absurd and the irrational, the elevation of instinct over reason, and the search for "the secret power of the word." All these features mark *Mysteries* as a significant, pioneering novel.

Sources for Further Study
Gustafson, Alrik. "Man and the Soil," in *Six Scandinavian Novelists*, 1940.
Larsen, Hanna Astrup. *Knut Hamsun*, 1922.
McFarlane, J. W. "The Whisper of the Blood: A Study of Knut Hamsun's Early Novels," in *PMLA*. LXXI (1956), pp. 563-594.
Næss, Harald. *Knut Hamsun*, 1984.
——————. "Who Was Hamsun's Hero?" in *The Hero in Scandinavian Literature*, 1975. Edited by John M. Weinstock and Robert T. Rovinsky.

Karen Kildahl

THE NAME OF THE ROSE

Author: Umberto Eco (1932-　　)
Type of plot: Mystery
Time of plot: November, 1327
Locale: A monastery in the Italian Apennines
First published: Il nome della rosa, 1980 (English translation, 1983)

Principal characters:

　　WILLIAM OF BASKERVILLE, a fifty-year-old Franciscan monk
　　　　and a detective
　　ADSO OF MELK, an eighteen-year-old Benedictine novice,
　　　　William's disciple and scribe
　　ABO, the abbot
　　ADELMO OF OTRONTO, a master illuminator
　　BENNO OF UPPSALA, a scholar of rhetoric
　　BERENGAR OF ARUNDEL, an assistant librarian
　　BERNARD GUI, a seventy-year-old Dominican inquisitor
　　CARDINAL BERTRAND DEL POGETTO, the head of the papal
　　　　delegation
　　JORGE OF BURGOS, a blind former librarian
　　MALACHI OF HILDERSHEIM, a librarian
　　MICHAEL OF CESENA, the Minister-General of the Order of
　　　　Friars
　　MINOR, a supporter of Emperor Louis IV
　　NICHOLAS OF MORIMONDO, a master glazier
　　REMIGIO OF VARAGINE, a fifty-two-year-old cellarer
　　SALVATORE, Remigio's friend and assistant
　　SEVERINUS OF SANKT WENDEL, an herbalist
　　UBERTINO OF CASALE, the sixty-eight-year-old leader of the
　　　　Spirituals and a close friend of William
　　VENANTIUS OF SALVEMER, a translator of Greek and Latin
　　　　manuscripts

The Novel

In his old age, Adso of Melk recalls a momentous week in November, 1327. With William of Baskerville he reached an abbey somewhere along the central ridge of the Apennines. William's mission was to mediate between delegations from Pope John XXII and Michael of Cesena, which would be meeting there. The purpose of this gathering was to ensure Michael's safe passage to and from the papal palace at Avignon, where he hoped to secure endorsement for various church reforms.

Upon arriving at the abbey, William received a second charge, as well: to solve the mysterious death of Adelmo, whose body had recently been discovered outside the monastery walls. The abbot, Abo, wants to know how and why Adelmo died, not only because he is concerned about the welfare of the monks but also because he does not want the papal delegation, led by the inquisitors Cardinal Bertrand del Pogetto and Bernard Gui, to use the suspected murder as an excuse for investigating the abbey.

Despite William's efforts, the mystery is still unsolved when the legations arrive. In fact, it has become even more puzzling. Two more monks have died: Venantius has been discovered with his head in a pail of pig's blood, and Berengar has drowned in a bath. Moreover, Severinus, the herbalist who has been aiding William, is killed on the morning of the meeting, and Malachi dies shortly afterward.

As the abbot feared, the papal inquisitors take advantage of these occurrences to learn that Abo has been harboring monks who once followed the condemned heretic Fra Dolcino. Bernard Gui is convinced that Salvatore and Remigio, former Dolcinians, remain heretics and are responsible for the murders. He also makes clear in the course of the brief trial that Michael of Cesena will not succeed in gaining support for his views; the Church has no use for reformers who challenge its hegemony.

William's first mission, to guarantee the safety of Michael if he visits the Pope, has failed, and Abo dismisses him from his second mission, as well. Since the inquisitors have made their discoveries, he fears that anything William learns will only damage further the reputation of the abbey and consequently his own standing. Despite Abo's order, William persists in his investigation, spurred on by his love of knowledge and perhaps a certain intellectual pride. A few hours after Abo dismisses him from the case, William solves the mystery.

As a young man, Jorge of Burgos left the monastery and returned to his native Spain to secure books for the library. Among those he brought back was a unique copy of the second book of Aristotle's *Poetics*, which treated comedy as the first book dealt with tragedy. Regarding laughter as the worst heresy, Jorge locked the volume away in the most inaccessible part of the abbey's labyrinthine library, where it remained for decades.

Somehow, Berengar, the assistant librarian, found the book and persuaded Adelmo to have sex with him in return for the chance to examine the rare work. Driven by remorse for his carnal sin, Adelmo killed himself by leaping from the monastery walls. Venantius and Berengar also killed themselves, in a sense, for Jorge had poisoned the pages of the book to guarantee its continued unavailability. As a reader licked his fingers to turn the damp pages more easily, he ingested the poison. Because Berengar had taken the book with him when he fled to the baths next to the herbarium to seek relief from the toxin, Malachi, Jorge's ally, had to kill Severinus to retrieve the volume. Then, overcome by curiosity, Malachi, too, succumbed to the lethal pages.

Although William finds the book and correctly traces the murderous actions of Jorge and the others involved, his victory is temporary. Rather than allow anyone else to read Aristotle's work, Jorge begins eating the pages. A scuffle ensues in the library, Jorge knocks over Adso's lamp, and the entire monastery is destroyed by fire.

The Characters

In addition to challenging the reader to solve the mystery of the monks' deaths, Umberto Eco presents a second puzzle. *The Name of the Rose* is a *roman à clef*; many of the characters resemble well-known real or fictional figures. William of Baskerville, a tall, thin English detective with a fondness for a substance that induces lethargy, needs only a pipe, deerstalker cap, and cape to be the perfect double of Sherlock Holmes, whose use of cocaine is legendary. Adso resembles Holmes's faithful and not overly bright historian, Dr. Watson. The blind Spaniard, Jorge of Burgos, bears the features of the Argentine writer Jorge Luis Borges, who also created labyrinths and imaginary libraries. Just as Dante, a contemporary of the events related in the novel, peopled *The Divine Comedy* with his fellow Florentines, so Eco adds thinly disguised figures from postwar Italian politics to his novel. For example, Renato Curcio, the leader of the terrorist Red Brigades, resembles the radical reformer Fra Dolcino, who turned to violence the more rapidly to achieve a peaceful world.

Characters may thus be read allegorically, each figure in the book corresponding to another in a different book or in life. In medieval fashion, they may also be read anagogically, representing metaphysical concepts. William can stand for reason, Adso for mysticism, Jorge for the power of evil, and Abo for complacency. The novel then takes on yet another medieval guise, the psychomachia, or war of ideas, as it pits these characters against one another. Unlike the clear resolution of medieval conflicts, Eco's ending is uncertain. William solves the mystery by exposing Jorge. He also, however, becomes Jorge's accomplice by destroying the Aristotelian treatise in the fire that results from his determination to unravel the monastery's riddles.

Themes and Meanings

Such ambiguity is fitting for a book about uncertainty. In the typical mystery, detective and reader must interpret a series of signs to find the identity and motive of the criminal. The signs in such works may have several possible meanings, but only one is correct, and only the right reading will lead to the truth. *The Name of the Rose* shuns these conventions. Clues may be understood in various ways, and a false hypothesis nevertheless leads to the solution. As William tells Adso at the end of the book:

I arrived at Jorge through an apocalyptic pattern that seemed to underlie all the crimes, and yet it was accidental. I arrived at Jorge seeking one criminal for all the crimes and we discovered that each crime was committed by a different person, or by no one. I arrived at Jorge pursuing the plan of a perverse and rational mind, and there was no plan.

William believes that signs "are the only things man has with which to orient himself in the world," but he knows that one can never be certain about the relation among signs. The uncertainty begins with the book's title, which Eco says he chose because it "rightly disoriented the reader, who was unable to choose just one interpretation." The opening paragraph of Adso's memoir further warns of the impossibility of certainty. Adso begins by quoting the first verse of the Gospel of John: "In the beginning was the Word, and the Word was with God, and the Word was God." In this world one sees God, and hence the Word, whether in the form of language or other signs, as through a glass darkly.

Sensory perception and even logic are therefore untrustworthy. From a distance, the octagonal monastery appears to be a tetragon, and the heptagonal towers look like pentagons. On the mountaintop, Adso cannot tell whether the fog descends from the sky or ascends from the valley, nor can he decide whether the monastery contains holy or damned men. Signs can deceive: The lion and the serpent represent both Christ and Satan.

William, and so Eco, does not deny that truth exists, nor does he deny that one can sometimes read signs properly to reach that truth. The novel opens with a clever bit of deduction, as William determines from a knowledge of literature, and the presence of several agitated monks, broken branches, and horsehair, that the abbot's favorite horse has escaped from the monastery and is hiding nearby. Signs are not, however, always as clear as hoofprints in the snow. When a friar is condemned as a heretic, various spectators comment on his behavior. "He is a madman, he is possessed by the Devil, swollen with pride," some say. Others maintain that "he is not a saint, he was sent by Louis to stir up discord among the citizens." A third group disagrees: "All Christians should be like him." Given such confusion, the proper course is good-natured tolerance. As William tells Adso, "The only truth lies in learning to free ourselves from insane passion for the truth."

Critical Context

The Name of the Rose is filled with Latin phrases, literary allusions, medieval history and theology, and deconstructionist and semiotic theory. It has enjoyed wide acclaim despite its complexity. A critical success, it won the Strega Prize and the Viareggio Prize in Italy and the Médicis Prize in France. Before its translation into English, it sold half a million copies in Italy. It has been on the best-seller lists of Italy, France, Germany, and the United States, and in 1986 it was adapted for film.

Such response reveals the irony of Eco's claim in the preface that the story is "gloriously lacking in any relevance for our day, atemporally alien to our hopes and our certainties." Not only do late twentieth century characters appear thinly disguised, not only does the book reflect late twentieth century skepticism, but also, in its plea for tolerance, it offers a nuclear world its best and last hope for survival.

The novel is no more exclusively a twentieth century book than it is medieval. The eighteenth century novelist Henry Fielding, defending the realism of his characters, observed that not only were they living as he wrote, they had been alive for the past two thousand years. So, too, with Eco's characters. The historical background helps clarify the plot, but it also reveals how history repeats itself. Each period has its orthodoxy and its heresies, which may well change places in the succeeding age. Indeed, at any moment it may not be clear which is which. When Nicholas of Morimondo says he would be willing to destroy those who are "enemies of the people of God," William asks, "But who today is the enemy of the people of God? Louis the Emperor or John the Pope?" Eco's claim to atemporality thus contains some validity; like all classics, it stands outside time because it speaks to all ages.

Sources for Further Study

Eco, Umberto. *Postscript to "The Name of the Rose,"* 1984.

_____. "Reflections on *The Name of the Rose,*" in *Encounter.* LXIV (April, 1985), pp. 7-19.

Reichardt, Paul F. "*The Name of the Rose*: The Sign of the Apocalypse," in *Publications of the Missouri Philological Association.* IX (1984), pp. 1-7.

Yeager, Robert F. "Fear of Writing: Or, Adso and the Poisoned Text," in *SubStance.* XIV, no. 2 (1985), pp. 40-53.

Joseph Rosenblum

NAOMI

Author: Jun'ichirō Tanizaki (1886-1965)
Type of plot: Comedy of manners
Time of plot: The 1920's
Locale: Tokyo and surrounding areas
First published: Chijin no ai, 1924-1925, serial; 1925, book (English
translation, 1985)

> *Principal characters:*
> Jōji Kawai, a young company employee
> Naomi, a café waitress; later Jōji's mistress and wife
> Kumagai, Naomi's lover
> Hamada, Naomi's rejected lover

The Novel

Naomi is an ironic account of a seemingly proper gentleman in his mid-
twenties who meets a young girl named Naomi, who is working as a waitress
in a café. The story is told by its protagonist, Jōji Kawai. Fascinated by her
Western-sounding name and her sensuous beauty, which reminds him of
American silent film star Mary Pickford (highly popular in Japan in the
1920's), Jōji decides that he intends to marry Naomi; soon he falls into a
Pygmalion-like relationship as he attempts to tame this selfish and willful
creature. Jōji gives Naomi money for English and voice lessons, only to learn
that she is less talented than he had first supposed. She refuses to do any
work in the house, buys extravagant clothes, and manipulates Jōji into bor-
rowing money under false pretenses from his doting mother, who lives in the
country.

Naomi next takes up Western dancing and forces Jōji to accompany her to
her lessons and to Tokyo dance halls. There he realizes that she has developed a whole coterie of younger male friends unknown to him. The young
student Kumagai in particular speaks with Naomi in a fashion which suggests
that they have been intimate. Jōji's illusions shatter; his work suffers, and he
begins to lose control of himself.

At Naomi's suggestion, Jōji decides to rent a cottage for the summer in
the resort town of Kamakura, south of Tokyo. He commutes from there to
his job in Tokyo. Naomi seems happy with this arrangement, but Jōji learns
one evening that she has been carrying on an affair with Kumagai, abetted
by Hamada and her other student friends. Horrified, Jōji finally manages to
demand that Naomi leave him, which she does. Later, talking with Hamada,
Jōji realizes that Naomi has duped that young man as well; together, they set
out to locate her. Naomi, it appears, now goes from lover to lover, some of
them Japanese, some Westerners. When she eventually does return to Jōji,

he is so glad to see her that he easily gives in to her demands that they now live only as "friends," and he endures as well her sexual and psychological titillations. A slave to her outrageous desires, Jōji disposes of his family property, buys a huge Western-style house in the foreign community south of Tokyo in Yokohama, and lives on the periphery of his egotistical wife's existence, fully aware that his own life is now ruined.

The Characters

Jōji is a surprisingly complex creation and hardly a reliable narrator of the story he sets out to tell. Although he prefers to see himself as an upright young Japanese gentleman of the old school, he is prone to unrealistic fantasies concerning Naomi in which she is at least outwardly a docile and fashionable wife, and he attempts to manipulate both her and his mother. That Jōji fails to achieve any control over Naomi in line with those fantasies is certainly not from any want of trying. Naomi represents for Jōji a kind of Westernized, ideal figure who can fulfill his yearning for the sort of emotional relationship which is actually impossible for him to find in real life. Jōji provides a running commentary on all of his rueful adventures, revealing all too clearly how he distorts the truth, both to the reader and himself. Jōji reveals some of the same human weaknesses that appear in many of the young heroes of seventeenth and eighteenth century Kabuki plays and popular novels, men who throw themselves away on wild romantic flings. In attempting to break out of his staid life, Jōji, like his literary predecessors, leaves behind the prison of convention only to achieve a more private and personal hell.

Naomi, who has been described as a kind of Japanese "Carmen," is a perfect 1920's flapper. Beautiful, narcissistic, self-indulgent, she knows exactly what she wants and she gets it. However dubious her behavior, at least as described by Jōji, Naomi has the courage of her convictions, the very thing that he lacks. She leads him on because he wants to be led, and her teasing, however thoughtless and cynical, can occur only because Jōji foolishly worships her in all the wrong ways.

Kumagai, Hamada (who is also infatuated with Naomi), and a host of other incidental characters are nicely and satirically sketched, but they exist only to fill in the edges of Jun'ichirō Tanizaki's central cartoon, the battle between Jōji and Naomi.

Themes and Meanings

In this novel, Jun'ichirō Tanizaki provides an ironic account of a "fool's love" (as the Japanese title promises), but his story, given the setting he has provided, also suggests certain overtones applicable to a rapidly Westernizing Japan. Naomi is attractive to Jōji not only because she is a beautiful woman but also because she seems to have all the mysterious glamour of the West.

Yet despite its Western sound, her name is written with the usual Sino-Japanese characters, as Tanizaki is quick to point out. At one point, Jōji manages to convince himself that Naomi has actually become a Western woman, but his illusions are soon destroyed. There are a number of scenes in the novel that suggest that all Japan, like Jōji, is infatuated with a false view of Western culture, a state that can only result in frustration and disappointment. Tanizaki himself, although he never went abroad, loved Western art, literature, and ways of life as much as any writer of his generation; he was well aware at the same time, however, that his compatriots' pursuit of a dream lying outside everyday cultural contexts could provide the basis for a mordant and wry chronicle of the times. The battle of the sexes in *Naomi* serves as a highly effective tool that Tanizaki uses to poke fun, sometimes with good humor, sometimes with cruelty, at the foibles and dreams of his generation.

Critical Context

Naomi was Tanizaki's first popular success, which he soon followed with another highly regarded novel, *Tade kuu mushi* (1936; *Some Prefer Nettles*, 1955). In his works, he examined with trenchant irony the mixed cultural values that he detected in his contemporaries, caught between Eastern and Western ideals of behavior and morality. Later, Tanizaki explored traditional Japanese culture in his brilliant 1939-1941 translation into modern Japanese of the eleventh century classic *Genji monogatari*, by Murasaki Shikibu. Tanizaki then went on to write his own elegy to more traditional Japanese values in his majestic *Sasame-yuki* (1949; *The Makioka Sisters*, 1957). Tanizaki's postwar writings continued to explore cultural and erotic themes in both modern and historical settings, often revealing a profound understanding of traditional Japanese cultural and aesthetic values. Although *Naomi* is an early work, set in the twentieth century, in it the author first revealed his skill at dealing with themes that were to occupy him for the rest of his creative life. *Naomi* can thus be seen as a highly suggestive, and altogether successful, prelude to a long, insightful writing career focused on the ultimately mysterious relationships between men, women, and the cultures to which they owe allegiance.

Sources for Further Study

Kato, Shūichi. "Tanizaki Jun'ichirō and Other Novelists," in *A History of Japanese Literature*. Vol. 3, *The Modern Years*, 1983.

Keene, Donald. "Tanizaki Jun'ichirō," in *Dawn to the West: Japanese Literature of the Modern Era*, 1984.

Petersen, Gwenn Boardman. *The Moon in the Water: Understanding Tanizaki, Kawabata, and Mishima*, 1979.

Rimer, J. Thomas. "Tanizaki Jun'ichirō: The Past as Homage," in *Modern*

Japanese Fiction and Its Traditions, 1978.

Seidensticker, Edward. "Tanizaki Jun'ichirō," in *Monumenta Nipponica*. XXI, nos. 3/4 (1966), pp. 249-265.

Ueda, Makoto. "Tanizaki Jun'ichirō," in *Modern Japanese Writers and the Nature of Literature*, 1976.

J. Thomas Rimer

NARCISSUS AND GOLDMUND

Author: Hermann Hesse (1877-1962)
Type of plot: Philosophical romance
Time of plot: The late Middle Ages
Locale: The German Empire
First published: Narziss und Goldmund, 1930 (*Death and the Lover*, 1932;
  better known as *Narcissus and Goldmund*)

> *Principal characters:*
> GOLDMUND, a student, a wanderer, and an artist
> NARCISSUS, a teacher, a monk, and an intellectual

The Novel

Narcissus and Goldmund is a tale about the vagrant and erotic adventures of Goldmund (golden mouth) and his quest for the meaning of life and death. The novel, written in the third person, contrasts Goldmund's spontaneity and sensualism with the scholarly Narcissus' orderliness and rationalism. Hermann Hesse also provides historical insights into the medieval monasteries, the artistic guilds, the persecution of the Jews, and the Black Death.

As the novel begins, the naïve eighteen-year-old Goldmund is sent by his father to the Mariabronn cloister, where knowledge of the arts and sciences is passed from one generation to another. Goldmund, an extroverted adolescent, becomes an eager student because he is attracted to his teacher, Narcissus, a young man of keen perception and analytical thinking. Goldmund is also drawn to Abbot Daniel because of his saintliness. As a result of his regard for these men—the humble abbot and the brilliant scholar—Goldmund finds himself pursuing the idealistic but unachievable goal of emulating both, thereby causing himself much suffering. Narcissus, sensing in Goldmund his own opposite and complement, wants to guide him in his confusion, but he holds back, aware that his jealous brethren might accuse him of falling in love with a pupil. His duty is to educate the mind, not to become emotionally involved.

One night, some students persuade Goldmund to sneak out to the village, where they are to meet some girls. Goldmund only observes, but when leaving, he is kissed by a girl. Later, he forgets the excitement of sneaking away from the cloister, but he cannot forget the girl's kiss. Troubled and undecided about life in the cloister, Goldmund is sent out to the fields to contemplate nature and pick flowers, where he fortuitously meets a young woman who teaches him about the nature of love. Exhilarated by this new experience of life, he bids farewell to the monastery and to Narcissus and returns to the woman. He tells himself that he is not leaving because of her. On the contrary, he has abandoned the shelter of the cloister because he is no longer a child or a student; he is now a man.

Goldmund ventures into the world, enduring its hardships and relishing its freedom. He does not want to think too much but wants simply to take things as they come. Many women of high and low rank love him briefly and then return to their husbands and homes, unwilling to give up everything, even an abusive husband, for the wandering life. While Goldmund feels a general guilt, which he identifies as the burden of Original Sin, he does not feel the personal guilt of adultery. He is often lonely yet he cherishes his freedom.

During one miserable winter, Goldmund meets and travels with Viktor, a shrewd vagrant who tries to rob and murder him. In self-defense, Goldmund kills him. This experience gives rise to meditation about death and about the fact that a man could exist and then be gone without a trace. Perhaps, Goldmund thinks, the fear of death is the root of all art; since artists themselves are transitory, they want to create something that will outlive them.

Goldmund becomes a student of the well-known artist Master Niklaus and tries to create, in art, the sorrow and joy that he has experienced in life. He wants to re-create the universal mother of men, the source of life, the face of all the women he has known. His best achievement, however, turns out to be a statue of Saint John, the artistic embodiment of his friend Narcissus. During this period as a disciplined artist, Goldmund is still much desired by women and unpopular with men. For Goldmund, love and ecstasy give life its value; ambition, power, and materialism are unimportant. Despising the spoiled burghers who live for money and routine, he leaves his artistic post to taste more of the beauty and horror of the world.

The horror is soon evident in the plague, the Black Death. He learns that the plague is indiscriminate and ugly, but at the same time it is sweet and motherly, an enticement. He and his female companion Lene set up house in the forest, away from the plague-stricken city. Soon he kills again; the victim this time is a rapist who was attacking Lene. After a while, Goldmund knows that he has had enough of the domestic life and must move on. Lene dies of the plague, and Goldmund is again liberated.

Caught with the count's mistress, Goldmund comes face-to-face with his own death when he is sentenced to hang. He wants to accept his death, but he is still unwilling to leave everything and every woman. Regardless of whether there is an eternity, he wants this insecure and transitory life, even if it means that he must kill the priest who will hear his last confession and escape in the priest's clothes. He recognizes the priest as his old friend Narcissus, who has brought Goldmund a pardon for his sins.

Narcissus, now the abbot of the monastery, gives Goldmund a workshop where he can continue his artwork. After completing an art project, Goldmund feels empty; his life is in disorder. He is no longer young and attractive to women. Growing old and full of suffering, he leaves the cloister only to return before the winter. In the hope that dying will be a happiness as great as love, Goldmund finally welcomes death, his mother.

The Characters

In Greek mythology, Narcissus is the youth who rejected love from others and, as a consequence, contemplates only himself. He falls in love with his own reflection in a pool and eventually turns into a flower. In *Narcissus and Goldmund*, Narcissus represents one pole in the dichotomy of human nature, the mind. Hesse writes, "All was mind to him, even love; he was unable to give in to an attraction without thinking about it first." His home is the world of ideas rather than of experience and the senses. Even as a novice in the monastery, he was singled out as the disciple of Aristotle and Saint Thomas, as a man worthy of teaching his peers.

Narcissus is attracted to his opposite, the sensual Goldmund, but he knows that they will never understand each other completely. Yet Goldmund teaches Narcissus that there are many paths to knowledge, that the path of the mind is not the only one. Narcissus also learns that the artist translates thought into art, thus re-creating God's order. Narcissus has been enriched by Goldmund, but at the same time he has been weakened: "The world in which he lived and made his home, his well-constructed edifice, had been shaken and now filled with doubt."

Although at peace with the spiritual life in the monastery, Narcissus is challenged by Goldmund: "But how will you die when your time comes, Narcissus, since you have no mother? Without a mother, one cannot love. Without a mother, one cannot die."

Goldmund, named for the golden-mouthed preacher Saint John Chrysostom, is the main character and the complement to Narcissus. Whereas Narcissus is "analytical, a thinker," Goldmund is "a dreamer with the soul of a child." Something they have in common bridges those differences; "both were refined; both were different from the others because of obvious gifts and signs; both bore the special mark of fate." Goldmund is more than simply the opposite of Narcissus; he is a complex figure who, at different times, plays the pliable student, the sensual vagabond, and the disciplined artist.

Goldmund takes his character from his mother, whom he lost at an early age. He is forever trying to recover her in women, nature, and death. He goes through several stages in his search, and in each he experiences both joy and suffering. He learns that death and ecstasy are one. Eve, the mother of life, is for Goldmund "the source of bliss as well as of death; eternally she gave birth and eternally she killed; her love was fused with cruelty." Goldmund discovers that the ecstasy of love brings the suffering of birth; the sensual life gives birth to the painful creation of art. Throughout his life, Goldmund attains temporary understanding of the polarization of the world.

Still, he is not satisfied. He continually quarrels about "God's imperfect creation," but in the end, he accepts life's dichotomy.

All the minor figures in the novel appear as archetypes, basically unperturbed by life. For example, Abbot Daniel is a saintly ascetic in his own spiritual kingdom who belongs neither to the world of the mind nor to the world of the body. The women all belong merely to the world of the senses: The peasant woman is lusty, the daughter of the knight is aloof and unwilling to forgo her inheritance, and the middle-class Lene is satisfied simply to have a man and a house. Viktor, who exploits friends and society, represents the evil side of the vagabond. Master Niklaus is an artist who is so driven by the ordered discipline of art that he misses out on life.

Themes and Meanings

A central theme in *Narcissus and Goldmund* is the conflicting dichotomy present in the world and in every man: good and evil, life and death, joy and sorrow, thinker and dreamer, male and female. Hesse has polarized the worlds of the spirit and the senses with the examples of Narcissus and Goldmund. If one such as Narcissus rarely leaves the pole of the spirit, conflicts are minimal. Narcissus is satisfied with this partial existence. Others such as Goldmund are forever trying to bridge the two worlds. At first Goldmund believes that he can fuse opposites through love and then through art, but in each attempt, he fails to attain a permanent synthesis. Finally, he accepts himself the way he is. Though one never maintains a perfect balance between mind and body, one can reconcile oneself to this dichotomy.

The topics of death and the transience of life receive special emphasis in the novel. Death in the monastery is no threat because it is only the beginning of an eternal reward. Only in the world is death a tragedy, especially death by murder, the plague, or some other unexpected form. Goldmund is repulsed by the finality and violence of death and by his inability to understand or to conquer it. Only at the end of the novel does he come to terms with the other side of death, the joy of being received by mother earth: "My mother called me and I had to follow. She is everywhere. She was Lise, the gypsy; she was Master Niklaus' beautiful madonna; she was life, love, ecstasy. She was also fear, hunger, instinct. Now she is death . . . I'm glad to die; she makes it easy."

According to Goldmund, a work of art is the union of the father and the mother worlds, the spirit and the senses; it is eternal. Art may originate either in the heart or in the mind and then lead to the opposite; it is "a merging of instinct and pure spirituality." For Goldmund, true art is born of the senses; he produces his art only after he has the experience of love. Art alone, however, is not the answer to a happy life. If one devotes oneself single-heartedly to art, one soon becomes a prisoner to routine, loses one's freedom, and then the lust for life dries up.

Critical Context

Narcissus and Goldmund appeared in 1930, following three successful novels by Hesse: *Demian* (1919; English translation, 1923), an examination of psychoanalysis and the subconscious; *Siddhartha* (1922; English translation, 1951), a meditation on Eastern philosophy; and *Der Steppenwolf* (1927; *Steppenwolf*, 1929), the story of a man torn between middle-class respectability and his baser instincts. Structurally and thematically, *Narcissus and Goldmund* fits between *Demian* and *Siddhartha*: Goldmund continues the personality crisis of Demian, yet he does not find the harmony that Siddhartha finds. *Narcissus and Goldmund* is lighthearted and clear, a natural counterpoint to the depressing and dreamlike *Steppenwolf*. Both novels concentrate on the "natural" or "female" side of man.

Since Hesse's own philosophy was closer to that of the thinker Narcissus than that of the sensualist Goldmund, the escapades in the novel cannot be traced to Hesse's life. Still, several of Hesse's personal conflicts are evident: his departure from Maulbronn seminary, his doubts about faith, his relationships with teachers and peers, his flights into Freudian and Jungian psychology, his disgust with World War I, and the breakup of his own marriage.

Some critics claim that this novel is Hesse's best work, while others see it as too unstructured in form and too simplistic in theme. They believe that Hesse is more interested in expressing his ideas about polarization than in forming plausible characters. Whatever the judgment of the critics, *Narcissus and Goldmund* has become Hesse's most popular novel. It can be enjoyed both as a medieval romantic quest and as a philosophical tract.

Sources for Further Study
Boulby, Mark. *Hermann Hesse: His Mind and Art*, 1967.
Digan, Kathleen E. *Hermann Hesse's Narcissus and Goldmund: A Phenomenological Study*, 1975.
Field, George Wallis. *Hermann Hesse*, 1970.
Mileck, Joseph. *Hermann Hesse: Life and Art*, 1978.
Ziolkowski, Theodore. *The Novels of Hermann Hesse: A Study in Theme and Structure*, 1965.

James Schmitt

THE NATIVES OF HEMSÖ

Author: August Strindberg (1849-1912)
Type of plot: Naturalism
Time of plot: The late 1800's
Locale: The island of Hemsö and environs, on the Stockholm archipelago
First published: Hemsöborna, 1887 (*The People of Hemsö,* 1959; better
known as *The Natives of Hemsö*)

Principal characters:
JOHANNES EDVARD CARLSSON, the newly hired manger of the
farm
ANNA EVA FLOD, the widow who owns the farm, who
becomes his wife
GUSTEN FLOD, the son of Mrs. Flod
ERIK NORDSTRÖM, the pastor of the community

The Novel

Johannes Edvard Carlsson arrives from the mainland to the island fishing
village of Hemsö to manage the farm of an old widow, Anna Eva Flod. His
ignorance of things nautical and of the folkways of the small community provokes the disdain of Mrs. Flod's son, Gusten.

Carlsson dreams big, however, and does know about managing a farm and
about asserting his superiority. In no time, he works his way up, literally,
from sharing a bed in the kitchen to enjoying the solitary attic room. He sees
great promise in the terrain and livestock. He quickly becomes not only
indispensable but also revered by everyone but Gusten. Carlsson gives fervent Bible readings on Sundays too inclement for the household to get to
church, wins over the farmhands through trickery, spruces up the big summerhouse to accommodate a professor and his family as paying summer
guests, and then flirts with their pretty cook, Ida. Although Norman, another farmhand, also woos Ida, Ida is Carlsson's partner at the July hay-
making and dancing festivities, and when they sneak away hand in hand, the
widow looks longingly after them.

In the fall, the professor's family moves back to the city, Ida goes with
them, and Carlsson pines after her. One stormy night when Carlsson has
gone to the city to get supplies (but, more important, to see Ida), the pastor,
Erik Nordström appears, drunk and voicing the rumor that Carlsson will
marry Mrs. Flod. Carlsson returns, spurned by Ida, and proposes to and is
accepted by Mrs. Flod. At the news, the community feels hostile toward
Carlsson, because he is an outsider coming into possession of "their" property through marriage. Gusten even persuades the pastor to postpone the
wedding for six months, and the winter passes quietly. The professor's family

returns in the spring, but Ida is no longer with them. Once the banns are read and Carlsson is unshakably sure of himself, both he and the widow begin to fight bitterly.

The day before the wedding, Gusten rows to Norsten, a small, rocky islet that is a familiar fishing haunt of the Hemsö folk. Pastor Nordström joins him, and as the men drink and smoke, Gusten reveals that he will not attend the wedding because he wishes to shame Carlsson. The two plot to get Carlsson so drunk that he will be unable to take his bride to bed. Meanwhile, Carlsson learns that the pair is at Norsten and concludes that they are plotting mischief, so he plans his own revenge.

At the wedding, the vows are interrupted by the crash of glass: The beer bottles have burst in the hot sun, and the bride is distressed at the bad omen. After the ceremony, the pastor toasts Carlsson again and again. Gusten finally arrives, and he and Carlsson make tentative peace during a round of toasts and good cheer. Ready to begin eating, the guests discover the pastor, very drunk, in the outhouse, carrying on a spirited debate with the professor. When the pastor returns to the festivities, he gives a speech in honor of Christmas before keeling over. At dawn, after the dance, steaming glögg is to be drunk, the first glass traditionally given to the pastor. Carlsson discovers that the pastor is occupying the bridal bed, so he flings him out the window into a patch of stinging nettles and then into fish-gut slime at the water's edge. When the crowd arrives, Carlsson pretends that he has heroically rescued the pastor from drowning.

In the fall, the widow, now Mrs. Carlsson, gives birth to a stillborn child and Carlsson's ship is hit by a gale. Undaunted by these misfortunes, Carlsson prepares for the future; he builds a new house, becomes a homebody, convinces his wife to prepare a will in his favor, and reads to her biblical passages about death.

Shortly before Christmas, Carlsson flirts with the household cook, Clara. One night as they sneak out for a tryst, Mrs. Carlsson follows them, falls through the ice, and becomes deathly ill. After instructing Gusten to burn her will and make funeral arrangements, she dies, and Carlsson and Gusten bitterly argue about who is in charge. Five days later, in a desperate effort to remove Mrs. Carlsson's body to the church for burial, the men battle ice and slush with hooks and axes. Their boat, however, capsizes, and the coffin sinks into the sea. Gusten and Carlsson, separated on a remote island from the rest of the crew and the boat, are caught in a whirling snowstorm. Gusten successfully battles waves and ice to reach the pastor's house, but Carlsson's weight and lack of endurance defeat him. The marooned Hemsö boat is rescued the next day, but the bodies of Carlsson and his wife are not found. The novel concludes with the pastor conducting an improvised burial service for two, and with Gusten, the new master of Hemsö, rowing home on the fickle Sea of Life.

The Characters

For several summers in his early twenties, August Strindberg spent what was perhaps the happiest time of his life vacationing on Kymmendö, on the Stockholm archipelago. The novel, written quickly to make money, is in part a peaceful memory of island flora and fauna but more important an unsentimental chronicle of the bawdy, colorful, comic, and proud island inhabitants. It is naturalistic in its depiction of an individual's unsuccessful struggle against life, and Strindberg seems uncharacteristically to side against the individual and with society. There are no large ideas here, only small, specific vignettes of real people leading uncomplicated and not very admirable lives.

Carlsson is an ambitious and clever entrepreneur, but he is also a rogue and an interloper. Unlike most of Strindberg's main characters, he is free of inner conflict and psychological turmoil. He is so self-assured that he has an easy time convincing others to trust him. He is not maliciously manipulative but merely savvy enough to live by his wits. If he profits from the fruits of his economical ruses, so do the people of Hemsö. While they never forget that he is an interloper, and at times hate him for it, they cannot deny that he has managed money and position well.

A drifter and jack-of-all-trades from the mainland, Carlsson may lack roots and nautical knowledge, but his good humor and survival skills allow him to adapt well to various situations and people. He is spirited, confident, and lucky, and Strindberg admires those traits in him. His downfall is merely an unhappy twist of fate. Because Strindberg uses primarily the third-person, limited-omniscient point of view, his readers largely gain entrance only to Carlsson's mind. While Strindberg's characters are all of a piece, no other stands out in so many dimensions or communicates so much personality and information as Carlsson does.

The widow is seen, by turns, to be trusting and warm, even coquettish in the early stages of courtship, but gullible in listening to her heart rather than her mind and capable of bitter anger. After two years of widowhood, she relishes the prospect of marriage. Yet, both before and after the wedding, Carlsson's philandering is her undoing. She is justifiably suspicious of her younger husband, though proving his infidelity leads to her death.

Gusten, Strindberg makes clear early, is easygoing and lazy. His aimless drifting at Norsten is typical of his lack of direction and immaturity for most of the novel. Yet he is loyal to societal and familial ties. He is the first character to be suspicious of Carlsson. His knowledge of the sea is the critical advantage that he holds over Carlsson; Carlsson defers to him in this throughout the novel, and he dies because he does not possess it. At Carlsson's death, when Gusten is ready to assume the position of command and his rival can no longer threaten him, Gusten calls himself by his last name and even voices some charitable thoughts about Carlsson. The novel is a tale of Gusten's coming of age.

Strindberg's other characters are a sociable, very human lot who are prone to drunkenness and bawdiness, holding grudges and kicking up their heels. They are ribald and uncomplicated, taking the world as it is and making the best of it.

Themes and Meanings

A major theme in all Strindberg's novels is the quest for identity. In *The Natives of Hemsō*, however, the quest is not for self-knowledge but for experience of every sort of human activity. In Strindberg's other novels, the major character is engaged in psychological introspection or anguishing self-analysis, but here Carlsson lives very much on the surface. He cavalierly, but not ruthlessly, manipulates people to turn a profit for himself. The person who gains the most identity, finally, is Gusten, who simply grows up.

In addition, the novel explores the implications of an interloper integrating with and usurping land and possessions which are not his by birth. By turns, the Hemsö natives are receptive, puzzled, jealous, hostile, and grateful to Carlsson for his intrusion. His sociability and good humor draw them in, and, while they never really embrace him as one of their own, they are charmed by and profit from him. The widow, however, admonishes Gusten on her deathbed to marry one of his own kind.

At one time or another, each of the major characters experiences isolation, setting himself apart from or against the main group, which results in some disaster. Carlsson is the first to do this, claiming, in his pride, the attic room, and once there, being overcome with hallucinations. Gusten's reluctance to attend the wedding haunts him at his mother's deathbed. Pastor Nordström's drinking bouts lead to his being physically ejected from the group by Carlsson. Mrs. Carlsson fans her jealousy by pursuing Carlsson on his amorous trysts.

The large theme of life and death emerges against a more specific backdrop of seasonal rise and fall over the three-year span of action. There are alternating periods of good fortune and defeat for the Hemsö community and, specifically, for the main character. Spring brings promise, as Carlsson arrives in April. Summer brings fruition, with the wedding in July. Fall brings crisis and disappointment in the crash of a feldspar mine nearby. Winter brings the death of the Carlssons and their child.

Embellishing the larger themes are several strands of symbolism. The sea is a gauge of reality and truth. Carlsson, the interloper, knows nothing about the sea, and, though he smokes Black Anchor tobacco and gazes long at the rippling surface of the sea in his depression over losing Ida, his attempts to master nautical ways are futile. The sea and the creek are described several times in the novel as mirrors in which all the main characters, through gazing, gain some insight.

Light and darkness are important in setting the mood, in revealing or concealing information, and they alternate more frequently than the seasons do. Carlsson first sees Hemsö in the twilight, and he himself soon becomes a shining light to the natives. The widow feels that Carlsson has lit a flame in her breast; as their engagement progresses, tempers seethe, and the sun is hot. Light imagery abounds at the wedding: Sun reflects off bottles, Japanese lanterns decorate the yard, and blue flames rise from the glögg. In his drunkenness, the pastor heedlessly douses his lantern light, and he erroneously extols the Festival of Lights. A luminescent fire rises out of the sea where Mrs. Carlsson lies buried, and the funeral takes place at dusk. Clouds set in, marking the onset of misfortune.

The isolated rural folk are superstitious and believe in folk medicine. Sorcery is practiced on people and animals, and money is hidden under a rock to ensure a good herring catch. Water is divined with a rod, and good weather is prophesied. The pastor wears small leaden ear hoops as a charm, and an attempt is made to bleed him when he gets drunk.

Music, a motif of secondary importance, is used to emphasize Carlsson's status as an interloper. He is a nonmusician; in contrast, Norman courts Ida with an accordion, Gusten yodels a schottische when tempers flare, the professor plays violin with the royal orchestra, and the pastor leads the singing of several hymns.

Perhaps the most pervasive stylistic device Strindberg uses is cataloging. He emphasizes and examines the surfaces and appearances of things, because his characters and his story are very much on the surface. Feelings are open, blunt, and obvious, and the details of things carry more weight than their overall significance. Strindberg's descriptions have a richness and precision, because detail is layered upon detail: The pier, rooms of the farmhouse, the flora and fauna of the islands, depictions of the haymakers, and mementos of the summer guests re-create with clarity a place and people very alive in Strindberg's memory. The surfaces he portrays are sensuous, immediate, and accessible. His sensitive use of impressionism presents a model of simple, uncomplicated life.

Critical Context

Strindberg is universally recognized as one of the progenitors of modern drama, but outside Scandinavia, his reputation as a writer of fiction is scarcely known. He did write a dozen novels and many volumes of short stories and tales. This novel is one of his earliest, written during a stage in his career when he was concerned with realism, predating the other important stages marked by symbolism, myth, and experimental form. Strindberg called this novel an "intermezzo scherzando in between major engagements," and in tone and subject matter, it is a literary respite between two more darkly profound works: *Fadren* (1887; *The Father*, 1899), a play that Strindberg labeled his tragedy, and *Le laidoyer d'un fou* (1893; *The Confession of a*

Fool, 1912), an autobiographical novel about a bitter marital relationship which illustrates Strindberg's concept of "psychic murder." This work was therapy for its author and remains an anomaly among his other major works, which tend to be tense, introspective, and tortuous, depicting evil and a suffering humanity.

Strindberg's interest in psychology led him to explore the self in depth in his drama, but here an unambiguous, one-dimensional hero is exploring instead how to have a good time and make some money. Here, the character is defeated not by subjective mental anguish but by a very objective physical storm. Although Strindberg used the setting of the outer Skerries in other works—notably the later novel *I havsbandet* (1890; *By the Open Sea*, 1913) and several tales—nowhere else is the treatment so picaresque and undidactic, the characters so realistic, and the philosophy so obviously un-Rousseauistic. This novel of local color is worlds removed from the "inferno" period of hallucinations, religious mysticism, and pseudoscientific experiments that darkened his life soon after.

Strindberg has called the novel his sanest book. It was written in typical Strindberg fashion—quickly, with little attention to revision. He characterized the book as art for art's sake and, when he saw it in print, thought it was insignificant. It is his most objective novel and his most conventional work of fiction. It is also his most popular, hailed as a success when it was first published and seen today as a masterpiece of naturalistic fiction. The novel is uncluttered, unself-conscious, and joyful, showing off Strindberg's knack for storytelling, his ear for dialogue, and his painter's eye.

Sources for Further Study

Gustafson, Alrick. "Strindberg and the Realistic Breakthrough," in *A History of Swedish Literature*, 1961.

Johannesson, Eric O. *The Novels of August Strindberg: A Study in Theme and Structure*, 1968.

_____. "The Problem of Identity in Strindberg's Novels," in *Scandinavian Studies*. XXXIV (February, 1962), pp. 1-35.

Paulson, Arvid. Foreword to *The Natives of Hemsö*, 1965.

Tennant, P. F. D. Introduction to *The People of Hemsö*, 1959.

Jill B. Gidmark

THE NAZARENE

Author: Sholem Asch (1880-1957)
Type of plot: Historical realism
Time of plot: The first century
Locale: Palestine
First published: 1939 in English translation (*Der Man fun Notseres*, 1943)

> *Principal characters:*
> PAN VIADOMSKY, a twentieth century Polish scholar, an expert
>   on the ancient Near East
> CORNELIUS, a Roman commander in Jerusalem under Pontius
>   Pilate
> JESUS OF NAZARETH
> RABBI NICODEMON, a devout Pharisee
> JUDAS ISCARIOT, a disciple of Jesus who also betrayed him
> MARY, the mother of Jesus
> MARY MAGDALENE, a prostitute who became an intensely
>   devoted follower of Jesus
> THE NARRATOR, a young Jewish scholar who is assisting Pan
>   Viadomsky
> JOCHANAN, a disciple of the Rabbi Nicodemon

The Novel

The Nazarene is an attempt to capture the drama and meaning of the life of Christ in its historical and cultural context from several perspectives. Jesus is particularly viewed from the vantage points of a high-ranking Roman officer, Judas Iscariot, and a devout student of the Rabbi Nicodemon. Many other perspectives are depicted as well. Jesus is seen differently by the ruling Sanhedrin; by his mother, Mary; by Mary Magdalene; by Rufus, a young student who will eventually join the "Messianist" sect; and by the masses of devout Jews in Jerusalem.

As a unifying device and to show the historical significance of his subject matter, Sholem Asch uses the concept of reincarnation to bring three of his first century characters to twentieth century Poland. Their discussions and lengthy narratives then provide the vehicle to tell the story. Asch also uses the device of a "recently-discovered manuscript" to relate the events of the Gospels from the perspective of Judas Iscariot.

The novel is divided into three parts. The first part is a rather convoluted effort to depict a twentieth century scholar, an expert on the ancient Near East, Pan Viadomsky, as the reincarnation of the Roman officer Cornelius, who arrested Jesus in the Garden of Gethsemane. His arrogance and pragmatic ruthlessness are portrayed convincingly in both roles. Asch uses the

Roman soldier as a means of describing for his readers the cultural setting of ancient Jerusalem in intricate detail. Indeed, the novel is worth reading simply for the many insights it gives of first century Jewish life and customs, derived from material gathered over a thirty-year period. One wonders occasionally, however, whether Asch is describing first century Palestine or that of the early twentieth century. (Asch visited Palestine in 1908 and again in 1914.)

Part 2 takes the reader back to twentieth century Poland, where Viadomsky unveils a secret manuscript by Judas Iscariot written in the first person, in which Judas tries to understand his rabbi, becomes convinced that Jesus was indeed the promised messiah, and then, in contrast with the Gospel accounts, decides that he must betray Jesus in order to force the Messiah to demonstrate his supernatural power to deliver the subjugated Jews from the domination of the Romans.

Part 3 returns to modern Poland again where, astonishingly, the young Jewish student who has been helping Viadomsky read the Iscariot manuscript discovers that he himself is the reincarnation of Jochanan, a disciple of the Rabbi Nicodemon. He is then able to recall in a fascinating narrative what it was like to be a young Jewish lad learning from the devout Pharisee who went to inquire of Jesus "by night." Nicodemon aided in the burial of Jesus and apparently was a "secret disciple." His spiritual pilgrimage is used to show Jesus from yet another perspective.

The Characters

Asch is particularly vivid in his narrative, and his characterizations are convincing and realistic. From the leaders of the Sadducees and Pharisees to the individuality of each disciple to the fascinating charm of Mary Magdalene or the integrity and courage of Rabbi Nicodemon, Asch depicts real and lifelike characters with human struggles and dilemmas. Judas Iscariot is an intense zealot, but the rationale for his betrayal of Jesus lacks plausibility. There is a certain ambiguity, though, in Asch's development of his character. At one point, for example, he writes of a conversation between Jesus and Judas in which the Rabbi tells his disciple:

> Judah, thy heart is restless; it is like a lost ship in a stormy sea. Why canst thou not find rest, like my other disciples?"
> And I answered, saying:
> "Rabbi, perform now one of thy wonders and strengthen my faith in thee."
> And my Rabbi answered: "Even for this did I pray now, Judah, for thou couldst have been my most beloved disciple.

Cornelius was an agent of Pontius Pilate who, according to Asch, plotted the arrest and execution of Jesus. In sharp contrast to the historical record in the Gospels, the Romans pushed the Jews to ask for the execution of Jesus, rather than their having pressured Pilate to do so. Asch here seeks to modify the anti-Semitic European tradition that viewed all Jews as "Christ-killers." Orthodox Christian doctrine has always taught the universal guilt of mankind and Christ dying in redemption for that guilt. The historical record in the Gospels shows both Jews and Romans as having been guilty of Christ's crucifixion. Nevertheless, the charge has been a convenient rationalization for anti-Semites for nineteen hundred years.

It may well be that in Nicodemon, Asch is showing something of his own ambivalence in viewing Jesus. Both remained Jews. Both greatly respected Jesus and saw him as a great Jewish leader. Asch later said:

> I couldn't help writing on Jesus. Since I first met him he has held my mind and heart. . . . For Jesus Christ is to me the outstanding personality of all time, all history, both as Son of God and as Son of Man. Everything he ever said or did has value for us today and that is something you can say of no other man, dead or alive. There is no easy middle ground to stroll upon. You either accept Jesus or reject him. You can analyze Mohammed and . . . Buddha, but don't try it with him. You either accept or you reject. . . .

Nicodemon never became a follower of Jesus as Messiah; he saw the new sect not as a threat to traditional Judaism but as another way of reaching the same God. A Jew, according to him, could follow the traditional way of the Mosaic law and the Torah or follow the new way through Christ.

Asch identified emotionally with many of his characters, and his intensity reflects that empathy. He respected the intellectual, the wealthy, the powerful in society, but his sympathy was with the simple folk who live honestly and conscientiously at a more intuitive level.

Themes and Meanings

Asch considered *The Nazarene* to be his most important novel, "the main product of my life-work," as he expressed it. He planned for it and studied historical and cultural background for thirty years in preparation. He sincerely wished to reconcile, not unite, Jews and Gentiles through this medium. He saw Jesus as an important Hebrew prophet who was carefully following the Old Testament law, seeking to fulfill "every jot and tittle." It was preposterous to him to think of Jews and Christians as worshipping two different Gods from the same Old Testament Scriptures. How could they read "the same Psalms in two language to two Gods"? For Asch, if an accommodation could be reached between Jew and Gentile in the matter of religion, perhaps they would be reconciled culturally.

Narrating a story from multiple perspectives is often an effective and insightful literary device, but the shifts in time and action from first century Palestine to Warsaw of the 1930's are distracting.

Critical Context

Most of the bitter criticism that Asch encountered came from fellow Jews. He was the first Yiddish writer to gain international, worldwide fame. His deviations from literary traditions, including his sympathetic treatment of Jesus, antagonized some of his contemporaries, especially those in competition with him for public acclaim. Every Yiddish newspaper but one closed its pages to Asch. Liberals considered the novel too orthodox and the orthodox thought it too imaginative. Two million Americans, however, read *The Nazarene* in its first two years.

Christians, too, had problems with Asch's ideas. Many found the novel intriguing and the many cultural insights fascinating, but they realized that Asch looked upon Jesus as superhuman, perhaps the greatest leader in history, but still less than a deity. A few realized that Asch's theology, if logically pursued, would reduce Christianity to merely a sect within Judaism. In theological terms, then, Asch was a Judaizer.

Historians in general paid little attention to the novel, but the ones who did saw that Asch sought to be historically accurate as well as culturally correct. Jesus' sermon in the synagogue was a composite, and Asch rearranged the chronological sequence of events, but so did the New Testament writers; after all, the New Testament accounts give glimpses into only some 150 days in the thirty-three years of Jesus' life.

Sources for Further Study

Asch, Nathan. "My Father and I," in *Commentary*. XXXIX (January, 1965), pp. 55-64.

Bates, Ernest S. "The Gospel in a Modern Version," in *The Saturday Review of Literature*. XX (October 21, 1939), p. 5.

Colum, Mary M. "Re-Creation of New Testament History," in *Forum and Century*. CII (December, 1939), pp. 261-262.

Madison, Charles A. "Sholem Asch: Novelist of Lyric Intensity," in *Yiddish Literature: Its Scope and Major Writers*, 1968.

Siegel, Ben. *The Controversial Sholem Asch: An Introduction to His Fiction*, 1976.

William H. Burnside

NETOCHKA NEZVANOVA

Author: Fyodor Dostoevski (1821-1881)
Type of plot: Memoir
Time of plot: The early 1800's
Locale: St. Petersburg
First published: 1849 (English translation, 1920)

> *Principal characters:*
> ANNA "NETOCHKA" NEZVANOVA, the narrator, eight or nine
>   years old when the story begins and seventeen when it ends
> YEGOR PETROVICH YEFIMOV, her stepfather
> PRINCESS KATYA, the younger daughter of Prince Kh——y,
>   who adopts Netochka when her parents die
> ALEKSANDRA MIKHAILOVNA, Katya's older sister, with whom
>   Netochka lives after the Prince's family moves to Moscow
> PYOTR ALEKSANDROVICH, Aleksandra's husband

The Novel

Netochka begins her story with a brief account of her stepfather's life, a narration, she explains, which is intended to help the reader understand her own story. Netochka is to learn of the short and disappointing career of her beloved stepfather much later, from a fellow musician known only as "B." Netochka's story begins with her earliest memories of living in a crowded garret with her stepfather and her ailing mother, who is too embittered to show her little daughter any affection. Yefimov is a talented, arrogant, but failed musician; he blames his lack of fame and success on his sick and ill-tempered wife. Closely observing everything around her, Netochka also lives in her imagination and fantasy, siding with her stepfather, who makes wild promises to her. The musician begs money from everyone to support his drinking habit. He even forces Netochka to give him the few kopecks with which she has been sent to the store. Yet Netochka loves him and tries hard to please him, and she fears her miserable mother, whose only sign of tenderness and affection toward her daughter is given shortly before she dies, when she calls her by a pet name.

The first part of Netochka's memoir ends when her mother dies in such strange circumstances that the reader must suspect that she was murdered by her husband, though Netochka is too horrified and bewildered to grasp fully what is happening. The child and Yefimov rush out of the garret, he tricks her into going back to retrieve something, and she then sees him rushing away from her. Yefimov dies shortly thereafter in a fit of madness.

Prince Kh——y happens to be nearby when Netochka is running after her stepfather. The Prince has long been interested in the troubled musician, has tried to help him, and, pitying the little girl, takes her into his home. The abrupt and extreme change of environment and the numerous shocks that she has experienced cause Netochka to fall ill. She recovers too slowly to be a satisfactory companion to Princess Katya, who abuses Netochka, tormenting and teasing her and even allowing her to suffer severe punishment for a misdeed that she herself actually committed. Gradually, however, the two girls become friends, and a strong relationship develops between them, so passionate that Katya's mother, who has never liked Netochka, separates them. Soon afterward, the family moves to Moscow, and Netochka is sent to live with the Prince's older daughter, Aleksandra.

The third and final part of the memoir concerns Netochka's quiet and serene life, as she becomes devoted to the gentle and loving woman whose abrupt changes of mood, inordinate devotion to her husband, and evident misery puzzle the young girl. She senses a mysterious sorrow in her adoptive mother and an inflexible cruelty in Aleksandra's husband, Pyotr. Gradually, as Netochka develops her imagination and intellect by reading and observation, Aleksandra withdraws more and more from her, immersed in her own mental illness. Occasionally, however, she renews her involvement with Netochka, and it is during one of these times that she discovers the girl's musical talent; as a result, Netochka begins voice lessons.

All goes well for a time. When Netochka is sixteen, however, she is afflicted with an inexplicable apathy and withdraws once more into solitude. She begins to recover only when she discovers the reasons behind Aleksandra's puzzling behavior and the extent of Pyotr's jealousy and malice. He comes upon the girl in the library, holding a letter which he suspects is from a lover. Only when Pyotr has accused her of deceit and sinfulness does he discover that the letter was actually written to his wife many years ago, at the end of an affair for which, he insisted at the time, he had forgiven her, though clearly he has not. The book, which Dostoevski did not finish, ends with Netochka's impassioned confrontation with Pyotr. Denouncing him for his cruelty toward his wife, as well as toward herself, Netochka reveals her strength, courage, and depth of feeling, which even the hardships of her early life could not subdue.

The Characters

As the narrator, Netochka is the only character who is consistently present and whose qualities are revealed in some detail and depth. A timid, fearful, and neglected child, she tries to understand and help her weak and wretched stepfather. It is clear that despite the privation and misery of her childhood, Netochka longs for love and bestows it on a man who takes advantage of her undeserved devotion. Dostoevski portrays Yefimov harshly and pitilessly, showing him to be a bitterly disappointed man who can forget his failures as a musician and as a husband and stepfather only in drink.

After the death of her parents and her adoption by the Prince, Netochka is very ill for a long time, and her grief and despondency annoy and puzzle little Katya, a lively, mischievous, and spoiled child. As Netochka begins to recover, her loving but timid nature is not recognized by Katya, but eventually the child realizes that Netochka is bravely and selflessly devoted to her. Their girlish and essentially innocent attachment to each other ends suddenly, but Netochka suffers from the separation much more than does the flighty and frivolous Katya.

Netochka's second set of foster parents, Aleksandra and Pyotr, provide her with a comfortable and quiet life, but she is often bewildered and hurt by their strange relationship and their strange treatment of her. Pyotr is rarely at home, but Netochka's immediate antipathy toward him is later justified as she discovers how spiteful and vindictive he is. Aleksandra's character is portrayed with more complexity but no less mystery. Quite undependable in her moods—sometimes childish, sometimes motherly, at times gay and cheerful, at other times gloomy and despondent—Aleksandra realizes her weakness, endlessly begs forgiveness, is tender and suspicious by turns, but has been so demoralized by her secret sorrow and her husband's hateful treatment of her that she loses her will to live.

When the story is brought to its abrupt end, Netochka's courage and capacity for love, qualities which have always been dormant within her, are clearly and admirably revealed in her nascent willingness to act on all that she has experienced and observed.

Themes and Meanings

Dostoevski's completion of this carefully planned novel, broad in its intended scope, was interrupted by his imprisonment and forced labor in Siberia. After his release, he never again worked on *Netochka Nezvanova*. The ideas which he meant to express in this work, however, are clearly suggested. These include the arduous and hazardous life of the artist, as exemplified by Yefimov and his opposite, the hardworking B.

Another theme that is undeniably important is the victimization of innocent children, shown in the suffering of Netochka. In contrast to the pampered and privileged Katya, it is the selfless, sensitive nature of the deprived and mistreated narrator that suggests the ennobling effect of what she has had to endure. The unbearable suffering of impoverished and abused children was a theme that Dostoevski was to use again and again in his later works.

Finally, the pity and compassion that the author showed for Netochka's mother and for Aleksandra also form a motif in this and other novels. The helplessness and sickness of these women, one from the poorest class and the other from the aristocracy, were also to typify many of his female characters.

Critical Context

In *Netochka Nezvanova* can be found the precursors of the memorable characters that people Dostoevski's major works, such as *Prestupleniye i nakazaniye* (1866; *Crime and Punishment*, 1886) and *Bratya Karamazovy* (1879-1880; *The Brothers Karamazov*, 1912). In these later novels, he achieved much more control over his complex material and expressed with increasing clarity and depth the psychological and spiritual significance of his themes. Nevertheless, the potential for his later greatness is undoubtedly present in what must be recognized as an impressive indication of what was to come. As one critic has commented, "*Netochka Nezvanova* was the epilogue to Dostoevski's literary youth," but in it he established himself as "a portrayer of the dangerous path of the artist, creator, and seeker."

One of the nineteenth century's giants of Russian literature, Dostoevski has had no equal in his understanding of and compassion for the troubled, the weak, and the downtrodden; of men and women and especially children; and of the sources and nature of vice, as well as virtue. Although undeveloped and incomplete, *Netochka Nezvanova* is an important and valuable part of Dostoevski's work. In itself, the novel must be recognized as a vivid, moving, and absorbing account of Russian society in the early part of the nineteenth century, as seen through the eyes of an appealing and unforgettable young girl.

Sources for Further Study

Frank, Joseph. *Dostoevsky: The Seeds of Revolt, 1821-1849*, 1976.
Grossman, Leonid. *Dostoevsky: A Biography*, 1975.
Hingley, Ronald. *Dostoevsky: His Life and Work*, 1978.
Magarshack, David. *Dostoevsky*, 1963.
Welleck, René, ed. *Dostoevsky: A Collection of Critical Essays*, 1962.

Natalie Harper

NIAGARA
A Stereophonic Novel

Author: Michel Butor (1926-   )
Type of plot: Impressionistic realism
Time of plot: A year during the 1960's
Locale: Niagara Falls
First published: 6,810,000 Litres d'eau par seconde: Étude stéréophonique,
   1965 (English translation, 1969)

Principal characters:
   THE ANNOUNCER, who guides the tour of Niagara Falls
   THE READER, who meditates upon Chateaubriand's words
   "JUST MARRIEDS," whose names begin with A and B
   OLD MARRIED COUPLES, whose names begin with C and D
   BLACK GARDENERS, whose names begin with E and F
   OLD MADAMS, whose names begin with G
   GIGOLOS, whose names begin with H
   VILE SEDUCERS, whose names begin with I
   EASY PREY, whose names begin with J
   YOUNG MEN ALONE, whose names begin with K
   YOUNG WOMEN ALONE, whose names begin with L
   WIDOWERS, whose names begin with M
   WIDOWS, whose names begin with N
   BLACK WIDOWERS, whose names begin with O
   BLACK WIDOWS, whose names begin with P
   QUENTIN, a Frenchman and visiting professor at the
         University of Buffalo

The Novel

Niagara both epitomizes the French New Novel of the 1950's and 1960's and bewilders readers expecting traditional plot and character development. It is a work in which very little happens in the usual sense of novelistic action; structure towers over substance and the medium itself is one of the principal messages. Simply put, over the course of a year, groups of representative and interchangeable characters visit Niagara Falls, take the usual tours (on the *Maid of the Mist*, for example), speak to one another or to themselves, observe the local attractions, and leave. The human action in the novel follows predictably from one chapter (which spans a month's time) to another and is as constant as the flow of the falls.

On another level, the novel's action takes place in the mind of the individual reader, who must participate in the work by making judgments, listening, adjusting the volume of what is heard, and remembering the words of an announcer, a reader, and the other characters, as well as the sounds of the falls and the tourists. Each reader must produce his or her own version of a radio broadcast, complete with sound effects: This production, the act of the mind producing this broadcast, is the primary action of this experimental "open" novel. One object of this action is stichomythia, as one seeks "to hear how, within this liquid monument, a change in lighting will cause new forms and aspects to appear."

The physical actions of the groups of characters form the important and necessary basis of the broadcast. Actions such as touring and tending the flower gardens mark a contrast between motives for action (tourism and work), between socioeconomic classes, races, and classes within the races. The description of the descent down the rocks in the elevator (June) provides an example of temporary unity and solidarity, since all who go must strip off the clothing they have worn, don orange rubber suits, and descend together, all looking alike. Yet this action is also an isolating event: No one can be heard above the roar of the cataract, and each is encased not only in rubber but also in solitude. This isolation within communion is the burden of much of the novel's action, an isolation that is reinforced by the principal action of producing the broadcast alone and in the silence of reading, while hearing and processing the words and sounds communicated by the printed page.

Motivating, complementing, and sometimes thwarting human action is the action of the natural world, both the cycle of nature and the human life cycle. The novel begins in April, the sweet season when folk long to go on pilgrimages in Chaucerian terms and also the cruelest month in Eliotic terms, which mixes memory with desire in yet another contemporary wasteland. As the year progresses and festivals pass, the weather and climate change from the warmth and fertility of spring to the heat and torpor of summer, then to the melancholy of autumn, and finally, to desolation of winter, which brings the novel into March. This change of seasons finds its parallel in the appearance of new types of characters: the widows and widowers; the solitary young men; the lonely young women; the seducers and their easy prey; and, in a single appearance in the Coda (March), the homesick Frenchman who has, like the year and the other characters, reached bottom.

As in T. S. Eliot's *The Waste Land* (1922), each of the characters is locked within the prison of himself. The key to unlocking the prisons of Eliot's poem lies in what the thunder said. In *Niagara*, the key is also the word—in this case, the cascade of words drawn from Chateaubriand that constitutes the human action which complements and competes with the natural action of the falls, making sense of experience, reordering it, capturing it, organizing it, and involving the reader in a participatory action of communication.

What the falls said and what Chateaubriand said both open the action of the novel and conclude it. While Chateaubriand's opening remarks about the falls are from a historical, political, and moral essay on ancient and modern revolutions, his concluding remarks describing the same scene are drawn from his Romantic novel *Atala* (1801; English translation, 1802), which has as its subtitle "The Love of Two Strangers in the Wilderness." In the midst of desolation, then, the action concludes in a subtly positive way with words— Chateaubriand's, Butor's, and the reader's—surviving the author's orchestrated failure of communication and communicating anew in the action of the mind reflecting upon experience and communicating it.

The Characters

The characters, with the possible exception of Quentin, are actually character types with little variation within their groupings. The "just marrieds," for example, seem as interchangeable as all the other characters, so that the Abel and Betty of May could as easily be married to the Bettina and Andrew of July. They communicate in fragments and are only beginning to learn how to share with each other, to discover the likes and dislikes, the aspirations, the personalities, and the habits of their partners. The old married couples mark the passage of time, recounting their first visits as newlyweds or the poverty that prevented a honeymoon visit, remarking upon the ways in which their lives have changed and how everything has changed. They speak in interrupted fragments, talking past each other increasingly as the months go by and couples succeed each other. Remarkably absent from the cast are young children and teenagers, who are usually present in abundance at Niagara Falls, especially in the amusement parks that postdate the novel. Nevertheless, the absence of children may be seen as a pointed commentary on the married couples' unproductive marriages or their empty nests.

The black gardeners, widowers and widows, and tourists all serve to highlight both personal and societal alienation and discrimination. They also accent the more general social tensions between blacks and whites in the racially turbulent 1960's, particularly in the years just preceding the novel's publication, at the dawn of the Civil Rights movement. The old madams (mutton dressed as lamb), accompanied by gigolos young enough to be their sons, are presented as faded women who wish, in part, to dominate their young, paid-for, and generally spineless escorts. These pairs, along with the vile seducers and their easy prey, represent one of the more sordid aspects of the great tourist centers of romance: physical intimacy that remains merely physical, that is essentially a limited and disconnected form of communion and communication. These people, too, are seekers after something that does not exist, or, if it exists, does so imperfectly. In the same way, the young men and young women alone circle each other, afraid to ask an overwhelming question, each more isolated than the isolates who are there in couples.

Michele Butor makes a guest appearance as Quentin, separated from his homeland and loved ones by a gulf more immense than Niagara. He is separated from them by his profession (words) and seeks to express his separation and to overcome it by and in words. Two other characters coordinate and arrange words, the announcer and the reader, who occupy central positions in the set directions. The announcer speaks in a consistently loud voice and introduces aspects of physical geography, history, artifacts, and the scene in general; the reader presents a yearlong meditation on Chateaubriand's two texts. These characters guide the external and internal order of experience for the unnamed character who produces each version of *Niagara*, the individual holding the book.

Themes and Meanings

Set at Niagara Falls, the honeymoon capital of North America, this stereophonic novel must be heard as it is read and is susceptible to a variety of hearings or readings. The directions for hearing the novel include adjusting seven volume settings, controlling left and right speakers, and listening to certain voices on both speakers. There are two major tracks, a short one which instructs listeners to skip parenthetical material in thirty-four segments (for example, the first parenthesis of May) and a long one in which nothing is skipped; there are also eight intermediate tracks which allow for a great variation in each reading and listening experience. These ten tracks are labeled A through J. In the second chapter, which is set in May, tracks ABC skip the parenthetic material, tracks DEF read "Memories and Tulips" (the first parenthesis) and omit Abel's and Betty's lines, and tracks GHIJ read everything. This pattern changes in each of the chapters.

While the changes in each chapter make variable readings possible, there are several constants. Each chapter begins at a specific time of the day or night and each is heralded by a specific stroke on the Westminster's carillon. A constant narration of portions of Chateaubriand's descriptions of Niagara from his *Essai sur les révolutions* (1797; *An Historical, Political, Moral Essay on Revolutions*, 1815) and from his novel *Atala* surfaces in each chapter and also opens and closes the work. Chateaubriand's commentary is interrupted by specific guided tours of Niagara Falls landmarks, the boat and bus tours, flower gardens, bridges, promenades, descriptions of gift shops and their wares, and the history of shooting the falls. The most significant constant, which also holds within itself the widest possibility of variation, is the speech of the character in the dialogue, monologue, and interior musings. These voices, juxtaposed and self-interrupting, tell the stories of the novel and are set against the sounds of the falls, the traffic, and machinery in what is at times a polyphony of voices, ancient and modern, set against the cacophony of modern tourism and its trappings.

Butor's technique suggests an extraordinary complexity that blends into a simplicity and liquidity more commonly associated with musical compositions than with novels. From the music of the Westminster chimes, to Johann Sebastian Bach's "Von Himmel Hock" in December, to the bass of the cascade and the polyphonic nature of the speakers' choruses, music abounds in what is, after all, "a stereophonic novel." A useful approach to the text is to treat it as a fugue. This is quite consistent with a theory—propounded by Johann Wolfgang von Goethe, seconded by Charles-Augustin Saint-Beuve and Charles Baudelaire, and voiced in English by Walter Pater—that all art aspires to the condition of music.

Thematically, the novel is concerned with flux, the passing of time, the isolation, the difficulty of communication, and the necessity to believe that words can effectively communicate meaning. It is also possible to view the work as an example of art for art's sake, given the highly organized structure Butor has created. To do so is to appreciate the artistic intricacy but to miss the fundamental concerns about meaning and unmeaning.

Critical Context

Butor has called *Niagara* a novel, but its classification as such has been questioned. It may be called a long fiction, a prose poem, a meditation, a radio drama, or even a play about a radio broadcast. It may also be called a "postnovel." Nevertheless, it is a novel, an important example of the French New Novel that rejected the traditional novelistic formula of a history (a continuous action or series of actions carried out by a principal character) or a depiction of a character's growth, sensation, and ideas. Butor's experimentation with form and content in this novel reflects his lifelong experimentation with narrative, which began with his first novel, *Passage de Milan* (1954), and continued with *Mobile: Étude pour une représentation des États-Unis* (1962; *Mobile: Study for a Representation of the United States*, 1963) and his even more "open" works, *Résean aerien: Texte radiophonique* (1962), a radio play, and *Votre Faust: Fantaisie variable genre Opéra* (1962), an operatic fantasy in which the audience chooses its directions and outcomes.

Butor's work, both before and after *Niagara*, has included poetry, novels and postnovels, and volumes of essays. Heralded early in his career by Jean-Paul Sartre, Butor is known outside France principally for his early New Novels. The scope of his work is such that he has become not only a premier novelist but also a more universal man of letters. He remains an active force in intellectual life, both in France and well beyond his native country.

Sources for Further Study

Aubral, François. *Michel Butor*, 1973.
McWilliams, Dean. *The Narrative of Michel Butor: The Writer as Janus*, 1978.
Mercier, Vivian. *The New Novel: From Queneau to Pinget*, 1971.
Spencer, Michael. *Michel Butor*, 1974.
Sturrock, John. *The French New Novel: Claude Simon, Michel Butor, Alain Robbe-Grillet*, 1969.

John J. Conlon

1934

Author: Alberto Moravia (Alberto Pincherle, 1907-   )
Type of plot: Philosophical realism
Time of plot: 1934
Locale: Capri, Italy
First published: 1982 (English translation, 1982)

> *Principal characters:*
> LUCIO, the twenty-seven-year-old narrator, a writer
> BEATE/TRUDE MÜLLER, a nineteen-year-old actress
> ALOIS MÜLLER, her middle-aged husband
> PAULA, an actress, Beate/Trude's lover
> SHAPIRO, an art collector
> SONIA, a Russian émigré, Shapiro's curator

The Novel

As the book opens, Lucio is sailing toward Capri from Naples. On the island he intends to complete a translation of Heinrich von Kleist's novella *Michael Kohlaas* (1810) and work on a story of his own in which the hero, like Kleist, commits suicide. By disposing of his character in this way, Lucio hopes to "stabilize" his own despair and so avoid killing himself. Among his fellow passengers on the boat is a German couple. The woman captures his interest, for in her eyes he reads a mood similar to his own. Without exchanging a word, they seem to carry on a conversation; by the time the boat docks, Lucio is in love.

He wonders how he will be able to continue this romance, since he knows neither the woman's name nor her destination. Fate favors him when the husband tells him that they are staying at the Pensione Damecuta on Anacapri. Lucio follows them and continues his silent wooing at dinner by showing the woman two lines from Friedrich Nietzsche's *Also sprach Zarathustra*: "But every pleasure wants eternity—/—wants deep, deep eternity." Shortly afterward she replies silently with another book, Kleist's letters, with a bookmark indicating Henriette Vogel's last communication to Ernest Friedrich Peguilhen, dated November 21, 1811: "The loyal friendship you have always shown me till now awaits a wonderful test, for the two of us, namely Kleist, whom you know, and I, find ourselves here at Stimmung, on the Potsdam road . . . *shot*," the victims of a double suicide.

Lucio believes that Beate Müller, whose name he learns from the concierge, intends for the two of them to make love and then kill themselves just as Kleist and his mistress did. In the course of their one brief conversation, she virtually confirms these suspicions when she promises to come to his room after midnight, if he in turn will do something for her, something she has already told him with the Kleist book. Although he does not want to die, he resigns himself to carrying out Beate's plan. In the end, though, she never appears and he thus survives.

Beate has told Lucio that she is returning immediately to Germany but that her twin sister, Trude, will soon take her place on the island. That very evening Trude appears at the hotel with her supposed mother. While she looks exactly like Beate, they are otherwise total opposites. Beate, who grew up in Germany, is an ascetic: She hardly eats, and she shuns Lucio's advances. Trude, who was reared in Italy, is an aesthete, gorging herself and practically throwing herself at Lucio. She seems unable to get enough of life and frequently repeats pleasurable experiences. Soon she, like Beate, promises to come to Lucio's room, following a late-night radio speech by Adolf Hitler that she wants to hear.

Like Beate, however, Trude disappoints her would-be lover and does not come to his room. Instead, Paula, who has merely pretended to be Trude's mother, tells him that Beate and Trude are one person and that the Müllers contrived with her to play a joke on Lucio as a way of teaching Italian men that they are not as irresistible to women as they believe.

Lucio leaves the island the following day. A month later Lucio learns that the joke played on him had its serious side. On the night of Hitler's speech, Alois Müller was killed by the Nazis. Beate/Trude and Paula learned of his death the next day and left the hotel together. A peasant found them on a beach overlooking the sea, victims of a Kleistian double suicide.

The Characters

In 1934, the twenty-seven-year-old Alberto Moravia was living on Capri with his wife, Elsa Morante, who was also a writer. Like Lucio, he abhorred the Fascist regimes in Italy and Germany and faced an uncertain future. While the first-person narrator derives in part from Moravia's autobiography, he also resembles the many effete middle-class intellectuals who appear in Moravia's fiction. Lucio is working on a translation and a novel, but he finishes neither. He wants to make love to Beate and then to Trude, but neither relationship is consummated. He contemplates sex with Sonia, who would willingly go to bed with him; again, nothing comes of his desire. Lucio remains aloof, and the reader last sees him hiding at his parents' home in the Italian countryside.

Lucio is a spectator rather than a participant in life. This attitude is most clearly revealed when he rows out to an island and the Müllers follow. While Lucio watches from behind a rock, Alois takes nude photographs of Beate. Since Lucio's boat is plainly visible, the Müllers know that he is nearby, and at length Alois invites him to photograph the two of them. Throughout the scene, Lucio merely observes from behind a screen, whether that screen is a boulder or a camera lens. His aloofness may save his life, but without passion is he truly alive?

Sonia suggests that the answer is no. In a lengthy interpolated story, she tells Lucio about her life in Russia before the Revolution. A member of the Revolutionary Socialist Party, she fell in love with Evno Azev, ostensibly a fellow revolutionary but in fact an agent provocateur. When the central committee discovered Azev's identity, it ordered Sonia to kill him, thereby eliminating a traitor and demonstrating her own loyalty to the cause. She refused to obey. Instead, she fled Russia by herself, disgusted by the behavior of her party and Azev. Though she survived, she tells Lucio that when she left her homeland at the age of twenty-seven, which is, significantly, Lucio's age, she died spiritually, because she had lost everything she had believed in and loved.

Her employer, Shapiro, is also spiritually dead. Modeled on Bernard Berenson, he looks at and purchases pictures, but he does not create art. Whatever passion he once had for beauty seems to have evaporated. When Lucio asks Shapiro for advice, the best he can offer echoes William Shakespeare's arch-villain Iago's statement, "Put money in thy purse." Shapiro is more concise: "Get rich." For companionship, he recommends Sonia to Lucio, even though he knows that she is incapable of a serious relationship.

In contrast to this detachment from life exhibited by Lucio, Sonia, and Shapiro, is the German hypersensitivity of Beate/Trude and Paula. Both are actresses who stage an elaborate charade to teach Lucio a lesson about vanity. They are also deeply in love. Beate/Trude kills herself because she does not want to exist without her husband, and Paula joins in the suicide because she cannot live without Beate/Trude. Whereas Sonia chose separation in life, the two Germans prefer union in death. Neither alternative is happy, but Moravia offers no other.

Themes and Meanings

1934 opens with the question, "Is it possible to live in despair and not wish for death?" Moravia probes possible answers through the actions of the various characters. For the Germans, the answer is clearly no. Sonia remains physically alive but tells Lucio, "I am a dead woman." Lucio hopes to arrive at a different answer through his writing, but Shapiro refers him to Johann Wolfgang von Goethe's character Werther, a young man who kills himself because of unrequited love. Shapiro adds that Lucio may be able to stabilize his own despair because he is not living deeply: "If you were really in despair, you wouldn't come here to tell me so."

Is Lucio playing a role? Is he as much an actor as Paula or Beate/Trude, differing from them only in that he deceives himself rather than others, or does he respond to despair as a life-loving Italian, whereas Werther, like the Germans in *1934* and like Kleist, is a typical Nordic romantic? Such questions of interpreting reality dominate the novel. In the opening scene, Lucio reads in Beate's eyes and shaking head the negative answer to his riddle about despair and life. Yet he must confess that her sad look could be the effect of nearsightedness, and she might be shaking her head to discourage his flirtatious stares. Or she might be sad because he has taken so long to notice her, and shaking her head might be a silent reprimand to his inattentiveness.

Later, as Lucio rides to Anacapri, he reflects on the landscape. The ocean appears calm and soothing, while the mountains seem menacing. Yet he realizes that the hills will not harm him, whereas he could easily drown in the sea. He believes that Beate/Trude is two women and is completely taken in by her masquerade. He is convinced that Beate will come to his room for sex and suicide. He never suspects that Beate/Trude deeply loves her husband; in fact, he believes that she loathes him. Similarly, he cannot gauge the strength of Paula's affection for her companion.

Moravia's is a confused and confusing world. As the character Michele observes in Moravia's first novel, *Gli indifferenti* (1929; *The Time of Indifference*, 1953), "Now one's head was in a bag, one was in the dark, one was blind. And yet one still had to go somewhere." Moravia ponders the question of whether one can pierce through the shadows into reality.

Critical Context

Increasingly, the modernist answer to this query is negative. As R. W. B. Lewis has remarked, "sadness is . . . the supreme emotion in the Moravian universe," and that emotion certainly pervades *1934*. The historical setting lends credence to the dominant feeling of despair, as the world seemed increasingly to be falling under the domination of ruthless dictators. Personally, too, the 1930's were bad for Moravia, who has said that "the years between 1933 and 1943 . . . were, from the point of view of public life, the worst of my life; and even today, I cannot remember them without horror." Moravia also noted that the book reflects the time of its composition in the early 1980's, commenting in a 1983 interview, "Communism is going badly, and so is capitalism."

1934 suggests, then, that uncertainties are less the product of an age or political system than of the human condition. For Moravia, as for his contemporary existentialist writers, that condition is one of isolation, of an inability to relate to any reality outside oneself. Lucio has trouble finding Beate/ Trude's message in the volume of Kleist's letters; a month passes before he discovers the suicide note she left for him during their final night on Capri. In an effort to overcome their loneliness, people will huddle around a radio to listen to a familiar language and voice, even if the speaker is Adolf Hitler, or they will consent to lovemaking even at the cost of life itself. Like Lucio during his last night on Capri, they think they are waking up to reach out in the dark to embrace reality, but instead they find that they clasp the void.

Sources for Further Study

Brose, Margaret. "Alberto Moravia: Fetishism and Figuration," in *Novel.* XV (Fall, 1981), pp. 62-75.

Heiney, Donald. *Three Italian Novelists: Moravia, Pavese, Vittorini,* 1968.

Lewis, R. W. B. "Alberto Moravia: Eros and Existence," in *From Verismo to Experimentalism: Essays in the Modern Italian Novel,* 1969.

Pacifici, Sergio. *The Modern Italian Novel: From Pea to Moravia,* 1979.

Joseph Rosenblum

NO LONGER HUMAN

Author: Osamu Dazai (Tsushima Shūji', 1909-1948)
Type of plot: Autobiographical fiction
Time of plot: From the 1910's to 1930
Locale: An unnamed village in northeastern Japan and Tokyo
First published: Ningen shikkaku, 1948 (English translation, 1958)

> *Principal characters:*
> YOZO, the narrator-protagonist, a college dropout and artist
> HORIKI, a college student, artist, and Yozo's friend
> FLATFISH, a family friend and guardian of Yozo
> YOSHIKO, Yozo's girlfriend and, later, his wife

The Novel

In *No Longer Human,* the first-person narrator, Yozo, traces his development and experiences from childhood through his twenty-seventh year. Using the device of a journal kept by the narrator which has been recovered and is being read by someone else, the author has made this book a revelation of his innermost self and a confession of his increasing alienation from society. In fact, the book is highly autobiographical and belongs to the "I novel" genre, a style popular in Japan.

Yozo learns very early as a child that he is apparently quite different from the people around him, and he consequently fears these people. Yet he wants to be accepted, so by constantly playing the role of clown, he makes himself popular. He observes in general that people live in mutual distrust and are insincere. On the way home from a political rally sponsored by his father, he overhears family friends saying how idiotic the meeting was; these same friends then congratulate his father on a "wonderful meeting."

After going away to high school, Yozo learns that his clowning and posturing are easier now that he is away from family and familiars. He discovers that he loves painting and wants to make it his profession. His art parallels his public and private selves: He paints standard "pretty pictures" for others to see and odd self-portraits, which he calls "ghost pictures," for his private amusement. While in high school, he also discovers that he gets along better with women and finds them easier to clown for, even though he finds them rather difficult to understand.

Although Yozo wants to go to art school, his father makes him go to college. There, Yozo meets Horiki, who introduces him to the world of drinking, smoking, and prostitution. Yozo finds Horiki's friendship (such as it is) necessary because he is afraid to get around Tokyo on his own, and Horiki consequently becomes a crutch, for he is very accomplished in all the skills needed to survive in a big city. Yozo also begins attending student Communist meetings while in college, but he has no liking for Marxist economic theory. He merely prefers the personality of the Communist movement; it exists, as he does, on the margins of society.

After several years, he must leave the comfortable house in which he has been staying and move to a room in a lodging house. He is now on a tiny monthly dole from home and has real financial worries. He drops out of school, neglects his painting, and ceases to attend the Communist meetings. He rarely sees Horiki but spends most of his time with a succession of girlfriends and prostitutes, and he becomes a heavy drinker. He finds a waitress in a Ginza café who is as unhappy as he. They both decide that there is no hope living in an upside-down society in which they are so miserable, and they attempt a double suicide which leaves the girl dead but Yozo still alive.

The suicide attempt embarrasses his relatives, and his father forces Yozo to live with a family friend whom Yozo calls Flatfish. Yozo is quickly disgusted with Flatfish's lack of straightforwardness and leaves. He eventually lives with Shizuko, a woman journalist, and her daughter. Flatfish reaches an agreement with the woman whereby Yozo severs all relations with his family and takes Shizuko as a common-law wife. This arrangement does not work, and he drifts into a relationship with Yoshiko, a seventeen-year-old girl, virginal, innocent, and trusting, who works in a tobacco shop. Yoshiko, so completely unlike other people in society, enchants Yozo and he marries her.

Yozo is very happy with her, but his happiness is short-lived, for she is raped by a man who takes advantage of her innocence. This event completely shatters Yozo, not because of her physical defilement but because of the defilement of her trusting nature. He tries to commit suicide with sleeping pills but is unsuccessful. By now, he is coughing blood and has become addicted to morphine. Flatfish and Horiki offer to put him into a hospital for a cure. Yozo wants to be helped so he lets them do this, but they have tricked him—the hospital is really an insane asylum. Yozo believes that he is not insane, but there is nothing he can do—he has been officially branded as mad. This marks his ultimate disqualification as a member of society. He has utterly ceased to be human.

The Characters

In the Japanese style of autobiographical fiction, readers expect to see a portrait of the author, and Osamu Dazai provided in Yozo an artfully contrived view of himself, his problems, and his outlook on life. Yozo is highly sensitive to beauty and pleasure, and one of the circumstances of life which gives him most pain is the dull, prosaic aspect of things in the world. As a child, he was fascinated by the beauty and poetry of bridges and subway trains until he discovered that they were constructed for strictly utilitarian purposes.

What causes Yozo the most pain is the greed, insincerity, and hypocrisy of humans. He has a dread of other people and adopts a mask of camaraderie and extroversion, although he is constantly afraid that someone will discover his real self. He comes to a gradual realization that the rules and regulations of society have a cold and cruel logic. He sees that society actually consists of each individual, and survival means being victorious in a series of conflicts between individuals. Virtue and vice were invented by humans for a morality also invented by humans. He further becomes aware that he is attracted to the disorganized and somewhat silly Communist meetings because of the irrationality of the students involved. For Yozo, this irrationality and the possibility of going to jail are preferable to the dread "realities of life" found in society at large.

Yozo has a vague awareness that drink, tobacco, and prostitutes are a means of dissipating his dread of humans. Although he eventually stops seeing prostitutes, he continues to have a number of relationships with other women. For his part, he feels more secure with women because they have no ulterior motives. The women apparently see in Yozo a gentle and tortured person beneath the antics and drunkenness on the outside. It is through these various relationships that the revelation is made that Yozo is actually more human than anybody else. He leaves Shizuko and her daughter immediately when he realizes that he is interfering with their mutual happiness. He is especially shattered and reaches his lowest point when his wife is raped. Yozo himself has trusted little in others and marvels that Yoshiko can be so trusting. Her rape merely confirms his conviction that no one who relies on trust can survive.

Horiki and Flatfish are representatives of the society which is so threatening to Yozo. Horiki, although leading virtually the same wild life-style as Yozo, turns out to be petty and cruel. He insults and mortifies one of Yozo's earlier girlfriends because he detects an "air of poverty" about her. This treatment contributes to her eventual suicide. He sadistically makes sure that Yozo stumbles upon his wife in the act of being raped so that he will get the maximum shock. Flatfish is a respectable businessman, but he is never honest with Yozo. It is Flatfish who takes advantage of Yozo's weakness and has him committed to an asylum.

Yoshiko is typical of the women who can get along with Yozo. She accepts Yozo and his weaknesses, but it is her complete trust and innocence which make her memorable. When Yozo tells her that he has quit drinking and then comes home drunk, she insists that he is not drunk but is playacting. She trusts a complete stranger who then rewards her trust by raping her. She never understands that Yozo's later addiction to morphine is harming him. She is unfit for survival in a cruel world.

Themes and Meanings

For Dazai, post–World War II Japanese society is an utter wasteland. In order to survive in this wasteland, one must lie, cheat, and be an aggressive fighter against one's "fellow humans." This state of affairs is too much to bear. An existential laugh of despair is all that he can manage. To be weak (and Yozo is primarily a weak person) is a sign of goodness, not evil. On the contrary, the evil ones are those who have no sympathy for human weakness. These weak people are all too painfully aware that their sufferings and sometimes wild behavior are really attempts to ward off the ugliness and filth of life. Dazai sees a very basic human depravity and is moved by the experiences of those who suffer because of the depravity.

Both men and women suffer because of evil and their knowledge of the nature of society, but men generally want to commit suicide while women generally want to live. It seems that women are more capable of understanding evil and are also stronger. In Dazai's previous novel, *Shayō* (1947; *The Setting Sun*, 1956), the heroine, Kazuko, determines to have a baby out of wedlock at the end of the book, in effect defying the standards of society. In *No Longer Human*, Yozo tries to commit suicide numerous times, prefiguring Dazai's own answer to the problem: He himself committed suicide less than a year after finishing the novel.

Although the bulk of the novel consists of the discovered journal, there is a framing device at the beginning and the end. Initially, a person is looking at three pictures of someone taken as a child, teenager, and adult. All three pictures show a bewildered and bizarre person, who turns out to be Yozo. At the end of the novel, a woman who knew Yozo and who possesses the journal comments that he is nice and is even an angel. This remark directly contradicts the portrait Yozo gives of himself as a drunken and inhuman person and confirms the impression that Yozo is perhaps the most human person in the book (therein lies the irony of the title), who suffers precisely because he is too human. Another device which lends emphasis to the theme is the prose style, which matches the bizarre, Kafkaesque world of Yozo. Some paragraphs are several pages long; others are one sentence. Narrative logic jumps frequently and approaches the stream-of-consciousness technique in places.

Critical Context

No Longer Human is Dazai's last and most important book. It is regarded as the most outstanding example of Japanese autobiographical fiction, or *shishōsetsu* ("I novel"). A concern for the author and his or her personal revelations has a long history in Japan, going back to the female diary literature of the 800's and 900's. The "I novel" itself, which appeared in the 1920's, was not only a recounting of events in the author's life but also a merciless exposé in the style of a confession, with the emphasis on fact, not fiction or art. Dazai took this form and stretched it by placing far more emphasis on art. He suppressed some facts of his life, rearranged others, and paid far more attention to the demands of narrative than did previous "I novel" writers.

In the 1940's and after his death in the 1950's, Dazai was the most popular writer in Japan, especially among younger people. First with *The Setting Sun* and then with *No Longer Human*, he chronicled Japan's postwar atmosphere of degradation, despair, and nihilism, especially among those who had lost their money and their place in society. A new term entered the Japanese language based on Dazai's fiction, the "setting sun tribe," describing those people who scarcely felt human.

Sources for Further Study

Keene, Donald. "Dazai Osamu and the *Burai-ha*," in *Dawn to the West: Japanese Literature of the Modern Era*, 1984.

Lyons, Phyllis. *The Saga of Dazai Osamu: A Critical Study with Translations*, 1985.

O'Brien, James A. *Dazai Osamu*, 1975.

Rimer, J. Thomas. "Dazai Osamu: The Death of the Past," in *Modern Japanese Fiction and Its Traditions*, 1978.

Ueda, Makoto. "Dazai Osamu," in *Modern Japanese Writers and the Nature of Literature*, 1976.

James Muhleman

NO PLACE ON EARTH

Author: Christa Wolf (1929-   )
Type of plot: Philosophical realism
Time of plot: June, 1804
Locale: An estate near the town of Winkel on the Rhine, Germany
First published: Kein Ort: Nirgends, 1979 (English translation, 1982)

> *Principal characters:*
> KAROLINE VON GÜNDERODE, the Romantic poet who, early in
>   1804, published her first volume of poetry under the
>   pseudonym "Tian"
> HEINRICH VON KLEIST, the Romantic writer and dramatist,
>   who is recovering from a physical and mental breakdown

The Novel

No Place on Earth is Christa Wolf's vision of an imaginary meeting between the almost forgotten, though in many ways modern, German poet Karoline von Günderode (1780-1806) and the famous German writer and dramatist Heinrich von Kleist (1777-1811). They meet at a tea party at the estate of a merchant, Joseph Merten. Many of Germany's great young minds are present. The entire action takes place in one long afternoon in June, 1804. For several hours, the guests move back and forth in Merten's spacious living room, conversing and occasionally clustering around the tea table. Large windows overlook sloping, tree-covered meadows and a few rustic houses. At a distance, one can see the sluggish waters of the Rhine. As the clock strikes five, the guests decide to go outdoors for a walk along the river.

The novel has the dramatic intensity of a two-act play. The characters move within two sets. Their initial gathering in the living room permits a rapid introduction of all participants. Their individuality is established by showing them interacting with one another. Once outside, the action, such as it is, focuses entirely on the two main characters, Günderode and Kleist, who separate from the group. The merchant's invitation reads "Tea and Conversation," yet the omniscient narrator, while recording some actual conversations, prefers to concentrate on the unspoken thoughts of Günderode and Kleist. The narrator presents the protagonists' observations in a strictly balanced narrative, alternately writing from each character's point of view. The reality of the situation is enhanced by the inclusion in the text of quotations from the poetry of Günderode, Clemens Brentano, and Friedrich Hölderlin, and from Kleist's and Günderode's letters.

The French Revolution lies ten years in the past. Napoleon Bonaparte will soon bring profound changes to Germany. The Enlightenment as the dominant worldview is being challenged by Romanticism. The philosopher

Immanuel Kant and the great Johann Wolfgang von Goethe inspire both admiration and antagonism in the young, restless Romantics. The unfettered individualism of these new artists grants them an artistic freedom previously unknown, yet it imposes on them a burden of personal responsibility. Art is no longer clearly defined by a well-established society. The talents of women writers are beginning to be recognized in Germany, and Romantic individualism is about to extend to educated women privileges and burdens equal to those of men. The Romantics face a time of transition. They perceive their world as chaotic. This period of German Romanticism (c. 1796-1832) provides the intellectual background for *No Place on Earth*, and the conversation at the party centers on Romanticism's main concerns.

The Characters

No proof exists that Günderode ever met Kleist, but it is a fact that Günderode knew Merten. She stabbed herself to death at his country estate in 1806. Günderode spent her life in a convent for impoverished daughters of the nobility. In 1804 and 1805, she published two volumes of poetry under the pseudonym "Tian." By 1804, Kleist had resigned his Prussian army commission, failed in his effort to become a civil servant, broken his engagement to Wilhelmine von Zenge, and quarreled with his sister Ulrike. Influenced by Immanuel Kant's *Critique of Pure Reason* (1781), he became deeply depressed, destroyed portions of his second drama, *Robert Guiskard* (1808; English translation, 1962), and suffered a physical and mental breakdown which brought him under the care of Dr. Georg Christian Wedekind, in Mainz. Kleist committed suicide in 1811.

The guests at Wolf's imaginary tea party include the poet Brentano and his wife, the writer Sophie Mereau. Also at the gathering are Brentano's two sisters: Bettine von Arnim, who, in 1840, published her correspondence with Günderode, and Gunda von Savigny. Savigny's husband, Friedrich Karl von Savigny, a renowned German jurist who for several years maintained a precarious personal relationship with Günderode, is also present, as are Christian Nees von Esenbeck, a noted German botanist, and his wife, Lisette Mettingh, a woman of impressive intellectual ability and Günderode's closest friend.

All the major characters are historically significant, with well-known biographies to which there are constant allusions in the novel. The author, however, is not as interested in historical accuracy as in the circumstances which may have shaped these characters. Joseph Merten, the successful merchant, exudes self-satisfaction and is happy to live in an enlightened world which "curbed the baser passions and elevated reason to a position of power." Esenbeck, though sickly, is the confident modern scientist who seeks salvation through scientific progress. Dr. Wedekind is a dedicated physician who, while not insensitive to the needs of his patient Kleist, finds it necessary to apply proven methods of healing rather than to probe the depth of a tormented soul.

On the side of the Romantics, Savigny is a kind of mediator between opposites; he avoids committing himself to any cause. Savigny enjoys being the object of Günderode's passion but does not wish to become passionately involved. Lisette Mettingh is tormented by her lesbian infatuation with Günderode, who, in turn, sees Lisette as nothing more than a friend. The famous Brentanos, Clemens and Bettine, remain almost as obscure as their lesser-known sister Gunda. All three of them are self-assured, vain, and extroverted. They speak with the fluency of highly conceited people, in sharp contrast to Kleist, who stutters until, in his intimate conversation with Günderode, his stutter disappears.

Kleist is alone. He does not know anybody at the party except for Dr. Wedekind. His illness, his mental instability, is in its acute stage, while Günderode's similar affliction has reached a chronic state. Wolf describes Kleist as a machine running at full speed with its breaks applied. His life is the constant struggle of a man torn between the creative élan of a gifted individual and the need to conform to the demands of a society to which he is inevitably bound.

While for Kleist the party represents a difficult hurdle to be cleared in order to make possible a return to life and to his vocation as a writer, Günderode is taking leave. She no longer has the desire to be part of society. She has reached the point at which flirting with death produces not only dread but also intense joy. Secure in her decision to abandon the world at a point convenient to her, she finds it natural to carry a dagger with her and has had a physician show her the exact place where she must stab herself.

Themes and Meanings

The Romantics were the first to show fascination with the human psyche and, in particular, its darker and more mysterious aspects. Accordingly, the destinies of the protagonists are revealed through recurring dreams. Both find themselves torn by attraction to and alienation from other human beings and from themselves; both feel unable to verbalize their thoughts and emotions because "words are incapable of depicting the soul." The pivotal arguments of the novel ensue while the guests are about to leave for their walk outside (a symbolic step away from the confining atmosphere of the Enlightenment into the open spaces of a new Romantic era). The arguments are of an aesthetic as well as a political nature. Their meaning rests with the author's basic position that German Romanticism was the harbinger of a new age of freedom in which the individual, man and woman alike, as well as poetry and the arts could flourish as never before. While the rear guard of the Enlightenment continued to wage war to restrain humanity's irrational impulses, Romanticism's newfound emphasis on irrational cognition was meant to enhance rather than to replace reason. Imagination was not supposed to supersede realistic representation in art but was supposed to allow a vision beyond realism. As Kleist points out: "That which can be thought ought to be thought." Such a pronouncement may be read as applying to artistic freedom only, but it is more likely to be a plea for political freedom as well. Indeed, in the novel, Kleist's pleas for an end to oppression in his own country, Prussia, sound more like a cry for help coming from a disillusioned contemporary writer in East Germany than from a Prussian nobleman.

Merten, the merchant, and Esenbeck, the scientist, represent the forces of the Enlightenment, while Kleist struggles to express the Romantic worldview. The merchant and the scientist argue for an ordered universe that is ruled by reason. They show no understanding of the "lamentations of the literati." Kleist enters the argument with a question about the role of beauty in this orderly world, then continues: "Our modern day civilization is steadily expanding the sphere of the intellect, steadily restricting that of imagination. We have almost reached the point at which we can predict the end of the arts." It is highly unlikely that the real Kleist ever uttered these words. The lament is Christa Wolf's, who speaks out of an artist's frustration in a world devoted to technology and, in East Germany, to five-year economic plans.

When Günderode enters the argument by accusing Savigny of having a "masculine brain" and of knowing only "curiosity concerning that which is incontrovertible, logically consistent, and soluble," she, too, expresses the author's views. Throughout the novel, Wolf acquaints her readers with her ideas on the relationship between the sexes. She finds her own thoughts expressed in Günderode's poem "Change and Constancy," read by Brentano in the novel. The male of the species has a need to examine an argument and to judge its merits after mature consideration, while women acquire most of their knowledge more directly and more efficiently through a highly developed intuitive sense. The artist, male or female, works with both, intellectual and intuitive powers.

Kleist, in 1804, is still immature as a writer because his masculine pride conflicts with his developing sense of femininity, his poetic sense. He feels antagonistic toward Günderode and misjudges her until both find a common ground; as poets, they share the male and female traits which make for an organic whole. In the course of the novel, Kleist, unhappy in the exclusively masculine sphere dominated by the men who believe in the Enlightenment, is slowly drawn into the female ambience of the Romantic age. Günderode, on the other hand, is secure in her Romantic female sensibility but engages in an enervating struggle against the enlightened masculine world which would not grant her a position outside the traditional feminine role.

Critical Context

Personal experience is an element common to all Christa Wolf's work before 1979. The autobiographical stories, told neither chronologically nor in a confessional manner, recall single significant events in the context of her generation's destiny and the development of East Germany. Her critical examination of the position of women in a Communist state began with the publication of three short stories in the collection *Unter den Linden: Drei unwahrscheinliche Geschichten* (1974; under the linden: three improbable stories). The last of these is called a self-experiment and seems to mark the end of Wolf's blatant use of her own experiences. *No Place on Earth* could be considered a turning point in the author's development as a writer. In it, Wolf continues to take a strongly feminist position, yet she departs from the auto-biographical tradition with which she was previously identified.

Sources for Further Study

Abel, Elizabeth. "(E)Merging Identities: The Dynamics of Female Friend-ship in Contemporary Fiction by Women," in *Signs*. LI, no. 3 (1981), pp. 413-432.

Altbach, Edith H., ed. *German Feminism: Readings in Politics and Lit-erature*, 1984.

Fehervary, Helen. "Christa Wolf's Prose: A Landscape of Masks," in *New German Critique*. XXVII (1982), pp. 57-87.

Meyer-Gossau, Franke. "Culture Is What You Experience: An Interview with Christa Wolf," in *New German Critique*. XXVII (1982), pp. 89-100.

Rita Terras

THE NON-EXISTENT KNIGHT

Author: Italo Calvino (1923-1985)
Type of plot: Fable
Time of plot: During the reign of Charlemagne, 768-814
Locale: France
First published: Il cavaliere inesistente, 1959 (English translation, 1962)

> *Principal characters:*
> CHARLEMAGNE, the King of the Franks
> AGILULF, a non-existent knight
> RAIMBAUT, an idealistic youth who desires to avenge his
>   father's death
> TORRISMUND, a young, cynical knight
> BRADAMANTE, the Amazon who loves Agilulf and is loved by
>   Raimbaut
> SISTER THEODORA, the narrator and author of the story

The Novel

As its title suggests, Italo Calvino's *The Non-existent Knight* is a work of fabulation. It begins, simply enough, as a comic fable, a parodic satire on the medieval romance and all that that literary form implies about heroes, holy wars, and chivalric ideals. It soon becomes apparent, however, that, for all of its comic brevity, Calvino's novella is more complex and far-reaching than its opening pages suggest. Gradually, characters are added and authorial intrusions begin to break the narrative flow, until it becomes clear that the subplots and digressions constitute integral and parallel parts of the larger whole. Calvino's simple story becomes a narrative mare's nest, the untangling of which may be, if not quite impossible, ultimately beside the point, as the reader comes to understand that the tale being told is of no more, and no less, importance than the postmodern tale of its telling.

The novella opens with Charlemagne reviewing his troops shortly before they are to do battle against the Saracens in one of a seemingly endless, and perhaps pointless, series of holy wars. At the end of the review comes Sir Agilulf, a non-existent knight: nothingness within a suit of pure white armor. It is not his non-existence that makes Agilulf unpopular with the other knights but his scrupulous attention to all military and chivalric rules. He does manage to gain one follower, the youth Raimbaut, who is intent on avenging his father's death by killing the Saracen Isohar in battle. Raimbaut is very nearly disabused of both his idealism and his desire for revenge when he actually experiences the absurdity of battle conducted according to Calvino's burlesque set of chivalric codes. These rules include a Superintendent of Duels, Feuds, and Besmirched Honor, as well as interpreters to translate oaths and insults for the benefit of all the besmirched knights and Saracens who are not bilingual.

The temporary defeat of the Saracen army—in Calvino's tale everything is temporary—signals the real beginning of his fabulous story. It is at this point that another fatherless knight, Torrismund, not only besmirches Agilulf's honor but also undermines the already problematic existence of this non-existent knight when he reports that the royal virgin whom Agilulf saved fifteen years ago, in the act for which he was made a knight, was not a virgin but rather Torrismund's mother.

With Torrismund's disclosure and Agilulf's subsequent consternation, the tale becomes, in the narrator's words,"a mess of crisscrossing lines" as the various parallel stories branch out. Agilulf goes in search of what he hopes is a virginal Sophronia, expecting in this way to prove that he is what he claims to be: a non-existent knight. Torrismund, the self-proclaimed bastard, goes in search of his non-existent father, one of the knights of the Holy Grail. Raimbaut goes in search of the Amazon Bradamante, who has herself gone in search of the only man she believes she can ever love: Agilulf, a man who does not exist.

As these narratives flow from a common center, they eventually return to it. Agilulf finds Sophronia, rescues her in the nick of time, and leaves her in a cave while he goes to fetch Charlemagne, to vouch for his honor, and a midwife, to vouch for Sophronia's virginity. Meanwhile, Torrismund has found the knights of the Holy Grail, who turn out to be considerably less than his idealistic vision of them; intent upon the sacred vision, they perpetrate all kinds of violence on those whom they consider less pure. Abandoning his quest for his father, Torrismund wanders the world, eventually arriving at the cave, where he falls in love with Sophronia. They become lovers, and Torrismund does not discover who she is until Agilulf returns. In despair over his incest, Torrismund plunges into the woods only to return a moment later, realizing that because she was a virgin until a moment ago she could not be his mother. This revelation comes too late for Agilulf who, unable to bear his shame, becomes truly non-existent. He bequeaths his armor to Raimbaut, who is then mistaken for Agilulf by Bradamante. She makes love with Raimbaut, with her eyes closed, and discovering her mistake, disappears. She returns in the last chapter, as Sister Theodora discloses her true identity, or, rather, the other half of her double identity: She is Bradamante. That disclosure occurs just as Raimbaut arrives at the convent on horseback to take her away.

The Characters

It should hardly come as a surprise that in a work in which the plots are so numerous and so bizarre, characterization and, indeed, individual characters should play a decidedly secondary role. Moreover, because *The Non-existent Knight* is so clearly a work of fabulation rather than realism, its minimally drawn characters are necessarily sketched along allegorical lines. Agilulf, for example, is quite simply "the non-existent knight," the proof that "in Charlemagne's army one can be a knight with lots of names and titles and what's more a bold warrior and zealous officer, without needing to exist!" Lacking a sense of irony, he is chained to the letter of the law and to whatever is literally true, or, rather, to whatever is believed to be literally true. He is, in short, the complete realist, and, paradoxically, the character in the novella who is least touched by physical reality.

Although "a model soldier," Agilulf is understandably "disliked by all." Although it is true that "he exists without existing," he is nevertheless the story's most memorable character and thus the proof of Calvino's, and Sister Theodora's, powerful imagination. As something of a joke, Charlemagne assigns Agilulf a squire who is his complete opposite, "a man without a name and with every possible name," Gurduloo, to choose but one of his appellations. He is a figure whose name and being change according to whatever his immediate environment happens to be. Gurduloo exists but does not know that he exists, whereas Agilulf does not exist and believes that he does. They represent the poles between which an identity must be found: protean formlessness and empty rigidity.

The remaining characters comically and unsuccessfully try to work out compromises with their similarly divided selves. Raimbaut, for example, burns with the desire to avenge his father's death, but his efforts to do so only lead him to realize how rigid and absurd is the chivalric code by which he wishes to live. Torrismund is equally divided, being in some ways the innocent Raimbaut's double and in other ways his opposite. Torrismund is cynical about war and about Agilulf, whom he judges a baseless fiction: "Neither he exists nor the things he does nor what he says, nothing, nothing at all." The reader might agree, until it becomes clear that this non-existent knight forms the substance of the novella. Just as the reader must necessarily, and provisionally, believe in Agilulf's existence, as well as his non-existence, so Torrismund finds it necessary to believe in his own baseless fiction about the purity of the knights of the Holy Grail, a belief and a fiction he must eventually come to reject. Finally, there is Bradamante, who was driven "to the life of chivalry due to her love for all that was strict, exact, severe, conforming to moral rule and . . . exact precision of movement," though Bradamante is herself a slattern. Bradamante is not only divided within herself but also double, both a character in the story and, as Sister Theodora, its teller. This point is withheld by the ever-intrusive Theodora until the last two pages of a novella that is itself divided and double, its narrative flow disrupted by Theodora's frequent "authorial" comments which, in effect, add to the tale being told the tale of its telling.

Themes and Meanings

In *The Non-existent Knight*, Calvino's many narrative lines spread out in various directions only to return to a common center. In similar fashion, Calvino posits the separation and subsequent, though problematic, combination of art and life. As Raimbaut learns, in war nothing is as it seems, and, as Sister Theodora's duplicitous telling of her tale proves, in art nothing is quite as it seems either. War itself is like a dead metaphor or an overused literary convention: entirely predictable and played according to rules so stale and rigid as to make the knights who participate in it appear absurd. Yet, as Raimbaut also understands, humankind needs rituals to keep from slipping into the void. The chivalric code forms one such ritual, and the rules of narration another. Sister Theodora's narrative method involves, first, the breaking of literary rules and, second, breaking into her own narration. Her repeated disruptions leave the reader both perplexed and delighted, the attention divided between tale and teller. She leaves the sources of her narrative uncertain; they include rumors, written accounts, eyewitness reports, her own imagination, and, as the reader comes to believe, her own experiences. She implies that the daily routine in the convent where she writes has managed to leave its impress on her tale of war and quests, and one suspects that something similar has happened with fact and fiction, history and imagination, each infusing and confusing the other. Less obviously, she transforms the knights' quests through their various dark woods into her own uncertain progress as author through the blank pages before her, which she must fill up as an act of penance given her by her mother superior. The reader, it should be noted, is engaged in a similar quest through the pages, with status similarly uncertain, for it is not the "Dear Reader" to whom she addresses herself but instead her apostrophized "Book."

Ultimately, Sister Theodora's purpose is to turn the reader into her art in, again, a double sense: to make the reader into her text, or vice versa, and to force the reader to deal with her text as an active participant, as something of a coauthor, rather than a consumer of goods. In this way she and her author, Calvino, hope to restore the reader to a sense of existence empowered by art, rather than existence, or non-existence, drained of meaning by baseless rules and dead conventions, whether aesthetic, military, or social. Calvino's parodic laughter is not an end in itself but a means for undermining all exhausted fictions which deny the uncertainty and open-endedness of life, exalting the few as kings and noble knights while condemning the rest to servitude and non-existence. Overly committed to one fiction, Agilulf must necessarily dissolve into nothingness once he, however mistakenly, believes himself deprived of the title that has defined him. The other characters, Sister Theodora included, prove themselves more adaptable, and therefore they survive—not as they have been but as they can become, as hopeful as they are uncertain. As Sister Theodora says,

A page is good only when we turn it and find life urging along, confusing every page in the book. The pen rushes on, urged by the same joy that makes me course the open road. A chapter started when one doesn't know which tale to tell is like a corner turned on leaving a convent, when one might come face to face with a dragon, a Saracen gang, an enchanted isle or a new love.

Critical Context

Having begun his career as a writer of neorealist fictions, Calvino gradually turned to the writing of postmodern fables, such as *Le città invisibili* (1972; *Invisible Cities*, 1974) and *Il castello dei destini incrociati* (1969, 1973; *The Castle of Crossed Destinies*, 1977). Important in its own right, *The Non-existent Knight* takes on added importance when read as a transitional work or, better, the Calvino work that perhaps best embodies the twin sides of his genius: his preoccupation with social themes and his later preoccupation with a more nearly pure literary performance, an art of nonreferentiality. *The Non-existent Knight* is so satisfying a work largely because Calvino's social consciousness and growing love of postmodern playfulness support and deepen each other, proving, as Bradamante and Sister Theodora do as well, the compatibility of apparent opposites.

Sources for Further Study

Andrews, Richard. "Italo Calvino," in *Writers and Society in Contemporary Italy: A Collection of Essays*, 1984. Edited by Michael Caesar and Peter Hainsworth.

Cannon, JoAnn. *Italo Calvino: Writer and Critic*, 1981.

Carter, Albert Howard. *Italo Calvino: Metamorphoses of Fantasy*, 1987.

Olken, I. T. *With Pleated Eye and Garnet Wing: Symmetries of Italo Calvino*, 1984.

Robert A. Morace

NOVEMBER 1918
A German Revolution

Author: Alfred Döblin (1878-1957)
Type of plot: Social criticism
Time of plot: November, 1918, to the late 1920's
Locale: Berlin and the Weimar Republic
First published: November 1918: Eine deutsche Revolution, 1948-1950; first
   complete edition (including the novel *Bürger und Soldater*, which was
   originally published in 1939), 1978 (English translation, 1983): *Verratenes
   Volk*, 1948, and *Heimkehr der Fronttruppen*, 1949 (translated as *A People
   Betrayed* and *The Troops Return*, respectively, in *A People Betrayed:
   November 1918, A German Revolution*, 1983); *Karl und Rosa*, 1950 (*Karl
   and Rosa: November 1918, A German Revolution*, 1983)

> *Principal characters:*
> THE AUTHOR, an unreliable narrator figure
> FRIEDRICH BECKER, the protagonist, a former high-school
>   teacher and lieutenant in the German army who was
>   seriously wounded at the end of World War I and
>   discharged to his home in Berlin
> JOHANNES MAUS, his friend, also a former lieutenant in the
>   German army who was wounded in World War I and
>   discharged to Berlin
> HILDA, the nurse from Strasbourg who was in charge of
>   Becker and Maus's ward in the military hospital in Alsace,
>   part of a love triangle involving Maus and Becker
> FRIEDRICH EBERT, a German statesman and chairman of the
>   Social Democratic Party who succeeded as chancellor of
>   Germany in November, 1918, when Kaiser Wilhelm II
>   abdicated and went into exile
> WOODROW WILSON, the twenty-eighth President of the
>   United States, who was instrumental in getting the
>   Germans to sign a peace treaty and in establishing the
>   League of Nations
> KARL LIEBKNECHT, the leader of the Spartacus League and
>   the German Communist Party, who was murdered by the
>   military in January, 1919, after the revolution failed
> ROSA LUXEMBURG, a Polish-born Jew, Socialist leader, and
>   pacifist who is murdered, with Liebknecht, by the military

The Novel
   November 1918: A German Revolution, a novel in three parts, begins with
A People Betrayed (part 1) and *The Troops Return* (part 2), continuing with

Karl and Rosa (part 3), the story of Rosa Luxemburg and Karl Liebknecht, the leaders of the radical Socialist revolution which was defeated by government troops in January, 1919. Interwoven with the history of the lost revolution, a turning point in German history and a prophetic warning of the ultimate downfall of the Weimar Republic, are the trials and tribulations of the main protagonist, Friedrich Becker, who is presented as a kind of Faustian figure or German Everyman. He is characterized by Hilda, a nurse from Strasbourg, as the "most German thing" that she has encountered in her life, and she compares him to the German master builder of her beloved Strasbourg cathedral.

The novel plays on several levels. First, there is the level of the political history of the Weimar Republic, including the tragedy of Woodrow Wilson, whose vision of a League of Nations is defeated in his own country. Second, there is the level of the individual biographies of Friedrich Becker, Johannes Maus, and Hilda. Finally, there are the levels of Heaven and Hell, or good and evil. The novel ends with a metaphysical battle for Becker's soul between his guardian angel and Satan. Even though the outcome of the battle is left undecided for the other characters of the novel, Becker is saved and dies as a martyr of his time.

A People Betrayed, part 1 of *November 1918*, begins with the attack of the revolutionary masses on the Berlin police headquarters on November 22, 1918, planned in order to liberate political prisoners who had not been released on November 9, when a free German republic had been proclaimed. After his participation in the successful attack, Johannes Maus visits Becker, who has not yet recovered from his war injuries. Both of them were injured as lieutenants in the German army. After the armistice, they were returned to Germany from their ward in a military hospital in Alsace, where Hilda worked. When they meet again in Berlin, the city is under the rule of the workers' and soldiers' councils. Becker advises his friend Maus to join the revolution.

The leadership of the revolutionary movement is divided. The revolution is betrayed by the majority Social Democrats under the leadership of Friedrich Ebert, who is collaborating with the Army High Command to preserve law and order. It is Karl Liebknecht and the Spartacus League who try to reverse this counterrevolutionary development. The Ebert government and the council of people's commissars, who pretend that the revolution has gained its goals with the armistice and the removal of the monarchy, are plotting with the Army High Command to keep in check the revolutionary Left, organized by Liebknecht. A military putsch, staged by counterrevolutionary forces on December 6, 1918, leads to bloodshed among members of a Spartacus demonstration. Although Ebert is not responsible for the events of December 6, he appears to be in a secret alliance with the counterrevolutionary forces, while using violence against the revolutionaries. While the bloodshed of December 6 renders Maus a revolutionary, his friend Becker, who is troubled by his individual responsibility for the past war and its results, contemplates returning to his job as high-school teacher.

Part 2, entitled *The Troops Return*, begins around December 8, 1918, with the story of President Woodrow Wilson and his contribution to peace in Europe. Meanwhile, Hilda leaves her native Alsace, which has become French again after the defeat of Germany. She arrives in Berlin to join Friedrich Becker and nurse him back to health. Maus fails to persuade Becker to join the revolutionary cause. Instead, Becker takes refuge in Christianity. He has visions not only of the medieval German mystic Johannes Tauler, who gives him strength, but also of various messengers from Satan, a mysterious Brazilian gentleman, and a lion and a rat who drive him to suicide. At the last moment, Becker is saved by Hilda, who leaves him to take a job in a hospital. Becker considers returning to his teaching job, while Maus turns reactionary and joins one of the so-called volunteer corps (mercenary units, in reality) employed by the Ebert government.

The rest of part 2 tells the story of Woodrow Wilson's failure to establish a lasting peace in Europe and to obtain Senate approval for the League of Nations. The League of Nations is formed, but the Soviet Union is excluded, the United States excludes itself, and Germany is not admitted. Part 2 concludes with the cry of war, emerging from Satan's throat.

Part 3, *Karl and Rosa*, starts with the story of Rosa Luxemburg, who has been in and out of prison since 1915. She and Karl Liebknecht, the leaders of the Spartacus League, are the protagonists of part 3. While in prison, Rosa has visions of her young lover, Hannes Düsterberg, who has been killed in the war. His spirit attempts to assassinate her and assumes satanic features when he finally visits her shortly before her murder in January, 1919. After the armistice, Rosa is released from prison; on November 10, 1918, she arrives in Berlin. Meanwhile, Vladimir Ilich Lenin has had his revolution in Russia.

Friedrich Ebert is described as the obstructionist of the revolution. To stay in power, he relies on the support of the military, which is unable to suppress the sailors' revolt in Berlin. Because of Ebert's collusion with the military, the Independent Socialists withdraw from the government.

Meanwhile, Johannes Maus and Hilda accidentally meet on Christmas Eve and spend the night in a hotel. On New Year's Eve day, Maus proposes marriage, but Hilda is not ready, until she obtains Becker's approval. Becker returns to teaching, but his pacifism and lack of patriotism meet with much hostility from his students. When he refuses to join the witch-hunt against the homosexual director of his school, his continued employment is in danger. In search of a student who has joined the revolutionary forces because of an identity crisis, Becker finds himself fighting on the side of the Spartacists, defending the Berlin police presidium, the last stronghold of the revolutionaries, against the regular army. On January 12, 1919, the police presidium is stormed by government troops, and Becker is taken prisoner.

On December 30, 1918, the Spartacus League has reconstituted itself as the Communist Party of Germany. In opposition to Luxemburg and Lieb-knecht, who advocated participation in the elections for the constituent assembly, the membership has voted against bourgeois parliamentarism and in favor of revolutionary action. In spite of their defeat, Karl and Rosa remain loyal to their party. As they predicted and feared, the revolution of January 6, 1919, fails for lack of support from the masses and is crushed within six days by government troops, including the infamous volunteer corps, which Maus has joined. On January 15, 1919, Karl Liebknecht and Rosa Luxemburg are arrested and murdered by the officers who were supposed to deliver them to prison.

After Becker is released from prison, he discovers that Hilda and Maus have married, and the young student whom he tried to save has been killed in another revolutionary uprising. Becker has another vision of Johannes Tauler, who summons him to become a wandering preacher. He travels all over Germany to teach the word of Christ. His life is not free of temptation. Becker has another encounter with Satan, who dares him to make a bet that he would not be able to live with two souls in his breast, one criminal and one divine, without harm to his eternal salvation. He does become a thief and burglar, but he is saved after a final battle for his divine soul between his guardian angel and Satan, while his body is dumped into the Hamburg harbor.

The Characters

The author-narrator is a narrative device, employed by Alfred Döblin to emphasize the authorial impotence of the modern writer, who is neither omniscient nor able to master the plot and maintain the fiction of his work like a traditional novelist. The figure of the author repeatedly admits to having second thoughts. The author is part of the fiction of the novel, or *Erzählwerk* (narrative work), as Döblin preferred to call it. As a narrative device, the figure of the author justifies the deliberate fragmentation of the novel, causing abrupt changes in perspective and mixing historical documents with mystic visions.

Friedrich Becker, the main protagonist, is a Faustian figure. The end of part 3 contains a wager with Satan, reminding the reader of Johann Wolfgang von Goethe's *Faust* (1808, 1833). Goethe's Faust figure also has "two souls, alas! residing in his breast," he also concludes a wager with the Devil, which he loses, and his soul is also saved in the end. The use of the traditional Faust myth has a parallel in Thomas Mann's *Doktor Faustus* (1947; *Doctor Faustus*, 1948), which was written not only at approximately the same time but also in the same city. *Doctor Faustus*, as well as *Karl and Rosa*, was written in Los Angeles, California, where both authors lived in exile during World War II. It is doubtful, however, that these men exerted any influence on each other, because they were rather distant, if not hostile, toward each other. (Döblin, at least, was rather critical of Mann.) Döblin's main protagonist and Mann's Faust figure, Adrian Leverkühn, stand for modern Germany and its heritage. Both Leverkühn and Becker are symbols of Germany and its downfall at the end of the 1920's. Johannes Maus and Hilda do not display the same symbolic significance as characters, but to a large degree they are typical representatives of their generation.

The characters of Friedrich Ebert, Woodrow Wilson, Karl Liebknecht, and Rosa Luxemburg are historical figures and are based on extensive historical research conducted by Döblin. In fact, the novel is largely narrative history. This does not, however, prevent Döblin from adopting a critical perspective. This critical stance applies not only to Ebert and his followers but also to Karl and Rosa, who do not escape Döblin's criticism, even though he portrays them as martyrs of the revolution. Of special interest is the metaphysical dimension that Döblin added to the portrayal of Rosa Luxemburg. Her visions are totally fictional and perhaps out of character, especially when associated with Satan.

Themes and Meanings

November 1918 has all the weaknesses and strengths of Döblin's earlier masterpiece *Berlin Alexanderplatz: Die Geschichte vom Franz Biberkopf* (1929; *Berlin Alexanderplatz: The Story of Franz Biberkopf*, 1931). As a writer, Döblin wanted to present individual characters as a metaphor of the general population. He did not believe in nineteenth century individualism or in the individual confronting society. For him, the individual was an expression of the collective. The character of Friedrich Becker fulfills this function, as did Franz Biberkopf, the protagonist of *Berlin Alexanderplatz*. Both characters are representations of Berlin at a particular time in history. They do not have individual fates; their fates are reflections of the fate of the collective. Becker does not have the freedom to act but is driven by external events, subconscious forces, and mystic visions. Döblin combines two characteristics of the modernist novel: the loss of the individuality of man who becomes a type or part of the masses, and the analysis of the subconsciousness of an individual who functions as a metaphor for the collective. The novel is an attempt to reflect the totality of society and follows, in this respect, the tradition of the novel of social and political criticism established by Honoré de Balzac, Émile Zola, Leo Tolstoy, Fyodor Dostoevski, Upton Sinclair, and John Dos Passos.

In addition to these common features with *Berlin Alexanderplatz*, there are new departures in *November 1918*; among these are the function of narrative history, which supplies the chronology and realism of the novel, and the role of Christianity, which provides the metaphysical dimension to the realistic plot. To be sure, there are many religious leitmotifs in *Berlin Alexanderplatz*. *November 1918*, however, makes Christianity rather than socialism the ultimate value system, reflecting Döblin's dramatic conversion to Roman Catholicism in 1941. Although his sympathies are on the side of Karl Liebknecht and Rosa Luxemburg, his protagonist, Becker, follows the ideals of Christian mysticism and finds himself only by accident, not on the basis of a rational and political decision, fighting for the revolution. Döblin sides with the victims of his century. Friedrich Becker lives and dies the life of a Christian martyr of modern times.

Critical Context

A *People Betrayed* and *Karl and Rosa* are Döblin's most important works written during his exile from Nazi Germany from 1933 to 1945. The novels were written between 1937 and 1943 in Paris and Hollywood. Döblin returned to Germany in 1945 as a cultural officer of the French military government, only to leave Germany again for a second exile in France in 1953; he returned to a sanatorium in Germany to die in 1957. The original trilogy, as it is preserved in the English translation, grew into a tetralogy of four volumes which were not published in Germany until 1978. Only the shorter, three-volume version of 1950 was available until the final publication of the tetralogy in 1978.

The reasons for the abridged version were French censorship, which did not approve of the first part with its rather satirical view of the French in Alsace, and West German disinterest in exile literature, in general, and aversion to the November revolution of 1918, in particular. This intellectual climate of benevolent neglect was changed by the student movement of the 1970's, which brought about a new interest in German exile literature. This new interest made possible the final publication of the unabridged version in 1978, more than thirty years after its completion in manuscript.

Sources for Further Study

Hatfield, Henry. *Modern German Literature: The Major Figures in Context*, 1966.

Heilbut, Anthony. "A German Novelist of Revolution: *A People Betrayed: November 1918, A German Revolution*," in *The Nation*. CCXXXVI (May 21, 1983), p. 642.

Kort, Wolfgang. *Alfred Döblin: Leben und Werk*, 1965.

Osterle, Heinz D. "Alfred Döblins Revolutionstrilogie *November 1918*," in *Monatshefte*. LXII (1970), pp. 1-23.

Pawel, Ernst. "The Renaissance of Alfred Döblin: *A People Betrayed: November 1918, A German Revolution*," in *The New York Times Book Review*. LXXXVIII (April 17, 1983), p. 11.

Prawer, S. S. "The Way to Catastrophe: Alfred Döblin, *A People Betrayed* and *The Troops Return, November 1918—A German Revolution*, Parts I and II; *Karl and Rosa: November 1918—A German Revolution*, Part III," in *The Times Literary Supplement*. December 26, 1986, p. 1457.

Ehrhard Bahr

THE OATH

Author: Elie Wiesel (1928-   )
Type of plot: Parable
Time of plot: The early twentieth century to the early 1970's
Locale: Kolvillàg, a village in central Europe
First published: Le Serment de Kolvillàg, 1973 (English translation, 1973)

> *Principal characters:*
> AZRIEL, the only survivor of the Kolvillàg pogrom
> MOSHE, a mystic, Azriel's mentor
> SHMUEL, Azriel's father, the keeper of the *Pinkas* (the history of Kolvillàg)
> THE YOUNG MAN, a would-be suicide to whom Azriel tells his story

The Novel

In "The Old Man and the Child," the first of the three parts of *The Oath,* Azriel begins telling a young man a little about Kolvillàg, his native village, somewhere in central Europe between the Dniepr River and the Carpathian Mountains. Kolvillàg had been ruled by several nations but no longer exists. "I am Kolvillàg," says Azriel, "and I am going mad." His madness results from an oath not to tell the secret of his village.

The young man learns that Azriel is highly regarded for his extensive learning by a wide variety of people: "He made them understand what was happening to them; it was always more serious or simpler than they had imagined." Because Azriel cannot tell his friend more about Kolvillàg, he talks instead about his life after leaving there, about wandering through Europe during the years between the two world wars, and about Rachel, the only woman who has ever mattered to him.

The young man is tormented by memories of his mother, a survivor of the Nazi concentration camps who lost her first husband and son in the Holocaust. Because the young man has been contemplating suicide, Azriel decides to break his oath of fifty years: "I'll transmit my experience to him and he, in turn, will be compelled to do the same. . . . He must stay alive until he has transmitted his message." This message is contained in the *Pinkas,* the history of Kolvillàg kept over many generations, the last chronicler being Shmuel, Azriel's father, the official registrar of the community.

The events leading to the destruction of Kolvillàg are described in part two of *The Oath,* "The Child and the Madman." The trouble begins when Yancsi, a Christian youth and bully, disappears and is presumed killed. The Gentiles of Kolvillàg assume that Jews are responsible, but the Jews consider the thought of ritual murder in the twentieth century ridiculous. The Prefect of the village at first promises to keep the Jews safe but later says that a pogrom is inevitable.

The Oath then becomes the story of Azriel's friend and mentor, Moshe, who volunteers to be the scapegoat. Moshe is a religious scholar and mystic who claims to be able to read minds but chooses to live in isolation. He is satisfied to be thought a madman and to teach all that he knows to Azriel. The rabbis argue that Moshe's offer of self-sacrifice is pointless and is a rejection of God, but he goes to the police anyway and is savagely beaten. Davidov, the leader of the Jewish community, seeks help from the attorney Stefan Braun, a Jew who does not live as a Jew. Braun declines to help because, as he tells his son, "The era of crusades and pogroms is gone. Ours is dominated by humanism, liberalism."

Moshe's sacrificial offer is rejected by the Christian authorities, who are convinced, however, more than before that Jews are behind Yancsi's death. Addressing his fellow Jews at the synagogue, Moshe makes them swear an oath that whoever survives will not reveal what is about to happen since knowledge of previous atrocities has not stopped the pogroms over the centuries.

The ensuing slaughter is described in graphic detail in the final section, "The Madman and the Book." Shmuel passes the *Pinkas* on to Azriel, asking his son to be their witness. Before escaping, Azriel sees the Christians, driven mad by blood lust, turn against one another. He also sees Yancsi, who has returned in time to die. Azriel is the only survivor of Kolvillàg. *The Oath* ends with the young man assuming the memory of Kolvillàg.

The Characters

Azriel's motivations are complex. By giving him the *Pinkas*, Shmuel hands his son the values of memory, tradition, language, and community. Azriel increasingly respects these values as he grows older, but he is burdened by his duty to Kolvillàg, saying that the oath "ties me to a destiny that is not mine." He has become more a symbol than a human being: "My life does not belong to me. . . . All I can call my own is a forbidden city I must rebuild each day, only to watch it end in horror each night."

Moshe chooses silence and death, and, in abiding by Moshe's oath, Azriel is living a form of death even as Kolvillàg lives in him. In deciding to break the oath, he gives life to the suicidal young man and preserves the memory of his village. Azriel says that he is afraid only of indifference, and his story releases the young man from indifference to life: "Azriel knocked down the walls I had erected around myself. . . . By allowing me to enter his life, he gave meaning to mine."

Azriel may be the protagonist of *The Oath*, but the story is dominated by the mysterious and unpredictable Moshe, who responds to the indifference of man and God with silence and to sympathy with laughter. According to

Moshe, God understands silence; man does not. Silence bypasses man for a direct relationship with God. For the Jews of Kolvillàg, Moshe personifies "the combined virtues of the sage, the prince and the visionary."

Moshe is the opposite of his friend Shmuel, because he is concerned with eternity rather than history. He longs to transcend the world rather than transform it (as Azriel wants to do during a brief period as a revolutionary). Moshe is most significant for his effect on others, especially Azriel: "Thanks to him, like him, I fell under the spell of the inaccessible. . . . I aspired to trace new paths. I hoped to influence destiny." Through the oath, Moshe creates Azriel's destiny.

Themes and Meanings

The Oath examines conflicts between good and evil, man and God, destiny and human will. While depicting the ugliness and absurdity of death, it also shows how death creates a burden for the survivor: "Your contracts with the dead, the dead take with them, too late to cancel or modify their terms. They leave you no way out." Moshe chooses death, the young man contemplates it, but Azriel has seen too much of it. To save the young man is to sustain hope.

Moshe justifies the oath of silence by saying, "Man has only one story to tell, though he tells it in a thousand different ways: tortures, persecutions, manhunts, ritual murders, mass terror." Elie Wiesel clearly disagrees, for *The Oath*, despite its horrifying subject, is a celebration of the art and tradition of storytelling. Azriel even begins his story "Once upon a time, . . ." Both Azriel and Wiesel are concerned with turning history into legend. Wiesel is vague about the time and place because his story could be set anywhere at any time; the name Kolvillàg comes from the Hebrew *kol*, meaning every, and the Hungarian *villàg*, meaning village.

By juxtaposing stories from the *Pinkas*, Azriel's accounts of his life, Moshe, and the pogrom, stories told by Moshe, and the young man's commentary on all this, Wiesel emphasizes the need for memory, conscience, and imagination. The magical effect of storytelling is shown when the young man is transformed into a survivor. The narrative does not truly end, since it will change and grow as it becomes part of the young man's life and will continue to be altered as he passes it on, becoming more mythical with the passage of time.

Critical Context

Elie Wiesel was born and reared in an Orthodox Jewish community in a village in Transylvania. In 1944, he and his family were deported to the concentration camp at Auschwitz. Although Wiesel survived Auschwitz and Buchenwald, his father, mother, and younger sister did not. Liberated in 1945, he chose to go to France. In 1958, he published a memoir of the Holocaust,

La Nuit (1958; *Night*, 1960), sometimes described as a novella, although Wiesel himself has said that it is not a work of fiction. Since that time, Wiesel has published more than two dozen books, both fiction and nonfiction, all of which directly or indirectly reflect on the Holocaust. In 1986, he was awarded the Nobel Peace Prize.

Wiesel's preoccupation with the Holocaust and its meaning for humanity gives his work an exceptional intensity and unity. The theme of silence, for example, so central to *The Oath*, is prominent throughout Wiesel's work. In particular, his earlier novel *La Ville de la chance* (1962; *The Town Beyond the Wall*, 1964) should be read with *The Oath*. Both books, while acknowledging the claims of silence, ultimately affirm the responsibility to speak.

Also noteworthy in *The Oath* is the role of Moshe, a recurring character in Wiesel's works. Mystic and madman, he represents an essential dimension of human experience—one which needs to be balanced by rational discourse but which, if repressed, will resurface in a destructive form.

Sources for Further Study
Berenbaum, Michael. *The Vision of the Void: Theological Reflections on the Works of Elie Wiesel*, 1979.
Brown, Robert McAfee. *Elie Wiesel: Messenger to All Humanity*, 1983.
Estess, Ted L. *Elie Wiesel*, 1980.
Fine, Ellen S. *Legacy of Night: The Literary Universe of Elie Wiesel*, 1982.

Michael Adams

THE OGRE

Author: Michel Tournier (1924-   )
Type of plot: Philosophical realism and fabulation
Time of plot: The late 1930's and early 1940's
Locale: A French provincial city, the border on the Rhine, and East Prussia
First published: Le Roi des aulnes, 1970 (English translation, 1972)

> *Principal characters:*
> ABEL TIFFAUGES, a garage mechanic of gigantic stature
> NESTOR, his protector and mentor during his school days
> HERMANN GOERING, the Nazi field marshal
> STEFAN RAUFEISEN, an SS commander
> GENERAL COUNT VON KALTENBORN, an aristocrat
> EPHRAIM, a Jewish youth

The Novel

Michel Tournier's *The Ogre* is an unsettling work that relies on a range of narrative strategies to achieve its effects. Notable among these is the alternation between first- and third-person narration. The book opens with the "Sinister Writings" of the protagonist, Abel Tiffauges, a first-person narration, switches in sections 2 through 4 to a nonobjective third person, and in sections 5 and 6 alternates between first and third person. The very opening of the work is intended to shock:

> *January 3, 1938*: You're an ogre, Rachel used to say to me sometimes. An ogre? A fabulous monster emerging from the mists of time? Well, yes, I do think there's something magical about me, I do think there's a secret collusion, deep down, connecting what happens to me with what happens in general, and enabling my particular history to bend the course of things in its own direction.

This secret connection between events in the world at large and the workings of Abel's inner psychology is established through his journal, but then it continues even in the presentation of the third-person narration. This equation of the protagonist's psyche with the scale of world events makes for an unusual mix of conventional realistic description and fabulation.

Tournier's Abel is both an avatar of his namesake and a type of his patron saint, Saint Christopher. Misshapen and of gigantic proportions, Abel's fate will be to search for the most powerful master to serve. As the word "Christopher" comes from "Christ" and *phoria* (to carry), so Abel will find his vocation in *phoria* or carrying. As Abel's strange musings begin, he is trapped in an unsatisfying job as a garage mechanic. He has been judged unfit as a lover by his girlfriend Rachel because he cares too much for his own pleasure. Through Abel's own words, the reader learns that Abel eats raw meat, washes his head in the toilet, and bellows like an animal to maintain his sense of well-being. His first glimpse of his vocation for *phoria* comes when he lifts the wounded body of a young boy, Jeannot, who has been injured in the garage. This revelation leads Abel to seek out children whom he may carry and also to his practice of photographing and recording young children. His freedom to follow these instincts seems to come to an end when he is wrongly charged with the rape of a young girl, Martine. Yet here again, his fate acts to determine the course of world events.

While the external account of Abel's life seems to lead only to grim and rather tawdry experiences, his inner musings are what truly motivate the plot. It is Abel who philosophizes on his vocation of *phoria*, at the same time rewriting the book of Genesis to suit his beliefs. Nevertheless, it is the memory of his school friend, Nestor, that convinces Abel of his unique fate and place in society. Nestor was the obese child tyrant at the boarding school where Abel was reared. Of the many adventures on which Abel reflects, the central one is when Nestor carries the already oversized young Abel on his shoulders in a schoolyard game of horse and rider, defeating all the other boys combined. From then on, their bond is sealed. On a brief furlough at home awaiting the school's disciplinary action, young Abel has the fervent wish that the school should burn down. It does, and Nestor coincidentally perishes in the blaze. Awaiting trial years later for rape, Abel's destiny once more causes an incendiary outbreak, the beginning of World War II. Abel is instantly released and conscripted into the army, where his adult adventures begin.

Abel's freedom paradoxically increases immeasurably amid the constrictions of army life. Assigned to the communications sector, he is soon roaming the French countryside requisitioning pigeons for army communications. Captured by the Germans in the first series of engagements, Abel is sent with his fellow prisoners east to the bleak plains of East Prussia. Here as well, paradox is at work, and Abel's freedom actually increases. While his fellow prisoners toil miserably, Abel enjoys unofficial leaves in a deserted hunting lodge and entertains the visits of a blind elk (as oversized and misshapen as Abel). A forester discovers Abel, and before long, he is transferred to the service of the grand ogre of the region, Field Marshall Hermann Goering, at Goering's mythically inspired hunting lodge and domain. In Goering's service, Abel feels the strange atavistic pull that was at the center of Nazism, though at the lodge the prize is the stag hunt and the genetic experiments are on animals.

Through another twist, Abel is transferred at last to a Nazi elite youth training center, housed in an elaborate medieval castle. Here the SS commander, Stefan Raufeisen, trains the youths to be Nazi soldiers with the help of the titular head of the establishment and ancestral heir to the castle, the General Count von Kaltenborn. At first, Abel is in charge of provisions for the boys, who are between sixteen and eighteen years old. When the boys are mobilized and sent to the front, Abel quickly becomes the provider of young boys to replace those departed. In this role, mounted on his horse Bluebeard, Abel becomes the feared Ogre of Kaltenborn, the incarnation of Johann Wolfgang von Goethe's Erl-King, who in the poem of that title steals young children away from their parents. Yet once again, because the reader is privy to Abel's thoughts, there is a strange sympathy for his seeking out and subsequent attachment to these boys.

As the war moves toward its bloody conclusion, the leaders leave for the front, and Abel is left in charge of the castle. With the youths armed to defend the homeland, Abel, as it were, discovers for the first time the horrors of war. Various weapons backfire and explode, killing some of his young charges, and Abel receives a baptism of blood. He also discovers a young Jewish boy left for dead by soldiers leading a forced march from the death camps to the interior. The star-bearing child, Ephraim, is nursed back to health by Abel and in turn educates the protagonist about the dark underside of the war and the camp at Auschwitz. The book ends as the Russians overrun the castle of Kaltenborn. Abel fulfills his destiny as "astrophore," or star-bearer, by carrying the star-child away from the castle on his shoulders. When the reader last sees Abel, he is sinking into the alder marshes while gazing up at Ephraim.

The Characters

The protagonist of *The Ogre*, Abel, is also the lens through which the reader sees many of the book's key themes and events. A third of the novel is written in a first-person journal style in which Abel reflects in an eclectic manner on the significance of life and its symbolism. Abel gives the reader the key terms, such as *phoria*, around which the action of the novel turns. He is not only the novel's main character; he is also its first interpreter.

Through Abel's description, the reader sees the events of his childhood in boarding school and his central relationship with Nestor. Abel also tells of the events which lead to his arrest for the rape of the young girl Martine. In fact, were it not for the novel's major assertion that Abel's inner life operates on the course of world events, Abel would be a perfect example of the unreliable narrator. In the conventional novel, for example, the reader would be left wondering if he had raped Martine or not. As it is, the reader is forced to suspend disbelief and question instead the historiographical record of the time.

The central paradox of the novel is that Abel during peacetime is a societal misfit, whereas during the war, he can do no wrong. Although society is ready to put him in jail for pedophilia in normal times, in time of war, he is rewarded for his ability to track down young boys for the war machine. All the while, Abel's inner musings keep the reader off balance, because of their combination of weirdly obsessive logic and naïvely perceptive insight. The character who eats raw meat and covets the soft flesh of children is also the character who sets the model for the positive introspective values portrayed in the work.

All the other characters in the work serve primarily as foils for Abel's inner development, which is also the springboard for his destiny. His girlfriend Rachel first calls him an ogre. His childhood mentor and protector, Nestor, gives Abel a key insight into his vocation of *phoria*. Nestor is also an early model for the ogre and tyrant which Abel's wartime experience will multiply. The portrait of Hermann Goering is that of one of the central ogre figures in the novel. An opium addict with a fetish for the hunt and an insatiable appetite for physical pleasure, Goering is a mythomaniacal figure who makes Abel's ogreish tendencies seem benign. The SS commander Stefan Raufeisen is an important character because his flashbacks to his early life help to show the development of the Nazi mentality. The General Count von Kaltenborn, on the other hand, is a throwback to the old days of the aristocracy. He is Abel's main guide for interpreting the twisted symbols of the Third Reich and shows him how they point to ultimate catastrophe. The Jewish child Ephraim is the culminating link in the chain of child characters throughout the book. He also opens Abel's eyes to the reality of Nazi atrocities and is finally important as the symbolic star-child who fulfills Abel's vocation for carrying the heavens.

Themes and Meanings

With the dominant subjects of *The Ogre* being war and childhood, it is clear that Tournier's most important theme is the perversion of youthful drives and energies in the pursuit of geopolitical ends, particularly war. The way that he communicates this message is through the repeated use of paradox. That the protagonist is viewed as a marginal criminal during peacetime because of his pedophilia and is rewarded and given responsibility over children during war is one paradox. That he has more freedom within the constrictions of the army and as a prisoner of war is another. Throughout the work, Abel's strange pursuit of child-carrying, his interest in genetic features, and his attraction to atavism remain almost innocent. As he enters into the truly perverted world of Nazi leaders and doctors, Abel finds a dark mirror-world of his own obsessions.

A positive theme running counter to the theme of death and degradation in war is the unusual concept of *phoria*, or carrying. This theme shares in Tournier's well-known interest in proposing viable models of nongenital sexuality. In this view, the full range of bodily pleasure one may experience, practically from birth, is hampered by the societal imperative to procreation within marriage, which leaves genitally organized sex the only acceptable form of sexual pleasure. Here again, paradox is at work. Abel is viewed as a criminal by society because of his interest in children and child-carrying, but the course of the novel shows that society's own global perversions, war and the lust for power, are far more destructive to children.

One of Tournier's unique contributions is his framing of the narrative so that the protagonist is an active interpreter of symbols and events in the story. In this way, the reader is led through the strange and disturbing events of the story with an almost childlike innocence. Many things that normally appear disturbing thus seem benign, and the accepted views become disturbing. Tournier deliberately challenges the reader's preconceptions and urges him or her to think first before judging.

Critical Context

The Ogre is Michel Tournier's second novel, published after the award-winning *Vendredi: Ou, Les Limbes du Pacifique* (1967, 1972; *Friday*, 1969). *Friday* is the retelling of the Robinson Crusoe story from the perspective of Crusoe's manservant Friday and—like *The Ogre*—explores issues of social conditioning and sexuality in a mix of narrative strategies, including fabulation. *The Ogre* was awarded the prestigious Prix Goncourt for 1970 and solidly established Tournier as one of the leading writers of his generation in France. He has published several more novels and collections of stories, as well as some children's books.

The Ogre is an important work in many respects. Its innovative narrative goes beyond the often sterile manipulations of the New Novel practitioners in a way that has come to be seen as postmodern. The sympathetic stance for the experience of World War II on German soil is unusual for a French writer and demonstrates a generational break with the immediate postwar writers. *The Ogre* is, moreover, one of those epoch-defining works, such as Günter Grass's *Die Blechtrommel* (1959; *The Tin Drum*, 1961), which uses oneiric action and fabulous narrative to bring new understanding to the still-incomprehensible mysteries of Nazi barbarism.

Sources for Further Study

Cloonan, William. *Michel Tournier*, 1985.

Ellmann, Mary. "Recent Novels: *The Ogre*," in *The Yale Review*. LXII (March, 1973), pp. 465-467.

Engel, Marian. "*The Ogre*," in *The New York Times Book Review*. LXVII (September 3, 1972), pp. 7, 14.

Miller, Karl. "The Cyclopean Eye of the European Phallus: *G.* by John Berger, *The Ogre* by Michel Tournier," in *The New York Review of Books*. XIX (November 30, 1972), pp. 40-43.

Redfern, W. D. "Approximating Man: Michel Tournier and Play in Language," in *Modern Language Review*. LXXX (1985), pp. 304-319.

Peter Baker

OKTIABR SHESTNADTSATOGO

Author: Aleksandr Solzhenitsyn (1918-   )
Type of plot: Historical fiction
Time of plot: August through early November of 1918
Locale: Moscow, St. Petersburg, the Byelorussian and Ukrainian countryside, and Zurich
First published: 1984

> *Principal characters:*
>   GEORGII MIKHALYCH VOROTYNTSEV, a dedicated army career officer
>   ALINA, Vorotyntsev's wife, who is developing as a concert pianist while separated from her husband by the war
>   OLDA ORESTOVNA (PROFESSOR ANDOZERSKAYA), the lover and would-be mentor of Vorotyntsev, a scholar of history
>   ISAAKII LAZHENITSYN (SANYA), an idealistic young man who dropped out of the university to volunteer for the army
>   ARSENII BLAGODARYOV (SENKA), a natural leader in peacetime, serving as a soldier under Vorotyntsev
>   VLADIMIR ILICH LENIN, an aging, unpopular, would-be revolutionary, living in exile in Zurich
>   NICHOLAS II, the czar, a moody, stubborn man who is excessively dependent on his wife
>   FATHER SEVERYAN, an embodiment of the Russian Orthodox church in an age when religion has become unfashionable

The Novel

Oktiabr shestnadtsatogo (October 1916) seeks to re-create the processes that led to the 1917 overthrow of the czarist regime. Beneath the chaos, lines of fate are running to conjoin in a disaster, a universal pogrom of Russia itself. Competing groups, pursuing opposite goals, unwittingly work toward the same end. Once the chariot of revolution has begun to roll, like a runaway train, it cannot be stopped.

On the Byelorussian front, it has become clear to Colonel Georgii Vorotyntsev that Russia's continued participation in the Great War will destroy her, regardless of who wins. Vorotyntsev takes a brief leave from the battlefront with the desperate objective of presenting his views to Aleksandr Guchkov, who as Secretary of the Duma (parliament) appears to be Russia's most courageous statesman. On his way to see Guchkov in St. Petersburg, Vorotyntsev stops overnight in Moscow to visit his long-neglected wife, Alina. He placates her with a solemn promise to see her again on his way back (in less than two weeks), on her birthday. There is a tacit feeling that the continuation of their marriage will depend upon his keeping this promise.

In St. Petersburg, however, Vorotyntsev is immediately distracted from the purpose of his journey by a fascinating woman, Olda Orestovna (Professor Andozerskaya). The "wooden" soldier sinks into a lush new world of sensual eroticism and while away his entire leave. Vorotyntsev meets the elusive Guchkov only on his last day in St. Petersburg, and then quite by chance (although this meeting may have been arranged by Guchkov, for whom Vorotyntsev has been leaving messages).

Guchkov is seriously contemplating a coup, preferably bloodless. All he needs is a handful of officers to take over the General Staff headquarters at a moment when the henpecked czar, Nicholas II, is bivouacked there. Vorotyntsev, whom Guchkov has visualized as exactly the kind of iron-willed man who is needed, is unable to participate, however, because he does not dare to miss his wife's birthday. Thus the coup is postponed. More important, Vorotyntsev is unable to make even Guchkov, Russia's most enlightened politician, understand the danger that underlies all of their fates: The war is destroying Russia. When Czar Nicholas is finally overthrown by a broad coalition of the Russian intelligentsia, it will be in large part because of rumors that the czar himself was moving toward a separate peace with Germany.

Meanwhile, the much-proclaimed endurance of the Russian people has been sapped by the incessant call-ups of useless recruits, uselessly dying, which depopulates and demoralizes the countryside. This side of Russia, invisible to the urban populace, appears very early in the novel and is personified in the good soldier, Arsenii Blagodaryov (Senka).

Just at the moment that Senka becomes eligible for home leave, the high command denies all leaves for soldiers (timing this prohibition to coincide with the harvest is typical of the regime, which also exempts the politically radical proletariat, largely employed in war-related industry, from military service). A young officer, Isaakii Lazhenitsyn (Sanya)—himself of peasant stock—tries to get Senka a special leave. As the novel's focus shifts to Vorotyntsev's travels, Senka's leave is still pending. He is left behind as a somewhat pathetic figure: homesick for the farm and getting worried about his wife.

Midway through, when the novel's wheel completes its first revolution, Senka reenters, but now he is seen from a strikingly different perspective— as the backbone of a peasant family and a pillar of his community coming home to a warm celebration.

There appears, however, to be a problem with his wife, Katyona. When they are alone, she asks him to beat her. Senka assumes that she is asking to be punished for infidelity, and he complies. In fact, she is acting out an erotic fantasy that she nourished during his long absence. When she finally makes him understand that she is innocent and only wanted to "feel his will," he remorsefully carries her "like a child." This last gesture completes her fantasy: It was something for which she could not ask, but now she is content.

In a parallel scene, though under more refined and gentle circumstances, Vorotyntsev's lover has induced him to rock and swing her, like a child. When these two very different couples are shown in consecutive scenes, the Professoress (in bed) expounds her dazzling theories of Russian history and the need for a czar; down on the farm, Katyona keeps up a stream of chatter about the field in which she is a recognized authority: geese.

Encompassing the novel as a whole, a bigger circle is drawn which begins and ends with the Russian church, as embodied in Father Severyan, an anomalous figure in an age of unbelief. Sanya first meets Severyan on a painful night of doubt and disgust. Even Tolstoyanism is failing him. Severyan willingly polemicizes with the young officer. According to the priest's novel theory of war and peace, in which Sanya is able to find some comfort, the sum total of evil impulses in the world is always the same. War channels most of the evil of a country into a single direction: Therefore war is not the worst form of evil. In fact, "the dilemma of peace/war is the superficial dilemma of superficial minds."

When another priest, Father Alonius, appears at the end of the novel, it is in a similar role. In a running subplot (also counterpointing the Vorotyntsev-Andozerskaya affair), a bright, precocious, eccentric young woman, Zinaida Rumnitskaya, has played out the seamier side of the adultery poeticized by the Professoress. Zinaida saves her sanity by confessing to Alonius, putting herself in the worst possible light. The comfort that Alonius offers to this inconsolable woman is biblical, and closes the novel: "Who can tell another: 'Do this, but don't do that.' Who can order you not to love, when Christ said: There is nothing higher than love. And He did not exclude any love—any kind of love at all."

While personal relationships are life's most serious business, considerable humor is added to the novel by the events of history: The minutes of the Duma, quoted verbatim in separate chapters, are a tragicomedy; the internal monologues of the czar and czarina provide macabre humor when they reverently touch upon "Our Friend" (that is, Grigory Rasputin); and sustained irony is created by the mere recitation of the words and deeds of Vladimir Ilich Lenin. Convinced that the Russians are too meek to revolt, Lenin pins his hopes on a Marxist revolution in Switzerland. His tiny group of rebels calls itself "the Bowling Club," as if overturning governments were like knocking down tenpins.

Once a mass movement begins, however, Lenin, like a boy with a toy train, is confident that he alone knows how to drive it: "to brake on those turns in time, sometimes steering left, and sometimes right, foreseeing up ahead where the twisting road of revolution threatened to plunge."

The Characters

Following the classical Russian tradition, Aleksandr Solzhenitsyn's chief protagonist, Georgii Vorotyntsev, is a good man, but he is an antihero rather than a positive hero because of his flaws and weaknesses and ultimate inability to control events. Also in the Russian tradition, however, the hero's weaknesses can be interpreted as the obverse of his moral goodness and potential for growth. All the major characters are put through a forced growth of spirit and personality. After unquestioningly accepting the rather strange Professor Andozerskaya's sudden passion for him, Vorotyntsev blissfully assumes that he now has two adoring women granted to him by a generous fate: his uncomplaining wife, Alina, and the exciting Professoress.

Vorotyntsev is forced to metamorphose when he finds that his wife is shattered by this, his first infidelity after ten years of marriage. In helping Alina to put her mind back together, Vorotyntsev is further distracted from playing his role in history. (That a part in the revolution is still ahead of him, though, is hinted at by his name, which is from the root word meaning "turn.")

Katyona, who comes closest to being one of the novel's positive heroines, regards the marriage bond as being supremely important in her life. Yet her perception does not relegate her to an inferior status: Solzhenitsyn's male characters are also at their most positive and human when they appreciate the same bond. Solzhenitsyn painstakingly evokes a woman's world of exquisite, small cares and beauties—created out of love with little money. While this world is the opposite of the masculine one, it is equally important: The novel's male protagonists misprize it at their peril.

Among the characters with a nonfictional basis, Czar Nicholas and Lenin are the most fully developed. Nicholas II's saving grace, in this novel as in history, is his dedication to being a good father and husband. For all of his foolishness, Nicholas slowly acquires a certain moral stature as the novel progresses. Although the ultimate antihero, as a private human being the czar takes his place among the novel's positive characters.

Applying the same litmus test to Lenin, Solzhenitsyn finds him badly lacking. Lenin is an appalling husband, whose wife, Nadya, is a victim with no basis for moral revolt, being herself an unprincipled revolutionary. They take vacations *à trois* with Lenin's mistress, Inessa. While having no respect for his devoted Nadya, Lenin masochistically humbles himself before his capricious Inessa because "there is no humiliation, before her."

Solzhenitsyn shows all of his major characters both in a process of growth and in-the-round. The two contrasting spheres in which they move are the masculine-dominated, outer world of action and the woman-controlled, private world of feeling.

Themes and Meanings

Krasnoe koleso (*The Red Wheel*), the trilogy of which *Oktiabr shestnad-*

tsatogo is the second part or "knot," is a highly thematic work. Solzhenitsyn underscores his themes by developing them in contrasting contexts and from contrasting viewpoints. A major theme is derived from the age-old folk wisdom that disorder in the family will inevitably bring about disorder in the state. Like Boris Pasternak, and his and Pasternak's common predecessor, Leo Tolstoy, Solzhenitsyn uses the capacious form of the Russian novel to bind history to the spontaneous acts of private individuals. In a sense, all three of these great Russian novelists have used the historical novel to produce "antihistory." The academic and journalistic abstraction of history is shown to be meaningless: The organic process of events is best reflected by a complex art that is itself like a process of nature.

The process of revolution is very aptly symbolized by a wheel, which runs over people's lives and, having reached a certain momentum, cannot be stopped. The wheel is red, not only because of the Bolshevik associations but also because it is on fire (the symbol of destruction, passion, and pain). The hesitant conspirator, Vorotyntsev, watches a patriotic fireworks display in the shape of a wheel with the national colors:

> The silver grew thin, then the blue, and both went out; but not the all-embracing red: It spun and spun on the rim in a solid mass. Red. Scarlet. Ox-blood. Fiery. Then it crumpled, scattering sparks.

The wheels of a vast clockworks spin invisibly, generating the "vibrating minutes" of time itself.

Alina, Vorotyntsev's pianist wife, highlights the subtheme of music. The movement of events, like music, is circular. Similar events are repeated, but in different keys. Similar ideas are picked up by one mind after another, but in different styles, at different speeds. As in classical music, Solzhenitsyn's motifs always come full circle: Their meaning is realized upon their reemergence, after numerous modulations through the entire scale. Music reflects the rhythm of reality.

Solzhenitsyn presents a complexly interconnected world, one in which politics, religious conflicts, futuristic technology, and the experiments of intellectuals playing at conspiracy all contribute to the catastrophe of 1917. Indeed, if even one element had been missing, Solzhenitsyn implies, that most extraordinary revolution could not have taken place. Hence very limited personal action can indeed affect history; the "rub" is that in history's orchestra, the pressure on the individual to repeat the most deafening motifs is overwhelming.

Critical Context

Like his major novels of the 1960's, *V kruge pervom* (1968; *The First Circle*, 1968) and *Rakovy korpus* (1968; *Cancer Ward*, 1968), Solzhenitsyn's trilogy *The Red Wheel* aims for a universalist depiction of society. The settings for his previous works—the vast Soviet prison system and a large hospital— were natural grids for capturing a broad cross section of Soviet society, drawn from every region and every class. Life offered this vast range to Solzhenitsyn (who certainly did not volunteer to live in such settings), and the earlier novels are autobiographical. The events of *The Red Wheel* predate both Solzhenitsyn's personal experience and the Soviet system. Re-creating pre-Soviet Russia in the round is an important stage in Solzhenitsyn's moral and aesthetic reclamation of a country and its language and culture that he perceives as tragically despoiled.

From the parallels to be drawn with Fyodor Dostoevski's prison memoirs to the polemics with Tolstoy in *Oktiabr shestnadtsatogo*, Solzhenitsyn's work has always demanded comparison with that of his great predecessors. In *Oktiabr shestnadtsatogo*, different classical authors form part of the consciousness of several key characters. The Professoress (Olda Andozerskaya) is a passionate proponent of Dostoevski; she is also an antiheroine, however, whose enthusiasms may be questionable. Sanya, naïve but earnest, moves from committed Tolstoyanism to total disillusionment with everything for which Tolstoy stood. The luckless Zinaida seduces a married man whom she describes only as looking "Chekhovian" (for a girl of the time, irresistible).

Solzhenitsyn warmly endorsed Dostoevski's vision in his Nobel Prize speech. The primacy of moral issues in Solzhenitsyn's writing puts him in the tradition of Dostoevski; so does the open, impassioned polemicizing of Solzhenitsyn's characters. While Tolstoy appears increasingly rejected as Solzhenitsyn's intellectual forebear, however, Tolstoy's approach as a novelist can be very strongly felt in Solzhenitsyn's grappling with man and nature, peace and war. Like Tolstoy, Solzhenitsyn wishes to have his characters trodding firmly on the earth and fully illuminated in strong, natural light. Dostoevski's intellectual openness is continued, but not his love of the shadows and the eerie suggestiveness of only partial illumination. When Solzhenitsyn's evil genius, Lenin, is fully lit up, his mystique vanishes: Seen from all sides, the menace is ultimately comical.

In *Oktiabr shestnadtsatogo*, far more than in *Avgust chetyrnadtsatogo* (1971, revised 1983; *August 1914*, 1971), the preceding volume of the trilogy, the authority whose wit and wisdom Solzhenitsyn quotes most often is not literary at all. By far the most conspicuous outside "source" consists of popular sayings and proverbs, representing the voice of the people. Solzhenitsyn sets these apart, as if each sagacious utterance of the people were worth a whole chapter-full of its own. He thereby affirms the Russian language and all of its creators as his most important source.

Sources for Further Study
Burg, David, and George Feifer. *Solzhenitsyn*, 1972.

Kodjak, Andrej. *Alexander Solzhenitsyn*, 1978.
Krasnov, Vladislav. *Solzhenitsyn and Dostoevsky: A Study in the Polyphonic Novel*, 1980.
Moody, Christopher. *Solzhenitsyn*, 1976.
Scammell, Michael. *Solzhenitsyn: A Biography*, 1984.

D. Gosselin Nakeeb

THE OLD MAN

Author: Yury Trifonov (1925-1981)
Type of plot: Psychological realism
Time of plot: 1973, with flashbacks beginning in 1917
Locale: Russia
First published: Starik, 1978 (English translation, 1984)

> *Principal characters:*
> PAVEL EVGRAFOVICH LETUNOV, the old man and protagonist
> SERGEI KIRILOVICH MIGULIN, a hero of the Russian
>   Revolution, later proclaimed a traitor
> ASYA, Migulin's wife and Pavel's childhood friend
> VLADIMIR (VOLODYA), Asya's cousin and first husband, also
>   Pavel's childhood friend
> SHURA, Pavel's uncle
> VERA, Pavel's daughter
> RUSLAN (RUSKA), Pavel's son
> OLEG VASILEVICH KANDAUROV, a government executive vying
>   for the same *dacha* (summerhouse) that Pavel's children
>   want

The Novel

While the thrust of Yury Trifonov's plot in *The Old Man* concerns Pavel Letunov's recollections of certain events during and after the Russian Revolution of 1917, there is a complementary subplot in which Pavel is at odds with his own family regarding the acquisition of a *dacha*. It is 1973, and Pavel, the old man of the title, is spending the summer at his *dacha* near Moscow. He receives a letter from an old friend, Asya, which triggers his memories of the impetuous and violent days of the Russian Revolution and the civil war that followed.

Through kaleidoscopic digression, Pavel reconstructs the events which led him, Asya, and her cousin Volodya to join the Bolsheviks, who eventually were to seize power and set Russia into a frenzied spin culminating in the bloody civil war. It was during the civil war that Sergei Migulin, a prominent revolutionary leader and hero, became the vortex of events embroiling Pavel and Asya, then Migulin's wife; although a respected hero, Migulin was labeled a traitor and executed. Asya's letter, years later, compels Pavel to search his memory to find the "truth" regarding Migulin's trial and execution.

Pavel's quest for the truth of these events leads him to other "truths" as well. His search for the ultimate truth becomes the leitmotif of the novel: What is truth? Is there a generic truth? Does truth exist a priori or a posteriori? Is truth based on ideology, or is it situational, depending on specific times and places?

In his youth, Pavel was infatuated with Asya and vied for her attention even though he was too young to warrant her notice as anything other than a good friend. Pavel, Asya, and Volodya were inseparable before and after the Revolution. Together they roamed the streets of Petrograd, caught up in the excitement of the Revolution: the protests, marches, proclamations, and meetings. The ideals of Pavel's romantic revolutionary uncle Shura and of his activist mother stirred them. Those were heady times, but the memory of Migulin overshadows Pavel's reflections.

Migulin was viewed as a counterrevolutionary and declared an outlaw and a traitor for disobeying orders. He was condemned and sentenced to death. Although the sentence was repealed, he was later executed.

In his youth, Pavel supported Migulin out of loyalty to the Revolution and to Asya. Yet as secretary of the revolutionary tribunal which condemned Migulin, Pavel admitted that Migulin had led his men to the southern front although he had been ordered not to undertake such an action, thereby admitting that said action was counterrevolutionary and treasonous in time of war. Thus, Pavel helped condemn Migulin to death. Did he feel justified in doing so because Migulin had won Asya's love? In order to redeem himself, Pavel later wrote a favorable article restoring Migulin to his historical role as a revolutionary hero.

Fifty years later Pavel receives a letter from Asya. He visits her and asks why Migulin led the march to the southern front in 1919. Her answer reveals the "truth" as she knows it, or, more important, as it matters to her: She never loved anyone as much as she loved Migulin; all the other "facts" about him are long forgotten.

The subplot of the novel centers on the acquisition of a *dacha* that belonged to a woman who had no heirs at the time of her death. Pavel is irked by the way his daughter Vera and son Ruslan have become wrapped up in their quest for material gain. Their lives seem to revolve around the competition to get the summerhouse, which they think will make them happy— the answer to all of their problems. Their continual hounding of Pavel to use his influence as a venerable member of the Communist Party to help them win ownership of the *dacha* drives him to escape deeper into his recollections of a time when one's concerns were of consequence. Pavel's memory serves not only as an escape valve but also as a search for the truth behind others' and his own actions.

Oleg Kandaurov, the principal rival for ownership of the contested *dacha*, is a cynical and amoral pragmatist whose selfish motives define his "truth." Eventually he succumbs to an illness and is forced out of the competition despite his manipulations. As an ironic Chekhovian denouement, the government requisitions the land that the cluster of *dachas* occupies in order to build a residence for government workers. All of Pavel's family's and Kandaurov's efforts have come to nothing.

Although Pavel mourns the lost years and time wasted, he rejoices in a life well lived, rich in experiences, and in the fact that he has survived, in spite of his trials. A graduate student, writing his dissertation on the Migulin affair, interviews Pavel and realizes that the latter conveniently forgot about his role in condemning Migulin, which, in a sense, illustrates that truth and belief are so closely related as to be difficult to distinguish one from the other.

The Characters

For the most part, the characters in *The Old Man* are personifications of various shades of "truth," that is truth as each one sees or perceives it. Thus Shura, Pavel's uncle, is not blinded by Bolshevik ideology but searches for the ultimate truth of his conscience by refusing to participate in the kangaroo court deliberating Migulin's fate. In contrast, Bychin, a minor character, lets revenge color his truth in his dealings with counterrevolutionaries. Kandaurov's truth is pragmatism, self-aggrandizement, and unequivocal cynicism. Others, such as Volodya, have misconstrued ideology as the real truth, thus making the ends justify the means.

All forms of truth are rationalizations—a mental game. One form of truth, however, is based on feelings and intuition. It is interesting to note that Yury Trifonov, like Boris Pasternak before him in *Doktor Zhivago* (1957; *Dr. Zhivago*, 1958), imbues his female characters with a "female" intuition or sixth sense which transcends "male" logic and sees truth through the medium of feelings. After all that has happened, it is love that has sustained Asya and that is all that counts, no matter what the deductive reasoning regarding Migulin's innocence or guilt may be. In another case, Asya's mother, whose family has been all but decimated by the Revolution and the civil war, finds no comfort or solace in such "logical" platitudes for the cause of her distress as "historical necessity," for they do not alleviate her pain and anguish. Her truth is the experience of bitterness and resentment. Thus truth is not to be found in documents or accounts, either actual or distorted, for these sources render only part of the total truth; not to include the feelings of all the participants leads to a perverted truth.

Themes and Meanings

The story is a kaleidoscopic journey through the mind of Pavel, whose memory shuttles back and forth not unlike Marcel Proust's in *À la recherche du temps perdu* (1913-1927; *Remembrance of Things Past*, 1922-1931), with the senses evoking a series of emotions which trigger memories of seemingly forgotten events. In recapturing an ideological and fervent past, Pavel reveals a drab present with decaying morals.

For all of its faults, the older generation—the generation of the Migulins and Shuras—was vibrant, and people were busy being alive and trying to stay alive in order to create a new and better society. The new generation, however, is materialistic and morally corrupt, as portrayed by Pavel's children, who agonize over such mundane decisions as securing a summerhouse, and by Kandaurov, whose proclivity for the amoral and cynical reminds one of Fyodor Dostoevski's Svidrigailov in *Prestupleniye i nakazaniye* (1866; *Crime and Punishment*, 1886). There is little left of ideology, the driving force in the early days of the Soviet Union. Instead, complacency and banal materialism set in. The hunger for ideals has been satisfied by burying it in the weighty folds of deliberate forgetfulness. It is precisely for this reason that Pavel sets out on his quest for truth, his Holy Grail: By concentrating on a particular historical incident—the Migulin affair—he slowly exposes Soviet history to scrutiny. The microcosm of Pavel's mind is a reflection of the Soviet society at large, for to understand the present one must dig up the past, the ensuing "dirt" notwithstanding. Thus, the Soviet Union must clean its Augean stables if it wants to refresh and reinvigorate its "true" ideology and moral premises.

Critical Context

In *The Old Man*, Trifonov elaborates on the general theme of his earlier works, in which his characters reflect the gradual loss of idealism in modern Soviet society. Included in this group are *Dom na naberezhnoi* (1976; *The House on the Embankment*, 1983), *Utolenie zhazhdy* (1963; the quenching of thirst), and his trilogy: *Obmen* (1969; *The Exchange*, 1973), *Prevaritalnye itogi* (1970; *Taking Stock*, 1978), and *Dolgoe proshchanie* (1971; *The Long Goodbye*, 1978). What was once a revolutionary, vibrant world has gradually acquiesced to the bromides of conformity, self-satisfied commonness, and vulgar banality. A full belly does not a revolutionary make, or, as the German playwright Bertolt Brecht has said, "Erst kommt das Fressen, dann kommt die Moral" (first gobble up your food and then talk about ethics). The hunger for change and improvement has turned into selfishness and complacency. Trifonov's theme is not unlike Anton Chekhov's portrayal of the emptiness and dullness in Russian society of the 1890's.

Trifonov's stream-of-consciousness technique is a seemingly disjointed sequence of images, reflections, and ideas linked together through association with similar reflections and images, triggered by the five senses. In other words, the "smell" or "feel" of an object may conjure up a similar smell or feel from one's past experience. This style has been used since the turn of the century by such writers as Proust, Henry James, James Joyce, Virginia Woolf, and William Faulkner, not to mention Leo Tolstoy's so-called interior monologue technique.

Sources for Further Study

Brown, Deming. *Soviet Russian Literature Since Stalin*, 1978.

Brown, Edward J. *Russian Literature Since the Revolution*, 1982.

Terras, Victor, ed. *Handbook of Russian Literature*, 1985.

Woll, Josephine. "Trifonov's *Starik*: The Truth of the Past," in *Russian Literature Triquarterly*. No. 19 (1986).

Nicholas Vontsolos

ON THE EVE

Author: Ivan Turgenev (1818-1883)
Type of plot: Psychological realism
Time of plot: 1853
Locale: Moscow, the surrounding countryside, and Venice
First published: Nakanune, 1860 (English translation, 1871)

> *Principal characters:*
> ELENA STAHOV, an idealistic twenty-year-old woman
> ANNA STAHOV, her wealthy, ineffectual mother
> NIKOLAI STAHOV, her emotionally distant father
> DMITRI INSAROV, a twenty-five-year-old Bulgarian patriot
> exiled in Russia
> ANDREI BERSENYEV, a twenty-three-year-old graduate of
> Moscow University with scholarly ambitions
> PAVEL SHUBIN, a twenty-six-year-old sculptor
> ZOYA "ZOE" MULLER, Elena's attractive, eighteen-year-old
> female companion
> YEGOR KURNATOVSKY, a successful Russian official and
> Elena's suitor

The Novel

A romantic story of ill-fated love, *On the Eve* is set against the background of the social concerns of Russia in the 1850's. As is typical of Ivan Turgenev's love stories, the relationship between the lovers is rendered with sensitive but intense emotion. The action is structured around the heroine, Elena Stahov, a serious, idealistic young woman searching for a commitment which can give shape and meaning to her life.

One of the social concerns of the 1850's was the political role of women in society, and Elena represents the determined but frustrated young woman of the day. Like many of Turgenev's other strong heroines, she is presented first within the context of her home surroundings: The novel opens at her family's summer home in the countryside outside Moscow in 1853 (a significant summer because it is just before the outbreak of the Crimean War). Although Elena appears to be tranquil, she lives an intense inner life which does not find expression in the outer world. She yearns to be doing good works but has no avenue to the larger world to fulfill this desire, and the other members of her family do not provide her with direction. She lives with her mother, Anna Stahov, who loves her daughter but is an ineffectual woman who can barely manage the household and her own frustratingly empty life; a companion, Zoya "Zoe" Muller, a physically attractive but shallow young woman more interested in her dress than in the larger concerns of the age;

and slothful Uvar Stahov, an elderly relative who spends his days on the couch digesting his dinner. Elena has little patience with her father, Nikolai Stahov, who is staying with his mistress in Moscow against the wishes of her mother; Elena detests deceit in any form and consequently is not close to him. The one character who does possess an alert energy to match her own is Pavel Shubin, a talented young sculptor, a distant maternal cousin, who lives with the family and is being supported by Elena's mother. Yet Shubin and Elena are not compatible; they remain friends, but he is a sensually self-indulgent young man who has affairs with the local peasant girls. With the emotional temperament of the artist, he does not have the seriousness of purpose for which Elena yearns.

Shubin does have a friend, however, a recent graduate of Moscow University who lives on a neighboring estate. A reticent, serious young man, Andrei Bersenyev is committed to intellectual ideas, and he interests Elena. Although Andrei is physically awkward, when he speaks to Elena about the intellectual issues of the day, he becomes eloquent. In a series of scenes between Shubin and Andrei, which are related in masterly dialogue—Turgenev was also a great playwright; he wrote the classic *Mesyats v derevne* (1885; *A Month in the Country*, 1924)—the charming loveliness of Elena as a woman is conveyed. Shubin confesses his love for Elena to Andrei, but, unfortunately, she caught Shubin kissing the arms of the attractive Zoya, and thus Shubin knows that Elena will never return his love. He has observed Elena and Andrei together, however, and he is convinced that Elena is falling in love with Andrei.

Just as the relationship between Andrei and Elena is beginning to evolve, the novel takes an unexpected twist. When Elena asks Andrei if he knows of any remarkable men at the university, he replies that he knows of no Russian who qualifies but there is a foreign student who is deserving of the term "remarkable." After this conversation, Andrei invites the foreign student, Dmitri Insarov, out to his lodgings for the summer. Insarov is a Bulgarian patriot who is committed to overthrowing the Turkish rule in his country; when he was a child, his mother was violated and killed by a Turkish official, and when his father tried to avenge her, he also was killed. Insarov is now in exile in Russia, a poor student attending Moscow University while preparing to return to his country for an armed revolution. When Andrei introduces Insarov to Elena, she does not at first find him to be remarkable, but during later visits she discovers that his passionate commitment as a patriot matches her own idealistic nature, and she becomes increasingly attracted to him.

On an excursion to view the scenery around Tsaritsino Castle, Insarov displays the characteristics of the man of action. All the members of Elena's household—except her father—join in the sightseeing, accompanied by Andrei and Insarov. In a setting which contains rich, clear detail, the party picnics on the historic grounds and then goes boating on a nearby lake. (The boating scene is a masterful demonstration of the delicate mood that Turgenev can evoke with language.) When the party is preparing to leave, however, they are accosted by some drunken Germans. When the largest—a giant of a man with bull-like strength—refuses to move aside so that Elena's party might pass, Insarov suddenly takes command of the situation, quickly manhandling the German into the lake. Insarov's bold action stands in contrast to the artistic sensibility of Shubin and the moral steadfastness of Andrei; it matches Insarov's passionate commitment to his ideals. Soon after this incident, as Elena is writing in her diary, she realizes that she has fallen in love with Insarov.

Andrei comes to the realization that he loves Elena, and he despairs of his lost opportunity, as Shubin had earlier, but Andrei, like Shubin, remains a faithful friend to Elena and aids her in whatever way he can. Another concern of the age was the role of self-sacrifice in an individual's life, and Andrei, like Elena and Insarov, illustrates this concern. When Elena learns that Insarov is leaving to move back to Moscow, she goes by herself to Andrei's lodgings—a bold move for a woman in this culture—to see Insarov. When it begins to rain, she dodges into a roadside chapel, and shortly afterward, she sees Insarov walking down the road. In a moving, romantic scene, Elena confesses her love, and Insarov admits that he was leaving because he had fallen in love with Elena and feared that this love would distract him from his patriotic duties. As the rain falls about them, the two embrace, committing themselves to each other as they vow to marry.

Because of Insarov's lower social position, the lovers keep their commitment to each other secret. Shortly afterward, Elena's father returns to the summer house, since his mistress has left on a trip. While in Moscow, her father found a suitor for Elena, a man named Yegor Kurnatovsky, who is a successful bureaucrat. During his visits, the suitor adopts a condescendingly superior attitude toward Elena. She cannot help but compare him to Insarov, and indirectly, Turgenev draws a similar comparison for the reader: Although Kurnatovsky is an efficient administrator, he does not measure up to Insarov, for he lacks the ability to make a passionate commitment. He is without the burning desire to lead men toward a common goal. Unlike Insarov, he is not a remarkable man, not a man capable of heroic action.

Before Insarov and Elena can marry, he suddenly falls ill and hovers between life and death for eight days. During his long, slow recuperation, the Crimean War between Turkey and Russia breaks out, and Insarov plunges into support for his fellow Bulgarian patriots, working very hard although still ill. During this period, after her family has returned to Moscow for the winter, Elena and he secretly marry. Before their departure for the Bulgarian war zone, Elena tells her parents of her secret marriage; they strongly disapprove, her mother actually falling ill from the news. Although Anna finally forgives Elena, Nikolai refuses to do so. When the time comes for the loaded sleigh to pull away, however, he unexpectedly arrives with champagne for a farewell toast, and, in a moving scene, he blesses the marriage.

By April, Insarov and Elena have traveled as far as Venice, Italy, but Insarov's illness is steadily worsening; he has tuberculosis. While waiting for a boat to take them across the Adriatic Sea, one evening they attend an opera by Guiseppe Verdi. (Turgenev himself was in love with an opera singer for most of his adult life, and his description re-creates the artistic effect of the performance with compelling detail.) Turgenev also portrays the beautiful, unique city of Venice as the couple moves through it in a gondola. They spend their days waiting in a hotel, where Insarov's illness takes a turn for the worse. Just before the captain of the boat arrives, Insarov suddenly dies.

The novel ends as Elena boards the ship with Insarov's coffin. Her parents receive a letter from her saying that she is committed to Insarov's cause and will not return to Russia. In the closing chapter, Turgenev relates that Elena's father went to the war zone and searched for her, but she had disappeared; there were rumors of a woman accompanying the battle forces, but those could not be substantiated. The attractive but shallow Zoya has married Elena's former suitor, Yegor Kurnatovsky the bureaucrat; it is a suitable match, meeting her expectations of a husband and his of a wife. Shubin has moved to Rome and is a promising sculptor, and Andrei is a professor who travels widely at government expense. Although Elena's father has parted from his mistress, he now keeps an attractive housekeeper who dresses suspiciously well for a person in her position. Obviously, she is his present mistress.

The Characters

Elena is a charming, courageous, proud young woman. Considered a novelist's novelist, Turgenev is a master of the technique of developing character: Elena is presented not only through the narrator's relaying her direct thoughts, and through her diary, but also through the responses of the other characters to her. Shubin is a delightful character in his own right, with his quick insight into other people, but his response to Elena creates an added dimension to her. The same is true of Andrei: Not only is he a separate, well-drawn portrait of the man who is intellectually committed to ideas—who lives ideas, as Turgenev did himself when a graduate student in philosophy— but also his serious response to Elena gives yet another dimension to her character. This technique is of central importance in drama, and, like good drama, Turgenev's dialogue also makes the characters come alive for the reader.

The one major character who is not completely successful is Insarov. Too much the stereotypical hero, Insarov is without those human traits that could make him a fully believable figure. Although Elena represents one type of the universal Russian woman, with her ability to sacrifice her own well-being for her ideals, Insarov remains merely the man to whom such a woman devotes her life rather than a full-bodied character in his own right.

Other characters would be as well-suited to a drama of the mid-nineteenth century as to this novel because of their easily recognizable traits: Elena's mother remains the kind but ineffectual landowner; Elena's father is the typical man whose chief interest in life is chasing women; Zoya is the shallow, attractive young woman (a blonde) whom successful, middle-class men wish to marry. Turgenev's accomplishment in creating such characters lies in his giving life to their individual moments, so that even though they are subordinated to Elena, they have an integrity of their own.

Finally, there is Uvar Stahov, the paternal relative, a typical Slavophile— that is, a Russian who rejects all Western European influences. At the same time, in his slothful mannerisms and in his taking a long look at life yet not participating actively in it, he represents another character type, modeled on the title figure in the novel *Oblomov* (1859; English translation, 1915) by Ivan Goncharov.

Themes and Meanings

In the 1850's, Russia was moving into an age when the traditional ways of the landowning aristocracy were being questioned. Turgenev captured the spirit of those social concerns in writing about the members of the aristocracy whom he knew so well; he himself was a very wealthy man who inherited a large estate, and he personally faced the problems of that class. Those concerns are evident in the title, for the novel was written "on the eve" of one of the most significant events in the history of Russia: the freeing of the serfs in 1861. Until that time, the peasants who worked the land were considered to be the property of the landowner. This reform was but one manifestation of the social and intellectual activity which began in Russia during the decade of the 1850's; the political role of women in society and the nature of idealism and of self-sacrifice were also being considered, as is reflected in the thoughts and actions of the characters.

The fact that Andrei knows of no outstanding Russian of the period is significant, for indirectly, it suggests that, in general, contemporary Russian men were not capable of leading the revolutionary social and political movements of the age. Turgenev viewed most Russian men as the "superfluous man"—ineffectual, uncommitted, but deeply sensitive men who were not capable of decisive action. In his story "Dnevnik lishnyago cheloveka" (1850; "The Diary of a Superfluous Man"), Turgenev assigned the term to a long line of such characters in Russian literature. Turgenev believed that men of action were needed to accomplish the transition to a more enlightened society and also those women—such as Elena—who could emotionally support such men. Although Turgenev believed in Russia's movement toward progressive Western ways—he considered himself to be a Westerner, one who believed in the ways of Europe—he was not radical in his actions, and, in fact, radicals of the period attacked him for his moderate position.

The importance of romantic love in a person's life is a theme which Turgenev explored repeatedly in his work. Turgenev's lovers always experience the most exquisite aspect of life in their loving, but, as in this novel, their happiness is almost always ill-fated.

Critical Context

As *On the Eve* illustrates, Turgenev's genius as a novelist was to harmonize all the various elements of the novel into one artistic focus. He was always in control of his material, continually setting one brilliant scene against another with a minimum of authorial intrusion, so that the story unfolds like a play before the reader's eyes. After this novel, Turgenev went on to write his masterpiece, *Ottsy i deti* (1862; *Fathers and Sons*, 1867), in which, like *On the Eve* and his other longer works—*Rudin* (1856; *Dimitri Roudine*, 1873; also known as *Rudin*, 1947), *Dvoryanskoye gnezdo* (1859; *Liza*, 1869; also known as *A House of Gentlefolk*, 1894), *Dym* (1867; *Smoke*, 1868), and *Nov* (1877; *Virgin Soil*, 1877)—he consciously looked outward to social concerns as well as to the inner, personal lives of his characters.

Because of his artistic control, Turgenev achieved a place for the young Russian novel that it had not previously held. If Turgenev's best novels do not possess the epic scope or the compelling intensity of the longer novels of his younger contemporaries Leo Tolstoy and Fyodor Dostoevski—both of whom Turgenev encouraged and influenced—they nevertheless exhibit a clarity of scene and language and a delicacy of structure and mood that place them among the best works in the tradition of the novel. Turgenev influenced a large number of novelists, including such American realistic writers as William Dean Howells and Henry James. His character of Elena, in her strong-willed desire to do good, was a forerunner of Dorothea Brooke, the heroine of *Middlemarch* (1871-1872) by George Eliot, a British writer who greatly admired Turgenev.

Sources for Further Study

Dessaix, Robert. *Turgenev: The Quest for Faith*, 1980.
Freeborn, Richard. *Turgenev: The Novelist's Novelist*, 1960.
Gutsche, George. "Turgenev's *On the Eve*," in *Moral Apostasy in Russian Literature*, 1986.
Ripp, Victor. *Turgenev's Russia: From "Notes of a Hunter" to "Fathers and Sons,"* 1980.
Yarmolinsky, Avrahm. *Turgenev: The Man, His Art, and His Age*, 1959 (revised edition).

Ronald L. Johnson

ONE DAY IN THE LIFE OF IVAN DENISOVICH

Author: Aleksandr Solzhenitsyn (1918-   )
Type of plot: Historical realism
Time of plot: One day in January, 1951
Locale: A Soviet labor camp
First published: Odin den Ivana Denisovicha, 1962 (English translation, 1963)

> *Principal characters:*
> IVAN DENISOVICH (SHUKOV), the title character, who is serving time in a Soviet forced-labor camp
> FETYUKOV, a hapless fellow prisoner who is disliked by the others and doomed to extinction
> CAESAR MARKOVICH, a prisoner with packages of food for whom Shukov does favors
> ALYOSHKA THE BAPTIST, a religious inmate whom Shukov likes but does not understand
> TYURIN, the boss of Shukov's work gang

The Novel

One Day in the Life of Ivan Denisovich is the story of a typical day in the life of a prisoner in a Soviet labor camp. It is set in 1951, near the end of the rule of Joseph Stalin, and is, on one level, an exposé of Stalin's brutal forced-labor camps, a central but suppressed fact of modern Russian history. The novel follows the title character during the course of a not-unusual winter day, in the process eliciting great respect for a simple, unreflective man and offering a commentary on life in a totalitarian society.

Ivan Denisovich (Shukov) is awakened with the rest of his work gang at five in the morning on a January day. The temperature hovers around twenty degrees below zero. His first thoughts, as always, are of what he can do to increase his chances for survival. The time before breakfast is precious to him not only because he can find ways to obtain a bit of tobacco or extra food but also because, for a short while, his time is his own to use as he pleases.

After what passes for breakfast, Shukov stops on his way back to the barrack to try to get on the sick list for the day. Camp (Soviet) bureaucracy, however, dictates that no more than two prisoners will be sick each day, and, even with a fever, Shukov is too late to be one of those two. While waiting in the cold to march out of camp to work, Shukov sees Caesar finishing a cigarette. Shukov wants very much to have the butt that Caesar will leave but, significantly, will not beg for it, or even stare at Caesar while he smokes, both of which the wretched Fetyukov does. Caesar demonstrates the code of the camp by giving the butt to Shukov, not to Fetyukov.

Because of the negotiating skill of their work gang leader, Tyurin, the gang has the relatively easy job that day of building a power station. Shukov ruminates on the importance of a gang leader to the survival of the prisoners and on their allegiance to him. After the morning's work in the snow and cold comes the noon meal. Meals are the single most important part of the day, although they are pathetic, consisting, for example, of a small allotment of bread and a soup made of water and oats and an occasional fish head. It is crucial, however, that one not be further weakened by missing any of this meager repast. Shukov shows his cleverness in getting two extra bowls of soup for his work gang and is rewarded by having one of them allotted to him.

The afternoon is spent building a wall in the power station. The men, except for the shirker Fetyukov, begin to work with enthusiasm. Momentarily forgetting the circumstances of their lives, they work faster and faster, feeling both the camaraderie of common effort and a reminder of their own abilities. During this time, they also come to the aid of their gang leader when a supervisor threatens to get him in trouble. In his desire to finish his bricklaying and to contemplate for a moment his craftsmanship, Shukov risks being late for the return to camp and being punished. His friend, Senka, takes the same risk by waiting for him, but the two men make it back without trouble.

Shukov manages to smuggle back into camp a piece of metal that he found during the day. Once inside, he runs to the place where packages are handed out so that he can save a place for Caesar, who, unlike Shukov, often gets packages. Shukov is rewarded for his efforts when Caesar does receive a package and tells Shukov to eat his evening meal for him.

Shukov helps his gang get their soup and bread, again playing all the angles in order to increase his own share. He meditates on the sacredness of eating and its centrality to the life of the prisoner. As he eats, he observes the others, noting especially an old man whose many, many years in prison have not destroyed his spirit, though they have ravaged his body. After the meal, Shukov goes to buy some tobacco from another inmate. Back in the barrack, he watches Fetyukov enter, in tears and with a bloody face. Shukov speculates that Fetyukov has been beaten again while trying to scrounge an extra bowl of soup and surmises that the man will not last in the camp, because he simply does not know how to survive. Despite the efforts of the gang leader, the Captain is led off to begin his ten-day sentence in solitary confinement, a punishment that he may or may not survive in the January cold. Shukov helps Caesar keep his package of food from being stolen during the night count and returns to his bed feeling very good about his day.

Unable to sleep immediately, Shukov talks to Alyoshka the Baptist. Alyoshka tries to persuade Shukov to see the time in prison from a different perspective and suggests that one should even thank God for being in prison, because it keeps one from being misled by the false values of the outside world. Shukov likes Alyoshka but does not understand him. Shukov falls asleep recounting the day to himself, with its many small victories, and he decides that it was "almost happy." The reader is then offered the bleak reminder, "There were three thousand six hundred and fifty-three days like this in his sentence, from reveille to lights out."

The Characters

If the plot seems to be composed of largely trivial things, it is intentional. Aleksandr Solzhenitsyn wants nothing to be spectacular in his depiction of a typical day in a Soviet labor camp. He wants neither moral heroism nor sensational cruelty, because though each exists in the camps, these qualities do not define the daily experience. What Solzhenitsyn wants instead is for the reader to follow as closely as possible the thoughts and actions of one very unexceptional prisoner, Ivan Denisovich. Shukov is not particularly intelligent or even reflective. Instead, he spends almost all of his time thinking of ways to get an edge against extinction. A piece of metal becomes a potential tool with which he can earn extra food or tobacco. A favor done for another prisoner will earn a favor in return that will make his life a little longer and a little easier.

For all his ordinariness, however, Shukov is a character that the reader comes to admire. He is a survivor—crafty and courageous in small things when necessary. Also, very important in Solzhenitsyn's world, there are things that Shukov will not do. He will not beg, unlike the pathetic Fetyukov. Nor will Shukov take bribes, a telling virtue in a society in which the oppressive bureaucracy has made under-the-table transactions the accepted way of life. In many ways, Shukov is a man of integrity, who knows intimately what he must do to survive and is determined to do so, but not at the cost of his humanity. Shukov is no dissident or rebel. He does not rail against the system or think of ways to change it. In a sense, he is Solzhenitsyn's common Russian, a man more interested in finding a way to stay alive and out of trouble than in involving himself in any causes. His great qualities are perseverance and common decency.

Shukov's foil is Fetyukov. Fetyukov is not an evil man, only an ignorant and weak one. He lacks not only Shukov's knowledge of how to survive but also Shukov's self-respect. When he begs Caesar for his cigarette butt, Fetyukov puts himself in the same class as those who lick their bowls after eating, those who have begun to lose their sense of worth as human beings, a sure prelude to physical demise as well.

None of the characters in the novel, apart from Shukov, is fully developed. The reader catches glimpses of them as they cross paths with Shukov, but they do not develop into more fully realized characters. This may be the result of Solzhenitsyn's decision to present this day through the eyes of one man. Because Shukov spends most of his time looking for ways to survive, he is primarily interested only in those aspects of the others that might contribute to his goal.

Themes and Meanings

How does one retain one's full humanity in a social system that is designed to debase it? This question is just as pertinent to people in the West as to those in totalitarian societies, for the forces of dehumanization are strong in all modern societies. Solzhenitsyn offers Shukov and his fellow prisoners as a partial answer to this question. Most important to their survival is their ability to retain their dignity under the worst possible circumstances. Given numbers in place of names, made to undergo humiliating and arbitrary rituals (for example, repeated "counts"), forced to do often-meaningless labor and compete for inadequate resources, the prisoners somehow manage, nevertheless, to maintain a sense of themselves as individuals and, on key occasions, to help one another. This last activity underscores another key part of Solzhenitsyn's answer, the role of camaraderie or community as a defense against inhumanity. Despite Shukov's comment that the other prisoners are often one's worst enemy in the fight to survive, the reader sees many examples of mutual dependence and even selflessness.

The key scene in the novel illustrates the importance of both dignity and community. In working together on the wall, the members of the work gang discover both their own ability to do something of value and the encouragement of a shared goal. Ignoring the danger of being late, Shukov stops to look at the wall he has laid: "Not bad. He went up and looked over the wall from left to right. His eye was true as a level. The wall was straight as a die. His hands were still good for something!" In turning to leave, Shukov finds Senka waiting for him in a dangerous act of friendship: "He wasn't the kind to leave you in the lurch. If you were in trouble, he was always there to take the rap with you."

Yet nothing is taken for granted by Solzhenitsyn. These values are seen only in the cracks of an otherwise bleak and soul-killing existence. Many of these men will not survive. In this life, at least, justice often will not prevail. Shukov goes to sleep delighted with his day, but the reader is left to wonder about how bad this life must be when such seemingly minor victories can be considered the cause for near happiness, especially when this day is only one of thousands in his sentence. Perhaps the ultimate value that comes out of *One Day in the Life of Ivan Denisovich* is perseverance.

Critical Context

One Day in the Life of Ivan Denisovich is the book which brought Solzhenitsyn from total obscurity to worldwide fame. Its publication was a central event in Russian political as well as literary history. The late 1950's and early 1960's were known as the time of "the thaw," a period when intellectual and artistic restrictions were temporarily loosened in an attempt to move beyond the terror and repression of the decades under Stalin. Solzhenitsyn's novel dealt directly with events which touched the life of every Russian family and yet which had never been spoken of publicly even after Stalin's death.

The publication of *One Day in the Life of Ivan Denisovich*, therefore, was a sensational event in the Soviet Union, selling out large editions in a matter of hours. Within a short time, however, the Soviet leaders decided that allowing criticism of the past set a dangerous precedent for criticism of the present, and the book was withdrawn. So began Solzhenitsyn's conflict with Soviet officials. The appearance of his novels *Rakovy korpus* (1968; *Cancer Ward*, 1968) and *V kruge pervom* (1968; *The First Circle*, 1968), published in the West but not in the Soviet Union, led not only to his winning the Nobel Prize in Literature in 1970 but also to his eventual exile from his country in 1974.

Sources for Further Study
Clement, Oliver. *The Spirit of Solzhenitsyn*, 1976.
Ericson, Edward E., Jr. *Solzhenitsyn: The Moral Vision*, 1980.
Kodjak, Andrej. *Alexander Solzhenitsyn*, 1978.
Moody, Christopher. *Solzhenitsyn*, 1976.
Scammell, Michael. *Solzhenitsyn: A Biography*, 1984.

Daniel Taylor

OUR FRIEND MANSO

Author: Benito Pérez Galdós (1843-1920)
Type of plot: Social realism
Time of plot: The late 1870's
Locale: Madrid
First published: El amigo Manso, 1882 (English translation, 1987)

> *Principal characters:*
> MÁXIMO MANSO, a scholar, philosopher, and teacher
> DOÑA JAVIERA DE PEÑA, an attractive middle-aged widow,
> who is Máximo's neighbor
> MANUEL DE PEÑA, Doña Javiera's son and Máximo's student
> DOÑA CÁNDIDA DE GARCÍA GRANDE, a pretentious widow,
> who was a friend of Máximo's mother
> IRENE, a beautiful, intelligent young girl, Doña Cándida's
> niece
> JOSÉ MARÍA, Máximo's brother, who made his fortune in
> Cuba
> LICA, José María's Cuban wife

The Novel

Máximo Manso meets his neighbor, Doña Javiera de Peña, one night in the summer of 1878, when a fire alarm forces the residents to leave their building. Doña Javiera is a warm, expansive woman who owns a lucrative meat business. She takes an interest in Máximo and stops by his apartment often to talk or to bring him a cut of meat. A woman of low origins and little education, Doña Javiera is in awe of Máximo's vast knowledge. He, in turn, is impressed with his neighbor's perceptiveness and common sense.

Doña Javiera asks Máximo to take charge of the education of her twenty-one-year-old son, Manuel, whose indolence has his mother worried. Doña Javiera does not expect Manuel to become a scholar, but she would like him to receive a basic education in the humanities that would allow him to function in society. Máximo soon charms Manuel with conversations and excursions; the two become good friends and the boy makes excellent progress. Although he does not care for philosophy and never displays talent for writing, Manuel enjoys history and expresses himself well orally.

Doña Cándida de García Grande is another frequent visitor to Máximo's apartment. Her husband, now deceased, had been a businessman and minor politician. With his death, Doña Cándida fell into dire economic straits. Vain and pretentious, she talks constantly of her aristocratic friends and her property, while at the same time begging Máximo for handouts. Máximo, who feels obligated to the woman because of her former friendship with his deceased mother, gives her money. Often Doña Cándida does not come in person but sends her orphaned niece Irene, who lives with her. Irene is a well-mannered child who shows interest in Máximo's books, although the teacher soon realizes that her primary preoccupation is far more basic: food. Frequently, he gives her reading materials and candy, and on one occasion he buys her a pair of shoes. As time passes, Irene grows up and stops frequenting Máximo's house. She enters a teachers' institute, where she excels at her studies.

Manuel becomes involved with a young woman from the Vendesol family and begins to spend more time courting her than studying. Doña Javiera is delighted, since the Vendesols are a wealthy, respectable family who also made their fortune in the meat business. The relationship, however, does not last.

Máximo Manso's calm is shattered by the arrival from Cuba of his brother José María and his wife, Lica, their three children, Lica's mother and sister, a mulatto nanny, and a black servant. José María rents a house for his large, boisterous family and decides to run for Congress as a representative from Cuba, then still a Spanish colony. Soon the house is full of politicians, poets, and journalists. Among them is Manuel, whose oratorical skills promise to launch him into a position of political prominence. Public life demands that José María impose a more urban veneer on his wife and children, whose relaxed, unpolished behavior is unacceptable in Madrid society. Máximo suggests that his brother hire Irene as a governess.

Family etiquette demands that Máximo dine at his brother's house almost daily. There he comes into frequent contact with Irene, with whom he falls in love. Máximo and Irene spend a large amount of time together, supervising the children's lessons and strolling through Madrid. On several occasions, Máximo notices that Irene is flushed and exuberant. After some time, however, she confides that she is not happy at José María's house.

José María wins the election and becomes engrossed in his career. Lica gives birth to their fourth child, whom she names Máximo, after his godfather. José María, more and more convinced of his own importance, has little time for his family and often belittles Lica, whose Cuban customs and vocabulary he finds embarrassing. Soon, Lica learns that he is womanizing and that his prime target is Irene. Máximo is furious.

Doña Cándida announces that she has come into some money and intends to move into a better house. She will take Irene with her, since she believes that it is not fitting that the niece of a woman in her position work as a salaried governess. Máximo suspects that Doña Cándida is lying, and sure enough, he learns that José María is paying for the new apartment in order to have access to Irene. Trapped by her conniving aunt and a rich, ambitious politician, Irene confides in Máximo, who confronts his brother and threatens to create a career-damaging scandal.

Having eliminated his rival, Máximo is now in a position to court Irene himself. He soon learns, however, that she is in love with Manuel de Peña. Sick with grief at the realization that his dear disciple is his competitor, he interrogates Irene, who admits that she is not interested in studying or in having a career, but wants to marry Manuel and get away from her aunt. Máximo struggles with his emotions but finally takes the side of the young lovers. Doña Javiera opposes the marriage because the girl is "just a teacher," but Máximo convinces her to give her approval, and the couple are married. Doña Javiera becomes more attentive than ever to Manso, and she seems a likely mate for him. Máximo, however, falls ill and soon dies.

The Characters

Máximo Manso, whose name translates roughly as "great meek one" or "maximum gentleness," appears to be a self-sacrificing soul of whom people take advantage. He constantly yields to the demands of others. He himself comments repeatedly on his tractability: "When will my painful efforts on behalf of others cease?" he laments. "Fortunate is he who lights one candle to charity and another to selfishness." As is often the case in Benito Pérez Galdós' novels, the character's name is ironic. On the one hand, Máximo is kind and mild mannered. On the other, he is self-righteous and intolerant. Like Don Quixote, a literary creation that greatly influenced Pérez Galdós, he wishes to mold the world in accordance with his own ideals. When Irene fails to conform to his image of her, he is sorely disappointed.

Máximo is the embodiment of Krausism, a philosophy that was popular in nineteenth century Spain. Krausism taught that reality progresses toward higher internal unities. God includes both nature and humanity, while transcending both. Man is the highest component of the material universe. Each individual person is like the cell of a body. The progress of society depends on the perfection of its components; therefore, by educating the individual, one works toward the improvement of society. Máximo sees education as the tool through which he will mold Manuel and Irene. Yet he fails to take into consideration the role of the emotions and the pressures of society. Although Máximo is credited with being a great scholar in search of the truth, his idealism blinds rather than illumintes him. It is obvious to the reader far earlier than to Máximo that Manuel, not his middle-aged teacher, is a likely match for Irene.

In *Our Friend Manso*, Pérez Galdós attempts to break away from naturalism, a literary current that stresses the dominating influence of heredity and environment on human life. To this end, he identifies Máximo as a literary creation from the beginning. The novel opens with the words, "I don't exist," and the first chapter relates how the character is drawn out of the author's pen and given its own life. At the end, after his death, Máximo continues his narrative from Heaven. By depriving his character of a personal past, Pérez

Galdós tries to endow him with independence and free will.

Pérez Galdós, however, is not completely successful. In *Our Friend Manso* the characters are more archetypes than individuals. Thus, José María is a classic example of a breed of newly rich Spanish males: ambitious, shallow, egocentric. Manuel de Peña is a flamboyant orator with nothing to say, a type that, in Pérez Galdós' opinion, plagues Spanish politics. Doña Cándida is the penniless social climber who feeds her illusions of grandeur by forcing herself into moneyed circles. Doña Javiera is the rich businesswoman who, although of humble origins, becomes increasingly pretentious and socially ambitious. Lica is the sweet, indolent Cuban, and Irene, the materialistic young woman who, in spite of her intellectual potential, craves the comfort, security—and emptiness—of a place at the side of a rising young politician.

Themes and Meanings

Two main themes dominate *Our Friend Manso*: education and society. Máximo's conversations with Doña Javiera, Manuel, and Irene provide Pérez Galdós with ample opportunities to set forth his theories of education. Máximo provides Manuel with a well-rounded, humanistic education by stressing experience rather than dry book-learning. He understands that it is impossible to force intellectual curiosity, so he stimulates his student by engaging him in debate, taking him to the museum, and strolling with him through Madrid, where daily life provides ample material for discussion. Since Manuel does not possess a good knowledge of Latin, Máximo emphasizes modern authors, and since Manuel writes poorly, Máximo emphasizes oral communication. His system discards rigid pedagogical norms, replacing them with a pragmatic approach. The teacher builds on his student's strengths, while at the same time trying to correct his deficiencies. Most important, he understands that "no teaching is possible without blessed friendship, which is the best conveyor of ideas between one man and another." Máximo's success depends on his ability to win Manuel's trust and love, which makes it possible for him to convey to his pupil his own enthusiasm for learning.

Máximo encourages the education of women, although he stresses that it should be limited to "that which is appropriate to [their] sex." He is delighted that Irene, although apparently eager to study, shows a distaste for erudition in women and contempt for those who try to compete with men.

While Pérez Galdós sees Máximo's pedagogical theories as valid for the most part, he demonstrates that it is impossible for the individual to mold others according to his own ideas, through education or otherwise. Máximo prides himself on being a man of reason who "suffocates little passions." Yet emotion is as much a part of the human reality as intellect, and feelings can interfere with man's best-laid plans.

Like Pérez Galdós' other novels, *Our Friend Manso* provides a richly detailed overview of Spanish society. During the nineteenth century, many nobles lost their fortunes, while a prosperous new middle class began to exercise power. That resulted in a certain social leveling; Pérez Galdós comments that Spain was becoming as democratic as the United States. Yet, rather than abolishing the social hierarchy, mobility facilitated the establishment of a new elite. Material wealth provided the burgeoning bourgeoisie with an entry into the upper echelons of society. Patrician lineage, traditionally a requirement for membership in the aristocracy, became less important as wealthy businessmen purchased titles of nobility. José María represents a new type—the commoner who returns from the New World with a considerable fortune. With hypocrisy that Pérez Galdós sees as characteristic of the politician, José María preaches democracy and lauds the proletariat, while at the same time attempting to acquire the title of marquess.

With the growth of the middle class comes material progress and increased economic, political, and educational equality. For many, this is a period of optimism and hope. Yet, Pérez Galdós shows that the widening social base also fosters mediocrity, superficiality, and crass materialism. Intellectually and artistically, standards are low. José María's poet friend Francisco de Paula de la Costa y Sainz del Bardal is a bad writer and a pompous idiot. The theater production that Máximo attends with Irene and her pupils is tiresome and tasteless. Society is filled with vulgar, presumptuous people, such as Doña Cándida, who claim to be arbiters of taste, and of undiscriminating nouveaux riches. As always in Pérez Galdós' novels, reality is multifaceted.

Critical Context

The nineteenth century Spanish novelists prior to Pérez Galdós were mostly regionalists or *costumbristas*, writers who described the picturesque and folkloric elements of life. Pérez Galdós, who was a practicing journalist, revolutionized the novel by using his gift for observation, his political acumen, and his knowledge of history to create a narrative that penetrates deep into the national psyche. Although Pérez Galdós is usually classified as a realist, his characters are sometimes caricatures, exaggerating traits associated with particular social types. All Pérez Galdós' works are an attempt to understand Spanish society—how it is, and how it became that way. Pérez Galdós' first novel, *La fontana de oro* (1868), contained both *costumbrista* and historical elements, and each succeeding work was a new attempt to comprehend the interelation between history and personal experience.

In 1873, with the publication of *Trafalgar* (English translation, 1884), Pérez Galdós began the first series of his "national episodes," or historical novels. Three years later, he published *Doña Perfecta* (1876; English translation, 1880), the first of his "Spanish contemporary novels." Although Pérez Galdós appeared to be moving in opposite directions at once, the historical and contemporary sequences were actually complementary. The first represented an effort to comprehend contemporary Spain by following the course of history from the past to the present. The second allowed the author to construct archetypes in order to reach a deeper comprehension of contemporary Spanish society.

Doña Perfecta was followed by *Gloria* (1876-1877; English translation, 1879) and *Marianela* (1878; English translation, 1883). All three depicted the intolerance of the inhabitants of the small towns of rural Spain. With *La desheredada* (1881; *The Disinherited Lady*, 1957), Pérez Galdós created the city novel and entered a new period in which he depicted the perverse commitment to material wealth and social climbing at the time of the Bourbon Restoration (1874). *Our Friend Manso* forms part of the second period of "Spanish contemporary novels." In it, Pérez Galdós continues to examine the distortion of values of the new Spain that was emerging during the second part of the nineteenth century. While its predecessor explores the determinism imposed by history and heredity, *Our Friend Manso* attempts to introduce an element of free will into the narrative. That Pérez Galdós does not completely succeed does not diminish the significance of the novel. *Our Friend Manso*, although not Pérez Galdós' best work, is a step toward the creation of his masterpieces, *Fortunata y Jacinta* (1886-1887; *Fortunata and Jacinta: Two Stories of Married Women*, 1973) and his four-volume *Torquemada* series (1889-1895), in which he reaches a synthesis of the historical and the individual, of the deterministic and the independent.

Sources for Further Study
Bly, Peter A. *Galdós' Novel of the Historical Imagination: A Study of the Contemporary Novels*, 1984.
Dendle, Brian. *Galdós: The Mature Thought*, 1980.
Eoff, Sherman H. *The Novels of Pérez Galdós*, 1954.
Gilman, Stephen. *Galdós and the Art of the European Novel: 1867-1887*, 1981.
Pattison, Walter. *Benito Pérez Galdós*, 1975.
_____. *Benito Pérez Galdós and the Creative Process*, 1954.
Rutherford, John. "Story, Character, Setting, and Narrative Mode in Galdós' *El Amigo Manso*," in *Style and Structure in Literature*, 1976. Edited by Roger Fowler.
Woodbridge, Hensley C. *Benito Pérez Galdós: A Selective Annotated Bibliography*, 1976.

Barbara Mujica

OUR LADY OF THE FLOWERS

Author: Jean Genet (1910-1986)
Type of plot: Impressionistic realism
Time of plot: The late 1930's and early 1940's
Locale: Fresnes prison, Paris, and the provinces
First published: Notre-Dame des Fleurs, 1944; revised edition, 1951 (English
   translation, 1949; revised edition, 1963)

> *Principal characters:*
> THE NARRATOR, Jean Genet himself, a prisoner
> DIVINE, a transvestite queen
> OUR LADY OF THE FLOWERS, a youthful homosexual, thief,
>   and murderer
> DARLING, a pimp and Divine's lover

The Novel

The world portrayed in Jean Genet's *Our Lady of the Flowers* is shocking
and unsettling in many respects. Though he deals with characters who are
pimps, transvestites, and petty murderers, he describes them in the language
of heroism, poetry, and even sainthood. Written by the narrator—Genet
himself—in a prison cell awaiting sentencing, the novel features characters
that are for the most part the pure creation of the narrator's whims and
desires. He treats them, in turn, with cruelty, openly expressed physical
desire, and brilliant lyricism.

The book opens with a brief description of several famous murderers of
the period, saying of them: "It is in honor of their crimes that I am writing
my book." The key terms that the narrator develops in the novel are glory
and abjection. By reaching the lowest or most abject state, Genet's characters attain a sort of sainthood. By daring to commit the most heinous
crime of murder, they attain their ultimate glory. To prepare for the story of
the young assassin, Our Lady of the Flowers, the narrator first presents the
saintly—because abject—life of the leading character, a drug addict and
male transvestite prostitute named Divine.

The story of Divine begins and ends with her death (the transvestite characters in the book are all depicted through the use of female pronouns).
Moving in and out of the present in his prison cell, the narrator weaves a
series of fantasies concerning his main character, who is also a version of himself. Divine's great love is a pimp, Darling Daintyfoot. Before the narrative
reaches their first night together, however, the reader learns about Darling's
life and physical attributes as well as Divine's youth as Louis Culafroy. Like
Genet's own complicated feelings for his mother, Lou's relationship with his
mother, Ernestine, is troubled, with Ernestine all the while fervently wishing
for her son's death.

Divine meets Darling on the street and brings him back to her attic flat overlooking Montmartre Cemetery. Darling, with his proud bearing and masculine physique, quickly casts his spell on Divine, moves in with her, and becomes her pimp. Their life together is described in lyrical detail, even down to their fights and Darling's sexual domination of Divine. In the fractured narrative, there are passages of Divine's youthful reminiscences, as well as the narrator's present experience in prison. The most extended narrative sequence describes a tea Divine gives for Darling and her most serious rival, Mimosa. Darling deserts Divine to live with Mimosa, but one night all three meet on the street, and the two queens have a fight in which Mimosa badly beats Divine. Darling takes this as a sign of Divine's devotion to him and moves back in with her.

After this extended development of the narrative, the title character makes his appearance: "Our Lady of the Flowers here makes his solemn entrance through the door of crime. . . ." A sixteen-year-old vagabond youth, Our Lady, for no apparent reason, murders and robs an aging homosexual. The murder is described as a solemn, even heroic event, through which Our Lady accedes to his ultimate glory. Shortly thereafter, he meets Darling in a train station. When Our Lady loses his wallet with the stolen money, Darling retrieves it and offers to return half. Thus begins their friendship, which also includes Our Lady moving in with Darling and Divine. Darling is a restless sort, however, and soon disappears; Our Lady is similarly erratic in his behavior and is gone for long stretches of time.

During this period, the focus is on Divine: flashbacks to her youth and first homosexual experience with Alberto; her love affair with a young soldier, Gabriel; and her meeting with a black pimp, Seck Gorgui. Seck Gorgui is based on the narrator's memories of a black murderer whom he knew in prison, Clément Village, so he also tells of Village and Village's murder of a young prostitute. Seck Gorgui moves in with Divine and is still there when Our Lady returns from one of his exploits. The three of them establish a ménage together, with Divine serving as lover to each. This situation continues happily until a transvestite ball, when the young Our Lady, dressed for the first time as a woman, falls for Seck. This provokes Divine's jealousy, and she eventually enlists Mimosa's help to get rid of Our Lady.

Darling, meanwhile, has been caught stealing from a department store and imprisoned. The story of Darling's capture and humiliation by the police serves as a bridge to the story of Our Lady's downfall, because Darling hears the story in prison. Our Lady had been living with another youth and dealing cocaine. When the police arrest him, he is tortured and inexplicably confesses to the earlier murder. The trial of Our Lady allows the narrator the full range of his rage against what he views as the oppression of normal society. The judge, the lawyers, and the jury are pious, self-serving morons who act together to condemn the saintly and angelic Our Lady to death. The only moments when the veil of hypocrisy opens are when Our Lady makes his pointed and vulgar remarks in his distinctive slang.

After Our Lady is condemned and executed, the story winds down quickly. Divine is an aging shadow of herself and sinks more heavily into drugs and self-parody. She even kills a young child, out of despair for not having the courage to kill herself. Her actual death scene and thoughts during it are explored in great detail. The narrator ends with his own thoughts on his upcoming sentencing and with a letter to Divine from the imprisoned Darling.

The Characters

All the characters in *Our Lady of the Flowers* are seen through the perspective of the narrator, who is Genet himself or a version of himself. Perspective is not a strong enough term, for the narrator states that his characters are his own fantasies, which he develops for his own onanistic purposes. The fractured narrative which results is interwoven with the narrator's own prison experiences, past and present. All the other major characters, then, are primarily versions of himself.

This fact is especially true of the book's central figure, Divine. From the unhappy childhood and borderline murderous mother to the vagabond adolescence, the background for Divine's character is artfully modeled on Genet's own. Divine's true uniqueness, on the other hand, lies in her ability to transform reality by living a willed fantasy. Her transformation into a woman is at every moment subject to external abuse and pressure from a hostile society. Nevertheless, she is somehow able to transcend these impossibilities and bring not only a sort of poetry into her world but also a kind of love.

Darling is the male fantasy counterpart to Divine—that is, he is the desired male figure that the narrator creates to be Divine's lover so the narrator can enjoy him vicariously. Darling's key attributes are all external: his physique, his manner of smoking a cigarette, even his bodily functions. He has little interior development and little personality other than a sovereign disdain for the morality of normal society. This disdain and the actions it allows him to perform contribute to the heroic aspect which his physical beauty suggests.

Our Lady is the most enigmatic character in the book. He is so young that he seems to undertake the most serious actions with a sublime lack of reflection. In fact, that combination of murderous action with a blank interior state accounts for what the narrator terms his glory. Our Lady is the type in the book for other killers known by the narrator in prison. His sublime indifference and blind courage are part of the mystery of the assassin that Genet wishes to explore in the book.

The rest of the characters in the book serve primarily to give depth to the past and inner experience of Divine. From her childhood as Lou Culafroy, these include her mother, Ernestine, who will be truly happy only when Lou is dead; Alberto, the snake catcher, who first shows Lou the physical aspect of love; and the young Solange, Lou's only experience with a woman. Seck Gorgui, the black pimp, and Gabriel, a young French soldier, are Divine's other important lovers. Mimosa is her primary rival and, with the other queens, serves to establish the atmosphere and milieu in which Divine lives.

Themes and Meanings

Genet's fiction is both an assault on the sensibilities of ordinary society and a desperate attempt at communication. Literally written in prison on prison-supplied brown scraps of paper, his voice comes from a dark nether-world that most people will never see. He succeeds, as though through a miracle, in transforming the world of prisons and the marginal underworld of pimps, killers, and prostitutes, into a fabric of dream and fantasy. The lowest form of degradation becomes a religious exercise, and the worst forms of violence are exalted in poetic raptures.

Names are a central facet of this dream transformation: Lou Culafroy becomes Divine, Paul Garcia is Darling, and Adrien Baillou is Our Lady of the Flowers. The inversion of masculine and feminine pronouns similarly helps to cast the spell. In Genet's dream fantasy of Divine, it is often unclear whether Divine's experience is real, or if she is inventing her own dream. In the prison world of the narrator and the harsh outside world of the characters, these fundamental imaginative acts create their own system of values.

Crime is a value in *Our Lady of the Flowers* but only under certain circumstances. Accomplished with a sublime indifference, murder can become the ultimate glory. As the narrator says in describing Clément Village's murder of the prostitute Sonia: "Men endowed with a wild imagination should have, in addition, the great poetic faculty of denying our universe and its values so that they may act upon it with a sovereign ease." In Genet's universe, such men overcome the tawdry and ugly world in which they live. Tried and condemned for murder, they are unlike the others in prison and rise above them in a form of heroism that transcends ordinary life and judgment.

To understand this attitude on the part of the narrator toward the heroic indifference of the killer, one must also understand the abjection of the lowest criminal. In Genet's world, anything is allowed. Betrayal is saintly, as is the fact of being dominated and abused sexually. All the men who are real men in Genet's work are strong and beautiful in order to fulfill the narrator's desire to be dominated by them. The narrator gives his emotional identification to Divine, because Divine is in the position of the weakest, always offering herself to be used and abused. Through this constant abjection, Divine attains sainthood, in a strange but oddly coherent transformation of Christian typology. From the bleakest reality of deprivation and violence, Genet creates a universe of values which is poetic and internally coherent in its mirror inversion of the world that most people know and recognize.

Critical Context

Our Lady of the Flowers is Genet's first novel, published in an extremely small edition in 1944 and reissued in 1948. Along with his second novel, *Miracle de la rose* (1946, revised 1951; *Miracle of the Rose*, 1966) and his autobiographical *Journal du voleur* (1948, 1949; *The Thief's Journal*, 1954), it helped to create a nearly instant celebrity for Genet. Praised for their innovative narrative strategies as well as their startling depiction of marginal society, these early prose works assured Genet's literary reputation. This reputation in turn aided a group of leading French intellectuals, including Jean-Paul Sartre, in arguing successfully for Genet's release from prison, where he was serving a life sentence as a so-called incorrigible offender.

Genet's subsequent career was primarily as a playwright whose works participate in the experimentalism of the 1950's, along with other writers such as Samuel Beckett and Eugène Ionesco. Genet's plays, *Le Balcon* (1956; *The Balcony*, 1957), *Les Bonnes* (1947; revised, 1954; *The Maids*, 1956), and *Les Nègres* (1958; *The Blacks*, 1960), are avant-garde theater classics. Like his prose works, they explore issues of sexual and political domination, interpersonal power struggles, and life-and-death role-playing.

Our Lady of the Flowers is thus the earliest sign of Genet's genius and a groundbreaking work in its own right. Extending the innovative narrative practices of writers such as Marcel Proust and Louis-Ferdinand Céline, Genet's novel also confronts the ordinary reader with a shocking vision that inevitably calls into question his own universe of values. Its unmatched lyricism creates poetry out of sordid reality and establishes startling models for modern-day saints and heroes.

Sources for Further Study

Coe, Richard. *The Vision of Jean Genet*, 1968.
Knapp, Bettina. *Jean Genet*, 1968.
MacMahon, Joseph. *The Imagination of Jean Genet*, 1963.
Sartre, Jean-Paul. Introduction to *Our Lady of the Flowers*, 1963.
Thody, Philip. *Jean Genet: A Study of His Novels*, 1968.

Peter Baker

PAN

Author: Knut Hamsun (Knut Pedersen, 1859-1952)
Type of plot: Psychological romance
Time of plot: 1855-1861
Locale: The Norwegian seacoast town of Sirilund and an adjacent forest
First published: 1894 (English translation, 1920)

> *Principal characters:*
>> LIEUTENANT THOMAS GLAHN, the first narrator, an out-
>> doorsman who falls in love with Edvarda Mack
>> EDVARDA MACK, the spoiled daughter of a successful trader
>> HERR MACK, Edvarda's father, the town's wealthiest man
>> THE DOCTOR, one of Glahn's rivals for Edvarda
>> EVA, a blacksmith's young wife who gives herself to Glahn
>> THE SECOND NARRATOR, Glahn's hunting partner in India, who
>> shoots him

The Novel

Pan depicts the stormy romance between the vacationing Lieutenant Thomas Glahn and Edvarda Mack, the beautiful daughter of the most influential businessman in the Nordland region. The story is narrated by Glahn himself, who, two years after the events of 1855, has decided to write down his memories, as he says, for his own amusement. A second narrator, Glahn's murderer, relates the events of 1861 leading up to the fatal act.

Glahn's narration is prompted by a mysterious note that contains two green feathers. Although he feigns indifference, his emotions are stirred by these tokens. As the reader comes to learn, they are the belated and nearly final interchange in his volatile relationship with Edvarda.

Glahn had journeyed to this wild, northern region in order to indulge his passion for nature's magnificence and for the independent life of hunting and fishing. Beginning in the late spring, he lived with his dog, Aesop, in a simple hut, occasionally venturing into the nearby coastal town of Sirilund. On one of those visits, Herr Mack, his landlord and a wealthy trader, introduces him to the Doctor, a lame older man who seems to have been chosen by Herr Mack for his daughter, Edvarda. At first, Edvarda makes little impression on Glahn, but soon he is fascinated by her beauty and manner.

Their mutual attraction is enormous, but each is willful and perverse. Edvarda is sometimes vulnerable, often coquettish, and at times disdainful. Glahn can never be sure where he stands with her, and yet this unpredictability continues to attract him, even while he senses that he is being played for a fool. The mixture of serenity and awe that Glahn feels during the long summer days in this magnificent setting is counterpointed by the complexity of his anxiety-ridden affair.

Part of the complication grows out of Glahn's own nature. Socially awkward, his courtship of Edvarda puts him in situations which show his worst side. On one such occasion, he gives her two feathers of the kind that he uses to make fishing lures. Only a short time later, he disgraces himself by impulsively throwing her shoe into the water. Further social engagements trigger irresponsible, insulting actions that embarrass Edvarda while making Glahn less and less welcome to Herr Mack. The stubborn pride in both characters makes apologies and forgiveness difficult. Drawn to each other by an overpowering erotic magnetism, they routinely destroy each other's happiness. In fact, their egoistic actions are finally self-destructive.

Glahn is attracted to other women, partly as a consolation for the wounds that he suffers at Edvarda's hands. After all, she measures him against her father's favorites: first the Doctor and then the Baron. Eva, the young wife of the blacksmith, provides Glahn with uncomplicated comforts. She gives while asking nothing in return, while Edvarda, a social creature, is her antithesis.

Herr Mack, aware of Glahn's fondness for Eva, tries to irritate him by making Eva's life difficult. As her employer, he assigns her arduous tasks for long hours. Unsure of his control over Edvarda, Herr Mack plans a series of slights, threats, and ugly incidents to drive Glahn away. In his perverse way, Glahn enjoys countering Herr Mack.

As Glahn's humiliation at the hands of Edvarda grows, he becomes more and more irrational. At one point, in a fit of jealousy, he shoots himself in the foot in order to win sympathy and to resemble the limping Doctor. To get back at the Mack family and all they represent, Glahn drills holes beneath a boulder in preparation for sending it crashing down on the Sirilund dock, the site of Herr Mack's trading enterprises. Glahn believes that Herr Mack, who seems to have discovered this plan, may have set fire to the hut. When Glahn ignites the powder packed into the drilled holes, the boulder not only does its damage but also kills Eva, whom Herr Mack had assigned to work there.

Meanwhile, Edvarda has her own battle. On the one hand, she recognizes Glahn as her spiritual soul mate, turning to him again and again when he least expects affection from her. On the other hand, she is flattered by the attentions of the respectable suitors whom her father has encouraged. Furthermore, she resents Glahn's periods of independence as well as the hold he has on her emotions. Each waits for the other to find the means of saving the relationship, but neither is able to do anything but watch and contribute to its disintegration.

As Glahn prepares to leave the territory and Edvarda's marriage to the Baron is planned, she makes an outlandish request: She asks Glahn to give her Aesop, his most valued personal possession. Stunned, once again, by Edvarda's unpredictable charm and her seeming admission of their special relationship, Glahn agrees. Remembering her past cruelties and his need to assert himself, however, Glahn shoots Aesop and sends her the grotesque gift of the corpse. Soon after, Glahn leaves and his narrative ends.

A brief second section of the novel is presented as a paper written in 1861 explaining the death of Lieutenant Glahn. The writer, a man who had become Glahn's hunting companion in India, describes a haughty, reckless Glahn who goes out of his way to irritate others. Attractive to women, Glahn steals Henriette, a beautiful native girl, away from the narrator and, in so doing, seems to invite retaliation. Glahn's behavior becomes more and more self-destructive, as though the memories of his affair with Edvarda have never given him peace.

Glahn receives a letter that the reader assumes is from Edvarda, once again testing or tormenting him in some way. He becomes sullen and even more reckless. By provoking his hunting partner a number of times, Glahn makes it clear that he fully intends to have himself killed. His last act is to fire purposely a gun inches from the narrator's head, and then insist that the enraged rival take his revenge—which he does, putting Glahn out of his misery once and for all.

The Characters

Knut Hamsun's intent is to demonstrate the power of irrational forces at work in his characters. Like other late nineteenth century European writers, such as August Strindberg and Fyodor Dostoevski, Hamsun creates character studies that seem to anticipate the theories formulated by Sigmund Freud and his followers. In particular, Hamsun demonstrates how the subconscious precipitates actions that are contrary to an individual's conscious motives and acknowledged self-interest.

The case is especially clear with Glahn. As much as he is attracted to Edvarda, he resents the intrusion of this uncontrollable element into his life. He is a man who thrives in isolation, living by and for himself. He feels compromised by relationships and social codes. Once drawn into the world of courtship and social convention, he becomes uneasy. Without knowing the reasons, Glahn does impulsive things that mark him as a dangerous eccentric: He throws Edvarda's shoe into the water, he speaks abusively in polite company, he shoots himself in the foot, he dynamites a boulder which destroys a dock, killing Eva, he spits in the Baron's ear, and he shoots his beloved dog.

The reader can understand this behavior, in part, as a kind of survival instinct, the means by which Glahn extricates himself from a relationship and forces himself into the isolation in which he thrives. Yet Glahn's ego and his passion for Edvarda lead him, on the conscious level, to attempt to master situations in which he finds himself rather than run from them. Though his subconscious breaks through in these embarrassing and often painful ways, Glahn does not heed these warnings. He is at war with himself.

Hamsun underscores his intentions by identifying Glahn with Pan, a mythological figure associated with the forest, hunting, sexual energy, and a consequent magnetism. The identification is made most pointedly by the image of Pan on Glahn's powder horn, and in this way, the destructive potential is foreshadowed: Glahn will use his rifle powder as a tool for a vengeance that is in part sexually motivated. Pan is often portrayed as goat-footed, a detail that may be psychoanalytically translated into both lameness (without normal foot formation) and sexual potency (goatlike). Hamsun brings these associations together through the lame Doctor, Glahn's rival, who tries to tame Edvarda by constantly correcting her speech, and through Glahn's act of identification through self-mutilation. Above all, Pan is a phallic deity, and many of his legends are stories of seduction. Glahn's actions toward Eva and Henriette dramatize this aspect. These women parallel the nymphs and shepherdesses of Greek mythology.

Edvarda is another matter. With her somewhat masculine name and boyish figure, she is a confused character in her own right, unable to choose successfully between her social needs (Freud's superego) and her id's passion for Glahn. The choice she makes—her father's choice, one assumes—is made out of spite and brings her no happiness, as her periodic correspondence to Glahn demonstrates. Her habit of domination has been learned, as the daughter of the town's wealthy leader, and this habit conflicts with another, more submissive, part of her personality.

The other characters exist largely as aspects of Glahn and Edvarda or as the means to reveal these two more fully. They are treated more as types than as individuals: The Doctor is an intellectual bully, the Baron is an aristocratic snob, and Eva is the incarnation of idyllic, passive femininity.

Themes and Meanings

Hamsun's purpose in this and other novels is not so much to interpret but to dramatize convincingly the role of the irrational and the subconscious in human behavior. In *Pan*, Hamsun employs mythological allusions as well as dream material to universalize Glahn's plight. He recognizes that man's inability to discover and to reconcile the full range of human motivation often leads to tragedy.

Dreams and musings involving obscure legendary figures—Iselin, Diderik, Dundas, and Stamer—give the reader access to Glahn's thinly disguised sexual wishes. In these passages and others, Hamsun uses an evocative, poetic style. He allows the suggestions of his rich imagery to conjure the direction and intensity of his characters' longings. Hamsun's pursuit of subjective truths makes such a style appropriate, and he is a master of it.

Similarly, Hamsun's decision to have Glahn tell his own story rests on the subjective orientation. One feels the experience as Glahn remembers it, but one also sees Glahn more clearly than he sees himself. One purpose of the second narrator is to give the reader another perspective on Glahn. This device succeeds, even though one must filter one's perceptions through an extremely biased source. With two subjective perspectives on his main character, both of them self-interested and self-justifying, Hamsun has insisted that there is little certainty. The texture of passionate experience, however, has been convincingly rendered.

Critical Context

Hamsun's works published before 1890 are of little interest. Beginning with the publication of *Sult* (1890; *Hunger*, 1899), however, he became recognized as one of Europe's foremost innovators in a new genre later to be called the lyrical novel. Rebelling against the prevailing rationalism of his day and against the convention of novels focused on society, Hamsun explored the terrain of the human psyche in all its complexity and inconsistency. With *Mysterier* (1892; *Mysteries*, 1927) and *Pan*, he continued to fashion a series of attractive, somewhat tragic nonconformists. The nihilistic spirit of these works aligns him with the work of Friedrich Nietzsche, the great German philosopher. In fact, Nietzsche's conception of the contrast between the Apollonian and Dionysian spirits provides a handy orientation for understanding the tensions in *Pan*.

Hamsun's poetry and his later novels maintained but did not surpass the high standard of the 1890's, a period of high achievement which concluded with *Victoria* (1898; English translation, 1929). The one exception is *Markens grøde* (1917; *Growth of the Soil*, 1920), for which he was awarded the Nobel Prize for Literature in 1920. By the time Hamsun had written this work, his heroes were no longer rootless vagabonds but people wedded to their labors.

Hamsun's work has been widely praised by André Gide, Thomas Mann, and other giants of modern world literature who recognized Hamsun as a towering, iconoclastic genius both in his perception of the human spiritual condition and in his crafting of a flexible, highly evocative style. *Pan* is the novel in which this genius was fully realized for the first time. Though far less known than these writers in England and the United States, Hamsun stands with them.

Sources for Further Study

Ferguson, Robert. *Enigma: The Life of Knut Hamsun*, 1987.
Gustavson, Alrik. *Six Scandinavian Novelists*, 1940.
Larsen, Hanna Astrup. *Knut Hamsun*, 1922.
Næss, Harald. *Knut Hamsun*, 1984.
Sehmsdorf, Henning K. "Knut Hamsun's *Pan*: Myth and Symbol," in *Edda*.
    LXXIV (1974), pp. 345-393.
Vige, Rolf. *Knut Hamsun's Pan*, 1963.

Philip K. Jason

PASSING TIME

Author: Michel Butor (1926-   )
Type of plot: Detective
Time of plot: 1951-1952
Locale: Bleston, an industrial city in the north of England
First published: L'Emploi du temps, 1956 (English translation,1960)

> *Principal characters:*
> JACQUES REVEL, a French diarist working in England for a
> year
> GEORGE BURTON, a mystery writer under the pseudonym
> J. C. HAMILTON, who is nearly killed
> LUCIEN BLAISE, Revel's countryman who becomes engaged to
> Rose Bailey
> ANN BAILEY, to whom Revel is first attracted until he meets
> Rose
> ROSE BAILEY, Ann's attractive sister, whom Revel loses to
> Blaise
> JAMES JENKINS, Revel's coworker who becomes Ann's fiancé
> HORACE BUCK, a black pyromaniac who befriends Revel

The Novel

The principal action of the novel is Jacques Revel's physical and mental journey through the labyrinthine ways of Bleston, an industrial town in the north of England, where he has come to do translation work for a year. From his arrival in the early hours of October 2, 1951, through his departure on September 30, 1952, the major events of his story are recorded in his diary. This record of events begins ominously, with a missed train, a postmidnight arrival in rainy Bleston, the first of many confused wanderings in the city's streets, and, to add to his inauspicious arrival, the necessity of sleeping in a railway station. The oppressive gloom of the city, the omnipresent falling of fine soot and ash, the limitations of its inhabitants, and the confusion of places and streets conspire to give Bleston such an atmosphere of hostility that the city itself becomes a sinister character seeking to overcome Revel and suffocate him.

Revel's encounters with the city's inhabitants range in significance from habitual misunderstandings with merchants, shopkeepers, and bus drivers to important meetings with the few who befriend him, chief among them James Jenkins, the Bailey sisters, Lucien Blaise, Horace Buck, and George Burton. His chance meeting with Burton, who, as J.C. Hamilton, wrote a mystery novel, *The Murder of Bleston*, leads him into an odd sequence of events. He comes to suspect a cover-up of an actual fratricide and the attempted murder of Burton by Jenkins, to whom Revel reveals Burton's true identity. At the same time, Revel is also trying to fathom the mystery of the city and its inhabitants' obsession with the fratricidal Cain depicted in the stained glass of the Old Cathedral. A series of fires of mysterious origin, perhaps set by Horace Buck, perhaps even set by Revel, who engages in four ritual inciner-ations, adds to the aura of fear, anxiety, and uneasiness that overshadows the city and Revel.

Revel first seeks to escape Bleston and the oppressive confinement that both repels and attracts him by trying to walk beyond its precincts into the countryside; this, however, proves impossible. His escapes to the oases of amusement parks that move from one section of the city to another are short-lived and unsatisfactory. His refuge in the cinema, which screens travel-ogues of distant countries, is necessarily temporary and reinforces his sense of imprisonment. He partially succeeds in escaping the present by exploring Bleston's past and encountering representations of the mythic detective prob-lem solvers Oedipus and Theseus. His most successful escape, apart from his departure on September 30, comes when he begins his diary and seeks ref-uge in the act of writing. This is ironic, since he can escape his physical and temporal confines only by immersing himself in them to record them.

His immersion in Bleston's events, monuments, and people involves his probing maps, examining buildings, such as the cathedrals, and following Burton's fictional guide to Bleston, *The Murder of Bleston*. In all these ex-plorations, Revel is conscious that he is wandering through his internal wasteland, and on a quest for the meaning of his own life, as well. Although he probes the original Bleston murder in this City of Cain, he does not solve it. Nor does he solve the attempted murder of Burton. He remains a mys-tified, suspicious outsider, changed and overcome by Bleston.

The Characters

Jacques Revel is Michel Butor's masterfully produced central character, the diarist-narrator of the work, who records his impressions, meetings, and journeys in Bleston. Self-absorbed, he cannot go beyond himself to join in either a deep or a permanent way with any of the characters who befriend him during his yearlong confinement in the unreal city. Revel's attempts at closeness, first with Ann Bailey and then with Rose Bailey, are awkward and superficial crushes he can communicate only imperfectly. His acquaintance with Horace Buck and with George and Harriet Burton never becomes real friendship. His companionship with Lucien Blaise, the only other Frenchman to arrive in Bleston, becomes strained when Lucien and Rose announce their engagement. His friendship with James Jenkins, uneasy from the first, cools when James begins courting Ann and breaks off when he suspects James of attempting to kill Burton in a fit of hatred for the writer. Revel himself remains enigmatic, largely because of his inability to overcome Bleston and his own isolation.

Jenkins is also enigmatic in his alternations between guardedness and openness with Revel. A self-described Blestonian who has never left the city, he both analyzes the superstitious nature of the inhabitants and shares that trait. He comments that detective writers avoid setting their novels in Bleston for fear that their make-believe may turn into grim reality. Jenkins is Revel's chief suspect in Burton's attempted murder. He realizes and accepts as his heritage the darker and more primitive origins of Bleston and appears intent on both protecting and preserving them in his own life.

Burton, whose discourses on the nature of murder and detection and on the role of the writer/detective reflect Butor's own activity as a writer, creates multiple masks to shield his identity out of a justifiable fear for his life. Burton reveals his identity to Revel, an outsider who carries his book, with the stipulation that he tell no one; Revel betrays his confidence to the Bailey girls and to Jenkins, whose family was linked to building the New Cathedral Burton had derided in *The Murder of Bleston*. A successful popular novelist using one pseudonym for his best-sellers and another for novels written in collaboration with his wife, he chooses a third for *The Murder of Bleston*, in which a detective sets out to find a murderer, just as Burton himself may be writing to flush out a murderer.

Horace Buck, a stranger like Revel, lives at the fringes of Bleston and embodies the burning hatred of an outsider doomed to remain there. He seeks Revel's companionship but also frightens him with his intensity. Their meetings usually happen by chance, but also with some consistency, as they become drinking companions united by their common hatred of the city. Buck, one suspects, is the pyromaniac responsible for the Bleston fires.

The Bailey girls, Ann and Rose, are not fully realized characters. They are presented vaguely through the eyes of Revel. In one sense, Ann is Revel's Ariadne, who guides him through the maze of Bleston, and Rose is his Phaedra. The sisters attract Revel, but he is incapable of forming more than a casual relationship with either of them, unable to express the affection he feels.

Themes and Meanings

Butor blends a wide variety of themes into the highly structured narrative he has called *L'Emploi du temps*. The title delineates the principal theme of temporality in several important respects. Translated as "passing time," it could mean the passage of time, time's flight, or killing time; it could also be translated as "the schedule," clearly identifying the constraints of railway scheduling that begin the novel inauspiciously and end it abruptly. The structure of the work reinforces its title and the theme of time: It is divided into five parts, like the acts of classical French plays, each part corresponding to the month in which it is written. Begun on May 1, the diary's subject for May is the preceding October. By June, Revel is writing about the events of

November and also contemporaneous June events. July expands to include December, May, and July. In the final part, "Farewell," he writes of September, February, March, July, and August and recalls every other month's events as he reads the pages written since May, so that the year's experience finds its iteration and culmination in September. This fluid process of moving back and forth across time follows a sometimes rigid and sometimes interrupted schedule of writing on most weeknights, so that each part is divided into five sections, each of about five days' duration. Despite all the work's infrastructure, Revel is frustrated by the nearly impossible task of telling his story, reordering experience, and reflecting on earlier experience modified by later revelation.

Within the framework of passing time, ancient and modern figures, events, and themes coalesce. Revel, for example, is a modern Odysseus who likens Bleston to Circe's island. He is also a modern variation on Theseus, for whom Ann Bailey is his Ariadne and Rose his Phaedra. Burton likens the detective, and the writer, to the son of the murderer Oedipus who answers a riddle and kills the one to whom he owes his title of detective. Above all is the shadow of Cain as depicted in the Murderer's Window of the Old Cathedral. In Cain's shadow is *The Murder of Bleston*, the actual and fictional victim, the fictional detective and the actual writer/detective, and Revel as detective manqué. Bleston itself has an origin that reinforces its mysterious present, an origin in a Roman outpost called "Bellista," from "Belli Civitas," the city of war. It is a city at war with its inhabitants and visitors.

Among the other themes Butor brings together in the novel are unrequited, because unexpressed, love, the outsider's abiding sense of alienation, the dark family secrets of murder and revenge, the supremacy of place over person, and the uneasy necessity to hide one's true identity even as others seek to discover it. These, together with temporality, the inability to capture it, and the reenactment of the past in the present, combine to underscore one of Butor's primary artistic concerns: the power of the word either to communicate experience and meaning or to withhold their expression. Thus the novel's format itself—the division of labor into five months of commenting on the previous seven as well as on the present, and of combining the elements of all twelve months into the last—emphasizes the act of writing for the purpose of communicating. That the communication is often unclear, incomplete, misleading, and circular suggests that Revel has only a provisional understanding of those around him and of himself.

Critical Context

Passing Time, his second novel, gained for Butor national recognition in France in the form of the Fénelon Prize in 1957. During the same year, he published and won the Théophraste-Renaudot Prize for *La Modification* (1957; *A Change of Heart*, 1959). Firmly established in the avant-garde as an advocate for and writer of the "New Novel" of the 1950's and 1960's, Butor experimented with the structure of the novel as well as the presentation of characters and the interiorizing of action. Like his first novel, *Passage de Milan* (1954), *Passing Time* is a work of extraordinary technical virtuosity that foreshadows his later and bolder experiments with form in *Réseau aérien: Texte radiophonique* (1962) and in the long narratives variously called postnovels or novels, *Mobile: Étude pour une représentation des États-Unis* (1962; *Mobile: Study for the Representation of the United States*, 1963), *6,810,000 Litres d'eau par seconde: Étude stéréophonique* (1965; *Niagara: A Stereophonic Novel*, 1969), and *Boomerang* (1978).

Passing Time, experimental though it is, falls recognizably within the category of the novel. Butor's later writings seek to transcend the form in such a way as to become "open" works, susceptible to a variety of readings, not confined to the printed page but aspiring to the condition of music. His diverse poetry, his operatic work with Henri Pousseur in producing *Votre Faust: Fantaisie variable genre Opéra* (1962), his travelogues as novels, his essays, and his continuing work as a writer and lecturer place him among the few great literary figures of the last half of the twentieth century.

Sources for Further Study
Grant, Marian. *Michel Butor: L'Emploi du temps*, 1973.
McWilliams, Dean. *The Narratives of Michel Butor: The Writer as Janus*, 1978.
Spencer, Michael. *Michel Butor*, 1974.
World Literature Today. LVI (Spring, 1982). Special Butor issue.

John J. Conlon

THE PATH TO THE NEST OF SPIDERS

Author: Italo Calvino (1923-1985)
Type of plot: Psychological realism
Time of plot: 1944
Locale: An unnamed town and the surrounding countryside, on the coast of
   Liguria in the northwest portion of the Italian peninsula
First published: Il sentiero dei nidi di ragno, 1947 (English translation, 1956)

> *Principal characters:*
> PIN, a teenage boy
> RINA (the DARK GIRL OF LONG ALLEY), his older sister
> RED WOLF, a young Communist partisan
> COUSIN, a member of a partisan band

The Novel

It is Italy in the year 1944: The Germans are locked in combat with the Allied forces advancing from the south, while the countryside is roamed by partisan bands, ambushing German convoys and disrupting their supply lines. Overhead, Allied bombers pass by on their way to the destruction of cities and factories, while at sea the low, dark shapes of warships patrol the coasts.

The convulsion of a world at war is lost on Pin, a young, foulmouthed urchin who is both precocious in worldly ways and almost touchingly naïve. He smokes, cadges drinks from men in the local bar, sings them dirty songs and tells them filthy jokes to win their approval, but despises them so thoroughly that he inevitably turns on them with his cruel, accurate wit. The men turn on him with their fists and boots and kick him out into the street. For Pin, however, adults are his only companions; he cannot get along with boys his own age.

Pin lives with his sister, Rina, who is known as the Dark Girl of Long Alley. Rina's current boyfriend is a young German sailor; there have been many others, and Pin contemptuously dismisses his sister as a whore. Their mother is dead and their father has deserted them.

Pin is plunged into the complexity of the war through accident, almost on a dare. The drinkers in the bar become excited when a partisan recruiter passes through town, and, although their commitment is limited to some loud and indiscreet talk, they convince Pin to steal a pistol from Rina's German sailor. Pin takes the weapon when the two are making love, but instead of turning it over to the men he buries it at his secret place, a stretch of grassy riverbank where spiders build their nests.

On his way home, Pin is arrested, beaten during interrogation, and lodged in a former English villa that is now a prison. There he meets Red Wolf, the legendary young Communist partisan. Even Pin, who is indifferent to the war, has heard of this young bridge destroyer and Nazi fighter. Perhaps, Pin thinks, he has at last met someone with whom to share the secret of the spiders' nests. Red Wolf and Pin escape, but before Pin can reveal his treasure the two are separated.

Pin meets Cousin, another partisan, who takes Pin with him to his detachment. It is a ragged group, a combination of misfits, and the partisan commanders always station it far from actual fighting during battles. Pin finds these adults no better than the wine drinkers back home. As he follows them he resumes his old behavior, mocking the men with his coarse, uncomfortably accurate jokes, while watching them narrowly for any signs of weakness or fault. Only Cousin, who, like Pin, expresses contempt and scorn for women, wins his approval. Finally, disgusted beyond endurance, he leaves the band to return home.

Pin finds that his sister is now the mistress of a German officer; nothing has changed at home, so he leaves. Down by the river he searches for the hidden pistol among the nests of spiders. Throughout his adventures he has often thought of it and feared that others might have found it. At last, he unearths it. Cousin comes along and Pin shows him the spiders' hidden homes. As the book ends, the two go off together across the fields.

The Characters

The central character of *The Path to the Nest of Spiders* is Pin. All the other characters and events of the novel are filtered through his perceptions. These perceptions are skewed, however, because of Pin's situation and personality. Living without a father or mother, and with a sister whose morals are distinctly casual, has hardened and coarsened Pin. Beyond this, Pin seems to be suffering from severe anxieties relating to sexuality; partly, no doubt, these stem from his own developing sexual nature, but the severity and depth of his condition often seem much more than can be attributed to adolescent uncertainty.

Pin is well acquainted with the mechanical aspects of human sexuality; during the escape with Red Wolf he irks the young Communist by drawing obscene pictures on the side of a wall, instead of the proletarian propaganda Red Wolf expects. Elsewhere in the novel, Pin is able to score cruel and accurate hits on others with his jokes and songs aimed at their sexual foibles or frailties. He clearly has a thorough, if gutter-level, education in the topic of sex.

Yet the relationships between men and women baffle him. He cannot understand why the two desire each other, and this ignorance leads to fear and a vibrant hatred of females. The main appeal of the young partisan known as Cousin is that he, too, scorns women. Cousin wastes no occasion to disparage women, and at one point concisely states his philosophy to Pin: "Of course, behind all the stories with a bad ending there's always a woman, make no mistake about that. You're young, just listen to what I tell you. War's all due to women. . . ." It is little wonder, then, that Pin is drawn to Cousin, the only person to whom he can show the nests of spiders. Still, Cousin is flawed, just as Pin is, and the novel leaves unresolved their future development.

Within the world of Italo Calvino's novel, all characters are flawed. There are obvious moral failings, such as those of Pin's sister, Rina, and there are other, more ambiguous faults, which are somehow darkly connected with sex. Dritto, the commander of the inept partisan unit, seems an excellent leader in his potential but continually wastes opportunities in combat and destroys his reputation with the higher command. During the climactic battle toward the end of the book, Dritto renounces his command to Cousin and remains behind to make love with the young wife of the unit's cook. Pin, who has stayed behind to spy on the couple, receives fresh confirmation that the sexual bond between man and women is a base and destroying union, rather than a loving and creative one.

Other motives fare no better in the bleak view of the boy. Red Wolf, who entered Pin's life as a shining hero, proves to be a humorless, doctrinaire Communist, who finds all of his answers in the Party line. At one point he dismisses another character as a "Trotskyist," explaining the word to Pin by quoting the title of a work by Vladimir Ilich Lenin: "Left-wing Communism, an infantile disorder."

The boozy drinkers in the town bar, the misfits of the partisan band, the brutal but inefficient members of the Fascist guards, all of these are flawed and lacking. Some of this is a result of the novel's setting in wartime Italy, where human nature is degraded by circumstance and condition. More of it, however, comes from the view of the world as seen by Pin, a deeply troubled young boy.

Themes and Meanings

Relationships between people is the central theme of *The Path to the Nest of Spiders*. How do human beings connect, how can they reach out to one another? These are Pin's unspoken but deeply rooted questions. Throughout the novel he searches for someone who is worthy of his trust and admiration, someone to whom he can reveal the symbolic secret nest of spiders.

Pin's puzzlement is exacerbated by his developing sexuality and the chaos and danger of war. Although he can make clever, if crude, jokes about sex, he does not fully understand it. He is aware of its powerful hold over men and women, but he does not yet feel this tug of passion himself, so it both confuses and angers him to see its effects in others.

Pin seems almost antisexual, and his rejection spills over into a profound contempt for all human weakness. He has fantasies of winning the approval and applause of adults, but, significantly, his daydreams generally revolve around acts of violence directed at those same adults. For Pin, violence and sex form a binary combination.

Such a combination is well expressed in the context of war. During war, relationships are severely tested. Will one's comrade prove to be worthy of trust on the march, in battle, or during interrogation by the enemy? Can one trust another to keep one's identity secret, or will one be betrayed to the Fascists in the Black Brigade, or their masters in the Nazi Gestapo? Because the wartime situation emphasizes these concerns, it is an apt choice for a novel about relationships between persons.

War is also a telling metaphor for Pin's internal condition, as he is torn between the world of childhood and the adult world, and fits well into neither of them. Few things make him happy, and his one great pleasure—the nests of spiders—cannot be shared with anyone in the flawed, dirty world around him. Each time Pin reaches out to another, he finds some fault in his would-be companion. His sister is a whore, the men in the tavern are loudmouthed braggarts, Red Wolf is a humorless automaton, the partisans are bumbling malcontents. Only Cousin, who has also rejected sex and women, is worthy of admiration and friendship.

Pin rails and storms against a world that is base and ruled by lust and passion, and seeks out an ally who shares his contempt for all that is weak and defiled. Pin and Cousin deliberately limit themselves to a narrow, circumscribed existence. Together they form a small, dedicated partisan band, determined to resist the unruly world around them.

Critical Context

The Path to the Nest of Spiders was Italo Calvino's first novel and was published in 1947, only two years after the end of the war. In a sense, the book is a literary counterpart to Vittorio De Sica's film *Ladri di biciclette* (1948; *The Bicycle Thief*), which also probes the ravaged, precarious lives of the common men and women in war-torn Italy. Both works, the novel and the film, present life in gritty, uncompromising terms and focus on the fundamental passions which govern human life. Life, they say, is a struggle for sex or bread, a battle in the hills between Fascists and partisans or between the poor and homeless in the streets.

On the surface, then, *The Path to the Nest of Spiders* would seem to be pure neorealism, a bleak and unblinking depiction of the harsh truth of Italy during World War II. Boys join the Fascists so they can carry machine guns; women sleep with German sailors and officers to have ersatz chocolate and jam to eat; and the partisans, far from being the sterling heroes of myth, are a ragtag collection of misfits, parroting Communists, and confused youths.

This work stands in marked contrast to Calvino's other writings. There is little humor and no fantasy in this book, while both of these elements are essential qualities of his more mature efforts such as *Le cosmicomiche* (1965;

Cosmicomics, 1968), *Ti con zero* (1967; *T Zero*, 1969), or the lyrical, enchanting *Le città invisibili* (1972; *Invisible Cities*, 1974). In this first novel, Calvino sketches a solid, earthy and earthbound narrative, one that is grounded firmly in the sordid reality of a war's unraveling and a young boy's sexual awakening.

Still, there are touches which reveal the Calvino to come. The choice of the spiders' nests as a critical, central symbol, and the deft, almost poetic description of those nests, is an indication of the neorealistic, nonliteral tendencies which would become more prominent as Calvino's career progressed.

On the one hand, it is clear that to Pin the nests are a secret, a talisman whose revelation to another is the only certain test of comradeship in an otherwise unfriendly and untrustworthy world. On the other hand, the intricate, almost magical nature of the nests, with their woven round doors on gossamer hinges, hints at a reality beyond the mundane. In the books which followed this first novel, Italo Calvino steadily moved away from the realm of mere realism to that of the enchanted symbol.

Sources for Further Study
Andrews, Richard. "Italo Calvino," in *Writers and Society in Contemporary Italy: A Collection of Essays*, 1984. Edited by Michael Caesar and Peter Hainsworth.

Calvino, Italo. *The Uses of Literature*, 1986.

Carter, Albert Howard. *Italo Calvino: Metamorphoses of Fantasy*, 1987.

Olken, I. T. *With Pleated Eye and Garnet Wing: Symmetries of Italo Calvino*, 1984.

Michael Witkoski

PATTERNS OF CHILDHOOD

Author: Christa Wolf (1929-   )
Type of plot: Social realism
Time of plot: 1932-1947 and 1971-1975
Locale: L. (Landsberg, Germany; later, Gorzów Wielkopolski, Poland);
   Mecklenburg, in the Soviet Occupation Zone; and the German Democratic
   Republic
First published: Kindheitsmuster, 1976 (*A Model Childhood*, 1980; reissued as
   Patterns of Childhood)

> Principal characters:
> NELLY JORDAN, the narrator, a woman who grew up in
>   Germany during the Fascist period
> CHARLOTTE JORDAN, her mother
> BRUNO JORDAN, her father
> LENKA, her fifteen-year-old daughter

The Novel

   Patterns of Childhood is an intricate interweaving of three narratives: Nelly Jordan's childhood under National Socialism; her trip with her husband, daughter, and brother to her former hometown (now in Poland); and the difficult process of recollecting and recording her unsettling memories. In July, 1971, a two-day trip to L., which the narrator has not seen since fleeing with her family in late January, 1945, sets off a string of associations, dreams, and memories about her childhood. She is unsuccessful in organizing these recollections until November, 1972, when she begins to write about her childhood self in the third person, namely as Nelly Jordan, and about her remembering and writing selves in the second person. Only in the last pages of the novel do these selves coalesce.

   Nelly's earliest memory is of herself as a three-year-old in 1932 sitting on the steps in front of her father's grocery story and repeating the word "I" over and over. The momentous political events of the following year hardly affected her happy childhood. Despite the economic crisis, her father successfully opened a second store, and her parents were probably too busy with business to take notice in the newspaper of the curtailment of personal freedoms or the opening of the Dachau concentration camp in March, 1933. In the summer, the Nazi Standard Bearer Rudi Arndt accused Nelly's father, Bruno Jordan, of having connections with the outlawed Communists, but Bruno was able to appease him with the promise of a sack of flour and sugar for the next Party meeting. One day in the fall of 1933, Bruno appeared in Nelly's room proudly wearing his new peaked, blue naval storm trooper cap. "See! Now your father is one of them, too," exclaimed her mother in a "happy voice." Although they had previously voted for the Social Democrats, Nelly's parents voted for the Nazis in the November elections, along with most of the other citizens of L.

In 1937, Elvira, the family's maid, revealed to Nelly that four years earlier Elvira and her family had stayed home and wept when the Communist flags were burned in the town, for her family were Communists. Only thirty-five years later, in the State Library, which had old copies of the newspaper from L. on file, did the narrator learn the background information on what had really happened in the town. Now, the narrator can only speculate on Nelly's family's reactions to the day of the flag burning, March 17, 1933. Neither can she be sure of why Nelly realized that she had to keep Elvira's secret to herself. She does know that Nelly started asking fewer questions, that somewhere around this time Nelly dreamed or thought for the first time that "it's all wrong," that Nelly's sense of guilt increased as the realm of her secrets grew, and that the family did not talk openly about certain "glitter words" ("alien blood," "sterilization," "hereditary diseases," "a eugenic way of life"). The narrator now wonders whether one solution to the problem of living under a dictatorship is to restrict one's curiosity to areas that are not dangerous.

During Nelly's first year in the girls' school on Adolf-Hitlerstrasse, she tried assiduously to live up to the expectation of Herr Warsinski, her religion and German teacher. Remembering it now, the narrator finds it difficult to explain to her daughter, Lenka, how Nelly could so eagerly submit to her teacher's demands for unflinching obedience and faithfulness to the Führer. During this period, Nelly's family was building a new house and store on the outskirts of town near two barracks, one of which was just being constructed. With the growing number of soldiers in the area, it proved to be a very favorable location. These "peacetime" years were good years for Bruno Jordan and his family. Bruno became active in the buyers' cooperative, his account book grew thin, as people could now pay with cash and not on credit, and he purchased a picture of the Führer from his Party friend Leo Siegmann.

When the purity of an aunt's ancestry was questioned, Nelly's response was that she did not want to be Jewish. She did not need to be concerned, for her family had no Jewish, foreign, or Communist relatives, friends, or connections, no mental diseases, and no subversive tendencies. An uncle took over the candy factory abandoned by an escaping Jew. Nelly went to see the remains of the Jewish synagogue in town the day after it had been destroyed during the Crystal Night of November 8, 1938. Soon after, she made little prisons for ladybugs, her favorite creatures, and covered them sadistically with sand when they tried to escape.

When a mailman brought Bruno's draft notice in late August, 1939, a week before the German invasion of Poland, Charlotte called out on the stairs: "The hell with your Führer." Nelly's father, however, was soon home again after the successful completion of the Polish Campaign in October. A few weeks later, when Leo Siegmann called Bruno to tell him that their unit had executed five Polish hostages, Leo remarked that it was too bad that Bruno was not there. Bruno's face became ashen. "That kind of thing is not for me," he said later. Nevertheless, he remained in the reserves for the rest of the war, and his wife, Charlotte, took over the daily running of the business.

Nelly excelled at sporting events sponsored by the Hitler Youth in the local stadium. She even pushed her way into serving with the Jungmädel League; it was far more interesting than sitting around home or the store, and it made one tough. It also protected her from fear and self-doubt. Yet, for all the time she spent in her Jungmädel unit, the narrator has no memory of a single face or name from its mass of activities. What the narrator does remember precisely is Nelly's history and German teacher, Julia Strauch. Julia was single and the sole female intellectual Nelly knew. Nelly fell in love with Julia, but her love was a kind of captivity and was never returned. Nelly was thirteen at the time and had begun to steal candy from the store. She had also started to read surreptitiously her parents' copy of the SS magazine and to tear up her fingernails.

In 1943, the adolescent antics of her friends behind the altar at their confirmation and Herr Andrack's hypnosis demonstration at the party afterward left a stronger impression on Nelly than reports of the German defeat at Stalingrad or Joseph Goebbels' voice on the radio proclaiming total war. In 1944, refugees began to arrive in town, and Charlotte had to wake her children every night as bombers flew overhead on the way to Berlin. On January 29, 1945, when Russian troops were approaching the town, Nelly fled with her aunts, uncles, and grandparents in a truck belonging to her Uncle Alfons' employer. Her father had already left with the French prisoners of whom he had been put in charge and would soon be captured. Charlotte decided to stay behind at the last minute to settle their affairs, leaving Nelly and her younger brother, Lutz, in the care of the other family members.

It took two weeks for the twelve family members to reach the town of Wittenberge on the Elbe River, several hundred kilometers due west of L. There, in the school where they were housed, Charlotte miraculously caught up with them. The family soon moved to a hotel in a village west of Berlin, then in late April, was forced to flee again, this time to the northwest by foot. They heard of Hitler's death and met survivors from the concentration camps, one of whom, a Communist, said to them, "Where on earth have you all been living," a sentence which years later was to become a kind of motto for Nelly.

Eventually they settled in a small village in Mecklenburg, which was then occupied by Russian troops. From her teacher, Nelly "discovered that she'd been living under a dictatorship for twelve years, apparently without noticing it." In 1946, she contracted a mild case of tuberculosis a few months before her father, hardly recognizable, returned from a Russian prisoner-of-war camp. She spent the following winter in a sanatorium and was released in April, 1947, weighing 165 pounds.

During the two-day stay in L. years later, the narrator and her family avoided contact with the Polish inhabitants of what is now G. Her family's houses and stores, the school, the bathing area on the river, the church, the stadium, the barracks, the factories, the train station, an overgrown cemetery, and the sandy hills outside the town all provided access to forgotten images, conversations, people, and events. Lutz is far less troubled by the past than his sister, but Lenka repeatedly asks disturbing questions as the very ordinary narrative of her mother's life under Hitler begins to be told.

The Characters

In a brief foreword, Christa Wolf warns the reader that the characters and events in the novel are the inventions of the narrator and that anyone who "detects a similarity between a character in the narrative and either himself or anyone else should consider the strange lack of individuality in the behavior of many contemporaries." Almost all the characters in the novel sacrificed their individuality during the Nazi era out of fear, duty, opportunism, idealism, or indifference. In contrast, the narrator and Lenka, by questioning authoritarian behavior patterns in themselves and others, are able to break out of such patterns and develop as unique individuals. Readers are thus challenged to examine critically their own lives in order to see to what extent they, too, are susceptible to the "universal loss of memory" and "terrifying lack of individuality" that are characteristic of the modern age.

Halfway through the novel, the narrator has grave second thoughts about her character young Nelly. The girl she describes seems helpless, manipulated, strange; she calls her "nothing but the product of your hypocrisy." The narrator now blames herself for not directly confronting that of which she is ashamed and defensive. The year is 1942, Nelly is thirteen and has begun eating candy while reading the SS newspaper. She has been swept along by events and fully indoctrinated into the Nazi educational and youth organizations. She is only marginally aware of the war of Nazi racial policies and has long since stopped asking painful questions. Her acquiescence in the daily routine of a small town under Fascism is virtually complete. Unlike the main characters of most other East German novels about the Nazi era, whose heroes are resistance fighters or rapid converts to socialism, Nelly begins to gain a new social identity slowly, during the flight from L. and the resettlement in the Soviet Occupation Zone.

Late in the novel, the narrator quotes Johann Wolfgang von Goethe without comment: "I have done much writing, in order to lay the foundation for memory." She feels compelled to write about her childhood not only because of the trip to L. and her daughter's probing questions but also because no other book on World War II or Fascism can adequately explain her own experience. "Woe to our time, which forces the writer to exhibit the wound of his own crime before he is allowed to describe other people's wounds," she notes in a chapter that opens with a quote by the Austrian writer Ingeborg Bachmann ("With my burned hand I write about the nature of fire") and the statement: "The craving for authenticity is growing." Authenticity, honesty, and integrity are the goals that the narrator sets for her writing in the hope that such relentless self-exposure will show how Fascism is not a phenomenon to be studied only in others but a latent tendency which everyone must confront.

Lenka is typical of the children of parents who lived under National Socialism, children who do not understand, despite all the books, films, and history lessons on the subject, how one could submit to the horrors of such a regime. Her function in the book is twofold: to keep the question of her mother's complicity always in front of her and to keep open the possibility of greater personal involvement and social responsibility for her own and future generations. She is uneasy with what she finds in the present-day German Democratic Republic, a "pseudo-people, a pseudo-life," she says. The Poles leave a positive impression on her, for they seem spontaneous and not obsessed with efficiency, discipline, and order. For her mother, Lenka is a constant reminder of the need for an honesty that would allow one to speak more openly and precisely about what was and is.

Of all Nelly's relatives, only her parents and brother did not eventually flee to West Germany. Much more than her less cautious and more opportunistic and enterprising husband, Charlotte realized the unstable ground on which the family's prosperity during the 1930's was based. A "Cassandra behind the counter of her store," she dared to tell several customers in 1944 that the war was lost, after which she was visited by two men in trenchcoats, to whom she denied the incident. After the war, Charlotte was the only family member with sufficient conscience and sensitivity to reach out beyond her own circle. When Bruno returned in 1946, she was devastated by his transformation—"with a single blow she had lost herself and her husband."

Themes and Meanings

The opening sentence of the book provides the key to its meaning: "What is past is not dead; it is not even past." In fact, it is a dangerous delusion to believe that the German past has been overcome and that 1945 represented a clean break with Fascism. In the mid-1970's, the narrator finds variants of Fascism in Greece, Chile, and the American treatment of Vietnam (aside from criticism of Joseph Stalin, the Soviet Union and Eastern Bloc countries are spared direct criticism). Despite the Socialist revolution in the German

Democratic Republic, the novel shows that disquieting attitudes persist: A cabdriver is defensive about German war guilt, an East German youth group sings Nazi songs outside Prague, and even Lutz displays an anti-Polish bias and would prefer to forget about what happened between 1933 and 1945. In order to overcome such repression and memory loss, particularly in her own case, the narrator insists on seeing the process of remembering as an endlessly repeated moral act. Yet her writing can only partially and tentatively answer the haunting question, "How did we become what we are today?"

When they joined their respective Nazi organizations, both Nelly and her father "opted for the thousands" and against themselves. The narrator's lengthy struggle to become accountable for her childhood self—to learn to say "I" rather than "she"—exemplifies Wolf's search for subjective authenticity. By becoming so intensely aware of the patterns of conforming behavior in herself and those around her—the "patterns of childhood" that are extraordinarily difficult to change, fear, hate, deception, duty, obedience, bondage to authority—the narrator is able to gain insight into the "ghastly secret of human beings in this century," how one can be witness to such events and yet ignore them, to be there and yet not be there at the same time. When Bruno returned from captivity, he asked "What have they done to us[?]" It never occurred to him to ask himself what role he played in the disaster, how he was personally responsible for what happened.

The complex structure of the novel, with its nonlinear narration and tightly woven fabric of personal reminiscence, meditative essay, and factual evidence, reflects the seriousness of Wolf's undertaking. Yet, no matter how honest one tries to be about one's own life, there will always be distortion and falsehood. The "fantastic accuracy" that would occur if "the structure of experience" were to coincide with the "structure of the narrative" is an unreachable goal. Although the narrator wonders whether it is possible "to escape the mortal sin of our time, the desire not to come to grips with oneself," in the end she affirms the beauty of change and dreams and declares, "I shall not revolt against the limits of the expressible."

Critical Context

Patterns of Childhood was published in the German Democratic Republic within weeks after Wolf, along with her husband and ten other prominent East German writers, protested publicly against the expulsion of the controversial songwriter and poet Wolf Biermann from the country. Despite the fact that she was looked upon with official disfavor, *Patterns of Childhood* was received positively by the critics in her country, and the first edition of sixty thousand sold out within two months. Her third novel, it represented a departure from *Der geteilte Himmel* (1963; *Divided Heaven*, 1965) and *Nachdenken über Christa T.* (1968; *The Quest for Christa T.*, 1970), both of which dealt with contemporary problems in the German Democratic Republic. Wolf next investigated the problems of self and authenticity in the context of German Romanticism in *Kein Ort: Nirgends* (1979; *No Place on Earth,* 1982) and of Greek myth and feminist theory in *Voraussetzungen einer Erzählung: "Kassandra"* and *Kassandra* (1983; *Cassandra: A Novel and Four Essays,* 1984). *Störfall* (1987; breakdown) is her report of a day in April, 1986, when news of the Chernobyl reactor disaster reached her at the same time her brother was undergoing an operation for brain cancer.

More than other recent memoirs and fiction dealing with the Fascist period, *Patterns of Childhood* achieves the formal richness and thought-provoking depth of such postwar masterpieces as Thomas Mann's *Doktor Faustus* (1947; English translation, 1948), Günter Grass's *Die Blechtrommel* (1959; *The Tin Drum,* 1961), and Heinrich Böll's *Gruppenbild mit Dame* (1971; *Group Portrait with Lady,* 1973). In the German Democratic Republic, only the dramatist Heiner Müller has dealt so uncompromisingly with the remnants of Fascism in the present. Critics have repeatedly compared Wolf's novel to Alexander and Margarete Mitscherlich's psychological study, *The Incapacity to Mourn* (1977), in which they uncovered many of the same taboos and behavior patterns in West German society.

Sources for Further Study

Ezergalis, Inta. *Women Writers: The Divided Self, Analysis of Novels by Christa Wolf, Ingeborg Bachmann, Doris Lessing, and Others,* 1982.

Frieden, Sandra. "'In eigener Sache': Christa Wolf's *Kindheitsmuster,*" in *The German Quarterly.* LIV (1981), pp. 473-487.

Lamse, Mary Jane. "*Kindheitsmuster* in Context: The Achievement of Christa Wolf," in *University of Dayton Review.* XV (1981), pp. 49-55.

Love, Myra. "Christa Wolf and Feminism: Breaking the Patriarchal Connection," in *New German Critique.* XVI (Winter, 1979), pp. 31-53.

_____. *"Das Spiel mit offenen Möglichkeiten": Subjectivity and the Thematization of Writing in the Works of Christa Wolf,* 1984.

Wendt-Hildebrandt, Susan. "*Kindheitsmuster*: Christa Wolf's 'Probestück,'" in *Seminar.* I (1981), pp. 164-176.

Peter West Nutting

A PERFECT PEACE

Author: Amos Oz (1939-   )
Type of plot: Historical realism
Time of plot: From the end of 1965 to the beginning of 1967
Locale: Israel, especially Kibbutz Granot
First published: Menuhah nekhonah, 1982 (English translation, 1985)

> *Principal characters:*
> YONATAN LIFSHITZ, the protagonist, a young man who is
>   bored with life in Kibbutz Granot
> RIMONA, his wife
> YOLEK LIFSHITZ, Yonatan's father, the secretary of Kibbutz
>   Granot and once a national political force
> HAVA, his wife and Yonatan's mother
> AZARIAH GITLIN, a strange young man who is received into
>   Kibbutz Granot and then into Yonatan's home
> LEVI ESHKOL, the Prime Minister and Minister of Defense of
>   Israel
> SRULIK, the music conductor of Kibbutz Granot and later its
>   secretary

The Novel

Divided into two parts, "Winter" and "Spring," *A Perfect Peace* begins in the winter of 1965 and ends at the beginning of 1967. Although Yonatan Lifshitz is the central character, almost all the other main characters help to carry the story forward by their thoughts or their writings or a combination of these. The principal action occurs in and around Kibbutz Granot, a collective settlement in Israel. Yonatan has lived in the kibbutz all of his life and now, at the age of twenty-six, he plans to leave his wife and home. Having long felt hemmed in by the kibbutz and by his years in the army, he longs to be free to do what he wants, though he cannot say for certain what that is. He has already hinted to his father how discontented he is, and before very long he tells his wife, the quiet and passive Rimona, that he will be leaving. Rimona has taken to dreaming yearningly of faraway places and great natural beauties; this longing is probably a consequence of her having recently suffered the birth of a stillborn child, her second failed pregnancy.

Into the life of Kibbutz Granot, and especially the lives of Yonatan and Rimona, comes Azariah Gitlin. Azariah is a young man who sometimes seems little more than a boy, although he is old enough to have survived the Holocaust, wandered across Western Europe, read widely (but not necessarily deeply), and served a number of years in the Israeli army. Seeking a home, companionship, and a family, he asks to be admitted into the kibbutz.

In a short time he makes a place for himself there, although at first he is considered a nuisance and a bore. Almost without knowing what is taking place as it happens, Yonatan and Azariah become friends, housemates, and then, with Yonatan's approval, lovers of the same woman, Rimona. Seeing this turn of events as a circumstance that will allow him, finally, to get away, Yonatan gathers a few items for the road and, very early one morning, leaves, hitchhiking to the border with Jordan.

Although it should be clear to his parents, Yolek and Hava, that he has left of his own accord, they blame each other for his disappearance. Yolek is angrily self-persuaded that Benya Trotsky, who has for decades been the center of dispute between Yolek and his wife, has arranged for Yonatan to join him in Miami, where he has acquired millions of dollars from various business ventures. Years before, Benya had been in love with Hava but had had to leave Kibbutz Granot after a violent, but failed, attempt on the lives of Yolek, Hava, the kibbutz bull, and himself. From afar Benya has, at various times, "volunteered" to be Yonatan's father; so intense is his argument, however unlikely, that he is his father that both Benya and Yolek are ready to believe that it is so. In a letter and through an agent, Benya lends his support to the search for Yonatan, which by now has also been taken up by members of the army unit in which Yonatan served. Even Levi Eshkol, the Prime Minister and Minister of Defense of Israel, is enlisted in the effort to locate Yonatan.

The story moves back and forth between life in the kibbutz and life, for Yonatan, on the road. Srulik replaces Yolek as kibbutz secretary; Azariah cares for Rimona during her third pregnancy; Hava becomes a stabilizing force throughout the kibbutz when her husband's health fails; Stutchnik the milkman dies; Azariah prophesies war; and, at about the time of the birth of Rimona's child (whose paternity is uncertain), Yonatan comes home and takes up his former life again.

The war that Azariah had foreseen comes and—being the Six Day War—goes. Both Yonatan and Azariah return from it as heroes and life goes on. Srulik implies in a journal entry which ends the novel that the only course one can take is to do what one can do and then, for the rest, wait and see.

The Characters

Amos Oz proves convincingly that, as Ernest Hemingway taught, an author writes best when he thoroughly knows the world about which he writes. Having lived continuously on a kibbutz from the age of fourteen, Oz knows of the experiences and the individuals peculiar to such an existence. His characters owe their lifelikeness in part to the fact that he is writing from semiautobiographical materials. Like Yonatan, he was a soldier who served on active duty in the Israeli army; like Azariah, he is outspoken and creative; like Srulik, he is steady and dependable, reflective, and profoundly intelligent. A master observer and a student of human behavior, Oz so selects and orders the parts of the narrative as to make them stand out dramatically. The reader of *A Perfect Peace* comes to know Kibbutz Granot as a real place inhabited by real people. With the modern history of Israel as their back-drop, the characters—the fictional ones and the one from real life, Levi Eshkol—seem to be realistically drawn.

What helps give the major characters wholeness and individuality is that they are tellers of their own stories; they advance the narrative by thinking or, as with Srulik, by writing down what has happened around them. The lesser characters, too, have their voice, a collective one, speaking at times (especially early in the novel) in the way the chorus speaks in an ancient Greek play; this point of view is a device used to perfection by Oz to take the place of omniscience. Oz appears to be hardly present, in fact, except as a kind of stage manager who cues the players in the drama in their entrances and exits.

Themes and Meanings

Set in a small settlement in a small country, *A Perfect Peace* is about, for one thing, seeking freedom from containment. One who is unfulfilled at home dreams of magic and beauties to be found in another place; the adven-turer wanders; the philosopher propounds and prophesies; the political has-been rages against new generations. The Promised Land is always ahead; the unpromising and undesired one, always current. How to live with the fact of containment—and its claustrophobic consequences for some—is another concern of the novel. The author's view is likely that of Srulik: to make the best of things. One way to make the best of things is to learn to live with others; the novel demonstrates the possibility of community among mixed peoples, disparate not only in nationalities but also in ideas and life-styles. Kibbutz Granot is a microcosm of Israel, a land struggling to find unity and purpose.

Opposed to Israel's well-being as a nation are internal political, philo-sophical and religious factions and, outside, perpetual threats of war. Azariah, a man of peace, prophesies war, but anyone could have done so, for war in Israel is constantly at hand. From the first words of the novel, Oz, with the facts of the modern history of Israel in sight, ironically dramatizes a period of peace before a time of war. The presence of Sheikh Dahr, an aban-doned Arab settlement near the kibbutz, is a reminder of past wars and of the likelihood of future ones.

War, however, is not the private lot of the Jewish people; it is as universal and as elemental as nature itself, occurring in a quiet and lovely place as well as in a menacing location. Nature, nevertheless, is indifferent to the comings and goings, the wars and times of peace, of human beings. Only human be-ings can make or cause war, or peace. The title of the novel is from a phrase in the Jewish prayer for the dead. The interpretation of the word "peace," however, depends on the individual perspectives of the characters. Yonatan goes in search of the peace of solitude and of freedom from responsibility. Azariah, on the other hand, seeks the very peace that Yonatan leaves behind, that which comes from domestic serenity, security, and acceptance. Yonatan has already had what Azariah has wanted to have, a wife and a home and a community; Azariah has already been what Yonatan has wanted to be, a free spirit and a wanderer. How does Yolek find peace? He does not: Until the time when, because of his poor health, he can no longer think or do for himself, he relives the past of bitter experiences. His personal wars go on forever, if only in his thoughts. He gives a special meaning to generational conflicts by warring with both youth and the past. Hava comes to terms with her husband by coming to terms with herself; when she no longer needs the self-assurance that comes, often, from being loved and appreciated by others, she is able to forget herself and find peace in helping others, including the man, her husband, with whom she had fought so many verbal battles. Rimona's peace is the result of her first successful childbirth. Peace for Srulik comes—as one might expect—on its own, without anxious seeking, in the normal course of events. Peace is available to those who wish it, Oz makes clear, and any kind of peace may be a perfect peace.

Critical Context

Oz began *A Perfect Peace* in 1970, laid it aside until 1976, and completed it in 1981. Doubtless, then, the narrative and thematic directions of his novel had to be changed from his original intentions. It is certain that as time passed his view of modern Israel past and present and future changed also; from the perspective of the past Oz writes with prophetic, even godlike, knowledge of the way to achieve universal peace. A member of the Peace Now organization and a spokesman for Palestinian rights, he has been writing since the mid-1960's from the context of Jewishness: its culture, its politics, its history. Dispossession, isolation, alienation, and hostility, however, are found not only in Israel but also in all the nations of the world; in an effort to promote understanding among people separated from one another by their boundaries and beliefs and fears, then, Oz maintains an international vision that is reflected by life in Israel. In an unending stream of essays, articles, short stories, novels, and speeches, Oz demonstrates over and over that community is an answer to the worst ills in the world. Kibbutz Granot may be a small settlement in Israel, but it is made up of both native Israelis and European immigrants representing a large segment of civilization. Peace in a microcosm is translatable to peace everywhere.

The growing importance of Israel as a world nation lends force to the voice of Amos Oz, but he is a writer whose passion, vision, and art would make him a singular influence anywhere.

Sources for Further Study

Alter, Robert. "The World of Oz," in *The New Republic*. ÇXCIII (July 29, 1985), pp. 38-39.

Lyons, Gene. "Every Man Is an Island," in *Newsweek*. CVI (July 29, 1985), p. 58.

Shechner, Mark. "The Uncircumcised Heart," in *The Nation*. CCXL (June 8, 1985), pp. 709-711.

David Powell

A PERSONAL MATTER

Author: Kenzaburō Ōe (1935-   )
Type of plot: Realism
Time of plot: The 1960's
Locale: An unnamed Japanese city
First published: Kojinteki na taiken, 1964 (English translation, 1968)

> *Principal characters:*
> BIRD, the protagonist, a cram-school teacher
> BIRD'S WIFE
> BIRD'S FATHER-IN-LAW
> BIRD'S MOTHER-IN-LAW
> KIKUHIKO, Bird's newborn son
> HIMIKO, Bird's former girlfriend

The Novel

A Personal Matter tells the story of a conflict between duty and desire. At the beginning of the novel, the protagonist, who is known to the reader only by his childhood name, Bird, is waiting for his wife to produce their first child. Bird is less than enthusiastic about the prospect of fatherhood. He fears that it will interfere with the realization of his dream, to travel throughout Africa in order to test his courage and, more practically, to enable him to gather material for a book.

Unfortunately, when the baby is born, it is defective. Diagnosing a brain hernia, the doctors predict that if it does not die, it will be a vegetable. At the suggestion of his wife's mother, Bird does not tell his wife the extent of the baby's condition.

Bird's response to his problem is typical. Just as he dropped out of graduate school for an extended period of drunkenness immediately after he was married, so he again runs away from responsibility when he must deal with his son's defect. After his sympathetic father-in-law gives him a bottle of whiskey, Bird takes refuge with a former girlfriend, Himiko, with whom he spends a drunken night. Appropriately, Himiko has dropped out of society, spending her time in a messy apartment, where she entertains lovers and broods over her husband's suicide, and from which she emerges at night for wild rides in her sports car.

Reporting for work after his night with Himiko, Bird vomits in front of his class and leaves, certain that he will be fired. At the hospital, he learns that the baby, whose death he desires, is stronger. Again he returns to Himiko, who now insists that Bird has no more responsibility for his child's malformation than she did for her husband's suicide. Captivated by Bird's dream and encouraged by her lesbian friend and by her father-in-law, Himiko urges

Bird to remove the baby from the hospital, see that he dies, and then run away with her to Africa.

Bird agrees with Himiko's plan and picks up the baby, who now seems to be his enemy, the person who has been born to thwart Bird's hopes. As Bird and Himiko drive through the rain with the screaming child, however, Bird cannot believe that he will ever be happy, even in Africa, knowing that he has betrayed his own child. Himiko's reminder of Bird's earlier betrayal of a friend, Kikuhiko, disturbs Bird, and when he names his son Kikuhiko, the present deed fuses with the past. After Bird and Himiko leave the baby with an unscrupulous doctor, ironically they encounter their old friend Kikuhiko, who attributes his present unsavory life in part to Bird's treatment of him. At this point, Bird realizes that the treasure which he believed he was protecting from his baby-enemy was only an illusion, that all of his life he has been fleeing from responsibility in friendship, in marriage, and in fatherhood. Despite the arguments of his mistress Himiko and his friend Kikuhiko, Bird leaves to reclaim his child.

In the epilogue, Bird and his wife are leaving the hospital with their son, whose brain hernia was rediagnosed as a less serious tumor, for which an operation may have left the baby normal. In any case, Bird has accepted his responsibilities. While Himiko has gone to Africa, taking Bird's dream for her own, Bird is resigned to being a guide for tourists from other parts of the world rather than seeing the world for himself. He has changed from a child who deserved to be called by a child's name to an adult who can respect himself and be respected by others.

The Characters

All of the other characters in *A Personal Matter* are seen through Bird's eyes and are important because of their relationship to his central conflict. His wife, her parents, and his son all demand that he mature. Because of his past irresponsibility, his wife and her parents have no reason to trust him. His father-in-law, formerly the chairman of an English department, saw Bird disintegrate after marriage, quitting graduate school and indulging in a long period of drunkenness. It was the father-in-law who arranged Bird's present job, which Bird does not even attempt to retain after his misfortune in class. Although the mother-in-law does not rebuke Bird, it is obvious that she, not Bird, is the wife's support during labor and recuperation from childbirth. Bird's wife at one point tells him that he has never thought of anyone but himself; when the time comes, she predicts, he will be neither responsible nor courageous. Bird, she knows, will let her down. Looking at the baby, Bird feels curiosity, not tenderness. He is convinced that either in the act which produced the child or in some act which will destroy him, he will let down his son as he has his wife and her parents. None of these characters who need to depend on Bird is really individualized; instead, they constitute four voices who attempt to call forth Bird's adult self but, until the end of the novel, find him to be only a child.

Three characters, themselves deniers of responsibility, encourage Bird to run away as they have done. Kikuhiko appears briefly as the proprietor of a gay bar. His answer to the besetting fears of his own childhood has been to reject the demands of society. Himiko's lesbian friend has also learned to avoid guilt by refusing to be committed to anything. The most vivid of the characters who counsel flight, Himiko, is particularly interesting because she has constructed an elaborate philosophical argument which permits her to detach herself from the results of any act which she has performed. Bird suspects that her philosophy, as well as her promiscuous and purposeless life-style, is the result of her unresolved feelings about the suicide of her young husband. As Himiko talks, her own insecurity is revealed, and as she engages in desperate sexual exploits, her unhappiness is plain.

Finally, Bird must choose between the two sets of characters. The revelation of Himiko's dissatisfaction with her own life is important, because it indicates that Bird made the right choice when he rejected her and her values.

Themes and Meanings

The title *A Personal Matter* suggests the central theme of the novel: that the choice among life's options is one which must be made by every individual. To a child, all things are possible. To Bird, whose childish nickname suggests his nature, both marriage and freedom have seemed possible, and like a child, he strikes out at another human being, his own helpless son, when life interferes with his plans.

Bird's name also suggests the childish response to unpleasantness, flight. When his friend Kikuhiko showed fear, Bird deserted him, as if to fly from another's fear would prevent one's own fearfulness. Later, Bird ran from life to alcohol. Such flights are both negations of the self, as is the ultimate negation, suicide, an important motif in the novel. It is significant that Bird's own father committed suicide after the child questioned him about death. Himiko, whose husband killed himself, and whose own sexual life is more destructive than creative, points out that Bird, too, has a predisposition toward suicide.

The theme of negation is supported by the literary allusions in the novel. Remembering Tom Sawyer's experience in the cave, Bird says that he is looking for an exit from his own cave; at the end of the story, he has rejected that search, understanding that the only exit from life is death. References to Ernest Hemingway, particularly to his novel *The Sun Also Rises* (1926), also underline the theme of negation.

When Bird accepts life and its responsibilities, he is able to accept himself. The epilogue makes it clear that in giving, Bird has found meaning. The baby's successful operation has demanded Bird's sacrifice of his own blood. Knowing that the baby may need further medical care, Bird is willing to sacrifice the money which he had saved for a trip to Africa. Even what Bird believed was freedom, time to loaf and to dissipate, has been sacrificed for his new family, whom Bird will now work to support. At the end of the novel, it is clear that Bird can accept and respect himself because of the choice he has made among life's options.

Critical Context

Contemporary Japanese fiction is preoccupied with the relationship between tradition and the modern world. From a hierarchical society in which behavior was governed by a strict and unchanging code, Japan has changed to a Westernized culture in which for many people there are no moral and social guides. Some novelists now emphasize the need for retaining traditional Japanese values and customs even in a changing society. Others, such as Kenzaburō Ōe, accepting the loss of the old society, follow their characters in a search for individual standards.

The winner of both the Akutagawa Prize, while he was still a student, and later of the prestigious Tanizaki Prize, Ōe has been critically praised for his work in various genres, including essays, short stories, and novels. His first significant work, the short story "Shiiku" ("The Catch"), published in 1958, revealed a sympathy with the outcast: The story deals with a black American airman whose plane crashes near a Japanese village during World War II. In 1963, Ōe's first child was born with a severe disability requiring surgery not unlike that described in *A Personal Matter*. Images of estrangement and deformity recur throughout his fiction, often in connection with the threat of nuclear annihilation—a foretaste of which Ōe had when he went to Hiroshima in the early 1960's to write about survivors of the atom bomb. Because he addresses problems which affect young people throughout the world, it is not surprising that Ōe is becoming increasingly well-known in the West.

Sources for Further Study

Falke, Wayne. "Japanese Tradition in Kenzaburō Ōe's *A Personal Matter*," in *Critique: Studies in Modern Fiction*. XV, no. 3 (1974), pp. 43-52.

Kimball, Arthur G. *Crisis in Identity and Contemporary Japanese Novels*, 1973.

Wilson, Michiko N. *The Marginal World of Ōe Kenzaburō: A Study in Themes and Techniques*, 1986.

Yamanouchi, Hisaaki. *The Search of Authenticity in Modern Japanese Literature*, 1978.

Rosemary M. Canfield-Reisman

PEŠČANIK

Author: Danilo Kiš (1935-   )
Type of plot: Psychological realism
Time of plot: World War II
Locale: Northern Yugoslavia
First published: 1972

>   *Principal characters:*
>   EDUARD SAM, a retired railroad official
>   THE NARRATOR, his son

The Novel

In *Peščanik* (hourglass), Danilo Kiš returns to the loss of his father in World War II, a theme with which he began working in an earlier novel, *Bašta, pepeo* (1965; *Garden, Ashes*, 1975). Although not considered to be strictly autobiography, the novel has enough autobiographical elements in it to justify connecting it with the author's personal life. This interpretation, however, is not absolutely necessary for an understanding of the novel. Eduard Sam (called Eduard Scham in *Garden, Ashes*), a Jew and a retired railroad official, figured in *Garden, Ashes* as the youthful narrator's often-absent but still-dominating father. The focus in *Peščanik* shifts to Sam himself, even though the narrator of *Garden, Ashes* is once more present. By shifting his focus, Kiš allows Sam to tell his own story, so that his last days are seen from a slightly different perspective from that of the earlier book. This dual vision is symbolized by a drawing in the novel of a white hourglass silhouetted against a black background, the sides of the hourglass clearly showing the contours of two faces confronting each other.

Peščanik begins with a detailed, realistic account of a man lost in a snowy wilderness, attempting to find his way ("Pictures from a Journey"). This passage is followed by the musings and ravings of an unidentified person—who turns out to be Eduard Sam ("Notes of a Madman")—and by an examination of Sam carried out in a police station ("Investigation" and "Investigation of Witnesses"). These chapter headings recur several times. The novel ends with the last letter written by Sam, which supposedly gives the final version of the sequence of events that led to his death.

The story of the novel unfolds as these chapters alternate. First, the external circumstances of the wanderings and Sam's escape attempts are given in minute, realistic detail as pictures from a journey. Although disconnected and seemingly unrelated, these tableaux all pertain to the movements of a hunted man. Chapters on the notes of a madman show the persecuted protagonist's emotional reactions to the mental torture to which he is subjected, while in the chapters on the investigation, the most tangible details about

Sam's activities and "transgressions" are to be found. Even in these more concrete sections of the book, many details seem disconnected and unrelated because of the well-known habit of criminal investigators of circling around the main topic and returning to the same questions in a slightly different form. Sam seldom loses his composure, although he comes very close to it. He gives straightforward, believable answers, to the displeasure of the investigators, who seek an admission of guilt, justifiable or not. The outcome is a foregone conclusion, from which Sam, like the protagonist of a classical tragedy, cannot escape.

The last chapter, Sam's letter to his sister, is a litany of the sorrows inflicted upon him and his family by unfeeling relatives. It is a picture of utter despair, though couched in civilized tones. The letter also demonstrates that a man can be hunted like an animal by his own kin as well as by his enemies. Sam ends his letter fatalistically by comforting himself, "It is better to be hunted than hunters."

The Characters

Eduard Sam is the only character who deserves discussion. The book's attention never strays from him, in contrast to *Garden, Ashes*, in which the narrator's childhood experiences receive considerable attention. The other characters in *Peščanik* are minor, their only purpose being to sharpen the focus on Sam. Sam's chief traits are the same as those highlighted in the previous novel. He is a dreamer, highly impractical and seemingly incapable of providing for his family, despite his best efforts. He is utterly naïve in dealing with other people, most of whom, especially his relatives, take advantage of him whenever they can. During the investigation, it is revealed that he has had wide contacts with a large variety of people, many of whom are now suspected by the authorities. These contacts eventually bring about his demise, although clearly they are used only as a pretext; the primary reason for his persecution is that he is Jewish.

Sam's reaction to persecution changes noticeably in this novel. In the previous novel, he was almost optimistic and buoyant; now he seems resigned to his fate, an attitude only glimpsed earlier. Sam is also more attentive to the needs of his family in this book. Earlier, he adopted a devil-may-care attitude toward his wife and children; now he is more concerned about their welfare. The results are the same, but his involvement is markedly different. Furthermore, while in *Garden, Ashes* he still hoped to publish his poetry and his railroad schedule as his life's achievement, in *Peščanik* he seems to be resigned to failure; he seldom mentions his artistic endeavors in this book. Clearly, he has become the ultimate victim. Somehow the designation of a specific person—Eduard Sam—persecuted for a specific reason—being a Jew—has been muted; instead, he has become a symbol of humanity's endless suffering.

The role of the narrator, presumably his son, has been reduced to that of an observer and not a totally objective one, although in the descriptive chapters, he is as detached as possible under the circumstances. As previously mentioned, the narrator is now satisfied to let Sam tell his own story, either directly or through the police investigations.

Themes and Meanings

The two main themes in *Peščanik* are the persecution of the Jews in World War II and the more universal suffering that runs throughout human history. Persecution has become Kiš's main theme. In *Peščanik*, however, as always, he is less concerned with the concrete description of persecution than he is with the impact it has on its victims. Eduard Sam is just as innocent as all the other Jews who perished in the Holocaust, but somehow his demise bears even greater pathos. He is an intelligent, gifted, harmless man who benefits mankind, if in no other way simply by being different from most people— always a refreshing phenomenon. The fact that he knows in advance of his fate and does nothing to prevent it speaks for his innocence and basic inability to commit violence. Describing the Four Horsemen of the Apocalypse as four gendarmes on white horses, he is convinced that "they will come, for sure . . . I hear the neighing of their horses. And I hear as the plumes on their black hats flutter in the wind." A short time later, he laments, "Everything else will be wiped out by the night, and my letter will not be sent, my handwriting will be dead at dawn in the dead sea of time, a decomposed papyrus in the decayed swamp of the Panonian Sea." These fatalistic utterances speak for the millions senselessly slaughtered in the twilight of demented gods.

Eduard Sam's sacrifice stands for much more than the persecution of the Jews in World War II. Kiš sees in it a universal theme: the tragic suffering of humans in the struggle against one another, be it caused by race, religion, politics, or greed. Whenever people forsake understanding, compassion, and respect for individual human beings, suffering is inevitable. This implicit message is unobtrusive yet just as poignant as the more explicit one. The author is willing to let his personal tragedy serve as a constant reminder that the step between civilization and barbarism is often a small one, that the victim can be the most innocent person, and that the persecutor can be found where he is least expected.

Critical Context

The virtues of *Peščanik* lie in both its themes and its artistic excellence; the universality of the main themes is accompanied by a style that is both bold and accomplished. Kiš employs a distinctive approach in which the subject is seen from three different angles. First, the scene is set by a realistic description in a style which resembles that of Rembrandt van Rijn: Every motion, sound, and sight is recorded as if on a canvas or a tape. This approach represents reality as it is seen at first glance, without any attempt to analyze or penetrate it. Kiš's second technique consists of diary notes written by Sam, in which he records his reactions, both mental and emotional, to outward stimuli. This diary also gives him an opportunity to voice his opinion on various matters—the only chance he has amid general distrust and mutual disregard. The third approach is employed in the chapters on the investigation in the police station. In a highly dramatic technique of rapid questions and answers, the reality, only described in the first approach and mused upon in the second, is mercilessly pierced and torn asunder, revealing the unspeakable tension under which every moment of the protagonist's life is spent. Kiš approaches his subject from these three angles because he believes that only in such a way can the truth be obtained. In addition, the book's versatility and changes of pace make for lively reading, though they also make the novel somewhat more complex, demanding the active participation of the reader.

Approaching the form of the novel in such a complex and demanding manner, Kiš exhibits the qualities that make him one of the most sophisticated and prominent writers in late twentieth century Serbian and Yugoslav literature. It is no surprise, therefore, that he has been one of the most translated writers in Yugoslavia.

Sources for Further Study

Czarny, Norbert. "Imaginary-Real Lives: On Danilo Kiš," in *Cross-Currents*. III (1984), pp. 279-284.

Gavrilović, Zoran. "Intelektualni lirizam Danila Kiša," in *Književna kritika*. IV (1973), pp. 89-94.

Georgijevski, Hristo. "Roman *Peščanik*," in *Delo*. XIX (1973), pp. 692-697.

Matillon, Janine. "Entretien avec Danilo Kiš: Qu'est-ce qu'un écrivain yougoslave à Paris?" in *La Quinzaine littéraire*. No. 317 (January, 1980), p. 17.

Vitanovic, Slobodan. "Thematic Unity in Danilo Kiš's Literary Works, " in *Relations*. Nos. 9/10 (1979), pp. 66-69.

White, Edmund. "Danilo Kiš: The Obligations of Form," in *Southwest Review*. LXXI (Summer, 1986), pp. 363-377.

Vasa D. Mihailovich

THE PLANETARIUM

Author: Nathalie Sarraute (1900-   )
Type of plot: Psychological realism
Time of plot: The late 1950's
Locale: Unspecified, probably Paris
First published: Le Planétarium, 1959 (English translation, 1960)

> *Principal characters:*
> ALAIN GUIMIEZ, the protagonist, a young would-be writer
> GISÈLE, his wife
> GERMAINE LEMAIRE, a writer and salon celebrity
> PIERRE GUIMIEZ, Alain's father
> AUNT BERTHE, Pierre's sister

The Novel

The plot of *The Planetarium* is demarcated not by physical events but by the perceptions of the characters. The action is thus almost exclusively in their minds and feelings and is initiated by a line of dialogue, another character's gesture, or a detail of place or time which impinges on the characters' observations. Because Nathalie Sarraute abjures plot in the traditional sense, the "story" is only obliquely realized and is almost absurdly trivial. The action opens with Aunt Berthe's obsessive concern with decorating her apartment. She fusses over curtains and color schemes, even door handles, as if they were at the center of her existence, driving the workmen from her apartment with her fastidiousness, which verges on madness.

Her apartment is the overriding concern of her nephew, Alain, as well. Newly married, something of a failure, and anxious to create a successful image for himself, Alain covets his aunt's spacious, lavishly appointed rooms and tries to get her to leave them. Alain expects his father to cajole Aunt Berthe at first, then goes to her himself, relying on his aunt's love for him and his own ability to wheedle. In the beginning, Aunt Berthe refuses to give up her apartment, knowing very well the spoiled, acquisitive nature of her nephew and his spaniel-hearted wife. Defiantly, Alain threatens to sue his aunt and to apply pressure on her landlord. In the end, Aunt Berthe surrenders, content to leave Alain to his own misguided values.

Aunt Berthe's apartment is only one of Alain's obsessions. He is also infatuated with a famous writer, Germaine Lemaire, and visits her salon soon after his marriage. Germaine is an intoxicant to him; he adores her not so much for her sexuality as for her fame, her beautiful life-style. When he sees her surrounded by hangers-on and would-be admirers, he immediately becomes frustrated and inarticulate. Unable to impress her, he convinces himself that he has behaved like a fool.

Alain's perceptions of Germaine—of her world of art and gossip and idle wit—complement the action revolving around Aunt Berthe and her apartment. The two units merge at the end when Germaine is invited to Alain's "new" place and is given a tour. Alain points out the pieces of furniture and the examples of artwork, but Germaine is politely unimpressed. The book ends, as it began, with a catalog of things in the apartment, items which have taken the place of vital human relationships.

The Characters

Alain Guimiez is too much the dandy to be a cad, too much the weakling to be mean, too shallow to be likable. He is interesting only because of a series of perceptions and observations which push him to the verge of paranoia. Alain sees his relationships—with his wife, with his aunt, and with Germaine—as adversarial. He is continually on the defensive, ready to apologize; continually bracing himself for the blow to his self-respect; constantly balancing between the emotional retreat and the verbal thrust.

Though still a young man, Alain is already something of a failure. He has been working on an academic thesis for a number of years, but it is obvious that he will never finish it. His father, Pierre, waits expectantly for him to secure a position, but Alain's laziness and his reliance on his father's and his aunt's money permit him to live a life of decadence. He has been pampered by his aunt and has become selfish, petulant, and insecure.

Gisèle, Alain's wife, evokes the passive Victorian bride in a romantic novel. Devoted to Alain, she has few thoughts which do not concern her husband, and her own goal is to please him, to respect his wishes, especially with the furniture (she does not want the leather chairs that her mother gave them as a wedding gift, for example, because Alain thinks they are in bad taste). Gisèle is absolutely convinced of Alain's genius; when her mother warns her about Alain—a "queer" young man unlike others of his age—she merely smiles and insists that she loves him for his very peculiarity.

Aunt Berthe is the most interesting character in the novel. Though she is prepared to leave Alain a small fortune in her will and thus perpetuate his aimless life-style, she is not necessarily blind to her nephew's true character; she senses Alain's weakness and realizes that he will probably never amount to anything. In contrast, she is unquestionably loyal to her brother. In her eyes, Pierre possesses all the strengths of character lacking in Alain. Near the end of the novel, brother and sister view each other with renewed respect. Indeed, Pierre admires Berthe for her intelligence and hardihood. He recognizes her shrewdness in financial matters and notes sarcastically her seeking his advice when he knows that she has already made the right investments.

Despite her strengths, however, Aunt Berthe maintains a skewed sense of reality. The opening section of the novel, in which she obsessively reflects upon the decorations in her apartment, suggests that things themselves have become the focus of her daily life. Her furnishings, like her investments, are what keep her in touch with the world; they have become the axis around which everything else—her relationships, her feelings—revolves.

At the center of her own universe is Germaine Lemaire. The title of the book, *The Planetarium*, effectively and metaphorically defines her position and importance in the lives of the other characters and in the novel itself. Germaine is, like the sun, the foremost luminary in the local universe of would-be writers and failed literati, such as Alain. The first scene in which she appears evokes the image of a comic solar system, in the center of which she sits, serenely enthroned, while around her the "ape-like" René and other members of her coterie spin in her reflected light.

Though Germaine thus exerts a controlling influence on Alain—impelling him to impress her, to succeed with her where he has failed in his own career—she herself, like the sun, is but a mediocre star. Her work has some popular appeal, but it does not claim any critical importance. Germaine enjoys the attention of Alain and her other admirers, but she has nothing important to say. When, at the novel's close, she presents Alain and his wife with a copy of a Greek vase as a gift for their apartment, Alain immediately perceives her superficiality. Like Aunt Berthe, like Alain himself, she is entangled with the material and the commonplace, which in this case make a pretense of art but which are actually dull, empty, and lifeless.

Themes and Meanings

As an antinovel, a work of fiction whose avowed purpose is the virtual annihilation of standard plot and characterization, *The Planetarium* nevertheless makes a statement about the fragility of human relationships and the difficulty, if not impossibility, of direct communication between people. None of the characters makes a commitment, none acts in a positive way. Instead, each questions personal perceptions, evaluates feelings, anatomizes observations, appearances, and statements, until all the characters seem almost paranoically insecure. At best, such insecurity is merely stabilized by a concern for material things. In an attempt to anchor themselves to the only solid ground of which they are certain, the characters preoccupy themselves with the trivial, the worldly. Spiritual values do not exist; only physical sensations exist.

In this context, the novel may be observed—as through a telescope—as a sort of comedy of manners, each character marshaling his or her inchoate actions and conversations in pursuit of a particular goal: the acquisition of goods, the wheedling of an apartment, the palliation of a wounded ego. Such comedy permits the reader brief views of the world of the literati, a closed society of would-be writers with nothing to say. It also allows the reader to glimpse the nearer world of shallow bourgeois values.

Critical Context

The Planetarium is Nathalie Sarraute's most popular novel and her most "readable" in terms of traditional plot and structure. The work exemplifies her theory of "tropisms" while still maintaining a controlled sense of action or at least of "preaction." As early as 1939, Sarraute had established her literary method with her first book, *Tropismes* (1938; *Tropisms*, 1963). Hardly a novel, *Tropisms* was a series of sketches or vignettes, in which characters revealed themselves in a series of images (tropisms, as she called them) which evoked sensations, reflexes, "subconversations" just below, behind, or before the spoken word.

Like Marcel Proust, her near-contemporary, she seeks to examine the emotional content of experience which lies just beneath the conscious perception and which determines the course of physical action without being part of it. Sarraute is also interested in what James Joyce called an "epiphany," a showing forth, that moment of instantaneous illumination, of acute emotional awareness, that occurs to the sensitive human being. Unlike the work of Joyce or Proust, however, Sarraute's is peculiarly synthetic. A sense of nature—flowers, mud, rain, the color of the sky—is missing in her books, and locale is only vaguely comprehended. The characters operate in the private worlds of their own minds.

Sources for Further Study

Beja, Morris. *Epiphany in the Modern Novel*, 1971.

Besser, Gretchen Rous. *Nathalie Sarraute*, 1979.

Knapp, Bettina. "Nathalie Sarraute: A Theater of Tropisms," in *Performing Arts Journal*. I (Winter, 1977), pp. 15-27.

Minogue, Valerie. *Nathalie Sarraute and the War of Words*, 1981.

Peyre, Henri. *French Novelists of Today*, 1967.

Rahv, Betty. *From Sartre to the New Novel*, 1974.

Sontag, Susan. "Nathalie Sarraute and the Novel," in *Against Interpretation and Other Essays*, 1966.

Weightman, John. *The Concept of the Avant-garde: Explorations in Modernism*, 1973.

Edward Fiorelli

THE POLISH COMPLEX

Author: Tadeusz Konwicki (1926-　　)
Type of plot: Philosophical and psychological realism
Time of plot: The early 1970's, with flashbacks to earlier rebellions
Locale: Warsaw, with imagined episodes elsewhere
First published: Kompleks polski, 1977 (English translation, 1981)

> *Principal characters:*
> KONWICKI, the narrator, a well-known Polish writer
> KOJRAN, a man who knows Konwicki's books and who
> stalked him for three weeks in 1951 with orders to kill
> DUSZEK, a large man who pursued Kojran and was his
> jailer
> ZYGMUNT MINEYKO, a revolutionary of the 1863 uprising, to
> whom a large part of the book is addressed in a narrative
> historical fantasy; the narrator identifies with him
> ROMUALD TRAUGUTT, a Polish patriot who was appointed
> leader in the same 1863 uprising

The Novel

　　The Polish Complex centers on one of the constants of contemporary
Polish life—waiting in line. In this case Poles are waiting outside a jewelry
store in Warsaw for gold rings to arrive from the Soviet Union. The entire
novel takes place in this line, although there are vivid interludes at other
sites—a remote forest in Lithuania, for example, and a hotel room in
another city. In these partly surrealistic and dreamlike episodes, a historical
journey takes place as well as a geographical one. The episodes re-create
scenes from the unsuccessful Polish rebellion of 1863; the sense of defeat,
disappointment, inevitable doom, and eternal struggle suffered by the main
characters of these episodes provides a psychological glue that binds past and
present, determining individual and national identity. Tadeusz Konwicki
himself was a revolutionary, fighting against the Soviet troops who took over
his native area of Lithuania in the 1940's. Like Zygmunt Mineyko, the 1863
revolutionary, Konwicki was unsuccessful in his attempt to keep his homeland free, but his identification with Mineyko in defeat and blighted hopes
blurs the temporal distance between the two characters and explains something of the present psychological state of the Konwicki protagonist.

　　As Konwicki waits in line for the order to arrive from the Soviet Union,
he makes the acquaintance of a number of other people. The two major
characters he meets are Kojran and Duszek, standing behind Konwicki in
that order. The order is symbolic, for these three have followed one another
in the past. Kojran followed Konwicki with a death order for a time after
Konwicki had dropped his revolutionary sympathies in favor of Socialist

leanings. Duszek, in turn, pursued Kojran to torment and imprison him. Now, however, the three men join in a kind of begrudging camaraderie, even going off to have a drink together. They share an unspoken disillusionment over the value of intense political feeling, a sense of futility, and the feeling of being jaded with life, with politics, with experience; their shared feelings render the past almost humorously negligible and enable them to accept their differing roles and past hostilities.

Trivial episodes occur while they wait in line. A woman pretends to be old in order to get ahead in the line. A peasant woman suddenly tries to sell veal. A young man turns out to be a French anarchist who, ironically enough, has fled to Poland to find true freedom. Street musicians play Christmas tunes. There are also periodic announcements by the manager of the store. The three men temporarily leave the line to go for a drink. A girl walks barefoot through the December snowstorm in a dressing gown. A group of Soviet tourists get preferential treatment and go to the head of the line, although why they want to buy Soviet gold rings in Poland is never explained. The manager announces that the awaited rings have not arrived and that the shipment consists of samovars instead. Konwicki daydreams and muses and philosophizes about himself, about his identity, his career, his connection with Poland, his native land, his place in the universe. During the course of the evening he feels the symptoms of a heart attack and subsequently experiences a mild attack. When he comes to, he finds himself with Iwona, a salesgirl, and makes love with her. The episode begins in a gloriously romantic, passionate mood—Iwona is described in beautiful images drawn from nature—but degenerates into the tawdry as the lovers recognize the inevitable futility of their relationship and the manager angrily bangs on the door of their backroom trysting site.

As the novel approaches its end, there is another scene of a defeated revolutionary. This time it is the final good-bye between Romuald Traugutt and his wife in a strange hotel room. They are clearly aware that in assuming leadership of the People's Government, Traugutt is deliberately marching to his death. Yet he must go. Their last night together is neither romanticized nor idealized, interrupted as it is by news that Traugutt's passport has been seized by the police and by sounds of rowdy behavior in the adjacent room. This domestic good-bye prepares the reader for the less intimate farewells and dispersal of the people waiting in line. Konwicki rejects the invitation of a lonely woman to spend the night with her, and he heads back to his home. Yet where is home? It cannot be his native land, for Wilno has been seized and there is no freedom there, so it must be the small apartment where his wife presumably awaits his return. Despite the indifference of the universe, he feels the great potential of Poland—Warsaw is a "great massif" and houses "caves full of sleeping knights." This is the Polish Complex—reality and vision.

The Characters

The major character in the novel is Konwicki himself. As the narrator-protagonist, he indulges in reveries and philosophical musings that are interrupted by the pedestrian events involved in waiting in line in front of a store for goods that never arrive. The novel depicts the human mind shifting without explanation or transition from the real world to the world of imagination and speculation. Konwicki identifies with failed, historically authentic revolutionaries of the nineteenth century, and the cycle of defeat and thwarted ambitions colors his sense of himself and his sense of Poland. The historical dimension brings psychological depth to the narrator, for it justifies and explains his sense of futility and despair.

All aspects of the narrator's life are brought under scrutiny. Perhaps most important are his politics. Like the failed revolutionary, he wonders if it was worth it. Political opposites can now be superficial friends, and there is no suggestion that anything more is desired or desirable. Politics are meaningless although unavoidable in Konwicki's depiction of contemporary Poland. Konwicki's writings are reconsidered. Kojran and Iwona are familiar with his books. Yet what difference does that make? Konwicki takes no pleasure in their recognition. Indeed, he says that he hates his own books and laments the inadequacy of language for true communication. So strong is his sense of man's alienation from man that he no longer writes to communicate but only to ward off total nihilism through an existential act. His personal life is under scrutiny. There is no haste to return home on Christmas Eve, and he engages in adultery. Romance degenerates into lust, and his stirrings of desire for a woman blend with those imagined ones of a revolutionary a century ago. His nationalism is examined. He wonders why the critics label him a Polish writer. What is the source of one's ethnic identity? Waiting in line provides the narrator with the personal space he needs for introspection.

It is significant that the novel takes place on Christmas Eve and that these characters, a microcosm of the people of Poland, are waiting. They are waiting for material goods, waiting for gold of all things, that most symbolically materialistic of goods, the standard measure of wealth. The fact that it is Christmas Eve marks the degeneration of the Polish spirit compared to the triumphant waiting for the Christ child centuries ago. The implication is that modern Poles inhabit a spiritual wasteland. Yet Konwicki insists that he is waiting for a miracle, and the word is used throughout the book, evoking the quiet faith that a miracle can happen. Despite the narrator's obvious satiety with life, despite his resigned despair, his halfhearted hope for a miracle betrays a residual and understated hopefulness that lingers regardless of the reality of both contemporary and historical Poland.

The other characters, who represent common types in Poland, share in the narrator's individual and social malaise, but they find different responses. Some attempt to lie and cheat their way through life. Some, like the student and the French anarchist, fail to see the reality of present-day Poland, their lack of insight symbolized by the Frenchman's physical blindness. Any evidence of compassion, such as the student's allowing the old woman to cut in line, becomes reason for ridicule; she has worked on their sympathies and they are fools, but the worst thing about it is the understated way in which her hoax is subsequently revealed. Nothing is made of it—no outburst, no anger, as if it were to be expected that kindness and generosity would turn out to be absurd in this absurd world. There is grumbling and complaining. People waiting in line are selfish and greedy. They are caught up in the pettiness of everyday life. If they were waiting for something necessary, such as meat or milk or even needed clothing, they would be more sympathetic characters. Instead, they are waiting for gold rings, that most useless of commodities that soothes only one's vanity or hedges one's security.

While the reader of *The Polish Complex* becomes immersed in the psyche of the narrator-protagonist and is sensitized to how he thinks and what he feels, the other characters are not so fully realized. Indeed, they are almost caricatures, each vividly portrayed but representing a clear stereotype. The effect is that a reader feels exposed to the broad range of Polish society. Antagonistic or compassionate, honest or lying—these are merely superficial manifestations although they turn out after all to be universal. All cultures have such types; it is the human condition. Yet these characters are also distinctly Polish. It is the bedrock of Polish history and the collective Polish experience that make the Polish character unique.

Themes and Meanings

Episodes in contemporary Polish life (waiting in line) and historical episodes (the two long flashbacks on the nineteenth century revolutionaries) are juxtaposed to Konwicki's philosophical musings and analyses in the book. Even a letter, thinly disguised as being from someone from another country, is inserted into the book. The people who are waiting in line seem to be a random assortment of individuals. They have little purpose, certainly no long-term goals, just as the novel has no conventional plot. The evening progresses and the action seems pointless. Because there are no transitions in the novel, no introductions or explanations of gaps in time, character, or mode, the effect is fragmentation and loose ends. Life is a kaleidoscope of vividly depicted and intensely realized scenes, but it has little meaning.

What replaces a sense of meaning in life is Poland—not the real, but the ideal, the possible, potential Poland. Defeated, humiliated, and debased as far back in history as one cares to look, there yet remains the faintest spark of hope for a better future. This hope for Poland is revealed not directly or explicitly, but in some of Konwicki's most lyrical passages, where he warmly describes domestic scenes and evokes Polish customs, such as the breaking and sharing of the wafer on Christmas Eve. The anonymous "friend" writes,

> When inwardly I say that one short word "Poland," a wistful exaltation arises in me, something clear, free, soothing; Poland, homeland of freedom; Poland, lair of tolerance; Poland, that great garden of rampant individualism. Where people greet each other with a smile, where a policeman lifts a rose instead of a club, where the air is made of oxygen and truth. Poland the great white eagle in the center of Europe.

Contrast with the tawdry reality of contemporary Poland is inescapable, yet the longing for what might be persists to lift the spirit and encourage perseverance. The dream for Poland is freedom. The Christmas miracle that Konwicki awaits this cold Christmas Eve, standing in line outside a jewelry store, may well be that Poland somehow achieves the freedom it has sought throughout its history.

The interplay between the nation and the individual is an important theme in *The Polish Complex*. National character is shown to determine individual identity. That is one reason the historical interludes are so lengthy and so important. Defeat, abandonment of ideals, and disillusionment are not unique to Konwicki; they were suffered by countless revolutionaries before him. They constitute the history of Poland and as a result color the Polish national character. This in turn affects every Pole alive, regardless of the particular shading provided by his own personality. Repeatedly Konwicki writes of the similarity between nations and individuals. National fortunes and misfortunes are like individual fortunes and misfortunes, he says. Some nations are lucky, some unlucky. For some individuals everything turns out well; for others, everything inexplicably goes wrong. Situations in which individuals sometimes find themselves are like situations into which a nation can fall. The kidnapped victim who must behave and speak as though everything is all right demonstrates the plight of the nation that is controlled by a larger power. The view that Konwicki offers is that history shows Poland to be a loser, but that the spark of hope for a miracle endures. This hope is what keeps the real Poland going. "The Polish complex" is that strange combination of real defeat and visionary hope that exists for Poland as a nation as well as for the Polish people.

The book presents the autobiographical, introspective search of Tadeusz Konwicki. It suggests that no Polish individual can solve the enigma of his own identity without simultaneously probing the national character. There is another perspective in *The Polish Complex*: the cosmos. Earth is only one planet in one system. The cosmic perspective prevents the self-searching of *The Polish Complex* from appearing ridiculous or pompous. The serious philosophical inquiry is no Quixote battling windmills, but eternal questions that all human beings must ask. What does it mean to be human? Where do lying and cheating as common modes of human behavior come from? Are they indigenous to the species? Or do they derive from one's very Polishness?

The Polish Complex presents more questions than answers. Its fragmentary structure and the absence of plot as conventionally understood, the banality of situation and randomness of the individuals gathered together, the unrootedness of individuals—all contrive perfectly to ask the questions Konwicki asks. It is the reader who must provide the answers. The section on Traugutt, which appears near the end of the book, is enclosed by a statement that undercuts it. The episode "could have happened" as Konwicki depicts it. Yet did it? Can one ever know? Does historical authenticity matter? In this book of individual and national Polish identity, psychological and philosophical authenticity are much more important Yet, like the characters of the novel, psychological and philsophical strands disperse in different directions. *The Polish Complex* is a powerful book that asks questions important not only to Poles but to the world community of human beings as well.

Critical Context

The Polish Complex marks a dramatic change from the kind of writing which first earned for Konwicki a literary reputation in Poland. In 1954, his Socialist Realist novel *Władza* (power) appeared and won the State Prize for Literature. Two years later he published *Rojsty* (1956; marshes), a book which he had actually written in 1948 but which could not be published until censorship restrictions were eased. *Rojsty* points in the direction of *The Polish Complex*; it satirizes a young man who is trying to become a hero fighting against the Soviet invasion of Poland. *Rojsty* marks a turning point in Konwicki's value system; he had sided with the Communists for a time because he believed that industrialism was the wave of the future for Poland, but he became disillusioned with socialism and turned in other directions. *Rojsty* was the first work to show the kind of writing that would make Konwicki a major literary figure.

Sennik współczesny (1963; *A Dreambook for Our Time*, 1969) brought Konwicki an international reputation. Almost immediately it was hailed as a major literary sensation. Konwicki depicts in the book a nightmarish world of torment, fear, evil, guilt, and alienation. A terrifying book, it has a surrealistic aura and a pessimistic view of life. These qualities also obtain in *The Polish Complex*, which was officially banned in Poland. First published in the samizdat, the novel shows the dismal realities of everyday life in Poland—the boredom, the disillusionment, the sense of a bleak future that seems shared by everyone. What makes the book perhaps even more devastating than Konwicki's earlier work is that the problems are not idiosyncratic; they cannot be dismissed as one person's peculiar combination of circumstances and identity, but are endemic to the country. Furthermore, the shaping of individual character by national history is inevitable and inescapable. Thus the condemnation is all the stronger.

Konwicki's subsequent works have continued his vivid portrayal of a grim

Polish reality and strong condemnation of the moral and spiritual condition of the country through techniques of fragmentation and collage. *The Polish Complex* confirmed that Konwicki is a powerful and intense writer whose reputation on the international scene is well justified.

Sources for Further Study

Anders, Jaroslaw. Review in *The New York Review of Books*. XXIX (March 4, 1982), p. 16.

Baran, Henry K. Review in *Library Journal*. CVII (March 15, 1982), p. 650.

Barańczak, Stanisław. "*The Polish Complex*," in *Partisan Review*. LI, no. 3 (1984), pp. 433-441.

Krzyzanowski, Jerzy R. "*The Polish Complex*," in *Polish Perspectives*. XXV (1979), pp. 98-110.

Paula Kopacz

THE POOR CHRIST OF BOMBA

Author: Mongo Beti (Alexandre Biyidi, 1932-   )
Type of plot: Satirical realism
Time of plot: The 1930's
Locale: Southern Cameroon, the small village of Bomba and several yet smaller villages throughout the forest
First published: Le Pauvre Christ de Bomba, 1956 (English translation, 1971)

> *Principal characters:*
> FATHER DRUMONT, the archetypal, aging Catholic missionary, who founded Bomba, remaining for twenty years
> DENIS, the fourteen-year-old, unreliable, first-person African narrator and naïve protagonist, who ironically echoes Drumont's Christianity
> ZACHARIA, the adult protagonist, Drumont's materialistic African cook, who explicitly opposes Drumont's views
> VIDAL, the French colonial administrator of the region, who uses forced labor to build roads
> CATHERINE, a young African girl, Zacharia's mistress, who also seduces Denis
> CLEMENTINE, Zacharia's wife, who beats Catherine to defend her belief in Christian monogamy

The Novel
Structured through the device of a young teenager's daily journal, *The Poor Christ of Bomba* records the tour of a French Catholic missionary, Father Drumont, and his two assistants—Denis, Drumont's "boy" and the narrator, and Zacharia, the cook—through a dozen tiny villages in the forest of the Tala region. Bomba, itself a small village surrounded by the forest, teems with activity, sustained primarily by the mission's *sixa*, a home for the prenuptial training of young women to encourage monogamy among the traditionally polygamous Talas. These women stay several months at the *sixa* and provide free labor for various workshops, plantations, and an elementary school. In contrast, the Tala villagers in the forest, who have become familiar with Drumont's evangelism over the past twenty years, not to mention the German missionaries before him, have remained largely resistant to his faith, despite his practice of soliciting conversions through fear and misery. While nominally accepting Christianity, the Talas have done so only to the extent that the European faith has provided access to what the Talas regard as the secret power of colonialism: money. Ironically, converted Talas have left their villages for those such as Bomba which are scattered along the new colonial roads; motivated by cash rather than Christ, these Talas staff

the mission, serving as counterparts to the forest people, who live by essentially traditional customs, integrally bound to the forest's natural cycles and resources.

Drumont's tour results from the Talas' negligence in paying their church dues. Having been absent for three years, Drumont decides that he has "punished" them long enough by withholding his spiritual guidance. As Denis duly echoes Drumont's bombastic language, the reader soon realizes that the narrator's voice consists of sustained comic irony. In village after village, chapels have decayed to ruins and the forest people listen obediently but uncomprehendingly to Father Drumont's sermons, which are composed of alien—to the Africans—biblical rhetoric and anecdotes. Polygamy and "pagan" dances continue, even while Drumont rails against them on his one-day visits to village after village. Zacharia, meanwhile, is joined by Catherine, his mistress from the *sixa*, and continues his illicit affair with her just as he had done in Bomba. Night after night, Drumont sleeps obliviously next door to Zacharia and Catherine.

Drumont's aloof blindness to his failure to convert the Talas cannot continue. Stern and stubborn, he struggles to maintain his delusion of successful evangelism, but too much to the contrary confronts him. In a parody of baptism, Drumont is nearly drowned while crossing a river. Catherine seduces Denis, who confesses his sin, and his pleasure, to Drumont. Clementine, Zacharia's wife, arrives to expose his adultery and beats Catherine to demonstrate her belief in monogamy. Catherine's fiancé arrives and soundly beats Zacharia. The greatest blow comes to Drumont's confidence as Clementine reveals that Catherine belongs to the *sixa*. Vidal, the administrator in the region, visits Drumont in the effort to recruit laborers from among the fruits of Drumont's new evangelical harvest. When Vidal finds that the father superior is failing, he urges the father to stay, threatening to impose a blatant condition of slavery on the Talas if Drumont returns to France as he contemplates doing. Over the course of only two weeks, Drumont's twenty-year delusions of the spiritual achievements of Christianity in Tala country have utterly collapsed. He retreats hastily to Bomba.

When Drumont returns, the scandals only grow more pervasive and more serious than he had realized on his tour. The *sixa* has been used for years as a brothel, making his loyal catechists little more than rich pimps. As the widespread pandering comes to light through Drumont's inquiries of the *sixa* women, who confess under the duress of whippings directed by Drumont himself, the African supervisors and catechists flee Bomba; the *sixa* women name more and more of them in their "confession," parodying those of the Catholic ritual. Worse, Drumont's "Number One Boy," Daniel, has introduced syphilis into the *sixa*; consequently, many of Bomba's men and their wives are afflicted with the venereal disease. Drumont, demoralized at the fragility of Christian values among the Talas, quickly completes his plans to

return to France. He returns Denis to his father and·sends the *sixa* women
back to their home villages—still infected with syphilis and gonorrhea.

Despite the missionary's promises to write, Denis hears nothing from
Drumont. Three weeks after his return to France, Bomba is deserted. Rumors surface of men and women being "driven into the labour gangs" under
"a real reign of terror" by Vidal's soldiers. With the Talas abandoned and
crippled physically and spiritually, Denis, fearing for his own safety, must
awaken to the colonial realities which threaten him. Any hope of continuing
his Christian education or even hearing a Mass now gone, Denis decides to
escape from the countryside for the more "civilized" servitude of working for
a Greek merchant in a larger town. Drumont, called Father Jesus by the
young boys of the once-thriving mission and the Cunning One by the forest
Talas, has left Africa to suffer not only the degradation of self-destruction
but also the oppression of colonial tyranny.

The Characters

Within the insistently ironic voice of the narrator, Mongo Beti subtly
develops a gradual opposition between the seemingly inextricable viewpoints
of Drumont and Denis. While Drumont realizes slowly his failure to convert
the Talas to Christianity in any authentic sense, Denis realizes slowly that
Christianity has destroyed rather than saved his people. Because Denis often
says just the opposite of what the author means and because the narrator's
amply detailed description of the mission, villages, forest, and customs is factual rather than ironic, the characterization of the two seems at first nearly
static. As the pace of comic events becomes more rapid as the novel progresses, Drumont's disillusionment appears somewhat sudden, yet, as he
himself suggests, the reality of his failures has been emerging over several
years. Denis, on the other hand, maintains his naïve stance until the last
pages of the novel, even though the reader senses the waning of the irony in
his voice from the point of his first sexual experience. By the end of the
novel, what initially seemed a genuine spiritual alliance between Drumont
and Denis becomes an irreconcilable conflict between the colonial Christianity of Drumont and the rootless coming-of-age of a modern African boy.

In Beti's use of an innocent vision to shape a web from which all other
characters speak for themselves and to one another, a second conflicting
tension develops. Because Denis records an increasing amount of dialogue as
the novel unfolds, the reader can discern two sets of characters who hold
contrasting viewpoints on the significance of the mission. The first group,
those such as Denis, see the evangelism at work from the inside and depend
on the omission of details (such as the flagrant pandering), on discrepancy,
and on extreme hyperbole to show the irrelevance of a faith so deeply antagonistic to African values. The vicar, Jean-Martin Le Guen, has just come
from France, but, an insider, he is as blind as Drumont to the mission's spiri-

tual poverty. Catherine, while understanding her sins nominally, chooses complicity in the schemes in order to gain easier work assignments and relative freedom in the *sixa*.

The second set of characters, much greater in number, see the mission from a detached viewpoint, although many of them are employed at the mission. Zacharia is the protagonist for this colonized African viewpoint: He sees that a central source of the mission's income is derived from the inflated baptism fees of unwed mothers, despite Drumont's condescending sermons against premarital sex. While Denis is aware of the discrepancy, Zacharia understands clearly the implication of the Father's high fees: Making money is making money. Raphael, the supervisor of the *sixa*, understands similarly how the mission prostitutes its own existence, taking the contradiction as license for his own pandering of the *sixa* women. Consequently, the two groups share materialistic values, but the insiders use their bankrupt spirituality to control African wealth; the outsiders, all Africans who recognize their lack of power as a lack of wealth, pursue directly their own acquisition of wealth—and hence control of it—by any means available.

To Beti's credit, his attack on Christianity is tempered by restraint in his condemnation of European missionaries. Drumont, for all of his sins, seems genuine (if ignorant of his role as an agent for colonial control) in his concern for the spiritual health of the Talas. He believes earnestly in his own values, blind as he is to their disruptive consequences for the Africans. When he realizes that his twenty years of missionary work have depleted the Talas of both Christian and traditional values, he muses over the validity of the traditional values and, at least, has the good sense to do no further harm: He leaves. Conversely, Beti refuses to glorify his African characters beyond credibility. Save for the traditional Talas, who remain in the descriptive background and from whom not even a minor character emerges fully, Beti's outsiders are largely self-serving in their actions, whatever their motives or circumstances may be. Sanga Boto, or Ferdinand (depending on what opportunity arises), is a sorcerer and baptized polygamist who quite willingly plays whatever role will enhance his private reputation. To do so is good for the sorcery business. Clementine's brutal demonstration of her belief in monogamy suggests that she is more interested in Zacharia's benefits from the mission than in nurturing the intimacies of marriage. Zacharia, after all, represents a consistent source of material goods. In Beti's evenhanded treatment of both blatant flaws (Vidal's racism) and subtle ones among both European and African characters, he enhances his portrait of a people on the edge of social and spiritual chaos.

Themes and Meanings

Although Beti's novel debunks the relevance of Christianity to traditional Africa with wit and comedy, the larger and more serious charge against

Christianity is that it paves the road of colonialism with a spiritual chaos that softens the resistance to colonial exploitation. In the metaphor of Christianity as a venereal disease that spreads quietly through the countryside, the Talas lose their capacity for not only resistance but also self-determination. Implicitly, Beti argues the negritude movement's position that sensuality is superior to rationality, that emotion determines human relationships much more powerfully than does reason. Left without a coherent set of emotional principles for guidance, the Talas are deprived of the basis of their identity with a larger community. Drumont preaches constantly against sexuality not simply because he represents a theology that espouses sexual repression but also because to forbid sex among traditional Tala practices is to undermine a crucial element of Tala morality. Socially, the destruction of polygamy, the superficial imposition of alien ritual, and the absence of young men and women from the traditional family (a result of Christian education and the introduction of technology into village life) all combine to divide the Talas between those who pursue a European commercial life-style along the roads and those who cling to a pastoral, agrarian life-style in the forest. Consequently, a nascent class system built on sexual practices, values, and race begins to characterize a previously complex kinship system of social organization.

Without either African traditions or viable Christian values to sustain a united community, the Talas are left without the power of wealth, leadership, or numbers to resist the intrusion of Vidal and his soldiers into their midst. To the colonial administrator, the modernized Africans mean only an underemployed service sector of society that can be counted on to perpetuate the paternalistic, benevolent image of the colonial state, precisely because they are dependent on French revenue for their material survival. Even if they emigrate to large towns, as Denis plans to do, and work for other Europeans, such as the Greek merchants, they will still be second-class citizens in their own country. The forest Talas, without European technology and weaponry, cannot resist being herded into road gangs that will only open more of the forest to colonial expansion, thereby providing even greater wealth for the colonizers. Vidal, then, under the guise of the biblical curse on Ham, is more than happy to trot out the racist argument that God ordained white men to rule black Africans. When Vidal encourages Drumont to stay, he is fully aware that the mission's presence makes his conquest that much easier.

Not even the emerging class structure is lost upon Vidal. When Drumont rejects Vidal's argument based on the sons of Ham, Vidal turns to the Communist threat as a pretense for colonial rule: "According to our informers, there are already certain subversive groups in the towns who follow Marxist-Leninism and I don't know what-all. To my mind, the best weapon we have against that thuggish philosophy is Christianity." Moreover, Vidal cares little about what role Christianity plays as long as it supports a benevolent pose for colonial conquest: "Cook up some kind of Christianity for the Africans, it doesn't matter what, but don't go away and leave us."

In summary, Vidal represents the paradigm that characterizes African colonial history: The Church, operating under the false assumption that spiritually the Africans are a blank slate, seeks to "save" them; the colonial administration follows, seeking to "civilize" them; when the economic exploitation subsequently creates an underclass, the colonizers use the threat of left-wing totalitarianism which would destroy religious freedom as the pretext both for an implicit demand of the Church's cooperative silence in the face of brutalities and for an explicit excuse to impose military domination. Beti's novel suggests, then, that Drumont fails as the Poor Christ of Bomba because his belief in Christ as a spiritual force who "has mingled us all in the same love" is not reflected in the everyday reality of the mission. Colonial Christianity, in short, is Christianity without love. Around and within it is only materialism. Drumont is doomed to failure because European materialism and greed spawn African materialism and greed, which, in turn— whether in the *sixa* or along the roads—further perpetuates the greed of both races. The price for deception and delusion is, for both races, the loss of love.

Critical Context

For more than three decades, Alexandre Biyidi (Beti's real name) has used comic satire, precise observation, and incisive analysis to create a continual record of Cameroon's transition from a colonial state to an independent nation. While *Ville cruelle* (1954; cruel town) was a failure critically, even to the point that Biyidi dropped the pseudonym of Ezra Boto forever, *The Poor Christ of Bomba*, his second novel, earned just praise, although it was translated much later than his two subsequent novels, *Mission terminée* (1957; *Mission to Kala*, 1958) and *Le Roi miraculé* (1958; *King Lazarus*, 1960). After these early novels, which helped create the genre of the francophone anticolonial novel, Biyidi, continuing to write under the name of Mongo Beti because it provided limited safety from persecution, turned his darkening vision of colonial Africa to a satirical attack on Cameroon, *Tumultueux Cameroun* (1959; tumultuous Cameroon). Having returned from France as his country prepared for independence only to be jailed briefly as a political suspect, he left Cameroon to return to France, living in exile and teaching French literature. After a decade of silence, he began where he had left off, publishing a scathing attack on the ruling elite of Cameroon, *Main basse sur le Cameroun* (1972; the plundering of Cameroon), which was suppressed in both Cameroon and France. Almost as if to complete a circle, Biyidi, still writing as Beti, turned again to fiction, examining the position of women in postcolonial Cameroon through two subsequent novels.

In addition to affording a measure of political distance, Biyidi's pen name has helped him establish an intellectual distance that was once rare among modern African writers. He spares no race or nationality in his early satires, yet the absence of bitterness and self-pity that Beti achieves through his wit, humor, and racy dialogues constitutes the emergence of the African comic novel. While Biyidi might be said to have created a singularly thorough and successful record of the failure of French West African colonialism and independence, it is the ring of laughter from an otherwise grim period of African history on which the reputation of *The Poor Christ of Bomba* will endure.

Sources for Further Study

Britwum, Kwabena. "Irony and the Paradox of Idealism in Mongo Beti's *Le Pauvre Christ de Bomba,*" in *Re: Arts and Letters*. VI (1972), pp. 48-68.

Cassirer, Thomas. "The Dilemma of Leadership as Tragi-Comedy in the Novels of Mongo Beti," in *L'Esprit Createur*. X (1970), pp. 223-233.

Chase, Joanne. "Saints and Idiots: The Fanatic Mentality as Depicted in Mongo Beti's *The Poor Christ of Bomba,*" in *ACLALS Bulletin*. V (1980), pp. 86-97.

Lambert, Fernando. "Narrative Perspectives in Mongo Beti's *Le Pauvre Christ de Bomba,*" in *Yale French Studies*. LIII (1976), pp. 78-91.

Porter, Abioseh Mike. "The Child-Narrator and the Theme of Love in Mongo Beti's *Le Pauvre Christ de Bomba,*" in *Design and Intent in African Literature*, 1982.

Michael Loudon

PORNOGRAFIA

Author: Witold Gombrowicz (1904-1969)
Type of plot: Philosophical realism
Time of plot: During World War II
Locale: German-occupied Poland
First published: 1960 (English translation, 1966)

> *Principal characters:*
> WITOLD, the narrator
> FREDERICK, the narrator's companion and the instigator of many of the novel's incidents
> HIPPOLYTUS S. (HIPPO), the landowner whom Frederick and Witold visit
> KAROL, a young Pole with whom the two men are obsessed
> HENIA, Hippo's daughter, whom Frederick and Witold wish to match up with Karol
> ALBERT, a distinguished gentleman engaged to Henia
> LADY AMELIA, the owner of the estate that Frederick and Witold visit
> SIEMIAN, a soldier in the Home Army who is murdered by Karol at Frederick's instigation

The Novel

Frederick and Witold are two older men who visit the country estate of their friend Hippolytus S. They soon become obsessed with two young people, Karol and Henia, and scheme to bring them together as lovers. Frederick is the motivating force in this erotic plan, and Witold is his passive and somewhat distrustful ally. No precise reason is given for Frederick's interference in the lives of others, except that he seems to derive his pleasure from manipulating others. He has no beliefs. He is an atheist who kneels in church only because that is the behavior required of him in that setting. He performs the act of kneeling so carefully that it looks as though he really is a believer. His actions are so correct that for the moment (Witold speculates) Frederick may actually believe in the act he is performing. Similarly, to Frederick, Karol and Henia, who are about the same age and who have grown up together, seem to be made for each other. Frederick and Witold regard Albert (Henia's fiancée) as an older man who is not fit to have her.

Frederick and Witold conspire to contrive situations in which Karol and Henia are thrown together. Witold is somewhat surprised when he finds that Henia is no innocent and has had other men. Karol, too, is no innocent and shocks Witold when he lifts the skirt of an old woman. Nevertheless, Witold and Frederick are never shaken in their belief that Karol and Henia belong together, and the conspirators achieve their goal when they manage to have

Albert see what appears to be an erotic meeting between Karol and Henia.

Much of the satisfaction Frederick and Witold seem to derive from the Henia-Karol coupling has to do with their apparent dislike of growing old, although they never say so. They are clearly rejuvenated by their creation of a love affair between the young people. They also obtain a thrill by disconcerting the mature Albert, who has never doubted Henia's constancy. In the end, Albert contrives his own death by assuming the identity of Siemian, a Home Army soldier who has lost his nerve and who therefore must be murdered before he reveals vital information to the German occupiers. Hippo, Frederick, and Witold have agreed on the murder and persuade Karol to do it, but Karol mistakes Albert for Siemian and murders him. At the end of the novel, Frederick and Witold and Karol and Henia find themselves united in recognition of Karol's error. Witold's last words indicate the satisfaction he and Frederick share with this young couple they have made their own: "They smiled. As the young always do when they are trying to get out of a scrape. And for a split second, all four of us smiled." For an instant, at least, Frederick and Witold have succeeded in becoming young again.

The Characters

Frederick is Witold's source of fascination. Witold knows that his middle-aged companion is attracted to the young for lack of a belief in anything else. The visit to the countryside does not really have much appeal to either Frederick or Witold. They remain only when they discover Karol and Henia, seeing them as playthings. The other characters have little real interest for Frederick and Witold. Hippo is the imperceptive country gentleman, who believes that his daughter is a good match for Albert and who welcomes an alliance with a good family. Albert (Witold acknowledges) is an accomplished and elegant man, but Albert's air of confidence only incites Frederick and Witold to prove that it is a sham and that it can easily be shattered. Siemian is a fascinating character, a courageous underground soldier who has succumbed to fear, but in Frederick's and Witold's eyes, that only means that he should be eliminated without any moral anguish.

Lady Amelia, however, excites Witold's curiosity because she is the exact opposite of Frederick. She is a devout Catholic and a wise old woman. She seems entirely secure in her faith and her way of life. Yet Frederick bothers her, and she attempts to impress him. In the end, like Albert, she proves to be unstable. She dies in mysterious circumstances, having engaged in some sort of struggle with a young intruder. Her behavior suggests hysteria and perhaps some kind of sexual need. Has her grappling with a young man been an effort to defend herself or in some sense to possess him, as Frederick and Witold have tried to possess Karol and Henia? Her motivations are not clear, but there is no doubt that she has not lived the life of repose that her calm demeanor suggests.

Themes and Meanings

Pornografia, despite its title, is not a pornographic novel; it does not provide graphic scenes of sexual activity or dwell on the physical aspects of love. It is, however, an erotic novel which suggests that the basis of human behavior is not intellectual or religious but sensual and secretive. People hide as much or more than they reveal. By and large, people are motivated by impulses they try to mask with a veneer of reason and cultivation. Frederick is an exception because he lives his life according to the feelings most people suppress and fail to act upon. He realizes that most people do not grow up, even though this is the professed goal of most human beings. In his preface to *Pornografia* (included in the Grove Press paperback edition) Witold Gombrowicz notes that if one of man's goals is "fulfillment" and "total maturity. . . it seems to me that another of man's aims appears, a more secret one, undoubtedly, one which is in some way illegal: his need for the unfinished . . . for imperfection . . . for inferiority . . . for youth. . . ." Youth, however, is not idealized in *Pornografia*. It is, rather, a state of being which Frederick and Witold secretly wish to enjoy, for they find the demands of adulthood trying and pretentious. They lack any sort of belief in the church, the home, or the family. They are not patriots and show little concern with the Home Army organized by Poles to fight the German invaders.

This theme of a fascination with the immature seems to be autobiographical. Ewa Thompson has quoted from Gombrowicz's published journal to show that during his exile in Argentina (beginning in 1939) the author sought out "young, unrefined, and unadulterated" people. While not much of this aspect of the author's life is known, it is clear that he rejected the Argentine literary establishment and preferred to consort with a generation younger and less cultivated than himself. Frederick and Witold are also in a kind of exile from Warsaw and are drawn not to figures of their own age but to a younger and seemingly inexperienced couple. By giving the narrator of *Pornografia* his own first name, the author has encouraged this autobiographical reading of his work. At the same time, however, he places himself in Poland during the period he was in Argentina. Gombrowicz did not set foot in Poland during the war. It would be hazardous, therefore, to identify too many connections between the author's life and his work.

Critical Context

In his preface to *Pornografia*, Gombrowicz states that the novel "springs from *Ferdydurke*" (1937; English translation, 1961). In his words, this earlier novel is about the way "youth, biologically superior, physically more beautiful, has no trouble in charming and conquering the adult, already poisoned by death." In *Ferdydurke*, the author says he struggled against immaturity and tried to show through humor and sarcasm the ridiculousness of an obsession with youth. In *Pornografia*, on the other hand, it could be argued (he suggests) that he is "in love with immaturity." In the latter work he has "given up the distance lent by humor. It is not a satire but a noble, a classical novel." The themes of the two novels are virtually identical, but *Pornografia* is more profound, Gombrowicz implies, because he has admitted that he himself is the source of his theme. It is not something he has observed outside himself.

By adopting the guise of personal confession in his preface, and by calling his narrator Witold, Gombrowicz paradoxically creates another kind of fiction, which is more real precisely because he admits that it comes out of his own experience. Yet he is surely having some fun with his reader and putting distance between himself and his creation when he uses his preface to become his own critic: "The novel of two middle-aged men and a couple of adolescents; a sensually metaphysical novel. What a disgrace!" The exclamation mark, the value judgment, are terms that would never be used in the novel proper. The preface's critical terms, in other words, provide a clever way of distancing the author from his fiction even as he proclaims that it is the product of his own obsessions.

Gombrowicz has also suggested in his preface that *Pornografia* is an attempt "to renew Polish eroticism." He refers to recent Polish history as "composed of rape, slavery, and boyish squabbles." In effect, he suggests that there has been an immaturity in Polish life that is apparent on both the private and public levels. Frederick and Witold have tried, in a sense, to rape and enslave Karol and Henia. Frederick and Witold have wanted to master the younger generation, and in postwar Poland that generation has suffered the indoctrination of a government that would manipulate it just as obscenely as Frederick and Witold manipulate Karol and Henia. By suggesting that *Pornografia* is "a descent to the dark limits of the conscience and the body," Gombrowicz holds in his preface that much more than ideas, political and otherwise, must be considered in explaining Polish destiny. Rather, he advises his readers to look to the impulses of the body, to the fact that all philosophy is grounded in the erotic, and to ideas that cannot be "desexualized."

Sources for Further Study

Boyers, Robert. "Aspects of the Perversion in Gombrowicz's *Pornografia*," in *Salmagundi*. XVII (1971), pp. 19-46.

Fletcher, John. "Witold Gombrowicz," in *New Directions in Literature: Critical Approaches to a Contemporary Phenomenon*, 1968.

Jelenski, Constantin. "Witold Gombrowicz," in *Tri-Quarterly*. No. 9 (Spring, 1967), pp. 37-42.

Miłosz, Czesław. *A History of Polish Literature*, 1983 (second edition).

Thompson, Ewa. *Witold Gombrowicz*, 1979.

Carl E. Rollyson, Jr.

PORTRAIT OF A MAN UNKNOWN

Author: Nathalie Sarraute (1900-   )
Type of plot: Experimental fiction
Time of plot: The late 1940's
Locale: Paris and an unnamed Dutch city (probably Amsterdam)
First published: Portrait d'un inconnu, 1948 (English translation, 1958)

> *Principal characters:*
> THE NARRATOR, a sensitive man who looks for the unconscious
> "movements" behind people's words and actions
> THE DAUGHTER, a strange old maid who has a difficult
> relationship with her father
> THE FATHER, an old miser who believes that his daughter is
> trying to rob him
> LOUIS DUMONTET, an employee of the Finance Ministry who
> becomes the daughter's fiancé

The Novel

Portrait of a Man Unknown has no plot in the traditional sense. It describes the narrator's search for reality, his attempts to discover the truth about the relationship between an old man and his daughter. Like a detective, he spies on them and even imagines scenes between them at which he is not present.

The narrator's method of exploration consists of seeing and imagining what Nathalie Sarraute has called "tropisms." In her introduction to *Tropismes* (1938; *Tropisms*, 1963), she defined tropisms as movements, "hidden under the commonplace, harmless appearances of every instant of our lives," which "slip through us on the frontiers of consciousness in the form of undefinable, extremely rapid sensations." These movements "hide behind our gestures, beneath the words we speak, the feelings we manifest, are aware of experiencing, and able to define." She called them tropisms "because of their spontaneous, irresistible, instinctive nature, similar to that of the movements made by certain living organisms under the influence of outside stimuli, such as light or heat."

The novel explores the theme of the "mask," or false face, which the father puts on every time he sees his daughter. The narrator compares it with the mask worn by Prince Bolkonski in Leo Tolstoy's *Voyna i mir* (1865-1869; *War and Peace*, 1886) to hide his powerful love for his daughter, Princess Marie. The prince's mask slipped once on his deathbed when he called Marie "my little friend" or "my little soul"; no one heard exactly what he said. The narrator wonders why the prince would need to hide his love from his daughter, who was perfectly pure and innocent—or was she? The old man's daughter was probably not perfectly innocent, even as a baby. She seemed like a monster to him as her strident cry and "tentacles" made him "secrete" the mask the first time. Prince Bolkonski and Princess Marie are real characters in a real novel—solid, defined, explained. The narrator wishes that real life were like that; then he could feel confident, secure.

At the urging of his parents, he goes to see a specialist (psychologist? psychiatrist? literary critic?) who convinces him that tropisms do not exist, that he is oversensitive and neurotic, suffering from "introversion." The doctor suggests that he take a trip to complete the cure.

On a visit to an art museum in Holland, he rediscovers the painting whose name provides the title of the novel. "The Portrait of a Man Unknown," also called "The Man with the Waistcoat," is doubly unknown. Not only is the man's name unknown, but the name of the artist is unknown as well. This unfinished picture exercises a mysterious charm over the narrator, who is fascinated by the groping, uncertain lines which seem to have been drawn by a blindman. It appears that the artist was interrupted in the process of creation by a sudden, fatal catastrophe. Only the eyes of the portrait still seem alive to the narrator. He feels them calling to him.

The narrator returns to Paris and continues imagining tropisms about the father. In front of his table, reading children's schoolbooks, the old man feels secure, but behind his apparent serenity and feeling of detachment is an anxiety which wakes him up in the middle of the night. The narrator imagines him suffering because he believes that his daughter is draining the life from him, sucking away his substance. Barefoot, in his nightshirt, the man rushes to the kitchen to verify that his daughter has cut off and stolen part of his bar of soap. Tormented by these thoughts, he is unable to go back to sleep all night.

In the longest and most important scene of the novel, which the narrator presumably imagines, the daughter and the father, compared to two dung beetles, lock horns in an epic battle. She has come to shame him into giving her money for medical care. He believes that she is being taken advantage of by charlatans who want to bilk him of his money. When he seems to be losing, the father asks her why she does not get married and have someone else support her. She unexpectedly replies that she is engaged. He pushes her out of the room and locks the door, but she begs and grovels until he spitefully throws some money at her. Then she leaves, quite satisfied with herself.

The narrator's final encounter with the father and daughter is a chance meeting in a restaurant where they are dining with Louis Dumontet, the daughter's fiancé. Dumontet is a "real" character with a name and a complete physical description. He resembles the father and even has a bunion on his toe like him. Dumontet is powerful and sure of himself. In his presence all the tropisms vanish. When the daughter leaves with Dumontet, the narrator returns home to find that things are clean, smooth, solid, and pure. His world has taken on the serene look of dead people's faces. Without tropisms everything is dead.

The Characters

The subject of this novel is how to create characters in a literary work. Sarraute started with a situation worthy of a traditional novel, the relationship between a miser and his old maid daughter. This is the same subject, Sarraute points out, as that of Honoré de Balzac's *Eugénie Grandet* (1833; English translation, 1859). Balzac, however, begins his novel with a thirty-page description of the town, street, and house where his characters live in order to explain their personalities. Then he moves on to describe them psychologically and physically in great detail, including the wart on Grandet's nose which inspired Dumontet's bunion.

Sarraute gives very few details of the miser's house, only a brief description of the wallpaper and an incidental mention of a leaky pipe. With the exception of Dumontet, who is intended as a parody of traditional characters, none of her characters has a name. The protagonists are referred to as "he," "she," and "I." Sarraute's characters are constantly changing as the narrator gains new insights into their personalities. In the interminable warfare between the father and the daughter, neither the narrator nor the reader is certain who is telling the truth. Possibly the doctors are charlatans and the daughter is trying to pry her father's substance from him; possibly the daughter is the innocent victim of an egotistical miser. As in life outside novels, the reader can never know for sure.

The narrator longs to know the truth. He wants to give people names, to make them into the characters of a traditional novel—smooth, solid, and finished. He wants to put labels on them, to call her a maniac and him a miser. He suspects, however, that things are not as simple as that, that this solid mass is really a veneer which will crack, or that it is a mask built from the clichés and commonplaces of language. From behind the mask or through the crack oozes the disgusting liquid which is life.

The painting called "The Portrait of a Man Unknown" illustrates how Sarraute thinks characters should be formed: with the unsteady, groping hand of a blindman. Characters should not be pure, smooth, solid, and finished but uncertain, changing, vacillating with the rapid movements called tropisms. Only the eyes of the unknown man are alive. A work of art should shine with the life and power of those eyes.

Themes and Meanings

This novel can be understood on at least three levels. On the simplest level, it is the story of a snoopy, sensitive man who wants to find out what is happening in the lives of two other people. This man, who shares his hypersensitivity with the daughter and to some extent with the father, fears tropisms and wants to be convinced that they do not exist. Yet he enjoys his "visions," as he calls the scenes in which he imagines the protagonists. He shares a mystical link with them through these scenes, and he is strangely sad when it is cut by Dumontet.

The second level of interpretation of *Portrait of a Man Unknown* is as the story of language and how it is used to oversimplify and obscure reality. Language is a phenomenon which is shared by a group. Groups of people who hold the same values, expressed as clichés, interact constantly with the main characters. In the epic battle between father and daughter, each is surrounded by a classic chorus of invisible supporters—a group of victimized women for the daughter and some businessmen for the father.

Throughout the novel the characters move from identification with a group to individual defiance of the group and back to identification with the group. Individual experience never fits exactly into the words that are offered by the group to cover it, so the individual tries to define himself better by rejecting the group labels. Ultimately this proves impossible and the fear of solitude pushes each individual back to the group for the warmth of kindred spirits.

In addition to the interaction of tropisms among individuals and groups, Sarraute also studies the interplay of two registers of discourse. The first register, which she calls "conversation," realistically and sometimes ironically imitates the banal clichés that people exchange in everyday life or in the dialogues of a traditional novel. The second register, called "subconversation," contains the images (such as the dung beetle) that convey the tropisms that occur behind ordinary conversation.

The most complex interpretation of the novel is as the story of an artist, the narrator, who not only describes but also creates the people out of his own imagination. The narrator wants to create authentic people; as he discovers how difficult that is, he constantly seeks refuge in generalizations, simplifications, and the solid characters of a traditional novel. When the portrait of the unknown man inspires him to try again to create authentic characters, he imagines the most powerful scene of the novel: the confrontation between the father and the daughter.

This interpretation of the novel suggests that the narrator fails to capture life because Dumontet kills the tropisms, but the narrator's failure is Sarraute's success, for she has created the authentic characters filled with life which he could not.

Critical Context

Sarraute's early works, *Tropisms*, *Portrait of a Man Unknown*, and *Martereau* (1953; English translation, 1959), received almost no critical attention until the late 1950's. By that time, the literary movement called the New Novel had awakened the French reading public to the possibilities of experimental fiction. The republication of *Portrait of a Man Unknown* in 1956 co-incided with that of a collection of critical essays called *L'Ère du soupçon* (1956; *The Age of Suspicion*, 1963), which explored the evolution of the novel form.

Along with Alain Robbe-Grillet, Sarraute came to be considered a leader and a theorist of the New Novel movement. This movement challenged tradi-tional concepts of plot and characters in a novel, seeing them as outmoded and in need of renewal.

Portrait of a Man Unknown illustrates the principles expressed in *The Age of Suspicion* and forms a transition between *Tropisms* and *Martereau*. Like *Portrait of a Man Unknown*, *Martereau* has a first-person narrator who per-ceives the tropisms. After *Martereau*, Sarraute moved beyond the first-person narrator to fragment the central consciousness, dispersing it among all the "characters."

Portrait of a Man Unknown contains the seeds of all Sarraute's subsequent novels. In its preoccupation with the relationship between the artist and real-ity, it squarely poses the dilemma which she examines in her later works. As one of the first New Novels, its experimentation with novelistic techniques was a useful example for younger writers who developed the "New Novel" into the "new New Novel." Finally, its critique of the banality of conversation and its examination of other issues surrounding the use of language contrib-uted to the structuralist and deconstruction movements of the 1960's and 1970's.

Sources for Further Study
Besser, Gretchen Rous. *Nathalie Sarraute*, 1979.
Mercier, Vivian. *The New Novel: From Queneau to Pinget*, 1971.
Minogue, Valerie. *Nathalie Sarraute and the War of Words*, 1981.
Temple, Ruth Z. *Nathalie Sarraute*, 1968.
Tison-Braun, Micheline. *Nathalie Sarraute: Ou, La Recherche de l'authenti-cité*, 1971.

Lucy Schwartz

THE QUEST FOR CHRISTA T.

Author: Christa Wolf (1929-   )
Type of plot: Philosophical realism
Time of plot: The 1940's to the 1960's
Locale: East Germany: Freideberg, Leipzig, Berlin, and Mecklenberg
First published: Nachdenken über Christa T., 1968 (English translation, 1970)

> *Principal characters:*
> THE NARRATOR, a writer who has undertaken to put together a
> biography of her friend Christa T.
> CHRISTA T., an ordinary East German woman who dies from
> leukemia at the age of thirty-five
> JUSTUS, Christa T.'s husband, a veterinarian

The Novel

The Quest for Christa T. is an attempt to capture the quality of a life—the life of an ordinary, unheroic woman. Christa T. is an adolescent as World War II ends; she is educated, teaches, marries, has children, and dies young from leukemia in the German Democratic Republic (East Germany) of the 1950's and the 1960's. The unnamed narrator's quest in writing the biography of Christa T. encompasses her own memories of her friend; Christa T.'s diaries, letters, poetry, and occasional writings; the memories of Christa T.'s family; imagined reconstructions of incidents; and interviews with friends. As much as the book purports to be a quest for Christa T., it is also a quest for the way to compose such a memoir and how to find a justification for its existence.

In the "prelude" to the book, the narrator expresses her need to find some way to preserve the life of Christa T., a year after her death. Having read her friend's papers, she dismisses her own memory as deceptive; she fears the illusory quality of recollection but feels obliged to rescue Christa T. from oblivion. She realizes that "the compulsion to make her stand and be recognized" comes from the need of those who live on, a "we" in which she includes herself and the audience of readers.

The narrator recounts her first memories of Christa T. as a sixteen-year-old schoolgirl in the Hermann Goering School in Freideberg. Christa is the new student whose independent superiority undermines the authoritarian attitude of the teachers, provokes the gossip of her fellow students, and annoys the narrator. One day, after the all-clear signal following an air raid, Christa T. rolls up a newspaper and lets forth with a loud shout which shatters the repressive quiet of the Nazi town. This action jolts the narrator into a new awareness with its exuberance: "[S]uddenly I felt, with a sense of terror, that you'll come to a bad end if you suppress all shouts prematurely." The narrator's initial friendship with Christa is, however, short-lived as the Christmas holidays are eclipsed by the defeat of the Nazis, turning the townspeople into refugees. The narrator gathers impressions of Christa's flight from a diary which also contains her earlier childhood scribblings and poetry.

The two friends meet again in a university lecture hall in Leipzig seven years later. Christa has spent the intervening years as a manual laborer and, later, as a grammar-school teacher. The narrator finds their reunion miraculous, as if they both had been resurrected from the dead. A spontaneous outbreak of laughter as they part at a bus stop reveals to the narrator that Christa can still elicit the joy of surprise. Yet she has become timid, afraid of disappearing without a trace and afraid of labeling herself and thus putting boundaries around her life.

As a student, Christa is erratic and careless, dependent on her classmates for support, which they willingly provide with a trace of exasperation. Her imagination seems to fuel their quest for a perfect society, which they believe to be imminent. Yet she is the first to question the nature of such change. She asks, "What does the world need to become perfect? First of all, and for quite a long time, it needs perfect love." Christa has an intense love affair with a fellow student, Kostia, which ends not when a blonde, Inge, is brought into their relationship as a "little sister" but when Kostia's friend, Günter, falls apart over the "loss" of Inge. Christa contemplates suicide and writes a letter which the narrator would like to suppress but cannot; in it, Christa divulges that she is unable to find a purpose in her life.

She returns to her home village and spends the summer recuperating. During this period, she consults a psychic, "the General," who intimates that she will die young. Christa believes him but tells no one. Instead, she sets herself a plan of study, turning to the nineteenth century literature of fine but simple feeling, of clarity, of celebration of small things—and turning away from her first attraction, the multifaceted, complicated world-weariness of Thomas Mann and his contemporaries. As the topic of her graduate thesis, she chooses Theodor Storm, the lyric poet and tragic novelist. The narrator has requested Christa's thesis from the university and is surprised by the lack of stridency in the writing, a tone she remembers in herself and other members of her generation of students. The work is gracefully and personally written and seeks to understand "how, if at all, and under what circumstances, can one realize oneself in a work of art." It is Storm's *Sehnsucht* (longing to see and understand) with which Christa particularly identifies. The thesis is finished in 1954; Christa has not quite nine more years to live.

After leaving the university, Christa teaches in a high school in Berlin and explores the city. The city belongs to her in its multiplicity of human experience, but she soon senses that she is pretending at self-sufficiency, so she decides to marry Justus, a veterinarian from Mecklenberg who has long loved and wooed her.

In the six months between the decision to marry and the official ceremony, Christa continues to live in Berlin. The narrator perceives her as radiant with happiness, "beautiful and strange and happy." After finally committing herself to Justus on a Sunday visit to his small town, she begins to refashion herself for him. Her diary writing ceases except for recipes and household accounts. She takes great satisfaction in domestic skills and activities. She and Justus travel, sometimes drüben (over there), to West Berlin to visit Justus' relatives, where they are quite appalled by the rampant materialism of his cousins' lives and their philosophies. On one of these visits, Christa's pregnancy is observed. Subsequently, she and Justus are officially married in the courthouse.

On their wedding night, she becomes ill. She enters the hospital the next morning, suffering from an old complaint which the doctors say her pregnancy has aggravated. When the narrator visits her, they discuss the woman in the next bed, a streetcar conductress who is in the hospital as a result of her husband's beating. The narrator and Christa share the bitterness of being unable to help the woman because she will not consent to having her husband prosecuted. Immediately following the account of the conversation, the narrator raises the issue of the Hungarian uprising, connecting the disparate events with the same feeling of bitterness. The narrator describes this bitterness as "the fruit of passion." Christa's child, Anna, is born, and Christa joins Justus and settles into domestic life.

The narrator's memories of her subject from this period forward are brief, as she and Christa did not see enough of each other. She has letters and scraps of notes that Christa has written to herself, mostly on the backs of envelopes. In one of her infrequent letters, she finally labels herself "veterinary surgeon's wife in a small Mecklenberg town." She has chosen a role and realizes that the time of unlimited possibilities is over. Another child, Lena, is born two years after Anna. The narrator remembers most clearly that Christa was always tired. Nevertheless, she and Justus decide to build a house on a lake; it is a house Christa has imagined into being, planning every small detail and taking on the responsibility for all the arrangements. When the narrator suggests to her that she will be burying herself, Christa replies that, on the contrary, she is digging her way out. Despite her preoccupation with the house, Christa believes that she is losing consciousness of herself in the constant round of domesticity. In order to revalidate her sensations, she has an affair with a young forester, which ends only with her decision to have another child.

When the narrator visits Christa's old home for the last time over the New Year's holidays, Christa hosts a party that is warm, easy, and comfortable, largely because of her solid and uncalculating relationship with each guest. Only in the small hours of the morning does Christa speak of what the narrator calls her difficulties, her need for nothing to be fixed or still, for her life to keep on"originating. . . . One should never, never let it become something finished."

Christa's dying takes a year. First she is overcome by perpetual exhaustion. When she collapses and enters the hospital, the doctors diagnose her leukemia and declare that the case is too advanced for a cure. She rallies and spends the summer in the new house. The narrator visits her in July and is shocked by the change in her, a change which Christa calls "aging." The narrator envisions Christa dreaming her third, yet unborn child's life into existence as she looks over the lake. The baby, another girl, is born in the autumn, and Christa takes the child's health as a pledge of life, a pledge that is broken when she again collapses. She dies one February morning and is buried near the lake. The narrator finally affirms the need to re-create her life for those who will come later and seek to know who she was.

The Characters

The narrator and Christa T. come into being through a kind of dialogue that the narrator-writer creates with her readers. There is an element of autobiography in the narrator's book. Christa Wolf has said that the impetus for the novel was the death of someone close to her who died too young. She wrote the novel as a search for some means to "defend herself" against this death, as a kind of discovery. This reaching toward understanding is the major characteristic to be discerned in the character of the narrator. The German *Nachdenken* does not literally translate as "quest" but rather as "a thinking toward" or "a thinking in accordance with." The narrator is involved in this process by writing the memoir of Christa T. It is a kind of identification that allows her to accept her subject's life as fully lived and to understand the significance of her life.

The narrator is delineated by her reactions to and her reflections upon Christa's character. As a young girl, she is initially attracted to Christa's spontaneity and candid opinions, unclouded by any ideological cant. She retains her affection for her friend as a university student but is critical of her seeming irresponsibility and headlong passions. When Christa becomes a teacher, the narrator describes the responsibility she has for her students to become humanized and inquiring as a responsibility she takes perhaps too seriously and somewhat naïvely. Later, the narrator worries about the domestic box within which Christa finds herself during her marriage and is frustrated by the fragments of writing, unfinished stories, and lists of titles that Christa has left behind. Nevertheless, she is convinced that Christa's life was fully realized and needs to stand as an exemplar.

By reflection, the narrator is then judged to be an intelligent, responsible, and productive member of society who yet continues to question her own choices and carries traces of a commitment tinged by disappointment and some cynicism. To some degree, she lives the life that Christa did not choose.

Her subject is important to her because, while Christa distrusted commitment, she disavowed cynicism and continued to question her life until she
died.

The narrator describes other characters only in their relationship to
Christa. Justus, her husband, is a good man, who falls in love with Christa
when he first sees her, and he wins her love because he allows her to choose
him. Kostia, by contrast, is passionate but vain; he is afraid of Christa's independence and candor. Günter is the committed Socialist who is attracted by
Christa but disapproves of her lack of purpose. None of these characters is
fully realized, for the book is not a history or a narrative of Christa's life but
rather an exploration of the process of "coming-to-oneself" experienced by
the narrator in her association with Christa.

Themes and Meanings

"When, if not now?" is the final question asked by the narrator. It is a
question that echoes throughout the memoir. Christa asks it in the letter that
she writes to her sister when she is contemplating suicide. The question
probes not only toward the purpose of a life but also toward the enjoyment
of a life. Christa resists identification and labeling because she enjoys the
idea of possibilities, of choices. Choosing or, more essentially, naming closes
off possibilities and fixes reality. She longs to write but fears the definiteness
of the act. The process of seeing anew is all-important to her—in her academic career, in her family, in the construction of her house, in her writing,
and in her living.

This ambivalence about the nature of the word, of language, and of naming necessarily translates itself into the task of the narrator. She also must
resist labeling Christa in the process of re-creating her life. The life of
Christa, an unheroic woman, is crucial because the narrator discovers in her
life an openness to experience and a refusal to categorize that are the
underpinnings of a noncoercive search for life's values within oneself. The
narrator involves the reader in this learning toward self-awareness. The fragmented, analytical discourse and thoroughly subjective stance of the narrator
further serve to underline and affirm the restless, questioning nature of
Christa T.

Critical Context

Although Christa Wolf had received from the German Democratic Republic both the Heinrich Mann Prize and the Nationalpreis for her previous
novel, *Der geteilte Himmel* (1963; *Divided Heaven*, 1965), *The Quest for
Christa T.* was banned from publication by East German censors for two
years. When it was published, it appeared in a limited edition to be sold only
to those professionally involved in literary matters. East German critics
attacked its pessimism and individualistic psychological orientation. It was,

however, received with universal critical acclaim in the West.

The Quest for Christa T. anticipates themes developed in Wolf's later novels. *Kindheitsmuster* (1976; *A Model Childhood*, 1980; reissued as *Patterns of Childhood*, 1984) is an autobiographical novel in which Wolf seeks to come to terms with her Nazi childhood. She attempts to re-create herself by present reflection on her past history. Through an imagined encounter between the nineteenth century poet Karoline von Günderrode and the dramatist Heinrich von Kleist in *Kein Ort: Nirgends* (1979; *No Place on Earth*, 1982), she explores the alienation of the artist, particularly the female artist, from a society that grants her no identity. *Voraussetzungen einer Erzählung: "Kassandra"* and *Kassandra* (1983; *Cassandra: A Novel and Four Essays*, 1984) retells the Greek myth of the Trojan prophetess as a feminist parable about the recovery of humane values in a world besieged by corruption and war.

Always concerned with the possibilities of self-realization in a historical context, Wolf transcends the question of life in a Communist society in *The Quest for Christa T.* The context is present in the novel, but the issues of Christa T.'s life are of universal concern. This novel, with its discursive prose style, highly subjective stance, and wide thematic concerns, gained for Wolf her international reputation.

Sources for Further Study

Cicora, Mary A. "Language, Identity, and the Woman in *Nachdenken über Christa T.*: A Post-Structuralist Approach," in *The Germanic Review*. LVII (Winter, 1982), pp. 16-22.

Ezergalis, Inta. *Women Writers: The Divided Self, Analysis of Novels by Christa Wolf, Ingeborg Bachmann, Doris Lessing, and Others*, 1982.

Love, Myra. "Christa Wolf and Feminism: Breaking the Patriarchal Connection," in *New German Critique*. XVI (Winter, 1979), pp. 31-53.

Stephan, Alexander. *Christa Wolf*, 1979 (second edition).

Wolf, Christa. "Interview with Myself: 1966," in *The Reader and the Writer: Essays, Sketches, Memories*, 1977. Translated by Joan Becker.

Jane Anderson Jones

THE QUEST OF THE ABSOLUTE

Author: Honoré de Balzac (1799-1850)
Type of plot: Psychological realism
Time of plot: 1812-1832
Locale: Douai, France
First published: La Recherche de l'absolu, 1834 (*Balthazar: Or, Science and Love*, 1859; better known as *The Quest of the Absolute*)

> *Principal characters:*
> BALTHAZAR CLAES, a wealthy, middle-aged genius
> JOSEPHINE DE TEMNINCK CLAES, his aristocratic wife
> MARGUERITE CLAES, their oldest child
> GABRIEL CLAES, their oldest son
> FÉLICIE CLAES, their second daughter
> JEAN BALTHAZAR CLAES, their younger son
> EMMANUEL DE SOLIS, a schoolmaster
> PIERQUIN, a notary and a friend of the family
> LEMULQUINIER, Balthazar's valet

The Novel

 The Quest of the Absolute is the story of an obsession. At the beginning of the novel, Josephine de Temninck Claes is heartbroken because she believes that her husband, the magnetic Balthazar Claes, has ceased to love her after many happy years of marriage. Although he is not unkind, he ignores her and their four children, spending most of his time locked up in a laboratory.

 Josephine feels even more insecure because, although beautiful, she is lame and deformed. She could hardly believe her good fortune when the handsome, wealthy young Balthazar, hearing of her virtue and beauty, sought her out and fell deeply in love with her. To Josephine, Balthazar is almost a god. Three years before the opening scene of the novel, however, Balthazar became preoccupied with a scientific quest. Shutting himself up in the laboratory with his valet-assistant Lemulquinier, Balthazar has deserted his family, which does not even know the object of his quest.

 As the novel progresses, Josephine tries to be a loyal wife. Persuading her husband to explain his search, which is an attempt to find the single element which is the basis of all matter, Josephine reads scientific materials and pretends enthusiasm, concealing as long as she can the family's desperate financial situation. When at last Josephine must tell her husband that they can no longer pay their debts, Balthazar repents and promises to give up his experiments. When his frustration and despair seem to threaten his life, however, Josephine returns his promise, and once again, he returns to the laboratory. It is Josephine who pays for his obsession with her life, for, driven by worry, she sickens and dies, bequeathing the responsibility for the family to her oldest daughter, Marguerite.

Realizing that he has caused his wife's death, Balthazar once again gives up his work, but when he threatens to kill himself, Marguerite, like her mother, sacrifices the welfare of the children for that of the father and gives him the little money that she has left. Again Balthazar experiments; again he gives up his search, this time taking a paying job. It seems that the family can now recoup its fortunes. Under Marguerite's leadership, the little remaining property is increased. Gabriel marries an heiress; Félicie marries the notary, who is financially well off and anxious to ally himself with an aristocratic family; and Marguerite marries her kind, practical schoolmaster. Nevertheless, Balthazar's obsession will not release him, and he squanders all the property which Marguerite has reclaimed for him. At the end of the novel, he dies penniless, in his last words insisting that he has found the absolute.

The Characters

The tension in *The Quest of the Absolute* results from two kinds of conflicts: between characters and within characters. At the beginning of their relationship, Josephine and Balthazar had a conventional nineteenth century marriage. Balthazar was in charge; he cherished and provided for Josephine, and in return, she obeyed and loved him. Two events bring problems and conflict: Balthazar's insistence on putting his work ahead of both his marriage and his family, and Josephine's realization that she has a responsibility for their children which in this case conflicts with her duty to obey her husband. In addition to this disruptive disagreement, Balthazar is torn between the demands of his genius and his love for his family, and Josephine is torn between her love for her husband and her love for her children.

Honoré de Balzac describes Balthazar as a forceful, brilliant man whose features remind one of those of a dedicated priest. Certainly he has inherited his single-minded devotion to duty from an ancestor who died in the cause of freedom. (Because Balzac spent his own life obsessively pursuing various commercial ventures in quest of wealth, thereby losing all that he made by his writing, he could understand Balthazar's similar personality.) Other characters are affected by this trait as well. Copying his master, the valet Lemulquinier is possessed by the idea of the absolute, and his increasing quarrels with the other servants reflect the disintegration of his own character as well as the household disorder which results from Balthazar's experiments.

In contrast to Balthazar and Lemulquinier, Josephine, her strong daughter Marguerite, and the other children represent the sensible, everyday world, which balances one need against another and compromises in order to satisfy partially as many needs as possible. None of them can understand Balthazar's single-mindedness. On the other hand, Balthazar refuses to face financial reality, leaving his wife or children to pay the debts which he irresponsibly incurs.

Josephine and Marguerite are alike in their love for Balthazar. To Josephine, he is the prince who rescued her from unpopularity. Uncertain of herself, she is all the more dependent on his love for a sense of her own identity. When she believes that she has been replaced by his quest, she is lost. Always hoping that she can once again be the center of his life, she believes him, forgives him his coldness and his extravagance, and sacrifices her children for his love. Although Marguerite, who is Josephine's successor as protector of the family, does not fear the loss of love, she is too compassionate to see her father suffer or even possibly kill himself when he is deprived of his work. Therefore, though for different motives, she softens and indulges him as her mother had.

Balzac's treatment of the two suitors is interesting. Neither of them is a simple character. Emmanuel de Solis, the intelligent, honest schoolmaster whom Marguerite finally marries, though idealistic, is willing to conspire in order to save the family fortunes and even to lie in order to keep Balthazar from taking Marguerite's last remaining funds. Pierquin, the notary, is also complex. Although at first he seems interested in Marguerite only because of her parents' wealth, at the end of the story, when he marries Félicie, primarily because of her aristocratic ancestry, he commits himself to aiding the family, showing more human warmth than he had displayed earlier in the novel.

Themes and Meanings

In this novel, Balzac attempts to define genius and to trace its effects on those who live too close to its flame. At one point, he compares genius to vice in that both involve excess. The difference is that vice is selfish, while genius is self-consuming. Certainly Balthazar hopes to attain wealth by discovering the secret of the universe, and he frequently assures his family that he will compensate them for their sacrifices. Nevertheless, it is clear that any wealth that he acquires will be merely a by-product of his success. His mistress is not wealth but science. It is evidence of Balzac's own genius that he can sympathize with Balthazar, understanding that men such as him have been responsible for the progress of mankind, while also understanding that the families of such dreamers have often suffered and that the geniuses themselves have frequently been destroyed by their own intensity.

Balzac also examines the nature of love. Josephine's feeling for her husband is based upon a compound of gratitude, insecurity, and real devotion. Unfortunately, the intensity of her love for him, which in its own way resembles his love of science, weakens her. Even to save her children, she cannot deny this passion.

In their relationship, which is just as affectionate as that of her parents,

Marguerite and Emmanuel are far wiser. Neither sacrifices his identity or his reason for the other. If they avoid the appealing but destructive love which Josephine evinces, however, it should be remembered that these more fortunate lovers live in the real world, not in the world of genius.

Can love exist in the same environment with genius? When Josephine weeps, the scientist Balthazar recites the formula for tears; when she is dying, he resents the interruption to his work. Only occasionally does he become aware of anyone's suffering. Not until the end of his life, when children throw stones at him and his assistant, shouting that they are madmen or sorcerers, does he catch a glimpse of the way in which the real world views him. Thus Balzac presents his problem and asks his question. As a realist, he describes results. He does not solve the problem of love versus genius, nor does he suggest a basis for their coexistence.

Critical Context

The Quest of the Absolute was published only five years after Balzac's first successful novel; it is in the series which he called "Philosophical Studies," one of three major subdivisions of his vast lifework, *La Comédie humaine* (1829-1848; *The Human Comedy*, 1895-1896, 1911). Although it is a relatively early work, it does not show indications of immaturity. Critics praise the novel for its realistic detail in both description and scientific fact. It has been noted that Balzac used the care of a scientist in referring to the scientific knowledge of his time, as well as the insight of a psychologist in revealing the fluctuations of the human heart.

As a study of monomania, *The Quest of the Absolute* is in the vein of Balzac's masterpieces: stories of obsession such as *Eugénie Grandet* (1833; English translation, 1859), *Le Père Goriot* (1835; *Daddy Goriot*, 1860; also as *Père Goriot*), and *La Cousine Bette* (1846; *Cousin Bette*, 1888). Indeed, referring to Balzac's "Philosophical Studies," V. S. Pritchett observes that it is "above all" *The Quest of the Absolute* which "contains the theme of a destiny that is the directing force in his imagination."

Sources for Further Study

Bertault, Philippe. *Balzac and the Human Comedy*, 1963.
Lawton, Frederick. *Balzac*, 1910.
Maurois, André. *Prometheus: The Life of Balzac*, 1965.
Pritchett, V. S. *Balzac*, 1973.
Saintsbury, George. *A History of the French Novel to the Close of the Nineteenth Century*. Vol. 2, 1919.

Rosemary M. Canfield-Reisman

THE QUESTIONNAIRE
Or, Prayer for a Town and a Friend

Author: Jiří Gruša (1938-   )
Type of plot: Poetic realism
Time of plot: From the onset of World War II through the early 1970's
Locale: Chlumec, a richly historical town in Bohemia, Czechoslovakia
First published: Dotazník, aneb modlitba za jedno město a přítele, 1978
   (English translation, 1982)

Principal characters:
JAN CHRYSOSTOM KEPKA, the narrator, an unemployable
   citizen of Socialist Czechoslovakia
EDVIN KEPKA, Jan's father, who is noted for his good looks
ALICE VACHAL KEPKA, Jan's mother, a carrier of ancient
   traditions
ERNA KLAHN, the girl next door
MIRENA KLAHN, Erna's mother, a music teacher
UNCLE BONEK, Edvin's brother, collaborator with both the
   Nazis and the Socialists
UNCLE OLIN, Alice's cousin and Jan's eccentric mentor
MONSIGNOR ROSIN, the local pastor and historian

The Novel

In ironic answer to an employment application, the unemployable Jan Chrysostom Kepka attempts a full explanation of his life for the benefit of the faceless bureaucrat, Comrade Pavlenda. Jan's life began before he was born, is played out on multiple levels of reality, and continues after his death. His keenly recollected conception occurred in 1938, during a tryst between an army deserter and an unmarried schoolgirl. Just before Jan's birth, his parents marry, in the ancient Church of St. Barbora. The medieval martyr Barbora, and Jan's entire Chlumec ancestry, form part of the consciousness of both Jan and the other inhabitants of Chlumec. Jan's paradisaic childhood unfolds among playful, affectionate people. Their warm, sane atmosphere surrounds him like a protective transparent bubble, through which, though untouched himself, he sees the insanity and ugliness of outside events with a crystal, preternatural clarity.

From early childhood through late adolescence, Jan is erotically obsessed with little Erna. While still young enough to be pulled in a cart by his dog Astor, Jan married Erna several times. "I clicked my tongue at Astor, waved my rosemary sprig, and I was off to see my bride." A real union with Erna eludes him. To be near her, Jan takes music lessons from her mother, Mirena, but it is Mirena, widowed by the "comrades," who becomes his first lover.

The liaison ends when Jan is called up for military service. The experience consists chiefly of painting propaganda posters and sleeping in a dog kennel. His commander, a former hangman, goes mad, in one of many bizarre incidents that reveal the dark side of life as exquisitely as the sanity and peace of Jan's home life show the light.

Everything happening to the people whom Jan knows happens, in a sense, to Jan as well. This is particularly true of events in the life of Uncle Olin, a former brewer, French legionnaire, and perpetual rebel and survivor. It is also true of Monsignor Rosin, whose *History of Chlumec*, though awkward and prosaic, blazes with fresh detail and psychological insight in Jan's imagination. Jan obsessively re-creates the last days of Rosin, who was finally herded into a Nazi death pit for preaching about "the city which cannot hide."

Jan and Olin seek to evade defeat by the repressive forces around them. They are mystics, who try to outfox these forces on some higher plane. Their weapons are imagination, magic, local lore, astrology, and (most important, but most unconscious) old-fashioned Czech humanism. The repressive forces, though evaded, are observed coldly and plainly. The novel's last event is the East Bloc invasion of Czechoslovakia in 1968. "I pulled up the blinds and saw a row of bugs crawling down the road from Hradek and Svetlice toward Chlumec." Jan retrieves an exhibition of puppets that he has set up in the town square and is roughed up by soldiers.

> I reached out to get my suitcase back, but two other soldiers reached out for me first, spun me around—direction Hradek—prodded me in the back with their rifle butts to make me gasp and jump. Then they shot me dead.
> They shot me full of holes. But I kept walking. Even with bullets plopping out of little holes in my body. I was light as air. Back inside Alice. I glanced at my watch to see the precise time of my death.
> It was 10:57, precisely as per ephemeris.

The novel concludes with the effulgences of Jan's vivid, prophetic, but now disintegrating consciousness.

The Characters

Jan Chrysostom Kepka has the freshness of perception of a child. Ironically, the older he gets, the more childlike he becomes. Jiří Gruša does not wholly identify with Jan, by any means. He hints that Jan is slowly going mad, no matter how rich and enticing Jan's perceptions may be. The other side of Jan's childlike vision is his emotional immaturity. After a very promising start, even amid the abysmal external conditions of the Nazi Occupation and the Soviet liberation, Jan begins to slide backward around the time that Czechoslovakia becomes Socialist. He only barely restrains himself from actually telling young Erna that he has become involved with her mother.

After military service, he can find nothing more productive to do than breed cats—and not even successfully, since his "Ma Fille" turns out to be a "Mafius." He carries on a long-distance flirtation with a female cat-owner in Germany, a relationship consummated in a comical and outrageous fantasy. His devotion to Alice continues in full force to the end. Yet his is not a true Oedipal complex, because there is no sense of rivalry between his father and himself. He views Edvin with a mixture of good-humored condescension and tenderness.

Alice is the most realistic, vibrant, and consistent character. She is spotlighted by Jan's love but has enough personality to stand on her own: dry humor, courage, wholeness, stubborn patriotism, and a mouth "that says what must be said." She is not described as beautiful, but her beauty is never in doubt. She is the bearer of "four-beam," "equatorial" eyes, inherited from a well-hidden Jewish ancestor. She is thus the center of a complicated historical subplot which is also part of Jan's life. Edvin and Olin, like Alice, are whole, harmonious characters with emotional integrity. They are touchstones of normalcy and natural goodness.

In the Czech tradition, Gruša is reluctant to strip humanity from characters who are simpleminded, immoral, or crude. His Russian liberators, hilarious in their crudity, are drawn with just enough naturalism so that they stop short of being caricatures. The despicable Uncle Bonek, a greedy collaborator with both Nazis and comrades, is given human motives and a human consciousness—although Gruša's description of his macabre end is gleeful. Only the former hangman, Lieutenant Mikit, leaves the human realm.

Themes and Meanings

The Questionnaire stands as an answer to the dessicated simplicities of a bureaucratic state. Life is so multifaceted and interconnected that it overflows all categorical boundaries—including those between humans and other life forms, and between the quick and the dead. The larger Czech rebellion against dehumanization is by no means complete. When the Nazis fall, there is an orgy of recrimination against the remaining Germans that is itself dehumanizing. To Jan's childish mind, all the Germans are "Amdas" (so named after the one he knew, and whom he had no reason to like). Yet Gruša's adult repugnance at the postwar excesses rings out in the exclamation: "'Mr. Hajek,' said one of the Brothers, his eyes averted from the screaming, upside-down Amdas, 'you have hung him on the Tree of the Republic!'"

Gruša has a strong sense of the long, continuous history of Bohemia. A large part of Jan (and many of the other characters) is the history of Chlumec, going back to medieval times. Without that larger past, they simply do not exist. This is more than conventional homage to a national heritage.

Gruša lends a poetic and mystical focus to concrete reality. Examples abound in his portraiture, such as the depiction of Edvin's smile through the affectionate, ironic eyes of his son Jan:

> At such times the face of Edvin the Handsome radiates a magic triangle, for in accordance with the law of Pythagoras (transmuted into the law of Edvin the Handsome), two beams of light emanating from the eye sockets engender a third bolt emanating from dental ivory, disarming and conquering all.

Life itself is magical, and to be approached with wonder. The novel is subtitled "Prayer for a Town and a Friend": Its spirit of reverence (for life as well as for something at the furthest limits of life) accords with that genre, as well.

Critical Context

Although *The Questionnaire* was not officially published until 1978, when it was issued by an émigré publishing house in Toronto, Canada, founded by exiled Czech writer Josef Škvorecký, it first appeared in Czechoslovakia in 1974, in samizdat. At that time, Gruša was arrested and charged with "initiating disorder"; he subsequently emigrated to West Germany. *Doktor Kokeš Mistr Panny* (1984; Doctor Kokes, master of the virgin), his first novel after *The Questionnaire*, was, like its predecessor, published in Canada.

The Questionnaire continues in the tradition of Czech humanism that goes back to the medieval allegorist Jan Ámos Komensky, and continues in the twentieth century with myriad Czech writers. At least from the time of Karel Čapek (coiner of "robot") onward, Czech humanism has been combined with a love of modernism, sometimes carried to an extreme. Gruša's prose is further enriched by the kind of innovative imagery more characteristic of twentieth century Czech poetry such as that of Josef Hora or Jaroslav Seifert.

The Czechs have been especially at home in the modern medium of filmmaking. Gruša's choice of puppet making as a skill for Jan is a nod to Jiří Trnka, a pioneer in using puppets in animated films whose mute masterpiece, *The Hand* (1965), made a strong plea for the rights of creative man (and by extension, Everyman) to flourish organically and peacefully, without interference from the heavy hand of the state.

To be a humanist—a follower of a very old tradition, and Gruša is steeped in tradition—is, paradoxically, to be as modern as possible, since human nature does not change. The special feature of Czech humanism, from the Middle Ages through Gruša, has been to affirm human nature precisely as it is, with its weaknesses and absurdities, and to see true evil as a deviation from what is human. Gruša was among those who had to leave Czechoslovakia permanently, when the East Bloc turned down the Prague movement for

"Socialism with a human face." As a major statement of Czech humanism, *The Questionnaire* deserves an international audience. Its excellent English translation, by Peter Kussi, may help to ensure that readership.

Sources for Further Study
Banerjee, Maria Němcová. Review of *Doktor Kokeš Mistr Panny* in *World Literature Today*. LIX (Spring, 1985), pp. 286-287.
_____. Review of *The Questionnaire* in *World Literature Today*. LVII (Spring, 1983), p. 314.
Gruša, Jiří. *Franz Kafka of Prague*, 1983.
Soete, George. Review in *Library Journal*. CVII (August, 1982), p. 1480.

D. Gosselin Nakeeb

THE RADIANCE OF THE KING

Author: Camara Laye (1928-1980)
Type of plot: Philosophical surrealism
Time of plot: Unspecified
Locale: "Adramé" (a trade city in the North) and "Aziana" (a forest village in the South) in precolonial Africa
First published: Le Regard du roi, 1954 (English translation, 1956)

> *Principal characters:*
> CLARENCE, a middle-aged white man who is in Africa for unexplained reasons
> THE BEGGAR, an old African who guides Clarence to the South and sells him into slavery
> NAGOA and NOAGA, the two mischievous grandsons of the ruling Naba in Aziana
> AKISSI, Clarence's African wife who is frequently indistinguishable from the women of the Naba's harem
> SAMBA BALOUM, the eunuch of the Naba's harem
> THE MASTER OF CEREMONIES, a stern, legalistic man who envies Clarence's role as stud to the harem
> DIALLO, the blacksmith who helps Clarence to clarify his social role
> DIOKI, an old woman who lives with snakes and interprets visions

The Novel

Opening *in medias res*, *The Radiance of the King* is narrated in the third person but from the point of view of Clarence, a white man whose limited perceptions reveal ironic discrepancies between what he experiences and what he comprehends. He waits for the black "king of kings" in the midst of a crowded esplanade in Adramé, a fictional African city in the North, hoping that he can find employment in the King's service. Gradually, the novel relates Clarence's background. He was nearly shipwrecked while crossing a reef to enter this unnamed country; reaching Adramé, he then lost his money by gambling with other Europeans, resulting in his humiliating eviction from a European hotel and his subsequent residence in a ramshackle African inn where he also cannot pay his bills. While waiting for the King to make his rare ceremonial appearance, Clarence meets an old black beggar and two unruly boys, Nagoa and Noaga, whom he cannot tell apart. When Clarence expresses his desire to have an audience with the King, the beggar dismisses the request as impossible. Clarence responds by asserting his presumed superiority: "I am not 'just anybody.' . . . I am a white man."

The beggar, however, seems indifferent; white men are not permitted to see the King and do not usually mingle with the natives. When the King appears, Clarence is overwhelmed with awe at the sight of a frail, white-robed, gold-braceleted boy. Clarence accepts the beggar's offer to plead his case before the King, but while the beggar is gone, Clarence hears screams. Nagoa claims that they come from the King's sacrifices of his unfaithful subjects, although Noaga says that the cries come from devoted subjects, who alone are worthy of sacrifice. When the beggar returns, having failed to gain an audience for Clarence, he responds to Clarence's confusion by denying that there have even been any screams or sacrifices. Unable to clarify the events in which he is enmeshed, Clarence, obsessed with seeing the King, agrees to accompany the beggar to the South, where the King is expected to make his next appearance.

Returning to the inn to retrieve Clarence's clothes, the party shares a feast and gets drunk on palm wine. During the conversation, Clarence perceives only ambiguity and nonsense in the Africans' customs; nevertheless, he is determined to see the King, and he is too mortified by his debts to return to the Europeans. Because Clarence cannot pay his bills, he reluctantly settles his account by surrendering his suit coat to the innkeeper. As the party prepares to depart for the South, Clarence is arrested for theft. The trial proceeds from one absurd *non sequitur* to another, while Clarence attempts to use rational persuasion to argue his innocence yet fails. Unknown to him, the boys have stolen back his coat, but Clarence's self-defense is regarded as evidence that he is inherently a liar and should therefore be imprisoned. Panic-stricken, Clarence allows the beggar to help him escape. Just as he is about to be apprehended by the guards after a wild chase through "the street of Africa," Clarence is rescued by a topless dancer who offers him sanctuary in her home. Her father, Clarence realizes, is the judge from his trial, but the judge acts as if there had never been a trial. He hosts a jovial feast before Clarence, the beggar, and the boys depart on their journey to the South.

As far as Clarence is concerned, the travelers wander for days in circles through a dense rain forest. Disoriented by the odor of tropical plants that seem to drug him, he almost gives up hope of ever seeing the King when they arrive at Aziana, a village surrounded by the forest. The local ruler, the Naba, is the boys' grandfather; seemingly, he generously provides Clarence with a hut and a wife, Akissi, while the visitor waits for the King. Actually, however, the beggar has traded with the Naba; in exchange for an old woman and a donkey, the beggar has sold Clarence as a stud to the Naba's harem. Each night, Clarence is drugged by the scent of white flowers and fails to realize that he sleeps with a different woman from the harem. Gradually, through friendships with Samba Baloum, the eunuch who supervises the harem, Akissi, who treats him as she would an African man, and the boys,

Clarence becomes part of village life, shedding his clothes, learning to weave, and inventing towels and a shower. He does not, however, understand his role, and he feels ashamed of his sexual appetite and lack of work.

Jealous of Clarence's sexual prowess, the Naba's humorless Master of Ceremonies reveals to Clarence his actual role. Yet even after Clarence sees the many mulatto children in the harem, he refuses to accept the truth. The Master of Ceremonies is punished for telling Clarence about his secret role, but Clarence, failing once more to comprehend any logic in African justice, stops the public whipping out of pity. Rather than admire Clarence's compassion, the villagers, including the Master of Ceremonies, consider Clarence's intervention a travesty of justice: By disrupting the sentence, he has undermined the completion of justice, thereby creating lingering shame for the Master of Ceremonies and introducing guilt into the village as a whole for failing to sustain its principles.

Understanding finally that he cannot alleviate his self-revulsion for being the village stud by disrupting the rituals of Aziana, Clarence feels unworthy to see the King, should he ever come. He does not understand, moreover, why Diallo, the blacksmith, is making his finest ax for the King, who, in fact, may not even want it. Clarence slips deeper into depression and confusion, dreaming of Fish-Women who pursue him. In desperation because of his obsession to see the King, yet seized by his own sense of degradation, he visits Dioki, a sorceress who lives with snakes. She agrees to show him the future, and, while she couples erotically with her snakes, Clarence has a vision of the King beginning his tour to Aziana.

In Clarence's confusion of dream and reality, he becomes certain only of the King's arrival. Goaded by the Master of Ceremonies, he convinces himself that he is unworthy to see the King, that he is sinful and useless. When the King does arrive, Clarence hides naked in his hut. As the King receives his subjects and accepts their gifts, Clarence cannot bring himself to look at him for long. Then, suddenly, Clarence senses that the King's eyes are searching for him. He begins to walk toward the King; the walls of his hut having "melted away," Clarence, "ravaged by the tongue of fire, but alive still," kneels before the King. Beckoning Clarence to come closer, the King opens his arms, and Clarence kisses his heart while the King embraces him "for ever."

The Characters

In order to portray Clarence's quest for spiritual salvation undeterred by cultural conflict, Camara Laye inverts the archetypal story of the African's alienation in Europe that was begun in his first autobiographical novel, *L'Enfant noir* (1953; *The Dark Child*, 1954), and continued in his third novel, *Dramouss* (1966; *A Dream of Africa*, 1970). Clarence, however, undergoes much more than a difficult adaptation to an alien culture: He represents an archetypal parody of African history in its subordination to the colonial empires of Europe. Instead of black slaves being taken to the New World (the symbolic North of European values), Clarence is sold into slavery in the South. Without understanding language, values, or culture, he is expected to assimilate the customs of a community in which he has no role except reproduction, thus satirizing the Western tendency to associate sensuality with blackness. Simultaneously, it is precisely that sensuality with which Clarence must come to terms, if he is to be saved by the King. His technological contributions, the rational inventions of the towel and shower, are, symbolically, the "cleansing" remnants of the Cartesian categories to which he unsuccessfully tried to cling while in Adramé. Yet, however much the historical exploitation of Africans by the West weighs in the allegory, Clarence, through Laye's sympathetic, limited point of view, is never mistreated or even labeled a slave. Instead, he enjoys the tolerance and patience of his fellow villagers. He appears to himself to be a beast only when he discovers his role as stud—the Africans treat him with the respect accorded to his humanity.

Gradually, this respect permits Clarence to shed not only his clothes but also his fear of sexuality. Every other person in Aziana has a specific role; as Clarence comes to accept his own participation in the communal harmony of the village, he is less and less egocentric in his disgust at his erotic impulses. From his Western point of view, he is a lecherous sinner; in the tolerant view of the Africans, however, he is creating life, affirming sexuality as the origin of life, which is sacred. Consequently, his shame is genuine, but overcoming his repression is also, because of that shame, the source of the humility which he must have in order to be accepted by the King. Accepting the beauty of open sensuality prepares Clarence, ironically, to believe in the transcendence of the body. To revel without rational constraint in the natural world's lush vitality is to overcome the very limits of appearance: The last enclosing structure of his mind, his hut of shame, melts away in order to permit Clarence to embrace the grace of the King.

Clarence, then, represents the light that emerges from the spiritual strength of African darkness. His name, unusual at best in French West African fiction, suggests the combination of *clarté* (clarity, light) and *clair* (light, lucidity, comprehension) and forms an implicit pun on his white skin. To move from the outcast status of a poor white among Europeans in Adramé to the fusion with the radiance from the King's gold, symbolic of "the purest kind of love," is to move from an alienating reason that is based on class hierarchy to a balance between spirit and body that is the radiance of salvation. Clarence, in short, despite the comic digressions resulting from his confused self-identity and cultural ignorance, finds the universal power of human love and overcomes both his racism and his repression.

In his quest, the other characters help Clarence to accept ambiguity, learn tolerance, and comprehend the limits of his own egotism. In the North, the judge adheres strictly to the rules, sentences him, and then celebrates his escape. In the South, the Master of Ceremonies develops the judge's rigid, legalistic thought, while Samba Baloum provides development for that side of the judge which is jovial companionship. Clarence learns both to reprimand and to laugh at himself. Nagoa and Noaga, perhaps suggesting a parody of the white stereotype that "all blacks look alike," embody a natural joy in exposing the superficial categories of rational thinking; they consistently undo the Western rigid sense of language. As dancers, they constitute an oral performance that spontaneously disrupts the logic of written texts. As Clarence comes to know the two boys, he perceives acutely the details of nature and culture but with a decreasing need to fit those perceptions into his patterns of moral abstraction. Akissi, who enables the harem women to sleep with him, teaches Clarence that sexuality is sharing rather than possessing love. Each of these characters, however, is human; each is subject, like the beggar, to a mixture of dignity and crudity, kindness and cruelty. While uncorrupted by colonialism, none of the characters is portrayed as an idealistic "noble savage." Dioki, for example, is demeaning and terrifying even while she provides Clarence with the vision of the King that brings him hope in the midst of his despair. The comic social dynamic of Aziana, rather than idealizing Laye's characters, reveals the author's humanistic affirmation of the universal need for grace. All Aziana waits for the King; all need love to quash the xenophobia.

Themes and Meanings

Although *The Radiance of the King* follows the white man's attempt to comprehend an alien culture and to adjust to a nonrational mode of thought, the novel also suggests a traditional conception of community that rivals the individualistic isolation of modern society. Clarence, through much of the novel, is lost either in the maze of streets in Adramé or in the dense vegetation of the rain forest. He cannot understand how the Africans await such a brief appearance of the King with so much uncertainty about when and where he will next appear, especially given that his power, like the Naba's, seems whimsically arbitrary. Physically and socially, Clarence finds little experience that is subject to rational analysis. The King is irrelevant to daily life, not even communicating with his subjects. While rulers impose only a few laws through mediators, such as the Master of Ceremonies, even those minimal laws seem all but ignored by the people, who act primarily upon their own desires. Both the ruler's authority and the individual's submission within the community, however, are constrained by ritual. Tradition governs political authority, and that tradition gives equal status to both human and natural worlds.

The culture of Aziana and its governing principles are based on the

respect for and the immediacy of the natural world, on emotion and sensuality, and on chance and custom, unlike the mechanistic, determined rational
world of the West. In Aziana, the individual's identity and needs are defined
and met by the traditions within the larger community, including the natural
world. Defining the self in order to belong to the community is unthinkable
for those in Aziana, who belong by right of birth and have their identities
proscribed by ritual and talent. Clarence's identity crisis is as puzzling to the
Africans as their customs, thought, and dress are to him. Consequently, as
Clarence adapts to village life, he also becomes attuned to participating in
the physical world. He learns to trust the vagaries of nature and to trust
dreams as revelations of thought greater than logic.

Laye, by unraveling the mystical experience of Clarence from his seemingly surrealistic adventures in Africa, affirms the belief in the transcendence
of human reality, whatever its cultural coding, in creating the peace of divine
union. While the King's gentle beckoning suggests that he is a savior much
like Christ, his figure also suggests Allah as an unknowable, aloof God. In
Laye's privileging of dreams and visions, he suggests the animism of the
Manding people's ancient beliefs. Drawing, in addition, upon the Sufi mystical rituals which his father practiced, Laye suggests yet another spiritual
tradition's thread in his tapestry. All these diverse traditions, however, suggest a single path to unity with a divine presence: Clarence, like any human
being who pursues the classic mystical quest, must first reject reason, then
the senses, and finally his own ego, even to the point of annihilating race,
history, and culture, before he can experience the grace of divine peace.
What begins as a parody of the white man's cultural conquest develops into a
serious inquiry into the universal means of enlightenment, destroying the
very premises and inversions of race which initiate the novel.

Critical Context

The Radiance of the King unites the technical elements of African traditional literatures and the modernistic surrealism of the European novel. The
society of the archetypal African village evokes the thirteenth century kingdom of Soundiata, and the King resembles the kings of medieval Mali in that
the processions and remote governance are, loosely, historically based. Just
as the *griot*, the storyteller-historian, served as the intermediary between
ruler and subjects, at whatever level of feudal bureaucracy, Laye mingles
dream and fable, present reality and fragmented legend, to ground his novel
in the traditional tale. Repetition of phrases and motifs and the use of stock
figures such as the trickster (the beggar), the seductress (the dancer), and
the unfaithful wife (Akissi) are common characteristics of the oral tradition.
In traditional stories, time and place are frequently left unspecified; characters, such as the two boys, Dioki, and the Fish-Women, often undergo
metamorphosis, changing because there are no absolute categories of being.

Juxtaposed to the traditional fabric of the novel are the comic absurdities of Franz Kafka's novels, but, while obvious influences and correlations have been cataloged by critics, Laye's use of Kafka is to transform the nightmares of modern bureaucracy from the pessimism of existentialist anguish into the dreams of an African spirituality that is essentially optimistic about human nature. From the impersonal brutalities of Kafka's bizarre state Laye creates personal hope within communal harmony.

The influence of not only Kafka but also European surrealism in poetry contributes to but does not limit Laye's affirmation of the negritude movement's espousal of African sensuality and harmony with the natural world. Insofar as negritude asserted sensual, emotional well-being as the center of African metaphysics, then Laye's novel embodies those moral principles as communion among all things, with the primary value bestowed upon the community. Yet unique to *The Radiance of the King* is its ultimate rejection of negritude's limits: Race and culture as determinants of value and judgment are undercut by the novel's emphatic conclusion, which gives superiority to mystical vision and the transcendence of those very values upon which negritude based its aesthetic claims. In a period when negritude dominated African writing, Laye's genius was to affirm yet question its assumed monopoly over sensual, mystical experience and fiction.

Sources for Further Study

Deduck, Patricia A. "Kafka's Influence on Camara Laye's *Le Regard du roi*," in *Studies in Twentieth-century Literature*. IV (Spring, 1980), pp. 239-255.

Harrow, Kenneth. "A Sufi Interpretation of *Le Regard du roi*," in *Research in African Literatures*. XIV (Summer, 1983), pp. 135-164.

King, Adele. *The Writings of Camara Laye*, 1981.

Obumselu, Ben. "The French and Moslem Backgrounds of *The Radiance of the King*," in *Research in African Literatures*. XI (Spring, 1980), pp. 1-25.

Salt, M. J. "A Literary (and Social) Context for *The Radiance of the King*, by Camara Laye," in *Lore and Language*. III (1979), pp. 62-72.

Michael Loudon

THE RAT

Author: Günter Grass (1927-   )
Type of plot: Social criticism
Time of plot: 1984
Locale: Germany, Sweden, and Poland
First published: Die Rättin, 1986 (English translation, 1987)

Principal characters:
THE NARRATOR, an observer who closely resembles Günter
  Grass
OSKAR MATZERATH-BRONSKI, a film and video producer
THE RAT, a doomsayer

The Novel

Set in large part during the Orwellian year of 1984 (also the Chinese "Year of the Rat" and the six hundredth anniversary of the legendary pied piper of Hamelin), *The Rat* is informed with an air of eschatology and doomsday. Yet it is also ironic and self-parodying, something of a swan song for Günter Grass himself because it was written as he approached the age of sixty. His previous works and their characters are here united and come full circle to their beginnings.

Oskar Matzerath-Bronski, the protagonist of Grass's first novel *Die Blechtrommel* (1959; *The Tin Drum*, 1961), now reappears in time for his sixtieth birthday. He has become a motion-picture producer, whom the narrator engages to make a silent film about acid rain and the death of the forests. For this film, Oskar decides to parody fairy tales and the Walt Disney style, bringing together all the fairy-tale figures to save the forest from the monied interests and corrupt officials who are destroying it.

Meanwhile, Oskar's grandmother, Anna Koljaiczek, still lives in Poland and is approaching her one hundred seventh birthday. She extends an invitation to Oskar and to the other members of her far-flung family to help her celebrate it. The visionary Oskar prepares a video in advance of the event which shows the birthday party. He and his chauffeur, Bruno, his former guard at the asylum in *The Tin Drum*, load his Mercedes with gifts for the Polish relatives (including a population of small toy Smurfs for the children) and set out.

Interwoven with these strands of narrative is an account of five women, including the narrator's wife, Damroka, who embark on a scientific expedition into the Baltic Sea to study the link between pollution and a population explosion of jellyfish. Along the way, however, Damroka secretly consults with a speaking flounder, a reference to Grass's novel *Der Butt* (1977; *The Flounder*, 1978). Off the coast near Gdansk, the women are led by the fish to the site of a legendary sunken city which was ruled by women.

Yet another narrative, also interesting to Oskar as a potential film script, concerns a certain Lothar Malskat, a painter convicted of art forgery in the 1950's, who confessed to having completely repainted the ceilings in Gothic buildings rather than having merely restored the (almost nonexistent) originals. Oskar believes that his film about Malskat will open eyes, especially the eyes of young people, to the fraudulent nature of the whole postwar era and of its legacy, the global arms race.

Other narratives concern rats, who, having survived such calamities as Noah's Flood, know that humanity is again bound for destruction. They, along with other natural creatures such as jellyfish, venture forth in large numbers in mute protest demonstrations. There are also cultural warning signs of imminent collapse, such as the phenomenon of punkers, children who apply cosmetics to one another so that their skin has pallor of death and who, full of presentiment, mark themselves with the green of corpses. Fittingly, they adopt rats as pets and follow various pied pipers.

In one subplot, the tale is told of the children of Hamelin led away by the pied piper. A maid of Hamelin, Gret, is impregnated by her pet rat, Hans, and gives birth to a new race of rat-humans. They travel to the same sunken city in the Baltic to which the flounder leads the women in the boat.

In the main narrative, a female rat stands on a pile of human refuse to say the human race is gone and that only its refuse survives. As the rat relates the end, "Ultimo," as she calls it, the narrator circles the earth in a space capsule and watches the events happening before him on his video screen.

Ultimo occurs at noon on a Sunday, just as the five women on the boat are preparing to descend into the underwater city. The women and the wooden superstructure of their boat are vaporized. The steel hull drifts aimlessly across the Baltic.

The bombs fall just as Oskar's video reaches the point at which the guests at the party are watching a video of the guests at the party watching a video. Oskar seeks refuge under the skirts of his grandmother—he has always wished to flee from evil times by returning to the womb—but he is reduced by radiation to a shriveled gnome. His grandmother lives on for a time but eventually dies, and the rats move the mummies of Oskar and his grandmother to Gdansk, placing them on the altar of St. Mary's Church. There she becomes a kind of fertility goddess to the hungry rats, a grotesque new Virgin with Oskar as the child, the role he played in the same church in *The Tin Drum*.

There is, however, one final element in this nightmare. Shortly before they are vaporized, the five women dock at Visby on the Swedish island of Gotland and go ashore for the afternoon. They join a group protesting the use of animals in medical research and follow the crowd to a building on the outskirts of town. Rocks are thrown, glass is shattered, and the animals escape. The women return to their boat and cast off in haste before the police arrive, but they have left the boat unlocked.

From his vantage point in orbit, the narrator watches a hulk moving under its own power into the harbor of Gdansk, now called Danzig. When it docks, strange stowaways emerge: rat-humans are on board, a product of gene manipulations in the laboratory at Visby. Called Manippels, they are also known to the rats as Watsoncricks after the discoverers of DNA. They are blond, blue-eyed, hominoid dwarves with the heads of rats and the language of Smurfs. These monsters trace the stages of human development: They reinvent fire, drink beer, and march in formation.

Gradually, they conquer the entire area. Naturally these new hominoids begin to exploit and consume the rats and to build concentration camps for them. Strengthened by having put behind them their national and their religious differences, however, and united under the banner of the Polish labor movement Solidarity, which was taken from a museum, the rats finally eradicate this last monstrous creation of the human race.

In the end, the tale of the rat is only a dream. Oskar returns safely from Gdansk, as does Damroka. Humanity has a second chance. The narrator dreams that there may be at least a glimmer of hope that humans can act humane after all.

The Characters

Oskar Matzerath-Bronski is Grass's most famous character. In *The Tin Drum*, Oskar is both the victim and the documenter of the evil principle under Adolf Hitler, personified in the person of the Black Cook. He is someone who reported on the era as it wrote its awful history on the pages of his own life. In *The Tin Drum*, he is always at crucial places at crucial times: He witnesses the first shots of World War II in the attack on the Polish post office in Danzig in 1939 and the first shots of the invasion at Normandy in 1944. His return in the present as a clairvoyant harbinger of World War III suggests that the situation in the world is again in crisis, again teetering on the brink of destruction.

Grass's female rat, like the fish in *The Flounder*, may appear to be less a character in the traditional sense than a convenient zoomorphic platform standing outside the human race, existing outside human time, from which Grass lectures humankind about its foibles. Yet she and the flounder really are interesting characters in their own right. They know much, but they are not omniscient, and they often distort the story to make themselves look more important. They are interesting manifestations of the author's own personality, microcosmic reductions of typical human beings.

The narrator, too, first appears to be only a slightly fictionalized Günter Grass. Yet he is more than that, as he suggests when he refers to himself as a helpless human god to the rats. Powerless to help the rats from his orbit in space, he can only observe their efforts to rid their microcosm of evil: nationalism, religious bigotry, weapons of war, and the belligerent monstrosities represented by the rat-humans.

He learns that unlike the humans and their monstrosities, however, the rats survive because they have learned how to change and have learned how to cooperate. When he awakens from his nightmare, he realizes that even if a god in space is powerless to help humanity, humanity *can* help itself. Now the narrator, having learned from the rats in his microcosmic dream, is ready to begin.

Themes and Meanings

Though *The Rat* appears to be a conglomeration of disparate subplots, each of these, in fact, is closely related to the whole. One underlying theme is that when human beings engage in fraud—whether it be in the "restoration" of Gothic churches, in giving deadly nuclear weapons euphemistic names such as "Peacekeeper," in disposing of wastes in the Baltic, or in covering up the death of the forests for political reasons—they all contribute, at least symbolically, to the ultimate calamity: Ultimo.

Failure to respect nature, as demonstrated by his attacks on gene manipulation, and failure to heed the warning signs in nature, even in human nature, which is fundamentally peaceful and nurturing, Grass argues, will contribute to mankind's and to the earth's demise.

Just as Grass portrayed in *The Tin Drum* the rise of dictatorship, war, and the Holocaust under Hitler as the accumulation of many small sins of commission and omission on the part of many, he portrays the ultimate holocaust as the culmination of avoidable error. Yet Grass's arguments cut both ways: If many immoral acts by many people can cause a holocaust, then many moral acts by many can prevent it.

Critical Context

Grass had used talking rats to comment on human calamity in his earliest play, *Hochwasser* (1957; *Flood*, 1967). Oskar, again, is his most celebrated character from *The Tin Drum*. The grotesque caricature of dehumanized hominoids, here called rat-humans, is an echo of the robotic sculptures created in the image of humans by the gifted artist Eddi Amsel in Grass's grand novel *Hundejahre* (1963; *Dog Years*, 1965).

Grass's *Aus dem Tagebuch einer Schnecke* (1972; *From the Diary of a Snail*, 1973), with its admonitions to society to move ahead peacefully and slowly, avoiding violent revolutionary leaps, is memorialized in *The Rat* in the form of mutant flying snails, which the peaceful rats must subdue in order to survive. His all-inclusive lesson about the violent, male domination of world history in *The Flounder* is invoked when the five women, all of whom are characters in that novel, here board their ancient boat, named *The New*

Ilsebill after the central fairy-tale figure of *The Flounder*.

Grass's work with the film director Volker Schlöndorff, who filmed *The Tin Drum* and is described in *Kopfgeburten: Oder, Die Deutschen sterben aus* (1980; *Headbirths: Or, The Germans Are Dying Out*, 1982), is evoked by Oskar's occupation as a filmmaker and by Schlöndorff's appearance at Oskar's sixtieth birthday party.

Reviewing the scope of Grass's oeuvre from the vantage point of this culminating tale, it is clear that the artist has, for more than three decades, consistently portrayed what he sees as the most dangerous insanities of the modern age. Yet out of it all, he has synthesized some very reasonable prescriptions for a sane and peaceful world. He knows that these prescriptions are probably futile. He knows he is a dreamer. He knows the chances for doomsday are increasing. Yet he does not give up; his very predictions of calamity are themselves valiant attempts to avert it.

Sources for Further Study

Butler, G. P. "The End of the World, and After," in *The Times Literary Supplement*. April 4, 1986, pp. 35-36.

Hospital, Janette Turner. "Postfuturum Blues," in *The New York Times Book Review*. XCII (July 5, 1987), p. 6.

Keele, Alan Frank. *Understanding Günter Grass*, 1987.

O'Neill, Patrick. "Grass's Doomsday Book: *Die Rättin*," in *Critical Essays on Günter Grass*, 1987.

Vormweg, Heinrich. *Günter Grass*, 1986.

Alan Frank Keele

THE RAVISHING OF LOL STEIN

Author: Marguerite Duras (1914-   )
Type of plot: Antistory
Time of plot: The 1950's and early 1960's
Locale: The resort towns of South Tahla and Town Beach
First published: Le Ravissement de Lol V. Stein, 1964 (English translation, 1966)

> *Principal characters:*
> LOL VALERIE STEIN, a young woman who has suffered a rejection by her fiancé
> TATIANA KARL, Lol's best friend during her school years
> DR. PETER BREUGNER, Tatiana's husband
> MICHAEL RICHARDSON, Lol's fiancé
> JOHN BEDFORD, Lol's husband, a musician
> JACK HOLD, a friend of the Breugners, the narrator of the novel
> ANNE-MARIE STRETTER, the wife of the French consul to Calcutta

The Novel

The plot of *The Ravishing of Lol Stein* focuses almost entirely on the passions of the central characters and on the narrator's attempts to understand the history of the enigmatic Lol. Stripped of climax and denouement, the story elevates memory and sexual tension over physical action.

Lol Stein, a reserved young woman, is engaged to Michael Richardson, a well-to-do young man. At a ball, he abandons Lol for a mysterious older woman, named Anne-Marie Stretter, with whom he dances all night, and with whom he finally leaves. Lol's friend Tatiana Karl tries to comfort her, but Lol is so shocked at this rejection that she faints and her mother has to come retrieve her. Michael later leaves for India with Anne-Marie, and Lol goes through a period of extreme depression. One day, while on a walk, she meets John Bedford, who is intrigued by her withdrawn behavior. He falls in love with her and proposes; she accepts and they move to Uxbridge.

After ten years of a relatively uneventful life, they move back to South Tahla. Lol spends most of her time setting up her house, much as she had at Uxbridge, but she begins to go out on long, meandering walks. The narrator says that he sometimes follows her on these walks, without her knowing it. While walking, Lol apparently reminisces about her tragic experience at the ball. One day she sees a pair of lovers pass and seems to recognize the woman. Later, she follows the man; he meets the woman, who turns out to be her old friend Tatiana, and the couple goes to a hotel (which Lol and Michael had frequented). Lol stays outside in a field, spying on the figures until after dark. Eventually, Lol decides to visit Tatiana, pretending not to have seen her earlier; at Tatiana's house, she also meets Tatiana's husband, Dr. Peter Breugner, and the man who is Tatiana's lover, Jack Hold. At this point, the narrator reveals that he is Jack, and the reader realizes that all along the narrator has been aware of Lol.

Later, Jack and Lol declare their mutual desire, and Jack says that he will leave Tatiana. Lol wants him to keep meeting Tatiana, however, so that she can spy on the two of them as she had earlier. The attraction between Lol and Jack intensifies, but they do not consummate their love and Jack continues to meet Tatiana while Lol watches. Although he is still drawn to Tatiana, Jack begins to tire of her, and Tatiana suspects that Jack is in love with Lol, a suspicion that he manages to allay. Then one day Lol asks Jack to accompany her on a trip to Town Beach to relive the loss of her fiancé. The journey there heightens their intimacy, and finally Lol and Jack visit the ballroom where the initial catastrophe occurred. Lol faces the past and overcomes her fear of the place. Realizing that it is too late to return to South Tahla, Lol and Jack decide to stay in Town Beach, and, in a hotel room, the couple finally make love. The next day, however, Jack has scheduled a rendezvous with Tatiana, and Lol insists that he keep the appointment. Tired from the journey, Lol falls asleep in the field outside the hotel.

The Characters

Although its central character is clearly Lol Stein, the novel channels the story through Jack Hold and thus filters all details and perceptions through his obsession with Lol. Unlike the omniscient narrator of most realistic fiction, Jack cannot penetrate Lol's mind, and so he must rely on information from Tatiana, Lol's recollections, and his own observations. He attempts to piece together all these perspectives, rejecting everything that he believes to be biased or inaccurate. He uses the present tense frequently, presenting events as they occur, with little reflection or commentary. As a result of its perspective, then, the novel tends to depict its characters reticently, with little concern for a careful detailing of motives. In general, the main characters do not seem unmotivated or arbitrary; rather, the reader must deduce the motives from the minimal information supplied.

Lol herself is at various times distant, cool, passionate, unpredictable, and tragic. Practically nothing is known of her childhood; nothing prepares the reader for Lol's extreme depression and withdrawal when Michael Richardson has left her for another woman. Their romance is presented in matter-of-fact terms, as is Lol's paralysis during the dance, followed by her screaming fit when her mother attempts to make her leave. Lol's subsequent madness, her meeting with John Bedford, and her marriage are also described undramatically, and the narrator glides over her ten years of married life in Uxbridge. Lol appears to have returned to normal, though she has a tendency to impose an extreme order on her life as a compensation for her lost passion and as an escape from her suffering. When Lol spies Tatiana after ten years of absence from her birthplace, however, she begins to relive and to try to control her past by following Tatiana's lover. For Lol, Jack seems to represent the chance to relive her affair vicariously. Lol substitutes Tatiana for herself and directs Jack to meet Tatiana so that Lol can watch their lovemaking. As a voyeur, Lol can experience passion without rejection or pain. Her return to Town Beach and the consummation of her love for Jack might mark a progress away from her fixation on the past, but the next day she expects Jack to keep his appointment with Tatiana so that she can watch from her position of security. The novel ends without a definite resolution or any indication of Lol's independence from the past.

Equally enigmatic is the narrator, Jack Hold. His love for Lol seems genuine, yet at the same time, he continues to be attracted to Tatiana, occasionally with added fervor knowing that Lol is watching. In fact, he obeys Lol's instructions faithfully, with no hope that he will ever be rewarded; after he has finally made love to Lol, he is happy but hardly more intimate with her. Like Lol, he is still burdened with understanding the past by his obsession with gathering and interpreting correctly her story, her life.

Tatiana Karl and the other minor characters seldom rise above types. Tatiana exemplifies a woman drawn into a relationship that offers no ultimate satisfaction, but she is also a woman jealously holding onto that relationship. The betrayed husbands, John Bedford and Peter Breugner, are shown to be somewhat complacent; Bedford is treated rather sympathetically, but the reader learns little of either man's inner lives, such as how Bedford has reacted to his wife's threat to leave him. Most enigmatic of all, perhaps, is Anne-Marie Stretter, the older woman with a mysterious power over Michael. She and Lol Stein appear in other works by Marguerite Duras, including *Le Vice-consul* (1966; *The Vice-Consul*, 1968). Duras has commented that the works involving Lol and Anne-Marie are open in that she is still writing their stories and allowing their characters to evolve. The lack of a formal ending for *The Ravishing of Lol Stein* and the novel's refusal to categorize and analyze all the motives of its central characters maintain this openness and freedom.

Themes and Meanings

The central theme of *The Ravishing of Lol Stein* is the power of memory to control one's life in the present. Memory is not presented as simply destructive or beneficent; rather, the novel takes a more detached attitude toward the influence of memory. Although the past continues to involve Lol in the voyeuristic triangle with Jack and Tatiana, a life without memory, as represented by the quiet domestic life that entrapped Lol before she returned to her hometown, is hardly preferable. Perhaps the contact with pain can one day prove to be therapeutic.

Closely related to the theme of memory is that of love and passion. Lol, Jack, and, to some extent, Tatiana are seeking a fulfillment beyond the bonds of memory; each attempts a connection that, by effacing identity, will liberate him or her from memory but still allow consciousness to survive. In particular, the moments of passion between Lol and Jack are erotically charged (at least from Jack's perspective), especially the moments of communication. Indeed, the consummation itself is described unemotionally, as though the real significance of their passion lies in the alternation between closeness and tension.

The Ravishing of Lol Stein comments implicitly on the form and value of novels. It avoids an omniscient, godlike narrator who conveys a didactic evaluation to the reader and who represents characters as being easily capable of dissection; the narrator's obsession replaces an objective, and the characters remain throughout mysterious, elusive, open. Such a strategy forsakes the illusion of authorial omnipotence in order to force the reader to become involved in the creative process.

Critical Context

In its lack of violence or crime, the plot of *The Ravishing of Lol Stein* differs from the plots of other Duras novels. The novel is typical, however, in its focus on love and memory. As noted above, several of Duras' other works, including the novel *The Vice-Consul* and the play *India Song: Texte-théâtre-film* (1973; English translation, 1976), develop in more detail some of the characters from *The Ravishing of Lol Stein*, particularly Ann-Marie Stretter and what happened after she went to Calcutta with Michael Richardson. These recurring characters are not limited to the time frame of a single book but exist in time, subject to change.

In addition to her concern with the themes of memory and love, Duras shares the interest of other writers of the New Novel in breaking down the boundaries of the traditional novel, especially the requirements for characters with a stable, fixed identity; plots with a clearly delineated chronology; and a consistent point of view, often embodied in an omniscient, godlike narrator. At the same time, Duras infuses her novels with a strongly felt passion and a frequently erotic tension. In *The Ravishing of Lol Stein*, the narrator's quest for understanding the truth of Lol's history finds no single satisfactory explanation, paralleling his obsessive attraction to her and her obsession with dominating the past, which fails to lead to any final erotic release. Duras' novels, like their characters, are impelled onward in time, and memory, with all of its gaps and misreadings of the past, is ever seeking to impose a shape on that flow. In its unrelenting analysis of memory and passion and in its honesty and rigor of form, the work of Marguerite Duras constitutes a unique and significant achievement in twentieth century fiction.

Sources for Further Study

Cismaru, Alfred. *Marguerite Duras*, 1971.

Kristeva, Julia. "The Pain of Sorrow in the Modern World: The Works of Marguerite Duras," in *PMLA*. CII, no. 2 (1987), pp. 138-152.

Murphy, Carol J. *Alienation and Absence in the Novels of Marguerite Duras*, 1982.

Schulz-Jander, Eva-Maria. "Marguerite Duras' *Le Ravissement de Lol V. Stein*: A Woman's Long Search for Absence," in *Symposium*. XL (Fall, 1986), pp. 223-233.

Willis, Sharon. *Marguerite Duras: Writing on the Body*, 1987.

Steven L. Hale

A RAW YOUTH

Author: Fyodor Dostoevski (1821-1881)
Type of plot: Psychological realism
Time of plot: The 1870's
Locale: St. Petersburg, with flashbacks to Moscow
First published: Podrostok, 1875 (English translation, 1916)

> *Principal characters:*
> ARKADY DOLGORUKY, the narrator and the "raw youth" of the
> title
> ANDREI VERSILOV, the father of Arkady, an entrepreneur of
> noble background
> MAKAR DOLGORUKY, a religious pilgrim, the legal father of
> Arkady
> SOFIA DOLGORUKY, the legal wife of Makar, who lives with
> Versilov
> KATERINA AKHMAKOVA, a society woman, loved by both
> Versilov and Arkady

The Novel

A Raw Youth is divided into three sections, each of which relates the events of three days. The narrator of the three sections is Arkady Dolgoruky; the narration takes the form of an autobiography unintended for readers.

The first section of the novel is in the form of a flashback as Arkady relates the events of the previous year. It contains a self-description of Arkady as a schoolboy, especially the evolution of his "idea": to become a Rothschild. The acquisition of money, however, is not an end in itself; the power which accompanies money is the real goal. At this time Arkady makes his first real acquaintance with his father, Andrei Versilov.

Arkady is initially portrayed as resentful of his illegitimate birth, his father's seeming indifference to the fate of his son, and the taunts of his peers concerning his low status on the social ladder. To make matters worse, he has heard rumors, confirmed by almost unimpeachable sources, that his father has behaved dishonorably on a number of occasions, thus bringing even more shame to the boy.

The section concludes, however, on a completely different note; Arkady realizes that his father not only is not guilty of the many misdeeds attributed to his name but also is a very good person with high ideals and a rigid code of honor. As the new image of his father takes shape in his mind, Arkady changes his attitude from hatred to boundless admiration for his father. Arkady discovers that his father was not the sire of an illegitimate child by the crippled daughter of Katerina Akhmakova, but only offered to marry the unfortunate girl out of love and compassion for her mother. Arkady also realizes that Versilov has not propositioned another girl, but was seeking to come to her aid during a period of extreme financial distress. Finally, Versilov's voluntary surrender of an inheritance, won only after a lengthy court wrangle, convinces Arkady of the inherent goodness in his father. Arkady's feelings of spite and resentment disappear, and he begins a new life based on his resurrection from the depths of depression.

The second section of the novel depicts Arkady's initiation into "the good life" of St. Petersburg society and his further knowledge of his father. His previous idea—to become a Rothschild—is replaced by the search for the beauty and dignity of life. Arkady falls in love with Katerina Akhmakova, an elegant society woman, who is much older than the youth; he also learns that his father has an obsessive passion for the same woman, based upon a curious love/hate combination. The second section ends in disaster for Arkady; he is unceremoniously expelled from an illegal but fashionable gambling den because of false charges of theft, of which he is eventually exonerated. He passes out in the street, a victim of fever, and remains unconscious for nine days.

The third and final section of the novel recounts the violent clash of the currents which surfaced in the second section. A letter which would compromise Katerina's position with her father, threatening to put him under court supervision because of suspected senility, occupies a central place in the drama of this section. The characters, with Versilov now occupying center stage, are depicted in the light of their attitudes toward the fateful letter. A picture of chaos is drawn for the reader, and Arkady's newly found peace of mind is destroyed as the whirlwind of events proves too much for him. At this point, Makar Dolgoruky arrives upon the scene as a personified antithesis of the way of life among the upper class which not only permits but is conducive to this disorder. Makar, however, solves nothing; he merely presents, through the example of his life, an alternative way of living. At the end of the novel the misunderstandings are solved. While the characters are visibly changed for the better, the reader remains unconvinced that their lives will be peaceful for long.

The link between the three sections is Arkady, the narrator. Although the central position in the novel is surrendered to Versilov in the final section, the reader views the events and characters of all three sections through the eyes of Arkady. For example, the original negative impression of Versilov changes only when Arkady's impression of his father evolves from bad to good. Throughout the novel one is aware of Arkady's gradual, painful, and confusing change from a resentful adolescent into a balanced, optimistic young man. The climax of this development is Arkady's recognition of the double within himself, two aspects of the same personality often working at cross purposes.

Arkady's adjustment is not the only evident evolution of personality; Versilov himself is apparently cured of the afflictions caused by his dual personality. Father and son solve their problems at the same time.

The Characters

Fyodor Dostoevski's novels tend to emphasize characters rather than plot; many of his works seem to be character studies with only a veneer of action to glue the various personalities into a coherent whole. At the beginning of *A Raw Youth*, Andrei Versilov is a complete mystery to his son and to the reader. As Arkady begins to unravel the complex personality of his father, the reader begins to comprehend the enigmatic Versilov.

The first clue to Versilov's character is a childhood remembrance of Arkady's, as he eavesdrops upon his father practicing lines from a play. The child adores the rehearsing father, who appears as a heroic figure revolting against the hypocrisy, anti-intellectualism, and gossip of high society. As Arkady grows older, however, these feelings are balanced by a long period of parental neglect and ostracism by schoolmates, causing the boy great emotional distress. As a result, he begins a period of solitary dreaming and growing hatred toward his father.

When Arkady rejoins his family as a young adult, he gradually becomes close to Versilov and his hatred is balanced by his worship of the good qualities in Versilov's character. Eventually the hatred is extinguished as Arkady realizes that his father is also consumed by an idea: a paradise without God, an earthly utopia. The sympathy and respect which Arkady and the reader feel for Versilov at this point are indications of the author's sympathy for the father, even though Makar's role in the novel is to demonstrate the ultimate failure of the nonreligious worldview. At a crucial moment, however, Versilov breaks an icon to demonstrate his lack of religious belief, and the author permits Versilov's lack of faith to stymie all of his good deeds and idealism. For Dostoevski, this is the essence of Versilov's tragedy.

Arkady is in many ways his father's son. He permits the all-consuming passion of becoming a Rothschild to warp his personality; only when Arkady begins to appreciate the religious worldview of Makar does the youth achieve a semblance of peace. Arkady's illness for nine days is symbolic; in Dostoevski's novels internal chaos is often accompanied by physical disorder. The lengthy sickness signals the death throes of the internal battle; Arkady awakens to find Makar, the symbol of integration, at his bedside, and new life presents itself to the distraught youth.

Makar, whose young wife was seduced by Versilov, wanders through Russia, begging alms and visiting religious shrines. Meek and humble, Makar radiates the happiness which signifies peace of mind. His peace and joy present an antithesis to the chaos and unhappiness reigning in the Versilov household. His happiness anticipates the paradise without God to which Versilov aspires, and he does not need the Rothschild idea to prove that he is a human being with value.

Sofia Dolgoruky, Versilov's mistress and the wife of Makar, takes little part in the action except to serve as a constant source of strength for Versilov. She suffers the hardships of her life because it is necessary to do so; her sufferings will expiate her sin toward her legal husband and assure her eventual salvation. For Sofia, a very religious person, salvation—not paradise on earth or money—is the ultimate goal, and this belief redeems her in the eyes of Dostoevski. Despite her irregular position, she is the only character who brings out feelings of love and tenderness within Versilov and Arkady at their worst moments; she alone brings an acquaintance with happiness.

Themes and Meanings

A common theme in Dostoevski's novels is the prevailing disorder in Russian society of the late nineteenth century. In this novel the chaos is represented by two ideas which seem to be at opposite ends of the spectrum: a selfish goal (Arkady's desire to be a Rothschild) and a selfless goal (Versilov's paradise without God). The meeting point is the passion both men feel for Katerina; both men forget their ideas and lead disordered lives, causing themselves and their loved ones great pain. Arkady, through this process, realizes the duality of his nature and sees it reflected in the actions of his father.

Both of these ideas, which are not strong enough to sustain Versilov and Arkady, are countered by the idea of Christian love, personified by Makar. The serenity of this faith allows the integration of body and soul, the much sought-after unity between the two aspects of the human personality. For Dostoevski, this unity cannot occur without belief in Christianity.

A secondary theme, although closely aligned with the general tenor of the first, is the role of the family. Family feuds and irregular family situations crop up throughout the novel, and the author uses the phrase "an accidental family" many times to portray the haphazard relationships among the characters. Dostoevski believes that the chaos in the family unit is symbolic of the disorder in society in general; this theme is evident in many of his novels. The implication is clear that the disintegration of society affects the family, and the disintegration of the family can only lead to greater chaos in society.

Critical Context

Dostoevski's life as a writer and thinker revolves around one great subject: the role of freedom in human existence. The author comes to the conclusion that free will is the most precious possession, but abuses of that freedom, such as the conscious choice of evil, lead to chaos. In *Idiot* (1868; *The Idiot*, 1887), Dostoevski portrays the preoccupation with money leading to the disintegration of families and society, but only in *A Raw Youth* does he dwell upon the antidote to such chaos—a return to Christian belief.

In *Besy* (1871-1872; *The Possessed*, 1913), the author portrays disorder on a societal level, but he drops this theme to return to the family in *A Raw Youth* and *Bratya Karamazovy* (1879-1880; *The Brothers Karamazov*, 1912). *A Raw Youth* is not considered one of Dostoevski's great works, but it is valuable because it isolates one of Dostoevski's themes—Christianity versus other ideas and ideals—and gives readers a clear idea of his beliefs concerning religious faith. Even good characters, such as Arkady and Versilov, cause and suffer from chaos because they have rejected religious belief. In *The Brothers Karamazov* this particular theme is developed further in the character of Ivan and, in general, the religious dimension is dealt with at great length.

While *A Raw Youth* may be slighted by critics and historians of literature, it is an important step in the development of Dostoevski's central theme and clarifies his thought concerning the eventual rejuvenation of Russian social life through religious renewal.

Sources for Further Study
Jones, John. *Dostoevsky*, 1983.
Leatherbarrow, William J. *Feodor Dostoevsky*, 1981.
Mochulsky, K. V. *Dostoevsky: His Life and Work*, 1967.
Rzhevsky, Nicholas. "*The Adolescent*: Structure and Ideology," in *Slavic and East European Review*. XXVI (1982), pp. 27-42.
Wasiolek, Edward. *Dostoevsky: The Major Fiction*, 1964.

Philip Maloney

LA REGENTA

Author: Leopoldo Alas (Clarín, 1852-1901)
Type of plot: Psychological realism
Time of plot: The late 1870's
Locale: Vetusta, a fictional city in Spain
First published: 1884, 2 volumes (English translation, 1984)

> *Principal characters:*
> ANA OZORES, a respectable woman of the cultured middle
> class in Vetusta
> VÍCTOR QUINTANAR, her husband
> ALVARO MESÍAS, the man with whom Ana has a brief love
> affair
> FERMÍN DE PAS, a priest, Ana's confessor
> PETRA, a servant in the home of Víctor and Ana
> FRIGILIS (FRILLITY), a close friend of Víctor

The Novel

La Regenta (the magistrate's wife) is the history of three years in the life of Vetusta, a small city in northwestern Spain, the fictional counterpart of Leopoldo Alas' native Oviedo. The narrative begins with an event that will become the focus of the novel. Ana Ozores, a beautiful, cultured woman married to the ex-magistrate of the city, Víctor Quintanar, makes her confession to Fermín de Pas, the priest who has just been assigned to her as spiritual guide. Ana reveals her frustration with her husband, who cannot give her a child, and her attraction to Alvaro Mesías, a handsome bachelor who has a reputation in the city as a ladies' man.

As the novel progresses, Ana develops a dependence on Fermín as her savior from her sexual frustration and her unfulfilled longing for a child. Fermín tries to help Ana control her desires, which conflict with her strong sense of duty and responsibility to her husband. In the process of performing his priestly duties, however, Fermín falls in love with her. Víctor spends his evenings in his bedroom, reciting passages from seventeenth century Spanish plays, imagining himself in the role of the betrayed husband who avenges his honor by killing his wife and her lover. Alvaro, meanwhile, becomes aware of Ana's attraction to him and pursues her, at first discreetly, then more openly.

The members of the prominent social circle in which Víctor and Ana move become aware of the competitive struggle for Ana's attention waged by Fermín and Alvaro. As they begin to take sides, the impending crisis of Ana's downfall becomes a topic of general conversation, and Ana finally succumbs to Alvaro's advances. Víctor, still unaware of his wife's infidelity, fires

Ana's maid, Petra, because he is afraid that she will reveal that he has flirted with her. To get revenge, Petra tells Fermín that Ana is having an affair with Alvaro. In a fit of jealousy, Fermín persuades Petra to set Víctor's alarm clock ahead an hour so that he will wake up for his daily hunting trip in time to see Alvaro leaving Ana's bedroom.

When Víctor realizes that, like the heroes of the Spanish dramas, he has been deceived, he challenges Alvaro to a duel. In spite of Frigilis' attempts to get Alvaro to leave town, thus averting a tragedy, the duel takes place and Víctor is killed. Alvaro flees Vetusta, leaving Ana widowed and disgraced, banished from society by the Vetustans and from the Church by Fermín.

The Characters

The first half of this seven-hundred-page novel, which covers only the first three days of the story's three years, is devoted to the presentation of the four central characters and a portrayal of Vetusta and its inhabitants. Although the narrator's point of view is omniscient, the characterization of Ana Ozores, Fermín de Pas, Alvaro Mesías, and Víctor Quitanar is developed almost entirely through the characters' self-awareness, through their own perspectives on their existence.

In the first volume of the novel, Ana reflects on her childhood, a time when she had the energy to resist the influence of the cold, unfeeling, capricious people who took care of her. Now, trapped in the same kind of environment, she fears that she is no longer able to survive. She longs for the fulfillment of love and for the experience of bearing a child, longings that intensify her attraction to Alvaro, in spite of her strict belief in morality and marital fidelity. Ana also develops an intense attraction to Fermín as her spiritual counselor. Her inner conflict grows as she is torn between her sensual desires and her self-image as a devout, pious sister of the Church, devoted to her husband.

Fermín de Pas also reflects on his youth and his close relationship to his mother, who sacrificed her own happiness to help him fulfill his strong ambitions in the Church. His sudden awareness of his attraction to Ana creates in him a moral and political dilemma. He must guide Ana through her moral crisis and, at the same time, suppress his sexual feelings for her if he is to succeed in his quest for recognition in the city as a significant spiritual guide. Thus, the possibility of Ana's adultery takes on a dual meaning for him. Ana's infidelity would represent Fermín's failure as a priest, and it would also signify his inability, as a man, to keep her faithful to the frustrating relationship with him that his religious vows impose.

Alvaro and Víctor are portrayed primarily through their self-identification with literary characters. Alvaro cultivates the opinion that the citizens of Vetusta have of him, that he is a dashing, heroic Don Juan figure. Aware of the legend that has grown up around him, he plays the role with an intense cynicism, thinking that it will help him get what he wants. Víctor, on the other hand, is unaware of the extent to which his life has begun to parallel that of the characters in the honor plays of the Golden Age dramatist Pedro Calderón de la Barca. Night after night, he acts out the roles and imagines how he himself would act if his wife were unfaithful to him. Yet, when he sees Alvaro leaving his wife's bedroom as he stands in the plaza, shotgun in hand, he is unable to act. He realizes that the drama of honor is pure fiction, that the reality of the situation is not heroic, but ugly and humiliating.

Themes and Meanings

The most pervasive theme of the text of *La Regenta*, the interpenetration of life and literature in the society of Vetusta, is evident in Alvaro's cynical self-identification with the Don Juan figure and in Víctor's immersion in the Golden Age dramas. A significant part of the novel is devoted to a portrayal of the minor characters who gather in the public meeting places and spend much of their time discussing the literary works that they have read. Consciously or unconsciously, they form concepts of themselves in relationship to the literary creations. Saturno Bermúdez, for example, combats his innate shyness by idealizing himself as a romantic hero platonically enamored of married women.

The interplay of life and literature is most evident in the scene in which Ana and Alvaro sit together watching a performance of the Romantic drama *Don Juan Tenorio*. As the play's action unfolds, paralleling to a large extent the events taking place in the reality of Vetusta, Ana identifies with the tragic protagonist of the play, Inés, while Alvaro concentrates on finding the right moment to touch Ana's leg as the first step in seducing her.

The different perspectives of Ana and Alvaro on the action of the play, her romantic idealization of her predicament and Alvaro's pragmatic opportunism, are related to the theme of power that is developed throughout the text. Much of Ana's conflict is a result of the disadvantaged position of women with respect to a society that allows men much more freedom to satisfy their needs and still remain within the bounds of social acceptance. It is very clear in the novel that Ana is a typical nineteenth century woman in that she is dependent financially and emotionally on men. Her choices are all male oriented: a continuation of her barren marriage to Víctor, an affair with Alvaro, or a celibate, devout subjugation to the influence of Fermín. The theme of power is further developed in the treatment of Fermín's conflict. His attempt to save Ana from her impending doom, though rooted in his own sexual feelings for her, is primarily a struggle to maintain and increase his influence in Vetusta and in the Church. When Ana falls, Fermín's vengeance is not only because of his jealous rage but also because of the public humiliation of his failure to preserve her devotion to the moral values of the Church.

The themes of power and the interpenetration of life and literature are part of the larger theme of the novel, the search for individual freedom within the restrictions of society. Alas portrays Vetusta as a social world made up of mediocre, hypocritical individuals trapped in their own boredom, escaping their environment by idealizing their existence according to the fictional world that they find in literature. The two characters in the novel who have the potential of rising above the mediocrity, Ana and Fermín, are defeated by their emotional responses to their predicament. Ana succumbs to Alvaro's advances because she sees the adulterous relationship as the triumph of love over the restrictiveness of a situation that she cannot change. Fermín compromises his aspirations to power by allowing his feelings of love for Ana to interfere with his duty as her confessor. Because his commitment to his religious vocation is primarily a quest for power, he becomes the instigator of Ana's ultimate destruction.

Critical Context

Although Leopoldo Alas published a number of short stories and one short novel, he produced only one major work of fiction, *La Regenta*. His principal contribution to the literary scene of the late nineteenth century, other than *La Regenta*, was as a critic. For many years, "Clarín" (the pseudonym used by Alas in his literary criticism) was the most respected, and the most feared, commentator on the literary and social scene in Spain. His reputation was such that he was able to destroy the prestige of a writer through a single unfavorable review, and he spent his career satirizing the mediocrity and pretensions of those who considered themselves members of the elite class.

Alas' attitude in his critical writing is reflected in his treatment of the society of Vetusta in *La Regenta*. Ignorance, mediocrity, stupidity, and dishonesty are rampant in Spanish society, and they should be exposed and destroyed. The function of criticism is to refine society, separating the truly excellent from the pretentious and inferior.

Sources for Further Study

Durand, Frank. "Characterization in *La Regenta*: Point of View and Theme," in *Bulletin of Hispanic Studies*. XLI (1964), pp. 86-100.

————. "Leopoldo Alas, 'Clarin': Consistency of Outlook as Critic and Novelist," in *Romanic Review*. XLI (February, 1965), pp. 37-49.

————. "Structural Unity in Leopoldo Alas' *La Regenta*," in *Hispanic Review*. XXXI (October, 1963), pp. 324-335.

Rutherford, John. Introduction to *La Regenta*, 1984. Translated by John Rutherford.

Schyfter, Sara E. " 'La loca, la tonta, la literata': Woman's Destiny in Clarín's *La Regenta*," in *Theory and Practice of Feminist Literary Criticism*, 1982.

Edited by Gabriela Mora and Karen S. Van Hooft.

Valis, Noël M. *The Decadent Vision in Leopoldo Alas*, 1981.

——————. "Order and Meaning in Clarín's *La Regenta*," in *Novel*. XVI (Spring, 1983), pp. 246-258.

Gilbert Smith

RETURN TO REGIÓN

Author: Juan Benet (1927-   )
Type of plot: Antistory
Time of plot: The 1920's to the early 1960's
Locale: Región, a fictional town in Spain
First published: Volverás a Región, 1967 (English translation, 1985)

Principal characters:
NUMA, the guardian and protector of the mountains
GAMALLO, a Nationalist officer
MARRÉ GAMALLO, his daughter
MARÍA TIMONER, Gamallo's girlfriend
DANIEL SEBASTIÁN, a doctor who runs an almost empty clinic
in Región
THE BOY (later, THE YOUNG MAN) who becomes Dr. Sebastián's
only patient

The Novel

Return to Región is not a traditional novel with a conventional plot. It consists of integrated situations that are referred to throughout the work but that are never completely developed. The book is divided into four parts. In the first, the author describes in detail the landscape of Región and introduces Numa, the mythical guardian of the town, whom no one has ever seen and who does not actually appear in the novel. Numa's presence dominates Región, although the townspeople are not certain who he is. Numa "protects" the town by killing anyone who ventures into the forest which borders it, thereby maintaining a state of order by keeping out intruders. Yet during the Spanish Civil War (1936-1939), a period of national disorder, an intruder does appear. He is a gambler who plays with a gold piece that miraculously wins for him every time. Gamallo, a Nationalist officer, becomes obsessed with winning the gold piece and loses María Timoner, his girlfriend or fiancée (the relationship is not clearly defined), to the gambler, who runs off with the woman and stabs Gamallo in the hand. The gambler's intrusion into the town sows disorder and the decline of Región is attributed to his presence. Independent of this incident, the town's liberals attempt to organize around Mr. Rombal or Rubal (the spelling of his name varies throughout). Also early in the novel, the mother of the boy (whose name is never stated) abandons her son for undisclosed reasons.

The second, third, and fourth parts of *Return to Región* consist of exchanges between Marré Gamallo, the daughter of the dishonored soldier, and Dr. Daniel Sebastián, who runs a clinic in the town. Events mentioned in the first part are partially described but never completely clarified. As a child, Marré received an upper-middle-class convent education but then rebelled against authority. Now in her forties, she has come to Región in search of María's son and Dr. Sebastián's godson, Luis I. Timoner, who is a Republican captain. Luis and Marré were lovers until, during the war, Luis fled into the mountains. Afterward, Marré spent time in a brothel, had a series of sexual encounters, and eventually wed (although her marriage was marred by an overbearing mother-in-law). Dr. Sebastián's childhood was dominated by a pretentious, tyrannical mother and a father who was obsessed with the mystical powers of the telegraph wheel which he used to read the future. After becoming a doctor at the insistence of his mother, he went to work in a clinic and married a woman whom he left alone for twenty years and with whom he never had sexual relations. At the time of his meeting with Marré, he runs a clinic with only one patient: the boy, now a man, whose mother abandoned him at the beginning of the novel.

Rather than "conversations" in the conventional sense, the exchanges in *Return to Región* are long soliloquies that are loosely tied together without constituting a coherent dialogue. Often it is not clear which character is speaking, to whom a character is speaking, or whether a character is speaking aloud or to himself. Occasionally, a character seems to be responding to a question that has not been asked or speaks with no obvious reference to what has been said before. Two other voices that intervene are that of the narrator, who is unidentified and does not participate in the action, and that of the editor, who, by means of footnotes, relates a version of Dr. Sebastián's marriage which is different from the one that the doctor himself relates. From these descriptions, ramblings, and notes, certain facts emerge, but these hardly constitute a story in the conventional sense, especially since the various voices often contradict one another, and the reader is never certain of the truth.

At the end of the "conversations," Dr. Sebastián's patient, refusing to believe that Marré is not his mother who has returned to fetch him, murders the doctor by smashing his head against the wall. Marré presumably leaves the clinic to search for Luis. The author does not describe her departure, but the book closes with the sound of Numa's shot, the punishment that awaits anyone who ventures into the wooded hills.

The Characters

Although Numa never appears, he is a pervasive presence throughout the novel. He reaches mythical proportions, transcending time and definition, for no one knows his origins, and no one has ever seen him. As befits a myth, he is the object of faith and conjecture—faith because the townspeople believe absolutely in his ability and authority to maintain order and conjecture because many stories circulate regarding his true identity. His domain is marked by a sign that reads: "No Trespassing—Private Property." Yet every year, Numa collects his tribute as some hapless tourist or explorer wanders into the hills and the townspeople, like participants in a sacred rite, gather to wait for the shot that will inevitably follow.

Like all mythic figures, Numa encompasses the values of those who create him. He is the archetype of the fierce, stubborn, and hostile shepherds who inhabit the area. As guardian of Región, he "protects" the decay and ruin, eliminating any challenge to the status quo. He is associated with death and silence, for the echo from his gun is followed invariably by an eerie stillness that announces the return to order. Some critics have identified Numa with General Francisco Franco and Región with Spain. Numa, however, is an ahistorical figure whose essence transcends the moment. He is symbolic of that area of human existence that humans cannot penetrate. He is guardian of the labyrinth of feelings that, if explored, kills the explorer with confusion and despair. The townspeople, who lead safe, ordered lives, know better than to venture into Numa's domain. Those, such as Marré and Luis, who defy authority and convention by giving free rein to their emotions, risk death.

Marré's journey to Región symbolizes her search for her own identity and, in a broader sense, man's search for himself. Since girlhood, she has been subjected to the iron will of others: in the convent, the nuns; during the war, the comrade Adela, "a robust woman, disciplined and intransigent"; after the war, Muerte (literally, death), the proprietress of the brothel; and finally, her mother-in-law, "an authoritarian and laconic lady." To Marré, life has been a constant struggle to find herself in the face of the demands of an established order. To her, all of her "guardians" are one: "If all those people are not one single person and only one it seems to me a waste of nature and society to employ so many people to fulfill a single function: watching over my behavior and trying by all means to keep me subject to the order they embody." Critics have identified Marré's guardians as Spanish society or as civilization in general. Her struggle is the struggle for the authenticity of the self in the face of pre-established norms. Her psychological health depends on her conviction that she can realize her "journey." That is why she tells Dr. Sebastián:

> You don't see me having the strength to continue the trip and I don't see myself as having the health to abandon it; once again because we're witnessing the same circumstance from two rather different points of view. Both are situated in fear, it's something both have in common; but I'm sure my fear is nothing but a package containing a conviction while the one you speak to me about is nothing but the last state before desperation.

Marré fears the selflessness that results in abandoning the search for the self; her determination to go on reveals a confidence lacking in Dr. Sebastián.

Dr. Sebastián lacks Marré's optimism. He exists on the brink of despair, fearful of overstepping the limits of equilibrium and plunging into the void.

Reared by an overbearing, destructive mother who threatened his sense of individuality, he became alienated. Medicine does not interest him, so he remains on the margin of his profession. His feelings of impotence are aggravated by his failure to please María Timoner, with whom he becomes infatuated while she is his patient, and by his marriage to a woman whom he does not love. Dr. Sebastián identifies three developmental stages: the age of instincts, the age of reflection, and the age of despair and alienation. To live peacefully, he argues, one must remain in the second and refuse to enter the third. Yet he is tormented by anguish and fear that push him to brink of crisis.

The abandoned boy who is Dr. Sebastián's only patient appears only sporadically. Still, it is he who illustrates most clearly the feelings of rejection and confusion that permeate the novel. Deserted by his mother before he has reached the age of reflection, the boy suffers from arrested development which prevents him from engaging in the kind of self-analysis on which the others embark. From childhood, he has lived in a state of permanent alienation which shrouds a primal rage that finally explodes. It is significant that the novel begins with the description of Región and the mother's departure and ends with the son's outburst. In a sense, the boy is a prototype who embodies all the pain that moves the other characters.

Themes and Meanings

The novel opens with a meticulous depiction of Región. The landscape is harsh, inhospitable, and unproductive. The winter is so severe that "the corpses of dogs who die in December don't decompose until the month of May," and the summer is so hot and dry that

> "the dogs who die during those burning months (and sometimes they die hanged, suspended from trees, like sacks of grain, their visceral mass all gathered in their hindquarters) are mummified in a couple of nights and are preserved like dried fish over the whole dry spell to serve as food for the creatures that come down from the mountains with the first snow."

The shepherds are savage and brutish, and the forested hills are so labyrinthine that they devour anyone who strays into them, subjecting him to the cruel and undisputed authority of Numa. The hostile setting, in which the individual is easily crushed, frames the struggle between the personality or spirit and outside forces, which is a major theme of the novel.

In Región, the individual is in constant danger of annihilation. Often that individual disappears. In the "conversation" between Marré and Dr. Sebastián, antecedents are often missing. Often it is not clear who is speaking. Some characters, such as the boy and the ferry woman, have no names. Mr. Rombal's name has numerous variations. Marré's name is mentioned so rarely that she seems almost without identity.

For Juan Benet's characters, the struggle for the self requires the subjugation of reason to emotion. Reason is associated with order, conformity,
compliance, while emotion is the chaos at the core of the personality. That is
why Marré's liberation requires that she rebel against authority and give vent
to the senses. In the urgent struggle to affirm the identity, however, the identity is often lost as the individual sinks into an abyss of explanations.

Benet's style, which is confused and often tedious, serves to emphasize the
disorientation and tedium of the characters. Like the traveler in Región, who
"will get to know the discouragement of feeling that every step forward is
only bringing him a little farther away from those unknown mountains," the
more the characters search and delve, the further they get from the coveted
goal of self-knowledge. Parenthetical phrases, often separated by dashes and
parentheses within parentheses, heighten the obscurity of the text. Fragments of information that promise to contribute to an understanding of the
action ultimately lead nowhere, while seemingly unimportant details become
relevant many pages later. The novel, like Región and like the human personality, is a labyrinth of tricks and traps. The "truth" is unreachable. *Return
to Región* offers no solution, no "way out." For Benet's characters, the search
ends only with death.

All Benet's characters are tormented by fear—a kind of primal terror
rooted deep in their personalities. In a hostile universe in which there is no
real caring, fear of rejection, of solitude, and of death dominates the individual. Sometimes Benet's characters seek release through sex or even madness,
but the existential angst is always there. They feel a "much more urgent
necessity to conquer fear than to reach love because fear is always real and
love [is] . . . a speculative invention to overcome the former without wishing
to fight it."

Such feelings are both personal and universal. They are personal in the
sense that they are individual and cannot be shared. That is why, although
Marré and Dr. Sebastián talk endlessly, there is no real communication between them. There is no coherent dialogue between any of Benet's characters. Typically, they are too alienated really to care about one another. One
of the adjectives most frequently used to describe people in the novel is
"indifferent." For these characters in search of the self, words are meaningless, for the self is buried below the layers of words that serve only to conceal
it. Marré recalls the words of her father's comrades as a kind of blur: "Almost everything was a string of abstract words for me, and I was scarcely able
to make out their ultimate meaning."

The primal fear that Benet's characters experience is what unites them,
for fear is universal. It transcends time. In *Return to Región*, chronological
time is obliterated. The soliloquies meander from one chronological context
to another without transition. For the characters, a moment in the past may
be more real and vivid—and, therefore, more "current"—than the present.

Dr. Sebastián explains that time is accidental; it is part of the external circumstance over which man has no control. To find peace, man must conquer time by becoming oblivious to it. Throughout the novel, there are references to Spain's historical past, which intermingles with the immediate past, defined by the Civil War. Although the Civil War is the backdrop for much of the action, *Return to Región* is not a political novel. On the contrary, the war is seen as a moment in a continuing struggle between order and life.

Critical Context

Trained as a civil engineer, Juan Benet began to write fiction while pursuing a successful career in that profession. *Return to Región* was his first major work of fiction. It attracted little attention until 1969, when his second novel, *Una meditación* (1970; *A Meditation*, 1982), won the Biblioteca Breve literary prize. With the publication of *Un viaje de invierno* (1972; a winter journey), which, like the first two novels, is set in Región, critics began to speak of Benet's trilogy. *La otra casa de Mazón* (1973; the Mazóns' other house) is also set in Región, and *En el estado* (1977; in the state) is set in a similar area which the author calls La Portada.

Because Benet is such an unconventional author, it is difficult and perhaps unnecessary to classify his literary production. He has worked in a variety of genres: the novel, the novella, the short story, and the drama. In all, he conveys a view of man that is unique and consistent. The critic Vicente Cabrera has called Benet's fictional world a "symphony of despair," for Benet depicts man as a solitary, alienated being whose fear and anguish lead inevitably to failure.

Sources for Further Study

Compitello, Malcolm Alan. "Language, Structure, and Ideology in *Volverás a Región*," in *Proceedings of the Fifth Annual Hispanic Literature Conference*, 1982. Edited by J. Cruz Mendizábal.

Herzberger, David K. "The Emergence of Juan Benet: A New Alternative for the Spanish Novel," in *American Hispanist*. I, no. 3 (1975), pp. 6-12.

_____ . *The Novelistic World of Juan Benet*, 1976.

Mantiega, Robert C., David K. Herzberger, and Malcolm Alan Compitello, eds. *Critical Approaches to the Writings of Juan Benet*, 1984.

Schwartz, Ronald. "Benet and *Volverás a Región*, 1967," in *Spain's New Wave Novelists, 1959-1974*, 1976.

Summerhill, Stephen J. "Prohibition and Transgression in Juan Benet," in *American Hispanist*. IV, no. 36 (1979), pp. 20-24.

Wescott, Julia L. "Exposition and Plot in Benet's *Volverás a Región*," in *Kentucky Romance Quarterly*. XXVIII (1981), pp. 155-163.

Barbara Mujica

RICKSHAW

Author: Lao She (Shu Ch'ing-ch'un, 1899-1966)
Type of plot: Melioristic realism
Time of plot: The mid-1930's
Locale: Peking
First published: Lo-t'o Hsiang-tzu, 1936 (English translation, 1979)

> *Principal characters:*
> HSIANG-TZU, a Peking rickshaw puller
> HU NIU, his wife and the daughter of Old Liu
> OLD LIU, the owner of the Jen Ho rickshaw agency
> MR. TS'AO, a professor who hires Hsiang-tzu
> HSIAO FU TZU, an ill-fated woman who misses her chance to
> become Hsiang-tzu's second wife

The Novel

Rickshaw recounts the story of a self-assured young rickshaw puller's arduous struggle for a gratifying and secure livelihood. Hsiang-tzu, the orphaned protagonist, is only eighteen years old when he abandons the drudgery of life in his native north Chinese village and treks to Peking, the nearest large city. Enchanted by the variety and splendor of the urban panorama, Hsiang-tzu realizes that he has finally found the abode of his dreams; he can never go back to the monotony of plowing fields in the countryside.

Determined to achieve the self-reliance that owning a rickshaw might provide, Hsiang-tzu pulls rickshaws rented from the Jen Ho agency over a period of three years, until he finally saves up the one hundred dollars required to purchase one. He continues to reside at the agency when not working stints as a private chauffeur, for the agency's proprietors, Old Liu and his firebrand daughter Hu Niu, have taken a fancy to the strapping young lad with the countrified airs.

Trouble shatters Hsiang-tzu's dreams one day when warlord soldiers are campaigning just outside the city gates of central Peking. Turning a deaf ear to tales about the military having impressed townsmen into the army and confiscated their wares, Hsiang-tzu impetuously agrees to take a high-paying customer outside the city gates to the northwestern suburbs. Along the way, a band of soldiers does indeed swoop down on Hsiang-tzu to confiscate his rickshaw and force him into servitude as a coolie. Taking advantage of the uproar during a nighttime attack on the soldiers' encampment later that month, Hsiang-tzu deserts and cannily leads three of the army's camels away with him. Though he sells them for merely one-third of what his rickshaw had cost him, rumors about Hsiang-tzu's remarkably adroit caper spread like wildfire when he returns to the rickshaw agency in Peking; his fellow rickshaw men even dub him "Camel Hsiang-tzu"(which is the title of the novel in the original Chinese version). Yet Hsiang-tzu takes no solace in this notoriety, complaining that he will need at least a year to recoup his losses and save up for another rickshaw. In fact, he now begins to violate his previously staunch code of fair play, stealing customers from rival rickshaw pullers and engaging in a wide array of other underhanded tactics. Why, fumes Hsiang-tzu, should he be on his best behavior in a world that has so unmercifully buffeted him?

A chance for moral regeneration arrives when Hsiang-tzu obtains a job as the private rickshaw man of a benevolent "fellow traveler" leftist professor named Mr. Ts'ao. Unfortunately, although Mr. Ts'ao manages to skip town after getting into serious trouble with the rightist political authorities, his hapless rickshaw man is cornered by a corrupt police detective who seizes every last penny of Hsiang-tzu's two-year-old nest egg.

Hsiang-tzu later manages to buy his second rickshaw with the help of his new wife, Hu Niu, but he has no choice but to sell it to pay for her funeral, after she dies in childbirth. His youthful zest for work and ideals of self-reliance have worn thin after so many reversals, but a reencounter with the recently exonerated Mr. Ts'ao rekindles his flagging hopes. Mr. Ts'ao offers to hire Hsiang-tzu as his permanent rickshaw puller and Hsiang-tzu's new sweetheart, Hsiao Fu Tzu, as his housemaid. At this point, Hsiang-tzu discovers to his horror that Hsiao Fu Tzu's drunkard father had sold her to a brothel, where in desperation she eventually committed suicide.

Believing that any goal he tries to achieve will be denied him in the end, Hsiang-tzu gives up all thought for the future and simply muddles through on a day-to-day basis. Soon a shiftless denizen of cheap dives who hobbles with a limp because of a severe case of gonorrhea, he abandons rickshaw pulling for disreputable sidelines requiring no such exertion, such as carrying placards in processions and informing on labor activists to the police. Hsiang-tzu eventually fades from the scene, an abject shell of a man totally broken in spirit.

The Characters

The protagonist is a composite of two 1930's Peking rickshaw men whose travails sparked Lao She's imagination. One had stolen three camels from some marauding soldiers to compensate for their confiscation of his rickshaw, while the other rickshaw man was forced by one calamity after another to pawn every rickshaw which he had bought, finally sinking into extreme penury. Hsiang-tzu's nickname and brief notoriety evolved from the first rickshaw man's camel caper, but the overall tenor of the protagonist's life resonates more fully with the string of bitter reversals that ground down the second rickshaw man.

A key irony in the harshness of Hsiang-tzu's fate is his long-standing obliviousness to the risks of establishing a place for himself in an unfamiliar urban environment: In his optimism that borders on foolhardiness, he has eyes for only the opportunities that the city offers. Hsiang-tzu once muses that even for beggars life holds far more opportunities in the city than in the country-side; urban beggars enjoy meat scraps now and then, while their rural counterparts may never savor the taste of meat. This windfall mentality makes him impatient with manual jobs such as street peddling that provide a reliable but meager income. Would it not be far better to work as a rickshaw puller, when one large tip from a wealthy customer might come to as much as a whole day's peddling? It is not until Hsiang-tzu is too overwhelmed by his reversals to continue striving for a decent livelihood that he sees through his naïveté; by this time, it is too late.

Hsiang-tzu resembles many north Chinese peasants in his stolid, taciturn manner. Unable to rely primarily on dialogue to sketch the contours of his personality and values, the author makes heavy use of interior monologue to enter the silent thoughts of Hsiang-tzu and the other major characters. The tour de force of Lao She's mastery of unlimited omniscience and interior monologue in narration occurs during Old Liu's grandiose celebration of his sixty-ninth birthday. Up to this time, Old Liu had favored Hsiang-tzu over all the other rickshaw men at the agency, but he grows more and more gruff as he notices his daughter flirting with Hsiang-tzu. When she decides to break the news of their engagement to Old Liu, the old man furiously berates her for having sullied the family name by chasing after a "stinking" rickshaw man. The author relates that even as Old Liu is mouthing this insult of Hsiang-tzu, Liu realizes within his heart that Hsiang-tzu is a good man. The true object of his anger is Hu Niu, who has shamed him in front of his birthday guests. Hu Niu had originally hoped to keep the love affair a secret, but she silently adjusts her strategy and lies, saying that she is already pregnant with Hsiang-tzu's child; she anticipates shocking her father into giving his assent to the marriage. Unfortunately, Old Liu is far more stubbornly proud than she anticipated, and he lays down an ultimatum that she choose either him or Hsiang-tzu. Hu Niu calls his bluff by storming out of the agency with Hsiang-tzu in tow, even though both she and her father are inwardly reluctant to part from each other. Rarely has one episode so powerfully rendered the dissonance between the inner thoughts and outward behavior of major characters.

Themes and Meanings

Hsiang-tzu would seem to be well equipped to flourish at rickshaw pulling: Brawny and strong-willed, he loves to work and is so frugal that he skimps on food while saving to buy a rickshaw. Though somewhat naïve, he has the presence of mind to win back part of his losses while escaping from the army. The fundamental factor behind his downfall, according to Lao She, is his idea that individual striving is the key to success in any endeavor. In an economically backward society lacking any sort of welfare safety net, aside from a few scattered soup kitchens, an individualist ethic of self-reliance is a dubious credo for manual laborers of the lower social strata.

An old rickshaw man tells Hsiang-tzu that he had watched helplessly while his grandson died in his arms from an illness because he could not afford the fees that doctors and hospitals charge. Lao She seems to suggest that there is something ethically bankrupt about a society that remains complacent in the face of true misery affecting a large segment of the citizenry. Yet Lao She puts forward none of the answers common in the 1930's, such as notions that a new political leadership or economic system would solve everything. Lao She views the problem of a lack of compassion for one's fellowman as generalized and diffused throughout all levels of society; late in the novel, as a condemned labor activist is paraded through the streets on his way to the execution ground, rich and poor alike throng the sidewalks to gape and jeer at a person whom they callously scorn as being no longer human.

Critical Context

Generally regarded as Lao She's masterpiece and one of the top three or four twentieth century Chinese novels, *Rickshaw* marked a new stage in his development as a meliorist writer. His earlier novels, such as *Li-hun* (1933; *Divorce*, 1948), generally pointed to the weakness of the individual will as a key factor preventing Chinese society from throwing off the traditional ways that have engendered the social stagnation of the age. By contrast, with Hsiang-tzu, one encounters a very strong-willed character whose spirit of self-reliance is punctured by so many reversals that it is ultimately ground flat by the corrupt society in which he moves. Lao She now turns from the discredited ethic of individualist striving to a new credo of collective struggle on the part of the downtrodden: The rickshaw man whose ill grandson died in his arms cites the parable of the locust, which when alone is helpless to prevent a small boy from pulling off its legs, but as part of a giant horde can sweep through entire regions unopposed, devouring everything in its path. No doubt more leftist in orientation than any of Lao She's previous novels, *Rickshaw* is nevertheless strikingly free of the obtrusive doctrinairism that mars so many other proletarian novels.

Sources for Further Study

Hsia, C. T. *A History of Modern Chinese Fiction*, 1971 (second edition).

Slupski, Zbigniew. *The Evolution of a Modern Chinese Writer: An Analysis of Lao She's Fiction*, 1966.

Vohra, Ranbir. *Lao She and the Chinese Revolution*, 1974.

Philip F. Williams

THE RIPENING SEED

Author: Colette (Sidonie-Gabrielle Colette, 1873-1954)
Type of plot: Social realism
Time of plot: One summer in the early 1920's
Locale: A summer house on the coast of Britanny
First published: Le Blé en herbe, 1923 (*The Ripening Corn*, 1931; better known
  as *The Ripening Seed*)

Principal characters:
>VINCA FERRET, one of the protagonists, a fifteen-year-old girl
> who is in love with Phillipe
>PHILLIPE AUDEBERT, the other protagonist, a sixteen-year-old
> boy who is in love with Vinca
>MADAME CAMILLE DALLERAY, the woman in white who
> seduces Phillipe

The Novel

The Ripening Seed explores the coming of age of its two main characters,
Vinca Ferret, a fifteen-year-old French girl with "eyes the color of April
showers," and Phillipe Audebert, a sixteen-year-old French boy in the "full
vigour" of youth and impatience. As the novel unfolds, the omniscient narrator moves back and forth between the thoughts and actions of Vinca and
Phillipe, revealing slowly the changes which turn these childhood friends into
neophyte adolescent lovers. This is the fifteenth summer that their families
have spent together in a house on the coast of Brittany, and much that occurs
is merely a continuation of the previous summers. Vinca and Phillipe spend
their days shrimping in the cliffside tidal pools, swimming or fishing in the
quiet waters along the beach, or hiking to their secret spots, where they can
sit and talk, or dream of the future, away from their parents' eyes. Underneath the familiar and comfortable routines of childhood, however, lurks an
uneasiness. Knowing that they are fated to marry each other, they find the
thought of waiting for five or six more years almost unbearable, and yet their
lives are programmed for them: Phillipe must finish school and then enter his
father's business, while Vinca will stay at home and perfect her domestic
role. Thus, while swimming, fishing, and hiking, they fall prey to melancholy,
self-indulgent fantasies and romantic melodramas.

One day, something intrudes upon their private world of waiting. Phillipe,
quite by accident, meets the "woman in white," Madame Camille Dalleray.
At first, she addresses him as "young fellow" when she sees him scrambling
through the sand wearing only a pair of shorts. Moments later, however, she
looks at him "like a man." Madame Dalleray tells Phillipe that she has lost
her way to *Ker-Anna*, her summer house, and Phillipe manages to stammer

out an answer, feeling both embarrassed and flattered by the attention. Just as the woman turns to leave, Vinca comes climbing up over the cliff demanding, with "anxious, jealous" eyes, to know with whom Phillipe was speaking. For reasons yet unknown to Phillipe, he gives Vinca a somewhat brief and ambiguous answer, keeping to himself some as yet unknown secret.

The next day, Vinca and Phillipe succumb to the gloom of a rainy day, aware that only three weeks of vacation remain. As they watch each other through the rain, their sadness deepens, and when a break in the storm comes, they take refuge on a protected ledge in the cliffs overlooking the darkened sea and sky. As they sit, lost in reveries of their forthcoming separation, Phillipe notices that Vinca "[w]ith eyes tight shut, . . . was slipping quietly, imperceptibly, deliberately, down the slope of the rocky ledge, so narrow that her feet were already dangling over space." Phillipe calmly yet firmly pulls her back onto the ledge, forcing her to choose life over death, waiting over having.

As the days continue, Vinca and Phillipe shift from "moody dramatics" to more normal behavior and back again. One day, they plan a picnic, taking along Lisette, Vinca's younger sister. Climbing over rocks and through fields of flowers, they reach a flat, sandy stretch and settle down for a picnic. Unconsciously, Vinca absorbs herself in "squaw-like chores," setting out the food, making sure that Phillipe and Lisette get what they want. She then proceeds to clean up after the three of them have finished, while Lisette runs off to play and Phillipe lies back, closes his eyes, and daydreams that Vinca is already his wife. At the same time, however, a naked and undefined form lurks in the recesses of his daydream.

Thus, at least for a short time, life seems to have resumed its normal routine, until one day, Phillipe, who is cycling back from the town, stops to rest beside the walls of *Ker-Anna*. Just as he begins to catch his breath, a shadow falls across his body. It is the lady in white, Madame Dalleray. She invites him in for a glass of orangeade, calling him "monsieur" as she had on that first day. Phillipe follows her indoors, feeling slightly dizzy, and encounters a room with drawn curtains and closed shutters. As Madame Dalleray hands Phillipe the glass, she dips her fingers into it and removes an ice cube. Again, Phillipe feels faint, noticing for the first time the subtle odor of incense and the deep reds and blacks that decorate the room, adding "to the atmosphere of nightmarish luxury, of startling uncertainty, of equivocal rape." He manages to stumble through some small talk, gulping his drink, and makes his escape. Down the road from *Ker-Anna*, he finds Vinca looking for him. When Vinca questions him as to why he was gone so long, he answers: "I was set upon . . . shut up in a cellar, given powerful potions to quench my thirst, tied naked to a stake, tortured, put to the test. . . ." Vinca laughs at his story, but Phillipe knows that he speaks the "truth."

From that day on, Phillipe is obsessed with thoughts of the woman in white and the room at *Ker-Anna*. He is both ashamed and excited by his memories, and he decides to repay her kindness by bringing her some flowers. He chooses the sea holly, which, ironically, is the same shade of blue as Vinca's eyes. Waiting for a day when Vinca remains indoors, Phillipe guiltily picks the holly and takes it to *Ker-Anna*. Madame Dalleray accepts the flowers, telling Phillipe to come the next time not bearing gifts like a repentant schoolboy but as a beggar for "another reason." Shame once again sends Phillipe back to the comfort of Vinca and their childhood, but now Vinca in turn notices a change in Phillipe, a "feminine presence" other than her own. He behaves like a guilty husband when faced with her silent stares, and he keeps his visits secret. On his fifth visit, he deliberately allows himself to be seduced with "slowness and calculated courage."

On returning to his home that night, Phillipe hears the clock strike two. He thinks of Vinca, asleep "like a child," and bursts into tears, succumbing to self-indulgent feelings of shame. Looking up, he sees the lights go on in Vinca's room, and he swears to himself, "never again." When he finally reaches his room, he falls into a troubled sleep and does not wake until he hears Vinca calling to him from below his window. She teases him about his pale face and fatigue.

Fighting an urge to remain in bed, he goes swimming with Vinca; as he watches her walk across the sand, he notices that she steps on and crushes a small crab and is shocked at her cruelty. Later, at lunch, Phillipe is sickened at the sight of her strong hands tearing away at a lobster claw. A few hours later, watching her trying to hook a conger eel and seeing the "spilt blood," he breaks down and sobs. Vinca, bewildered at first, listens to his sobs with an ear trained to "the new cadence" which gives meaning to his tears. Without a word, she turns and walks away.

Phillipe's visits to *Ker-Anna* continue, and with each visit he returns to Vinca, trying to regain his childhood friend and looking for a sign from Vinca that she "knows all" and will forgive, but finding nothing. Finally, one day, he receives a message that Madame Dalleray has left and does not know whether to be relieved or sad. As he walks back to the house in search of Vinca, he encounters his father, who begins to speak of Phillipe's future responsibilities: a job and a family. With these last words, Phillipe faints. When he recovers, he and Vinca take a walk, and she admits that she knows of his visits to the woman in white. Phillipe is ready to confess everything, but Vinca does not want his confession. What she does want is to know why he did not come to her, instead. Her words both surprise and frighten Phillipe, and Vinca mocks him for his prudishness.

Later that evening, after everyone else has gone to sleep, Phillipe and Vinca take a walk. Vinca leads the way through the dark, guiding Phillipe over and around obstacles. They make their way to a field of threshed wheat, and once again Phillipe allows himself to be seduced, surprised at Vinca's "feminine senses." The next morning, Phillipe's first thoughts are about how he can comfort Vinca, for he has heard that "they're always said to weep, after." His solicitous mood is shattered, however, when he sees Vinca smiling and singing on her balcony as she feeds the birds as usual. Phillipe grieves that he is "neither a hero, nor an executioner."

The Characters

Vinca, like many of Colette's adolescent heroines, moves from innocence to experience. She is closely linked to the colors and objects of nature: Her periwinkle eyes are the "colour of April showers," her tanned legs are the "colour of terra-cotta," her neck is "milk white," and her hair sticks out like "stiff corn-stalks." Vinca is also tomboyish: "[S]he was careful to fasten her blouses and jumpers over a non-existent bosom, she tucked up her skirt and knickers as high as she could when paddling with the unconcern of a small boy." She displays a feminine yet adolescent wisdom about becoming a wife and mother—already playing the part as she mends torn clothes, pours cof-fee, and serves food—while skillfully catching shrimp or fish, climbing rocks, and swimming. Nevertheless, although she moves comfortably between the physical worlds of tomboy and young girl, she is a bit wary when faced with the new world awaiting her, the world of physical love.

Phillipe is in a similar position: He is a young boy on the brink of man-hood who "made a weapon of everything that embarrassed him." He wants everything that Vinca wants, but he is less sure of himself and his future role as husband and overdramatizes first his virginity and later his virility. Phillipe retreats to fantasy worlds, where he plays the romantic and long-suffering hero. Longing for the freedom and pleasures of manhood, he is reluctant to give up the securities of childhood. Thus his movement between the two stages is more traumatic and, at times, more comically dramatic than Vinca's.

Madame Dalleray is the most static of the three characters, and in her role as the seductress, she is the antithesis of Vinca. The lady in white has no connection to nature. Her world is an indoor one of velvets, satins, and silks; she closes out the daylight, surrounding herself with reds, golds, and blacks. While Vinca and Phillipe move timidly toward sexual initiation, Madame Dalleray, at thirty, is well versed in sexual exploits. For Phillipe, she repre-sents both pleasure and shame; for Vinca, she awakens feelings of jealousy and competition.

Themes and Meanings

On the surface, *The Ripening Seed* is a love story with an old and familiar theme: the movement from innocence to experience. The novel also has a conventional plot line: the classic love triangle, in which the older woman initiates the younger boy, who then returns to the younger girl. Nevertheless,

Colette moves beneath these simple trappings, mainly with her use of symbols and her use of ambiguous sexual identities, to give her novel a deeper meaning.

Using Vinca and Madame Dalleray as opposites, Colette has put all that is positive into Vinca, with her naturelike simplicity, and all that is negative into Madame Dalleray and her calculated artifice. Vinca is the color of the sky, the sea, and the earth. Even her name is linked with nature: Vinca is the botanical name for the periwinkle, which is the color of the girl's eyes. She is at home in nature, moving through it freely, and even her sexual initiation takes place in a field of new-mown wheat. On the other hand, Madame Dalleray, although dressed always in white, shuns nature and surrounds herself with artificial light and rich, exotic colors. She seduces Phillipe indoors, substituting for the fresh smell of the sea and hay more potent odors, such as incense and perfume. In describing her seductions, Colette uses symbols of Phillipe falling or drowning, of him being overpowered by Madame Dalleray's sexual appetite. In contrast, when Vinca seduces Phillipe, they share a mutuality of desire and fear; "they lay, like brother and sister" before their legs "became interlaced."

As for the sexual ambiguities of the novel, they offer a unique look at how feminine and masculine roles overlap and blur. Vinca walks with a "firm step" and has "strong hands"; she has a "boyish, graceful figure," and her arms and legs are tanned and scarred. Phillipe, on the other hand, has "slender" arms and legs which might easily be "the pride of a girl in her teens." In addition, he often blushes and stammers, not knowing what to say. As much as their sexual identities blur, however, they also conform to normal limitations. Vinca knows "from the cradle" that she is destined to marry and rear a family, and even at fifteen, she knows how to be coquettish and submissive. As for Phillipe, he will finish school and work to support a family.

The protagonists' reactions to sexual experience, however, add symbolic significance to this male-female ambiguity. When Phillipe first meets Madame Dalleray, he is "overcome by an access of femininity," for she speaks to him "as a man might," and gazes at him openly. After his seduction, Phillipe looks like a "violated girl" with a smudge of red lipstick (red being the color of sexual initiation) across his face. Each time he encounters Madame Dalleray, he feels "suddenly tired, feeble and limp," and later has fits of crying and fainting. Vinca, however, after her first night of love wakes up in the morning unchanged. She smiles and sings, feeding the birds as always. The red flowers she waters on her balcony link her once again to nature, as she stares "fixedly in front of her," not seeing Phillipe hiding in the shadows of his room. For Phillipe, the act of sex will be tied up in memories of darkness and violence; for Vinca, it will be associated with nature's continuing cycle of birth and death.

Critical Context

Although *The Ripening Seed* was not Colette's first published work, this book marked the first time that she published under her own name rather than using her husband's. This novel, which was originally intended for magazine serialization (until the editors discovered that it ended with an adolescent love scene), falls into a common pattern of adolescent love triangles which involve older women. Nevertheless, like most of Colette's love stories, this novel is more, for it leads its characters, especially the adolescent heroine, on a search not only for the self but also for a sexual identity and equality within a traditional relationship. Without consciously addressing the issues of feminism, Colette explored them in a symbolic manner through her growing use of nature and sexual ambiguities. Regardless of this inherent symbolism, however, Colette's novels are set in the real world, a world in which society dictates male and female roles. Although there is a tendency to place Colette among the canon of women writers, such as George Eliot and Virginia Woolf, her characters and their struggles are limited by the very theme which they explore, love. Colette was aware of the traditions of French literary formalism, of the need for temporal unity and social realism, and she worked within these limits. Yet even within these limitations, she developed a style that was rich in sensuous imagery, very often using nature as her source.

Sources for Further Study

Eisinger, Erica Mendelson, and Mari Ward McCarty, eds. *Colette: The Woman, the Writer*, 1981.
Goudeket, Maurice. *Close to Colette*, 1957.
Marks, Elaine. *Colette*, 1960.
Richardson, Joanna. *Colette*, 1983.
Stewart, Joan Hinde. *Colette*, 1983

Deborah Charlie

THE ROADS TO FREEDOM

Author: Jean-Paul Sartre (1905-1980)
Type of plot: Philosophical realism
Time of plot: June, 1938, to June, 1940
Locale: France, Czechoslovakia, and New York City
First published: Les Chemins de la liberté, 1945-1949 (English translation,
    1947-1950): *L'Âge de raison,* 1945 (*The Age of Reason,* 1947); *Le Sursis,*
    1945 (*The Reprieve,* 1947); *La Morte dans l'âme,* 1949 (*Troubled Sleep,*
    1950; also as *Iron in the Soul,* 1950)

> *Principal characters:*
>   MATHIEU DELARUE, the protagonist, a professor of
>   philosophy
>   MARCELLE DUFFET, Mathieu's mistress and later Daniel
>   Sereno's wife
>   BORIS SERGUINE, Mathieu's student and disciple
>   IVICH SERGUINE, Boris' sister
>   LOLA MONTERO, a professional singer and Boris' mistress
>   BRUNET, a Communist activist
>   DANIEL SERENO, a homosexual friend of Mathieu and
>   Marcelle's husband
>   JACQUES DELARUE, Mathieu's older brother, a lawyer
>   ODETTE DELARUE, Jacques's wife, who is in love with Mathieu
>   GOMEZ, an artist turned general in the Spanish Republican
>   Army
>   SARAH GOMEZ, his wife
>   PHILIPPE GRÉSIGNE, an adolescent would-be poet and pacifist

The Novels

    The Roads to Freedom begins in June, 1938, with the first volume *The Age of Reason.* As the novel opens, Mathieu Delarue is visiting his longtime mistress, Marcelle Duffet. Because their affair has been going on for seven years, Mathieu has tired of Marcelle, but he continues to see her regularly, four times each week. Tonight, however, the routine changes, for Marcelle tells her lover that she is carrying his child. Without asking about her feelings and wishes, Mathieu immediately delcares, "Well, I suppose one gets rid of it, eh?"

    Because Mathieu wants Marcelle's abortion to be as safe as possible, he consults Sarah Gomez, who had ended a pregnancy some years earlier. Sarah gives him the address of a reliable but expensive doctor who will be leaving Paris for the United States in a few days. Mathieu must therefore quickly find four thousand francs. He goes first to his friend Daniel Sereno, who claims that he does not have that much money (though in fact, he has ten thousand francs in his wallet). Mathieu next turns to his brother but is again rebuffed. Jacques, too, has the money, but he disapproves of his brother's bohemian life. If Mathieu will marry Marcelle, his brother will give him ten thousand francs, but Jacques refuses to pay for an abortion.

Boris Serguine, Mathieu's student and admirer, is more sympathetic. Though he lacks such a sum himself, he knows that his mistress, Lola Montero, keeps seven thousand francs in her room. To his surprise, though, when he asks her for five thousand francs, she refuses him. The ensuing argument so distresses her that she takes an overdose of cocaine. Boris wakes up the next morning to find her cold and pale; thinking that she is dead, he flees the apartment.

Shortly afterward, he meets Mathieu and begs him to return to Lola's room and remove some letters, lest Boris be implicated in Lola's death. Mathieu agrees, and, at the same time that he takes the incriminating packet, he considers stealing the money which he needs. While he hesitates, Lola revives. He still has the key to her trunk, though, and later that day, with more resolution, he does take five thousand francs.

When he presents the money to Marcelle, however, she throws the notes in his face. She wants to keep the child, and Daniel, who for some time has been visiting her, has maliciously encouraged her belief that Mathieu will marry her. Rather than agree to an abortion and continuing her affair with Mathieu, she will marry Daniel, little suspecting that he is a homosexual who is taking her to humiliate both Mathieu and himself.

Mathieu returns to his apartment and finds Ivich waiting for him. He has lusted after her, but she has always remained aloof. Now that she has failed her examination at the *lycée* and must leave Paris for her native Laon, she is willing to give herself to Mathieu. Yet he cannot commit himself to her any more than he could to Marcelle. He tells her, "I mustn't touch you." As she prepares to depart, Lola enters, looking for Boris, whom she accuses of robbing her. Mathieu explains what has happened, and Daniel appears with the bank notes that Marcelle had refused. At the novel's end Mathieu is entangled with neither Marcelle nor Ivich, but, as he realizes, he remains "no freer than before."

When *The Reprieve* opens, three months have elapsed. In late September, 1938, Europe holds its breath while Neville Chamberlain, Édouard Daladier, and Adolf Hitler decide whether war will break out over the question of the Sudeten Germans in Czechoslovakia. As Jean-Paul Sartre observes of this novel, "All the characters in *The Age of Reason* . . . reappear . . . , only this time as lost people thwarted by a crowd of other people." In the partial mobilization that precedes the agreement at Munich, Mathieu is called up to serve. Boris, expecting war, enlists, and his sister returns to Paris from Laon to sleep with her boyfriend. Daniel and Marcelle have married and have left Paris to live at Peyrehorade.

Intersecting the stories of these major characters are accounts of numerous other figures swept up in what Sartre calls "the sense of disarray. . . at the time of the derisory reprieve that Munich offered." Philippe Grésigne rebels against his stepfather, a general, and resolves first to flee to Switzerland to avoid the fighting, then to become a martyr by staying in France to speak out against the war. Gros-Louis, an illiterate shepherd, wanders the streets of Marseilles, where he is beaten and robbed. Charles, an invalid, is reluctantly evacuated from his hospital. A number of villagers, believing that the mobilization is general rather than partial, leave their farms for the nearest army post. Gomez enjoys a brief respite of good food and a woman's bed before returning to the hopeless war against Francisco Franco.

Though war does not come in 1938, it engulfs France in 1940. *Troubled Sleep* examines the effect of the Nazi invasion on Gomez's family, Mathieu, Daniel, Philippe, and Brunet. Defeated by the Fascists in Spain, Gomez himself has fled to the United States. On June 15, 1940, he begins to work as an art critic; on that same day, the Germans enter Paris and Gomez's wife and child attempt to reach the relative safety of Gien. Their car breaks down, though, and the reader last sees them as refugees trudging along the dusty, crowded road.

Mathieu's unit has been in constant retreat, never stopping to confront the invaders. When they finally pause at a small village, every officer, from general down to lieutenant, flees, leaving the men leaderless. Most of the men take refuge in drink, but Mathieu joins a small detachment of soldiers resolved to resist the Germans. In the fifteen-minute battle, all the French except Mathieu are killed, and he is taken prisoner.

Philippe, despite his pacifist posing, joins the French army. After its defeat, he returns to Paris to visit his mother, only to find that she has fled. He then attempts to drown himself in the Seine but is rescued by Daniel, who has left Marcelle to enjoy the Nazi desecration of the French capital. Daniel takes Philippe to his Parisian apartment to begin a lengthy seduction.

Like Philippe, Brunet had opposed the war, though not because he considers himself a pacifist. On August 29, 1939, on the eve of the Nazi invasion of Poland, Brunet had written a lengthy editorial urging nonintervention, because Moscow had just signed a nonaggression pact with Germany. He thus follows the Communist Party line. Yet when Germany invades his homeland, Brunet enlists as a sergeant and is captured near Baccarat. In the prison camp, he begins to organize a Communist cell, and he continues his efforts to win recruits even as a train carries him and his fellow captives to slavery in Germany.

The Characters

Because *The Roads to Freedom* is historical as well as philosophical fiction, a number of characters are actual people: For example, Chamberlain,

Hitler, and Daladier all play minor but crucial roles in *The Reprieve*. Others are closely modeled on Sartre's friends. Ivich, for example, is based on Olga Kosakiewicz, and Paul Nizan served as the model for Schneider, whom Brunet meets in the German prison camp. Like Nizan, Schneider is a Communist who left the Party when it reversed its anti-Fascist stand in August, 1939. Mathieu closely resembles his creator. Like Sartre, he was born in 1905; moreover, both teach philosophy and ponder the meaning of true freedom. Still another set of characters derives from Sartre's study of nineteenth century French poets. Philippe suggests Charles Baudelaire, and Daniel bears some similarity to Arthur Rimbaud.

Sartre also uses his characters to exemplify types of people maintaining certain political or philosophical views. Like many of his contemporaries, Mathieu sympathizes with the Spanish Republicans but does nothing to support them. His brother reflects the widespread sentiment, "Better Hitler than (Léon) Blum," the Jewish premier of France; this attitude did much to undermine the French will to resist in 1940. Birnenschatz, a rich Jewish jeweler, typifies the assimilationist tendencies of his coreligionists in Germany as well as in France, calling himself a "Frenchman, not a Jew, not a French Jew" and opposing military intervention against the Nazis. Brunet represents the French Far Left, meaning well but far too willing to follow the various dictates of Moscow and more concerned with the current demands of the Soviet Union than with the needs of the French people. The fate of peasants such as Gros-Louis and members of the petite bourgeois such as Maurice demonstrates the plight of the masses caught up in forces beyond their comprehension and control.

Although Sartre thus uses his characters as representatives for various positions or for large groups, he allows his figures autonomy within the novels. In a review of François Mauriac's *La Fin de la nuit* (1935; *The End of the Night*, 1947) Sartre had criticized authorial omniscience, and in *The Roads to Freedom*, he uses dialogue and interior monologues that permit the characters to reveal themselves. Nor does he allow the reader to know more than the characters do. When Boris believes that Lola is dead, so does the reader. As Brunet is captured, Mathieu is fighting the Germans nearby, but since Brunet is unaware of his friend's proximity, Sartre does not draw attention to the coincidence. Concerned as he is with the individual consciousness, Sartre focuses on that element. By avoiding editorial comments, he lets his characters lead their own lives and so transcend their functions as spokesmen for their creator.

Themes and Meanings

At the same time that characters seem to act independently, they cannot escape the central issue implied in the title of their saga. "My intention is to write a novel about freedom," Sartre declared; in fact, he wrote three. More precisely, he wrote about ways to achieve freedom or the roads to that goal, for in the published trilogy, none of the characters, with the possible exception of Gomez, actually achieves the desired end.

Mathieu constantly thinks about and yearns for freedom. Early in *The Age of Reason*, he tells Marcelle, "I recognize no allegiance except to myself." Hence he shuns marriage or any other commitment, such as going to fight against Franco or joining the Communist Party, as his friend Brunet urges him to do. Although Sartre intended him to be the hero of *The Roads to Freedom*, he noted that Mathieu's initial attitude is not one that he himself could endorse:

> Mathieu is the embodiment of that total availability which Hegel calls terroristic freedom and which is practically the opposite of freedom. . . . He is not free because he has not been able to commit himself. . . . Mathieu is the freedom of indifference, abstract freedom, freedom for nothing, because he is always an outsider.

This aloofness manifests itself frequently, as when Mathieu and Ivich visit a Gaugin exhibit. Paul Gaugin represents all that Mathieu is not, for Gaugin abandoned his family and job to become an artist. Mathieu, however, will not commit himself to anything. Similarly, in *Troubled Sleep*, he remains sober while his comrades get drunk. Even within the confines of the small church tower he remains separated from his fellow soldiers, standing while they sit, surviving while they perish.

In fighting the Germans, Mathieu does at last commit himself, but he still does not attain true freedom, because his purpose is destructive. Moreover, he is not so much acting as reacting, shooting to erase "some ancient scruple." Hence, his behavior is, for Sartre, not freedom but its very negation.

Still, Mathieu remains more heroic than the characters who surround him, because of what Sartre calls his "lucidity." Mathieu is not free, but he recognizes that fact; he understands both what he is doing and the consequences of his actions. For example, toward the end of *The Age of Reason*, he concedes, "I have led a toothless life. . . . I have never bitten into anything. I was waiting. I was reserving myself for later on—and I have just noticed that my teeth have gone." When Mathieu fires on the Germans, he again recognizes that he is trying to compensate for his past, not to save France or protect his colleagues.

Such enlightenment, a prerequisite to attaining real freedom, eludes Brunet in these novels. Sartre shares the Communist's critique of capitalism, but he regards Brunet as too unthinking: "Man is free to commit himself, but he is not free unless he commits himself to being free." Brunet instead commits himself to following a Party line, whereas Sartre never joined the Communist Party because he wanted to think for himself. Schneider tries to educate Brunet. When Brunet begins to organize a Communist cell in the prison camp,

Schneider asks whether this action is appropriate: "What's the party up to? What orders has it issued, what directives? . . . If I were in your place, I should want to know." Brunet does not recognize the implication that he has acted previously only after he had received orders from Moscow.

Yet even Brunet is farther along the road to freedom than is Daniel or Philippe, who exemplify the exact opposite of the independent existential hero. Both of these characters want to turn themselves into objects and so commit metaphysical, if not actual, suicide. Daniel wishes "to be of stone, immobile, insensate, no sound, no movement, blind and deaf, . . . a ferocious statue with an empty stare, without a worry." When Mathieu looks at the statues in the Luxembourg Gardens and recognizes that he is becoming fixed and permanent like them because of his routine-filled life, he has the lucidity to be frightened. Daniel, though, would regard these statutes as his ideal. He welcomes the German Occupation of Paris, because he regards the city as now fixed in history, a dead monument rather than a living entity. He becomes religious because by believing in God he can regard himself as being observed: "I am seen; therefore I am" becomes his creed. He renounces his freedom, choosing, in Sartre's terms, to be rather than to exist. He fails to behave as Sartre would later urge in his *Critique de la raison dialectique* (1960; *Critique of Dialectical Reason*, 1976): "Man defines himself by his project. This material being continually transcends the condition made for him; he reveals and determines his situation by transcending it in order to objectify himself, through his work, his action, or his gesture." Daniel does not, cannot act, and so has no project.

Fittingly, Philippe vanishes into Daniel's apartment, for he, too, cannot define himself. Instead, like Daniel, he requires an observer to guarantee his existence. He runs away from home because he believes that his flight will make his mother think about him more and thus give meaning to his life. He imagines that others will flock to his hotel room as to a shrine. Although he considers himself a martyr, a witness, ironically, he behaves so as to be witnessed. Even his denunciations of the war do not reflect a commitment to pacifism but rather a desire for exhibitionism. He resolves to drown himself after he learns that his mother has left Paris and that the city is deserted; without anyone to see him, his life has no meaning. Once he finds an audience in Daniel, Philippe gives up his attempt at suicide, but he remains ontologically dead as long as he cannot assume responsibility for his own existence.

Only Gomez appears to succeed in achieving freedom. Like Gaugin, he leaves his family and his work to commit himself freely to a cause, in this case, to fighting in Spain. Hence, when Mathieu asks him about the future, Gomez can reply, "What difference does it make? I have lived." Through his self-reliance and his dedication to a worthwhile cause, he makes himself into the existential hero.

Critical Context

The first two volumes of *The Roads to Freedom* shocked France when they appeared in 1945, for they dealt freely with homosexuality, abortion, and nonmarital affairs. Yet the works proved as popular as they were controversial, going through numerous editions in French and in translation. With the passing of time, critics and readers alike came to recognize Sartre's achievement of bringing philosophy to life, an accomplishment that contributed to the Swedish Academy's decision to award Sartre the Nobel Prize for Literature in 1964.

The Roads to Freedom has taken its rightful place beside Marcel Proust's *À la recherche du temps perdu* (1913-1927; *Remembrance of Things Past*, 1922-1931, 1981) and Honoré de Balzac's *La Comédie humaine* (1829-1848; *The Human Comedy*, 1895-1896, 1911) as an epical record of its time, even though Sartre never finished his saga. He had indeed intended to write a trilogy, but the work grew as he progressed, so that "La Dernière chance," originally designed as the third installment, became the fourth, which remained incomplete at the time of the author's death. He had worked out the plot, which would allow Mathieu, Brunet, Odette, Philippe, and even Daniel to reach the end of their separate roads to freedom, but this concluding volume, to be set during the Nazi Occupation, never satisfied Sartre, because he regarded the choices facing his characters as too clear-cut: resist or collaborate. True to his philosophical calling, Sartre preferred to leave his readers with hard questions rather than with simple answers.

Sources for Further Study

Barnes, Hazel E. *Humanistic Existentialism: The Literature of Possibility*, 1959.

Bauer, George Howard. *Sartre and the Artist*, 1969.

Brosman, Catharine Savage. *Jean-Paul Sartre*, 1983.

Kern, Edith, ed. *Sartre: A Collection of Critical Essays*, 1962.

Planck, William. *Sartre and Surrealism*, 1981.

Thody, Philip. *Jean-Paul Sartre: A Literary and Political Study*, 1960.

Joseph Rosenblum

ROADSIDE PICNIC

Authors: Arkady Strugatsky (1925-   ) and Boris Strugatsky (1933-   )
Type of plot: Science fiction
Time of plot: The late 1990's and the early 2000's
Locale: The fictitious Canadian town of Harmont
First published: Piknik na obochine, 1972 (English translation, 1977)

> *Principal characters:*
> REDRICK "RED" SCHUHART, a roguish stalker from Harmont
>   who works for hire and for himself
> BUZZARD BURBRIDGE, an old stalker, who sends Redrick on
>   his final trip into the Zone
> KIRILL PANOV, a Russian scientist with the United Nations
>   team at Harmont
> DR. VALENTINE PILMAN, a Canadian and senior physicist at
>   the Zone
> RICHARD "DICK" NOONAN, a lazy, complacent bureaucrat, out
>   to stalk the stalkers
> GUTA SCHUHART, Redrick's wife
> "MONKEY" SCHUHART, Redrick's mutant daughter

The Novel

Roadside Picnic tells the story of humankind's dealing with the strange and sometimes quite dangerous leftovers from an alien "visitation" at six isolated spots on Earth. Thirty years after the event, a central bureaucracy has set up the International Institute for Extraterrestrial Cultures at the site of one such visitation at Harmont in Canada. There, scientists and their supporting local police and United Nations security forces compete with independent adventurers, called stalkers, for the abandoned alien artifacts, the workings of which still elude human understanding. The salvaging process poses many dangers, since the men have to enter the deadly terrain of the Zone, as the now-deserted ground has been named.

A radio interview with witty head scientist Dr. Valentine Pilman leads to Harmont, where native son Redrick Schuhart works as a laboratory assistant for Kirill Panov. Out of pity for the overworked and unsuccessful Russian scientist, Red (as his friends call him) proposes a trip into the Zone, where he knows about an artifact of interest for his employer. Kirill agrees to what is the novel's first of three excursions, even though Red has clearly compromised himself with his knowledge. As a former stalker who previously went into the Zone—which is off limits for all private citizens—Red sold his booty, called swag, on the black market; this illegal activity earned for him not only thorough knowledge of the deadly patch of stricken land but also a jail term and the suspicion of his antagonist from the police force, Captain Quarterblad.

In the Zone, Red guides his team through the perils created by the land's contact with the Visitors; "mosquito manges," centers of deadly enhanced gravity, and "witches' jelly," a man-eating slimy substance lurking in ditches and crevices, are all part of a vividly described and literally alienated yet terrestrial environment. At their destination, an abandoned garage, Red and Kirill salvage a magnetic trap holding a blue fluid; because of Red's oversight, his partner touches an alien substance, a silvery web. Returned to the safety of the Borscht, his favorite hangout, Red receives the news of Kirill's death. Drunk and enraged, he leaves the bar just in time to be caught by Guta, his girlfriend, who tells him she is pregnant. Despite known birth defects among children of men exposed to the Zone, they decide for marriage and against abortion—a fateful step which leaves Red with "Monkey," his ape-haired mutant daughter.

An illegal trip into the Zone five years later nets Red a bag full of swag and the loss of his legs while rescuing Buzzard Burbridge, a victim of witches' jelly. Dragged to safety by his companion, Burbridge promises Red the location of the Golden Ball, a seemingly magical alien leftover with the power to grant human wishes. Indeed, Burbridge's "wished" children, although they are brats, testify to the Golden Ball's potency. Pursued by Quarterblad after he has sold most of his booty to undercover officials who doublecross their own state bureaucracy, Red strikes a final deal with the agents before going to prison.

Three years later, at the time of Red's release from prison, bureaucrat Richard Noonan experiences great difficulties in stopping the stalkers' illegal salvage activity, which is, like its official counterpart, increasingly mechanized. Noonan and Dr. Pilman meet at the Borscht, and the conversation between commonsensical bureaucrat and top-notch unorthodox scientist reveals Pilman's belief that the Visitations were quite literally the high-tech equivalent of a group of humans' roadside picnics in a forest clearing, leaving behind their various debris ranging from discarded batteries to windup teddybears, all of which undoubtedly raise a stupid curiosity among the returning animals, who are far too primitive to begin to comprehend the human detritus. Indeed, humans have learned nothing from the alien artifacts in almost four decades of intensive studies. Valentine describes the use made thus far of the alien objects as analogous to using a microscope for a hammer.

Roadside Picnic climaxes with a turn of events slightly reminiscent of the biblical story of Isaac. On his last trip into the Zone, Red plans to sacrifice Burbridge's son Arthur to gain access to the Golden Ball, since the alien wishmachine is guarded by a "meatgrinder." Within sight of the alien artifact, Red has to make his decision. As he has planned all along, he lets Arthur run into the trap and thus opens a passage to the Ball. Red is shamed by the selflessness of Arthur's wishes, uttered seconds before his death, and he decides against his original plans when he shouts "Happiness for everybody, free, and no one will go away unsatisfied!"—which are Arthur's words.

The Characters

Red Schuhart's basic trait is his independence, which derives both from his extraordinary skills as an illegal explorer of the Zone and from his stubbornness. It is this strain of roguish autonomy and heroism in the face of a larger, constricting world which places Red in a long tradition ranging from the wandering hero of the Spanish picaresque novel in the Renaissance to the modern Jewish schlemiel. It is not difficult to see the Soviet reality behind the protagonist's struggles with his bureaucratic and formalistic environment.

Nevertheless, Red's independence is portrayed as being problematic. On the one hand, Red's special abilities award him the privilege of carrying out his naturally idealistic ethical behavior. Thus, in defiance of the regulations of authority, Red is able to bring up his mutant daughter, Monkey, and keep at his table the mute corpse of his father, which the forces of the Zone have strangely reconstructed. Red's individualism also has its bad side. Because he is accustomed to working alone, he fails to warn Kirill about the alien web which when he accidentally touches it causes the scientist's death. In his deal with the agents of the state, Red agrees against his better instincts to trade, for his family's sake, a small and well-secured portion of witches' jelly for dubious military research.

Roadside Picnic's finale is powerful because Red must face the principal problem embodied in his own character. As a loner, Red has decided to use Arthur as his key to personal happiness but has to fight his own better instincts. Throughout his last perilous trip into the Zone, Red tries to use language in order to minimize the moral impact of his murderous plan. He calls the boy "dummy" or "plastic" because he is his father's wished-for product of the Golden Ball, but the novel does not allow this easy way out. In the end, Red has to decide between individual happiness—which would finally elevate him above his life of private opposition to the forces of his bureaucratic, impersonal, and unresponsive society—and the greater common good; it is his choice of the latter that redeems him.

Kirill Panov, Red's Russian employer, is a fine example of the heroic yet deeply troubled human scientist, who has failed to catch even a glimpse of the principles behind the workings of the highly advanced alien technology. The irony of his situation is exemplified by his puzzlement over empty alien magnetic canisters: If he cannot understand even the obvious refuse of the Visitors, what else can be said about the state of human cognizance of the aliens' abilities?

Driven by an honest thirst for knowledge, Kirill represents both the best in human scientific endeavor, when it is undertaken for pure knowledge's sake at high personal cost, and the limit of human ambition. He is such a sympathetic character because of his sincerity and helplessness, two traits which earn for him Red's authentic respect. "Nope, a second Kirill hasn't been born," is Red's answer to Noonan's offer to have him work for "another Russian."

Among the secondary characters, Richard Noonan is given special attention in an in-depth study of a bureaucratic mind. In a finely crafted sarcastic doubling of the novel's title, the stalkers evade Noonan's hunt by disguising their activities with opulently celebrated picnics along a thinly supervised section of the Zone. Because *Roadside Picnic* offers such insight into Noonan's soul, it is also hard to dismiss this character as being entirely contemptible: Too much human material surfaces in him.

The other minor characters are well-chosen, well-drawn members of the community of Harmont, who all obliquely represent some aspects of contemporary Russian life in addition to serving their functions for the story. *Roadside Picnic* is full of intrepid pioneers, laboring scientists, rowdy adventurers, arrogant housing officials, and black marketeers put to use by a suspicious state.

Themes and Meanings

If it is true that science fiction has become the contemporary medium of myths, *Roadside Picnic* tells the age-old tale of a quest for knowledge intertwined with the conflict between individual happiness and responsibility toward the community. Embarking on a futuristic rite of passage, Red ultimately comes to terms with his existence as a societal being in a less-than-ideal community. His encounter with the Golden Ball can be translated as his final voluntary submission to the principle of collective well-being, when he sees that personal happiness is too selfish and too small a wish.

Kirill, the devoted "pure" scientist, fits this mythological pattern, as well as the sage Dr. Pilman, whose wisdom has shown him the limitations of exploration and knowledge but who nevertheless is able to live with the truth. His intellectual position of acceptance and Red's heroic act of self-denial are the answer to what could otherwise be seen as the deep pessimism of *Roadside Picnic*; even though the alien artifacts are mere refuse, humankind will be able to live with this fact and gain new strength out of the wonders of the Zone, which are wrought through the acts of its heroes.

Though the novel is set in the surreal Canadian town of Harmont, complete with Royal Air Force and Royal Tank Units, the atmosphere has a specifically Russian flavor. On one level, then, *Roadside Picnic* becomes a fascinating fable of the relationship between the extraordinary or fantastic and a bureaucratic society trying rigidly to control both exploration and exploitation of a strange and dangerous source of potentially beneficial material.

Critical Context

Roadside Picnic comes at a second turning point in the writing career of Arkady and Boris Strugatsky, who started out writing fairly conventional science fiction in the 1950's and early 1960's. Their work of that era, as it is collected in the anthology *Putna Amalteiu* (1960; *Destination Amalthea*, 1962), resembles such classic American science-fiction stories as Robert A. Heinlein's "juvenile" novels or Isaac Asimov's *The Foundation Trilogy* (1951-1953), which tell about man's future conflicts among the stars while keeping intact the beliefs of the ideology of the writer's home country.

When Soviet censorship became less stringent in the 1960's, the Strugatsky's tales turned darker and began to explore such hitherto taboo topics as the conflict between utopia and twentieth century experience. At the end of that cycle came *Ulitka na sklone* (1966-1968; *The Snail on the Slope*, 1980), a caustic satire on Soviet bureaucracy, which is also one of the most humorous pieces of science fiction yet written. With *Roadside Picnic*, however, the Strugatskys turn back to a more classical approach to science fiction, and their vision, although still bitter at times, becomes ultimately more gentle, as the hero is allowed a final moment of redemption, and absolute humanitarian values triumph, as they should, over petty bureaucracy and all-too-human limitations.

As a science-fiction novel, *Roadside Picnic* convinces because of its masterfully drawn technological background, out of which the larger intellectual questions organically arise. The Strugatskys' novel is a welcome presentation of the fundamental conflict between individualism and commitment to a higher societal good, which can demand the sacrifice of personal happiness; this intellectual content is convincingly built into the depiction of the protagonist and his environment, which have a definite taste of human reality. The novel served as the basis for Andrey Tarkovsky's much-praised film, *Stalker* (1981).

Sources for Further Study

Griffiths, John. "Retreat from Reality," in *Three Tomorrows: American, British, and Soviet Science Fiction*, 1980.

Le Guin, Ursula K. "A New Book by the Strugatskys," in *Science Fiction Studies*. IV (July, 1977), pp. 157-159.

Lem, Stanisław. "About the Strugatskys' *Roadside Picnic*," in *Microworlds: Writings on Science Fiction and Fantasy*, 1984.

Zebrowsky, George. "*Roadside Picnic* and *Tale of the Troika*," in *The Magazine of Fantasy and Science Fiction*. LVII (July, 1979), pp. 33-35.

Reinhart Lutz

ROSSHALDE

Author: Hermann Hesse (1877-1962)
Type of plot: Künstlerroman
Time of plot: The early 1900's
Locale: A manor house near Berne, Switzerland
First published: 1914 (English translation, 1970)

> *Principal characters:*
> JOHANN VERAGUTH, a famous painter
> ADELE VERAGUTH, his estranged wife
> PIERRE, his seven-year-old son
> ALBERT, his grown son
> OTTO BURKHARDT, his friend, a Malayan planter

The Novel

   Rosshalde is the story of an unhappy marriage, perhaps Hermann Hesse's own unhappy marriage. Written after his return from India, it may depict the incompatibility between him and his wife that led to his trip to the East in the first place. The manor house, Rosshalde, is based on the house of a deceased painter which the Hesses rented in 1912 just outside Berne. Adele Veraguth is patterned after Hesse's own wife, Maria. Yet the novel is more than an autobiographical fiction; it is also a thesis novel which argues that the artist is not suited for marriage, for his necessarily detached role as an observer and recorder of life renders him incapable of the kind of intimacy that marriage requires.

   Rosshalde is an account of a brief period in the life of a famous painter, Johann Veraguth, who because of incompatibility with his wife lives in a bachelor's studio on the grounds of his manor house. His wife, Adele, and their seven-year-old son, Pierre, the darling of both parents and the only link between them, live in the main house. Their older son, Albert, has been sent away to boarding school.

   Although Veraguth has been living apart from his wife for several years, this situation, which has become increasingly intolerable to him, comes to a head in the novel as a result of two factors: Albert, who is devoted solely to his mother and who hates his father, returns from school and Veraguth's old friend Otto Burkhardt arrives from his plantation home in India. Veraguth's awareness of the intensity of Albert's hatred for him and Burkhardt's efforts to convince Veraguth to come back with him to the East make Veraguth's dissatisfaction with his current situation more intolerable. It is little Pierre, however, who has kept Veraguth from leaving before.

   Veraguth tells Burkhardt that he is living among ruins and that Pierre is all that he has, to which Burkhardt argues that Veraguth has been living among dead things too long and has lost his contact with life. In his torment over trying to decide about leaving Pierre, Veraguth creates a large painting which reflects his situation; it depicts a man and a woman self-immersed and alien to each other and a child playing tranquilly between them. Burkhardt's invitation for Veraguth to return to India with him torments Veraguth, for although he feels his joyless existence coming to an end, he fears the loss of the boy.

This conflict intensifies when Pierre becomes mysteriously ill. Yet, in spite of Pierre's illness, Veraguth is primarily dominated by his sense that his life is driving toward the future and freedom for the first time in years. While Veraguth believes that he can begin living again, the prognosis for the boy is just the opposite; his sensitivity to sounds and smells leads the doctor to diagnose his illness as meningitis and to warn the parents that he does not have long to live.

Veraguth's first reaction to this news is despair, but then a new thought occurs to him—that the boy's death will be his ultimate suffering, that after his death nothing else will remain to bind him or hurt him, and that he will go forward with no peace and inertia but with a kind of all-consuming creative joy. Thus, when his wife promises him that if Pierre lives, then Veraguth may keep Pierre with him, the painter finds it absurd that the child should be his at the moment when he is doomed to die.

At the novel's conclusion when, after prolonged agony, the boy does die, Veraguth believes that he has never loved as much as he had during the boy's last days. Only his art remains for him now. Thus, Veraguth has the consolation of an outsider with the paradoxically barren yet fruitful passion to observe and to create. The residue of his existence will be the cold and lonely delight of art, which he will follow for the rest of his life without detour.

The Characters

The focus throughout the novel is on Veraguth; it is his psychological state in which Hesse is most interested. Veraguth, however, is not presented as a complex, multifaceted character. Rather, he is the artist *par excellence*—at least as Hesse sees the artist. Although Veraguth tells Burkhardt that Adele was never what he wanted from a wife, that she was too solemn and heavy rather than lively, it becomes clear that Veraguth's artistic temperament makes him singularly unsuitable for the intimacy that marriage requires. Burkhardt realizes that the dark springs of Veraguth's art are his inner loneliness and self-torment; it is this which constitutes the source of his power to create as well as the source of the strange sadness which one often sees in great works of art.

The fact that Veraguth can so easily accept the imminent death of his beloved son is one of the indications of the thesis-bound nature of this novel. Indeed, Veraguth senses as soon as the boy becomes ill that he must die, that his death will be that which will finally release him from any human involvement and will leave him free to be the observer and the creator only. His love for Pierre will now become fuel for his art. If Veraguth were presented as a complex and multifaceted human being in a realistic novel, rather than an embodiment of Hesse's views of the artist's relationship to life in what is basically the illustration of an aesthetic idea, then such a cold and fatalistic attitude would seem unbelievable.

Adele and Albert are closely aligned with each other. Although both are musicians, they are aloof and detached. Albert is filled with hatred for his father, although the novel never makes it clear why he hates him so much. Adele is overly possessive of her children and formal and reserved with her husband.

Although Veraguth is the central psychological focus of the novel, Pierre is also presented as a complex character, particularly after he becomes ill. His complexity, however, is more a result of his function as a symbolic figure who must be sacrificed for the sake of his father's art than of his inner psychological self. The illness makes him look prematurely aged, and indeed he seems preternaturally wise in the sense that he knows that his death and his father's departure will occur simultaneously. The other primary symptom of the disease—his sensitivity to smells and sounds, in short his inability to bear any input to the five senses—suggests a parallel to his father's life as an artist, for the father also cuts himself off from any real contact with the external world.

All the characters in the novel, therefore, seem primarily governed by the role they must play in the freeing of Veraguth from involvement with the world so that he may fulfill his life as an artist. They do not seem to exist in their own right; they exist as figures in a fable. Such an approach gives the novel a quality of simplicity and starkness that renders all the characters (with the exception of the victim Pierre) unsympathetic.

Themes and Meanings

On one level, *Rosshalde* is a domestic tragedy about incompatibility in which, inevitably, the children must pay the price. Albert's bitter hatred and coldness and Pierre's death are the emblems of guilt in a marriage that, for no specific reason, simply did not work.

This domestic drama, however, is merely a vehicle for Hesse's principal theme. Whether as self-justification for his artistic preoccupation or as genuine philosophic truth about what is demanded of the artist, Hesse's view that the artist must wrench himself free from marriage, family, and all other bourgeois attachments and give himself completely to his art is the obsessive message of the book. When Veraguth is offered the chance of escape to the East, he feels the surge of a torrent of unconscious and instinctual forces which have long been suppressed.

Although much of the work is filled with Veraguth's proclaimed love for

Pierre, Veraguth seldom seems to have time for the boy except for an absentminded pat on the head when the child comes to his studio. Much more of the novel is filled with what Hesse calls the "bitter joy" of the creator who can find the happiness of freedom only within an iron discipline and can only find fulfillment through an ascetic obedience to his artistic sense of truth. Although he believes that he has bungled his attempts at love and life, Veraguth also believes that he has almost succeeded in giving his art the richness his life has lost. The irony of the artist's position in the novel is that it is precisely through his anguish that he is able to create his finest work.

It is just this realization, however, that makes Pierre's death all the more poignant, for he seems the necessary sacrifice which will not only free Veraguth but also create the great sorrow which he will transform into a painting. In this sense, Pierre seems little more than a puppet who exists only to be immolated on the altar of art. When the child is dying, Veraguth feels the suffering burn in his heart with a "dark delight" that, even as it is unbearable, is pure and great. After the boy dies, Veraguth's final act is to sketch the dead child's features.

The theme of the novel is a relatively pure and simple one: The artist must stay removed from life, for every aspect of the artist's life exists for him only as subject matter and stimulus for his art. Thus, the true artist lives only within his art, for there is nothing for him; even those external elements of "real life" are either transformed by him into art or treated by him as if they were the elements of art.

Critical Context

Rosshalde marked a turning point in the Hesse canon, for in it he signaled his own freedom from efforts to divide himself between bourgeois family life and the demands of his work. After he returned from India, Hesse knew that his married life could last no longer; *Rosshalde* was written to exorcise that particular demon. Most critics find it to be one of the best of his prewar novels; it is certainly one of the most realistic and most structurally tight of his novels. Some critics find it to be the work of a playwright, because of the dramatic unities of time, place, and character that it embodies. The plot line is classically and tragically simple in its inevitability. Most of the story is carried by dialogue, with a minimum of description of the external world. In its straightforward style and the simplicity of its basic situation, it lacks the mysticism that made such Hesse works as *Demian* (1919; English translation, 1923) so widely popular in the 1960's in the United States.

The general critical opinion of the novel is that while it is the work of a consummate craftsman, it does not match the penetrating psychological portraits of such masterpieces as *Siddhartha* (1922; English translation, 1951) and *Der Steppenwolf* (1927; *Steppenwolf*, 1929). It is also inferior to his great *Künstlerroman*, *Narziss und Goldmund* (1930; *Death and the Lover*, 1932;

also as *Narcissus and Goldmund*, 1968). Consequently, although *Rosshalde* has an important place in the artistic career of Hermann Hesse, it lacks both the stylistic facility and the mystic profundity of the later works which made him one of the most widely read German authors of the twentieth century.

Sources for Further Study

Boulby, Mark. *Hermann Hesse: His Mind and Art*, 1967.
Field, George Wallis. *Hermann Hesse*, 1970.
Mileck, Joseph. *Hermann Hesse: Life and Art*, 1978.
Sorell, Walter. *Hermann Hesse: The Man Who Sought and Found Himself*, 1974.
Ziolkowski, Theodore. *The Novels of Hermann Hesse: A Study in Theme and Structure*, 1965.

Charles E. May

THE ROYAL WAY

Author: André Malraux (1901-1976)
Type of plot: Adventure
Time of plot: The early 1920's
Locale: French Somaliland, French Indochina, and Siam
First published: La Voie royale, 1930 (English translation, 1935)

> *Principal characters:*
> CLAUDE VANNEC, a French archaeologist sent on a mission by
> his government
> PERKEN, his friend, a Dutch adventurer
> GRABOT, Perken's former comrade and a deserter from the
> army

The Novel

The title of the novel refers to the route which links the ancient Cambodian city of Angkor and the lake region with the Me Nan river basin in central Siam. Claude Vannec, a young French archaeologist sent on a mission by his government, is drawn to the exploration of this route by a dual desire: to examine the archaeological treasures to be found along it and to profit from the sale of his discoveries. When he meets, in a Djibouti brothel, a Dutch adventurer by the name of Perken and later travels with him by ship to Singapore, Claude becomes convinced that he has found, in this older man, the ideal companion for his venture. Perken is a person around whom a legend has developed, because he has begun to create a kingdom in unpacified Laos. He views Claude's mission as a means of securing money for the purchase of machine guns in order to pursue his objective. Admiring Perken's scorn for convention and love of action, which reminds him of his revered grandfather's outlook on life, Claude discovers that he himself shares with Perken an obsession with death—not as a negative motivation but as a stimulus for savoring the exaltation of life.

Taking leave of Perken in Singapore, after having arranged to meet him later in Phnom Penh in order to organize their expedition, Claude continues on to the French Institute in Saigon and to the bungalow of the Deputy Resident in Siem-Reap to seek assistance for his undertaking. Both the director of the French Institute, Albert Ramèges, and the Deputy Resident try to dissuade Claude from making the trip into the jungle.

Undeterred, Claude and Perken set out on their adventure. Their party includes a guide; a male servant called Xa; and Svay, a Cambodian. The latter has been sent by the Deputy Resident ostensibly to recruit drivers for the carts which are to transport the archaeological treasures but his real assignment is to spy on the expedition. Perken's plan is to accompany Claude to the

Royal Way and then to make a detour through the unpacified area nearby where a former comrade of his, Grabot, is reported to have disappeared. Battling the heat and the oppressive plant and animal life of the jungle, the adventurers reach the Royal Way and eventually come upon the coveted sculptures, managing to load them on their carts.

During the night, however, their guide, Svay, and the cart drivers abandon them. Getting a new guide locally, but now having to drive the carts themselves, Perken, Claude, and Xa press on, with Perken still determined to find Grabot. A deserter from the army, Grabot had also sought to escape from the conformism of European life, expecting to realize in Asia his sexual fantasies and dreams of political power. Because the new guide is unfamiliar with the itinerary that the expedition had planned to follow, in order to reach Grabot the party must now traverse territory inhabited by the hostile Stieng tribes.

With the help of a Cambodian slave, Claude and Perken find Grabot in the hut of a Stieng village. Grabot has been blinded by his captors and is nothing but a slave himself, attached to a mill wheel that he circles like a beast of burden. Threatened by the tribesmen, who surround them, Claude and Perken nevertheless succeed in negotiating for their freedom and Grabot's, but in the process, Perken is wounded in the leg by a Stieng weapon: a bamboo splinter. From a Siamese town, Perken sends a telegram to the Siamese government reporting his encounter with the Stiengs. By now his wound, aggravated by the additional travel, has become infected, and his condition is diagnosed as hopeless.

Despite Perken's physical state, the expedition heads for Laos, which Perken considers to be "his" country, since he enjoys enormous political influence there. Claude has abandoned the sculptures in order to go with him. They reach a Laotian village, where Perken hopes to receive the assistance of Savan, a local chief. At the same time, the Stiengs are attempting to invest the village, aware that Perken is there. After having released Grabot, who was sent on to a Bangkok hospital, the tribesmen have been chased from their village and pursued by the soldiers dispatched in response to Perken's telegram. Perken sadly suspects that the punitive Siamese action may have an ulterior motive: to occupy militarily the whole of the unpacified region. Savan arrives for the meeting with Perken, but two Laotians who accompany him suddenly aim their rifles at Perken, blaming him for the presence of the Stiengs. Perken shoots first and kills them. He senses Savan's indifference, however, and notices that the chief, like Claude, looks at him as if he were already dead.

Claude and Perken set out for the mountains of northern Laos, whose chiefs Perken believes to be more loyal to him than is Savan. Close to death, Perken meditates on the solitude of dying and the need to make death a lucid individual experience. Even as Claude contemplates with compassion the agony of his friend, the Frenchman is permeated by a sense of his own ardent attachment to life. As Perken dies, Claude, in a desperate fraternal gesture, puts his arms around him, but Perken looks at Claude as if he were a being from another world.

The Characters

Claude presents an autobiographical dimension. André Malraux had led his own expedition into the Cambodian jungle in 1923 and made his way to the ruins of the Banteay-Srei temple, the removal of whose sculptures caused him to be arrested and put on trial by the colonial administration. Like Claude, Malraux had a grandfather whom he admired, and for some of the same reasons. Claude's characterization is nevertheless enriched beyond this autobiographical element. He, like Perken, is typical of the intellectual characters created by Malraux whose desire for adventure and revolt against convention are to be appreciated best on the metaphysical level. Their goal is to control their destiny, to pit successfully their will and determination against the order of the world. In contrast to Perken, however, Claude is the young, inexperienced beginner. As such, his role in the novel is often to stand as an admiring witness to Perken's actions.

That Claude's commitment to his friendship for Perken is sincere becomes evident when he agrees to journey with the fatally wounded man to Laos, although doing so means abandoning his precious sculptures. Yet Claude is destined to discover, at the end of his adventure, the tragic limits of fraternity. Once the hopelessness of Perken's condition is confirmed, the latter seems to read in Claude's look, despite their profound friendship, only the certainty of his own death. The conclusion of the novel only emphasizes the irreducible solitude of death: For the dying Perken, Claude is no longer a friend but simply a witness—and worse, a stranger.

Perken is by no means the ordinary adventurer, however worldly his grandiose political ambitions may be. His main concern is to live—and die—with absolute lucidity and, to the fullest extent possible, in response to the dictates of his own sense of the meaning of human existence. Nevertheless, once he senses that his death is imminent, Perken's concern becomes narrowly circumscribed: how to die with dignity, rebelling to the very end against the idea of death as something imposed from without, something issuing from an external order of things. Perken is fighting against insuperable odds, however, as his progressive physical deterioration makes him more and more the prisoner of his own body, undermining, at the same time, his intellectual communion with Claude. About to die, Perken strives desperately to affirm the autonomy of his individual consciousness. In his last words, he struggles to mark a forceful distinction between death as an abstraction and his personal, lucid experience of it: "There is . . . no death. There's only . . . I who . . . am dying." Given the tragic inevitability of Perken's death, these words do not register any real triumph.

Grabot's fate symbolizes a possible, extreme consequence of Perken's notion of political power gone awry. Though only briefly present before the reader, Grabot is more fully developed as a character through Perken's stories about him. To demonstrate Grabot's vengeful resolve, for example, Perken relates how the man deliberately infected and lost an eye merely to ruin an army doctor who had refused him sick leave.

Several of the minor characters in *The Royal Way* owe their vivid portrayal to their autobiographical source. Ramèges and the Deputy Resident derive their bureaucratic stuffiness from Malraux's personal contact with such colonial officials. In his own expedition, Malraux actually had a servant whose name was Xa.

Themes and Meanings

Malraux's preoccupation with man's fate in *The Royal Way*, as indicated by his characters' attempts to define meaningful human action and by the author's treatment of the themes of fraternity and death, gives the novel a depth lacking in the usual adventure story. An additional, unifying theme, characteristic of virtually all Malraux's writings, is the basic question of human communication. This theme is most strikingly illustrated in the case of Grabot, the most horrible aspect of whose degradation is his inability to communicate. Yet difficulty in communication is also evident between the whites and the native population. Here the problem stems not only from political tension but also from barriers that are at once linguistic, social, and psychological. Finally, even between Claude and Perken, friendship notwithstanding, communication is far from easy. Neither man is capable of fully expressing his thoughts on such complex matters as human destiny and death; at the end, because of Perken's illness, Claude can be neither a companion nor an interlocutor for him.

Since he wishes to focus on the human condition, Malraux's narrative technique is less concerned with highly individualizing the novel's main characters and displaying their complicated psychology than it is with underscoring their common revolt against the absurdity of human existence. Thus, instead of an omniscient narrator who explains these characters thoroughly and ensures the clarity of the plot development, Malraux creates a narrator who takes as his own in turn the respective points of view of Claude and Perken. The consequence of this method is twofold: an obligation on the reader's part to "fill in the gaps" and a subjective process of narration related to the characters' physical and psychological reactions. The reader knows, for example, that the moment of Perken's death is approaching not from any precise indication of the passage of time—the novel shuns dates or the chronicling of objective time—but from the fact that his leg has become so terribly swollen. Similarly, since Claude and Perken see the jungle primarily as an anarchic formlessness, it emerges symbolically as an obstacle to their determination to impose their own sense of order and coherence on external nature.

Critical Context

Appearing two years after Malraux's novel, *Les Conquérants* (1928, 1949; *The Conquerors*, 1929, 1956), a work also dealing with the tragic destiny of the European adventurer in Asia, *The Royal Way* belongs to the early phase of the novelist's career. Its will-to-power motifs and pessimism reflect both the particular influence of Friedrich Nietzsche, an author much admired by the young Malraux, and the general impact of World War I, which shook the spiritual and intellectual, as well as the social and political, foundations of Europe. Initially regarded by many critics as an inferior work, *The Royal Way* was subsequently appreciated for its merits—thanks to a more general acceptance of nonlinear but thematically and metaphorically coherent plot structures. Another factor contributing to this shift of critical opinion was the realization that Malraux's novels have only one plot: man's fate.

Later novels, such as his masterpiece, *La Condition humaine* (1933; *Man's Fate*, 1934; also as *Storm in Shanghai*), and *L'Espoir* (1937; *Days of Hope*, 1938; also as *Man's Hope*), sounded at times a more positive note, as Malraux dispensed with the adventurer and linked the actions of his heroes to the more laudable and tangible goals of political revolution against tyrannical regimes. Yet, to a considerable degree, these other works merely embroidered on the novelist's fundamental themes and stylistic devices as revealed in *The Royal Way*. Even their optimistic aspects were related in part to a strain of hope already marginally present in *The Royal Way*, the strain of hope implicit in the fact that Claude does survive the physical and metaphysical endurance tests of his jungle adventure.

Sources for Further Study

Blend, Charles. *André Malraux: Tragic Humanist*, 1963.
Fallaize, Elizabeth. *Malraux: La Voie royale*, 1982.
Frohock, Wilbur M. *André Malraux and the Tragic Imagination*, 1952.
Greenlee, James W. *Malraux's Heroes and History*, 1975.
Kline, Thomas Jefferson. *André Malraux and the Metamorphosis of Death*, 1973.

Norman Araujo

RUDIN

Author: Ivan Turgenev (1818-1883)
Type of plot: Psychological realism
Time of plot: The 1840's
Locale: A provincial estate in Russia
First published: 1856 (*Dimitri Roudine*, 1873; better known as *Rudin*)

> *Principal characters:*
> DMITRI RUDIN, an impoverished nobleman and progressive
>   thinker, about thirty-five years old
> NATALIA LASUNSKAIA, a young girl of marriageable age
> DARIA LASUNSKAIA, the mother of Natalia, a noblewoman
>   and leader of local society
> MIKHAILO LEZHNIOV, a local landowner and former classmate
>   of Rudin

The Novel

Ivan Turgenev commences his novel with an introduction to local society in a provincial backwater. Several scenes are presented with the sole purpose of introducing the reader to the various characters of the novel and the type of life they lead, isolated from the intellectual currents of the cities and fellow members of the nobility. Daria Lasunskaia is the center of social life in the area; her favor or disfavor determines one's position in society. She rules her household with the same heavy hand; her daughter is being reared very strictly at home, under the guidance of Daria and a prissy French governess. Natalia Lasunskaia, however, has a mind of her own; she reads current tracts about philosophy and social issues and seems ready to revolt against her narrow upbringing. Mikhailo Lezhniov is a neighboring landowner, as yet unmarried, and a university graduate who also loves working the land. He is an honest, direct person who does not like society life, especially the constricted sort found at Daria's estate. A number of minor local personages are introduced in the initial scenes: unmarried women, eccentric bachelors, tutors, and hangers-on. The picture presented is not flattering; life in the Russian provinces is boring, shaped by social constraints. The almost daily gatherings at Daria's are oppressive but represent the only social intercourse available to the local gentry.

Into this stagnant world appears Dmitri Rudin, ostensibly on business, but actually a vagabond who travels about from estate to estate until his hosts tire of him. Rudin is an idealistic radical whose stock-in-trade is witty conversation, full of social commentary and philosophical observation. The local gentry is electrified by his presence, which breathes life into their gatherings. Daria is amused by his wittiness, Natalia reveres him as an idealist and begins to fall in love with him, and other members of the circle react favorably to him as a breath of fresh air. The minority opinion is represented by one local landowner who resents not being the wittiest member of the circle any longer, and by Mikhailo Lezhniov, who remembers Rudin from university days. In fact, Rudin is intelligent and witty; he is superior to most of the local nobility, but his comments are delivered with gentleness and wit in order not to offend. Lezhniov does not explain his lack of interest in Rudin to his neighbors, and Rudin continues to dazzle the members of Daria's social circle. In a real sense, he is earning his keep by doing so; as long as he is viewed as a welcome addition to society and keeps its members amused and entertained, he will be supported by Daria, at whose home he is staying.

This situation begins to unravel as Natalia falls in love with Rudin. Rudin has recognized in her a desire for learning and freedom and is flattered by her attention. He encourages not only the infatuation but also her desire to revolt against her narrow intellectual training in the provinces and against the social mores of the nobility. With his apparent approval, Natalia declares her love to Rudin, stating that she is ready to run away with him and endure whatever fate has in store for them in their search for truth and freedom. At this point Rudin loses courage and delivers a homily on resignation to fate; since Daria will not allow the marriage, he cannot put Natalia in such an uncomfortable position. Despite Rudin's protestations, Natalia begins to see what Lezhniov has known all along: Rudin cannot act on his principles. Though Rudin insists that he does not want to hurt Natalia by making her act against the wishes of her mother, the girl correctly realizes that the prospect of action terrifies Rudin. While he excoriates Russian society and preaches revolt against social conventions in the name of freedom and honesty, he himself cannot do so. Instead, when faced with the possibility of real love and of turning theory into practice, Rudin preaches resignation. Natalia points out his weakness to him, which he realizes after halfhearted protestations.

With this turn of events, Rudin has worn out his welcome and leaves Daria's estate. As the affair becomes known, Lezhniov explains to his curious neighbors the background of his relationship with Rudin, and life returns to normal in the countryside. After a hiatus of two years, the author presents a glance at the local gentry. Lezhniov has married happily and is the father of a child, Natalia is about to be married to a local landowner with the consent of her mother, and the news is brought that Rudin has moved from family to family, alienating each in its turn.

At this point the author seems to have second thoughts about leaving Rudin in such a predicament. An epilogue is attached in which Lezhniov, traveling on business, meets Rudin in a hotel. Rudin has gone to seed and Lezhniov, feeling sorry for the indigent philosopher, invites him to dinner for old times' sake. The conversation is frank, as Rudin admits to his character defects, but Lezhniov also remembers the idealistic young man in Rudin who, for some reason, was unable to mature into a man of action. At the very end of the story the reader is informed that, in fact, at the end of his life Rudin did put his theories into practice by joining in the Paris revolt of 1848 and dying on the barricades for freedom.

The Characters

Dmitri Rudin, after whom the novel is titled, is the central character of the novel. Turgenev, one of the most renowned novelists produced by Russia, was not above using an old technique to emphasize the importance of the main character. Rudin is the dynamic outsider who intrudes upon the closed society of the countryside and produces a stir; he dominates conversation, provokes commentary on his origins and opinions, and steals the heart of a beautiful, thoughtful young girl. In his wake not much has changed; only Natalia seems to have learned a valuable lesson about human nature. After Rudin's departure, life returns to normal. A person such as Rudin leaves no permanent imprint upon people except memories, both positive and negative.

Daria and Natalia, on the other hand, are people of action. Daria is domineering, but she is also responsible for a large estate, rears her daughter without assistance, and acts immediately when the need arises. Her daughter has inherited this trait; when Natalia is enthralled by Rudin's ideas, she wants to begin to put them into practice. For some reason Turgenev sprinkles his novels with such women, while the men in his novels tend to be ineffective or shallow.

Lezhniov is an exception to the typically weak male character in Turgenev's fiction. He is almost an ideal character; he combines love of the land and hard work with respect for intellectual labor, seems to be an extremely stable person, and is an embodiment of the virtues of decency and honesty. His last visit with Rudin in the hotel symbolizes what Turgenev believed was the correct attitude toward Rudin: respect for his idealism and intellect, but criticism of his inability to do anything practical. While maintaining one's ideals, Turgenev suggests, one must be prepared to accommodate the demands of reality.

Themes and Meanings

During the 1850's Turgenev wrote a series of novels and tales which dealt with social themes, a common practice in Russian literature. Turgenev was a progressive liberal in his political and social opinions; he distrusted revolutionaries and reactionaries alike and preferred the path of reform to radical change. He also had a large dose of common sense about human nature and heaped scorn upon theories which seemed to be unrealistic and theoreticians who seemed removed from reality.

In *Rudin* the author deals with such a theoretician. Rudin preaches theories which lead to an almost utopian society but which are impossible to put into practice. The generation of idealists represented by Rudin wants radical change, but Turgenev believed that actual change could be achieved only in small increments. His belief was based upon two factors: First, the inherent conservatism of human nature resists change unless it comes about in moderate doses; second, large-scale radical change requires such an effort that most people are unable to effect such change. In *Rudin* both factors are at work: While Rudin can dazzle local society, his ideas are not really accepted except by Natalia and one minor character, the tutor Basistov. Further, the changes envisioned are so fundamentally different from the existing social order that even Rudin cannot act upon them. Thus the necessity of reforming the social order must be trimmed down to fit human capacities.

Turgenev also seems to be taking aim at German Idealist philosophy, which was popular among Russian intellectual circles at that time. Turgenev disliked theories which elevate the rational aspect of the human being and downgrade the nonrational aspects, such as the emotions and the will. In Turgenev's view, the entire human being has to be taken into consideration when planning change. In Rudin's case, the absence of willpower is evident; all of his energy goes into thinking about theories of change which are not based upon reality, and reality defeats him. If rational processes are not based upon reality, they lead nowhere.

Critical Context

During his youth Turgenev was heavily influenced by German romantic idealism. In *Rudin*, the first of the author's novels after a successful career as a writer of short stories, the central character is a typical romantic idealist. Turgenev seems to be engaging in self-criticism as he portrays Rudin to be a failure; that period of life is over, and the author repudiates his earlier views. By softening the portrait toward the end of the novel, perhaps the author demonstrates a lingering fondness for the character of the romantic idealist, if not for the ideas.

Turgenev may also be reacting to a heightened sense of Russian nationalism resulting from the Crimean War. When Lezhniov states that Rudin is not really malicious but rather a victim of his time who does not understand Russia, he seems to be rejecting a cosmopolitan sense toward which Turgenev is sympathetic in ordinary circumstances, and to which he returned in later life. In this sense, Rudin may represent an atypical period of the author's life.

Rudin is considered to be one of Turgenev's best short novels. In a sense it serves as a dry run for his later works, in which he dealt with the question of reform versus revolution. *Rudin* is one of the many works which Turgenev wrote about social and political issues during the 1850's, and the writer is given credit by historians for being influential upon the process of reform in Russia. Turgenev continues the tradition, begun by Alexander Pushkin, of portraying strong heroines who are disappointed by weaker men. Perhaps Turgenev's most lasting contribution is his ability to re-create life in the Russian countryside, exposing both its negative and positive aspects.

Sources for Further Study

Dessaix, Robert. *Turgenev: The Quest for Faith*, 1980.

Freeborn, Richard. *Turgenev: The Novelist's Novelist*, 1960.

Matlaw, Ralph. "Turgenev's Novels: Civic Responsibility and Literary Predilection," in *Harvard Slavic Studies*. IV (1957), pp. 249-262.

Pritchett, V. S. *The Gentle Barbarian: The Life and Work of Turgenev*, 1977.

Ripp, Victor. *Turgenev's Russia: From "Notes of a Hunter" to "Fathers and Sons,"* 1980.

Schapiro, Leonard. *Turgenev: His Life and Times*, 1979.

Philip Maloney

THE RUINED MAP

Author: Kōbō Abe (1924-   )
Type of plot: Mystery
Time of plot: 1967
Locale: An unnamed Japanese metropolis
First published: Moetsukita chizu, 1967 (English translation, 1969)

> *Principal characters:*
> THE NARRATOR, an unnamed private detective who specializes
>   in the investigation of missing persons
> NEMURO HIROSHI, a fuel dealer who is missing throughout the
>   novel
> NEMURO HARU, the wife of Nemuro Hiroshi
> THE BROTHER, the unnamed brother of Nemuro Hiroshi, who
>   is apparently involved in racketeering
> TASHIRO, a fellow employee of Nemuro Hiroshi
> THE CHIEF, the narrator's boss

The Novel

On the surface, *The Ruined Map* might be seen as a Japanese version of the American "hard-boiled" detective novel such as those authored by Dashiell Hammett and Raymond Chandler. Like Chandler's Marlowe or Hammett's Spade, the protagonist of Kōbō Abe's novel appears to be, in the beginning of the novel, a tough, smart, naturalistic survivor of the city's "mean streets" whose task it is to negotiate unfeelingly the labyrinth of crossed paths, conspiracies, and conflicted emotions that typify the genre. Yet, very soon, the reader of *The Ruined Map* notices that Abe's investigator is enormously sensitive to the details of the chaotic physical environment of a large, expanding city and obsessed with mapping its intricacies. The occasion for the narrator's activities in this regard is his employment by a young married woman, Nemuro Haru, who asks the narrator to find her husband, now missing for six months. The wife provides the investigator with little information about the details of or motivations behind her husband's disappearance: a book of matches, a photograph, a worn raincoat, and the fact that he vanished only hundreds of yards from his house while on the way to a meeting with his colleague, Tashiro. The narrator is immediately suspicious. Why has Nemuro Haru taken so long to seek the assistance of a private detective? Why does she provide so little information about her husband, his life-style, and his personality? The narrator's suspicions are increased when he learns that the missing man's brother has been "on the case" since the disappearance and has discovered nothing. The narrator wonders who this mysterious brother is, what he does for a living, and what his involvement might be with

Nemuro Hiroshi's disappearance—to the extent that he begins to doubt the brother's identity. Has the wife convinced someone (a lover? an enemy of her husband?) to pose as her brother-in-law in order to confuse the detective? What would be her motivation in doing so? Such enigmas, with their endless solutions, fill the pages of Abe's novel.

With little to go on, the narrator begins to investigate: He visits the restaurant whose name and telephone number appear on the matchbook; he goes to the wholesale fuel house where the missing man last worked; he "runs into" (clearly, not coincidentally) the mysterious brother; he frequently visits the mysteriously complacent wife; he meets with Tashiro, the man whom Nemuro Hiroshi was supposed to meet in a subway station before he disappeared.

As he proceeds in his investigation, the information begins to flood in and the narrator begins to formulate a number of theories about the disappearance. Perhaps, he thinks, the two brothers were working together on a corrupt business venture involving the sale of propane gas to new developers in the city when something went wrong, making it necessary for one brother to dispose of the other. Perhaps the missing man's penchant for nude photographs and his brother's involvement in a homosexual prostitution ring indicate that either a sex crime or connections with the city's underworld are responsible for the disappearance. On the other hand, it might be that the wife and the brother conspired to kill the husband, then hired a private investigator as a "cover." Tashiro has a packet of nude photographs which he says he was to give to Nemuro Hiroshi at their last meeting: Are these pictures (all of them shot from a peculiar angle so that the woman's face cannot be seen) of a prostitute, as Tashiro at first claims them to be, or are they pictures of the investigator's client, and how are they connected to the disappearance?

The crossed purposes revealed by theories about the disappearance are further complicated by the narrator's extraordinary perceptual awareness of the physical world to the extent that there is, in the novel, a continual sensory overload of information. At the same time, he is gifted or cursed with what might be called a "hypothetical imagination," a tendency to create in his mind multiple explanations of each event or possibility and to draw these out to their most extreme conclusions. The narrator's overly active imagination, coupled with his exaggerated attention to detail, suggests that Abe provides the reader with a parodic version of Edgar Allan Poe's Dupin, who uses both his empirical and artistic sensibilities to solve crimes. In any case, the narrator is lost in the labyrinth of the city. Ruined or incorrect maps, conflicting fragments of information, and a plethora of visual impressions combine to give the narrator the sense that he is cut adrift in a Borges-like world where the choice of direction seems infinitely open yet constricted by the materiality of the physical world: "One had no idea of the direction governing these walking people, where they came from, where they were going. Perhaps it was because, with the tiled floors and the tiled pillars, all the lines of the passageways and stairs converged here, and anyone could follow the line of his choice."

Yet, despite the confusion, things do "happen" in *The Ruined Map*. When the narrator visits a construction site where the brother, apparently, provides food and prostitutes to the workers, he witnesses the brother's brutal and senseless death at the hands of rival gang members. The investigator ferrets out a possible connection between a city councilman and corruption in the new developments, though he is not able to tie this into the disappearance. He is, at one point, beaten nearly senseless by a group of men in a restaurant (the same one identified on the book of matches) when it becomes clear that he is close to uncovering an illegal transportation ring. As he becomes more deeply implicated in the case, the narrator begins to feel identified with Nemuro Hiroshi, even to the extent of sharing his bed with his wife. Yet none of these events offers a way out of the labyrinth: By the end of the novel, the narrator has resigned his position in the detective agency and has himself, like his predecessor, disappeared into the city, anonymous and amnesiac. Thus, seemingly, the solution to this mystery lies with the assimilation of the detective/narrator's identity into that of the lost man.

The Characters

As is the case with many first-person novels, the only "real" character in the book is the narrator: Everything or everyone else is filtered through the narrator and is thus made a part of his own particular modes of perception and interpretation. The reflexivity of the novel is further complicated by the narrator's own sense of identity, and his merging with the dead or lost Nemuro Hiroshi. With the exception of one sequence, the reader learns very little about the past life or present circumstances of the narrator. He lives alone (he is recently separated from his wife) in a nondescript apartment, and his life is his work. He seems to have no memory or no past. In one scene, the narrator visits his wife at her dressmaker's shop in order to convince her not to divorce him, but even here, in what might be termed one of the most intimate scenes of the novel, the reader learns little of what the narrator's marriage has been like. Instead, externals are presented: details about the appearance of his wife's assistant, the clothes his wife is wearing, the kinds of clothing she makes. In short, the narrated world of *The Ruined Map* is almost wholly externalized, so that the usual attributes of character— emotions, reactions, habitual modes of speech or thought, memories, articulation or enactment of desire—are almost totally lacking. Even the infrequent dialogues between characters seem like tape-recorded transcriptions of what was said rather than the represented speech patterns and gestures of Forsterian, "rounded" characters. Thus, what is seen of the other characters in the novel is filtered through a narrative consciousness incapable of providing the "inward look" that would reveal the personalities, motives, or histories of those involved in the plot of the mystery. For example, after the narrator has made love to Nemuro Haru, she arises, and this description of "the client" is given:

> Somewhere—perhaps in the kitchen—she was humming in a low voice. Since I could hear only the higher tones, I could not tell what the song was. I put on my coat and began walking . . . and she too began to walk . . . when she crossed in front of the lemon-yellow curtains, her face became black, her hair white, and her lips white too, the irises of her eyes became white and the whites black, her freckles became white spots, white like dust that had gathered on the cheekbones of a stone image.

To the narrator, the lover is merely an image, a reversed black-and-white photograph, without depth or dimension. Similarly, for the narrator, the mysterious brother remains nameless: Like the other characters in the novel, he is a function of a plot (or, more often, an antifunction that halts and confuses the ongoing investigation) for which he, partially, bears responsibility, but over which he has no control. In any normative sense, character is absent from *The Ruined Map*.

Themes and Meanings

Perhaps the most revealing tack to take with a novel such as *The Ruined Map* is to see in which ways it parodies certain received themes and genres. Chandler's *The Big Sleep* (1939), for example, portrays a world just as confusing and labyrinthine as that of *The Ruined Map*; moreover, Chandler's detective, like Abe's, seems curiously ineffectual in his attempts to find a solution to the mystery, though there is one provided at the end of the novel. Yet, despite this, Marlowe still acts as a kind of moral agent in a corrupt world: He may not be able to change that world, but neither is he wholly complicit with it. For the narrator of *The Ruined Map*, there is no solution to the mystery; instead, as character or agent, he vanishes into the world of mystery he originally set out to explore, map, and explain. In the end, he is an antidetective as he makes the choice to disappear, rather than to discover himself or the victim of a crime. In terms of genre, Abe has written an "antinovel" which explores and explodes the assumptions of the mystery genre, which assumes either that there is a rational explanation for the world's mysteries or that rationality ("detection") can somehow come to terms with irrational motives and desires, even if it acts only as a moral counteragent to these. Like Alain Robbe-Grillet's *Les Gommes* (1953; *The Erasers*, 1964) or John Hawkes's *The Lime Twig* (1961), *The Ruined Map* posits the notion that rationality, as a way of knowing, is ineffective, and that an understanding of labyrinth or mystery can come only through a descriptive awareness, a phenomenological identification.

Thematically, *The Ruined Map* can be viewed as a naturalistic or existential novel that conveys the plight of the seeker after truth in the modern world of the city. The metropolis of Abe's novel does have its local, Japanese characteristics, but the style of the novel (at least in translation) renders the city virtually anonymous, so that it could be Paris or New York as well as Tokyo. The narrator of *The Ruined Map* is constrained by the prisonlike environment of the city, yet within these constraints, he discovers his freedom, even to disappear, if he wishes. Indeed, "freedom" in the novel, which connotes the liberty to investigate, to scrutinize, and to wander—in short, the freedom of the artist or philosopher—is intimately connected with death. In terms of plot, the narrator seeks truth only to find his own death (the disappearance of his identity); in this light, Abe's statement that "asking a novelist to talk about his writing is like asking him to describe his coffin" takes on a special poignancy. In *The Ruined Map*, the narrator's ability to perceive signs and surfaces—his activity as a *reader*—is clearly linked to his vanishing as a character. Thus, Abe's novel suggests that the search for meaning and the act of interpretation lead not to the portmanteau assertion of the reader/detective's identity, but to his "disappearance" into the externalized world of the novel—this is both his freedom and his fate.

Critical Context

Kōbō Abe is an extraordinarily diverse and prolific writer, and *The Ruined Map* represents both the height of his novelistic career and one of the finest examples of the New Novel, if one extends its presence beyond the borders of France. A graduate of medical school, Abe is a playwright, director, producer, and essayist, as well as a novelist: In 1973, his *Abe Kōbō zensakuhin* (the collected works of Kōbō Abe) ran to fifteen volumes. Other novels of the period of *The Ruined Map*, including *Suna no onna* (1962; *The Woman in the Dunes*, 1964), *Tanin no kao* (1964; *The Face of Another*, 1966), and *Hakootoko* (1973; *The Box Man*, 1974), reflect an ongoing concern with the psychology of the individual in the modern world, where the "self" is viewed as a series of masks or façades, as an organization of surfaces amid the surfaces of a palimpsestic contemporary existence that hides or erases the depths within. The cinematic quality of Abe's novels, which seem to be composed largely of a series of disparate images or "shots" taken from various angles, accords with his presentation of identity projected within acts of perception, rather than through action or the development of character. A superb stylist, Abe—along with other allegorists of the modern condition such as Franz Kafka, Robbe-Grillet, and Hawkes—has made a crucial imaginative contribution to an understanding of how perception and interpretation partially govern the construction of a contemporary reality.

Sources for Further Study

Kimball, Arthur G. *Crisis in Identity and Contemporary Japanese Novels*, 1973.

Montgomery, Scott C. "Reading Japan Through Its Writers: Abe Kōbō and Ōe Kenzaburō, the Problem of Selfhood in Contemporary Japan," in *Book Forum*. VII (1984), pp. 30-31.

Rimer, J. Thomas. *Modern Japanese Fiction and Its Traditions*, 1978.

Williams, Phillip. "Absurdity and Kōbō Abe's Art," in *Journal of the English Institute*. III/IV (1972), pp. 129-143.

Yamamoto, Fumiko. "Metamorphosis in Abe Kōbō's Work," in *Journal of the Association of Teachers of Japanese*. XV (1980), pp. 170-194.

Patrick O'Donnell

RUNAWAY HORSE

Author: Martin Walser (1927-   )
Type of plot: Psychological realism
Time of plot: c. 1978
Locale: A resort town on Lake Constance, Germany
First published: Ein fliehendes Pferd, 1978 (English translation, 1980)

>   *Principal characters:*
>   HELMUT HALM, a middle-aged German schoolteacher
>   SABINA HALM, his wife
>   KLAUS BUCH, a middle-aged German journalist and author
>   HELENE (HELLA) BUCH, his much younger wife

The Novel

   Schoolteacher Helmut Halm is vacationing with his wife, Sabina, as they have for the past eleven summers, in a little town by the water on the German side of Lake Constance. Sunburn, a fondness for food and alcohol, and a lack of exercise do not flatter his forty-six-year-old body or hers. The reader first meets them in a sidewalk café watching the passersby, whose appearance puts him to shame: He has not even managed a decent tan, and sunburn has brought out every wrinkle and blemish in his wife's puffed-up skin. Just as he decides to return to their lonely rented room, a trim, muscular, handsome, bronzed young fellow comes up beside them, accompanied by an equally stunning woman, both stylishly casual in blue jeans. Helmut, with distaste, imagines the man to be one of his former students, but the latter introduces himself, however improbably, as Klaus Buch, Helmut's long-forgotten boyhood companion. Klaus, though Helmut's age, appears a generation younger, thanks to a regimen of jogging, sailboating, health foods, mineral water, and abstinence from drink and tobacco. He and his strikingly lovely younger wife, Helene, obviously revel in their appearance, even as they excite Helmut's envy. Klaus professes great joy at this chance encounter and insists on renewing their friendship, despite reluctance on Helmut's part. In front of both wives, Klaus spins endless tales about their often embarrassingly sexual boyhood adventures. Helmut professes, not very convincingly, to remember virtually none of the details, and he even denies the basic truth of some of the incidents.

   Klaus asks that Helmut and Sabina lead a hike into the nearby mountains, but he sneers at the height that they finally attain: a mere hill. He laughs uproariously and mocks Helmut's inability to keep to the route, a failure scarcely diminished by a sudden downpour. At the summit, they dine at a restaurant, but Klaus objects to the poor quality of the food. During their descent, passing through a village, they come upon a runaway horse, with two men chasing it helplessly. Klaus, approaching it in a wide arc, daringly grabs its mane and mounts it. It races off anew but soon is seen returning, Klaus still astride. He claims to identify with runaway horses and maintains that the owner erred in approaching it head-on: "You must never stand in the path of a runaway horse. It must have the feeling that its path remains unobstructed. Besides: You can't reason with a runaway horse."

Klaus is the hero of the excursion. He even appears to be no longer pathologically afraid of the cold, wet nose of Helmut's gentle old spaniel, Otto, which formerly made him scream at its friendly touch—odd behavior in so virile a man.

More meetings ensue, during the course of which not only does Sabina flirt mildly with Klaus, but also Helmut, who has for some months forsworn sexual contact with his wife, begins secretly to covet Helene. They go sailing on the lake, which, for the Halms, is an unexpected delight. This experience sets the stage for the book's melodramatic climax. The two men, this time alone, set out for a second sail. The weather deteriorates; a vicious storm arises. Klaus, becoming somewhat crazed, refuses to turn back, almost determined to head for the storm's eye. The canvas tilts so close to the water as would seem inevitably to capsize the vessel. Only by leaning far out in the opposite direction do they avoid disaster. The logical Helmut demands that they head for shore. Klaus at least agrees to face the wind, thus momentarily righting the boat. He calls Helmut a coward but screams at him to seize the tiller and hold it tight between his legs. Helmut obeys clumsily, causing the boat to change direction. Klaus retakes control and recklessly allows the craft to heel over again. Waves break over the sides. Then, Helmut kicks the tiller out of his friend's hand; the boat, again heading into the wind, rights itself, but Klaus is knocked into the water and disappears. Eventually, Helmut manages to beach the craft, but Klaus is lost.

The next day, there is still no sign of Klaus. Three people are reported drowned during the storm. Helmut, curiously, proposes to Sabina that they go jogging in the forest. They will walk into town, purchase some running shoes, shorts, shirts, and two bicycles. As they prepare to exercise after their return, they find Helene at the door. She enters, begins to drink, smoke, and eat some rich homemade cake. She is no longer stylishly garbed. This is not the Helene they have known. Her arrival initiates a confession. Tearfully, she claims that Klaus was not at all the successful environmental journalist that he seemed. Often he suffered from writer's block, staring for hours at the blank page in his typewriter. He fought with his editors and publishers, and his career was about finished. He really worried that she (his second wife) no longer loved him. She could not communicate with him. Jealous of her early musical promise, he forced her to abandon a career as a pianist. Far from a success, he had sunk so far as to look upon Helmut as his only means of salvation.

They answer a knock at the door, and there stands Klaus, the survivor, come to take his wife home. Still drinking and smoking, Helene greets him, somewhat ambiguously says, "Let's go, genius, onward and upward," and leaves with him.

Helmut and Sabina now decide that they do not really want to go jogging. In fact, they will even leave the just-purchased bicycles with their landlord. If they ever return to the lakeshore another year, they can retrieve them. Instead, they will pack and head for some other town. The story ends aboard a train, where they find a compartment to themselves; Helmut looks upon his wife with rekindled desire.

The Characters

Since *Runaway Horse* is actually a novella, hardly more than a hundred pages, there is little space for character description and development. Only Helmut and Klaus receive full treatment. The introspective Helmut is given to hiding his real persona, uncertain of his calling as a teacher and troubled by memories, most of which he would willingly forget (and often does). He prefers the confines of his rented room to the world outside. (He actually enjoys its barred windows and misses them when he returns home.) Depicted as a man of reason, he is nevertheless patently neurotic and even irrational in his unease at Klaus's probing into their boyhood past. His uncertainties extend to his own self-image. He is gradually, if unwillingly, growing apart from his wife, unable to communicate sexually and torn by a sense of inadequacy. Not until the story's end does he succeed in achieving some satisfaction from his life and in reestablishing a sexual bond with his wife.

Klaus at first seems to be a successful and well-adjusted writer of health and environmental books, lean and tanned of body, admired by women, and in appearance twenty years younger than his boyhood friend. Yet he is far from this ideal. His wife accuses him of morbid jealousy, of being so insecure as to believe that the equally insecure Helmut can effect his salvation. If Helmut is the man of reason, then Klaus is the man of instinct, the runaway horse of the book's title and, as the storm incident bears out, an irrational force with which no one can reason.

Sabina and Helene, characters merely sketched, are more normal, foils for their respective husbands. Helene, though younger than Klaus, actually shelters and mothers him. She is unhappy, repressed but resigned, another survivor like her husband. Sabina is scarcely more than a good German hausfrau.

Still, Martin Walser is too professional to create cardboard stereotypes. Helmut is no unblemished hero who, unaware of his own basic strengths, miraculously saves both vessel and madman from his folly, finally solving his physical and psychological problems. In truth, he is mainly to blame for Klaus's being swept overboard and is experiencing well-deserved pangs of guilt over his friend's apparent death. Nor does Klaus end as a mere shell of the man he once was; only the disaffected wife offers a litany of his supposed shortcomings. It takes quite a man to survive a plunge into a storm-tossed lake. He returns, doubtless demythologized, as one critic has put it, and doubtless chastened, but hardly conquered.

Themes and Meanings

The story can be read literally for what it purports to tell: the tale of two middle-aged men suffering from change of life, the one (Klaus) gladly reliving his past because it represents happier times, and the other (Helmut) reluctant to recall painful childhood memories and equally reluctant to cope with his present inadequacies as a teacher and a husband. The storm incident will allow Helmut to realize his positive qualities, see the shortcomings of his envied friend, and finally, purging himself of his frustrations and uncertainties, achieve a measure of happiness.

Others eschew such a simplistic explication. They know that Walser is a Socialist sympathetic with East German Communism, an author who refuses to accept the benefits of the vaunted *Wirtschaftswunder* (economic miracle) that turned West Germany, a nation virtually destroyed in World War II, into a world leader in industry, admired for its high standard of living and its freedom from unemployment and inflation. Instead, like several other postwar German writers, he sees West Germany as a nation of soulless capitalists and disaffected losers. The characters in this novella are comparable to Xaver Zürn, the frustrated chauffeur of *Seelenarbeit* (1979; *The Inner Man*, 1984) or the protagonist of *Die Gallistl'sche Krankheit* (1972; Gallistl's ailment), who suffers from a mysterious malady characterized by unhappiness about himself, his family, and Germany in general. He blames his country for his symptoms, which are relieved only when he turns Socialist. Thus interpreted, Helmut's story illustrates the folly of refusing to acknowledge Germany's past. Helmut and Klaus both, along with their wives, are also guilty of selfishly living for themselves alone, heedless of the truth that salvation must lie in social commitment.

Finally, what of the curious name Buch (German for "book")? Some scholars would see it as a symbol for the book of German history in which Helmut must read the nation's truth. This might appear to be a farfetched interpretation if it were not for the fact that, although Helmut's last name is almost never mentioned, Klaus is called "Klaus Buch" constantly, almost obsessively, often several times per page. Walser would seem to be laying special emphasis on the importance of this surname.

Critical Context

Runaway Horse afforded Walser his first commercial success; it was a runaway best-seller. It continued the critical acclaim of his earlier novels, plays, and essays. With the death of Heinrich Böll, Martin Walser has become one of the two most prominent German novelists; like Günter Grass, Walser is eminent in several genres. No modern German writer is better at probing the inner recesses of characters beset by frustration and failure, and Walser accomplishes this without the exaggeration of Grass or the social preachments and frequent humorlessness of so many East German writers. Walser can be quite amusing. Not every critic has recognized the fine sense of humor that prevents tendentiousness and leavens almost all of his books, not least among them *Runaway Horse*. He can laugh at his protagonists, making the reader laugh with him and possibly at him. If his beliefs and biases inevitably color his fiction, whatever message he sends must be discovered. Rarely does he slip into applying obvious labels. Walser remains a thoroughly satisfying master artist.

Sources for Further Study

Clark, Jonathan Philip. "A Subjective Confrontation with the German Past in Martin Walser's *Ein fliehendes Pferd*," in *Martin Walser: International Perspectives*, 1987. Edited by Jürgen E. Schlunk and Armand E. Singer.

Pickar, Gertrud B. "Narrative Perspective in the Novels of Martin Walser," in *The German Quarterly*. XLIV (1971), pp. 48-57.

Sinka, Margit M. "The Flight Motif in Martin Walser's *Ein fliehandes Pferd*," in *Monatshefte*. LXXIV (Spring, 1982), pp. 47-58.

Thomas, Noel L. "Martin Walser Rides Again: *Ein fliehendes Pferd*," in *Modern Languages*. LX (1979), pp. 168-171.

Waine, Anthony Edward. *Martin Walser*, 1980.

Armand E. Singer

THE SAFETY NET

Author: Heinrich Böll (1917-1985)
Type of plot: Social criticism
Time of plot: c. 1978
Locale: West Germany
First published: Fürsorgliche Belagerung, 1979 (English translation, 1982)

Principal characters:

FRITZ TOLM, a newspaper owner who is elected President of the Association

KÄTHE TOLM, his wife

HERBERT TOLM, their son, who is linked to the "Alternate Society"

ROLF TOLM, their second son, a former political activist who lives with Katharina Schroter and their son Holger II

VERONICA ZELGER, the former wife of Rolf Tolm, who now lives with their son Holger I

SABINE FISCHER, née Tolm, the daughter of Fritz and Käthe, who lives with her husband, Erwin Fischer, and their daughter Kit

HUBERT HENDLER, a security guard assigned to Sabine Fischer, who becomes his lover

HELGA HENDLER, the betrayed wife of Hubert and the mother of their son Bernhard

HOLZPUKE, the officer in charge of security for the Tolm family

HEINRICH (BEV) BEVERLOH, an underground activist who is the lover of Veronica Zelger

BLEIBL, a powerful industrialist who has been married four times

The Novel

In *The Safety Net*, Heinrich Böll seems to be more interested in creating a situation than in telling a conventional story. Böll defines a national state of paranoia that creates, in turn, a state of mind that is extremely disturbing and distasteful, as his characters, whose privacy is invaded by the "safety net" that is cast over their lives, attempt to deal with family and professional crises. Their lives are dominated and controlled by cadres of security guards assigned to protect them against terrorist attacks, kidnappings, and assassination attempts. The development is entirely psychological. This is a story of terrorism that generally avoids incidents of physical violence. Instead, it focuses on administrative terrorism, the intellectual discomfort experienced by those who are constantly under surveillance.

The novel begins with a decision reached by a conference of top industrialists of the Federal Republic of Germany. The central figure, Fritz Tolm, an elderly, cultivated publisher, has just been elected to head this industrial syndicate, called the Association, replacing his predecessor, the steel magnate Pliefger.

As a figurehead for the nation's leading industrialists, Tolm knows that he will become the prime symbolic target for terrorists. Because of his influence and recognition as a respected and admired avuncular celebrity, Tolm has had reason to fear for his life: "Now it was no longer fear *of* something but fear *for*" his wife, Käthe, his daughter Sabine, and his sons Herbert and Rolf—the latter an erstwhile political activist.

Tolm's family is endangered by dissolution and fragmentation. One of his family estates, Eickelhof near Iffenhoven, for example, has already been sold for industrial development and economic exploitation. Looking toward a bleak industrial future, Tolm anticipates the time when all the family lands, including Tolmshoven, where he currently lives, will be taken over, the houses razed, the land raped.

If the family fortunes are insecure, so, too, are the lives of Tolm's loved ones. His daughter Sabine is locked into a loveless marriage with Erwin Fischer, a man lacking in tact and charm, a suspected philanderer, an indulgent playboy. As the story unfolds, the reader learns that Sabine has been conducting an affair with Hubert Hendler, one of her security guards. As a consequence, she is pregnant by Hendler, and the term of the pregnancy can be traced back to a time when her husband was out of the country for a three-month business trip. Her husband thinks that she is three months pregnant; in fact, she is six months pregnant, and she knows that she cannot hide her secret much longer. This marriage is, therefore, in the process of dissolving.

The organization of the novel is altogether psychological. Böll takes the reader into the interior consciousness of the characters. Fritz Tolm is the focal point, and his ruminations reveal that he is an old man who lives mainly in the past, though he cares deeply for his wife, children, and grandchildren. His thoughts are as much on the past as on the present. He does not believe himself to be fully in control of the publishing empire that he heads, and he is conscious of being controlled by his subordinates. His election to lead the Association was engineered by the unsavory Bleibl, a war profiteer haunted by war memories of "blood money."

The novel shows the life of a man who should be at peace with himself, a man who has been successful in the world of business and industry, a man who has earned a life of ease and comfort. Yet Fritz Tolm is a prisoner of his own success. His personal life and relationships are bound up by the "safety net" of surveillance and security. He does not trust his associates. Despite his financial security and the measures taken to assure his personal security, Tolm is not a happy man.

Käthe is concerned about his well-being and happiness, and she has reservations about his new responsibilities as figurehead for the captains of industry. The main action of this shifting internal narrative concerns Tolm's election to the Association's figurehead position and his subsequent return home to Tolmshoven. Concurrently, his daughter Sabine has packed her belongings and moved, with her daughter Kit, first to Tolmshoven, then to Hubreichen, within eighteen kilometers, in order to stay with her brother Rolf, a reformed subversive, his wife, Katharina, and their son Holger II.

The novel's conclusion is dominated by three events. Rolf's first wife, Veronica, sends his oldest son, Holger I, back to Germany from Turkey. Holger's stepfather, the terrorist Heinrich Beverloh, is captured in Istanbul and kills himself and others in the process. The homosexual Kortschede commits suicide and leaves a letter for Tolm that the guard Holzpuke and his superiors in charge of security, Dollmer and Stabski, decide not to show to him. In protest, Tolm refuses to attend his friend Kortschede's funeral and to give the oration, as the Association expects him to do. This decision also ends his one-day term as President of the Association.

At the end, Sabine elopes with Hendler, whose wife realizes that he must attempt to find happiness with the estranged Mrs. Fischer. Veronica, disguised as a Dutch relative of Kortschede, rides a bicycle rigged with explosives to the cemetery where Kortschede is to be buried, in order to prove that Beverloh's terrorist plot could have worked, despite the most sophisticated security precautions. She stops short of mass murder, however, and turns herself in to a German police officer.

Fritz and Käthe Tolm attend Beverloh's burial at Hetzigrath instead of Kortschede's funeral. A photographer is there to document Tolm's presence, assigned by those who manipulated Tolm's election the day before, so as to discredit Tolm. Meanwhile, Holger I, conditioned by his terrorist stepfather, sets the manor house on fire, but no one is hurt. The fire is of little consequence, since Tolm and Käthe are resigned to leave Tolmshoven and all that it represents—corrupt industrialization and a life without privacy or dignity.

The Characters

The Safety Net is overpopulated with characters. There are so many of them (more than seventy) that Böll provides a "List of Characters" in the opening of his narrative in order to help the reader. This list is useful, given the tangled and interwoven relationships.

The technique of narration is both subjective and omniscient. Böll advances the narrative by constantly shifting from the consciousness of one character to that of another, enabling the reader to understand the motivations of the central players in this sordid political drama. The central players, Fritz and Käthe and their daughter Sabine Fischer, are explored in depth at the outset, and Böll most frequently invades their consciousnesses. The son Rolf is also very important to the story, since he served time for subversive political activities, and his knowledge gives the family an understanding of the terrorist mentality. There is some doubt as to whether Rolf has been entirely rehabilitated.

On the other, adversarial side of the story, Böll takes the reader most frequently into the mind of Holzpuke, the officer in charge of security, the man who controls the "safety net." Böll also penetrates the mind of the notorious Bleibl, an apparently ruthless industrialist who is corrupt (as facts taken from his "denazification file" demonstrate) but who is also tortured by his guilty conscience. Bleibl is a reprehensible character, but at least he feels remorse, and his treatment of Tolm is even potentially decent: "Of course he had 'hoisted' Tolm into that position [as President of the Association], but not to destroy him, on the contrary, he wanted to lighten his load, wanted him to be released from the paper. . . to recover his health . . . to get well and live." This information, appearing late in the novel, comes as a surprise.

To provide a context for Sabine's embarrassing pregnancy, Böll also enters the mind of Hubert Hendler, the security guard who has made her pregnant, and that of his wife, Helga. At the end of the novel, Böll records the thoughts of Veronica, who is empowered to execute a terrorist bombing but chooses not to do so because of her sense of compassion and her human decency.

The psychological texture of the novel is extremely complicated and demanding, but it is ultimately rewarding. There are few novels that are so deft in the handling of psychological motivation. The shifting points of view in *The Safety Net* represent a narrative tour de force and an artistic accomplishment of the very highest order.

Themes and Meanings

Heinrich Böll's agenda in *The Safety Net* may be seen as an extended meditation on the same issue raised by his earlier, shorter novel *Die verlorene Ehre der Katharina Blum* (1974; *The Lost Honor of Katharina Blum*, 1975), which intended to show, per its subtitle, "how violence can develop and where it can lead." The villain of that novel is a yellow journalist, Werner Tötges, who represents a sensationalist newspaper that resembles Axel Springer's *Bild-Zeitung*. The fear of terrorism and the question of personal privacy are themes that *The Lost Honor of Katharina Blum* and *The Safety Net* share.

In *The Lost Honor of Katharina Blum*, Böll presents an ordinary citizen, not at all political, being victimized by the press and by the police state. In *The Safety Net*, he suggests that even the rich and powerful may be victimized by the very mechanisms that are established to provide for their security. Fritz Tolm is a newspaper magnate, but his private life is no more secure than that of Böll's earlier heroine, Katharina Blum.

The Lost Honor of Katharina Blum was a polemical attack that Böll launched after his own privacy had been invaded when he wrote an article for *Der Spiegel* criticizing the hysterical coverage of the Baader-Meinhof terrorist gang in West Germany. Böll had taken the unpopular position that the terrorist Ulrike Meinhof should be given a fair trial. Thereafter, Böll was suspected of being in sympathy with the terrorists. He was maligned in the *Bild-Zeitung* and antagonized by the police. *The Lost Honor of Katharina Blum* was an angry response to this developing frustration.

The Safety Net is far more detached, marked by a weary sense of resignation on the part of the central figure, who is dignified, relatively apolitical, elderly, frail, and world-weary. The subliminal anger of *The Lost Honor of Katharina Blum* impels the heroine toward an act of violence. In *The Safety Net*, Fritz Tolm is made paranoid, living with the constant awareness that, as a beloved figurehead, he could at any time fall victim to a terrorist assassination attempt, despite the bodyguards who are constantly assigned to watch over him and his family. *The Lost Honor of Katharina Blum* is a novel about violence in response to harassment. *The Safety Net* is not itself a violent story, and, like Böll's earlier novel, it is only marginally about terrorists and terrorism. *The Safety Net* is primarily about power, connivance, and manipulation—a response to a paranoid fear of terrorism. The establishment's reaction triggers a kind of psychological terrorism in the name of security.

Fritz Tolm is not a happy man when the novel begins. In the short period during which he serves as President of the Association, he comes to realize and to resent the fact that he is controlled by others, and that resentment leads him to a position of rebellion and integrity. At the end of the novel, after he has asserted himself and resigned his position, he has demonstrated a newfound courage and is at peace with himself and his family.

Critical Context

When Heinrich Böll died in 1985, Germany lost its most respected novelist, social critic, essayist, and translator. He was a Roman Catholic and an activist in the peace movement. Writing in the *Frankfurter Allgemeine Zeitung*, Franz Josef Görtz described him as "the ever-alert conscience of the State." As Richard von Weizsäcker, President of the Federal Republic of Germany, noted on the occasion of Böll's death, "He caused offense and generated respect."

The Safety Net was Böll's fourteenth book, his fifth since he had won the Nobel Prize for Literature in 1972. Böll has been described as a Christian moralist, disturbed by the way that the Christian ideal has been corrupted by the industrial world of postwar Germany. At the age of sixty-four, when he wrote *The Safety Net*, Böll was obsessed by the atmosphere of defensive paranoia that had come to dominate Germany under the threat of terrorist violence. Other continuing concerns in his later fiction are the sanctity of the individual and the need for personal privacy.

The Safety Net effectively satirizes contemporary German life. The novel was criticized by Lothar Kahn in *The New Leader* for being "too genteel," an unavoidable consequence of Böll's focus on the civilized sensibility of Fritz Tolm, perhaps, but the novel also describes characters who are disenchanted (Rolf), corrupt (Bleibl), and pragmatic (Holzpuke). These characters are not particularly "genteel."

Though the novel succeeds mainly as a meditation on postwar "divided loyalties, lost traditions," and "desperate rebellions" and as a psychological narrative, it is also a borderline polemic. One review criticized Fritz Tolm's last comment to his wife at the burial of the terrorist Beverloh: "You know I have always loved you. And there's something else you must know. . . . That some form of socialism must come, must prevail. . . ."

This affirmation of the Socialist cause has not been carefully anticipated by the psychological development of the novel, but it is consistent with Böll's political orientation. In 1983, *The New York Times* reported that Böll "came out in support of the fledgling, iconoclastic Green Party, praising them for bringing 'a new language into Parliament,' and concluding, 'The Greens are always my hope.'" If Böll had not moved that far to the left when he wrote *The Safety Net*, at least the tendency can clearly be seen.

Sources for Further Study

Crampton, Patricia, trans. *Heinrich Böll: On His Death*, 1985.

Ghurye, Charlotte W. "Heinrich Böll's *Fürsorgliche Belagerung*: A Bloodless Novel of Terrorism," in *University of Dayton Review*. XVII (Summer, 1985), pp. 77-82.

_____. "The Theme of Angst in Heinrich Böll's *Fürsorgliche Belagerung*," in *Research Studies*. LII, nos. 3/4 (1983), pp. 156-164.

Kahn, Lothar. "German Prisoners of Fear," in *The New Leader*. LXV (March 22, 1982), p. 20.

Reid, J. H. "Back to the Billiards Table?" in *Forum for Modern Language Studies*. XIX (April, 1983), pp. 126-141.

Sheppard, R. Z. "Eavesdropping *über Alles*," in *Time*. CXIX (February 8, 1982), p. 74.

James M. Welsh

THE SAILOR WHO FELL FROM GRACE WITH THE SEA

Author: Yukio Mishima (Kimitake Hiraoka, 1925-1970)
Type of plot: Philosophical realism
Time of plot: After World War II, perhaps the late 1950's
Locale: Yado Hill in Yokohama, Japan
First published: Gogo no eikō, 1963 (English translation, 1965)

> *Principal characters:*
> NOBORU KURODA, a thirteen-year-old boy
> RYUJI TSUKAZAKI, a sailor and Fusako Kuroda's lover
> THE CHIEF, a thirteen-year-old boy, Noboru's friend and
> leader of their six-member gang
> FUSAKO KURODA, Noboru's mother, a widow and owner of a
> clothing boutique

The Novel

The Sailor Who Fell from Grace with the Sea is as much a story about the sailor Ryuji Tsukazaki as it is about thirteen-year-old Noboru Kuroda, who shares many of the same dreams as Ryuji, witnesses his downfall, and even participates in his ritualistic death. The novel examines the young boy's and the older man's desire for glory, beauty, and control, and their connections, all too often, with betrayal and death.

As the novel opens, Noboru finds himself bored and alone in his mother's house. While rummaging through an old chest of drawers built into the wall between his bedroom and his mother's, he discovers a small hole in the wood which allows him a fairly complete view of his mother's room. From that point on, when his mother is severe with him, he begins spying on her at night. What he sees is a thirty-three-year-old widow, Fusako Kuroda, sitting in front of her mirror naked, with "scented fingers rooted between her thighs." As he watches her caress her body, his curiosity is more philosophical than sexual, and he associates the "zone of black" beneath her fingers with a "pitiful little vacant house," and his own empty world.

His mother's room also holds a different attraction for him, for her windows overlook the ships in the harbor. Noboru has a fascination for ships, and his mother takes him to visit a tramp steamer one day. Their guide is Second Mate Tsukazaki. Both Noboru and Fusako are attracted to him. The boy sees the sailor as a hero, a "fantastic beast that's just come out of the sea." Fusako, a lonely widow, sees him as a man and takes him as a lover. As Noboru watches them make love in his mother's room, the sailor, his mother, the sea, and Noboru, himself, achieve a sort of "universal order" signaled by the faraway scream of a ship's horn. This ideal harmony is the "miracle" of which Noboru has always dreamed, and he vows to let nothing destroy it.

Noboru, however, is not the only one with a dream. Ryuji is drawn to the sea because he feels "destined for glory," and he believes that the sea is the only place he could find it. Closely linked to his passion for the sea and for glory is the idea of death. Thus as he makes love to Fusako on that first evening, he, too, hears the wail of the ship's horn, and for him the woman, the sea, and death become as one. He spends three days with her, and during that time comes to the realization that the glory for which he is destined will never come. He is tired of waiting. He tries to tell Fusako about his dreams, but all that comes out are stories of his travels. She thinks of them as simple, pleasant tales, but when Noboru hears them all he can think about is the adventure of foreign travel. For him, Ryuji is a hero.

The image of the hero begins to falter for Noboru the next day, when he meets Ryuji walking in the park. The boy is with the Chief and the other four members of the gang. He has boasted of his mother's lover and is eager to show him off. Ryuji, however, makes a fatal mistake. He tries to win the boy's friendship with an "overbright and artificial" smile reminiscent of all adults wishing to "mollify" a child. To make matters worse, Noboru has lied to his mother about where he would be that day and with whom he would be. He asks Ryuji not to tell his mother where he saw him, and when Ryuji agrees, Noboru is disappointed at his eagerness, again, to please the boy.

Noboru has a reason to be worried, for he and the other boys are returning from a ritual murder and vivisection of a cat. Noboru and his friends consider themselves "genuises," boys set apart from the world and its rules. They meet in secret places, call one another by ranking numbers instead of names, and discuss a type of nihilistic philosophy. For them, the adult world, especially fathers, are the enemy. They are searching for some sort of "internal order" to the chaos in the world and seem to find it only in the sea and death, or control over death. On this particular day the Chief has decided to put them all to the test of their convictions, especially Noboru, boy number three. They find a stray cat and take it to a shed behind the Chief's house. There Noboru is told to kill it, after each boy has held it and caressed it. He flings the cat up against a log twice before it dies, feeling a "resplendent power" throughout his body. The other boys, all naked, stand watching and are "overjoyed at the spattered blood" of the cat. The Chief puts on a pair of rubber gloves, picks up a pair of scissors, and begins to dissect the cat. As Noboru stares at the entrails and the blood, he finds a "wholeness and perfection in the rapture of the dead kitten's large languid soul." Death has produced a "perfect, autonomous world." He has passed the test, and is now a man.

That evening as Fusako and Ryuji spend one last night together, Noboru is in his room contemplating the "crimes" Ryuji has committed: He smiled at him in a "cowardly" manner; he sprayed himself with cool water in the park like a common bum; and he kept his mother out all night, depriving Noboru of the pleasure of watching them make love. The next day when Ryuji leaves for another voyage, Noboru watches his actions closely. Ryuji manages to regain some of his lost stature when he behaves like the "perfect" sailor, "a man leaving a woman behind to voyage around the world." Ryuji boards the ship, leaving behind not only the woman but also the land on which he finally feels comfortable.

Several months pass before Ryuji returns. It is December 30, and Fusako is waiting for him. There is an unspoken agreement that when Ryuji returns he will stay in Fusako's house. When Noboru sees him, his first question is when will the sailor leave again. The boy is outraged when Ryuji replies "I'm not sure." With rage, Noboru enters this answer as another of Ryuji's "crimes," along with the fact that he returned in the first place. Over the next few weeks his anger grows as he realizes that Ryuji is planning to marry his mother and not return to the sea. For Noboru and his friends, Ryuji is about to commit the ultimate crime: He is about to become a father, Noboru's father. Further, in addition to renouncing the sea, he exchanges his sailor's clothes for a suit and tie and goes with Fusako to learn how to help manage her clothing store. When Noboru tells the gang what is happening, the Chief tells him not to worry, he will think of something that will, once again, return Ryuji's hero status to him.

The night Noboru hears about the marriage plans he crawls into the chest of drawers, hoping to watch his mother and Ryuji again. He falls asleep reading by the light of a flashlight, and in his mother's darkened room Ryuji sees the pinpoint of light through the wall and realizes that Noboru has been spying on them. When confronted, Noboru remains silent. Ryuji struggles over how to handle the situation, and as far as Noboru is concerned, he chooses the wrong decision. He reasons with Noboru instead of punishing him. Had Ryuji beaten him, it would have been better. Noboru is convinced that Ryuji is not the hero he once was.

In an emergency meeting of the gang, Noboru produces a list of eighteen crimes charged against Ryuji. The Chief decides that there is only one way to save him and gives the other six members specific instructions. Noboru is to invite Ryuji on an outing with the gang. The other members are to bring the following items: a thermos of hot tea, some rope, a gag and blindfold, some cups, and any kind of cutting tools they can find. The Chief will produce the sleeping pills and the scalpel. He tells them that this is their last chance to return "internal order" to the world.

The next day, Ryuji, pleased at the invitation and dressed once again in his sailor's clothes, follows the gang to a deserted hill overlooking the sea. As they sit beneath the tree, Ryuji tells them stories about the sea. His stories, however, fascinate him more than the boys this time, and his mind wanders back to his days of longing for glory. The boys take advantage of his inattention and prepare the drugged tea. Ryuji sits lost in his stories, looking out

over the sea and thinks: "I could have been a man sailing away forever."
Again his dreams of glory unite the sea, women, and death. Now, however,
he has abandoned those dreams. Noboru nervously hands him a cup, and,
"still immersed in his dream," the sailor drinks down the bitter tea.

The Characters

On the surface, Noboru is a normal thirteen-year-old boy. He is a good
student, obeys his mother as much as any teenager does, dreams of having
adventures, and likes to be with his friends. Underneath, however, Noboru
harbors some disturbing qualities and philosophies: He is convinced that he
is a genius; he believes that death is mankind's only goal; he believes that
authority is an enemy; and he practices "hard-heartedness" as a matter of
pride. His obsession with the sea leads him to think of his heart as a "large
iron anchor" which resists decay. He believes that the sea holds some sort of
answer for him that his "empty world" on land cannot provide. When he
meets the sailor Ryuji, he sees in him a mythological hero who follows the
sea and answers only to the wail of the ship's horn. The sailor represents
beauty, glory, danger, perfection, and death, and Noboru is drawn toward
what he considers a "universal order." Nothing else will do.

As for Ryuji, he has many of the same passions as Noboru: beauty, glory,
danger, and a love of the sea. He also feels the power of death tied up in his
dreams, but adds to that the power of a woman. Feeling destined for glory by
the time he was twenty, Ryuji left the unflexibility of land for the mysteries
and movements of the sea. Yet nothing ever happened. Even the dangers of
storms at sea and the exotic ports he visited soon became routine. Now he
uses a woman and sexual love as a substitute for the sea and glory. As a result
of this compromise, the sailor dies a fallen hero.

The Chief, a self-appointed philosopher, preaches to the gang about the
chaos in the world, the need to return internal or universal order to mankind, and the necessity of gaining control over death. He is the one who sets
up the bizarre rituals. His self-control and contempt for the world around
him are so strong that he has no trouble leading his gang in either their ideas
or their actions.

The woman who lures Ryuji from the sea is Fusako. She is a modern and
very Westernized Japanese woman. Most often she is described through her
physical surroundings and activities: a house without one traditional Japanese room; a clothing boutique specializing in expensive, Western-style fash-
ions; her own clothes, cashmere sweaters, silk stockings, fur coats, tennis
outfits; her habits of smoking in public and running her own business; and
her indiscretion at taking a lover.

Themes and Meanings

The desire to harmonize an external and internal world, the needs of the flesh and the spirit, and the qualities of modern and traditional values is a concern that runs through many of Yukio Mishima's novels, including *The Sailor Who Fell from Grace with the Sea*. This desire, which often leads to tragedy, is best illustrated through the character of the sailor, and, by association, through the eyes of Noboru. For both man and boy, the sea symbolizes beauty, power, glory, and death. When Noboru spies on Ryuji making love to his mother, the sailor is described in sealike terms: His muscles are like the ropes on a ship and they "ripple" down his chest; he is "cast from the matrix of the sea"; the gold flesh of his chest "rises and falls." As for Ryuji's own vision of himself, he dreams of glory "surging in to flood him," and he feels it "knifing toward him like a shark" through the water.

Both men also incorporate a woman, Fusako, into this picture of glory. On that first night, as Ryuji makes love to her and Noboru watches, the moonlight over the sea reflects through her bedroom windows, and she gives off a sweaty, "musky" fragrance. In a rare gesture, she wears a kimono, and as she undresses, the gown makes a "swishing" sound, like sails unfurling, as it falls to the floor. The wail of the ship's horn is noticed by both the sailor and boy, and each associates the woman with the sea, with glory, and with death.

Yet these are only illusions, for the internal order, the spirit, has its opposite side in an external order, the flesh. Ryuji is lured away from the internal order of the sea and its connection to man's spirit by the external world of land and its comforts. While Noboru has a strange link to the sailor's own desires, they are too abstract; thus, when Ryuji gives up the sea for the woman, it is proof that he has lost his heroic stature. The sailor fired Noboru's "imagination," which had up to this point been "helpless" and dormant, just as the sea had once fired Ryuji's imagination. Yet like a quasi-mythological sea creature, when he turns his back on the sea, in much the same way as the Greek hero Odysseus, he loses his "manliness" and is doomed. As in other of Mishima's works, the necessity to harmonize these opposing forces is a life-and-death struggle, with death usually winning. Death, too, is a symbol, not necessarily of defeat, but, as the Chief states, the only way to achieve "universal order" in a chaotic world.

Critical Context

In the West, Yukio Mishima is probably the most widely read modern Japanese writer. In the judgment of Donald Keene, the prominent Western scholar of Japanese literature, "Mishima was the most gifted and achieved the most of all the [Japanese] writers who appeared after the war." The range of Mishima's work (much of which has not been translated) is all the more remarkable given that he was only forty-five years old at the time of his widely publicized ritual suicide.

The Sailor Who Fell from Grace with the Sea, which Keene describes as one of Mishima's "most perfectly crafted works," shares with many of Mishima's novels the notion that youth is supremely valuable, and that to grow older is not to mature but to decay. This notion is central to Mishima's tetralogy *Hōjō no umi* (1969-1971; *The Sea of Fertility: A Cycle of Four Novels*, 1972-1974), where it is interwoven with Buddhist themes.

Sources for Further Study

Keene, Donald. *Dawn to the West: Japanese Literature in the Modern Era*, 1984.

Petersen, Gwenn Boardman. *The Moon in the Water: Understanding Tanizaki, Kawabata, and Mishima*, 1979.

Ueda, Makoto. *Modern Japanese Writers and the Nature of Literature*, 1976.

Yamanouchi, Hisaaki. *The Search for Authenticity in Modern Japanese Literature*, 1978.

Deborah Charlie

SAINT MANUEL BUENO, MARTYR

Author: Miguel de Unamuno y Jugo (1864-1936)
Type of plot: Philosophical realism
Time of plot: The late nineteenth and early twentieth centuries
Locale: Valverde de Lucerna, a legendary town in northern Spain
First published: San Manuel Bueno, mártir, 1933 (English translation, 1956)

> *Principal characters:*
> DON MANUEL, a priest who has lost his faith
> ANGELA CARBALLINO, the narrator, Don Manuel's spiritual
> daughter
> LÁZARO, Angela's brother, who returns to Valverde de
> Lucerna after living in America and becomes Don
> Manuel's friend, confidant, and disciple

The Novel

The story begins at the moment when the town of Valverde de Lucerna begins to promote the beatification of its beloved priest. Angela Carballino, whose real father died when she was a child, has always considered Don Manuel as her "spiritual father"; she recounts his life as a kind of confession, the nature of which is not clear until the end of the novel.

Angela first recalls Don Manuel as a robust, active priest of about thirty-seven who participated in every aspect of the life of the town. He was especially interested in children and often helped in the school, teaching not only catechism but also other subjects. He was moved by the death of any child and rejected the popular notion that an early death is a blessing because a dead child goes directly to Heaven. He routinely helped the poor, providing them with clean clothing. On one occasion, he intercepted a child whose father had sent him for firewood on a wintry day, sending the boy home and going for the wood himself. Rather than preaching the glories of Heaven, Don Manuel urged the villagers to enjoy life on earth; he encouraged them to give parties, to dance, to be happy. His most important function, however, was helping people to die. At the moment of a parishioner's death, Don Manuel offered comfort and strength.

Don Manuel became the spiritual mainstay of the village. Everyone loved him. Soon his reputation extended beyond Valverde de Lucerna. When Angela went to an out-of-town high school, the girls asked constantly about Don Manuel. Before long, he became famous for his miracles. On the night of San Juan, on which Spaniards celebrate the beginning of summer, the physically and emotionally ill would come from miles around to gather at the lake at Valverde de Lucerna, which Don Manuel turned into a healing pool. Sometimes, moved by Don Manuel's presence and his extraordinary voice, they would come away cured. Yet when someone asked Don Manuel for a miraculous cure, all he would answer was, "I don't have permission from the bishop to perform miracles." As Don Manuel's fame grew, he received opportunities to advance within the Church structure, but he refused to leave his parishioners. "How can I save my own soul if I fail to save the soul of my people?" he would say.

In the town of Valverde de Lucerna, everyone went to church, many simply to experience Don Manuel's charismatic presence. At Mass all would recite the Apostles' Creed, led by Don Manuel. When, however, the congregation came to the words, "I believe in the resurrection of the body and the life everlasting," Don Manuel remained silent. On Good Friday, when Don Manuel repeated Christ's words, "My God, my God, why have you abandoned me?" he did so with such conviction that he brought the parishioners to tears. Afterward, Blasillo, the village idiot, would wander through the streets crying, "My God, my God, why have you abandoned me?" and again, the townspeople would weep. Angela, observing Don Manuel's silences and anguished lamentations in church, as well as his obsessive need to keep himself busy, begins to suspect the priest's terrible secret.

When Angela's brother Lázaro returns to Valverde from the New World with progressive, anticlerical ideas, a clash between him and Don Manuel seems inevitable. Lázaro sees Don Manuel as an instrument of the primitive, theocratic feudalism that is holding Spain back. At the same time, he respects Don Manuel's intellect. "He is too intelligent to believe everything he has to teach," Lázaro concludes.

Instead of confronting Lázaro, Don Manuel takes him into his confidence. The two men become close friends. Don Manuel admits to Lázaro that he has lost his faith and that he has long been tempted by suicide, but he argues that the people need religion in order to endure their hardships. When Lázaro speaks of unionizing the workers, Don Manuel counters that new ideas will sow discontent. Since Lázaro is not a believer, Don Manuel cannot win him through faith. He uses reason to convince him that the people are better off with their traditional ways and faith than with new ideas that will introduce turmoil into their lives. It is at this point that the nature of Don Manuel's martyrdom becomes clear. He has sacrificed himself all these years in order to give the people the faith he believes they need in order to survive.

When Angela's and Lázaro's mother is near death, Don Manuel persuades Lázaro to promise that he will pray for her soul so that she can die in peace. Once brought into the fold through prayer, Lázaro becomes Don Manuel's most ardent supporter. He assists him in his work, not because he believes in life everlasting but because he believes in life on earth. Don Manuel has convinced him that it is better for the villagers to enjoy their lives as much as possible rather than torture themselves with philosophical questions. When Don Manuel dies, it is Lázaro who urges his replacement to give the people "religion," not "theology."

Neither Lázaro nor his sister reveals Don Manuel's secret until the bishop insists that Angela, now in her fifties, write her thoughts about Don Manuel in support of the beatification process. She produces a text that not only will bring down the myth of Don Manuel, the saint, but also reveals her own doubts.

The Characters

Both Don Manuel and Lázaro are partially autobiographical characters. Lázaro, the political and social progressive, reflects the preoccupations of the young Miguel de Unamuno y Jugo, who, in his early years, was drawn toward scientific materialism. Later in life, Unamuno experienced a spiritual crisis. Like Don Manuel, he was concerned with the problem of immortality, for it seemed to him that if there were no afterlife, life on earth had no purpose. Don Manuel incarnates Unamuno's spiritual anguish. His fear that nothing follows death leads to depressions that border on the suicidal.

Like all Unamuno's characters, Don Manuel is far more complex than he appears. Agonizing over his own doubts while protecting his parishioners from the truth, he seems a saint. Yet Don Manuel has a negative side. The author shows in many of his works that every act of charity is also an act of egotism. Citing the example of Cain and Abel—one of Unamuno's favorite themes—he argues that the virtuous Abel is actually cruel because he causes Cain to be tortured by guilt. Don Manuel, unable to believe in eternal life, uses the parish to cultivate the fame that will allow him to go on living—through his reputation—after his death. When he tells people that the bishop has not given him permission to perform miracles, he seems humble. Yet he does not actually deny that he can perform them. His refusal to leave Valverde de Lucerna for a more prestigious position reveals not only his love for his people but also his fear of abandoning the safety of their adoring eyes. Don Manuel is cultivating his reputation as a saint. His beatification, which would allow him to be venerated as a local holy person, is a step in the process started by Don Manuel himself.

Unamuno writes in many essays that an unexamined faith is invalid. Although doubt is painful, it is part of the human condition. Christ himself, in human form, spoke the words, "My God, my God, why have you abandoned me?" That is, Unamuno implies, Christ himself doubted. Yet Don Manuel denies his parishioners the right to doubt. He maintains them in a state of childlike dependency, creating a cult of which he is the center. The recitation of the Apostles' Creed, in which all affirm mechanically, "I believe," becomes a control tactic.

Don Manuel cultivates his aura of sainthood by performing good deeds which, in fact, often serve to protect him from the scrutiny of the masses. When a judge asks him to interrogate a criminal, Don Manuel responds, "Judge not, that you may not be judged," an answer against which the court official has no argument. By declining to help condemn the criminal, Don Manuel not only contributes to his reputation but also avoids the anger of the man's family, who might seek ways to discredit him. In his sermons, Don Manuel never inveighs against masons, liberals, or heretics. His tolerance is a result of his own unorthodoxy, but it is also a means of avoiding the opposition of these traditionally anticlerical elements. On the other hand, Don Manuel constantly preaches against envy, vengeance, and judgment of others; he himself fears the scrutiny of his parishioners.

When Angela questions Don Manuel about dogma and his own beliefs, he gives her orthodox answers, often quoting from the Bible, without really addressing the issues. He encourages her to read adventure stories instead of theology, in order to avoid her soul-searching. Yet Angela guesses Don Manuel's secret and begins the intellectual process that will lead her to doubt. She comforts Don Manuel, offering him solace by allowing him to believe that she still possesses the innocent faith of a child. In the end, however, Angela asks, "Do I believe?" Her confession—the book *Saint Manuel Bueno, Martyr*, in which she reveals Don Manuel's secret—is her own attempt at achieving immortality, for she is truly Don Manuel's "spiritual child."

Lázaro represents a threat to Don Manuel's domain. His pamphlets and progressive ideas risk stimulating the populace to reflect, to ask questions, and, finally, to reject Don Manuel's authority. If he were to confront Lázaro openly, Don Manuel would provoke a rift in the village. Lázaro would continue his campaign and his supporters would oppose Don Manuel. Since Lázaro is a pragmatist and a rationalist, Don Manuel appeals to reason to convince him that it is in the best interests of the villagers to continue in their beliefs.

Themes and Meanings

Although Don Manuel has his duplicitous side, his spiritual anguish is genuine. His emphasis on life and children results from his dread of the nothingness that lies beyond the tomb. Don Manuel's manipulation of the villagers is unconscious. He is a benevolent theocrat who tries to protect himself by protecting others. It is not clear to what extent he intuits the self-serving nature of his conduct. It is evident, however, that he does not see himself as Angela and the reader see him.

In Unamuno's view, Don Manuel's spiritual dilemma is that of all thinking men and women. In essays such as *Del sentimiento trágico de la vida en los hombres y en los pueblos* (1913; *The Tragic Sense of Life in Men and Peoples*, 1921) and *La agonía del Cristianismo* (1925; *The Agony of Christianity*, 1928), Unamuno articulates what he sees as the basic human predicament: Man—*homo sapiens*—is a being who thinks and who therefore seeks rational explanations, but at the same time, man is a being who feels, intuits, and craves immortality. Through reason, man cannot prove the existence of God; he must accept it on faith. Yet his faith is continually eroded by doubt, for the *sapiens* part of man—the part that demands intellectual certainty—demands proof. Thus, life is an internal war between the rational and the nonrational. Don Manuel does not allow his parishioners to deal with this conflict, but, like a protective mother—Angela calls him "matriarchal"—shelters them from pain. By doing so, he deprives them of what Unamuno sees as an essential aspect of human life.

Yet the question remains as to what extent the common people are capable of dealing with the issues that torment Don Manuel. At the end of the work, Unamuno writes that in the long run, the priest's good deeds are what is important to the villagers, for the masses are not interested in philosophical questions. If this comment seems to contradict what Unamuno has written elsewhere, it is because contradiction is the essence of life. Unamuno admits readily that he is inconsistent, but that is only because human beings are constantly growing, thinking, changing.

Faith and immortality are the most important of Unamuno's themes, and he develops them in countless ways in his essays, novels, plays, and poems. Another major Unamunian theme is the personality, which the author sees as so complex and deep that it is inaccessible not only to others but also to the individual himself. In *Saint Manuel Bueno, Martyr*, the author uses the metaphor of the lake and the mountain to elaborate these themes.

Surrounded by mountains, Valverde de Lucerna is on a lake at the bottom of which there is a medieval town. On the festival of San Juan, the bells of the submerged church ring at midnight. The lake and the mountains represent two aspects of Don Manuel. The mountain is a traditional symbol of faith, and Don Manuel, the priest, embodies faith in God and in the Church. For the townspeople, Don Manuel is a pillar of strength, like the mountains that surround them. In the depths of his soul, however, Don Manuel clamors in the night. The placid waters of the lake, like the serene, blue pools that are Don Manuel's eyes, hide an ancient reality.

Don Manuel's fear of death is a primal fear, older than man himself. It is evident in the eyes of trapped animals. It is echoed in the words of Blasillo, who repeats Don Manuel's anguished cry without understanding it. Blasillo is a creature of instinct and emotion who voices Don Manuel's most intimate forebodings. Like Don Manuel, he is an alienated being who lives on the margin of society. Blasillo is Don Manuel's other self. That is why, when Don Manuel dies, Blasillo dies, too.

Critical Context

Unamuno wrote *Saint Manuel Bueno, Martyr* in 1930, six years before his death. It is one of his best and most mature works. Encompassing so many contradictory aspects of human nature—the saintly and the diabolical, the magnanimous and the manipulative, the tolerant and the self-serving, the reasonable and the intuitive—Don Manuel has become a towering character in contemporary Spanish literature. Because of the work's complexity, it lends itself to diverse interpretations and has attracted much critical attention.

Unamuno called his prose fiction *nivolas*. Like everything in Unamuno's world, the *nivola* defies definition. Unamuno explains in *Niebla* (1914; *Mist*, 1928) that a *nivola* transcends genre and blurs the line between reality and fiction. For example, *Saint Manuel Bueno, Martyr* consists of a mere thirty-five pages and so is neither a novel nor a short story. At the end of the work, the author transcends his role of invisible storyteller to comment on the significance of the characters, especially Angela. By introducing a personal interpretation of his own work, Unamuno eradicates the boundary between reader and writer. He uses an even more radical technique at the end of *Mist*, in which the author enters the work and is confronted by one of his characters.

Unamuno has often been called a pre-existentialist. Like characters in existentialist novels, Unamuno's protagonists grapple with nothingness and the finality of human life. Unamuno explains in several of his essays that aside from the eternal life promised by the Church, there are two means to achieve immortality: through children and through art. That is why Don Manuel cultivates a "spiritual daughter" and Angela produces her "confession."

In his commentary at the end of *Saint Manuel Bueno, Martyr*, Unamuno says that he believes in Angela more than he believes in himself. For Unamuno the creation is more real than the creator because the work of art outlives the artist and attains a life of its own, as future generations reinterpret it. That is why, at the end of *Mist*, the author is unable to kill his character. That is also why Unamuno sometimes becomes a character in his own books; through art, he attempts to bestow immortality upon himself.

Thus, the creation process acquires transcendental significance. Just as the character creates the author in the sense that the author is not an author without his creation, so man creates God. Thus, *creer es crear*—believing is creating. By believing—in defiance of reason—an individual performs an act of will, an act of self-affirmation, that gives his own life meaning.

Sources for Further Study

Butt, John. *Miguel de Unamuno: "San Manuel Bueno, Mártir,"* 1981.

Carey, Douglas M., and Phillip G. Williams. "Religious Confession as Perspective and Mediation in Unamuno's *San Manuel Bueno, Mártir,"* in *Modern Language Notes*. XCI (1976), pp. 292-310.

Foster, David. *Unamuno and the Novel as Expressionist Conceit*, 1974.

Horowitz, Renée B. "Unamuno's View of Women," in *Letras femeninas*. I (1975), pp. 56-60.

Livingstone, L. "Unamuno and the Aesthetic of the Novel," in *Hispania*. XXIV (1941), pp. 442-450.

Longhurst, C. A. "The Problem of Truth in *San Manuel Bueno, Mártir*," in *Modern Language Review*. LXXVI (July, 1981), pp. 581-597.

Moon, Harold Kay. "Miguel de Unamuno: A 'Heretic's' Quest for Eternal Life," in *The Need Beyond Reason and Other Essays*, 1976.

Predmore, Susan. "*San Manuel Bueno, Mártir*: A Jungian Perspective," in *Hispanófila*. LIV (1978), pp. 15-29.

Turner, David G. *Unamuno's Web of Fatality*, 1974.

Wyers, Frances. *Miguel de Unamuno: The Contrary Self*, 1976.

Barbara Mujica

THE SAMURAI

Author: Shusaku Endō (1923-   )
Type of plot: Historical realism
Time of plot: 1612-1624
Locale: Edo, Nunozawa, and Tsukinoura, all cities in Japan; various places in
    New Spain; Seville and Madrid in Spain; and Rome, Italy
First published: Samurai, 1980 (English translation, 1982)

> *Principal characters:*
> ROKUEMON HASEKURA, the samurai of the novel's title, holder
>   of a small fief in northeast Japan
> LORD ISHIDA, Hasekura's feudal superior and patron
> MASAMUNE DATE, invariably called His Lordship, the daimyo
>   holding the district in which Ishida and Hasekura live
> FATHER VELASCO, Provincial at Edo for the Franciscan order,
>   the translator for the mission to New Spain authorized by
>   Masamune Date
> THE MAN IN TECALI, a Japanese Christian convert living
>   among the Indians in New Spain
> YOZŌ, Hasekura's faithful servant and companion

The Novel

Dealing with a relatively obscure mission to New Spain, today known as
Mexico, mounted by the feudal overlord of a district in seventeenth century
Japan surrounding the modern northeastern city of Sendai, Shusaku Endō's
The Samurai focuses on the fundamental effects of the Tokugawa period on
Japan, of Japan's association with European Roman Catholic missionaries,
and of its ultimate decision to close the country to all foreign influence.
Endō's interest in the episode arises from its relative obscurity and the lack of
surviving historical records. His imagination was stirred by the situation of
unsophisticated Japanese of the lowest rank in the samurai class being forced
to play large roles on the international stage.

The novel begins with descriptions of the two men central to the action of
The Samurai. The first is Rokuemon Hasekura, a samurai and the holder of
a small fief in the marshlands in Masamune Date's district. At home in his
estate and among the people who serve his family, Hasekura cannot imagine
a life different from the one he leads. He is of the land he tills, and he suffers
the privations of the peasants tied to it. The second man is Father Velasco,
Provincial at Edo (the older name of the modern city of Tokyo) for the Franciscan order of missionaries in Japan. Velasco is, in nearly every respect, the
apparent opposite of the samurai. An alien in Japan, having fought with the
Jesuits for control of missionary efforts, Velasco nurses the ambition of being

named Bishop of Japan and gaining control of the effort to Christianize its people. Two more different men could not be imagined, but Endō links their destinies in the novel.

Summoned by Lord Ishida, his feudal superior and patron, Hasekura is told to hold himself ready to undertake a mission at the direction of Lord Shiraishi, a leading figure in His Lordship's provincial council. Hasekura's elderly uncle is overjoyed at the news, believing that the family will regain the property from which they were dispossessed two generations before, when they found themselves on the wrong side in a political conflict. Hasekura is less optimistic about the prospect of leaving his native place. An occasional white swan flies into the marshes each winter, and he marvels at the fact that it has seen places he cannot even name. Hasekura thinks that he is unprepared for the mission when it materializes; he is instructed to join three other low-ranking samurai as envoys from Masamune Date to the government of New Spain. The four will board a Western-style ship, designed under the supervision of shipwrecked Spanish sailors, and seek to persuade the colonial government in New Spain to trade directly with Date's district of Japan. To that end, they are instructed to offer the prospect of uncontrolled opportunities for Christian missionary activity.

Attached as translator to the group of Japanese envoys as they embark on the *San Juan Baptista*, Father Velasco exudes self-confidence about the success of the mission. He sees in this effort an opportunity for the Franciscans to supplant the Jesuits as the prime group undertaking missionary activity in Japan. The journey, however, proves more difficult than he anticipated, and the Japanese envoys and their attendants are less easy to control than he thought. Velasco does make some converts among the group, in part because he demonstrates the political expediency of becoming a Roman Catholic, but, from the first, Hasekura resists Velasco's arguments. He finds the man Jesus Christ beyond comprehension, for his conduct is the antithesis of behavior which a samurai finds natural. "This ugly, emaciated man," Hasekura thinks, reflecting on the image of the crucified Christ. He continues,

This man devoid of majesty, bereft of outward beauty, so wretchedly miserable. A man who exists only to be discarded after he has been used. A man born in a land I have never seen, and who died in the distant past. He has nothing to do with me, thought the samurai.

Nevertheless, Hasekura accepts Christian baptism in the guise of political expediency. Arriving in New Spain, the Japanese envoys find the colonial officials unresponsive. Three of them, Hasekura among them, accept Velasco's advice to cross the Atlantic to appeal to the King of Spain and the Pope. In Madrid the three envoys become Roman Catholics, but Hasekura is overcome during the ceremony by feelings of guilt: "He felt a loathing like a woman must when she is forced to sleep with a man she neither loves nor trusts." Yozō, Hasekura's companion and servant, accompanies his master in this momentous step, but his acceptance of Christ is genuine and unreserved.

The political consequences of Hasekura's actions are momentous, but they are hardly the ones that he anticipated. The Spanish king sends the Japanese envoys on to Rome, where they linger about the city until they are granted a single audience with the Pope. The Roman Catholic church seems on the verge of endorsing the aims of the embassy and of naming Velasco's Franciscans the chief missionary group in Japan, but word comes from the Jesuits in Macao that the Tokugawa government in Edo has formed a trading alliance with England and that Masamune Date, who had sent out Hasekura's mission, has begun to persecute the Christians living in his district. Their mission unsuccessful, Hasekura and his companions retrace their steps, hoping only to return to Japan and to be allowed to live unobtrusively. Meeting Chusaku Matsuki, an envoy who turned back and did not accompany them to Europe, they are told that the government never intended the mission to succeed. It was merely a ploy to hide the government's intention to gain knowledge of European methods of shipbuilding. "That's why they didn't choose qualified people as envoys," Matsuki explains. "Instead, they appointed low-ranking lance-corporals who could die or rot anywhere along the way and no one would care."

The Characters

Abandoned by his patron, Lord Ishida, and no longer protected by the disgraced Lord Shiraishi, Hasekura comes to question the basic workings of Japan's feudal society. Ideally, it is built upon the fulfillment of mutual obligations, but Hasekura sees how easily an insignificant member of it, one such as he, can be sacrificed to the policy decisions of the social elite. Cautioned to live quietly, he is allowed to go home to his family. In the process of destroying everything in his possession that suggests Christian sympathies, Hasekura comes upon a manuscript thrust into his hands by a Japanese living with the Indians in New Spain. A convert to Roman Catholicism, the man has rejected institutional religion for a personal relationship with Christ. The Man in Tecali (he has no other name) "had wanted not the Christ whom the affluent priests preached in the cathedrals of Nueva España, but a man who would be at his side, and beside the Indians, each of them forsaken by others." Painfully aware of his own isolation, Hasekura turns to the Christ he rejected even at the moment of his own baptism. Arrested for having converted to Roman Catholicism during his journey abroad, Hasekura is tried and sentenced to death by a Japanese government intent on stamping out Western influences. Hasekura, on the way to his execution, accepts "emphatically" the import of Yozō's parting words: "From now on . . . He will be beside you."

If Hasekura's rejection of class and culture for belief in Christ is dramatic, Father Velasco's transformation is equally impressive. Barred by the Tokugawa regime from returning to Japan, Velasco slips into the country to continue the missionary effort that has gone underground since the prohibition of Christianity by the government. No longer does he desire to become Bishop of Japan; his motives are no longer political. Chastened by the collapse of the Japanese mission to New Spain, Velasco no longer believes in his own skill as a negotiator. He has a new humility. Captured and tried in Nagasaki, Velasco accepts the sentence of death and receives comfort from a Jesuit in his cell. Confessing his sins to this man on the eve of their execution, he says, "I confused my will with the will of God." When he learns of the deaths of Hasekura and his fellow envoy Kyusuki Nishi, he expresses joy at the prospect of joining them: "Only the wind and the sound of collapsing firewood could be heard. Finally from within the white smoke which enveloped Velasco's stake, a single cry rang out. 'I . . . have lived!' "

Velasco's words affirm his essential human dignity, and, as such, they represent Hasekura's achievement as well. Both men have broken through the limitations of roles imposed by culture and personality. Both recognize the essential isolation of the individual, and both realize the comfort to be derived from the Christ envisioned by the Man in Tecali. This man is a type of Christ, as is Hasekura's servant Yozō, for he seeks to serve the hopeless rather than to exploit them. Many of the other characters in Endō's novel are genuinely exploitive. Chief among them is the series of Japanese political leaders, starting at the top of the society with the *Naifu*, including Ieyasu Tokugawa himself, who use both Hasekura and Velasco to further their particular ends. The feudal structure is characterized by such inhumanity, Endō suggests, because it values the integrity of the group over that of the individual. The same point is made about the court of the King of Spain and the Roman Curia surrounding the Pope.

Themes and Meanings

On the surface, Endō's *The Samurai* is a brilliantly executed historical chronicle, capturing the flavor of life in seventeenth century Japan. One of the book's purposes is to expose "the samurai" to the broad sweep of the world beyond his marshland home, and Endō succeeds in conveying Hasekura's bewilderment and confusion at the sights and sounds of the larger world. He also manages to dramatize the process of adjustment that both Velasco and Hasekura undergo when they recognize the isolation of the human condition. Both men see the folly of relying on the institutions of this world, and both turn for comfort to Christ. The meaning of this act, however, is not the same for both men. While Velasco subsumes his egotism to something larger than himself, Hasekura achieves a personal autonomy apart from his role in Japanese society. *The Samurai* does not offer Christianity as the answer to problems, nor does it suggest that either Hasekura or Velasco genuinely emulates Christ. Despite the neatness with which he ends the novel, Endō is not suggesting that the two men achieve identity of purpose so much as that both the priest and the samurai renounce roles assigned them by their different societies. The cultures of Japan and Western Europe are not easily reconciled.

Endō clearly intends Hasekura and Velasco to be perceived as doubles. His initial presentation of the samurai in the snowy world of his marshland fief contrasts with his introduction of the priest in a closed, dark cell. Both men are seen in similar settings at the end of *The Samurai*, but Hasekura has gained awareness of the dark side of his culture while Velasco sees the light of Christ in submission to his fate. Endō clearly intends these motifs of light and darkness to function thematically in the novel, but they serve less as affirmation of a religious perspective than as evidence of the muted, tentative nature of the book's resolution. The sympathy for the emaciated man on the Cross that Hasekura develops is hardly more an affirmation of conventional religious belief than is Velasco's affirmation of his own existence. Indeed, the statements of both men come to little more than assertions of selfhood in an indifferent, if not hostile, world.

Critical Context

Given the fact that Shusaku Endō is a Roman Catholic who, after World War II, studied in France, becoming aware of the work of novelists such as François Mauriac and Graham Greene, it would be tempting to make a strong case for European influences on his fiction. Endō's work, however, despite the subject matter of many of his novels, deals more with the ways in which Japanese culture responds to Roman Catholicism than with the doctrines of the faith itself. The protagonist of *Obaka san* (1959; *Wonderful Fool*, 1974), for example, is a holy innocent named Gaston Bonaparte, but the focus of the novel is on the inability of people in contemporary Japan to recognize and value the virtue beneath Bonaparte's comic exterior. The decision of Father Cristovao Ferreira, the Jesuit missionary in Endō's *Chimmoku* (1966; *Silence*, 1969), to apostatize at the instigation of Japanese interrogators comes as a result of Ferreira's hearing Christ's voice instructing him to deny his faith as a way of relieving the suffering of his Japanese charges. There are European novels—those of Graham Greene come to mind— which deal with similar priests, but Endō's character acts from so strong a sense of group identity as to be uniquely Japanese.

The Samurai does not deal with a character who is as engaging as Gaston Bonaparte or as holy as Father Ferreira; neither does it have the concise construction characteristic of both earlier novels. *The Samurai* is bigger and bolder than Endō's previous fiction, and in it he struggles to get closer to the appeal that noninstitutional Christianity has for those isolated within their societies. Endō suggests the complexity of the appeal by giving the novel two focal characters and by treating them with equal seriousness. He might have chosen to cast Hasekura and Velasco as antagonists, and in their conflict he might then have suggested the ethical or spiritual superiority of Japanese or Western systems of belief. Endō chose, instead, to demonstrate the insensitivity of both systems and to use Velasco and Hasekura to point the way to a moral alternative to both. That *The Samurai* fails to dramatize and explore that alternative does not mean that it does not exist.

Sources for Further Study

Elliot, William. "Shusaku Endō: A Christian Voice in Japanese Literature," in *The Christian Century*. LXXXIII (September 21, 1966), pp. 1147-1148.

Howe, Irving. "Mission from Japan," in *The New York Review of Books*. XXIX (November 4, 1982), pp. 31-33.

Moynihan, Julian. "The Conversion of Japan," in *The New York Times Book Review*. LXXXVII (December 26, 1982), pp. 7, 27.

Ribeiro, Jorge. "Shusaku Endō: Japanese Catholic Novelist," in *America*. CLII (February 2, 1985), pp. 87-89.

Rimer, J. Thomas. *Modern Japanese Fiction and Its Traditions*, 1978.

Robert C. Petersen

SARRASINE

Author: Honoré de Balzac (1799-1850)
Type of plot: Psychological realism
Time of plot: The 1820's
Locale: Paris
First published: 1831 (English translation, 1899)

Principal characters:
THE NARRATOR, who knows the Lantys' secret
A YOUNG DANCER, who loves the narrator
ERNEST-JEAN SARRASINE, a French sculptor
ZAMBINELLA, an Italian opera singer
COUNT DE LANTY, an extremely wealthy resident of Paris
COUNTESS DE LANTY, his wife
MARIANINA DE LANTY, their daughter
FILIPPO DE LANTY, their son

The Novel

As the action of this short but intricately plotted novella begins, the narrator is attending an evening reception given by Count and Countess de Lanty. The narrator has a very pessimistic if not fatalistic view of life. For example, he sees many trees partially covered by snow in front of the Lantys' house. This tranquil winter scene, however, reminds him of nothing less than a "dance of the dead." He then describes the refined elegance of this party as a "dance of the living." The narrator affirms that such opposing realities as life and death, love and violence, and happiness and bitter frustration always exist side by side. He also states that one should not confuse appearance with reality. The story of Sarrasine and Zambinella will, in fact, demonstrate the tragic consequences of mistaking appearance for reality.

Many mysteries surround the members of the Lanty family, which is composed of the Count, the Countess, and their children, Marianina and Filippo. All four speak five languages fluently, and no one knows their country of origin or even the source of their immense wealth. They seem to be very happy, although each becomes extremely disturbed whenever an unidentified elderly gentleman, always dressed in black, comes unexpectedly to their parties. At this particular reception, the mysterious man appears while Marianina is singing an Italian concert aria. The Lantys all turn pale. The partygoers soon realize that this person holds extraordinary power over the Lantys, who fear him for reasons that others do not understand.

A young dancer and the narrator then begin to discuss this secretive family. He tells her that things are rarely what they seem to be at the Lanty residence. When the girl praises an exquisite portrait representing Adonis, he informs her that the model for this painting was a woman and not a man. The young dancer is mystified, but she does not ask him to explain this apparent contradiction. Only at the end of *Sarrasine* does she discover that the model was Zambinella, an Italian opera singer. The dancer entreats the narrator, whom she loves, to tell her and her friend Mme de Rochefide the story of the elderly man whom the four Lantys fear.

The name of this gentleman is Ernest-Jean Sarrasine. During his adolescence, Sarrasine studied sculpture. Bouchardon, his teacher, strove both to cultivate Sarrasine's artistic talents and to control the tendency toward violence in his pupil's character. For six years, under Bouchardon's direction, Sarrasine learned much about art, but, unfortunately, his personality never changed. During a visit to Rome, the young Sarrasine attended an operatic performance at which the celebrated Zambinella was singing. He so admired her ideal and classical beauty that he wanted to rush onto the stage in order to embrace her. His sole desire became to "possess" Zambinella, as he explained it to himself. While listening to the narrator's tale, the young dancer quickly realizes that Sarrasine's concept of love is both violent and dangerous.

The narrator's tale takes center stage in the novella, as events of sixty years before are "replayed": When Sarrasine finally meets Zambinella at a dinner party, he praises her physical beauty, but he remains indifferent to her feelings. At the party, she tries repeatedly to discourage Sarrasine, then becomes convinced that he will kill her if she rejects his love. Sarrasine learns from another dinner guest that Zambinella is not really a woman but rather a castrato, one who dresses as a woman and sings female roles in Italian operas. Sarrasine does not accept this explanation, and he hires criminals to abduct Zambinella. Zambinella, afraid of being beaten or raped by Sarrasine, finally admits the truth to the young sculptor. The egotistical and cruel Sarrasine spares Zambinella's life and then announces his decision to renounce all pleasures and human emotions for the rest of his life. At the end of this novella, the narrator states that Zambinella was the granduncle of Marianina and Filippo. The Lantys' fear of Sarrasine is thus perfectly understandable.

The Characters

The four members of the Lanty family do not differ appreciably from the numerous other wealthy men and women who people *La Comédie humaine* (1829-1848; *The Human Comedy*, 1895-1896), the integrated series of novels and short stories in which Honoré de Balzac sought to describe all levels of French society in the years immediately following the restoration of the monarchy in 1815. The four lovers in *Sarrasine*, however, are all fully developed characters with individual personalities. In this novella, Balzac contrasts very effectively these two sets of lovers. Sarrasine and Zambinella are both egotistical and superficial, whereas the urbane narrator and the young dancer by their wit and moral sensitivity create a favorable impression on Balzac's readers.

Unlike Sarrasine, the narrator never tries to dominate his beloved. Instead, he fully respects her freedom of choice. The narrator also has a very refined sense of humor. Tongue in cheek, he promises to tell her the story of Sarrasine if she will agree to sleep with him. The dancer understands that this is not a serious proposal, and she responds with a witty double entendre. She assures the narrator that she has "an ardent desire to know this secret." Her ambiguous rejoinder may refer either to the very private act of love or to the secret of Sarrasine. After answering the narrator, she leaves him and waltzes with others at the party. The following day, the narrator, with whom she has *not* slept, willingly tells her the story of Sarrasine. The narrator and the young dancer are morally responsible characters with whom the reader can identify. At the end of *Sarrasine*, both sympathetic lovers rejoice that moral progress has occurred since the singing days of Zambinella. Young men are no longer deformed so that they can interpret the operatic roles once sung by castrati.

The other lovers, however, are quite unsympathetic. Zambinella expresses general hatred for both men and women, and he views the world as "a desert" for him. From others Zambinella seeks nothing more than superficial companionship and conversation. Indeed, he frequently attends dinner parties primarily so that he will not have to think about his profound unhappiness. When Sarrasine asks him why he deceived him for so long, Zambinella explains that he did so only in order "to please his friends who wanted to laugh." It is only near the end of *Sarrasine* that the reader discovers why such a sensitive and gifted singer has become so cynical and superficial. Although Zambinella is a victim of physical deformation, his extreme bitterness makes it difficult for others, including the narrator and the young dancer, to comprehend fully the depth of his suffering.

Zambinella's pessimistic view of life is, at least, understandable. Sarrasine, however, is a totally cruel and irrational character. During his years of study with Bouchardon, Sarrasine developed no social graces and never learned how to treat others with respect. Upon hearing Zambinella sing for the first time, he decides "to be loved by her or to die," an extreme reaction with which no sensible reader can identify. Once Sarrasine has Zambinella abducted, he considers neither the severe legal consequences for his crime nor the terror which the victim will certainly feel. When he finally learns that Zambinella is a castrato, Sarrasine is so self-centered that he expresses no compassion. Indeed, Sarrasine thinks about only his own offended vanity. Sarrasine is an extraordinary grotesque whose cruelty has caused much suffering for three generations of the Lanty family.

Themes and Meanings

In *Sarrasine*, Balzac primarily concerns himself with the search for happiness and love on the part of the novella's eight principal characters. Only the narrator and the young dancer are satisfied with their existence, and they may attain true happiness in their love for each other. These sympathetic lovers, however, were not influenced in any way by Sarrasine's cruelty or by the castration of Zambinella. *Sarrasine* illustrates very powerfully the long-term and unintended effects of the injustice done to Zambinella almost sixty years before this evening reception at the Lantys' residence.

Zambinella has been scarred both physically and emotionally by his castration. Since he is so profoundly different from other men, Zambinella believes that he is "condemned to understand happiness, to sense it, to desire it, and, like so many others, to see it disappear at every moment." He never suspects that his grandniece, Marianina, also a talented opera singer, will feel an equally keen sense of frustration. The Lantys, in turn, are ashamed of Zambinella's castration. For this reason, they left their native Italy and spent years trying to suppress their past suffering. Feelings, however, can never be fully suppressed. Their profound and long-lasting unhappiness is revealed to others by their obsessive attempts to hide their background and family history from the public. In contrast, Sarrasine's bitterness can be attributed to his selfish and unpleasant personality. Balzac's readers, however, regret that Sarrasine's cruelty toward Zambinella has prevented the Lantys from attaining happiness. Despite their repeated efforts, the Lantys cannot free themselves from the damage done six decades earlier.

Critical Context

Honoré de Balzac wrote *Sarrasine* in 1831, near the beginning of his literary career. When he finally put the novels and short stories in *The Human Comedy* into specific categories, he included *Sarrasine* in his "Scenes of Parisian Life." Like other works in this series, *Sarrasine* is rich with details that evoke a particular time and place. A critic, however, should not stress too much the distinctively Parisian elements in *Sarrasine*, for this novella, with profound psychological insight, explores universal emotions.

Sarrasine was rescued from obscurity by the critic Roland Barthes, who devoted an entire book, *S/Z* (1970; English translation, 1974), to Balzac's novella. In *S/Z* , Barthes analyzes Balzac's text minutely, dividing the novella into 561 sections ranging in length from a single word to a dozen lines or more. Barthes undertook this project during the heyday of structuralism, with its aspirations to infuse literary studies with the rigor of the sciences, and *S/Z* bristles with talk of narrative "codes." As a brilliantly sustained act of reading, however, *S/Z* transcends critical dogma. Indeed, few works of literature in any language have enjoyed the loving attention which Barthes lavishes on *Sarrasine*; thanks to *S/Z*, Balzac's novella remains in circulation.

Sources for Further Study

Barthes, Roland. *S/Z*, 1974.
Bertault, Philippe. *Balzac and "The Human Comedy,"* 1963.
Festa-McCormick, Diana. *Honoré de Balzac*, 1979.
Hunt, Herbert J. *Balzac's "Comédie humaine,"* 1959.
Pritchett, V. S. *Balzac*, 1973.
Zweig, Stefan. *Balzac*, 1946.

Edmund J. Campion

A SCHOOL FOR FOOLS

Author: Sasha Sokolov (1943-   )
Type of plot: Phantasmagoric modernism
Time of plot: The early 1960's
Locale: Moscow and a nearby summer cottage settlement
First published: Shkola dlia durakov, 1976 (English translation, 1977)

Principal characters:

THE NARRATOR (also known as NYMPHEA ALBA and THOSE WHO CAME), a schizophrenic adolescent

THE NARRATOR'S FATHER, a state prosecutor who dislikes his abnormal son

THE NARRATOR'S MOTHER, a kind, unimaginative woman who serves as a buffer between father and son

PAVEL NORVEGOV (also known as SAVL), the boy's idolized, eccentric geography teacher

VETA ACATOVA, the boy's biology teacher and imagined beloved

ARCADY ARCADIEVICH ACATOV, Veta's father, a retired entomologist

The Novel

A School for Fools is a fictional autobiographical journey through the mental landscape of a nameless, schizophrenic adolescent, told with the assistance of an author-persona who may be the boy's older self. Through the kaleidoscopically chaotic prism of the teenager's schizoid mind, the reader sees incidents reflecting his bizarre perceptions and his attempts to come to terms with the surrounding world.

The boy's aberration has two primary features: doubling, and the absence of linear time. He perceives himself and several other characters as two distinct but related persons, each with his or her own name. Much of the narrative is either interior dialogue between the two halves of the boy's mind or interior monologue directed toward unidentified persons. He cannot perceive time, or events in time, in any fixed chronological order. Past, present, and future are random and intermixed. These peculiarities determine the unorthodox form of the novel. There is, in the ordinary sense, no plot. It is replaced by an ever-swirling verbal collage.

The boy's remembered experiences arise from his relationships with his parents, with residents of their vacation summerhouse community, with his doctor, and with staff members of the "School for Fools" that he attends. His prosecutor father is a caviling misanthrope of the genus *Homo soveticus.* The boy has spent several periods in a mental institution where he was treated by a Dr. Zauze, who sought to cure him by uniting the two halves of his personality. Allied with Dr. Zauze in the boy's mind are Perillo, the petty tyrant in charge of the School for Fools, and his deputy, Sheina Trachtenberg, who ominously stalks the school corridors dragging her clubfoot. The threat of being returned to the hospital hangs over his head.

Two other characters, both teachers at the special school, play major roles in the boy's fantasy life. Like the boy's family, they own summer cottages near Moscow. The first is Veta Acatova, his biology teacher, whom he loves and fantasizes as his bride. One of the story's two main, albeit very tenuous, narrative threads is the boy's imaginary romance with Veta. The second thread involves the boy's adored geography teacher, the eccentric Pavel (who is also called Savl) Norvegov, who has died at some point in the boy's school years. Most of the boy's recalled conversations with him postdate the teacher's death and are entirely imaginary, as are his conversations with Veta's father. The two teachers serve as focal points of the disturbed adolescent's efforts to grasp the fundamental human experiences of sex and death.

Much of the narrative is set within two very long, disjointed, imagined dialogues to which the boy returns again and again. One is with Norvegov, from whom the boy attempts to learn about sex. The other is with Veta Acatova's father, in which the boy, imagining himself a winter butterfly collector, seeks to apprentice himself to the old entomologist and asks for Veta's hand in marriage. These imaginary conversations are interspersed with other fantasies, such as the boy's rendezvous with Veta, and with distorted memories of real events, such as visits to his grandmother's grave and to his accordion teacher.

The boy's thought processes and narrative are so chaotic that any outline of events is hazardous. The first chapter, "Nymphea," opens with the two halves of the boy's mind arguing over stylistic questions in the description of the summerhouse district: the suburban train station, the pond, the wooded paths. On the train platform the reader meets the barefoot Norvegov, who has died two years earlier but is still very much alive in the boy's mind. Through this, the reader learns of the boy's "timelessness" and his inability to grasp the directionality of death. The reader also learns of his selective memory and tendency to lose his identity, to dissolve into objects of natural beauty. Sitting in a rowboat, he picks a white water lily and becomes so engrossed that he merges with it, assuming its Latin name, Nymphea Alba. After numerous digressive episodes, the young hero sets off on a night journey to the summer home of his unsuspecting love, Veta Acatova.

The Veta theme is continued in the "Savl" chapter which, however, focuses on Norvegov and the hated School for Fools, with its trivial regimentation and its deceitful goal of turning its "special" students into good Soviet engineers. The following chapter, "Skeerlý," takes sex as its theme. The boy visits his prospective father-in-law and through the folktale "Skeerlý" expresses anxiety over his sexual ignorance. A second imaginary conversation, this one with Savl in the school men's room, addresses the sexual question somewhat more directly, although Savl (already deceased) is more interested in trying to recall his own fate. "Testament," the final chapter, tells of Savl's skeleton, which he has bequeathed to the school biology classroom. Here the reader learns of the geography teacher's illness, suspension, and death. In the final pages the author-persona steps forward. After discussing a title and the possible inclusion of additional episodes, the author and his hero wander arm in arm down the street to buy more writing paper.

The Characters

The nameless narrator-protagonist invariably refers to himself as "we," and the two halves of his mind are in constant dialogue with each other. The main voice is that of his free fantasy, his delusions; the other, lesser voice, is that of rationality, which constantly intrudes, hectors, corrects, and accuses the first voice of trivial and fundamental fabrications. The rational voice asserts that Dr. Zauze has charged him with following the other personality and merging with him. Only in this way can the boy become normal. The price of normality is, however, submission to the repressive rules of society's institutions. The boy prefers the freedom of madness.

There are hints that the narrator's madness is feigned, or perhaps later cured. Chapter 2, "Now, Stories Written on the Veranda," contains twelve realistic ministories which deal with people mentioned en passant in the "deranged" portions of the text. These are apparently written by the hero, now in his twenties. The occasional intrusion of an author-persona to whom the boy tells his story also hints that the hero's schizophrenia may have been feigned. The ambiguity is intentional on the part of author Sasha Sokolov, who, like his hero, has little interest in an inevitably constricting reality.

The novel's characters, who flicker in and out of the boy's fantasized recollections, are aligned with the two halves of his personality. One group represents the repressive forces of society that constrain the freedom and creativity of the individual. These include the boy's prosecutor-father, Dr. Zauze, the psychiatrist, and Perillo and Sheina Trachtenberg, the school officials. All are creatures of the city. The positive characters, Norvegov and the Acatovs, are all associated with nature and the summer settlement in the Moscow countryside. They are the characters of spontaneity and freedom. It is Norvegov who counsels the boy to "live in the wind."

Most of the characters are "doubles" who exist in two variants, although they are not always easily identifiable. Pavel, who is also Savl, that is, Paul/Saul, takes his dual name from the iconoclastic biblical figure. A more obscure pairing is Veta's scientist father, Arcady Acatov, who appears in many scenes as Leonardo da Vinci, the scientist and artist. Mikheev, the elderly postman whose beard streams behind him as he rides his bicycle, is also the seventeenth century writer Silvestr Medvedev, and, perhaps, the legendary "Sender of the Wind." The villainess, Sheina Trachtenberg, often appears as the witch Tinbergen. Each of these "doubles," projections of the boy's schizophrenia, is a complex blending of elements from life and the boy's imagination.

Themes and Meanings

A School for Fools can been read as a sociopolitical indictment of Soviet reality, but this is far too narrow an interpretation. Russian literature has a tradition, largely associated with Fyodor Dostoevski, that links rationalism with political and social authoritarianism and with artistic sterility. The irrational, on the other hand, is identified with social and personal freedom and with artistic creativity. To many, Soviet society seems to embody the evils assertedly consequent upon a rationalist worldview. The question has implications for more than only the Soviet scene; it is universal.

Madness, the most extreme manifestation of the irrational (at least in its romanticized, fictional representation), permits Sokolov's hero freedom from the constraints of a drab institutionalized reality. His madness and selective memory even free him from the laws of time. Death, along with all else, becomes problematic. The hero can simultaneously be a snot-nosed, crazy schoolboy and a suave graduate engineer courting Veta in his own car. Norvegov can simultaneously be dead and alive. It should be kept in mind, however, that the boy, and also his idol Norvegov, pay a high price for their freedom, since it puts them in conflict with social reality.

The irrationality/rationality theme pervades *A School for Fools* in several dimensions: madness versus sanity; the individual versus the collective; nature versus social institutions; and a free, spontaneous art versus a dictated, institutionalized pseudo-art. These themes give shape and meaning to a seemingly chaotic tale.

A School for Fools should not, however, be read solely, or even primarily, as intellectual argument. Sokolov is a brilliant stylist, a language-obsessed writer. It is the whirlwind of language and sound that shapes the narrative and carries it along. This irrational, free, creative force of nature is embodied in the figure of "The Sender of the Wind," who inspires and defends the positive characters and threatens havoc on their enemies. Norvegov, its prophet, is nicknamed the "winddriver" and the "windvane." His schoolgirl mistress is Rosa Windova. The name of the boy's beloved, Veta, poetically derives from the Russian word for wind, *veter*, as do the names and sobriquets of all the affirmative characters. They are quite literally "children of the wind," who emerge from the verbal hurricane of the novel's stream-of-consciousness passages. Such poetic devices are the essence of Sokolov's literary style.

Critical Context

   A School for Fools, Sokolov's first novel, was written in the Soviet Union but published only after his emigration in 1975. Hailed by Vladimir Nabokov as "an enchanting, tragic, and touching book," it was an immediate critical success. Sokolov's subsequent novels, *Mezhdu sobakoi i volkom* (1980; between dog and wolf) and *Palisandriya* (1985; astrophobia), have established him as a major figure in Russian letters.

   Socialist Realism, the simpleminded, didactic literary dogma imposed by Joseph Stalin in the 1930's, had succeeded in all but destroying Russian literature by the time of the dictator's death in 1953. Both the great nineteenth century tradition of critical realism, associated with Leo Tolstoy, and the glittering modernist tradition, associated with Andrey Bely, had nearly died out. With Stalin's death, Russian literature began to resume its earlier traditions, particularly that of critical realism, typified by Aleksandr Solzhenitsyn. The modernist tradition was reinaugurated by Andrei Sinyavsky (Abram Tertz), whose 1956 samizdat essay *On Socialist Realism* called for an avant-garde, "phantasmagoric art." The revived modernist tradition, however, fared less well in the U.S.S.R. than its older rival, and almost all intellectually provocative and stylistically innovative prose remained either underground or émigré. Sasha Sokolov's *A School for Fools* is, along with his other writings, among the most brilliant responses to Sinyavsky's modernist imperative.

Sources for Further Study

Boguslawski, Alexander. "Sokolov's *A School for Fools*: An Escape from Socialist Realism," in *Slavic and East European Journal*. XXVII (1983), pp. 91-97.

Canadian-American Slavic Studies. XXI (Fall, 1987). Special Sokolov issue.

Johnson, D. Barton. "A Structural Analysis of Sasha Sokolov's *A School for Fools*: A Paradigmatic Novel," in *Fiction and Drama in Eastern and Southeastern Europe: Evolution and Experiment in the Postwar Period*, 1980. Edited by Henrik Birnbaum and Thomas Eekmàn.

Karriker, Alexandra. "Double Vision: Sasha Sokolov's *A School for Fools*," in *World Literature Today*. LIII (Autumn, 1979), pp. 610-614.

Moody, Fred. "Madness and the Pattern of Freedom in Sasha Sokolov's *A School for Fools*," in *Russian Literature Triquarterly*. XVI (1979), pp. 7-32.

The New York Times Book Review. Review. LXXXII (September, 1977), p. 41.

Newsweek. Review. XC (July 11, 1977), p. 75.

                                                              D. Barton Johnson

THE SEA OF FERTILITY

Author: Yukio Mishima (Kimitake Hiraoka, 1925-1970)
Type of plot: Psychological realism
Time of plot: 1912-1975
Locale: Tokyo, Nara, and Osaka in Japan; Thailand; and India
First published: Hōjō no umi, 1969-1971 (English translation, 1972-1974):
  Haru no yuki, 1969 (*Spring Snow,* 1972); *Homba,* 1969 (*Runaway Horses,*
  1973); *Akatsuki no tera,* 1970 (*The Temple of Dawn,* 1973); *Tennin gosui,*
  1971 (*The Decay of the Angel,* 1974)

> *Principal characters:*
> MATSUGAE KIYOAKI, an upper-class boy who is reincarnated
>   in each subsequent volume
> ISAO IINUMA, the son of Kiyoaki's tutor, the second incarna-
>   tion of Kiyoaki
> YING CHAN, a Thai princess, the third incarnation of Kiyoaki
> TŌRU YASUNAGA, an orphan of the lower classes, assumed to
>   be Kiyoaki's fourth incarnation
> SHIGEKUNI HONDA, Kiyoaki's schoolmate, later a judge and
>   lawyer

The Novels

The first volume of *The Sea of Fertility, Spring Snow,* introduces two schoolmates, Kiyoaki and Honda, at the Peers School, an exclusive academy. The exposition reveals Kiyoaki's background. His father, Marquis Matsugae, a wealthy man from an old samurai family, sends his only son to be reared in the aristocratic household of Count Ayakura. Kiyoaki thus grows up with Ayakura Satoko, a beautiful girl two years his senior. The main plot of the first volume is the love story of these childhood friends, which ends tragically with Satoko's retirement to a nunnery and the death of Kiyoaki at the age of twenty.

Though attracted to each other, Kiyoaki and Satoko reach their desperate ends through a series of willful misunderstandings. Kiyoaki's diary entries are important in forwarding the plot in two ways. First, they reveal his overly subtle and resentful attraction for Satoko. Second, the dreams that he records faithfully foreshadow events in the later novels and also serve as a unifying motif throughout the tetralogy. Letters play an important role in precipitating the romantic tragedy. Kiyoaki cannot help being attracted to Satoko, who seems to him the most beautiful of the girls of her class; still, he is infuriated by his sense that she is arrogant and condescending toward him. As a means of revenge, he writes her a cruel letter describing his unfulfilled sexuality and his consequent disillusionment with women. He later calls her, making her promise not to read the letter. He subsequently learns from her maid, Tadeshina, that she has already read his indiscreet letter, and he is piqued by her deception. When his parents tell him that a match with an Imperial prince might be arranged for Satoko and ask him if he wishes to claim her first, he proudly maintains that he has no interest in her. He burns the letters that Satoko sends him and refuses to speak to her.

The plans for the Imperial marriage continue; Satoko is so depressed by Kiyoaki's coldness that she loses all interest in her life. When the plans for the marriage have advanced so far that it would be embarrassing and even dangerous for Satoko to change her mind, Kiyoaki realizes that he does indeed love her. He forces Tadeshina to arrange a meeting with Satoko at an inn where the two finally consummate their passion. Their assignations continue, spiced by danger.

Satoko becomes pregnant, much to the consternation of both families. They arrange an elaborate scheme for her to have an abortion in Osaka and then to visit a convent in Nara so that no one will be suspicious. At the convent, however, Satoko seeks asylum, pleading her desire to renounce the world. Kiyoaki, distraught with love, borrows money from Honda and leaves school to join Satoko. She refuses to see him, though he travels repeatedly through the snow to the abbey until he becomes desperately ill. Honda comes to take him home to die. On the train ride home, Kiyoaki exclaims in a delirious dream that he will meet Honda under the waterfalls.

In the second volume, *Runaway Horses*, the focus shifts to Honda, now thirty-eight years old and a respected judge. He is asked to take the place of another judge at a kendō match, where he is attracted to an accomplished eighteen-year-old, Isao. When he later sees Isao playing under the waterfalls, he is intrigued at the sight of three moles under Isao's left arm—one of Kiyoaki's physical traits. Upset by this threat to his rational approach to life, Honda discovers that Isao is the son of Iinuma, once Kiyoaki's tutor.

Iinuma makes his living running a school for the fanatical right wing. Isao is a political purist, dedicated to sacrificing himself for the cause of restoring Japan to its glorious heritage and returning power to the Emperor. He and his group of young rightists target their hatred at the wealthy entrepreneurs who are perceived to have caused the corruption and misery in Japan. Isao is devoted to the ideals set forth in "The League of the Divine Wind," the story of the revolt of a band of samurai in 1876. A long excerpt from this story constitutes about fifty pages of the novel, inserting a tale of rebellion against modernization in the past into the story of Isao's attempted revolt against the governmental policies of the 1930's.

Isao and his dedicated followers formulate a plan to assassinate the most important capitalists, blow up the Bank of Japan, and then commit ritual suicide as a gesture of patriotism. At one point in his plotting, Isao meets an army lieutenant at the same inn where Kiyoaki and Satoko began their affair. Isao senses something familiar about the place but ignores what he cannot explain. Gradually Isao's group loses its powerful supporters, but the members remain determined to carry out their violent plan. They are betrayed and arrested by the police. On learning of this, Honda, motivated by the memory of his friend, resigns his judgeship to defend Isao. The dedicated patriotism of the young people keeps the tide of public sympathy in their favor, and Isao is able to return home to his jubilant family.

At a celebration dinner, his father reveals that he was the one who betrayed the group because his school survives on funds from one of the capitalists Isao had planned to assassinate. Iinuma advises his son to give up futile heroic gestures and to understand the value of compromise in achieving high goals. Shaken to the core by this treachery and the sullying of his purity, Isao wishes that he had been born a woman, for then he would not be subject to illusions. As Honda sees the distraught young man to bed on this traumatic night, he hears Isao muttering about warm lands to the south. The next morning, Isao takes a train to the home of one of the capitalists, assassinates him, and commits ritual suicide at the age of twenty.

In the third volume, *The Temple of Dawn*, Honda, now forty-six and a lawyer representing a Japanese firm in cases involving international law, is sent to Thailand to settle a dispute. He hears about a young Thai princess, Ying Chan, who is believed to be mad because she claims to be Japanese and demands to be taken back to Japan. She is the daughter of one of the Thai princes who attended the Peers School with Honda in his youth. Honda meets the child and asks questions about Kiyoaki and Isao which she answers correctly. Offered a bonus trip for his successful work, Honda chooses to go next to India, where his experiences at the Ganges River, watching the funeral pyres, have a profound effect on him, reviving his interest in reincarnation. Excerpts of his reading make up a large portion of the first part of this novel.

The second part of the third novel takes place nine or ten years later. Honda is now revealed as a voyeur. His marriage, though serene, is passionless. A wealthy man as a result of soaring land values in the postwar period, he builds a new home and installs a peephole in his study so he can watch the activities of his visitors in the adjoining guest room. Ying Chan, grown into a beautiful woman, is sent to Japan to study. Honda is captivated by her and desperately needs to know if she is the reincarnation of his friend. She can no longer remember her childhood obsession. Honda sinks to degrading intrigues to discover whether Ying Chan has the three telltale moles under her left arm. When he does manage to observe her through his peephole, he sees the three moles but also finds her involved in a lesbian interlude. The last Honda hears of Ying Chan is that she is bitten by a cobra, having returned to Thailand, and dies at the age of twenty.

The fourth volume, *The Decay of the Angel*, is the shortest of the novels. The title, translated literally, means "the five signs of the decaying angel."

This final volume opens with the observations of Tōru, a sixteen-year-old sentry at a signal station. One day Honda and his companion, the lesbian Keiko Hisamatsu, come to the station. During their brief visit, Honda observes that Tōru has three moles under his left arm. He decides, having no children of his own, to adopt Tōru. Honda hires tutors to help Tōru prepare for a university education and agrees to a proposal of marriage from a respectable but impoverished family. Tōru's diary entries reveal his delight in destroying the naïve people he meets. He has an affair with an older woman simply so that he can persuade his fiancée to write a letter filled with falsehoods to his mistress and then shows the letter to Honda; the marriage plans are consequently broken off.

Tōru dominates the household, brutalizing Honda into submission. Honda has never verified the exact date of Ying Chan's death, so there is a possibility that Tōru was born before she died and is therefore not a true reincarnation of Kiyoaki. Honda has allowed Tōru to take over, thinking that Tōru is doomed to die at twenty, as in the other reincarnations. To save Honda, Keiko tells Tōru about Kiyoaki's diary and the moles. She taunts him with his dilemma: If he is as special as he thinks he is, he will die when he is twenty. If he does not die at twenty, then he is only a common boy with delusions of the grandeur of evil. Goaded by this information, Tōru tries to commit suicide with poison but succeeds only in going blind.

Tōru is last seen married to a mad young woman who is pregnant by him. He evinces all the five signs of a decaying angel: The flowers in the room have no odor, his clothing is soiled, he perspires heavily, he has lost his personal fastidiousness, and has completely withdrawn from the world.

Honda, suspecting that he has a malignant cancer, decides, at the age of eighty-one, to go to Nara and see Satoko before he dies. Face-to-face with the aged abbess, Honda is startled when she politely denies knowing anyone named Kiyoaki; she suggests that such a person never existed or existed only in Honda's mind. She takes him to the empty convent garden, where Honda thinks to himself that he has finally come to a place that has no memories. The novel ends on this image: Honda and Satoko gazing out at nothingness.

The Characters

The two main characters in each of these novels seem to exemplify Yukio Mishima's own obsession with youth and his horror of growing old. The four young characters of the tetralogy reflect aspects of Mishima himself: the adoration of physical perfection which compelled him to turn his frail frame into a well-muscled body; the concern for the literary aesthetic above politics or religion; the devotion to the ideal of the manly warrior which led Mishima to kill himself in the painful Japanese ritual of seppuku.

Kiyoaki, in *Spring Snow*, is described as an elegant, extraordinarily beautiful young man. His character seems to forecast his fate. An intensely sensitive young man, prone to melancholy, he is attracted to Satoko because she is his equal in elegance. He despises the majority of his schoolmates, his parents, and the adults in his world for their crudeness and rude vitality. His death at twenty is inevitable for someone of his aesthetic sensibility, for only thus can the essential monomania of his nature be preserved. In the next volume, Isao is notable for his physical skill at kendō and his worship of traditional Japanese ideals, much like Mishima toward the end of his life. Isao's early death ensures that he will never compromise his need for purity. The third reincarnation, in the Thai princess Ying Chan, is glimpsed only through Honda's attraction to her exotic dark beauty. Her early death, from a snakebite, retains the flavor of an eroticized death so central to Mishima's life and work. The last young character, Tōru, is obsessed with clarity, a sense that he is special because he can see through the false surface reality of the world. By implying that Tōru may be a false incarnation, Mishima suggests that even a soul, like a body, degenerates with age.

Honda is in some ways the major character of the cycle of novels, for it is his point of view which comes to dominate. Mishima's theory that the longer people live, the less admirable they become is manifested in Honda, who gradually degenerates from the studious young man and loyal friend in the first novel to the cynical and perverted old man in the fourth. His faith in reason and logic is undermined by each successive reincarnation. He may represent Mishima's attempt to imagine one part of himself, the realistic man of the world, growing old. When Honda is forty-six, seeing his reflection in a mirror, he thinks that it is "the face of a man who has lived too long"—a suggestive remark, since Mishima committed suicide when he was forty-five.

Themes and Meanings

The title of the tetralogy comes, according to Mishima, from the name of one of the craters or "seas" of the moon, *Mare Foecunditatis*. That the craters of the moon are barren suggests the underlying theme of the tetralogy: The apparent fecundity of human life—the sea of life—is ultimately, like the craters of the moon, arid and meaningless.

The fascination with death so evident in this work is a recurrent theme in Mishima's writing, curiously complemented by the preoccupation with reincarnation. Though the idea of reincarnation links the four novels, Mishima's religious underpinnings in this tetralogy are shaky. The literary device of the three moles which helps Honda to recognize the various incarnations is brilliant technically, linking a pair of characters in each volume and unifying this epic work. It is harder to reconcile with the idea that the essence of a spirit, not a body, is reincarnated. Moreover, the slick ending, when Honda is forced to consider if he has not invented these recurring characters, casts the whole reincarnation doctrine into doubt. Mishima seems to have concluded that even this hope of life after death is illusory.

Critical Context

Mishima's final work cannot be read without considering the dramatic significance Mishima himself attached to the work. He publicly announced his intention of writing a cycle of novels that would include everything he had learned as a writer. When he finished it, he was known to have said that he would have nothing left to do but kill himself. Though he finished the writing in August, he deliberately wrote the date November 25, 1970, as the last line of the last volume—the day he killed himself, after a dramatic confrontation with the army.

The public reception of the tetralogy in Japan varied; the first volume sold well, the second not as well. The third was not well-received critically. Mishima's declining success may have related, at least in part, to politics. Though essentially apolitical, Mishima had associated himself with rightist groups since 1966, which did not earn for him the favor of the mostly left-wing literary establishment.

Mishima's friend and Nobel Prize winner, Yasunari Kawabata, considered the tetralogy Mishima's masterpiece. Its success is attributable, here as in most of the more than thirty books he wrote, to Mishima's ability to tell a fascinating story in an evocatively poetic style. He was a writer who valued the literary aesthetic above all else. Mishima's passion for tightly constructed plots, as well as the cosmopolitan literary background which informs his writing, makes him one of the best-known and most widely read Japanese writers of his time.

Sources for Further Study

Keene, Donald. "Mishima Yukio," in *Dawn to the West: Japanese Literature of the Modern Era*, 1984.

Nathan, John. *Mishima: A Biography*, 1974.

Petersen, Gwenn Boardman. *The Moon in the Water: Understanding Tanizaki, Kawabata, and Mishima*, 1979.

Ueda, Makoto. "Mishima Yukio," in *Modern Japanese Writers and the Nature of Literature*, 1976.

Yourcenar, Marguerite. *Mishima: A Vision of the Void*, 1986.

Shakuntala Jayaswal

THE SEA WALL

Author: Marguerite Duras (1914-   )
Type of plot: Psychological realism
Time of plot: The 1920's
Locale: The Pacific coastal plain of French Indochina and the colonial city of Kam
First published: Un Barrage contre la Pacifique, 1950 (English translation, 1952; also as *A Sea of Troubles*, 1953)

Principal characters:
MA, a struggling, widowed French homesteader
JOSEPH, Ma's frustrated and cynical son
SUZANNE, Ma's daughter, a pretty but rough young woman
MONSIEUR (JO) JOSEPH, Suzanne's suitor, the unattractive, wealthy son of a rubber planter

The Novel

The Sea Wall, which documents one form of colonial oppression by chronicling the intimate life of an idiosyncratic family, is a masterpiece of narrative strategy. The characters' intense, often abusive relationships are shaped by spiritually debilitating cultural conditions and defy conventional moral expectations.

The narrative begins when Ma and her two children have lived on their land concession for three years and recounts the family's history to date: Ma, widowed soon after moving to the colony, obtained the land from the colonial government with savings earned from many years of hard work as a cinema piano player. Her hopes of a comfortable income from rice farming have been worn away by the yearly floods on the land—the Pacific flooding which has driven several other families from the same concession. After the first flood, Ma gathered together the native plain dwellers and, with the halfhearted consent of the local land agents, planned and executed the construction of a great seawall to drain the land and make it arable. For all of their efforts, however, the annual flood came and destroyed the wall in a single night.

Since that flood, Ma, heavily in debt from her failed project, is obsessively preoccupied with building another, stronger wall and prevailing over the land agents, who will profit from her failure to cultivate the land by repossessing and then reselling it. Ma still maintains a subsistence banana crop, and her children have accommodated themselves to a bleak existence by entertaining passive fantasies in which a rich, attractive stranger of the opposite sex rescues them from the plain.

A stranger does appear on the plain, and while not attractive, he is rich and therefore desirable. Monsieur Jo begins his courtship of Suzanne in a seedy nightclub where he meets the girl and her family. This location sets the illicit tone which characterizes the whole relationship. Bearing gifts, the unpleasant man visits Suzanne alone in the family's bungalow, with Ma strategically positioned within earshot but not in view of the house. Joseph makes no effort to mask his contempt for the vacuous Monsieur Jo, which stems from his disgust at Suzanne's prostitution for the family.

Suzanne, increasingly aware of her body as a family asset and potential commodity, draws closer to her brother as her relationship with Monsieur Jo magnifies the economic and personal inequities already present between the two men. Comparing her aggressive brother to Monsieur Jo, she is repulsed by her weak suitor, who, although desiring Suzanne sexually, will not marry a woman of her low social position. Even after giving her a diamond ring, Monsieur Jo fails to seduce Suzanne. Instead, he is perfunctorily expelled from the family circle. Although, in obtaining the ring, Suzanne has executed the family's objective with Monsieur Jo, she is beaten for her pains by Ma, who encourages but cannot accept the family's moral debasement.

After the family has the ring, the scene of the narrative shifts to the colonial city where Ma, Joseph, and Suzanne travel to sell their acquisition. While Ma runs from one diamond dealer to another, desperately trying to get a higher price for the ring, Suzanne and Joseph separately wander the city, going to cinemas and fantasizing about what they see on the screen. Suzanne meets and rejects another suitor, Joseph Burner, an English wool salesman wanting a pure and submissive wife; Suzanne cannot sell a false representation of herself to a man who pales in comparison to her brother.

Meanwhile, Joseph disappears with a beautiful, wealthy woman, to whom he finally sells the ring—and from whom he returns, after a long tryst, with a sum of money and, bizarrely, the ring. Ma pays off her debts, only to suffer a great irony: No longer abjectly poor, she cannot give up the burden of her ambitions; she is now too solvent to justify acquiescing to the native's poverty level. Grown ill and in despair, Ma returns to the plain with her children.

The trip to the city has profoundly changed the family. Joseph remains on the concession only long enough to gather his possessions and soon departs with his lover in a sleek automobile. While Ma's health deteriorates, Suzanne achieves a certain degree of autonomy by taking a lover—the son of another homesteader named, not surprisingly, Joseph. The novel ends with Ma's death, releasing the family from its futile struggle to achieve affluence. At the same time, the terms of the children's psychological struggles are irrevocably altered. Their mother's death signals a release from obligation—and a mournful recognition of all that the absence of that obligation implies.

The Characters

The main characters in this novel suffer, paradoxically, for both their closeness to and alienation from one another. Much of the dialogue appears banal, and frequently irrelevant, but these trivial exchanges invariably contain greater, emotionally significant meanings. The family's inarticulateness prevents them from engaging in direct confrontations yet permits them to communicate in ways deliberately excluding outsiders. Thus, when Ma and her children first met Monsieur Jo, the family jokingly relates the story of the sea wall. He fatuously pronounces the family "formidably droll," not realizing that their hysterical laughter masks deep frustration.

Comprehending the innuendo employed by Ma's family requires an understanding of the characters' values. Ma, whose plans to build and rebuild the sea walls are inspired by her faith in reason, suffers a profound sense of betrayal at the hands of justice. A schoolteacher before her husband died, Ma retains a sense of class position which is continually at odds with a perverse desire to give up and sink into acute poverty. After her debts have been paid and her source of capital is returned to her, Ma simply sobs, "I don't have the strength to begin all over again." Surrendering to the knowledge that her idealism has failed her, she no longer battles the land agents, because she finally understands that her failure is not an anomaly, but an effect of their corruption.

Suzanne and Joseph never face the same moment of surrender because, although they apprehend Ma's sense of justice and class ambition, they do not share it. Born and reared after the days of the family's good fortune, the children compensate for the rough conditions by living in a rich fantasy world fueled by popular concepts of romance. That the beautiful, wealthy woman of Joseph's dreams does come to rescue him strongly suggests that the children's sense of reality, more than their mother's, is reflected in the novel. With a shift in narrative voice, Joseph himself tells the story of his affair with the woman in the city. By conceding narrative authority to Joseph, Marguerite Duras permits a determined unwillingness to adopt class pretenses to assume a dominant position over conventional bourgeois values.

Suzanne, like her brother, waits to be rescued from her mother's failed dreams, but Suzanne must first overcome the worshipful attitude toward her brother which threatens to paralyze her. Her fascination with Joseph constantly borders on incestuous desire, an effect emphasized by a juxtaposition of events. After she spurns Monsieur Jo, her first thought is to find Joseph and go swimming with him; after seeing a romantic film in the city, she wanders the streets hoping to encounter her brother, who has been absent for several days. Suzanne's fascination with Joseph is broken only when she takes a lover by her own will, desirable because "[y]ou might say he resembled Joseph." Although perhaps only transferring her desire, Suzanne finally gains sovereignty over her mind and body at the end of the novel.

The other characters in *The Sea Wall*—Monsieur Jo, Joseph Burner, Suzanne's lover Joseph (a liquor smuggler), and Carmen (a city hotel owner who practices prostitution to prevent boredom)—all serve to flesh out the portrait of colonial life and colonial enterprise. Honor never rests on the side of conventional legitimacy with these figures, reinforcing the reversal of conventional values which separates Ma from her children.

Themes and Meanings

The Sea Wall presents a compelling critique of colonial capitalism and the ideological means by which people such as Ma are exploited. Deceived by the promises of colonial profiteers, and despite material conditions to the contrary, Ma resists admitting that she is a pawn in a corrupt system. A white colonial, because she is not so abjectly poor as the native servants she employs or entirely bereft of capital, Ma is made an unwitting collaborator in her own exploitation. Capital, in the guise of a diamond ring (which unequivocally refers to its origins in another colonial economy), represents a paradigm of capitalist enterprise from which there is no escape, once one is blinded, as Ma is, by unwavering faith in an insidiously exploitative ideology.

Nevertheless, the narrative is more concerned with examining the ways in which characters are constructed than with theorizing about alternative economic systems. The anxiety of loss, as well as the struggle for separation in relationships between mother and daughter, brother and sister, resounds in the image of a barrier swept away by the engulfing sea, as much as that image also represents the capricious tides of economic adversity. Like the Pacific, Ma is a suffocating, all-pervasive force in her children's lives, defying them to leave her. For her children to gain identity, the hysterical mother must be rejected—but this rejection institutes a sense of longing for the lost whole of mother and child and is echoed in other relationships.

Suzanne's incestuous fascination with Joseph is, psychically, a potentially debilitating form in which such a desire is mediated. This desire, when finally translated into sexual desire for another man, heralds Suzanne's sexual maturity. It also codifies a pattern of displaced desire in adult sexual relationships which can be traced back to the initial mother-child separation. The narrative's dreamlike offering, without comment or explanation, of suggestive thoughts or emotions emphasizes the construction of sexual desire through pre-Oedipal longing and memory.

Critical Context

A prolific author of more than twenty novels, many plays and films, and several important essays, Marguerite Duras maintains an important position in twentieth century French and international literary and intellectual life. *The Sea Wall*, Duras' third novel, was the first of her works to be translated into English, and it won for her wide international attention. It was made into a film by René Clément in 1967.

Unlike some of her later works, which defy standard generic classification,

The Sea Wall is recognizably a novel, although its narrative structure, which lacks conventional characterization, plot development, and closure, is an important moment for surveying Duras' developing technique. The themes of absence, memory, and longing for a past love, occurring in a politically and historically significant context, are continually present and under revision in her work. Frequently, Duras' works make specific reference to one another (*L'Éden Cinéma*, a 1977 theater production, contains specific plot and character elements also present in *The Sea Wall*). Transgressing generic lines, or reinscribing characters and plot, the core of Duras' creative production is a fascination with the subject in process, which enables her works to be read as a reflexive continuum.

Duras allows personal psychic material to permeate and shape her work. Her childhood memories significantly inform the plot of *The Sea Wall* (like Ma, Duras' mother was a failed colonial planter in French Indochina). Duras' third-person use of autobiographical material in *The Sea Wall* suggests but does not yet achieve, the ambiguity of voice and blurred distinctions between self and other apparent in later works, most notably *L'Amant* (1984; *The Lover*, 1985).

Sources for Further Study

Blake, Patricia, "The Stronger Bulwark," in *The New York Times Book Review*. LXIII (March 15, 1953), p. 5.

Cismaru, Alfred, *Marguerite Duras*, 1971.

Kristeva, Julia. "The Pain of Sorrow in the Modern World: The Works of Marguerite Duras," in *PMLA*. CII, no. 2 (1987), pp. 138-152.

Murphy, Carol J. *Alienation and Absence in the Novels of Marguerite Duras*, 1982.

Pierrot, Jean. *Marguerite Duras*, 1986.

Willis, Sharon. *Marguerite Duras: Writing on the Body*, 1987.

Mollie A. Brodsky

THE SECRET HISTORY OF THE LORD OF MUSASHI

Author: Jun'ichirō Tanizaki (1886-1965)
Type of plot: Historical fiction
Time of plot: 1549-1559
Locale: The Mount Ojika and Mount Tamon castles, Japan
First published: Bushūkō hiwa, 1931-1932, serial; 1935, book (English translation, 1982)

> *Principal characters:*
> HŌSHIMARU, later TERUKATSU, the eldest son of the feudal chief Kiryu Terukuni, the Lord of Musashi
> TSUKUMA ORIBENSHŌ NORISHIGE, the eldest son of Tsukuma Ikkansai
> LADY KIKYŌ, the wife of Norishige and paramour of Terukatsu
> DŌAMI, a servant and jester of Terukatsu

The Novel

In his preface to *The Secret Life of the Lord of Musashi*, Jun'ichirō Tanizaki claims to have examined secret papers telling of the otherwise unknown masochistic sexual desires of the famous sixteenth century samurai, the Lord of Musashi. The purpose of his book, he explains, is to reveal the development of these sexual desires in the young Musashi. Tanizaki approaches his subject with formal respect, carefully placing Musashi in the context of other renowned and respected warriors who were known to have enjoyed cruel and unusual sex practices. The novel's material is then presented as a historical investigation; it is related in the past tense, and the point of view is third-person, with occasional first-person commentary.

The novel is divided into six books, each divided into chapters. Book 1 opens with an account of the author's two "secret" sources: "The Dream of a Night" was written by a nun named Myōkaku, who had apparently once been in the service of Musashi; "Confessions of Dōami" was written by a servant of Musashi and recounts sexual exploits that the servant not only witnessed but in which he was also forced to participate. As an occasional confidant of his master, Dōami also had learned from Musashi himself the history of his sexual appetites. Throughout the novel these two sources are referred to, quoted, and compared with other (genuine) historical accounts.

In the three chapters of book 2, the origin of Musashi's sexual perversion is explained. The scene is the castle on Mount Ojika, where Musashi—referred to as Hōshimaru during this stage of his life—is kept hostage by Lord Tsukuma Ikkansai, who has won power over Hōshimaru's father and apparently retains Hōshimaru as surety against rebellion from the father's clan. The castle on Mount Ojika is being besieged by the forces of a war-lord named Yakushiji Danjō Masataka. The year is 1549, and Hōshimaru is twelve years old. Restless and disappointed at not being able either to fight in the battle or to observe it, Hōshimaru listens to women of the castle who describe the action and is finally invited to observe the women at their nightly task of cleaning and dressing the decapitated heads of defeated war-riors. On observing this spectacle, Hōshimaru is entranced, and he becomes especially excited upon seeing a young woman combing and cleaning a "woman-head," which is a head whose nose has been removed. Hōshimaru learns that warriors, when unable to carry the head of a defeated enemy, will sever its nose in order to return to identify it at the end of the day. The thrill for Hōshimaru is watching the calm, often smiling face of the beautiful girl as she attends almost affectionately to the grotesquely defaced death's head. The vision of beauty, "spiced with the bitterness of cruelty" brings Hōshi-maru to ecstasy, and he even feels jealous of the head. Though surprised at his reaction, like a man who, "believing himself to be in robust health, discovers that he has a malignant disease," Hōshimaru is nevertheless driven uncontrollably by it, and it is this ecstasy that he attempts to duplicate in his sexual exploits thereafter.

Three of these exploits dominate the remainder of the narrative. In the first, Hōshimaru, desperate to observe again the dressing of one of the rare woman-heads, determines to take the head of Lord Masataka, the chief of the besieging army. Though only twelve, Hōshimaru is almost equal to the task. He manages to sneak into the enemy camp and slay the sleeping lord but cannot sever the head before he is pursued by guards. He does manage to sever the nose, which he takes with him in his escape. The consequences of his daring are great: Faced with possible disgrace, the besieging forces re-treat, fabricating a story of their lord's dying of an illness. Thus the twelve-year-old samurai-to-be brings about the defeat of an army but with the same stroke deprives himself of ever again observing what he most desires to see—the young woman dressing a woman-head.

The second exploit occurs when Hōshimaru—now called Terukatsu, hav-ing reached maturity (fifteen years old)—meets Lady Kikyō, daughter to the Masataka that Terukatsu had slain three years earlier, and wife to Tsukuma Oribenshō Norishige, son of the Ikkansai who had held Terukatsu hostage for more than ten years of his youth. Tormented with the suspicion that Norishige's father was responsible for her father's disgrace, Lady Kikyō has secretly employed men to remove her husband's nose in revenge. Terukatsu learns of her desire and does the job for her. As a result of previous careless attempts on his nose, Norishige has by now lost an ear and much of his upper lip also. Terukatsu becomes Lady Kikyō's lover, but his greatest excitement is watching her and her deformed husband together. This nearly surpasses the vision of the young woman dressing the woman-head, for Norishige is more hideously deformed, more grotesque than a woman-head, and lives to receive the continuing affections of his wife.

The third adventure includes the participation of Terukatsu's servant and jester, Dōami, and the lord's vivacious, innocent, and childlike wife, Lady Oetsu, known as Shosētsuin. For Terukatsu, the high point of his relations with his wife is when he has Dōami placed in a hole in a floor so that only his head protrudes and has Shosētsuin attend to it as if it were a decapitated head. Again, Terukatsu can feast on the vision of a young, beautiful girl's attentions to a death's head. Testing the loyalty of Dōami and the limits of his wife's cruelty, Terukatsu gets his wife drunk and asks her to sever the nose of Dōami. She agrees but cannot perform the act. Instead, Terukatsu has her drill a hole in the servant's ears. The following day a sober Shosētsuin is horrified by the memory of the evening, and Terukatsu loses interest in her.

The Characters

Miyamoto Musashi is well-known to Japanese readers as the historical samurai whose reputation has grown into legend. Tanizaki's formal introduction in his preface mirrors as well as mocks the care customarily exercised in handling a folk hero, and the novel itself is a grotesque parody of historical fiction. The story is dominated by its central character; other characters are significant only inasmuch as the protagonist can interact with them. If popular historical fiction lacks depth, however, in its drive to glorify its heroes, this parody provides that depth in its meticulous tracing of the origins of the disgraceful obsession that drives its protagonist.

The complexity of the central character is provided by a fusion of the heroic and the perverse. The young Hōshimaru is physically strong, alert, self-conscious, and impatient with the restrictions of his youth. Throughout the narrative the sense is conveyed of a power held back only by convention. The qualities that can bring success to the samurai warrior, however, can carry an abnormal intensity to everything else, so that it is not surprising that Hōshimaru's curiosities and desires fix themselves into obsession. Reared in a castle which is intricately structured with layers of internal, middle, and external chambers, Hōshimaru is equally attentive to the refinements and delicate beauty of the aristocratic seclusion at the center, represented by the women with whom he first interacts, as to the gory struggle, waged by sword-brandishing samurai, that daily moves closer to the center from the outer and middle layers. Hōshimaru's sexuality expresses this tension as he seeks to reexperience, repeatedly, the delicate woman loving a gruesome, defaced man.

Kikyō and Shosētsuin serve in similar ways the protagonist's sadism. Each provides the ideal contrast—as did his first love, the dresser of woman-heads—to the deformed males. Where Kikyō is the type of aloof, regal beauty delicate in her refined life as lady to a feudal lord, Shosētsuin is the type of youthful innocence, virginal, childlike, and delicate in her own un-familiarity with her husband's world.

Norishige and Dōami are a similar pair, as ideal victims of the protago-nist's sadism. Dōami is ideal for his skill at mimicking the decapitated head and for his slavish obedience. Norishige is, however, the superior victim for the contrast he represents as an exalted figure brought low by violence and hideous deformity.

Themes and Meanings

The pursuit of an unobtainable ideal is a theme that recurs in the fiction of Tanizaki, and, as in *The Secret History of the Lord of Musashi*, the pursuit often discovers cruel obsession and sadism, represented as profound currents that are as natural to humans as attachment and sexuality. The protagonist of this novel is not victim to erotic fantasies that can be fulfilled, and the very terms of the fetish here prevent the story from being merely erotic at any point. The protagonist's ideal is of an impossible union of beauty and grotesquery, of delicate life and ugly death, of pleasure and suffering. In the image of a woman making love to a noseless man—or, as originally per-ceived, a dead man's noseless head—the protagonist forces together these apparent opposites, and the impossibility of the consummation intensifies his desire for it, by putting it on an ideal, or fantastic, plane. That this ideal ex-ists only as the protagonist's fantasy makes him both persecutor and victim in a closed world. It is in this sense that his sadism is masochistic, and it is in this condition of a self-created and self-contained world that the broader is-sue of the relationship between reality and fantasy is suggested. In *The Secret History of the Lord of Musashi*, Tanizaki represents fantasy and reality as irreconcilables and portrays man as hopelessly abandoned between them.

Critical Context

Though not translated into English until 1982, *The Secret History of the Lord of Musashi* was originally published serially in 1931-1932 and in book form in 1935, placing it at the beginning of the second period of Tanizaki's lit-erary career. His first period had just ended with the publication of his col-lected works in twelve volumes. Where his first period of fiction consisted of traditional storytelling, in which Tanizaki wove his plots with a conventional mix of dialogue and objective narrative, the second period introduced experi-mentation in combining fiction with nonfiction and employing less orthodox storytelling. *The Secret History of the Lord of Musashi* is an excellent ex-ample of both these areas of innovation. The narrator begins by announc-ing his intention to record the undisclosed truth about the legendary samurai, and he liberally speculates during the narrative on the motives of its char-acters. By fabricating events in the story of his real-life protagonist, and fabricating as well some of his very sources, Tanizaki creates a parody rich in ironic humor. The humorous pretense running through the work is that the author is coolly objective and appropriately distanced from his historical material.

Interest in Japanese tradition and history, while not new in Tanizaki's writing, is another characteristic that dominates in this second period. *Yoshino Kuzu* (1931; *Arrowroot*, 1982), appearing only months before the serialization of *The Secret History of the Lord of Musashi*, depicts a writer who is investigating a fifteenth century imperial court outside Kyoto. Two other historical fictions of this period are "Ashikari" (1932; English translation, 1936) and "Shunkin shō" (1933; "A Portrait of Shunkin," 1936).

Sadomasochism and obsession with unobtainable beauty are elements so common in Tanizaki's work that they are regarded as two of its unifying characteristics. In *The Secret History of the Lord of Musashi*, however, these elements are brought together with Tanizaki's humor. The story's exaggerated perversity, with the protagonist's fantastically bizarre desire, creates a parody of Tanizaki's own fiction and presents the author as he comments humorously on his work.

Sources for Further Study

Howard, Richard. "Japanese Master," in *The Nation*. CCXXXV (September 4, 1982), pp. 183-184.

Keene, Donald. "Tanizaki Jun'ichirō," in *Dawn to the West: Japanese Literature of the Modern Era*, 1984.

O'Brien, Geoffrey. "*The Secret History of the Lord of Musashi*," in *The Village Voice*. XXVII (April 27, 1982), p. 47.

White, Edmund. "Shadows and Obsessions," in *The New York Times Book Review*. LXXXVII (July 18, 1982), pp. 8, 22-23.

Dennis C. Chowenhill